Conflict, and Revolution

The problem of politics in international political thought

Paul Kelly

 Press

Published by
LSE Press
10 Portugal Street
London WC2A 2HD
press.lse.ac.uk

Text © Paul Kelly 2022

First published 2022

Cover design by Diana Jarvis https://www.roamland-studio.co.uk/
Cover image: Severini, Gino (1883–1966): 'Armored Train in Action' ('Train
blinde' en action'), 1915. New York, Museum of Modern Art (MoMA). Oil on
canvas, 45 5/8 x 34 7/8' (115.8 x 88.5 cm). Gift of Richard S. Zeisler. 287.1986
Cover image credit: © Digital image, The Museum of Modern Art, New York/
Scala, Florence 2021. © ADAGP, Paris and DACS, London 2021.

Print and digital versions typeset by Siliconchips Services Ltd.

ISBN (Paperback): 978-1-909890-72-5
ISBN (PDF): 978-1-909890-73-2
ISBN (EPUB): 978-1-909890-74-9
ISBN (Mobi): 978-1-909890-75-6

DOI: https://doi.org/10.31389/lsepress.cwr

The full text of this book has been peer-reviewed to ensure high
academic standards. For our full publishing ethics policies,
see http://press.lse.ac.uk

Suggested citation:
Kelly, Paul. 2022. *Conflict, war and revolution: The problem of politics
in international political thought*. London: LSE Press.
DOI: https://doi.org/10.31389/lsepress.cwr License: CC BY.

To read the free, open access version of this book
online, visit https://doi.org/10.31389/lsepress.cwr
or scan this QR code with your mobile device:

For G. W. Kelly (1932–2018)

Contents

Extended contents

Preface and acknowledgements

All books have a story and the acknowledgements provide the opportunity to tell it. For much of my career I have worked on and published political theory in a broadly liberal-egalitarian idiom. This book is rather different and needs an explanation. After nearly a decade as a department chair and then pro-director at LSE – both roles I loved and where I got to work with some exceptional people – I returned to a regular academic role writing political theory and teaching brilliant students. But a decade without major writing is a long time, and I did not want to spend my sabbatical in the library reading for a project that would only see the light of day many years in the future. I needed to begin writing something quickly, so I thought of writing up a course I had been teaching for years, as a possible textbook. When Nicola Scally, LSE's librarian, suggested I write a book for the new LSE Press she was setting up to publish online and open access books, I could not but rise to the provocation. I had had a long-term interest in online publication but was sceptical of online open access books. I am grateful to Nicola for that invitation and to Patrick Dunleavy, the subsequent editor in chief of LSE Press, who made sure the ambition turned into a reality and that I delivered it. I had had the pleasure of working with Patrick before, editing a journal, and he remains one of the most entrepreneurial academics at the LSE and in UK social science.

When I started writing the book, I realised the project was far too ambitious. This book was already long, and I had planned 24 chapters! As I worked on the book it was clear that my interests were in a particular direction and the character of the book was becoming more realist in orientation. It turns out that the book ended up bearing the mark of three political theorists: the late Glen Newey, Matt Sleat and Edward Hall, my last PhD student before going over to the 'dark side', who is now an established political theorist in his own right. Glen had always been a sort of sparring partner as he gently ridiculed my liberal-egalitarianism. Although he is no longer with us, I still hear his realist provocations. Matt spent time at the LSE before going to Sheffield and I had come to know and respect his work. But it was only when I read his *Liberal Realism* book that I got drawn into thinking more about the problems of political realism. Finally, Ed Hall probably did most to challenge my liberal-egalitarian presuppositions and he finally killed off my plan to complete a book on Ronald Dworkin: I am grateful for that. I still remain a kind of liberal-egalitarian, but I see that position and those values in a very different light: one illuminated by these three former friends, colleagues and students and, because of them, the thinkers I write about in this book.

Beyond them, the list of intellectual debts is so vast that I will just thank all my former teachers and all those who I have worked with or whose work I have read over the last four decades. I should also thank my current LSE undergraduate students. Returning to the classroom to discuss interesting ideas with some of the most talented and brilliant of young people is a priceless privilege only the LSE's Department of Government can offer.

I need to thank Anne. She is always thanked for her support, but this time around it is different. Over the last decade she has published four books and exhibited and taught all over the world. Following her around with a laptop and my online library made this book possible. The chapters often have an association with a place that is also the story of her travels, with me in tow. The book was conceived in Farindola in Italy, where she had a residency in 2018. Subsequent chapters were written in Limoges, on the beachfront at Newcastle (NSW, Australia), watching surfers and drinking extraordinary coffee whilst writing about Hobbes, or in Nelson and Wanganui (New Zealand), writing about Carl Schmitt. Other chapters have English stories: Harrogate, Lincoln, Salisbury, Ruthin, Mansfield, Cornwall. The book was finished during lockdown, and those memories of travel invisibly imprinted in each chapter have been enormously important to me as our worlds have necessarily closed in. Throughout that time, I have seen and enjoyed what she produced; now she can see what I was doing all that time.

The book is dedicated to my father. He died in the year I started writing it. He was not an intellectual and he worked in a factory, but he read widely and loved politics. When I went to university in 1980, he bought me the Clarendon edition of John Locke's *Essay Concerning Human Understanding*, edited by P.H. Nidditch. He could have bought me a cheap version. I treasure that book. This one is for him.

CHAPTER 1

Introduction

Conflict, war, revolution and the character of politics

We live in interesting times! Apocryphally, this is a Chinese curse, although there is little evidence that the English version, 'May you live in interesting times', matches any precise Chinese aphorism. Be that as it may, the times we live in are interesting, in that many very recent political preconceptions and trends of history are being turned on their heads, and this is happening in both confusing and troubling ways, the victims and beneficiaries of which are unclear. When Francis Fukuyama published his famous article 'The End of History' in 1989, it coincided with the collapse of the USSR, the fall of the Berlin Wall and the end of the Cold War. Although too much triumphalism has been unfairly attributed to Fukuyama's subtle argument, the title certainly chimed with the age. It was also pretty much clear to everyone who the beneficiaries and losers of that historical moment were. Globalisation (and U.S. military power) defeated 'really existing socialism', and with the subsequent first Gulf War in 1991 the western military and economic order looked as if it had the blessing of history. This, coupled with what is often called the 'great moderation', the period of stable and steady economic growth in western developed economies unleashed by economic deregulation and globalised trade during the 1990s and the early 2000s, further vindicated globalised finance and the 'Washington consensus' on growth – an economic policy stance that is called *globalisation* by its supporters and *neo-liberalism* by its critics. In Europe and the European Union, many of the more enthusiastic EU backers saw a move

How to cite this book chapter:
Kelly, Paul. 2022. *Conflict, war and revolution: The problem of politics in international political thought*. London: LSE Press, pp. 1–28.
DOI: https://doi.org/10.31389/lsepress.cwr.a License: CC BY.

away from the model of nation states as the 'end of history' to a post-state order modelled on closer cooperation and integration: again. Although his argument is more subtle and qualified than this, we can see this optimism in the great German social and political philosopher Jürgen Habermas (Habermas 1998; 2005). Books were being written about the rise of 'cosmopolitan' democracy, world politics and the new political configurations needed to govern this new order.

Yet all was not quite what it seemed. The terrible events of 11 September 2001 unleashed the most significant attack on the continental USA in its history when a group of suicide bombers weaponised domestic airliners to bring down the World Trade Center in New York City and attack the Pentagon, headquarters of the U.S. Department of Defense. An essentially low-technology attack, by a previously little-known terrorist group, Al-Qaeda, had challenged the most technologically sophisticated military ever seen in history. The U.S.-led response in Afghanistan (where the Taliban gave succour to Al-Qaeda) and then Iraq (where Saddam Hussein did not) unleashed nearly two decades of struggle in the Middle East. A nuclear-armed USSR was replaced as the dominant enemy of 'the west' by an asymmetrical struggle against a jihadist enemy indifferent to the fear of death and which had no prospect of victory in any conventional sense. Al-Qaeda is not a military structure with a territory, government or a return address.

Other events quickly followed the triumph of neo-liberal globalism and the rise of global terrorism, with Al-Qaeda and then more recently ISIS/Daesh, ensuring that international affairs became even more 'interesting' and urgent. These included the global financial crash in 2007–2008, the rise of China as the default backer of the global financial order (as the largest holder of U.S. debt), the subsequent rise of populism in the U.S. and Europe with the election of a protectionist and nationalist President Trump, and the vote by the UK (one of the largest and most important economic and political players in the European Union) to leave the EU following a domestic referendum (Brexit). The global institutions considered necessary for a stable world order, and which had delivered the great moderation, were now seen to be lacking political legitimacy. They faced a concerted backlash from political forces on a scale that had not been seen since the 1930s, and which threatened the domestic political structures of states that were supposed to be exemplars of democratic stability.

This complex pattern of events spanning four decades thus saw the triumph of the west and the rise of the east; the triumph of globalisation and the resurgence of protectionism and economic nationalism; the end of the Cold War and the launch of the global War on Terror. The pace of change has been bewildering even in a new century that has seen unprecedented transformations in human affairs (to 2021). This shift from an historical trajectory of liberal dominance and global order might seem challenging, and it is, but is it unique? Or is it not just a case of history – which perhaps naively we thought had ended – forcing its way back onto the agenda? International affairs and the thinking about it have always fluctuated between periods of progressive optimism and revolution, retrenchment and irredentism. Whilst there remains much about which we should remain optimistic, the challenges of the present, and the echoes of past crises, raise questions about the ways in which we think about and frame political action and agency, and especially about the adequacy of the dominant paradigms of international political thinking.

In this book, in a timeframe spanning the ancient world to the present, I examine the sources of some of those intellectual paradigms by exploring the ideas of a number of significant figures who illuminate ways of thinking about the challenges of politics and the prevalence of crisis and conflict. By studying 10 paradigmatic thinkers – Thucydides, Augustine, Machiavelli, Hobbes, Locke, Rousseau, Clausewitz, Lenin and Mao, and Carl Schmitt – I examine important debates in international political thought. The particular focus here is on those who wish to challenge or qualify the hope of redemption and order in human affairs by overcoming politics, versus thinkers who address the ineradicable necessity and challenges of politics, war and conflict. This may sometimes look like a 'history' of what international theorists and international relations scholars refer to as a tradition of realism, but my purpose is different.

Positing traditions such as realism already presupposes an answer to the question of how to read these thinkers and assumes that they conform to a single narrative (cf. Doyle 1997), but this is a narrowly circumscribed canvass. This book sets these key thinkers in a wider context, using them to identify and explore different ways of conceiving of the activity of politics as an autonomous way of acting in the world. The concept of realism falls within that domain because some of the thinkers discussed have been seen by some scholars as adherents of versions of this view. But, as we shall see, describing all these thinkers as 'realist' in the sense used either by international relations or by international political theory raises questions about the value and scope of that concept (see Chapter 11 for more on this).

The other reason this book is not a simple 'history' is that it does not aim to be comprehensive. There are clearly other ways of conceiving of international politics, and other narratives that may better explain the development of doctrines in the western tradition and beyond. To write such a comprehensive overview would be a considerably longer book, and it would also raise questions about the idea of a single history, issues that I mostly deliberately avoid (but see chapter 11). It is sufficient for this book to present a canon of thinkers whose ideas and approaches inform and illuminate some of the central questions of international politics and its contemporary challenges.

Precisely because it paints on such a large canvas, international political thought is a peculiarly valuable approach to understanding some of the most important questions about politics. It also leaves open precisely the sorts of questions, concepts and approaches that the 10 major thinkers here explored. They all tackled fundamental questions about the nature of political activity and the vehicles through which political agency is exercised at different times and places – without privileging the development or priority of any particular mode of organisation, whether polis, empire, principality, multitude, state, nation, class or nomos.

The perspective of international theory helps transcend the narrow confines of domestic politics as the distribution of 'who gets what, where, when and how' (Lasswell 1936). Instead, it focuses attention on what might be called a meta-level where the real and fundamental work of delineating political agency takes place. In some standard introductions to political thinking, the explanation begins with human actors, then moves up to the state or political community level, and terminates with the way those communities interact in the international realm. This is the model of the domestic and the international so fundamental to standard international relations theory, but it is also commonplace in political theory courses.

Focusing on international theory allows one to look at the bigger picture out of which much domestic politics emerges. It does not presuppose the primacy of domestic politics and see the international as a problematic remainder. Instead, it conceives of the challenges of the international realm as, if not prior or autonomous, then at least co-present with the challenge of delimiting political communities and sites of political agency. It is not surprising that much political theory and philosophy regards the perspective of international theory as secondary or an afterthought. That is indeed the legacy of Hobbes's work on political thought and international relations, a legacy that can be seen echoed in the work of the most important late 20th-century political philosopher, John Rawls. But this was clearly not the view of Augustine and Machiavelli, to take only two examples, for whom this distinction between domestic and international would have made no sense.

The narrative in this book deliberately eschews the term 'history' because it does not attempt to provide an overview of all the approaches one may find in international political thought courses. Indeed, if one refers back to my list of modes of organisation of political agency above, I deliberately left out organising categories such as the individual, society or economy, all of which would feature in some way in a comprehensive account of international political thought in the western canon. This choice is perhaps controversial, but it is a deliberate attempt to range beyond reductive approaches that reduce politics to morality, or to the economy and society. Too much contemporary thinking about our current global predicament suggests that there is a progressive unfolding of order that culminates in the triumph of the modern Westphalian state system and its international institutions alongside a globalised market economy. These approaches to international politics privilege the individual person as a right-holder or bearer of a unique ethical dignity, or as an individual utility maximiser with a clear preference order. In much academic debate and in much political theory and science, this conception of the person has been taken to be a true account of moral and economic agency, and as the basis of all other political arrangements and groups. This has led to the prevalence of an unchallenged but apolitical cosmopolitanism that has marginalised some of the most fundamental challenges facing contemporary politics.

In this book, I do not seek to reject individualism or cosmopolitanism as systems of value. Indeed, elsewhere I have written to endorse a version of this perspective as liberal-egalitarianism (Kelly 2005). But in the current climate, with challenges to the conception of agency that underpins such an approach, I am more interested in the challenges to that world view that are arguably returning to centre stage. This individualistic and cosmopolitan view of the domain of the political has not only shaped contemporary political science and international relations. It has also done so to the exclusion of perspectives that force us to confront different ways of doing politics, exercising power, force and violence, and conceiving of the goals of political activity and its fundamental purpose. This book attempts instead to introduce political thinking and inter-national political theory without indirectly presupposing that political agency and institutions must have a settled character and structure that conform to moral individualism and converge on liberal constitutionalism as the best form of political organisation.

My purpose is to let a set of thinkers speak in their own voices rather than reducing them to a settled historical and cultural narrative, or to pre-established traditions such as realism, or ideologies such as liberalism. So, the linking narrative here must be abstract and general and stay at a high level. Nev-ertheless, there are important linkages between the chapters that explain the juxtaposition of these particular thinkers, as opposed to an alternative canon or narrative. All of them take as fundamental the role of violence, conflict and coercion. Violence and conflict are either the perennial experience of human-ity beneath the thin veneer of civilisation or an aspect of human experience that morality and society attempt to discipline and obscure but which remains the basic stuff of political action and agency. For others still, these experiences are characteristic of life beyond the protections offered by state sovereignty in the anarchic world of international or interstate politics. Some of the thinkers conceive of violence as an ineradicable problem. For others, violence is morally ambiguous as a feature of experience that can be manipulated and channelled to achieve different ends and goals. We tend to think of both violence and con-flict as bad things that must be avoided or mitigated. But at a more fundamental level one might also argue that these are merely natural forces that we can con-demn under some descriptions whilst also praise under others. After all, is it not the case that order entails coercion (for all except anarchists), as indeed does the law – as indeed (if we follow St Augustine) does peace? Finally, under the headings of war and revolution we find approaches to politics that channel vio-lence into pursuing goals that cannot be achieved by negotiation, deliberation and compromise. In the case of revolution, they use violence to remove the existing order so as to (in theory) make way for a world beyond the violence and coercion of politics.

Discussing and contrasting these paradigmatic thinkers provides a theoretical introduction to international political theory. But what precisely is international political theory and how, if at all, does it differ from the study of international relations, and its sub-division international relations theory, or from the study of the history of political thought? International relations theory and the history of political thought are recognised academic activities. So it is important to show that international political theory is not simply a confused renaming of an already-familiar activity, or a more primitive and less clearly defined version of academic sub-divisions. In the next two sections I make a substantial argument in favour of defending international political theory and distinguishing it from the history of political thought. But, before turning to that argument, I want to distinguish international political theory from international relations theory.

The distinction between international relations theory and international political theory developed over the last few decades as a consequence of the disciplinary development of international relations on the one hand and the growth of normative political theory and applied ethics in political science and philosophy on the other. Chris Brown provided the most compelling account of how international political theory separated out from mainstream international relations theory. He linked it to the development in social science of a dominant turn towards positivism, which is an explanatory form of enquiry assuming that the facts or objects of study are stable and can be examined in ways analogous to the natural sciences (Brown 2015; Brown and Eckersley 2018). This positivist turn is exemplified in the application of formal modelling and economistic forms of theorising (such as rational choice theory) to traditional questions of national and state interaction and bargaining, as illustrated by leading theorists such as Kenneth Waltz (Waltz 1979). According to Brown, international political theorists are authors who see this as an unfortunate departure from humanistic approaches to the study of international relations that characterised its early origins as a distinct form of enquiry.

However, the issue is not just a war of methods between quantitative and formal theory against qualitative or historical approaches. It also relates to the point and style of international relations arguments. The turn to positivism and the primacy of explanation at the expense of normative and prescriptive arguments coincided with a resurgence of normative arguments in political theory and applied ethics under the influence of major theorists such as John Rawls, Michael Walzer and Peter Singer (Forrester 2019). These thinkers launched debates or rekindled questions about distributive justice and state legitimacy, the justification of war and what obligations we owe to distant others in the face of famine or global poverty. All of these questions have an element that links them to the familiar intellectual territory of traditional international relations theory. But they also depart from it because they either challenge its apparent statist assumptions or attempt to provide normative and prescriptive accounts for what states or other international agents *ought* to do, irrespective of what they may be likely to do in relation to their interests. It is often the case that disciplinary development happens because of the recognition that something interesting and intellectually exiting was happening elsewhere, just beyond traditional disciplinary boundaries – see, for example, the way in which modern behavioural economics has turned to experimental psychology. That is also true with the development of international political theory. Yet, at the same time there is not simply a turn to familiar normative political thought, which is often poorly informed about the reality of international affairs and politics. It is precisely a critical engagement with normative and prescriptive arguments about the international domain that makes the study of international political theory important and vital. It also explains the particular selection of paradigmatic thinkers in this book. International political theory does not merely dismiss, or wilfully overlook, normative and prescriptive arguments as methodologically primitive, in the way it claims that standard international relations theory perhaps does. Rather, it brings them back to the forefront of engagement with the sorts of challenges that shape and unsettle our times. In so doing, international political theory also raises questions about the vocabulary, source and scope of approaches, languages and concepts – precisely what this book considers.

Texts, contexts, thoughts or thinkers?

Studying the work of groups of thinkers from the past is often referred to as creating a canon. The approach has been a recognisable part of the study of politics since the emergence of the discipline of political science in the late 19th century (Boucher 1985; Kelly 1999). For most of that time, a series of great thinkers were gathered together to illustrate the dominant story of the emergence of the modern state. Reflecting on those past thinkers was part of a forward-looking activity that suggested arguments, principles and institutional models that could then be contrasted with current developments – all with the purpose of legitimating or improving the contemporary liberal state system. Just as in early international relations, many arguments based on this kind of enquiry were both prescriptive and normative. As the modern discipline of political science developed in the post-World War II period, the importance of political thought gave way to the study of political behaviour, political institutions and the development of comparative politics. The broad and eclectic study of political thinkers came to seem intellectually crude as it either lacked the robustness of a method or else followed the dictum of the 19th-century Cambridge constitutional historian F.W. Maitland that political science is 'either history or humbug'. The new field had a method but it was one that already had an intellectual home in the discipline of history. For radical critics of the modern state, history also enabled the critique of the present by showing how contemporary political values and institutions were tainted by their origins in colonialism or patriarchy. With the subsequent development of normative political theory (exemplified by Rawls, Walzer and Singer), the study of past political ideas seemed a distraction. We should instead be 'doing our thinking for ourselves', to paraphrase Brian Barry, one of the most uncompromising of British normative political theorists (Barry 1965; Forrester 2019).

In this context, the revolution in the methodology of the history of political thought associated with Quentin Skinner and his colleagues claimed the whole terrain of past political thought for historians of thought. In magisterial essays – including 'Meaning and Understanding in the History of Ideas' (Skinner 1969) and his now-classic two-volume study *The Foundations of Modern Political Theory* (Skinner 1978), he set a benchmark for any credible history of political ideas and deprecated any alternative uses of 'historical' texts for studying political or international political thinking. Skinner's 1969 article provides a forceful criticism of both textualism and contextualism as appropriate objects of enquiries.

In his view, textualists are guilty of the mythology of coherence by claiming that a single book or text is the appropriate object of enquiry. This raises general questions about the appropriateness of reducing a writer's thought to a specific work, especially when many writers (including a number in this book) author a number of works. Not least amongst these questions is that about the coherence between earlier and later work. In the case of Thucydides, I focus on a single authoritative text, but by contrast both Machiavelli and Rousseau developed their arguments over a number of very different books. Does textualism impose a mythical uniformity across very distinct arguments?

The point can be more radical still if we question the coherence of an author's thought within a single text. Are texts, by which we normally mean books, constituted by a single argument or position? For Skinner, that begs the question of historical inquiry. By contrast, contextualists look beyond the boundaries of a book in order to understand its meaning. Books are seen as epiphenomena of broader social and economic forces, which in turn explain their meaning and power. For example, Skinner criticises C.B. Macpherson's interpretation of the English 17th-century philosophers Thomas Hobbes and John Locke as exponents of 'possessive individualism' or the rationalisation of the emerging class politics of early modern capitalism (Macpherson 1962).

The problem with this form of contextualism, however, is that it is reductionist. It shifts attention away from texts as autonomous worlds of ideas to their social context, but without adequately specifying the causal connection between these forces and the logic and form of a specific argument. In short, it says little about why Hobbes's arguments have the precise form that they do. After all, many contemporaries of Hobbes wrote books that do not rationalise the individualism associated with capitalism in the same way.

In response to the inadequacies of these rival approaches, Skinner offers his own methodology of linguistic contextualism, drawing on the speech-act theory of linguistic philosophers such as J.L. Austin and John Searle and the logic of question and answer underpinning the philosophy of history of R.G. Collingwood (Collingwood 1939).

Underlying Skinner's historical method is a claim about the priority of the historical approach to past political thought and an attempt to distinguish the authentic understanding of a past thinkers' utterances (speech-acts) from the impositions and distortions imposed on them by the ideological predilections of later interpreters. Utterances are a term of art derived from linguistic philosophy, but in Skinner's case these include the arguments, propositions and positions in complex works. So, Hobbes's *Leviathan* can be an utterance, as can his particular arguments about the state of nature, or indeed particular claims in those arguments that may be reducible to a passage or sentence. The historical question is one about what these utterances mean. This question is then answered by reconstructing the linguistic context, as opposed to a social and economic context. This step sets limits on what those utterances could have been understood to mean by the author's contemporary audience and thus in turn determine what the author could have been taken to be doing in making the utterance in the way he does (it is always a 'he' at this stage). Political language is always the result of someone's attempt to do something via speech and language. For Skinner, what that action is is an historical question and anything else is irrelevant.

Skinner's method has not been left unchallenged, and I will continue that challenge in what follows. Yet, the undoubted power of his arguments and intellectual agenda has transformed the study of past political thought and continues to be an inspiration for subsequent scholars. Aspects of his approach remain powerful tools of enquiry even if one does not accept his arguments for the priority of history. A variant of this linguistic-historicist approach has recently been extended into international theory in the work of David Armitage (Armitage 2012).

This book focuses on single texts, combinations of texts and in some cases combinations of thinkers who I argue make complimentary contributions to particular debates and perspectives. The chapters make little reference to linguistic contexts, albeit they also make little reference to other kinds of contexts as primary explanations, although each thinker is situated in an historical context. The arguments here also range beyond historically specific claims to assess the logical and trans-historical value of arguments and perspectives and the ways in which that thought is still deployed in contemporary debates and arguments. At best this might seem a crude and simplistic approach, perhaps suited to an introductory primer but one that should soon be put aside once serious enquiry begins. At worst, my approach may seem simply a category mistake, collapsing history into practice and advocacy.

In defending this approach and commending it to readers and students, I do not claim that Skinner's method of recovering historical meaning is incorrect, although I think it is too narrowly focused. Instead I want to reject Skinner's elevation of an historical use of past texts as the *only* intellectually respectable one. That position reinforces the idea that political thought and criticism cannot be liberated from the sources from which it emerges, and therefore cuts both of them off from the activity of political theorising. The consequent disregard for the arguments of past thinkers, now considered to be of only historical interest, has had a deleterious effect on contemporary political and international political theory. A narrowly historical account of political enquiry, especially one that effectively denies any authority to non-historical accounts of the meaning, scope and the fecundity of great political texts, seriously impoverishes our ability to engage with the challenges the world poses. Assigning priority to an historical approach to past thought only makes sense if this is the only credible way of approaching texts and thinkers from the past. That can only be shown to be right if there is something special about the historical-linguistic interpretation of meanings that Skinner advocates. If an historical-linguistic approach is only one amongst a number of valid ways of construing a text, then the special privileging of the historical over any other mode of interpretation does not hold and the possibility of creative interpretation remains part of political thinking.

Without getting into too technical a discussion at this stage, it is clear that the meaning of complex texts (even construed in the variety of ways that Skinner advocates) is not exhausted by the particular linguistic context of an utterance in the way that a specific verbal speech-act might be. Written texts are not exhausted by the range of meanings that an author might have consciously intended, or by a particular interpretation of the range of intentions that the discourse used might be interpreted to have. Because many texts are mediated through the passage of time, they accumulate meanings that are not simply imposed on a text but equally are not simply contained within the limits of a given linguistic context. Texts are not identical to spoken utterances, which are historically particular, contingent and fleeting. Texts have a life beyond the confines of their authors' lives, or the experiences of those who were the first readers. Linguistic contexts are themselves made up of constellations of speech-acts that in turn are parts of broader languages that transcend the historically local. This does not mean that anything goes in interpreting major texts, but it does problematise the issue of determining the linguistic context. My point is not simply that linguistic contexts are not self-identifying and determinate. I also want to claim that meaning in written texts is more than what is said in a particular context, as it is also shaped by readers, interpreters and critics even over long expanses of historical time. Furthermore, the historical-linguistic questions one can ask of a text are not the only questions. Ideological and philosophical use is an important part of what any particular reader could understand by the arguments of a text.

This is not to make the over-hasty claim of some postmodernists about the death of the author and the open texture of all texts, suggesting that anything goes. Instead, I want to follow Paul Ricoeur in asserting that there is surplus meaning in texts beyond authorial intention or the understanding of immediate audiences. So I make a claim for the idea of the *overstanding* of texts, which is associated with the American literary critic Wayne Booth (Booth 1979; 1988). Indeed, if we look at literary criticism it does seem ludicrous that the only relevant approach to the meaning of a text is a narrowly historical one. No one would make that claim of a literary canon. Of course, literary texts such as novels, plays and poems are different things to political texts, although that difference can be overstated and was not always seen as essential (Boucher 1985). The point I want to emphasise is that, just as with literary texts, the removal of improper readings (to use Booth's phrase) is not simply done by focusing on the specific historical context in which the text was situated. For Booth, the very idea of improper interpretations is not simply a problem to be eradicated but is actually part of the process of *overstanding* or arriving at interpretations that reflect the uses to which readers and critics put texts, uses that can in their turn withstand critical scrutiny. So, without diverting into a long theoretical discussion about the appropriate methodology of criticism (which Booth as a defender of pluralism and ethical reading denies can be given a single and final statement), we can identify intellectually credible practices and discourses that do not attach priority to an historical mode of understanding.

Whilst Skinner is correct to argue in his essays that many interpreters of political texts distort the meanings of thinkers they address, this is often done in the way any critic would operate, by critically engaging with the argument as opposed to a narrowly historical judgement. One can say a lot about the distortions of Hobbes as a possessive individualist without a linguistic contextual argument, and in doing so reinforce the view that quite a lot can be understood by careful reading, comparison and contrast with other texts and thinkers. Whilst it is easy to belittle careful reading – and Skinner does belittle the scholarship of John Plamenatz, just because he suggests we can make sense of a thinker's argument by careful and repeated reading – Plamenatz was not actually wrong (Plamenatz 1963). One can read Thucydides in translation and understand an enormous amount about the intricacies of his arguments about the significance of historical events and ideas. It would no doubt be better to be able to master him in the original Greek, but it is just false to suggest that, unless one reads them in their original languages and only alongside their contemporaries, one cannot properly understand an author's meaning and value as utterances. The concerns of international political theory are also normative, and in some cases prescriptive. For example, many arguments advocate as well as explain the idea of the right of war, and these are normative arguments that require normative criticism. In this way it is clear that our enquiry is not simply a form of literary criticism, unless of course that involves ethical and normative engagement.

I also reject the false binary between thinkers and texts. Some chapters below are focused on texts, some on a number of texts from the same thinker, and some compare two texts and thinkers as a way of introducing a broader theory or position. In so doing I am not making exhaustive arguments about the historical identity of a thinker or text and the theory or ideas contained therein. I limit historical claims to historical evidence and I am aware that all such interpretations are partial and incomplete, although that is true of any interpretation: it can never be final. Instead, these interpretations and critical engagements should be seen as akin to Weberian 'ideal types' and Kuhnian paradigms. They self-consciously place in brackets aspects of a complete description for ease of explanation and comparison, but they also account for the normative force of an approach to political agency (Kuhn 1962).

Thomas Kuhn introduced the idea of paradigms in his social epistemology of scientific understanding and theory-change, instead of providing a criterion of what counts as science such as Popper's falsifiability test (Popper [1934] 1959). For Popper, the mark of a genuine scientific claim is that it can, in principle, be falsified by experience and counterexamples, and, where it has not, that fact provides the measure of its credibility. Claims that could not in principle be falsified, especially those that include all possible counter arguments, are non-science propositions – such as religion, myth or comprehensive social theories such as Marxism. Kuhn adopted an account of science that he claimed was closer to the practice of science, where normal science is based around the working through of problems within the context of an overarching paradigm or conceptual framework. Scientific change is marked by the incremental accumulation of knowledge within a given paradigm, punctuated by the occasional revolutionary transformation that changes the overall framework in response to ineradicable anomalies within the previous paradigm. The idea is illustrated by the way in which Copernicus's heliocentric view of the universe changed the questions being asked by cosmologists and astronomers, and in turn enabled the new physics of Galileo and Newton to supersede the Ptolemaic universe of the ancient world. The Newtonian paradigm then served as a successful framework until Einstein and the quantum revolution of the early 20th century. In each case, Kuhn focuses on how the world view of a new paradigm reframes the normal practice of scientists, most of whom work on small incremental problems without considering the overall coherence of their work with that of all other scientists. It is the revolutions and paradigm shifts that provide the explanation of scientific progress and questions that are living and dead in normal science.

Kuhn developed his language of paradigms, and normal and revolutionary science, in the specific context of the sociology of knowledge and the practice of rigorous scientific enquiry. That said, the looser idea of paradigms as broad world views or frameworks that shape the structure of ordinary activity and understanding has meant that many scholars use it as a shorthand for self-contained intellectual frameworks that influence the way in which the problems and languages of activities can be characterised. In political and international theory, this allows for the framing of distinct ways of characterising what politics is, without falling into the trap of assuming that there is a single uncontroversial object of enquiry that is progressively revealed over the historical development or evolution of political theory. By characterising the texts, arguments and thinkers in this book as paradigmatic, I emphasise the way in which they provide frameworks for thinking about the nature of political agency and its institutional and territorial manifestation – without assuming that each thinker or argument is engaged with progressing beyond or overcoming the ideas of the previous thinkers in my narrative. These free-standing paradigmatic views may indeed be challenged and overcome by the ideas of other paradigmatic thinkers in this narrative. But their value is primarily as exemplifications of different ways of thinking about and organising violence, force and conflict as contributions to an understanding of the various challenges of politics. The justification for these ideal typical interpretations is how useful they are for the arguments that they are illuminating or exemplifying, and not whether they are simply accurate accounts of the intentions of particular historical figures, whether authors or their contemporary readers.

Traditions are not necessarily historicist

In one obvious sense, my reluctance to offer a history to underpin my identification of a 'canon' of major works (originally meaning sacred texts) is curious. After all, there is a chronological sequence here beginning with the ancient Greeks in the 5th century bce and ending with 20th-century thinkers such as Schmitt. If this narrative is not a history, what is? However, a chronology is just a list of texts in the order of their authorship or publication. It does not involve treating the past 'as past' by bringing it under any practical or philosophical mode of understanding in a way that emphasises the significance of its 'pastness' (Oakeshott 1983). I have argued above that the pastness of a text is not definitive of its interpretation and critical use. There is, however, another dimension of a history (as opposed to just a chronology), namely that the sequence is also ordered in terms of a philosophical category.

There are a number of possible ordering narratives that could be given for a canon that I explicitly reject, hopefully in an effective way – it will be for the reader to decide. For instance, we could interpret the movement through the chapters as a 'progress' in thought, a positive development from the Greeks to the modern state or its postmodern replacement. Many histories of political or international thought illustrate a progressive narrative, often referred to as 'Whig histories'. Historically, 'Whig history' is associated with the 19th-century historian Thomas Babington Macaulay, who saw the development of English constitutional politics as the historical triumph of the principles of the Glorious Revolution growing from 1688 to 1832. Whilst attractive for political and ideological purposes, such an approach subordinates the details and complexity of actual historical thought and events to a predetermined political goal, in the Whig case the triumph of English political liberalism. They claim that history has a purpose that led to and legitimates the dominant political order of the present. I am particularly sensitive to this risk. As the author of a book on political liberalism (Kelly 2005), it would be only too easy for me to fall into a trap of arguing that history supports the triumph of those values – in the same way that a crude reading of Francis Fukuyama's thesis about the end of history is supposed to show. Of course, Fukuyama's subtle argument did not actually argue for this sort of naïve historical determinism. Yet, many contemporary and historical neo-liberals, neo-conservatives and Marxists do hold such crude views about the logic of history and try to dress them up in the arguments of Hegel or Marx. Liberals assume the progressive triumph of constitutional states and free markets, whereas Marxists offer a mirror image of the progress through successive crises towards an ultimate socialist revolution supposed to overthrow all exploitation and conflict. Although the narrative is different, both approaches assume that history has a logic, one that leads to human redemption. The problems around progress, historical change and the idea of redemption are themes explored in a different way here. All the thinkers in this book challenge or repudiate and seek to overthrow liberal and Marxist theories of modernisation and redemption.

To avoid any confusion, then, let me state boldly that history does not have a logic, whether liberal, Marxist or otherwise. If one wants to defend liberal or conservative values, or democracy or authoritarianism, then those arguments have to be free-standing and cannot be read from the narrative of history. I would like to believe that some kind of 'improvement' justification can be given for pacific, liberal and humane values, but these claims need independent justificatory arguments. History can play a part in providing those justifications but it is not a complete argument. It is open to the possibility of alternative non-progressive narratives that deny the existence of any path of liberation from oppression and ignorance, and provide accounts of history as the continued unfolding of oppression and domination – with historical political ideas providing successive ideological justifications for that.

Another way of reading 'Whig' or progressive histories of thought, culminating in the triumph of human emancipation, upends them to show that the same people billed as advocates of liberty are at the same time justifiers of colonial expansion and domination, racial subordination and orientalism (Said 1979). History here only uncovers a narrative of domination and conflict. Advocates of decolonising the canon often point out that many early modern western political theorists such as Hobbes and Locke were associated with the colonial and imperial expansions of their countries, even if they did not explicitly defend final-stage colonial and mercantile imperialism. The history of colonialism and empire can provide an important interpretative context even if it does not explain what the author was trying to do. A more complex question is whether this association vitiates the arguments of such thinkers, especially when discussing their arguments that do not expressly support or justify colonial domination. If one is trying to defend a set of political values by building on the arguments of a past thinker, then it might well be the case that such a context challenges that case. But the wider social and economic context or the use to which a work is put should not necessarily determine the meaning of the work. This Janus-faced character of progressive histories has led postmodernists such as J.-F. Lyotard to reject all meta-narratives (Lyotard 1984). Just as the canon of thinkers here clearly eschews a progressivist reading of international political theory, it is also not endorsing a postmodernist critique, even though it clearly recognises the value in undermining naïve historical optimism.

Avoiding implicit meta-narratives is a challenge, but it is possible, unless one believes in a naïve historical reductionism that subordinates the actual ideas of individual texts and thinkers to such trans-historical ideas. By juxtaposing a series of thinkers, I intend to open a space for comparison and contrast, to enlighten debates about the nature and scope of political agency in the international realm, rather than to construct a pre-existing tradition such as 'realism' through which international politics should be understood. Meta-narratives such as realism, idealism, liberalism and Marxism are political constructions that take the ideas of thinkers or key concepts associated with groups of thinkers and combine them to serve the task of political motivation. This kind of political discourse is best described as ideological thinking (Freeden 1996). For many scholars of political thought, ideological thinking is disparaged as a false history, a category mistake, or a practical distortion of a thinker. This criticism can also be overblown. There is nothing intellectually disreputable about ideological narratives such as 'liberalism' or 'realism', as long as one does not make unjustifiable causal claims about them.

But, if one rejects any single ordering narrative and rejects ideological constructions of the canon, does that just leave us with a mere list of thinkers arranged in a crude chronology? More philosophically sophisticated histories of thought that do not wish to confine attention to the interpretation of particular thinkers often deploy the idea of 'traditions' in some kind of dialectical relationship, whereby different theoretical positions develop out of the conceptual oppositions between their implications and their 'negation' or antithesis: a classic example is the struggle between individualism and communitarianism. Here the history of thought is explained in terms of new perspectives developing as traditions in response to contradictions in the perspectives of philosophical predecessors. One can see this approach in the sequence of three traditions identified by Martin Wight, namely realism, rationalism and revolution – which he subsequently named, after thinkers exemplifying those stances, as the Machiavellian, Grotian and Kantian traditions (Wight 1994).

A more sophisticated and explicitly philosophical history of this kind is also offered by David Boucher with his distinction between empirical realism, universal moral order and historical reason. For Boucher, these constructions are not simply derived from groupings of pre-interpreted theorists, as is the case with Wight. Rather, they use philosophical concepts that derive from but are in turn vindicated by their contribution to the interpretations of those thinkers. These ordering concepts, in turn, have a philosophical standing. They explain the development of ideas not in terms of an external causal account of historical events but in terms of the dialectical movement between arguments overcoming their own internal contradictions. Such philosophical histories have a value in that they explain the paradigmatic importance of great thinkers within a canon by distinguishing them from minor or second-rate thinkers. They also acknowledge the significance of genuine philosophical dialogues between thinkers. For instance, whatever else he might also have been doing, Rousseau was indeed reacting to Hobbes. Triadic narratives (such as Wight's and Boucher's) are not the only ordering traditions. Although using it to order contemporary theorising and not the broad sweep of history, Brown proposes a similar dialectical confrontation between cosmopolitan and communitarian thinking (Brown 2002). And one could make a similar case between the familiar confrontation between realism and idealism that preoccupied international relations theory in the early years of that discipline. One interpretation of the canon in this book is that it outlines a 'realist' tradition that could be contrasted with others in just such a historical dialectic.

It is very easy to subvert the classical traditions of liberal or state-based progressivism by portraying them sublimated justifications of colonialism or cultural imperialism, which privilege the perspectives of western or white-occidental thinkers. A history of international theory (even a partial one covering a sub-tradition such as realism) that only includes white male thinkers raises a serious and genuine question about its claims to universality as the site of truth or reason. If the western canon is not the sole repository of reason and truth, then why does it not include non-western thinkers in its account of history? A simple, but hasty response, might be to qualify the history by geography and argue that there can only be partial histories – there can be no complete global history of international political thought. Even that position leaves open a question of inclusion. Any account that claims to provide a complete overview is always subject to the criticism that it includes some over others; it reinforces claims about importance, marginality and absence because of who is included and who is not. Some grounds for selective inclusion are benign because textbook canons are often constrained by the availability of accessible texts that students can use in the classroom. It is unrealistic to assume that any cohort of students can acquire the books (mostly in translation) that would allow a genuinely inclusive global curriculum of international and political thought. In other cases, selection is less benign because it assumes that there is an underlying rationale for creating a distinct canon of texts, not to merely illustrate the variety of thought but to converge on the right way of living and ordering politics and international affairs. In this version, common in political philosophy, the individual chapters are stages on the way to the truth or a right answer.

Selection poses a serious challenge to any author of a book like this one because merely denying that this is my self-conscious goal is never going to be enough. It will always be possible that the criteria of inclusion and the overall narrative contain implicit 'exclusions' or meta-narratives. Indeed, the much-maligned approach of 'deconstructionism' is concerned with precisely this issue: uncovering the ways in which conceptual languages always embody exclusions of various kinds. An obvious criticism, for instance, is that all the thinkers considered here are men.

Where are the women?

Is the omission of any women in my set of authors just an oversight or prejudice on my part? Have I left them out of this canon because of prejudices about the significance and sophistication of women thinkers? Am I working with a testosterone-fuelled view of international politics and affairs as overly conflictual, an approach that is primarily masculine – so where the high theory or important philosophising is done by men? I certainly hope that is not the case but this book remains an exclusively male canon of thinkers: that needs an explanation and justification.

The composition of the canon is not the only legitimate place to ask the question 'where are the women?' If we look at the arguments and texts of almost all those authors discussed here, the very place of women in the world they describe is at best problematic and at worst invisible. Thucydides' *History of the Peloponnesian War* contains no women amongst its cast of actors. There are no women generals, orators, demagogues or regular soldiers, and when they appear at all it is either to be slaughtered or sold into slavery as a class. Other historical or philosophically inclined thinkers (such as Machiavelli or Hobbes) fare no better. Women do not feature in any important way in the events, institutions, moral practices or conceptions of politics that are addressed by these exclusively male theorists. Alternatively, they do feature yet are subsumed under heavily gender-loaded categories such as 'man', which is supposed to just mean human but clearly does not. So, what is going on, and more importantly how can one explain and justify presenting a canon of enquiry that not only excludes women but seems also to deny the experience of approximately half or the human species?

To begin, I need to turn to feminist theory. Feminist theory is a relatively recent perspective, although there have been genuinely feminist political (if not international) theorists, such as Mary Wollstonecraft, since the 18th century. And of course there are many unjustly neglected women writers in earlier ages on some of the issues covered in this book (Owens and Rietzler 2021).

Amongst those early feminist theorists, often known now as first-wave theo-rists, the emphasis was on extending rights and privileges enjoyed by men to women, who had been traditionally excluded from such rights. Wollstonecraft, for example, argues that the rights of man popularised by Thomas Paine or the French Declaration should be extended to women. Later movements argu-ing for the extension of the franchise are similarly concerned with equalising a common set of rights, liberties and privileges rather than explaining under-lying structures of power that shape and dominate gendered identities. They are about opening access to opportunities, not addressing the shaping of those opportunities. First-wave theory was a corrective to the unequal application of traditional political theories of freedom and equality. It was not until the development of second-wave feminism and feminist theory from the 1950s to the 1970s that feminism began to mount a full critical assault on the con-cepts, theories and vocabularies that are used to understand social, political and international relations.

The legacy of first-wave feminism has done much to unlock the academy to women by equalising access to the resources of advanced education and aca-demic positions even if first-wave theorists have been most focused in domestic politics. The significance of these changes should not be underestimated but they do not address the whole problem. This can be seen in relation to the canon of thinkers. I need to show that I have not discriminated against women by focusing on male thinkers when equally qualified women authors are avail-able. Is there a canon of equally qualified women who could be included that I have merely chosen to overlook? This question is relatively easy to address in the negative – although it remains for the reader or subsequent student to decide whether they are ultimately persuaded by my choice (Zerelli 2008). Whilst there are exceptional female authors who wrote on politics, law and international affairs, these women are truly exceptional given the social, politi-cal and physical exclusion of women from education, politics and public life for much of western history (and indeed the history of most other recorded literary civilisations: patriarchy is not simply a problem for the west). Conse-quently, with honorary exceptions such as philosophers like Christine di Pisan and Mary Wollstonecraft, or travel writers and diarists such as Mary Wortley Montagu, there is no existing canon of major international theorists that I have ignored or discriminated against at least until the 20th century. Indeed, the fact of male power excluding women (or patriarchy, as it is known) fully explains the absence of significant women authors in this canon until the 20th century. This is not to ignore the fact that some exceptional women – Cleopatra, Eliza-beth I, Catherine the Great – did exercise political and military power.

The substance of the book is not an example of overt discrimination and exclusion of equally qualified voices, but is that a sufficient justification for this enquiry? Although I am not making this claim, a not uncharitable inference from what I have said would be that it will take millennia to find gender-balanced canons of historical political and international thought. Until then, male authors can just carry on with our gendered canon until female political and international theorists can catch up on the lost ground! Underlying this point is the assumption that the human experience, institutions and events captured in the theories and concepts examined in this canon are somehow universal. If so, the problem is merely one of who is writing about it, which can be addressed by randomly distributing gendered pronouns – as if the ideas were being developed and discussed by women, when that was clearly not the case. But, if we return to the example of Thucydides and the place of women in his *History*, primarily as victims of violence, we can see a greater issue of concern than simply exclusion from contributing to a philosophical canon. This is what is captured by second-wave feminists and feminist theorists and their turn to the discussion of patriarchy as a social construction of power.

From the 1960s and 1970s, the second wave of feminism has led to a sophisticated body of theory that addresses the underlying power structures that constitute gendered identities and their social and political consequences. As a result, the concepts that we use to think about the social and political world are shaped by the power relations between men and women. Complex power relations are exercised through language, discourse and theory, as well as being constituted by discourse. Thus, conceptual language about human nature and human rights can appear emancipatory, whilst at the same time presupposing conceptions of humanity that are essentially masculine and which therefore disadvantage and exclude women and contribute to their oppression. One way to characterise the relationship between first-wave and second-wave feminist theorists would be to see the latter as reacting against the former's view of emancipation as making women more like men and assisting women to compete in a competition that privileges masculinity. The criticism of first-wave feminists is that they see the problem as equalising opportunities rather than challenging the hidden power structures that create those gendered-opportunities in the first place. Feminist care theorists often criticise natural and human rights individualism as masculinist because it privileges autonomy and independence over moral considerations of relationality, care and empathy. Care theory can seem to reduce these perspectives to inherently feminine attributes that follow from women's biological role in nurturing and childrearing, in contrast to masculine identities of protector and provider. But care theory does not have to be biologically reductive. Even if some moral responses are socialised through gendered roles in caring, it might nevertheless be the case that these can be liberated from socially constructed women's experience, and used to challenge and reshape social and political relations that are unduly distorted by masculine moral categories that reflect the predominance of male power. Such a perspective is a valuable source of criticism of the paradigms of political agency discussed in this book. Yet, taking that further to excluding such theorists is not a denial of their importance but merely of their relevance given that the point of the book is not to provide a full critical survey of all the ways of under-standing political agency. As I have said earlier in this introduction, the canon here deliberately excludes perspectives that make the concept of 'the political' derivative of moral notions such as care or justice.

Second-wave theory has turned feminist analysis into a critical and norma-tive theory, which sees social and political relationships as social construc-tions that need to be analysed and transformed rather than as immutable facts. Power structures and discourses are malleable and can be transformed. Femi-nist gender analysis is a tool for that transformative politics which now ranges beyond the distribution of opportunities, rights, liberties and privileges and instead focuses on the power relations of domination and subordination that work through our conceptual and philosophical languages.

One of the implications of the success of second-wave feminist theory is the development of identity politics, which acknowledges the diversity of human identity and the power structures that are reflected in the plural nature of per-sonal identity. People are not just men or women; they also have racial, national, sexual, gender, age and class identities in combination that link them to social groups who may be the beneficiaries of power relations in some respects, whilst being victims of overt and covert oppression in other respects: think of young, black, middle-class, university-educated women and white, working-class, non-graduate older men. Power relations include and exclude, oppress and dominate groups in different ways, but none are totally free from the play of dominant power structures in society. For some identity theorists, this fact has downplayed the importance of feminism as an emancipatory project, because it is focused on one amongst many sites of oppression and domination. Yet there is something profoundly important and historically resilient about gendered oppression that many feminists capture through the idea of intersectionality, which emphasises the ways in which various sources of social and personal identity are irreducibly interlinked for the most marginalised groups and voices in society.

In light of this second-wave and identity-based critique, histories of thought cannot simply be a long list of male authors. Such histories are also gendered in the sense that the conceptual languages and discourse covered by these things will inevitably reflect gendered social relations and patriarchal dominance. At its most obvious, this will be seen in the absence of women as agents in Thucydides, or in the overt sexism of Machiavelli. But it is also present in the predominantly masculinist discourse of human nature, natural law and rights in Hobbes or Rousseau. Even radical thinkers such as Lenin and Mao reduce women's oppression to a mere epiphenomenon of the more real class relations that shape late capitalism. So described, might it seem that books such as this one are guilty as charged?

In response, I acknowledge the importance of the second-wave feminist cri-tique but do not think it vitiates the conception of the book. That the narrative of this book is open to feminist critique does not vitiate its point, because I am not offering a defence of the substance of each argument from all or any criticism. Work is being done on exploring a feminist canon in international relations and political theory, especially in the 20th century (Owens and Rietzler 2021). The task here is to show that there is no deliberate exclusion and also to recognise that the main questions are not in the choice of canonical texts but rather in how they are read. After all, there is no set of thinkers from the past who are free from gendered power relations, and there is no prospect for future theory that is also not in some way implicated in the social construction of discourse. Feminist theory, or any other criticism of this kind, is a second-order activity that operates upon pre-critical interpretations. A book of this kind that is designed to set out a number of distinct perspectives is therefore logically prior to this second-order activity. Reducing one to the other would not only result in a different book but would still leave open that prior activity of interpretation as ostension (the act of showing or presenting), after which criticism follows.

I do not offer a feminist study of international political thought, or speculate whether the approaches discussed in this book must collapse under feminist scrutiny. However, I acknowledge that the real challenge for this book will be how far it lends itself to critical engagement with the discourses of power that are immanent within the thought and thinkers discussed, and acknowledges the ways the theories and concepts discussed can reinforce or explain those relationships of power and domination.

Overview of the argument

The book comprises nine substantive chapters and a concluding essay. Each chapter is presented as a distinct paradigm of politics in the international realm, rather than a stage in the unfolding of a single narrative explaining or legitimising the current world order. Whilst these paradigms may rise and fall, the overall argument of the book is that they remain effective sources and structures for thinking about international politics and agency. None of them can be simply confined to the past as of no more than historical or antiquarian interest. I have followed a rough chronological order but this is not supposed to illustrate an unfolding historical development.

The book begins with the most famous ancient Greek writer on the modern field of international affairs. Thucydides' *History of the Peloponnesian War* is one of the few foundational texts in international political thought. The chapter introduces Thucydides' work and his influence on theory and history and considers his role as a theorist of realism. I examine the nature of and basis of realism as the default perspective of international politics. Thucydides also provides an account of the collapse of Athenian democracy under the pressure of war, so the chapter explores the themes of democracy, strategy and leadership in wartime. Thucydides gives an account of a system of Greek political communities (poleis) operating in the absence of an overarching hegemonic power. This is a model of international order that continues to dominate international affairs and diplomacy. It is an account of the dynamics of international politics that is still thought to have lessons for present-day international politics and a changing world order.

The second chapter turns to the late Roman period and the rise of Christianity in the work of Augustine of Hippo. Augustine is considered to be one of the most important thinkers of the Christian era. He is an important source of ideas about the nature of politics, war and peace and a critic of theories of historical progress. Augustine's political thinking is located in an overview of his theology and the impact of his understanding of the Christian story of redemption on thinking about the nature, scope and claims of political and moral authority. The central question is whether the fundamental teachings of Christianity tend towards a utopian and pacificist view of political relationships, or is the legacy of Christianity in politics and international affairs more properly understood as a form of realism? Augustine's thought is central in the development of 'just war' theory and had a big impact on the development of 20th-century Christian realism and the marked anti-utopianism of post-Cold War liberalism.

Machiavelli is tackled in Chapter 4. He is one of the most controversial of political thinkers because his ideas ran counter to many traditional conceptions of politics, such as the primary role of the common good and the need for political power to be constrained by moral or ethical obligations. In the context of international political thought, Machiavelli is presented as a realist and an originator of the idea of *raison d'état* (reason of state). I advance the stronger claim that Machiavelli challenges the idea of any stable political societies or peoples. Instead, he focuses attention on the founding or refounding of political communities in a world of constant change and revolution. Machiavelli is also concerned with the character of leadership and the ways in which temporary and fleeting political power should be exercised to create and maintain regimes. Rather than steering a careful path around the idea of ethics in politics, he explores the nature of political life outside of a moralistic, ethical and legalistic framework. In this way, he poses one of the most striking challenges to the conceptual framework of modern politics.

Thomas Hobbes is covered in Chapter 5. He is one of the first great theorists of the concept of sovereignty and of the modern state, and the original theorists of the state system that lies at the heart of contemporary international relations. His theory of the sovereign state is set out in *Leviathan* and the chapter explores Hobbes's place in modern international relations theory alongside his intellectual context and wider materialist philosophy of humanity. He offers an account of human nature and the state of nature, as well as a contractarian account of the origin of sovereign power. The nature and extent of Hobbes's account of absolutism is another focus, and his rejection of international political society derived from early modern papalism. He sees international relations as solely between sovereign states, explaining the way in which contemporary international relations theory has absorbed him into the tradition or realism and interstate anarchy.

The second of the great social contract theorists is John Locke. In contrast to Hobbes, Locke is considered an early liberal because he argued for a constitutionally limited conception of sovereignty that protects individuals' rights to life, liberty and property. The sixth chapter begins with an overview of Locke's social contract theory and his account of the constitutional sovereign state. On the state of nature, the law and right of nature, and the theory of consent, Locke differs importantly from Hobbes. He also formulated a right of revolution and a theory of property that is linked to trade and colonial acquisition. Locke's connection to colonialism and its impact on his theory has been highlighted by what is known as the 'colonial turn' in modern political theory. I also discuss Locke's state theory and his views on the normative status of non-constitutionally limited powers and the extent to which they should be recognised by legitimate states, Although he is often thought of as a source for liberal idealism because of his moralistic natural law theory, his relationship to the realism/idealism distinction is more subtle, and he defended a militant or crusading liberal order in the international realm.

The seventh chapter gives an overview of Rousseau's writings and his influence on international thought and theory. Once again, the central concept is sovereignty and its political and international implications. However, Rousseau's main arguments concern the idea of popular sovereignty, and how the concept of sovereign power can be maintained and exercised collectively by a free sovereign people who remain free citizens. In this respect, it is a criticism and a development of the concept as deployed by Hobbes or by Locke. Rousseau is critical of the concept of state sovereignty as a distinct juridical or law-like entity. Instead, sovereignty for him can only be a power of a people acting in accordance with a general will. In order to be a sovereign people, the citizens need to think of themselves as more than a multitude or collection of individuals trying to secure and protect their private interests. To maintain that idea of a sovereign general will, the people need a strong conception of identity and to avoid the corrupting power of commercial society and cosmopolitan engagement. Rousseau's arguments are a precursor of an inward-looking nationalism and anti-cosmopolitanism that has seen a recent recurrence in anti-globalisation movements, political and economic nationalism, national solidarity and the rise of identity politics.

Clausewitz is an unfamiliar figure in histories of political thought and, when he is discussed, it is mostly as a footnote to discussions of the state or as a marginal figure of interest only to a small professional readership concerned with strategy and military affairs. The eighth chapter focuses on Clausewitz's great work *On War*, a book as much a work of political theory as any of the other texts I discuss. I begin by situating Clausewitz in the climate of state and military theory that grew up in Prussia in response to the French Revolution, the idea of the rights of man and the citizen, and the consequent wars for national liberation. I explore the methodology of his military theory as a development of a new policy science, and discuss his account of the concept of war and the place of genius and friction, which aligns with a Romantic critique of crude Enlightenment rationalism. The concept of the 'paradoxical trinity' (which covers the interplay between the people, the army and the government) is examined next, especially the question of whether there are actually one or two 'trinities' at play in Clausewitz's work. The concept of the 'trinity' illustrates Clausewitz's analysis of the deep interplay of hatred, chance, and reason or policy as the dynamic forces that explain war and drive international relations. The chapter moves on to consider the priority of offence and defence in the conduct of operations and concludes with an extended discussion of Clausewitz's influence in a modern age characterised by violence and war.

Whilst Marx has undoubtedly had a significant impact on the development of social and political theory, it is through his followers, especially Lenin and Mao, that his doctrines have had the greatest impact on international thought and affairs. Marx theorised (or, for some, predicted) the revolutionary overthrow of capitalism, but it was actually Lenin in 1917 and Mao in 1949 who presided over the two great socialist revolutions of the 20th century. The ninth chapter explores their writings on the theory and practice of revolutionary politics that have had the most impact on international political thinking. A brief introduction to the Marxist framework precedes a discussion of Lenin's theory of the vanguard party as the vehicle for establishing a dictatorship of the proletariat, an idea he took seriously and placed at the centre of revolutionary struggle. Marx's theory of imperialism as the latest phase of capitalism and the role of violence in the revolutionary overcoming of the state is examined next. Mao's thought, in turn, transformed the legacy of Leninism in the specific contexts of the Chinese struggle against imperialism by theorising the peasant masses as a revolutionary class, which transformed his account of revolution. I also explore Mao's writings on revolutionary war and the role of guerrilla forces. The chapter concludes by assessing how both Lenin's and Mao's thinking about the practice of revolutionary politics has impacted on contemporary political and international theory.

Carl Schmitt rejects the optimism of the contemporary liberal internationalist view of the global order that has been dominant since the end of World War II. Reviewed in Chapter 10, Schmitt is an uncompromising conservative thinker who has influenced theorists of the left and right. He saw the international system of states as a bulwark against the violence and conflict that he saw as underlying the universalist and globalist tendencies of liberal and revolutionary politics. His ideas are a response to the decline of European power, the rise of Cold War ideological opposition, and the emergence of new global hegemons such as the United States. Schmitt both provided a critique of liberal optimism and globalisation and at the same time attempted to salvage essential concepts such as sovereignty, war and enmity as a way of disciplining politics and responding to the decline of state power. I cover Schmitt's criticism of liberal democracy, and the concept of 'the political' as an examination of what sovereignty is and where it now resides following the abandonment of liberal popular sovereignty theories and nationalism. Finally, I consider his critique of global liberalism and international law.

Each chapter is free-standing and can be read and understood on its own. However, the juxtaposition of these paradigmatic approaches to the nature, scope and organisation of international politics and agency also shows the importance of three linking issues that frame the overall narrative. These are violence and politics, temporality and change, and the meaning and significance of history. These issues recur across the distinct treatments of individual authors, and are also illustrated in the methodologies deployed in shaping the discussion of these issues, whether these are historical, philosophical or political-theological. The final chapter examines the re-emergence of realism as an approach to political theory and how this 'realist turn' illuminates or complicates international political theory, which has been suspicious of the hegemony of realism in the wider discipline of international relations.

Using this book

Each of the chapters on a paradigmatic thinker gives a free-standing introduction to their perspective on the international realm, and so I have deliberately avoided narrative themes that span multiple chapters. I hope that readers will want to read all chapters but also that it will be useful to students studying just some of the authors covered here, and to general readers interested in particular authors. Each chapter outlines the context that the thinker operated in, the structure of their argument, and its implications for their views of politics – as an activity prior to the challenge of critical analysis and engagement. Covering an author does not entail endorsement of any of their arguments, but rather highlights the need to understand their structure before they can be critically analysed or (more importantly) organised into a distinctive interpretative narrative such as political realism.

Each chapter also outlines an historical introduction to the relevant texts being addressed, looking at critical themes and debates that provide the interpretation of the argument. A thinker like Hobbes wrote a number of works, but I am concentrating on the argument in *Leviathan* (1651) and its implications. In the case of Rousseau or Schmitt, I link a number of works to identify their main arguments, but even here I am not providing a complete overview of all of the thinkers' works. Augustine, Machiavelli, Rousseau and Schmitt each have a large corpus (or body of work), not all of which is relevant for understanding the position set out here. My treatment does not presuppose that readers are already familiar with the thinker, nor do I require students to master all the intricacies of an individual's thought. Some scholars in political thought spend their entire careers working on a single author or a small part of one author's output. This book cannot cover everything. It will have achieved its purpose if it inspires readers to go back to the main texts or to become familiar with the continuing scholarly debates.

It is not necessary to read chapters in their chronological order. Indeed, I am explicitly not claiming that there is an unfolding historical narrative that informs an argument about the triumph of a particular way of organising politics or international affairs. In principle, the book's narrative could be read backwards, with later thinkers providing insights and questions that can be used to frame the interpretations of their predecessors. Whilst reading the past in light of the present is a familiar basis for philosophical critique, there is also paradoxically some scope for this at the interpretive level.

All of the interpretations and arguments set out here are built on a vast scholarship that exists in the case of each thinker and text. It would be easy and unhelpful to overload readers with summaries and lists of the scholarship on each thinker. Each sentence could be accompanied by extensive bibliographic referencing because the act of scholarly writing always involves a complex synthesis of what has been read or argued elsewhere. Some of the readings I offer will be familiar and potentially controversial because they involve my taking sides in interpretive and scholarly debates and reflect my own studies over a number of decades. I hope that readers will challenge and debate those readings in time. For that reason, each chapter has a minimum of internal references. Where they occur, these references are to key positions in debates and not simply sources of a specific idea that underpins my interpretation of paraphrase. I have tried, but not always succeeded, in reducing the references to the work of my peers as I try to focus attention on the main text.

The bibliographies at the end of each chapter identify some of the more important scholarly works I have drawn on, or which best address the issues covered in the chapter. They are not intended to be comprehensive – indeed, that would not be possible – but to help readers with university or public library access to follow up and question my exposition. For the main texts, I have chosen easily available scholarly editions that are also authoritative. I have quoted relatively extensively, subject to the normal constraints of scholarly fair use. The quotations are sufficient to guide the reader in making sense of the key arguments. That said, none of the arguments or claims made for any of the thinkers discussed depends upon a particular translation or edition and that is why I have not linked digitally to those text versions. Any available online version will be adequate to the task of building a first understanding and familiarity with the main thinkers. There are no references that are time-dependent and no data sets or empirical materials that need a direct link or which could become unavailable.

The end of chapter references also includes a brief bibliography of key secondary literature about each main thinker,

Finally, the LSE Press guide at the end of the book has some advice on finding open access versions of the main texts for readers without such backup.

Bibliography

Armitage, David. (2012). *Foundations of Modern International Thought*. UK: Cambridge University Press.

Barry, Brian. (1965). *Political Argument*. UK: Routledge and Kegan Paul.

Booth, Wayne C. (1979). *Critical Understanding: The Powers and Limits of Pluralism*. USA: University of Chicago Press.

Booth, Wayne C. (1988). *The Company We Keep: An Ethics of Fiction*. USA: University of California Press.

Boucher, David. (1985). *Texts in Context*. Netherlands: Martinus Nijhoff.

Boucher, David. (1998). *Political Theories of International Relations*. UK: Oxford University Press.

Brown, Chris. (2002). *Sovereignty, Rights and Justice: International Political Theory Today*. UK: Polity Press.

Brown, Chris. (2015). *International Society, Global Polity*. UK: Sage.

Brown, Chris; and Ainley, Kirstin. (2005). *Understanding International Relations*, 3rd edn. UK: Palgrave.

Brown, Chris; and Eckersley, Robyn. (eds) (2018). *The Oxford Handbook of International Political Theory*. UK: Oxford University Press.

Bull, Hedley. (2002). *The Anarchical Society: A Study of Order in World Politics*, 3rd edn. UK: Palgrave.

Collingwood, Robin G. (1939). *An Autobiography*. UK: Clarendon Press.

Doyle, Michael W. (1997). *Ways of War and Peace*. USA: Norton.

Forrester, Katerina. (2019). *In the Shadow of Justice: Postwar Liberalism and the Remaking of Political Philosophy*. USA: Princeton University Press.

Freeden, Michael. (1996). *Ideologies and Political Theory a Conceptual Approach*. UK: Oxford University Press.

Fukuyama, Francis. (1989). 'The End of History?' *The National Interest*, vol. 16, pp. 3–18.

Fukuyama, Francis. (1992). *The End of History and the Last Man*. USA: Free Press.

Gaddis, John Lewis. (2018). *On Grand Strategy*. UK: Allen Lane.

Habermas, Jürgen. (1998). *The Postnational Constellation*. UK: Polity Press.

Habermas, Jürgen. (2005). *Old Europe, New Europe, Core Europe*, ed. Daniel Levy, Max Pensky and John C. Torpey. UK: Verso.

Kelly, Paul. (1998). 'Contextual and Non-Contextual Histories of Political Thought', in J. Hayward, B. Barry, and A. Brown (eds) *The British Study of Politics in the Twentieth Century*. UK: British Academy, pp. 37–62.

Kelly, Paul. (2005). *Liberalism*. UK: Polity.

Kuhn, Thomas S. (1962). *The Structure of Scientific Revolutions*. USA: University of Chicago Press.

Lasswell, Harold. (1936). *Politics: Who Gets What, When and How*. UK: McGraw Hill.

Lyotard, Jean-Francois. (1984). *The Post-Modern Condition: A Report on Knowledge*. USA: University of Minnesota Press.

Macpherson, Crawford B. (1962). *The Political Theory of Possessive Individualism*. UK: Oxford University Press.

Moller-Okin, Susan. (2013). *Women in Western Political Thought*. USA: Princeton University Press.

Nye, Joseph. (2015). *Is the American Century Over?* UK: Polity.

Oakeshott, Michael. (1983). *On History and Other Essays*. UK: Blackwell.

Owens, Patricia; and Rietzler, Katharina (2021). *Women's International Thought: A new History*. UK: Cambridge University Press.

Plamenatz, John P. (1963). *Man and Society*, 2 vols. UK: Longmans.

Popper, Karl. (1959). *The Logic of Scientific Discovery*. UK: Routledge.

Said, Edward. (1979). *Orientalism*. UK: Penguin.

Skinner, Quentin. (1969). 'Meaning and Understanding in the History of Ideas' *History and Theory*, vol. 8, pp. 3–53.

Skinner, Quentin. (1978). *The Foundations of Modern Political Theory*, 2 vols. UK: Cambridge University Press.

Strauss, Leo; and Cropsey, Joseph. (1987). *History of Political Philosophy*. USA: University of Chicago Press.

Voegelin, Eric. (1952). *The New Science of Politics: An Introduction*. USA: University of Chicago Press.

Waltz, Kenneth N. [1979] (2010). *Theory of International Politics*. USA: Waveland Press.

Wight, Martin. (1994). *International Theory: The Three Traditions*, ed. Gabriele Wight and Brian Ernest Porter. UK: Leicester University Press.

Zerelli, Linda. (2008). 'Feminist Theory and the Canon of Political Thought', in John S. Dryzek, Bonnie Honig and Anne Phillips (eds) *The Oxford Handbook of Political Theory*. UK: Oxford University Press, pp. 106–124.

PART I

Conflict, war and government
before the state era

CHAPTER 2

Thucydides

The naturalness of war

Thucydides' *History of the Peloponnesian War* is one of the few foundational texts in international political thought. I introduce Thucydides'
work and his influence on international relations theory and subsequent history. I consider his role as a theorist of realism and examine
the nature of and basis of realism as the default perspective of international politics. Thucydides also provides an historical account of the collapse of Athenian democracy under the pressure of war, so this chapter
explores the themes of democracy, strategy and leadership in wartime.
Thucydides' account of a system of political communities (poleis) interacting in the absence of an overarching hegemonic power is a model of
international order that continues to dominate international affairs and
diplomacy. Its account of the dynamics of international politics is still
thought by many to have lessons for present-day international politics
and a changing world order.

Prior to the first Gulf War in 2003 it was common to find commentators and
scholars framing the debate about the war or its subsequent conduct through
reference to the Greek historian Thucydides. Perhaps this is not surprising from
classically educated journalists or academics writing 'op-ed' pieces, but references to Thucydides also extended into the western military itself. Thucydides

How to cite this book chapter:
Kelly, Paul. 2022. *Conflict, war and revolution: The problem of politics in international
political thought.* London: LSE Press, pp. 31–61.
DOI: https://doi.org/10.31389/lsepress.cwr.b License: CC BY.

remains part of the academic education of the officer class, especially (though not exclusively) in the U.S. Many leading figures (such as General Colin Powell) quoted (or misquoted) Thucydides as part of the intellectual justification of their strategy and doctrine. For makers of foreign policy, defending or challenging a war of choice, the lessons of Thucydides are no doubt too good to ignore. This is by no means a recent phenomenon. Soldiers and politicians as well as scholars, have drawn on Thucydides' history of a relatively short period of struggle between two dominant ancient Greek poleis, under the looming influence of the nearby Persian empire (Morley 2014). Of course, many great texts in history are used for the justification, clarification and exemplification of positions, ideas and principles that could not have been intended by the author. Yet there is something peculiarly powerful about Thucydides for those interested in international political theory (Boucher 2018). It is hard to read his argument – which goes well beyond just a narrative – without seeing it as echoing contemporary events, characters and choices. A particularly pertinent example is provided by the former dean of Harvard's Kennedy School of Government, Graham Allison, with his thesis of the 'Thucydides trap' as a way of framing the challenge for the U.S. of managing the inevitable rise of China to the status of a global power (Allison 2017).

A later thinker, Machiavelli, famously encouraged the study of ancient and especially Roman history for its lessons for the politics of his times – on the grounds that human nature is fundamentally constant and so the past contains a source of illuminating and still-relevant arguments and lessons. However, few people now read Machiavelli in that way. By contrast, Thucydides does seem to offer a window into politics of successive ages including our own. For this reason alone, Thucydides' *History* remains for me one of the most penetrating and provocative texts in any canon of international political thinking and one of the few books that never exhausts restudy. This is why he seems the appropriate place to start this book, in contrast to Herodotus, with whom Ryan begins his account of political theory (Ryan 2012, pp. 5–31), because Thucydides describes many of the problems that are taken to be canonical for international theory and for the tradition of realism in international relations. Whether the claim withstands scholarly scrutiny, Thucydides is widely thought of as the first and perhaps greatest international theorist.

About Thucydides' life we know relatively little, other than what is revealed by his authorship and his role in the events that he narrates. He was born sometime between 460 and 455 bce and when the war he describes began he was in his mid- to late twenties, not much older than many modern university and military academy students. He was born into a wealthy Athenian family of distinction (despite bearing a Thracian, as opposed to an Athenian, name). His high status or social class is reflected in his birth but also in his support for Pericles (one of the key figures in his account of Athenian politics and strategy), and his hostility to other figures such as Cleon, who are associated with populism and the vulgarity of 'new money'. This perhaps explains Ryan's reference to Thucydides as a conservative (Ryan 2012, p. 12) and Leo Strauss's sympathy for him, despite his not being part of the canon of philosophers (Strauss 1978, pp. 139–241). During the early war period, he served in a number of campaigns. He was elected general in 424 and commanded the naval force in the area of Thrace and its primary Athenian colony, Amphipolis. When Amphipolis fell to the Spartan general Brasidas, Thucydides was tried and convicted of treason and exiled. It was during this period of exile that he began writing his history. He did not give the book a formal title but it has come down to us in a variety of forms as the *War between the Peloponnesians and the Athenians* or in a more popular form the *History of the Peloponnesian War*. Thucydides lived to see Athens's final defeat at the hands of Sparta and the beginning of the collapse of the Athenian Empire, but he did not live to complete the work, which famously ends mid-sentence 'He first went to Ephesus where he made a sacrifice to Artemis …' (Book VIII, 109).

Thucydides contrasts his enterprise with that of mythologies like Homer's, and more recent mixed modes of writing such Herodotus' *History*. This effort makes his work one of the most important early exemplars of a distinctively historical style of writing. Yet, this achievement as a historian can also mislead and direct attention away from his contribution to political thinking. Without undermining his importance as an historian and contributor to the development of historiography, I chiefly consider here his contribution to thinking about international politics and political theory. Thucydides will be used to illustrate an important contention of this book, that historians are often some of the most sophisticated and important theorists (indeed philosophers) of politics and international affairs. However, Thucydides does not offer an account of the human good and the ideal political arrangements in which that can be realised, and so he does not fit with one dominant account of the task of political philosophy. This latter claim challenges the categorical distinction and hierarchical ordering of experience that preoccupies many who write about the history of political thought and international political theory (Oakeshott 1975; Boucher 2018).

Although both Herodotus and Thucydides are both widely described as the founders of history as a distinct form of enquiry, many subsequent scholars follow Thucydides' own claims to be a distinctive and rigorous historian as opposed to storyteller. He opens his book with reflections on the activity of what we now call historical enquiry, and gives a clear and forceful statement of it:

> I do not think that one will be far wrong in accepting the conclusions I have reached from the evidence which I have put forward. It is better evidence than that of the poets, who exaggerate the importance of their themes, or the prose chroniclers, who are less interested in telling the

truth than in catching the attention of their public, whose authorities cannot be checked, and whose subject matter, owing to the passage of time, is mostly lost in unreliable streams of mythology. We may claim instead to have used only the plainest evidence and to have reached conclusions which are reasonably accurate. [Book I, 21] (Thucydides 1972, p. 47)

By 'poets', Thucydides means Homer, and by 'prose chroniclers' he means his near-contemporary Herodotus. The commitment to facts and evidence that would be recognised by those who witnessed the events is an important basis for his claim to write a distinctively historical science. His stance has been praised by countless subsequent writers from the ancient world and early moderns such as Thomas Hobbes, to the present day. His empirical and factual approach is clearly exemplified in the detailed narrative of events, set out in a chronological sequence.

But his reliance on facts is also combined with other elements to support his claim to be the founder of history as a distinct form of literary enquiry. What counts as facts remains an important and philosophically controversial question for all historians. After all, one of the key elements of any historical narrative is to account for and justify the relevant facts. For example, 20th-century structuralist historians of the *longue durée* such as Ferdinand Braudel emphasised climate and geography as central factual evidence (almost to the exclusion of what particular actors did to each other). So, Thucydides makes much of a rationalistic naturalism in helping to determine what counts as facticity. Unlike Herodotus, he gives virtually no place to the gods or supernatural explanations. Whilst auguries (signs of what will happen in the future) are reported, neither they nor the gods are causal players in accounts of events. Similarly, the eruptions of Mount Etna are merely reported as background geological context. To his own contemporaries this was a significant point, because most would have still occupied a world that was shaped by supernatural forces. Indeed, Thucydides' account of the desecration of the Herms prior to the Sicilian Expedition illustrates how important religion and the supernatural in politics remained for the majority of the Athenian populace. His scepticism about supernatural causes is particularly clear in his treatment of the plague that hit Athens, which is described as a social and clinical fact and not as a sign from the gods. For Thucydides, whatever causal explanations he wishes to make, it is sufficient to base these on natural facts about individuals and the facts about the political communities and institutional cultures from which they emerge.

A further element of his history that has been praised by subsequent historians is his purported impartiality in explaining events. Thucydides was both an Athenian and a participant in the war, especially in the unsuccessful defence of Amphipolis. However, he managed to avoid writing as a supporter of the Athenian cause or (in his own case) using the history as a personal vindication of his actions and against his accusers. Finally, although the history contains much drama, it is densely written and not designed to entertain its readership. In clear contrast to Herodotus, with his interesting asides, speculations and local anecdotes, Thucydides has an almost relentless concentration on the events as they unfolded in their own terms. So much was this so that many subsequent readers took it as a failure of the work, because it limited its rhetorical and didactic usefulness as a training for future politicians. Thucydides is praised by the moderns for focusing on the events as they happened. Although he clearly thinks his *History* will have a lasting value for posterity, he writes as a scientist organising materials so as to reveal the truth.

All that said, one important feature of his enquiry has troubled subsequent modern theorists of scientific history – namely, his reliance on speeches. Approximately one-quarter of the text is comprised of direct speech, including some orations that have become the centre piece of the text for subsequent readers. If Thucydides aimed for a version of historical science, how can he place such reliance on speeches? As a contemporary and participant, Thucydides would have witnessed some of the speeches and may have even have had written texts to consult. But for many of the reported speeches he would have been relying on reports that are impossible to check, and maybe even on reconstructions after the event accomplished by collating testimony from witnesses. Some philosophers of history have criticised his method here for allowing philosophical speculation to drive the narrative, as opposed to a pure historical consciousness: hence R.G. Collingwood's preference for Herodotus over Thucydides (Collingwood 1993). Yet, even where Thucydides used speeches extensively, he was careful that these are not too didactic and that they do not distract from the narrative evidence of context. My purpose here is not historiography, or to study the development of historical enquiry, so it is ultimately irrelevant whether Thucydides provides or fails to provide a scientific history of the Second Peloponnesian War. It is sufficient that, whilst one can mount challenges to the historicity of his narrative (Kagan 2009), it is considered accurate enough for it still to be the primary evidence for the broad narrative of the Second Peloponnesian War in sources like the *Cambridge Ancient History* (1992).

Does including speeches as the systematisation of political platforms make Thucydides' narrative better as a source for political theory? Whatever else Thucydides is doing, he is not pursuing the sort of abstract philosophical enquiry one finds in Plato and Aristotle. So does that mean that Thucydides fails to be either a proper historian or a proper philosopher? The rest of this chapter argues that Thucydides' method and substantive arguments form a distinctive contribution to international theory that ranks alongside the great philosophical thinkers in the canon, but first I need to say something in general about Thucydides as a theorist.

For scholars of political theory, issues of demarcation are crucial in determining what their object of enquiry actually is. Contemporary analytical philosophy is fairly relaxed about what it is to be a philosopher or to think philosophically. Philosophy is not a science and therefore does not have a distinct body of knowledge appropriate to it. Rather, it is a form of intellectual discipline, which for analytical philosophers is marked by logical and linguistic analysis and criticism of arguments. On the other hand, scholars of the history of political philosophy, such as followers of Leo Strauss, take a substantive view of political philosophy as focusing on the good life for humanity and the appropriate institutions in which that form of life can flourish (Strauss and Cropsey 1987). Yet, even by their own standards, that approach seems an arbitrary and circular definition, as the inclusion of a chapter on Thucydides in the third edition of their book makes clear.

For those informed by the idealist philosophical tradition, such as Oakeshott and Boucher, philosophy is not merely the application of a set of mental tools but involves the categorical distinction of the activity from other forms of human experience. Consequently, for such thinkers, distinguishing between historians, political pamphleteers and philosophers is crucial. But the distinction is not the only issue since the hierarchy of modes of experience is also important. Mapping the distinction between modes of experience is one thing but assigning a superiority to the most abstract mode of experience is another. Abstraction is merely a tool of thought largely achieved by 'bracketing' predicates in statements, and it is not obviously a superior source of wisdom. Indeed, its claim to superiority is that it can provide the broadest and most comprehensive account of human experience, fitting all other distinct modes of experience together. In this respect, philosophy is a higher-order activity that explores the presuppositions of any other mode of experience or activity. And, of course, the conditions of philosophy itself is one of the primary questions of philosophy.

As an intellectual exercise, this may well be interesting, although it rests on a number of claims that are philosophically challengeable, but when applied to the categorisation of reflective thought it begs its own questions. If the task is simply distinguishing the ways of reading a text, then pretty much anything goes in terms of establishing a hierarchy of experience and it is for the reader to determine their own interest. However, hierarchies of this kind are also prescriptive and cast doubt on the importance of ways of thinking about the world. So they are themselves open to criticism for the ways in which they can distort or prejudge understanding. For example, if history and philosophy are categorically distinct activities, then Thucydides' method is a mixed mode that combines two approaches. But, if we challenge the categorisation underlying this interpretation, then, far from being a mix of two more primary methods, his approach offers a single integrated mode of reflection on the world that is prior to and, therefore, more fundamental to ways in which we might wish to characterise the argument. The categories of history and philosophy are themselves not pre-interpreted but are theorised out of experiences that are ways of both making sense of that experience and responding to that world of experience.

A claim for the superiority of a higher philosophical perspective on this question is itself an historical and philosophical abstraction from a conditional mode of experience. All such approaches thus have a hermeneutic basis, which is itself always an historical philosophical perspective. The superiority of Thucydides' argument and approach relative to more purely abstract theorising is always perspectival, but can be defended on the grounds that his method acknowledges the irreducible interplay between action and reflection. It is precisely this quality that continues to draw adherents to Thucydides' reflections on international politics and thought despite his covering events that took place two and half millennia ago.

Explaining the Peloponnesian War

Thucydides is not the only source of evidence about the war between the Peloponnesians and the Athenians in 431–405 bce or the events and characters that comprise its history. However, the significance and majesty of his book are that it largely defines the war for subsequent historians and theorists. This is not a trivial point as the account of the war spans 27 years, divided into two periods that are explicitly connected as parts of the same conflict (Book V, 5.26.1–2). It is also distinguished from an earlier period of conflict between Sparta and Athens that followed the earlier Persian War and invasion of 480–479 bce. It could be interpreted as part of a longer struggle or a series of distinct campaigns and conflicts, which are only loosely related.

During the Persian invasion of 480–479, Sparta was head of the Peloponnesian League and was also chosen by the Greek poleis that formed a coalition to be the leader of Greek opposition. (Throughout this chapter I use the term state as a translation of the Greek term polis, mindful of the significant differences between the polis and the modern nation state, which does not appear in European history for another 20 centuries.) To this extent, Sparta and Athens were allies against a greater common enemy, but Sparta was considered the leading land and naval power in Greece, or the hegemon. Sparta was a deeply conservative, militaristic and land-based power. It had a relatively small citizen body of *spartiates* (men of equal status) who were trained from an early age in tough military discipline, making them fearsome infantry warriors. This training cultivated physical strength and self-reliance, coupled with fierce loyalty. Male youths were brought up in a tough (spartan) regime that denied them comforts and sometimes food in order to cultivate self-reliance. They were also required to train in combat with adult warriors. The *spartiates* became a military aristocracy who dominated a larger helot or peasant class who sustained Spartan society. Women were even more invisible in Spartan politics than was the custom in the masculine world of Greek politics. The helot class was fiercely ruled and kept in order with periodic small-scale domestic wars. The Spartan constitution was famously attributed to Lycurgus the lawgiver and it was fiercely defended and rarely changed. The government of the *spartiates* was complex, with a dual monarchy of elected kings, an aristocratic council of 28 members and five ephors or magistrates, whose primary responsibility was to deal with foreign policy and the conduct of war. Finally, there was an assembly of all men over the age of 30: decisions in the assembly were made by acclamation (or shouting) as opposed to debate!

At the time of the Persian War, Sparta was the leading land power in the Greek world. Yet, during the years preceding the Persian War, Athens had built up the largest navy in Greek history up to that time, and this formed the core of the Greek fleet that destroyed the Persian fleet at Salamis in 480 and then again at Mycale in 470. The defeat of the Persians at Mycale coincided with Sparta's defeat of Persia in the major land battle at Plataea and raised the spectre, for the Spartans, of a new power in the Greek world. Whilst the Spartans had defeated Persia on land and forced its withdrawal from mainland Europe, they remained indifferent to the fate of the Greek poleis around the Aegean Sea that were still under Persian rule. This created an opportunity for the Athenians to expand their influence by liberating these poleis, or by supporting those that had rebelled against the Persians. These poleis allied themselves with Athens in what became the Delian League, and subsequently the basis of a new Athenian maritime empire.

Athens was the largest polis, with a citizen body of around 40,000 (compared to Sparta, with approximately 4,000 *spartiates*). Its constitution was democratic, although the citizen body excluded an even larger male population of over 200,000, which included slaves, foreign labourers (called metics) and those too poor to act as hoplites. These soldiers had to provide their own armour and weapons, and training for service was a condition of voting. Once again, women were excluded from the political class and they do not feature in Thucydides' account of Athenian democracy. Athens was a relatively open trading city, hence its large navy and focus on the Aegean and beyond, as opposed to a land empire in the Peloponnese. As a democracy, decisions were made by vote, with simple majorities determining the outcome. The 10 generals who were the chief officers of the Athenian state were elected, but most other administrative roles were chosen by lot, including membership of the Council of 500, who prepared the business for legislative decision. The assumption was that all citizens had sufficient capacity to exercise the common power of the demos and all took turns in ruling and being ruled, although inevitably some ended up serving in elected roles for successive terms.

The rise of Athens and its appearance as a second hegemonic power is seen as one of the causes of the War with Sparta and the source of the modern idea of 'the Thucydides trap', whereby the rise of a new hegemonic power will compel a war or challenge before the existing dominant power or hegemon is displaced. This idea of the struggle between rising and remaining powers is a key to understanding major structural changes in international politics according to Allison and is currently represented by the rise of China and the remaining power of the USA. Not all instances of the 'trap' result in war, but the study of such historical instances is important if war is to be avoided (Allison 2017). Some classical scholars contest whether it makes sense to speak of a 'Thucydides trap' or to generalise from the specific circumstances of the ancient world. For the rest of this section I want to focus on the specific (as opposed to the general) causes of the war between the Peloponnesians and the Athenians.

Spartan jealousy of the rise of the Delian league led to a series of armed quarrels that formed the First Peloponnesian War, from 460 to 445. It ended with the Thirty Years' Peace when each side recognised the other in its own sphere – Athens with its maritime empire and Sparta as the leading land power in the Peloponnese. It should be noted that the label 'Thirty Years' Peace' does not indicate how long it actually lasted but the intended length of the treaty. In fact, the peace endured over 10 years, until 431, when a series of conflicts that were considered treaty violations led to the Second Peloponnesian War or the War between the Peloponnesians and the Athenians, as described by Thucydides. The events that triggered the conflict are complex and Thucydides refers to the dispute between Corcyra and Corinth and the Megarian Decree, both smaller conflicts that involved allies of the main protagonists and which eventually drew Sparta and Athens into direct conflict.

As the dominant power focusing on the Greek mainland, Sparta was not much interested in cultivating allies. Athens was predominantly a sea power so the struggle between the two was the origin of a western tradition of rivalry between land and sea powers. Corcyra was an independent state but with a substantial fleet second only to that of Athens. The third largest fleet belonged to Corinth, which was allied with Sparta. Athens was keen to establish an alliance with Corcyra that would then dominate and neutralise Corinth and hence Sparta. The rivalry between Corcyra and Corinth came to a head at Epidamnus (on the coast of modern Albania). This saw Corcyra defeat Corinth but the Corinthians regrouped and sought to expand their fleet further for a second major confrontation. With Corinth becoming the second naval power, the Corcyreans made overtures to Athens. In the Athenian Assembly, both the Corinthian and Corcyrean diplomats made their cases, with the conclusion that Athens would volunteer a small fleet as symbolic support for Corcyra. However, this was too small to effectively support Corcyra and large enough to infuriate the Corinthians, who saw it as an act of aggression.

The challenge for the Athenian leader Pericles was do nothing and risk the collapse of Athens's maritime empire and the further rise of Sparta, with Corinth providing its naval power. Yet the Spartans faced a similar challenge. If they supported Corinth against Corcyra they indicated a clear desire to become a total power on land and sea and thus to dominate Athens. Yet if they did not stand by Corinth then they risked losing their one naval power, and also possibly indicating their submission to the new rising power.

Alongside this cause was the Megarian Decree of 432, which imposed a total economic boycott on the island of Megara because it 'dishonoured' Athenian temples by sheltering runaway slaves from Athens. Again, Pericles was forced into a corner. Abandoning the boycott would have weakened his leadership position in Athens and signalled to Sparta that they could damage Athens's possessions elsewhere. If Sparta failed to pursue this course of action, then the Spartan King Archidamus II would be seen to be putting personal friendship with Pericles above the city's interests. Both leaders were compelled by their own peoples to pursue policies that they each recognised were dangerous and destabilising. For both Thucydides and modern historians such as Allen, the problems of the trap arise even when leaders are aware of the dangers but where the circumstances compel them to act in ways that are otherwise irrational and dangerous. As Thucydides reports, following a vigorous debate, the war party within Sparta triumphed and voted for war, for fear of seeing Athens's power become greater in the Greek world.

Spartan forces invaded Attica and began devastating Athenian territory and property. The Athenian strategy under its leading general, Pericles, was to withdraw within the city walls and rely on its wealth and naval power to wait out the Spartans, and to harass them through marine assaults as opposed to pitched land battles. Pericles' strategy and leadership is one of the deep underlying themes of Thucydides' narrative. Pericles' 'Funeral Oration' and subsequent speeches are a celebration of Athenian wealth, power and political wisdom and an indirect defence of his conservative policy. However, in 430 Athens was struck by a terrible plague, which devastated approximately one-third of the Athenian population (Thucydides contracted the plague but survived, no doubt adding additional significance to his discussion of this event). The plague raised questions about the wisdom of Pericles' strategy. It exposes in a dramatic way important features of Athenian political culture that we will explore later. Following the plague, Pericles was removed from office and his opponents sought terms for peace with Sparta but these were rebuffed. As a result of this failure, Pericles was re-elected to office but in 429 he died as a result of the plague.

The rest of the first part of the war, from 429 to 421, and the Peace of Nicias were characterised by the struggle amongst the Athenian factions to provide leadership in the absence of Pericles, and the search for a new war policy. In 428, the city of Mytilene on Lesbos rebelled against the Athenians, which created a fear amongst them of a general unravelling of their empire. The Mytilenian revolt was unsuccessful but gave rise to a famous debate about the punishment of the Mytilenians (discussed in detail below). This debate introduces the character of Cleon, who became the leader of the war party. Cleon was a figure whom Thucydides clearly did not respect but he nevertheless presented as a representative of a more successful aggressive strategy that led to the victory at Pylos. This aggressive strategy continued under Cleon, and on the Spartans' side with their general, Brasidas. Their fortunes come together at the Battle of

Amphipolis in 422. Brasidas had led the initial capture of Amphipolis from the Athenians, whilst Thucydides himself was the general in charge of the nearby Athenian fleet. This loss led to Thucydides' prosecution for treason and exile from Athens allowing him to write his history. Cleon led an expedition to recapture Amphipolis from Brasidas but in the course of the battle he was killed along with Brasidas, despite the Spartans' victory. With the death of the two leading protagonists on either side, who supported an aggressive policy, the peace party in Athens (led by Nicias) sued for peace and this marked the end of the first part of the war, often referred to as the Archidamian War.

Although the Peace of Nicias lasted four years, it was never stable because its terms suited neither main party, and many of Sparta's allies refused to ratify the treaty. The conflict continued with the Athenian conquest of the island of Melos, which occasioned the Melian dialogue. However, the most significant act that brought the peace to an end was Athens's launch of a major campaign against Syracuse in Sicily. The Sicilian campaign, and the debate that it launched, introduced the character of Alcibiades, a nephew of Pericles, who played a controversial role in the subsequent war, at various times with Athens, then Sparta and even Persia.

The Sicilian campaign and the attempt to relieve the first expedition were a catastrophic failure that marked the beginning of the end of the Athenian Empire. Athens lost its navy and the resources to replace it. It also lost considerable prestige. The Spartans, for their part, allied with Persia to develop their own navy and exploit Athens's weakness. Much of the rest of the history covers the factionalism and politics of Athenian decline including the oligarchic coup of the 30 tyrants in 411. Despite some successes in their struggle to fight on, the Athenians never recovered the initiative. Following the destruction of their fleet by the Spartans at Agospotami, and the embargo and siege of Athens under the Spartan general Lysander, the war came to an end with defeat of Athens and its empire.

By way of a footnote, it is worth noting that the decline of the Athenian empire coincided with the growth and development of its mature philosophical culture. Plato's Socrates was involved in the struggle against the 30 tyrants, as was the historical character of Thrasymachus (who plays such an important role in the drama of Plato's *Republic*). Plato and his political thinking were thus also shaped by the legacy of Thucydides' War between the Peloponnesians and the Athenians.

This brief outline sets the context for the wider significance of Thucydides' book. Most discussions of Thucydides turn to the explanation of the war and draw heavily on his primary concepts of fear, honour and interest, and consequently whether Pericles or other actors in the narrative made the right decisions. In what follows I focus on a different line of argument and what I take to be the two most important lessons from Thucydides: his reflections on democracy at war and his apparent contribution to the development of realism in politics and international relations.

Periclean liberalism

Pericles plays a central role in Thucydides' text, and in many ways he is more important than any other character in its pantheon, because of what he represents as much as what he allegedly did in the narrative. Often described as the first citizen of Athens, he was the dominant political figure and leader of the democratic faction from 460 bce to his death from plague in 431 bce. During that time Athens rose to its role as a maritime empire that threatened the military dominance of Sparta.

Pericles is the source of three important speeches: the response to the Spartan ultimatum in Book I, 140–145; the Funeral Oration in Book II, 35–46; and the third speech, in Book II, 60–64, in which he defends his strategy to the Athenians following the plague (I defer the discussion of this speech until the final section). Throughout these speeches we are presented with a strategic leader who is central to holding the Athenian demos to its true nature, which is set out carefully in the Funeral Oration. Thucydides gives us more than an account of an actor whose conduct of events can be judged as successful or not from the point of view of the challenges he faces. Pericles is also presented as an ideal of leadership that completes the institutional structure of Athenian democracy and thus saves it from its tendency to collapse into populist rivalry and disorder. Many of the lessons from the Athenian conduct of the war in Thucydides history are about the central role of leadership and the way in which that manifests itself in a clear strategy, backed by a vision or ideology that can sustain a nation at war and justify the privations that war brings. That ideology, which following Athens's defeat is detached from its connection to democracy, becomes an important source of constitutional liberal ideas. For subsequent centuries until the late 19th century, democracy and liberalism remained in competition.

The first speech, in Book I, 140–145, is the Athenian acceptance of war with Sparta, following Pericles' rejection of the request to revoke the Megarian Decree, which imposed economic sanctions and a blockade against this ally of Sparta. In defending this response, he outlines the Athenians' strategy in terms of its long-term or overall aim or (to use Clausewitz's definition) 'the use of engagements for the object of the war' (Clausewitz 1976, p. 128). Pericles sets out what the Athenians want to achieve and how he, as the leading general, proposes to achieve that through conduct of war. The full account of that strategy relies on the vision of Athenian democracy set out in the Funeral Oration, so I will devote most attention to that speech, but the first speech does tell us something important about Athenians' strategic ambitions.

In accepting the challenge of war with Sparta, Pericles emphasises the maritime nature of the Athenian Empire and its outward and commercial character. Sparta is acknowledged as the dominant land power in Greece and therefore Pericles argues for a strategy of avoiding set-piece land battles or engagements, instead relying on its naval power to harass the Peloponnesian League and to ensure the safety of supply of Athens. In this way, Athens can frustrate Spartan power by denying it access to the field in which it is dominant. And, although this will involve costs to Athens, Pericles argues that these are easily absorbed given Athens's commercial wealth and power. As an agrarian power, Sparta has little surplus to spend on the war and every day campaigning in Attica is costly. The Athenians are not after territorial conquest in the Peloponnese, and have more than enough territory in the islands of its maritime empire. So their goal is achieved by securing their empire and the rising position in Greece, whilst allowing Sparta and the Peloponnesian League to exhaust itself financially and seek new terms.

Despite the subsequent narrative of events, not least the plague that follows from the concentration of the population behind the Athens city walls and the depopulation of its agricultural territory in Attica, Pericles' strategy is a coherent one. It sets out a clear goal for the war and consequent measures of success. It also emphasises Athens's peculiar strengths and advantages as a maritime power with the capacity to reach deep into the Greek world of its island colonies, as opposed to the narrow confines of a land-based power. Whether appropriate or not, similar arguments were made by Winston Churchill about Great Britain in 1940 following the collapse of France – they were no doubt deliberately intended to appeal to the classical political imagination of an American elite audience. Pericles claimed that damage to Athens's land territory would have little long-term effect on its power and ability to sustain conflict and secure its goals. At worst they would lose land and property, whereas life and liberty are most important. Alongside this, Pericles made the very important – and, in the context of subsequent events, poignant – remark 'what I fear is not the enemy's strategy, but our own mistakes' (Book I, 144). For a strategy to work it needs to be adhered to once in place. Although subsequent military theorists like Clausewitz warn of the need to adapt plans once the friction of engagement with an enemy is experienced, it is equally important at the highest level of strategic policymaking to take the long view and not change everything at the perception of damage and harm. Indeed, it is precisely democracy's tendency to do this that Thucydides is most concerned about.

Clausewitz's greatest teacher, Gerd von Scharnhorst, is reported to have spent much time puzzling over how the French had managed to turn their revolutionary armies from an undisciplined rabble into the extraordinary fighting force they became under Napoleon. Much was due to doctrine and organisation but he emphasised the transformation of the society that lay behind this with the emergence of a French nation (Howard 2002, p. 7). The idea of a nation is a modern one and will be explored in later chapters. However, in setting out Pericles' account of Athenian strategy it is difficult not to see the celebration of Athens in the Funeral Oration as anything other than its liberal ideological underpinning, especially as this vision is the explanation and justification for the heroic actions of those being celebrated in the oration, and the explanation of the love and patriotism that inspires Athens.

One needs to be careful of anachronism in representing Greek ideas, but there is a clear sense in which Pericles suggests the war is not just a clash of interests but is rather an ideological struggle between an open and liberal democracy and a closed conservative autocracy. Pericles says 'I declare that our city is an Education to Greece' (Book II, 41). He is not just celebrating how the Athenians feel about themselves but advocating the best form of government and defending the Athenian Empire's ideological presuppositions against other members of the Delian League, who were frustrated at what we would call the imperialistic ambitions of the Athenians in transforming the regimes of its allies. Just as contemporary liberals are unapologetic about the universal value of their political order, so it appears is Pericles with respect to the Greeks.

The Funeral Oration remains one of the great statements of a liberal constitutional order and it sets out principles and values that are peculiarly contemporary for 21st-century western readers:

> Our constitution is called a democracy because power is in the hands not of a minority but of the whole people. When it is a question of settling private disputes, everyone is equal before the law; when it is a question of putting one person before another in positions of public responsibility, what counts is not membership of a particular class, but the actual ability which the man possesses. No one, so long as he has it in him to be of service to the state, is kept in political obscurity because of poverty. And, just as our political life is free and open, so is our day-to-day life in our relations with each other … We are free and tolerant in our private lives; but in public affairs we keep to the law. [Book II, 37–38] (Thucydides 1972, p. 145)

In this passage we see democracy tempered by the rule of law, meritocracy (or access to offices based on ability) and social tolerance. These fundamental liberal values are then coupled with a celebration of wide (global) trade, openness, public wealth and economic responsibility. This economic and social theory of liberal constitutionalism is in its turn the source of creativity, culture and civilisation. The text does not provide a philosophical defence of these values, but Pericles does offer some justification for the Athenian way of doing things in terms of the material benefits that flow from this constitutional and economic order. In so far as trade allows not only for beauty and civilisation but also for an economic surplus that supports Athens's strategy in its struggle with Sparta, we can see a utilitarian cost–benefit analysis that again prefigures modern arguments from international political economy about the benefits of free trade and liberal constitutions.

Whilst Thucydides allows Pericles to offer one of the most striking depictions of the ideal of a liberal constitutional order, it is by no means clear that he endorses the claims offered or the idea that liberal democratic imperialism is the best way of conducting international relations. To this extent, he presents an account of the defects of liberalism in international affairs that could be endorsed by contemporary realists such as John J. Mearsheimer (Mearsheimer 2018). Mearsheimer's argument is about contemporary U.S. foreign policy since 1989, but it precisely echoes Thucydides' narrative in acknowledging that, for all of its attractiveness as a domestic social order, the projection of liberal democratisation is a profoundly destabilising policy. In both cases, the challenge is imposing liberal democratic values on non-liberal democratic regimes. As the discussion of the Mytilenian debate below shows, the transformation of status from a treaty ally to a tributary unit was particularly important in raising the challenge to Athens. What started as a league became an opportunity for the Athenians to impose a political order and identity, just as western liberal democracies are seen as imposing the correct form of political society on non-democratic and non-liberal regimes in the 21st century. There may be arguments in favour of liberal democratic values, but the consequence of a right set of values or a correct political order is that those who differ from them are seen to be in the wrong or be an enemy, whereas the problem for the liberal democrats or the Athenians is that, if they simply concede that they are one amongst many equal regimes, they risk damaging the legitimacy of their own form of rule. Pericles says, 'our system of government does not copy the institutions of our neighbours. It is more the case of our being a model to others' (Book II, 37). Athenian democracy is not simply one amongst many but is a model for others; this makes it a fighting creed, in contrast to the Spartan model, which is neither particularly attractive nor even something that the Spartans think should apply to anyone but themselves. The challenge that Thucydides leaves us with in the account of Pericles' strategy is the challenge that faces liberal democratic regimes in international affairs, namely how they reconcile their values with peace and order? As Thucydides shows, it is by no means clear that the domestic virtues of liberal democratic order are appropriate to the international realm and achieving peace: a thesis that adds to Thucydides' reputation as a founder or source of realism in international political thought.

Thucydidean realism

Realism is often described as the default theory of international relations since the emergence of the modern discipline studying the subject since World War II. Yet it is a notoriously slippery concept involving a variety of dimensions that are both analytical and normative. At its minimal analytical level, it comprises two main assertions, namely that states pursue their own interests (however conceived) and that the international domain is non-hierarchical, with no over-

arching power imposing order on the interactions of states or political communities. Of course, this leaves open the idea that a state might see its interest in
collaborative or alliance terms, or that there might be an incomplete normative international order, with norms or law-like rules winning some acceptance
but without any sanctioning power. This raises important normative questions
about the nature of law and authority. Analytical realism, therefore, is compatible with the idea of an international normative realm or incomplete order but
acknowledging the absence of a dominant power.

Yet, influenced by Hobbes, many modern realists make the negative normative claims that national interests are inherently conflictual, so that a law without sanction is 'merely words' and the non-hierarchical international realm is
not only anarchic but without any morality or law. Whether these are conceptual points or historical and empirical claims is one of the fundamental questions of international political theory and explains the centrality of Thucydides
to those debates, whether it is strictly appropriate to describe him as a realist
or not. Much international relations theory concerns distinguishing or collapsing analytical and sceptical normative realism and adding ever more refined
accounts of why realism provides the best empirical account of international
affairs. Whilst modern realism draws on many thinkers' ideas, Thucydides is
seen as an early pioneer of this approach to international affairs, and all who
construct a tradition or canon of international 'theory' begin with him. In the
rest of this section I examine three sources of Thucydidean realism, alongside
its supposed most significant lesson.

The plague

The discussion of the plague follows immediately upon Pericles' Funeral Oration in Book II, 47–55, and it clearly fascinated Thucydides, who contracted the
unidentified disease but survived. Much of the discussion provides a detailed
description of the symptoms and speculation about the origins of the disease in
Ethiopia. Following so close on the account for the Funeral Oration, the plague
is seen as an unfortunate consequence of Pericles' policy of gathering the population in the city and leaving the countryside to the Spartans, whilst relying on
naval power and trade for supply from Athens's imperial possessions. Although
Thucydides mentions that the plague caused people to remember old oracles,
his own discussion is surprisingly free of appeals to supernatural causes or
explanations. The most important part of the plague narrative, for the purposes
of the discussion of realism, concerns its impact on morality and lawfulness.
Thucydides writes:

> people now began openly to venture on acts of self-indulgence which
> before then they used to keep dark … As for what is called honour,

no one showed himself willing to abide by its laws, so doubtful was it whether one would survive to enjoy the name for it. It was generally agreed that what was both honourable and valuable was the pleasure of the moment and everything that might conceivably contribute to that pleasure. No fear of god or law of man had a restraining influence. As for the gods, it seemed to be the same thing whether one worshipped them or not ... As for offences against human law, no one expected to live long enough to be brought to trial and punished. [Book II, 53–54] (Thucydides 1972, p. 155)

Thucydides describes how morality and lawfulness break down in the proximity and shadow of unpredictable mortality. The unleashing of repressed urges is a common story in accounts of wartime privation or siege. But, more importantly, this section provides evidence for thinking about how moral and legal norms work and the important Greek distinction between *physis*, or nature, and *nomos*, or conventional law. The contrast between these two important Greek philosophical concepts was a major concern of sophists and philosophers because it raised questions about the nature and authority of morality, law and convention. This has a bearing on the scope and limits of laws or norms and therefore the question of whether there can be an authoritative normative system that extends beyond the local practices of morality. Thucydides does not offer a philosophical speculation on the authority of morality but shows how it is fragile and how easily it collapses under the pressure of mortality in wartime and the catastrophe of the plague. The norms of honour are ignored and people are liberated to bring hidden things into the open: he is certainly referring to the social norms that regulate respect for the dead and sexual propriety. But this is not merely the concern of a conservative moralist facing the disruption of social norms. Thucydides is also contrasting the breakdown of norms with the liberation of nature and its pursuit of pleasure and gratification. Morality and law (*nomos*) are concerned with disciplining nature (*physis*) and rendering possible the character of Athenians. Once those norms and conventions are weakened, the character of Athenians is also weakened and the high-minded motivations celebrated in the Funeral Oration are overcome by a much more fickle and unmanageable raw nature of immediate satisfaction. National character is fragile and a vulnerable achievement that shapes and gives specific form to an otherwise fickle nature. The unleashing of crude individualism undermines community and its power to create and sustain character and social conventions (something that we will see later in Hobbes). Although Thucydides does not make the argument explicitly, much of his account of the treatment of the Mytilenians, the Melians, the character of Cleon and the new men of Athens suggests a loss of character and a submission to short-term and baser instincts in the conduct of war and of policy as a consequence of plague.

Although Thucydides is not making a philosophical point, his account of the consequences of the plague supports the two main elements of analytical realism. Firstly, the account of liberated nature and immediate gratification lends support to the idea of egoistic interest being in an important and perhaps irreducible sense both fundamental and natural, and not just amongst Athenians. In a world without the conventions and social practices that discipline brute nature to support character and the virtues, we have an assertive and conflictual source of egoistic interest. Of course, we need to extend this argument from individuals to groups to get a conception of conflictual national interest. But, if human nature is appetitive and only disciplined by social norms, we have some reason to assume in the absence of those norms that groups manifest the characteristics of brute, human nature.

The second, and important, lesson that is illustrated in the Mytilenian debate and the Melian dialogue is that there is no international normative order that disciplines individual nature and interest and creates a conception of international obligation. Thucydides' *History* gives many examples of a putative international order with 'laws of war' such as those governing the treatment of the dead, armistices, declarations of combat and triumphs marking victory, as well as diplomatic treaties, embassies and other such rituals of an apparent international (inter-polis) order. Yet, it is equally clear that these are often observed more in the breach or at the convenience of stronger parties. Also, and most importantly, they exist in a realm without an authoritative power to sanction breaches. The weakness of the Greek international order is simply an extension of the insight that Thucydides identifies in the loosening of social order in Athens following the plague. His clear lesson is that law and moral norms only have authority in normal times and amongst people who recognise their authority because they share a common destiny and accept subjection to sanctions. Morality and normativity are local, and the further we depart from the conventions that support and discipline our brute natures, the less their authority holds and ceases altogether.

The Mytilenian debate

Book III, 1–50 opens with an account of the revolt of Mytilene followed by the Mytilenian debate in Athens, one of the most famous and controversial episodes in Thucydides' *History*. Mytilene was the most significant city on the island of Lesbos and a tributary of the Athenians as part of the Delian League. The revolt occurred when the Mytilenians took the opportunity of the opening of the campaigning season in Attica to both abandon their allegiance to Athens and to assert dominance over the whole island of Lesbos. A delegation was sent to Sparta to plead their case for admission into the Peloponnesian League and seek the promise of military support. The Athenians received prior warning and, fearful of the damage that a secession of one of their tributaries could encourage, they sent an expedition to frustrate the Mytilenians. However, when the Athenians' siege proved successful and the Spartans failed to send an expedition to support the revolt, the Mytilenian leadership planned a direct confrontation with the Athenian forces. But, when the Mytilenian people understood this plan, they, in turn, revolted against the authorities and sought terms with the Athenian general Paches. These terms allowed the Athenians to do as they saw fit to the Mytilenians and for the Athenian troops to enter the city. However, the Mytilenians were accorded the opportunity to send delegates to Athens to plead their case, with the guarantee from Paches that the population would not be enslaved, imprisoned or killed until the representatives returned.

The initial Athenian decision was swift and brutal. Despite previous undertakings, the Mytilenian leader, Salaethus, was immediately put to death and not only did the authorities condemn to death the other prisoners but they decided that all the adult male population should be killed and all the women and children were to be enslaved. A ship (trireme) was immediately dispatched to inform Paches of the decision. The debate proper begins the following day as the Athenians have second thoughts about the harshness of their original decision and the authorities agree to debate the matter again. The debate is interesting in that we are presented with two named characters, the demagogue Cleon and his opponent Diodotus. Cleon was an advocate of the original decision and Thucydides introduces him, saying:

> It was he who was responsible for passing the original motion for putting the Mytilenians to death. He was remarkable among the Athenians for the violence of his character, and at this time he exercised far the greatest influence over the people. [Book III, 36–37] (Thucydides 1972, p. 212)

Cleon's forceful argument has three main elements: the justice of the original death sentence; the demands of empire; and the failings of democratic deliberation. I will return to this last issue, of the failings of democracy, at the end the chapter and instead focus on the first and second elements, which have the closest bearing on the emergence of Thucydidean realism.

Cleon forcefully argues that the death sentences are the just response to the egregious crime that the Mytilenians perpetrated in conspiring with Sparta. This is an unprompted treason and an assault on the Athenians that they should not ignore; though the original sentence is harsh, he claims that it was just and, as such, it should be carried out. By appealing to justice, Cleon is invoking a normative consideration but he is also clearly not appealing to a norm of justice beyond that of the interest of the Athenians. Again, whilst Cleon is not developing an ethical theory – and, given his hostility to philosophical deliberation over strict compliance with the conventional law, that would be unlikely – he is asserting the convergence of justice and interest. It is for the Athenian assembly as a court to do justice for Athens (and against Mytilene) and apply the law. In this way, Cleon provides a very stark assertion of a realist view that justice is whatever is in the interest of the state. There is no higher principle or standard that state law must comply with in order to be just: there is no question of whether a state should measure its actions against a higher or external moral standard.

Indeed, Cleon explicitly rejects the idea that the Athenians should be compassionate and qualify their actions by minimising the violence of punishment, because this would actually be unfair to other allies and tributaries. In this respect, Cleon's argument advances the Thucydidean depiction of realism by going beyond the scepticism about the scope and extent of moral norms in the international environment that is prefigured in the account of the plague. Instead, we are presented with a clear realist ethic for international affairs that identifies the obligations of empire. According to this ethic, states will pursue their own interests so that nature and obligation, interest and duty become the same thing. But Cleon also reveals a further dimension of this ethic by claiming that empires have to act in peculiar ways that require the projection of force and the deployment of exemplary violence. Because the nature of imperial relations is marked by distance – and, in Athens's case as a maritime empire, often by long distances – the sanctions of obligation need to be clear and compelling. After all, Cleon argues starkly, 'your empire is a tyranny exercised over subjects who do not like it' [Book III, 37] (Thucydides 1972, p. 213). Either this tyranny is just, in Athens's terms as following from its national interest, or, as Cleon points out, it is unjust, in which case the Athenians deserved to face rebellion and should be punished for their unjust empire. Athens is offered a stark choice in the logic of its position. It can either be an empire, but then it must act like one, or it can abandon its imperial ambitions and limit its aspirations. If it is to be an empire, it needs to project force, and the harsh punishment for Mytilenian treason is part of that imperial ethic. Athenian freedom, in terms of being free from the domination of other Greek states or external powers such as Persia, requires it to be assertively individualistic. This is a normative position, but a realist one because it does not recognise the equal ethical claims of any other state.

The Mytilenian debate is a debate with another interlocutor, namely Diodotus, who challenges Cleon. Diodotus argues for less harsh punishment and his style is much less ferocious than Cleon's. However, in many ways he supplements Cleon's argument with a more explicitly realist argument. Firstly, he rejects the idea that the assembly should be acting as a court; instead, it should be a political assembly and deliberate politically in terms of the balance of Athenian interests as an imperial power. Whilst acknowledging the apparent injustice of imposing the death penalty on the whole male population of Mytilene, and thus on the democratic class there who were not involved in the revolt, his real argument concerns what is in the interest of maintaining Athens's imperial power and possessions. The real measure of action should be a careful consideration of the balance of benefits to Athenian national interest and not justice or compassion. Although the assembly accepts Diodotus' argument and dispatches another boat to countermand the original decision for the destruction and enslavement of the Mytilenian population, his argument is a colder and more calculating assertion of national interest as the overriding principle of action. This is a political decision only, rather than one of justice, principle or law. This goes to the heart of the claim that, by highlighting this episode, Thucydides presents a realist vision of politics and international relations: the only criterion for judging a state's actions is in terms of what suits its long-term and considered interest.

The Melian dialogue

The Melian dialogue occurs in Book V, 85–113 following the collapse of the Peace of Nicias and it serves as a prelude to the Sicilian Expedition, where the Athenian ethic of empire is tested to destruction. Although chronologically and politically separate from the Mytilenian debate, the Melian dialogue continues to clarify the realist ethic of empire that is pursued by the Athenians. Melos was an island to the south-east of Attica populated by a colony originally from Sparta, but which had asserted its neutrality in the conflict before being forced to respond to Athenian attacks. When the Athenian expedition arrived in 416, they sent representatives to the Melians to seek terms for capitulation. The Melian leadership chose not to discuss the matter publicly but only in front of the governing body. This might explain why Thucydides presents the dialogue as between 'the Athenians' and 'the Melians' rather than as a debate between named characters.

The Athenians are brusque and instrumental in their argument. They want to save themselves from battle but equally are uninterested in 'fine phrases' about their right to empire or the justice of their claim. Instead, they make perhaps one of the most famous statements of a realist position in international politics:

> when these matters are discussed by practical people, the standard of justice depends upon the equality of power to compel and that in fact the strong do what they have the power to do and the weak accept what they have to accept. [Book V, 89] (Thucydides 1972, p. 402)

In this terse statement, Thucydides has the Athenians assert that justice at best can be a principle of mutual advantage amongst equal powers. And, as the specific example suggests, in the international realm, whilst there are imperial powers there is no such equality amongst all states and therefore the idea of justice does not apply. But, even amongst major powers, that equality is precarious and rare, as indeed the rise of Athens suggests. The Thucydides trap suggests strong structural reasons within international relations, for justice as mutual advantage to be rare (Allison 2017).

The claim that justice is at best the mutual advantage of equal powers is, however, not the most important part of the claim. That is the point reinforced in Book V, 105 (Thucydides 1972, p. 404), where the Athenians say, 'Our opinion of the gods and our knowledge of men lead us to conclude that it is a general and necessary law of nature to rule whatever one can'. So, not only can the powerful pursue their interest over the weak; they also have a natural inclination to dominate where they can. When this is coupled with the claim that justice is the mutual advantage of the strong, we have a statement of the fundamental elements of a realist vision of international politics:

1. States are motivated to pursue their interests.
2. In doing so, states are motivated to exploit their power and dominate the weak when they can.
3. The international condition is one without an overarching power that imposes order or with a permanent dominant power.
4. Consequently, order is the exception and the natural condition of international affairs is one of conflict or war.

It is precisely this argument that the Athenians make against the Melians, suggesting that, for all their appeals to honour and justice, they would behave in exactly the same way if they were in Athens's position. Indeed, the argument is almost mechanical (although one needs to be careful in not overinterpreting what Thucydides is implying with the idea of a 'necessary law of nature') because the Athenians reject the argument that they should avoid exploiting advantage in case circumstances should change and they might need justice, which is precisely what happens in Book VIII during the failed Sicilian Expedition. The dialogue ends with the Melians failing to persuade the Athenians to treat them justly, the Melians heroically refusing to submit to the Athenians, and the start of a siege. In the end, Melos falls to the Athenians, who execute all men of military age and sell into slavery all the women and children: dialogue and discussion are defeated by power. This is a forceful moral for politics, to be contrasted with theories that assert the primacy of the moral good and the power of reasoned speech and the best argument.

The narrative of the plague, the Mytilenian debate and the Melian dialogue provide a clear and forceful account of the elements of a normative realist ethic and an explanatory account of a realist interpretation of the war between the Peloponnesians and the Athenians. Thucydides clearly emerges as the 'father' of realism and the founder of international theory. However, it would be incorrect to go on and claim that Thucydides explicitly endorses a realist ethic. It is also clear that he has very little sympathy for the demagogue Cleon or much sympathy for the wisdom of the Athenian's behaviour with respect to the Melians. Consequently, whilst Thucydides offers us many lessons, his realism is more appropriately confined to the explanatory context of interstate action, as opposed to asserting the expansionist ethic of imperialism that follows from Cleon's contribution to the Mytilenian debate and to the Melian dialogue.

Realism might well provide a good explanation of the conduct of international affairs but it provides a much less sure platform for states to decide how they should act in a world in which realist premises hold: it is one thing knowing that states will pursue what they perceive to be their interests but it is much less clear what a state's interest actually is in the wider historical context. Whilst realism might provide the best account of the circumstances of interstate conflict and the limits of norms, Thucydides does not offer realism as a normative account of how states (poleis) should act. His real message with respect to realism is that judging a states' interest requires cool and considered judgement, precisely what Pericles provided and what democracy tends not to provide.

Democracy, war and *stasis*

The third major theme for international political theory in Thucydides' *History* is the issue of democracy, in particular the thesis that democracies are unstable and tend to dissolve from the inside: what the Greeks called *stasis* or the tendency to civil strife. Thucydides' *History* was one of the primary sources for the hostility to democracy within the western tradition of political thought until the late 19th century and the emergence of representative democracies. His negative view is particularly interesting in light of the 'democratic peace' thesis, to which I turn next.

The 'democratic peace' thesis

The democratic peace thesis (sometimes also the liberal peace thesis) claims that democracies do not go to war with each other, so that the extension of democracy would tend towards a more pacific world order. It has been advanced by a number of scholars but most significantly in the work of Doyle (1983) in two important papers. These focus on liberal democratic regimes and in particular the ideas of the late 18th-century German political philosopher Immanuel Kant in the context of the balance of power' thesis. There are significant differences between Kant's world and that of Pericles and Thucydides, let alone the modern liberal order of contemporary politics. Nevertheless, in light of the vision of liberal constitutionalism in Pericles' Funeral Oration, as well as other features of Athenian political practice, it is worth briefly outlining the thesis as a point of reference for the discussion of Thucydides on democracy and war. I do not evaluate here whether it holds as a generalisation in international politics and history, or whether Thucydides' history provides a disconfirmation of the thesis.

The thesis emerges most clearly in Kant's *Perpetual Peace: A Philosophical Sketch* (1795), where he argues that, in order for there to be a duty to seek peace in the international realm, there has to be the possibility of international peace. He attempts to show this with a speculative history that shows tendencies towards global pacifism. This speculative history has been taken up by contemporary political scientists to test whether the undoubted growth in democracies has led to more pacific international relations. The conclusion is that liberal democracies tend not to go to war with one another but that they are willing to go to war with non-liberal democratic regimes. This claim is subject to considerable scholarly contention, both in terms of whether it actually holds and whether (if it does) this is the result of something that can be described as democracy, rather some other variable that might be doing the causal work. It is the preference for peace with similar regime types that is then used as a further normative case for advancing democratic regime change: the more democracies there are, the less there will be interstate war.

The reasons why democracies are unlikely to go to war with other democracies depends upon fundamental shared features of liberal democratic regimes. The most obvious of these is that democratic leaders are accountable to their people in a way that authoritarian leaders are not. When wars go well, this means there is glory and credit. But, because wars are complex, protracted and precarious ventures, democratic leaders are liable to being held responsible for the consequences of the war. A simple 21st-century example is that of the British Prime Minister Tony Blair and his decision to support the U.S. in the second Gulf War. Blair was a popular and generally trusted prime minister before the Iraq War and so had majority popular support for an intervention backing the U.S. and removing an externally loathed Iraqi leader (Saddam Hussein). Despite the immediate success in toppling the Iraqi regime, the long-term occupation of Iraq proved intractable and public support evaporated. The war was contested by critics at the time, and has gone into popular memory as an expensive diplomatic failure that has coloured Blair's subsequent reputation. A similar story could be told about President George W. Bush and the USA's fortunes in the same conflict, despite their initial overwhelming military victory.

The lesson from such examples is that public opinion is often fickle and that the populace is often unwilling to accept the consequences of their choices, instead placing all the culpability on leaders. In this near-contemporary example, the war was fought by liberal democratic states against an authoritarian dictatorship, a case that the thesis acknowledges is not ruled out by the institutional structure of a liberal democratic regime. However, the general point about leadership culpability is intended as a constraint on waging war in both elements of the thesis. Where liberal democratic states confront one another, the thesis asserts that they are more likely to rely on diplomatic institutions to settle disputes, for the same reasons that they rely on law and dialogue to settle internal political disputes between parties and regions within a state. The claim is that liberal democratic regimes prefer to replace violence and confrontation with discourse and deliberative politics. So they are likely to conceive of international disputes in diplomatic terms as normal politics beyond borders, rather than something that replaces normal politics (Ikenberry 2020). The task of politics and deliberation is to marginalise conflict and violence. When two regimes are structured to do this, as liberal democratic regimes are, then the tendency will be to see the interstate realm as one that can continue that marginalisation of conflict and violence. This is further demonstrated by the tendency of liberal democratic regimes to favour international law, mediation, arbitration and alliances – to the extent that Kant and his followers saw history as tending towards global pacifism and a world federation.

Because liberal democratic states are structured to discipline war, violence and conflict internally, and to rely on diplomacy externally, so with respect to the substance of politics they are unlikely to see matters of policy or doctrine as the basis of conflict and violence. The thesis contrasts the politics of non-liberal democratic regimes with their focus on aggrandisement, awe and expansion with the technical problem-solving welfare focus of liberal democratic politics. Different liberal democratic regimes might seek different policy solutions to similar sorts of problems in terms of fiscal policy, welfare provision and trade, but these technical differences do not create the circumstances for conflict and violence. No liberal democratic state will go to war with another such state on the grounds of differences over welfare policy or industrial policy, because these matters are not politically threatening. Even in the vexed case of trade disputes, liberal democratic regimes tend to rely on international institutions, adjudication and diplomacy, as economic competition is not categorised as threatening behaviour by their similar approaches to political economy.

A feature of liberal democratic regimes, given the greatest emphasis in the thesis, is that such states tend to be relatively wealthy and have a political culture that is focused on the accumulation of wealth and its secure enjoyment, precisely the things most vulnerable to war and conflict. This echoes the contrast between Sparta, and its focus on preparedness for war and martial virtue, and Athens, with its celebration of the benefits of trade, wealth and display celebrated by Pericles in the Funeral Oration. The potential threat that war and conflict pose to the accumulation and enjoyment of wealth raises the cost of war in any analysis. But it also draws attention to the fundamental character of liberal democratic societies, where economy, trade, culture and civilisation are the primary activities of human life – and those most disrupted by military campaigns that both threaten those activities. In addition, those people who carry the burdens of fighting are going to be diverted from their normal lives and this will weigh heavily on their own decisions to support conflict over peace. As this calculation takes place on both sides in a potential war between liberal democracies, the tendency, according to the thesis, is towards some other form of settlement. When it happens on only one side, there is likely to be a strong but not overwhelming case against war, hence the pacific tendency of democratic peace thesis only holds between similar types of states.

If these considerations do hold and are causally effective when taken together, they support the idea that the more regimes become liberal and democratic, the more there will be a pacific world order and war will be marginalised. The challenge for the thesis is threefold: does it indeed hold; if it holds, what are the causal mechanisms as to why; and, finally, does this provide an argument for a global campaign to extend democracy across all regimes? Answering these questions is beyond the scope of this chapter and even of this book – it is the challenge of contemporary international, diplomatic and military strategy – but it does frame the discussion of some of the challenges that Thucydides identifies in the democratic practice of Athens and the Delian League.

Thucydides on democracy

As with the previous issues that we have extracted from Thucydides' narrative, it is important to avoid anachronism and recognise the peculiarities of Athenian democracy and its differences from modern liberal representative democracies. That said, we also need to avoid defining away the possibility of comparisons and contrasts. Whilst Periclean Athens is very different in size and scale and institutional culture to the contemporary United States, the United Kingdom or France, it would be a peculiar definition of democracy that excluded Athens as described by Thucydides or as idealised by Pericles in the Funeral Oration. Indeed, if we follow the five basic criteria set out by Robert Dahl, one of the foremost post-war theorists of democracy, we can see that with a generous interpretation Athenian democracy meets four of the five. It fails on the inclusion of all adults because of slavery and the exclusion of women. Similar problems in liberal constitutional states have only recently disappeared with the emancipation of slavery during the United States Civil War, and full granting of civil rights to Australia's Aboriginal people in 1967. Similarly, the enfranchisement of women was delayed to as late as the middle of the 20th century in France (Dahl 2015, p. 38) and 1971 in Switzerland. The other criteria are effective participation, equality in voting, enlightened deliberation and control of the agenda, and on all of these a case can be made for the democratic qualities of Athenian practices, not just the Periclean ideal. Thucydides is an important source for thinking about democracy both because he provides an ideal account, namely that of the Funeral Oration, and because he is equally concerned to show how democratic politics worked in practice, thus providing something for both the political philosophers and the political scientists. The linking concept in both perspectives is the problem of equality.

As an institutional form, democracy presupposes the equal distribution of political power and this is particularly true in the case of Athens, but only as long as one ignores women and slaves. The male populace decided policy and served in public office, being drawn by lot from a pool including all electors for most offices. Even the most senior officers of state, such as the generals like Pericles, were elected. Pericles had no standing army with a right to command; instead, that right was given by the people and expected to be exercised through the power of rhetoric and personality. The latter is illustrated in all three of his great speeches in Books I and II. But it is equally clear that there is a tension between political equality and economic equality. Athens was not a society of economic equals, as is illustrated by the characters of Pericles, who was from an established aristocratic family, Cleon, who was a parvenu, from new money, but equally was not simply one of the people, and Alcibiades, who was another internationally connected aristocrat. All three were representatives of money and wealth, who used that to mobilise the democratic party amongst the Athenian populace. These divisions raise the challenge of what we now call populism as a modification of democratic rule, where factions use the language of majorities to capture power in the interest of a numerical minority. This situation is most common where the majority is simply that of the largest faction – what in terms of U.S. democratic politics would be called a plurality. A large enough faction can be 'the majority' if all other factions are unable to collaborate as a single alternative. Alongside this hidden class division within Athenian democracy there were clearly oligarchic forces who rejected democratic rule and who mounted a coup following the defeat of Athens during the Sicilian campaign. The narrative of Books VII and VIII is devoted to exploring the unravelling of Athenian democracy through a failure of dominant leadership and the unleashing of factional pressures in response to the significant turn of events. These divisions within regimes are also apparent in the members of the Delian League, where the struggle between the oligarchic forces and the democratic or popular forces was one of the underlying issues behind the Mytilenian revolt and the hostility of the Melians.

Throughout the *History* we see the challenges of democratic action and rule illustrated in the turn of events and, when read carefully, we see democracy through the prism of not merely values but temporality, where the key issues are progress, change and stability. How are states able to maintain stable rule in the face of internal dynamics of change, such as the contest for power amongst factions and groups, as well as maintain order and stability in the face of the external dynamics of politics including changing boundaries, alliances and configurations of power? The central challenge of democratic politics, then and now, is the character of leadership that can hold the demos together into a single unified body that pursues a coherent set of interests and a stable populace. These are the persistent themes of Thucydides' *History* and central to his concern about the challenge of empire to a democratic polity. In Book II, immediately following the incident of the plague, he presents Pericles' defence of his policy against the anger of the populace, which blames, censures and fines him for their misfortune. But then Thucydides writes, 'Not long afterwards, however, as is the way with crowds, they re-elected him to the generalship and put all their affairs into his hands' [Book II, 65] (Thucydides 1972, p. 163). The passage goes on to link the fickleness of the people and their failure to accept a considered strategy to the eventual defeat of Athens.

This theme is central to the arguments around the Sicilian campaign in Book VI and the account of its conduct in Book VII. Here we see the characters of Alcibiades and Nicias, both successors to Pericles as generals and leaders, yet neither of them able to manifest the character or power of personality needed to sustain a coherent strategy. The Athenians are persuaded to join the Sicilian campaign by one city there, the Egestaeans (who seek an alliance against another city, the Selinuntines), with the promise of riches and financial support for the cost of the campaign. Alcibiades, who is depicted as an unscrupulous opportunist, supports this case as a ground for enhancing his own power. Nicias, on the other hand, tries to discourage the expedition by arguing that it will be complex and costly and require a much greater commitment from the Athenians. However, this argument has the perverse effect of providing greater enthusiasm for the campaign and for Nicias's role as one of the generals assigned to lead it.

Despite his success in persuading the Athenians to support the expedition, Alcibiades was subsequently implicated in the 'desecration of the herms'. These were statues comprising a block of stone topped with a carved head and sometimes carved genitals that were used to mark boundaries and were often placed outside houses to ward off evil. Prior to the departure of the Athenian expedition, all the herms were damaged and this act of desecration was seen as an attempt to undermine the expedition and weaken the Athenians' confidence. Alcibiades was charged with complicity in this act but his trial was postponed so as not to delay the expedition. He was subsequently recalled, but absconded and defected to Sparta. Whether or not Alcibiades was involved in this curious act, the way the incident was used by his opponents further illustrates how factions permeated the Athenian demos and the precariousness of stable leadership.

With the failure of the Athenian expedition to Sicily, and the subsequent involvement of the Persians in latter stages of the war, we also see Alcibiades supporting the oligarchic coup against the democracy. The coup is ultimately unsuccessful as the oligarchy is itself deposed. But again, in a detailed discussion of the internal workings of Athens's politics, Thucydides provides evidence of the tension between populism as the temporary will of the majority and a principled commitment to an ideal of democracy. Both reality and ideal come into conflict, in the absence of principled and strong leadership that can unite the many factional and individual interests into a common people.

The precariousness of democracy is clearly linked to economic inequality and the concern of the wealthy to protect their interests against populist policies that squander or risk their wealth, just as the poorer classes see conquest and empire as an opportunity for personal enrichment and advancement. Yet there is another aspect to the weakness of democracy as a vehicle for effective international policy. This is illustrated by Cleon's critique of democracy in the Mytilenian debate. Alongside an argument for the lawfulness of harsh punishment, he spends much of his speech assailing the way in which artful and clever rhetoric can persuade the demos to change its mind and act against its own interest. Effective policy, as in the case of Pericles' strategy, requires commitment and not constant revision in light of shifts in the balance of events. What might prove a virtue in some matters of domestic policy risks undermining strategy and the cool pursuit of national interest. Ironically, Cleon is presented in a critical light for his impatience, forcefulness and vulgarity, but at least in this respect he voices a concern that is repeated throughout the account of post-Periclean Athenian strategy.

In the end, Thucydides suggests that democracy is neither well suited to war and international affairs, or the management of an empire. Indeed, we can also infer that the tendency to empire exacerbates factionalism and expedites the undermining of democracy. This might not seem such a problem now, assuming that the democratic peace thesis holds, but we should remember that Thucydides does give examples of democracies attacking other democracies and the thesis is complicated by the presence of imperial democracies such as Athens and possibly contemporary hegemonic states. If we try to refute Thucydides by alluding to the triumph of modern democracies in 'good' wars (Roosevelt and Churchill in World War II), we also see his point that democratic success depends as much on the character of leaders as on the primacy of social and economic equality. And even in those near-contemporary examples we can see how quickly the demos can change and how important it is to be led wisely. This moral is particularly compelling in light of the recent rise of populism within the established western democracies and the 21st-century challenges to the post-World War II international order. Contemporary democracies, particularly liberal or representative democracies, tend to resolve the problem of the simultaneous importance and elusiveness of wise leadership with careful institutional design, such as the balance of powers within a constitution, or periodic elections to change parties or ruling elites. Yet, even this turn to institutions depends upon the character and virtues of political leaders, since no political order can be a free-standing mechanism independent of the motives of its moving parts, whether these be individual leaders, social classes and factions or (in the international domain) relations between peoples or nations. At the very least, democracy assumes that leaders are motivated by the threat of shame or dishonour. When a leader turns out to be genuinely shameless, it is difficult to tame the exercise of executive power without a political balance.

I argued earlier that, although Thucydides is an historian, we can nevertheless find in his history contribution to international political thinking that is as relevant today as in his own time, about the importance of history as a test for theories and hypotheses. Although Thucydides tends to identify problems that have become central to subsequent debates, as opposed to offering theories that resolve them, in so doing he provides perhaps the greatest service to subsequent theorising about the international realm. It would be invidious to reduce his nuanced and subtle history into a series of perennial problems for later students. Yet it is nevertheless the case that it is the open and complex questions raised by great thinkers, as opposed to clever answers, that make a great text just that. Every epoch and generation must try to answer its own political questions, but the really great texts are those that continuously inform those challenges. The philosopher A.N. Whitehead wrote that '[t]he safest general characterisation of the European philosophical tradition is that it consists of a series of footnotes to Plato' (Whitehead 1929, p. 39). In the context of international theory anywhere, it is no exaggeration to make the bolder claim for Thucydides (and remove the regional qualification also).

Bibliography

Essential reading

Thucydides. (1972). *History of the Peloponnesian War*, trans R. Warner, ed. M.I. Finley. UK: Penguin.
Citations to this translation are given in brackets and with the page number, but I have also used the book and line number in square brackets so that any modern translation can be used.

Secondary reading

Allison, Graham. (2017). *Destined for War*. USA: Houghton Mifflin.
Bell, Duncan. (2018). 'Realist Challenges', in R. Eckersley and C. Brown (eds) *Oxford Handbook of International Political Theory*. UK: Oxford University Press, pp. 641–651.
Clausewitz, Carl von [1832] (1984). *On War*, ed. M. Howard and P. Paret. USA: Princeton University Press.
Collingwood, Robin George. (1993). *The Idea of History with Lectures 1926–1928*. UK: Oxford University Press.
Dahl, Robert. (2015). *On Democracy*, 2nd edn. USA: Yale.
Freedman, Lawrence. (2013). *Strategy: A History*. UK: Oxford University Press.
Howard, Michael. (2002). *Clausewitz: A Short Introduction*. UK: Oxford University Press.
Ikenberry, G. John. (2020). *A World Safe for Democracy*. USA: Yale University Press.
Kagan, Donald. (2009). *Thucydides*. USA: Viking Penguin.
Kant, Immanuel. [1793] (1991). 'Perpetual Peace', in H.S. Reiss (ed.) *Kant Political Writings*. UK: Cambridge University Press.
Lewis, David Malcolm; Boardman, John; Davies, John Kenyon; and Ostwald, Martin. (1992). *The Cambridge Ancient History, vol. 5*. UK: Cambridge University Press.

Mearsheimer, John J. (2018). *The Great Delusion: Liberal Dreams and International Realities*. UK: Yale University Press.

Morley, Neville. (2014). *Thucydides and the Idea of History*. UK: I.B. Tauris.

Strauss, Leo. (1978). *The City and Man*. USA: University of Chicago Press.

Strauss, Leo; and Cropsey, Joseph. (1987). *History of Political Philosophy*. USA: University of Chicago Press.

Whitehead, Alfred North. (1929). *Process and Reality: An Essay in Cosmology*. USA: Macmillan.

Suggestion for finding open access versions of Thucydides' texts

https://openlibrary.org/books/OL5471702M/History_of_the_Peloponnesian_War

This is the same edition that Professor Kelly recommends:

Thucydides. (1972). *History of the Peloponnesian War*, trans R. Warner ed. M.I. Finley. UK: Penguin.

CHAPTER 3

Augustine

The problem of peace in a violent world

Augustine is considered to be one of the most important thinkers
of the Christian era and an important source of ideas about the nature of
politics, war and peace and as a critic of theories of historical progress.
I locate his political thinking in an overview of his theology and explore
the impact of his understanding of the Christian story of redemption
on thinking about the nature, scope and claims of political and moral
authority. Augustine's central question is whether the fundamental teachings of Christianity tend towards a utopian and pacificist view of political relationships, or whether the legacy of Christianity in politics and
international affairs is more properly understood as a form of realism.
Augustine's thought occupies an important place in the development of
'just war' theory and had an impact on the 20th-century resurgence of
Christian realism and the anti-utopianism of post-Cold War liberalism.

'Blessed are the peacemakers; for they will be called children of God'
(Matthew 5:9).

For Christians, peace is not just relief from war and violence; it is mandated by
God as a necessary feature of the order He wills for humanity. In this way, Christianity is pacific in ways that Orthodox Judaism and Islam, or Hinduism and

---

How to cite this book chapter:
Kelly, Paul. 2022. *Conflict, war and revolution: The problem of politics in international
political thought*. London: LSE Press, pp. 63–104.
DOI: https://doi.org/10.31389/lsepress.cwr.c License: CC BY.

Buddhism (despite the way it is caricatured in the west) are not. Yet, the history of international politics in the west for most of the last two millennia has been one of war and conflict; wars and violence against heretics such as Donatists and Cathars, major international wars against Islam during the Crusades, and the modern international order in Europe emerging from the religious wars that characterised the Reformation and the birth of the modern state. Whether Christianity can be faulted for this history of violence is not the point, but it is undoubtedly the case that professed and committed Christians have been actively involved in the deployment of violence and war, as opposed to living in peace. Christian countries and politicians supported the criminalisation of religious-based conscientious objection during World War I, and came to an awkward accommodation on the issue only in World War II. This paradoxical state is also reflected in the prevalence of avowedly Christian thinkers such as Niebuhr, Butterfield and Wight amongst the critics of interwar idealism and as the founders of modern international relations theory. The place of war alongside peace is a vexed and challenging issue for Christians, most of whom seek to explain and reluctantly accept the violence of the world. For instance, in a country such as the contemporary U.S., which has been involved in war for most of the last 30 years, it has nonetheless been led by Presidents George H.W. Bush, Bill Clinton, George W. Bush, Barack Obama and Joe Biden, who are all avowed Christians. Indeed, President Obama even identified the Christian theologian Reinhold Niebuhr as 'one of my favourite philosophers'. I leave aside former President Trump, but even his administration contained vocal evangelical Christians such as Vice President Pence and former Secretary of State Pompeo, who were both 'hawks' on questions of foreign policy and defence. Yet, alongside Christians taking a realist view, there are also strict Christian pacifists dating from early martyrs, sects such as the Quakers, and contemporary theologians such as Yoder, Hays and Hauerwas (Hauerwas 2002; 2011), who insist that the rejection of violence is central to being Christian.

No Christian thinker captures this seemingly paradoxical situation better than Augustine of Hippo. A Catholic saint and Latin Church father, Augustine is revered throughout the history of Christian theology. He is acknowledged on both sides of the rupture in Christianity that occurred at the birth of modernity with the Reformation: both Luther and Calvin recognised him as an authority, whilst he also continued to be a key figure for the Catholic Counter-Reformation. Although he was not a political philosopher, or a theorist of international relations, Augustine's ideas have shaped the way in which people who have abandoned the fundamental core of Christianity continue to see the world of politics and international affairs. This is similar to the way that those like Niebuhr (who applied Augustine's theological insights directly to 20th-century international affairs) continue to be read by people without religious belief.

No thought can be completely timeless in the sense of being free from the particular context, culture and presuppositions in which it emerges. Yet, one challenge of Augustine's Christian thought is that it professes to be based on divine revelation, which claims precisely that universal and transcendent quality. It is the complete and final truth about the nature and purposes of the created order in which humanity resides. As such, Augustine claims to speak to us now in the 21st century just as he spoke to his contemporaries in the 4th century of the common era. In consequence, this chapter both explains the main features of Augustine's thought in relation to politics and explores the ways in which his legacy impacts on contemporary thinking about war, violence and history.

Divine order – Jerusalem to Rome

Augustine's thought has to be set against the backdrop of Christian revelation. As a Catholic Christian, Augustine claims that revelation is not simply the Bible but the lived experience of the Christian Church that followed the death and resurrection of Jesus Christ in the early years of the common era. The Church is important because it is the source of the authoritative witness that is recorded in the books of the Bible. Consequently, distinguishing what is essential to that revelation from other contemporaneous books that are not included in the Bible is a key task. This is particularly important for Christians such as Augustine because the Christian revelation is not simply a new set of laws and commandments akin to the Mosaic Law of the Hebrew Bible (or even the new law of the Koran). The Christian revelation is not simply the words and teaching of Jesus, important though they become. It is the record of his active ministry and then the story of his prosecution, execution by crucifixion and death (which Christians refer to as the Passion), followed by his resurrection from the dead, his eventual bodily ascension into Heaven, and the coming of the holy spirit at Pentecost. In this way the life, death and resurrection of Jesus are the source of the fundamental Christian truth of the Trinity or the threefold nature of God, and it is from this that all other things follow, such as Christian morality and law.

For Christians, revelation is an account of God's presence in the world of history but one in which that history of presence and engagement is ongoing – it will only be completed with the Parousia or 'second coming' of Christ in judgement, this time in triumph, at the end of time. This is the coming of the 'Kingdom', which Jesus claimed is not an earthly kingdom such as that of biblical Israel. Christian revelation radically transforms some familiar political concepts. For the earliest Christians, this apocalyptic culmination of history was expected to be imminent. Indeed, the very earliest Christians probably expected it to occur in their own lifetimes, but it did not happen. Thus, by the time of the writings of St Paul, which are hugely important for Augustine, there is a clear recognition of the challenge of a delayed Parousia and the unfolding of human history, a problem that becomes acute with the spread of Christian communities throughout the Roman Empire and their subsequent persecution.

As the Acts of the Apostles illustrates, very early in Christian history the action shifted from Jerusalem to Rome, with both St Peter and St Paul ending their lives there. This spread of the Christian community was accelerated by the sack of Jerusalem by the Romans, but perhaps more importantly by the transition of Christianity from a millenarian Jewish sect into a distinct community, open through conversion to Gentiles, or non-Jews. From its earliest Roman history, the Church was seen as an alien force that challenged traditional public religious cults and therefore suffered periodic and severe persecutions. These began with Emperor Nero's persecution of the Christians following the Great Fire of Rome in 64 ce. Major Empire-wide persecutions were instituted by Emperor Decius in 250 ce, culminating in that of Diocletian in 303 ce. This resulted in the schism of the Donatists, who refused the ecclesiastical domination of bishops who had compromised with the Roman authorities to avoid punishment. However, Christianity spread beyond its initial appeal to the class of slaves, traders and immigrants and continued to permeate all social classes. The Emperor Constantine I converted to Christianity in 312 ce. Christianity became the official religion of the Roman Empire during the reign of Theodosius I (347–395 ce). The conversion of Constantine and the apparent Christianisation of the Empire led some prominent Christian thinkers (such as Eusebius of Caesarea (260–340 ce)) to suggest that millennial prophecies about the triumph of Christ's Kingdom were being realised by a Christian emperor and a Christian empire. It is precisely this simple alignment of imperial history and divine providence (or Constantinianism) that Augustine rejects in his theological and pastoral writings.

Augustine of Hippo

Writing to a correspondent, Augustine describes himself as 'an African, writing for Africans, both of us living in Africa' (Brown 2000, p. 127). In his role as a Latin father of Christianity and a prolific late Roman author, it is easy and dangerous to forget this important feature of Augustine's biography. In most iconography he is depicted as European, that is, white; he was not. Similarly, although he lived in the Western Empire, Roman Africa was a distinctive and powerful culture in its own right, something that was fully recognised when he went to Rome and then to Milan. Augustine was born in Thagaste (in modern-day Algeria) in 354 ce. His father, Patrick, was a small landholder who made great sacrifices for his son's education, as did the family friend Romanianus, who was also a minor Roman official. Augustine's mother, Monica, who later was made a Catholic saint, was an active and observant Christian. She had a major impact on Augustine's personal and spiritual development, a fact immortalised in his most famous work, the *Confessions*. Written in 401, this work is a model for modern autobiography as it depicts the formation of a mind and character. For Augustine it was the story of his spiritual formation and conversion. It remains the best source of information on Augustine's life, but it needs to be read with care as this is obviously a story with a particular conclusion – the triumph of faith in his life. Augustine's education was in the Latin classics; he never mastered Greek. Nevertheless, his studies progressed sufficiently for him to move to Rome and then to Milan, the imperial capital, where he was Professor of Rhetoric at the age of 31. His studies and his move to Italy were originally intended as a preparation for entry into the Imperial Civil Service, with the wealth and prestige that would follow. However, his intellectual and ultimately spiritual quest took him in a different direction.

In Milan he fell under the influence of the Bishop Ambrose (another saint) and lost his Manichean 'faith', coming to appreciate the truth of Christian scripture – which he had originally found unpersuasive and vulgar in contrast to Manichean mysticism and Platonist metaphysics. Although Augustine is clear that his conversion is a matter of divine grace, Ambrose certainly assisted in the formation that would lead to the famous conversion experience recounted in the *Confessions*, where a childlike voice urging him to 'take up and read' resulted in him returning to scripture and the conversion event. After a retreat to Cassiciacum, near Lake Como, Augustine and a group of followers returned to Thagaste in north Africa to establish a form of monastic life: a community devoted to the study and discussion of truth, clearly led by the intellectually dominant Augustine. At the same time, this community was very different from the austere world renunciation of those Egyptian desert fathers who were inspired by St Anthony.

In 395 ce, Augustine was elected as Bishop of Hippo, the second largest port city in Roman north Africa, where he remained until his death in 430 ce. During this period, Augustine wrote on almost every aspect of theology and the pastoral care of his congregation. In so doing, he engaged with the challenges to the Church from within (such as the Donatists and the Pelagians), as well as the temporal challenges from external enemies (such as the Vandals, who threatened the Empire in north Africa in his final years).

Situating 'The City of God'

The City of God against the Pagans is Augustine's key text. It is an extraordinary work. In modern paperback editions, it is over a thousand pages of closely printed text, yet it was written at a time when the technology of writing, let alone publication and dissemination, was a major challenge. Movable type printing would not appear for a further thousand years. As a comprehensive Christian response to pagan thought, it is extraordinarily wide-ranging and therefore it cannot be reduced to any simple task. It was completed between 413 and 427 ce and closely follows the sack of Rome by the Goths in 410, so it is inevitable that the work is seen as a response to this event. The early books offer a polemical response to pagan thinkers and continue Augustine's long-standing defence of Christianity against the pagan learning that he had transcended in becoming Christian. The latter part of the work is more substantial and concentrates on developing a theologically informed account of history. This is often seen as Augustine's direct response to the supposed challenge to Christianity posed by the sack of Rome and the decline of the Western Empire. But it was also a corrective to those earlier Christian thinkers who had seen the conversion of the empire under Theodosius as a sign of a sign of the prophetic triumph of Christ's kingdom.

For the pagans, the sack of Rome allowed a non-Christian aristocratic elite to argue that the betrayal of the popular civic religion of Rome and its traditional practices by Christians had not protected the empire from the 'wrath of the gods'. As the traditional religion of the Romans was primarily a series of public cults, the defenders of these traditional 'gods' (hence pagans) did not have to believe in their reality. It would have been enough for these practices to serve as sources of social cohesion rather than ontological justification. The risk for Christians, such as Augustine, was that these critics could raise the question why the Christian God no longer seemed to be guaranteeing His Church and empire. This was unsettling for ordinary Christians, who expected to see the triumph of God's kingdom being revealed in historical events. Scepticism about divine providence was a sufficient challenge, whether or not it was accompanied by actual belief in the gods of traditional Roman religion, and it remained a serious challenge for Christian theologians and apologists in this era.

How does Christian eschatology, or the story of the final destination of humanity, fit with the patterns of historical experience? For early historians of Rome, such as the Greek thinker Polybius (264–146 bce), history has a cyclical structure of the successive 'rise and fall' of the fortunes of political regimes, and history does not have a direction or an end. This stance can be allied with the theories of ideal and corrupt regimes that are found in Plato and Aristotle and which can be used to explain the fortunes of political regimes, in the context of the philosophical knowledge of the ideal form of political experience. The challenge for the Christian is that the resurrection of Christ is supposed to be the culmination or end of human experience and therefore the purpose of history. Yet, history as the succession of events has not ended, nor did it appear to represent the triumph of Christ's church on earth when the institutional life of the Church was threatened and destroyed by barbarian invaders. For Christians, history cannot be the endless repetition of cycles of rising and falling powers or civilisations, and it cannot be the meaningless succession of events, because everything has a purpose in the divinely created order. But how do we discern that order in history and prevent simplistic identifications of historical events with God's providence? This is the fundamental challenge that Augustine sets out to address in *The City of God against the Pagans*, and in doing so he also develops his mature political theory.

Political theology versus political philosophy – Augustine's method

Augustine's thought represents a challenge. Although often included as a major figure in histories of political philosophy or political theory, a cursory acquaintance with his writings illustrates that these categories are an awkward fit for his thought. Augustine writes as a late Roman Christian convert who becomes a Catholic Christian bishop. Many writings are not simply on theological topics such as the nature of the Trinity or the soul and creation but rather address the pastoral care of a community besieged by schismatic Donatists and Pelagian heretics. They are also often more mundanely about ecclesiastical politics. Yet, at the heart of Augustine's thought is the centrality of Christian revelation and it is this that raises the most fundamental questions about his method and thought. In an important respect he is undoubtedly a philosopher. His early and formative works and the *Confessions* exhibit a philosophical engagement with the Platonist philosophy, from Plotinus via Porphyry, that places Augustine within any account of late Roman philosophy. But in another crucial respect he is not a philosopher and would have rejected that description.

The nature of philosophy is a perennial problem for philosophers from Socrates to the present. Philosophy is defined as a love of truth, but in practice it takes two main forms that we find in Plato. In the character of Socrates, we see philosophy as a quest or method of inquiry and in the early Platonic dialogues he interrogates experts to find out what, if anything, they know. Most of these dialogues reduce the claims of experts to a muddle of contradictions, such that real knowledge is reduced to Socrates' famous scepticism: 'he can only be truly certain of what he does not know'. This form of critical enquiry leads to scepticism about grand claims and fits our contemporary mode of philosophy as a method of critical analysis, rather than a science or body of doctrines. But Plato also presents us with a conception of philosophy as a body of knowledge through its access to the fundamental truths about the nature of world, revealed through rational enquiry. It is this legacy of Plato that leads to Roman Platonism and which influences Augustine and inspires his rejection of the more sceptical model of philosophy that can be seen in Cicero. However, his philosophy engages him with Christian revelation that provides a final and complete vindication of what Platonism can only intimate. For Augustine there can be no question of what if any truth can we know. We have the gift of the complete and final truth in Christian revelation and in its scriptures, which Augustine regards as a substantial replacement of the literature of pagan classical civilisation. Consequently, philosophy or any other humanistic science can only be a tool for the explication and dissemination of Christian truth. Where philosophy seems to challenge or contradict revelation, it is philosophy that is defective and in error. For Augustine, theology is not one more science to fit into the academic curriculum but the master science of truth that subsumes philosophy as one particular tool. For this reason, it is more appropriate to see Augustine's political thought as a political theology as opposed to a political philosophy. This is a model for a form of thinking about politics that continues to be distinctive from the Socratic ideal of philosophy that has dominated western thought since the European Enlightenment.

Augustine's legacy is still alive amongst contemporary political theologians. They claim that the relationship between theology and politics:

> is not a question of adapting to alien requirements or submitting to external agenda, but of letting theology be true to its task and freeing it from a forced and unnatural detachment. Political theology tries to recover for faith in God, Christ and Salvation, what scepticism surrendered to mechanistic necessity. (O'Donovan 1996, p. 3)

As we have seen, Christian revelation about the Kingdom of God is not a simple statement of law such that the task of political theology is fundamentally interpretive. It is not just ransacking scripture for theological images of politics, or for apparent statements of what Christ has commanded. Instead, it is a search for an understanding of political experience that is informed by fundamental Christian concepts and which weaves together as a single narrative the history of salvation and the history of human political experience. It would be a grave misunderstanding to seek secularised conceptions of politics in Augustine's theology. We should not look at his views of the Church or Christian community as an intimation of a modern conception of the state or the medieval Christian Empire. Although Augustine does have important things to say about the nature of political community, political agency and the extent of political power, this is from the perspective of fundamental theology and its account of the nature and purpose of human existence. Augustine's political theology is the vehicle through which philosophical history is conducted until the early modern period. His thought continues to affect the shape of that form of enquiry, even in contemporary thought, and even by those who may have abandoned the fundamental Christian beliefs behind his account of the meaning and structure of history. It is for this reason that he remains of interest to contemporary international thinkers, as well as to Christian theologians.

Manicheans, Donatists and Pelagians

Alongside his political theology, Augustine was also a significant controversialist at a time when Christianity was defining its fundamental doctrines. His status as a Latin father of the Church is an acknowledgement of his important role in this process. He is most famous for his engagement with three rival positions, one (Manichean beliefs) an alternative theology to Christianity that had shaped his early pre-Christian thinking. The other two were movements within the Christian community that threatened its distinctive order and truth, namely Donatism and Pelagianism. Because each of these beliefs provides a context for Augustine's own theological and political position, a brief overview of all of them will be useful. They are certainly no longer familiar currency within the history of thought, even amongst very well read Christians. In addition, the three approaches also provide models of political thinking that continue to reappear within our secularised political discourse, because much western political discourse is informed by the theological context from which it emerged.

Manichaeism had its origins in the writings of the 3rd century ce Persian mystic Mani, and was influenced by Jewish and Gnostic (Jewish and early Christian unorthodox ideas that were left behind by the subsequent development of the two traditions) ideas that permeated the late Roman and early Christian period. At its height, the influence of Manicheanism spread across the Roman Empire, through the Middle East and Central Asia, even reaching Song Dynasty China. It was also the spiritual philosophy that Augustine subscribed to as a young man in Italy when straying from his initially superficial Christian upbringing. Because Manichaeism was defeated in its struggle with Christianity and subsequently Islam in the Middle East and Central Asia, we have little direct evidence for its fundamental teachings except through the accounts given by its opponents such as Augustine. Even the history of ideas tends to be written by the victors!

The attraction of Manichaeism for Augustine was its dualistic cosmology that explained the possibility of evil alongside the idea of a soul that is eternal and shares an element of the divine. For Mani, the world is divided between two opposing forces: that of light, which encompasses the realm of truth and the soul, and a world of darkness embodied in the materiality of the body, with its earthly lust and urges. These two forces are in a constant struggle for dominance, and this contest is also part of the human psyche, with a similar conflict between the soul and the material body. So sin and evil are not part of the divine creation of the God of light but the result of the lesser god or demiurge that clashes with light. One consequence of this view, which was comforting (for a time) to Augustine, is that it explains the possibility of evil in the world. Problematically, however, it also frees the individual from responsibility for their compulsive evil actions, such as the tyranny of lust and the desires of the body. Once Augustine had come to abandon this early commitment under the influence of Ambrose of Milan, and had achieved a deeper appreciation of Christian scripture, he devoted much effort to attacking the metaphysics and cosmology of Manichaeism, because of Gnostic efforts to elide Manichean doctrines with Christianity. Although it was a separate religion or philosophy, and therefore not strictly a Christian heresy – that is, a false doctrine that emerges within the Church or Christian community – Manichaeism's perpetual struggle between light and dark or good and evil clearly denies fundamental Catholic doctrines concerning creation, sin, the finality of salvation and the nature of an all-powerful God. Although Augustine's anti-Manichaeism is central to his fundamental theology, it does have implications for his political theology and history, not least in Augustine's 'realism'.

Donatism. If Manichaeism is a heresy, Donatism is a schism, that is, a division occurring within the life and structure of the Church or Christian community. Clearly, such divisions have some doctrinal element, but it is their political and physical separation from and challenge to Church authority that are most important. Donatism preoccupied Augustine throughout his priestly and episcopal ministry because it was a largely African phenomenon. The Donatists were a group who separated from the main body of the Church (although in parts of Augustine's Africa they were the majority of Christians) following the final great persecution of Christians in the late Roman Empire. At this time, the Roman authorities in Africa had accepted the handing over and destruction of Christian texts as a compromise for the Christian bishops to avoid further punishment. The Donatists took a stand against the bishops and clergy who compromised in this way and rejected their authority when the persecution ended and these individuals returned to ecclesiastical office. The Donatists were ecclesiastical purists who would not compromise with the world, even when that was the result of an attempt to protect their communities and not merely the acts of weak individuals saving themselves. They could not accept compromise and denied not just the legitimacy of bishops who had compromised with the Roman authorities but that of all clergy who traced their ordination and authority back through those bishops.

Of particular interest amongst the Donatists' beliefs was the way that they saw the physical manifestation of authority in holy texts or 'holy water' used in liturgy. To non-Christian and modern ears, these claims seem hard to credit, but for the Donatists they were the basis for the armed rejection of non-Donatist authority (they, of course, denied that this was legitimate Catholic authority). The Donatists had their own militants, the Circumcellions, whom we would characterise as terrorists. They carried out attacks on persons and property in defence of their claims against Catholics such as Augustine, who narrowly avoided an ambush and death at their hands. As with modern religiously inspired terrorism, the Donatists' purism did not just mean their separation; it also denied the faith of, and declared enmity with, the ordinary Catholic community who were caught up in the struggle. Augustine's primary theological dispute with the Donatists concerned the possibility of a self-identifying pure Church within a corrupt human Church and the purist presumption that goes with it. He was also concerned with the dangers of religiously inspired violence and its tendency to be even more uncompromising than the disinterested brutality of imperial rule. Violence was a part of man's fallen nature and a central feature of Roman imperial rule, but the challenge of the Donatists and the need for Church discipline also drew Augustine into confronting the problem of violence and coercion in the Church and amongst those who claimed to be followers of Jesus.

Pelagianism. This was another heresy that dominated the later years of Augustine's career. Like Manichaeism, it was also rooted in the problem of the possibility of evil within a divinely created order. This heresy actually continued to resonate into the Reformation and in secularised form into modern political ideologies. It was first condemned by the Council of Carthage (418) following a campaign by Augustine. The belief's originator, Pelagius, was a British theologian who was influential in Rome and advocated an ascetic lifestyle at a time when monastic and personal asceticism was developing as a reaction to the public association of the Church with the Roman imperial order. However, the fundamental issue between Pelagius and orthodox Catholicism, represented by Augustine, concerned the doctrine of original sin. This was the very problem that had encouraged Augustine to flirt with Manichaeism as a young man, namely: how could a good and just God create a world marred by the existence of sin and evil (what subsequent theologians have defined as *theodicy*)? In contrast to Manicheans, Pelagius did not have recourse to a dualist cosmology and instead located the problem of sin in human free will and culpability. But this raised the problem of heredity in Augustine's interpretation of the Genesis story in the Garden of Eden, when Adam and Eve rejected God through disobedience in eating from the 'tree of knowledge'. The issue here is how could the act of the first humans condemn all mankind through all time with the stain of an 'original sin' that culminates in eternal damnation? The problem is theological and not historical (because for both Augustine and Pelagius the Genesis story is a theological narrative as opposed to a simple natural history). The issue here goes to the heart of God's nature and the place of justice in His creation. For Pelagius, the challenge of double predestination (the idea that God creates some people to be damned for eternity) threatened the idea of the goodness of God's nature and thus His purpose in creating the world. How could a good God predestine some people to damnation from the very earliest moments of creation? Surely this undermines the very idea of human agency, morality and the significance of our actions. In his account of salvation, Pelagius asserts the importance of personal goodness and righteous action. Through good works and personal piety one could merit salvation, and, equally, those souls who are damned must in some way deserve that.

For Augustine, the problem of salvation by good works threatened the essential gift of salvation through Christ's passion, and suggested that salvation could be a personal transaction between humanity and God. This issue of the place of 'works' versus 'grace' was at the heart of Luther's dispute with Rome at the commencement of the Reformation, and it has wider ramifications for western culture in terms of the issue of agency and personal responsibility. If wickedness or evil is not in some way inherent in all of us, then is it not possible that the corruption of our natures is actually the result of external circumstances such as lack of appropriate socialisation or education, or the result of poverty (the problem of moral luck)? If so, then would not a social order that corrected for these things be the key to achieving a peaceful and just social order, so that we could actually build a version of Heaven on earth? Augustine's response to each of these challenges shapes his considerable contribution to the subsequent history of Christianity. In addition, as each one casts its own shadow over modern politics through dualism and political and personal perfectionism, so equally Augustine's responses also still cast a similar shadow over contemporary political thought, amongst Christian and non-Christian thinkers alike.

Sin and evil

The problem of sin and evil is the central thread of all of Augustine's writings and his pastoral or political writings are simply extensions of this fundamental discussion. The challenge and response to sin and evil is central to the drama of each human life or soul (to follow Augustine's Christian and Platonist way of thinking), and it concerns the meaning of each person's life and their ultimate destiny. Augustine's own story is partly captured, beautifully, in his most famous work, the *Confessions*. In addressing the ultimate destiny of human beings and their relationship with their creator, Augustine is drawn into fundamental theological reflections on the problem of evil and the nature of sin. Indeed, one can read the argument of the *Confessions* as the conclusion to Augustine's intellectual struggle with the problem of evil or sin in a world created by a good God. The journey is one within a universe that is created and ordered by some divine power: atheism of the modern variety never appears on Augustine's intellectual horizon. Instead, the movement is through a series of philosophical religions (such as Manichaeism or Platonism) to reach the revealed religion of Christianity, which gives a psychological and personal reality to what only existed abstractly in the philosophy of Platonism. Yet the recognition of the universal prevalence of sin or evil in the world of human experience is also central to Augustine's vision of politics and of social life in human history. This is what makes his thought central to Christians seeking to make sense of a created order that is clearly marred by pain, suffering, violence and disorder. But it is also relevant for non-Christian readers who recognise the depiction of human experience as essentially tragic because of violence, war and error, even if they reject Augustine's ultimate explanation of that fact in his account of sin and the fall of humanity.

The problem of evil is relatively simple to state. Given that the world is the product of a creator and that creator is good, how is it that sin, evil or bad are possible? For Platonists, following Plato's metaphysics, the universe is a hierarchically ordered creation at the pinnacle of which is the sovereignty of the good. This structure is a complete rational order, so for Platonists the problem is identifying the rational point of suffering, pain and violence? For Christians, the story is simpler but more challenging. The Genesis story of creation recounts how God created all things. This story takes place over a series of days in which different elements of the world are created and acknowledged as good by God: He sees his creation and considers it good. As the source of all created things, God therefore must be responsible for the creation of evil, bad or sin. But, if God created a power of sin or evil, then either He is not good, which for Christians is either a blasphemous or a terrifying idea, or He was negligent in the creation process and therefore not omnipotent, that is, all-powerful and all-seeing. God cannot be weak and He cannot be wrong; to think otherwise is to conceive of God as being less than perfect. Possibly God created evil as a check on humanity of some sort, but again this leaves the idea of God as some kind of cosmic force playing an unnecessary game with His creation. Surely an all-powerful and good God could have created a world without the suffering and pain of cancer and drought, or without the human sources of pain from predators, tyrants, bullies and murderers.

The facts of experience challenge both the philosophers and the Christians with the problem of evil. Responses to that include the Manichaeism explained earlier. This cosmology posits a dual power in the universe in antagonism, namely a force of good or light, and a force of darkness, which are in perpetual struggle. The powers of light are associated in the human psyche with reason and the quest for truth, whereas the powers of darkness are associated with materialism and the body. Humans' psychic or spiritual life is a mirror of the larger cosmic struggle between light and darkness or the spirit and the soul. This dualistic psychology is a recognisable feature of many religions and for some Christians it also provided a way of making sense of some features of their religion such as the place of Satan or the Devil. He appears in the Genesis story as an evil personality and power complicit in the temptation of Adam and Eve and, again, in the temptation of Jesus in his wilderness period, prior to his active ministry, as recorded in the Gospels. There do indeed seem to be two powers at work here. How can Jesus, one of the three persons of the Trinitarian God, be tempted by a 'power' that must in some respects be part of His own creation? We will leave aside the idea of non-human spiritual beings (such as angels, devils and daemons), which were widely shared beliefs throughout the classical and early modern period and central to Christian thinking. The important issue for us is not whether such beings exist – Augustine shared the traditional view of his age, and subsequently of Christianity, that the created order included beings who are not material or bodily.

In Manichaeism there is incessant struggle between these two opposing forces, and the forces of darkness may crowd out the light, like a storm cloud obscuring the sun. As a 'religion', Manichaeism teaches that man can overcome this darkening effect of our material bodies by renouncing things of the flesh, and by abstaining from sex and certain types of food. Many features of Manichean dualism persist into the modern world. Practices of renunciation to achieve enlightenment are common both in contemporary religions and in many 'New Age' philosophies of life. The Manichean dualism also appealed to Augustine because it resonated with his own struggle between the things of the body and the intellect or mind. Some argue that traces of this body–mind dualism persist into Augustine's Christianity and its legacy for western thinking, particularly in relation to traditional Christian teaching on sex (Connolly 1993). However, the Manichean cosmology was unstable, as it presented a good God as ultimately weak and vulnerable, because of His unwillingness to use power to destroy the forces of darkness. Manicheans thus purchase cosmological coherence only at the expense of divine perfection.

Augustine achieves his liberation from Manichean dualism with the help of Platonist metaphysics, specifically the doctrine of substances. This allows him to realise that evil is not a thing in the world that exists of its own right and which can be seen as a rival force within a created order, or something whose existence needs explanation. Augustine's breakthrough was achieved by denying that evil is a thing or substance at all. Sin and evil are nothing – not a thing. But, in denying that there is such a thing as sin or evil, Augustine is making an ontological claim (that is, a philosophical point about what there is the universe), not an ethical or moral claim. Humans still suffer the experience of sin, evil, harm, pain and violence. However, we should understand these as absences or departures from the good and not substances in the world. In this way, the created order is ultimately good but its goodness is obscured by the absence of the complete goodness of that order in the world of human experience. This is a matter of degree, depending on the enormity of evil. Major evils such as genocide potentially obscure goodness completely, in that they may cause people to deny that the universe can contain, or be, good at all. Small sins or bads may not totally obscure the good, but cumulatively they crowd out goodness in the experience of an individual life. All departures from the good matter: we can illustrate this complex idea in simple terms if we think of injustice not as a separate force in the cosmos but as a lack of or absence of justice. Similarly, pain is an absence of pleasure, order or wholeness in terms of health and well-being. Augustine thinks we can account for all of the perceived evils in human experience in terms of this idea of departures from goodness. This philosophical reorientation certainly provides a way around Manichean dualism and the idea of divided and conflictual cosmos. Yet, Augustine still needs to explain how, if sin and evil are ultimately nothing (Evans 1990, p. 2), they are still such a huge feature of human experience. Augustine's answer to this question is the second important element of the Genesis story, namely its account of the 'Fall of Man'.

The story of 'the Fall', or how Adam and Eve turn their backs on God by disobeying his command to refrain from eating of the tree of knowledge, is a parable about how humanity is created by God with the capacity to know and to love Him as the source of good, but through the exercise of their free will they rebel against or disobey God. The source of sin is rooted in this fundamental act of disobedience. What is significant in this story is that sin or evil has its source in the exercise of human will against the good, as opposed to the specific act done. Of course, doing what God prohibited makes that act wrong, but it is the wilfulness of the act that signifies the sin or evil. Consequently, for Augustine the source of evil is not a power in the world acting on humanity but one that originates in the human will with its tendency to reject the truth or the good. Individual acts of wilfulness are the sources of particular evils or wrongs. But the fundamental and universal tendency for the will to overcome reason and the good is the primary source of evil or bad in the universe: it is not a part of the created order but a consequence of how part of that created order – humanity, and only humanity – acts against its creator. By locating the source of evil or wrong in the will, Augustine distinguishes it from mind or reason, where humanity is most close to its creator, and in so doing follows in part the Manichean hostility to the flesh or body. He rejects the materiality of human nature over which will is sovereign in a way that mind or reason is not, and shares the Platonic elevation of mind over spirit and desire, which are rooted in the body. This is also why Augustine has such a negative view of sexuality and especially its manifestation in lust, to the discomfort of modern readers since Freud. The problem of lust, for Augustine, is a paradigm example of the body and will crowding out reason and control. Lust is also a source of tyranny and control over others, who are forced to submit their bodies to domination, power and the will of the powerful. Sex is not just a means of procreation and even enjoyment or an expression of love; it is often a source of domination, control and destruction. Rape and sexual violence are constant features of war and explicitly gross acts of symbolic and actual violence.

The story of the Fall, for Augustine, is the origin of original sin, which is hereditary such that all humanity as the heirs of Adam and Eve share that taint. No one is born free from sin, and in the *Confessions* Augustine famously describes how this is exhibited in the behaviour and character of human infants or his own childish sinning (such as stealing fruit for the thrill of transgression). It is important to note that the capacity to sin and the wilfulness of our nature have been fundamental since the Fall – they are not things that we acquire in a social context, nor are they learned behaviour. All human beings are sinners, albeit that some are greater sinners than others. Throughout the account of original sin and its transmission through procreation, Augustine is still primarily concerned with the story of each individual soul or psyche and its relation with its creator. At the same time, this story has implications for society and history. The consequences of sin shape human history and account for its structure: history is the story of humanity since the Fall confronting the legacy of original sin and the consequences of individual sinning. This account of the tyranny of individual will shaping the disorder of history and political experience has proved attractive to realist thinkers into the present, even if they deny the biblical story of its origin, because it reflects the limitations of reason and our ability to accept rational direction in politics.

While the Genesis story explains the origin of sin in the world, its introduction is not the whole story for Christians like Augustine. Sin and evil are the tyranny that human beings create for ourselves by rebelling against God. But God does not give up on humanity. In the person of Jesus, God seeks to redeem us by becoming human in the incarnation so as to take on human sin in the passion and be crucified before rising again and ascending to Heaven. For Augustine, this redemption is by far the most important part of the story of humanity's relation with God because it involves God reaching out to His creation, and potentially to each person, to offer ultimate reconciliation between the created and its creator. This reaching out is the gift of grace, which Christians see as the consequence of Jesus' acting in our world and the bridge between that world and an eternal life freed from sin. The gift of grace is an opportunity to reconcile with God and for us to seek forgiveness for that fundamental wilfulness or rejection of God. The rejection of God is the embracing of sin or evil and being subject to divine punishment – the choice between Heaven and Hell. The source of grace is Christ, but the signs of that gift of redemption are not things that we can simply infer from behaviour and actions. As a gift, it is freely given but it cannot be earned or merited.

This doctrine is what gives rise to Augustine's extensive debates with the followers of Pelagius, who look at good acts and virtuous lives as meriting grace. Put simply and crudely, if good works are not a sign of the grace that is linked to good works or moral behaviour, then why be good, because it will not guarantee redemption? Similarly, if those who have died outside the Church before they could be baptised (such as infants) will be damned, does this not make God cruel and fickle? Finally, if grace cannot be freely sought through works and individual acts, then we confront the problem of double predestination that was to plague Augustine's theological writings in his final years, and which was to become so important to Protestant reformers such as Luther and Calvin. This is the idea that, because an omniscient and omnipotent (all-seeing and all-powerful) God knows and sees the destination of all creation from the initial moment of creation, He must be creating some men to be irredeemable sinners and therefore condemned to damnation. Would it not have been more perfect to have only created those who can be saved? Are we not back with the problem of sin from which we began: how can a good God create an order in which some are damned from the moment of creation whatever they do?

The problem of grace and the mystery of predestination is one of the significant legacies of Augustine to subsequent theology. However, there is one last part of God's revelation of Himself in history as a means of redeeming creation, and that is that the full redemption of humanity is not completed at the point of Christ's resurrection in historical time. (Christians believe that the passion narrative of the Gospels describes actual events that occurred sometime in the fourth decade of what we now describe as the common era (ce).) For Augustine and the Church, God's work of redemption is only completed with His promise of the second coming, where Jesus will end human history with the final judgement between the damned and the saved and the establishment of His new Kingdom. Whilst Augustine is clear that this too will be an historical event ending the secular order, or the time of passing away, he is equally clear that it is ultimately a theological matter that ends time as we know and experience it. This has the important consequence that Augustine is not prepared to identify signs of the end of time with signs that occur within historical time. It is for this reason that he is opposed the Constantinians, who saw the end of time with the unification of the Church and the Roman Empire following the conversion of the Empire under Theodosius. Like St Paul in the Epistle to the Thessalonians, he cautions believers against being deceived by those who offer themselves as signs of the second coming, or those who claim that they can accelerate the coming of the Kingdom. Instead, for Augustine, the followers of Christ are condemned to be pilgrims on a journey to that new Kingdom through the world where sin and its powers continue to hold sway. The fate of the Roman Empire at the hands of its own internal destructive forces, or the barbarians invading from beyond its borders, are just another set of obstacles on that journey, and not a sign of some acceleration towards the end times. History remains, for Christians, the time of faith and not the new Kingdom.

All that Augustine teaches about redemption is fundamentally theological and has a reality outside of the world of bodily experience that is subject to time and change. So it leaves the problem of historical experience open. Humanity awaits the coming of the final judgement, yet, because God is outside of time and change, and is therefore in an eternal present, He is not waiting for anything to happen or to unfold in the divine realm. The time of change is a problem only of human experience, and it remains an important problem for Christians. They must confront the historical challenges of pain and change whilst holding to their faith in the resurrection. These problems are particularly current and acutely present for Augustine and his contemporaries, with the threats and challenges to the peace of the Empire and the persistent wilfulness of humans. Even within the Church there are those, such as the Donatist schismatics or Pelagians, who confuse fellow Christians by disseminating different and conflicting accounts of how one must live in this time of change and overcoming – what Augustine refers to as the secular world or Saeculum.

Augustine's fundamental theological writings are intended to reorient humanity away from the trappings of sin and the consequences of evil, by showing that evil is not actually a thing, or a power, but is merely the consequence of humanity's corrupted will. This will is potentially redeemed by the possibility of grace, signified by God becoming present in the world in the person of Jesus Christ. Yet, Augustine never turns away from the world or ignores the challenge of living within that secular order while oriented towards the things of God. In this way, he becomes a political thinker by default rather than intention, by not accepting that Christians have the luxury of turning their back on history and experience. What they must not do is confuse the secular order with the unfolding of the individual redemption of their souls. It is this fact that is the key to understanding Augustine's thought about political authority, violence and war. This warning against seeing historical events as a sign of human redemption is also one of Augustine's legacies for contemporary politics, whether viewed from a Christian perspective or not.

The two cities: an Augustinian theory of government and politics

Augustine's theology of sin and redemption is not a political theory but it has profound implications for his account of the nature of political life and the institutions of government and coercion in the Empire. We might call this his theory of the state – but be mindful of the fact that the state as an entity is an early modern concept that only appears in modern form a millennium after Augustine's death. In the context of the sack of Rome, the theology of sin is important because it disrupts the simple link between theological history or eschatology and the human history of political events. This rupture does not entail that there is no connection between human historical experience and redemption, but it does entail two important lessons. Firstly, as Augustine's response to Pelagianism shows, we cannot infer a simple connection between good actions amongst men and the reward of Heaven, because this would make history itself the vehicle for redemption. Secondly, we cannot infer God's will from perceived patterns in history. To claim that political success measured by human goals (such as the military triumphs of the Roman Empire) is a sign of God's plan unfolding in history is a further example of the pride and sinfulness of human nature. Augustine reminds us that providence might be as well served by political failure as by human flourishing. In neither case is it appropriate for Christians to see a pattern in historical events as a further source of revelation. Theological time and human history are distinct. Augustine is aware that there is a natural and perennial urge for all Christians to seek comfort from patterns in human events, and not simply theologians and philosophers, This remains the fundamental challenge of the secular age as a period of passing away and impermanence, pending the final judgement.

The profound lesson of Augustine's political thought is that politics is appropriate to this secular age and it is not concerned with the fundamental good for man or with human redemption as a Christian variant of the classical goal of politics. Augustine's thought marks a fundamental rupture with natural law as it emerges from the classical sources of Plato, Aristotle and Cicero, and the idea that political action and political life is part of a truly human life. The secular realm is not concerned with achieving the fundamental good for humanity, because that cannot be achieved by human action alone, even when that occurs in a good polity. Instead, the secular realm is one in which the damned and the saved continue to live out their human lives, in the shadow of final judgement but before that judgement is given. As such, the secular realm is one characterised by sin and its consequences, and, whilst the Christian (unlike the Manichean) can now be sure that sin cannot ultimately triumph, it remains a constant challenge for Christians as they seek to live out their lives in fidelity to the cross and resurrection of Jesus. Thus, Augustine's political theory should not be seen as an account of the good life for humanity, nor is it about the ideal political community or constitution in which that good can be achieved. Rather, it is essentially a pastoral teaching directed to Christians struggling with the practicalities of living faithfully in a world marked by sin and its signs of violence and coercion: a kind of Christian prudence. This pastoral advice can take the form of specific advice to named individuals, given in letters about how they should act with respect to specific challenges. Alternatively, it can take the form of a larger story or meta-narrative about how Christians should see their position in relation to the received institutions of the Empire and politics – the things of Caesar – and against which they should orient their actions. The most striking example of this is Augustine's distinction between the two cities and the account of political society as 'a gathered multitude … united by agreeing to share the things they love' (1998, p. 960).

The two cities

The distinction between the two cities – the city of God and the city of man – has become the most familiar feature of Augustine's political thought. It can easily be confused with a distinction of jurisdiction between temporal (political) rule and ecclesiastical authority, especially as the latter was to have such importance in the medieval period. There were intense debates then about the necessary limits of *regnum* (political jurisdiction, associated with the Holy Roman Emperor) and *sacredotium* (or ecclesiastical rule, associated with the Pope and bishops), as well as amongst the thinkers of the Reformation. This jurisdictional issue is not Augustine's concern in the distinguishing the two cities, although conflicts of jurisdiction are addressed in exercising episcopal and pastoral authority. Instead, the importance of the two cities is an implication of the reorientation of political thinking from the classical focus on the good life for humanity and the place of politics within it. Augustine is quite clear that the idea of dominion or rule of some human actors over others is not natural; indeed, the natural condition at the time of creation is one of freedom. At creation, humanity is given dominion only over the beasts as irrational creatures: 'He did not intend that His rational creature, made in His own image, should have lordship over any but irrational creatures: not man over man, but man over the beasts' (Augustine 1998, p. 942). Similarly, the first just humans, such as the biblical Abraham, were 'shepherds of flocks, rather than kings of men' (Augustine 1998, p. 942).

Dominion (or the domination of one human over another) is only a consequence of sin. Political rule is linked with slavery, war and the punishment of sin. Whilst this can seem a deeply pessimistic view of human experience, it is accompanied by Augustine's refocus on sociability, which takes many forms and which is natural, albeit tainted in the fallen world. Human beings have a natural tendency to associate and form societies so as to achieve many different ends – from the most basic of companionship and procreation to more complex collaborative ventures such as education and collective defence, or robbery and murder. Societies are simply 'gathered multitudes' of people agreeing to share and pursue the things that they love. It is in the context of this plurality of forms of social ends that we can locate the distinction between the two cities.

> Two cities, then, have been created by two loves: that is, the earthly by love of self, extending even to contempt of God, and the heavenly by love of God extending to contempt for self. The one, therefore, glories in itself, the other in the Lord; the one seeks for glory from men, the other finds its highest glory in God, the Witness of our conscience … In the Earthly City, princes are as much mastered by the lust for mastery as the nations they subdue are by them; in the Heavenly, all serve one another in charity, rulers by their counsel and subjects by their obedience. (Augustine 1998, p. 632)
>
> I divide the human race into two orders. The one consists of those who live according to man, and the other of those who live according to God's will. Speaking allegorically, I also call these two orders the two Cities: that is, two societies of men, one of which is predestined to reign in eternity with God, and the other of which will undergo eternal punishment with the devil. (Augustine 1998, p. 634)

Augustine's distinction is based on two distinct orientations, and his teaching applies to persons as well as to societies, rather than to institutional structures or territories. And, whilst the plurality of societies and social goals is considerable, the important distinction for Augustine is the type or object of love, and whether those are things of God or of humanity. The objects of love for some social groups will necessarily fall on one side of this distinction. For example, the love of a society of robbers or pirates will necessarily be part of the city of humanity because there could not be a form of righteous or Christian piracy. But some other ends that might be pursued by a society (such as education) could be oriented towards either the city of humanity or the city of God. A straightforward example might be the contrast between a seminary and a business school. Yet even here it is the *ultimate* orientation and motive of those sharing the goal that really matters, and not the superficial institutional function. A seminary can end up producing students consumed by earthly ambition and pride, whereas the business school can produce those who advance the Kingdom of God. It is the kind of love and the orientation of that love that are at the heart of the distinction, and not the constitution, history or nature of rule that distinguishes the two cities. This fact transcends the simple distinction between the Church and the state or political community. Whilst the Church is the gathered body of Christians it remains a visible community of sinners. Some members will simply fall short of their calling, in the way that Reformation thinkers castigated the sins of medieval popes. But, at a more fundamental level, Augustine also sees the conflict between the city of God and the city of humanity operating within the Church in the disputes between Donatist schismatics or heretics, such as Pelagians. In their own way, each of these creeds substitutes the orientation towards love of God with love of humanity, in terms of intellectual pride or a sense of purity and moral superiority over others. Augustine is clear that the idea of the two cities is an allegory, and it is the orientation to love God, versus love of the things of the world, that is the fundamental underpinning of the distinction.

In this way, Augustine introduces an idea of social pluralism in terms of the ends and goals of association in society, whilst rejecting the hierarchy of pluralism amongst the virtues that is derived from Aristotle or more modern ideas of value pluralism. Social pluralism is the fact of human experience and is something to be celebrated and acknowledged. As an educated Roman with an experience of the regional and social differences across the Empire, as well as being aware of the differences of cultures and style of theology between Eastern and Western Christianity, it is unsurprising that Augustine does not privilege a narrow uniformity in human experience. Nevertheless, his core teaching about the value and significance of these social ends, as well as their ordering, is in terms of fundamental orientation. Pagan ways and practices are a denial of the truth, just as the common ends pursued by pirates and brigands are evil.

The contrast between the two cities can lend itself to a distinction between types of political community and political rule. Augustine even uses the orientation of princes towards the things of God and things of the earth as a way of distinguishing good and bad regimes; in the one, the prince is mastered by the lust for 'mastery', and in the other by 'charity'. But, again, the focus is on the character and orientation of the ruler and not the constitution or state as such. This allows Augustine to acknowledge that genuine Christians could, and have been, Roman emperors and steered the Empire towards the things of God, without conceding that the Empire itself was therefore a vehicle of divine providence. No political society in a fallen world can be simply identified with the city of God, because, in a world marked by sin and pending final judgement, the two cities will be constantly intermingled in ways that mere human judgement cannot ultimately untangle. This precludes any form of utopian politics in secular history, whether that is of a classical form of a Platonic or Ciceronian ideal republic, or an ideal and pure church free from sinners. Until the final judgement that separates the damned and the saved, human history and human society will always be made up of an intermingling of the two cities.

Justice and the Empire

Augustine's anti-utopianism (and assertion of the inseparability of the two cities before the time of final judgement) also explains his rather curious denial that the Roman Empire was ever a commonwealth or a genuine republic. In Book XIX, Augustine challenges Cicero's conception of the Republic as a multitude or community of 'friends', that is, a voluntary association unlike a family, united in 'common agreement as to what is right' (Augustine 1998, p. 950). For Cicero, this agreement on 'the right or justice' was primarily concerned with the administration of property and its defence, thus presaging the argument of Locke 18 centuries later. This Ciceronian republican ideal is one with a lasting resonance and is still captured in Rawls's famous statement at the beginning of *A Theory of Justice* that 'justice is the first virtue of social institutions' (Rawls 1972, p. 3). Augustine rejects this position because it repeats the false idea (inherited from Aristotelian thinking) that political society is natural and entailed by the idea of the human good. Augustine's critique of Ciceronian republicanism is twofold: firstly, he rejects the idea that the human good can be separated from the Christian idea of humanity's ultimate goal and purpose; and, secondly, he rejects Cicero's implication about the moral justification of the Roman Empire as a just republic, in order to challenge pagan criticism of Christianity in the face of the sack of Rome and the barbarian threats facing the Empire.

The fundamental argument against the justice of the Empire, and therefore its claim to be a commonwealth, draws on the place of pagan civic religion in Roman life, either through its early and classical history or in the form of a revived pagan civil religion that Augustine's critics were defending. No social order that demands the worship of false gods, or what Augustine calls 'demons', can be a moral order and thus by definition pre-Empire Rome cannot be a commonwealth. The argument is both a conceptual sleight of hand and a moral critique of the pre-Christian order. It is the former because Augustine denies that there can be a narrowly human or political morality that can be separated from the fundamental theological basis of moral virtues and concepts: he therefore rules out precisely what contemporary political liberals like Rawls (following Cicero) wish to assert, namely that justice is a 'political' value. And it is the latter genuine critique in that it reasserts Augustine's view that we cannot see any historical political community as necessarily good or just. However, we wish to describe what Cicero intended: by using the concept of 'republic' or 'commonwealth', we are not naming a genuine commonwealth because it is another version of the earthly city, rejecting justice by requiring the worship of idols or demons, by which Augustine meant the false gods of folk religion. Only a city oriented towards the worship of the true God could possibly be just in the way that Cicero's account of republicanism would require. That would require the Empire to be the city of God. Whilst some Christian thinkers identified the post-Constantinian Empire with providence, Augustine was clear that we cannot identify the Empire or any other existing or historical political society as the city of God, because all actual human cities remain an inseparable mix of the two cities. This point brings us back to the fundamental Augustinian insight about the nature of politics and history, namely that, until the final judgement at the end of time, the historical order is not and should not be seen as the unfolding of humanity's moral redemption or fulfilment. The historical order is the rise and passing away of orders and societies pending the final judgement, and that is ultimately how we must see the fate of the Roman Empire and all political societies: not as a sign of providence.

It would be possible to draw a deeply pessimistic conclusion from this rejection of historical teleology and the triumph of justice, by retreating from the world. Instead, Augustine does provide a qualified account of the 'first virtue' of political society with his doctrine of peace. We cannot shun or retreat from the world despite its sinful character, because that is the order into which we have been placed by God. To that extent, the political societies that are given within that historical order have a place in whatever God's providence turns out to be. In this respect, Augustine goes back to the injunction of Jesus to 'Render unto Caesar, the things that are Caesar's' (Matthew 22:21) and his teaching that his 'Kingdom is not of this world'. From this, Augustine infers that Christians are compelled to acknowledge the claims of political authority and to exercise political judgement, rather than retreat from the world. At the same time, they must not fall victim to the human tendency to conflate the good of political authority with justice and the moral good. Yet, if political authority is not redeemed by the concept of justice or the good, what is the fundamental good of political authority? Augustine answers this question with an account of peace as the first virtue of political society.

Peace and political order

Having rejected the primacy of justice as the value underpinning the claims of political authority, Augustine replaces it with the more fundamental idea of peace. In the extended discussion of peace in *City of God* (Book XIX, Chapters 12 and 13), peace is described as a good for humans in the fallen world, as well as being the central and final gift of human redemption. Yet, it is the good for the fallen world that is central to his account of the value of political authority. And, because the human good of peace is likely to be confused with the supreme Christian good of the city of God, Augustine distinguishes the latter as 'eternal peace'. Even those not oriented towards the 'eternal peace' of the city of God can nevertheless be oriented to (human) peace:

> Whoever joins me in an examination, however, cursory, of human affairs and our common nature will acknowledge that, just as there is no one who does not wish to be joyful, so there is not one who does not wish to have peace. (Augustine 1998, p. 934)

Peace is a value that underpins any form of society because it is the condition of order on which any social life depends. As such, it is a condition of the realisation of the good life of the city of God but equally it underpins the city of humanity. Those who pursue war and violence do so ultimately in order to achieve peace, either through the defeat of enemies who threaten their peace or in terms of conquest and aggression in order to impose a new peace from which they will benefit through the exercise of domination and power. Bands of robbers 'wish to have peace with their fellows, if only in order to invade the peace of others with greater force and safety' (Augustine 1998, p. 934). Augustine goes on to argue that, even when bands of robbers turn against themselves, the individual robbers and brigands will still want some peace for their family and children so that they can enjoy the gains of their activities. Whatever the direct motive of contemporary drug lords, gangsters and criminals is, they all presuppose some form of peace that can be ordered to their advantage. And, to pre-empt those who might argue that there are some who are so evil that they just revel in violence and disorder, Augustine introduces the mythical figure of *kakos*, the half-man:

> He gave nothing to anyone; rather, he took what he wanted from anyone he could and whenever he could. Despite, all this, however, in the solitude of his own cave, the floor of which reeked with the blood of recent butchery, he wished for nothing other than the peace in which no one should molest him, and a rest which no man's violence, or the fear of it, should disturb. Also, he desired to be at peace with his own body; and in so far as he had such peace, all was well with him. (Augustine 1998, p. 935)

Peace is the condition of any kind of good, even the most depraved goals of the earthly city. And even those who crave the absence of human society still want the absence of violence from others to pursue their anti-social ends. This desire for peace is the legacy of the loss of the peace of creation prior to the fall of humanity and it remains to be seen whether we are oriented towards the good of the earthly or heavenly cities. Consequently, it is the underpinning of the order in which those conflictual goals are pursued, and it is precisely this which for Augustine is the domain of politics.

The peace of the earthly city is a significant departure from the 'eternal peace' of the heavenly city, but on a scale of absence that ends with total chaos and disorder, or the completeness of sin as the absence of good. As long as it falls short of the complete absence of good, earthly peace retains some measure of goodness within the order of the fallen world, because it makes possible attaining some of the goods of the city of God in human history and before the final judgement. The measure of that peace is provided within the fallen world by the political imposition of harm, violence and coercion in order to limit the greater violence, coercion and harm of the conflicting wills and goals of the earthly city and of the city of God when faced by the challenges of sin and violence. The limited good of political order, judgement and power is not then the Ciceronian good of justice, or the Christian good of eternal peace, but it is a subordinate good in that it provides the peace that is a precondition of societal goods, whether those of the earthly city or the city of God. To that end, although political authority is not natural, it is part of the ordained order for fallen humanity. In this way, Augustine builds a theory of obligation to the political orders, kingdoms and empires of the fallen world. Along with all other subjects of the Roman Empire, Christians have a duty to submit to their political rulers, and rulers have a duty to rule wisely by exercising judgement in the use of force and coercion (including violence) to secure peace and order. The duty of submission is not conditional on the wise conduct of the rulers, but it is also not totally unconditional either. Because the task of political rule is securing peace in which the inhabitants of the city of God can pursue their goods alongside the goods of the earthly city, Christians have a duty to submit their judgement to the judgement of that political authority, knowing that ultimately all human judgement is conditional and ultimately subject to divine judgement. In this way, Augustine establishes the traditional Christian response to the challenge of tyrannical rule, namely that subjects should obey the ruler, but ultimately God will be the judge of that ruler.

In some cases where a pagan political ruler claims divine authority, Christians can be faced with the challenge of 'God or Caesar' and the prospect of martyrdom. Yet even here, Augustine is careful not to usurp divine judgement by suggesting that martyrdom is a general duty when faced with the challenges of the fallen world. Whilst celebrating the heroic martyrs of the early Church and their essential witness, his dealings with the Donatists show a realistic appreciation of the demands of Christian witness in a fallen world, and an impatience with Donatist zealots who are too quick to claim divine judgement in counselling martyrdom. Whilst the choice between God and Caesar is clear and unequivocal, Augustine remains profoundly realistic about the complexity of that judgement in ordinary political experience, given the necessity of engaging with the earthly city. As God has deferred the final judgement, it cannot be the right of individual believers to accelerate that judgement in their own circumstances by appealing to martyrdom as the first response to the challenges of the earthly city. Suicide, and willing one's own death, is a sin for Christians. An Augustinian response to the modern-day challenge of suicide bombers seeking martyrdom is clear: they commit the ultimate blasphemy in placing their own judgement over that of God.

The character of Augustine's political thought is, therefore, neither classically philosophical in its focus on outlining the good life and ideal city or polity nor institutional in the way of contemporary political science. The question of the good life or ideal city is not ultimately a political matter, because it is not something achievable in the fallen world. Politics is an activity peculiar to humanity's fallen nature in the domain of history. Therefore, building ideal states or cities does not arise as the origins of political communities is a product of secular history, and so they are all ultimately temporary and subject to decline. In so far as Augustine contributes to institutional or constitutional politics, it is not in terms of ideal judgements but in terms of the practical manipulation of institutional authority to achieve the end of order: the political task is how we can live together in peace, not how we recreate the world to serve our own view of justice. A number of things follow from this perspective. It assumes the world as it is, and the distribution of political authority and power as it is given in history, and that means the fact of a plurality of political authorities – although the dominant authority is the Roman Empire, given its scope and power. That said, the Empire was clearly being challenged, both from external powers, such as the invading Goths and Vandals, and by internal centrifugal forces separating the Empire between the East and West.

One must remember that the Empire in Augustine's day was not a single sovereign state on modern lines. The sites of political authority within it were diverse, often being divided amongst the armies of various regional individual powers. Constantine came to power in one such struggle within the Roman Empire by drawing on his northern army. In the Empire of Augustine's experience, there was no single monopoly of violence within a single clearly defined territory, to take Max Weber's account of the minimum conditions of political sovereignty. Furthermore, because there was no simple sovereign in Augustine's political world, we cannot make modern assumptions about the nature of international relations there, or about the contrast between the domestic and the international. Whilst important features of international relations such as trade and war do exist in Augustine's political universe, he was forced to follow the Roman practice of addressing the 'international' in terms of the relations between peoples or 'multitudes'. Some of these sets of people will have existed as distinct bodies within the Empire, in the same way that modern empires contained distinct nationalities. Others will have existed beyond the boundaries of the Empire, such as those who come under the idea of *jus gentium* (the law of nations or people). But, for Augustine, *jus gentium* is not a sign of an underlying natural law that governs politics; instead, it is a series of conventions that have evolved to enable minimal peaceful cooperation amongst different peoples who are brought into some form of social cooperation such as trade. As conventions, the law of peoples is not really law at all, since for Augustine law in the earthly city must be *lex* and not just *jus*. The concept of *jus* is a primarily moral notion that we can translate as *right* and which is linked to the concept of justice. But, as we have seen with Augustine's critique of Cicero and the Empire as a commonwealth, the law of the Empire, whilst being law, cannot be conflated with justice or right.

Augustine instead emphasises the idea of a clear, promulgated and sanctioned political will as the basis of laws. Laws are ultimately the enforced will of a political authority and they have a claim on the individual will because they are sanctioned reasons through the imposition of punishment. In this respect, law as *lex* is a political as opposed to a moral notion, because it is the judgements that the wielder of political authority chooses to enforce and sanction. In the absence of a distinct sphere of international relations and a universal political authority, there cannot be a place for an idea of international law going beyond any temporary conventions that develop amongst peoples who are brought into contact with one another, whether through conflict or through cooperation.

Consequently, Augustine develops a political theory as a conception of political judgement about how best to exercise power, violence and coercion in a way that is consistent with the protection of peace and the purpose of maintaining order. As with the pastoral judgements of a bishop, political judgements are always conditional and subject to revision in the circumstances of history, although they are always oriented towards seeking peace and reducing disorder. Final judgements on all things are the sole prerogative of God, and political rulers and philosophers always err when they substitute their judgement for this final judgement. This position does not entail that anything goes for rulers, but it does remind us that human practical wisdom is cumulative, fragmentary and ultimately never complete. The challenge and necessity of judgement (as opposed to certainty and perfect law) is an ineradicable feature of human experience before the final judgement. It is precisely this necessity for judgement that compels Augustine to address one of the greatest challenges to those committed to peace, namely the challenge of war.

The legitimation of violence and just war

As we have seen, prior to the final judgement the city of God persists within human history and politics, and its attendant concepts of coercion and violence remain part of that. Augustine is careful to avoid claiming that God wills there to be violence and coercion, and instead says that they follow on from man's fallen nature and the domain of the political within human experience. Violence is a consequence of sin and so not something that Augustine celebrates, any more than he celebrates the necessity of punishment. Consequently, one needs to be careful in attributing to Augustine a theory of just war or just punishment within society or the Church, despite the common claim that he is one of the founders of just war theory, and perhaps the first Christian just war theorist. The most important distinction between Augustine and later Christian just war theorists (such as Aquinas or Vitoria) is that his thinking is not located within the broader structure of natural law theory. The domain of politics (whether it be domestic, imperial or international) is not governed by a single law of nature, and therefore just war thinking cannot be an implication of that normative order. Instead, war and violence are a consequence of the absence of a normative order and can only be seen as a reaction to our natural imperfection. In fact, Augustine is not the first significant theorist of just war amongst the fathers of the Church, and the idea is more common amongst those thinkers who tended toward the Constantinian identification of the empire with the divine order. Instead, as with his discussion of violence and coercion, Augustine's teaching about war emerges from a pastoral direction of soldiers and a reflection on the challenges to peace from the gathering powers on the edges of the Empire. There is some truth in the argument that Augustine's writings on just war are designed precisely to limit the claims of a more enthusiastic just war discourse in early Christianity (Markus 1983) and that he does not have a formal theory of the justice of war. That said, given the importance of Augustine's thinking to subsequent Christian just war theory, I will characterise his arguments using conceptual distinctions that emerge later in Christian thinking as developments of his insights.

The pastoral dimension to Augustine's teaching on violence and coercion is clear in in his letters that discuss the necessity of persecuting the Donatists. But it should be remembered that in the Roman world there was no monopoly of violence as the exclusive preserve of the state. The administration of violence was shared between courts, the military, the Church and even households. As such, it was a direct concern of Augustine as a bishop, for whom the exercise of coercion was a personal and not merely an academic problem. His initial position is hostile to coercion or violence. He holds a Christian distaste for violence alongside a genuine worry that its exercise unleashes emotions and motivations that are contrary to those of the city of God. Persuasion, patience and example are all preferable to coercion and violence in the forms of torture and corporal punishment.

Yet, this initial attitude gives way in *Letter 93 to Vincentius* to a more realist and world-weary recognition of the need for coercive methods, especially when faced by the violence and uncompromising character of Donatist opponents. The arguments of the *Letter to Vincentius* were to become important in the early modern period in debates about religious persecution versus toleration. But it is important to note that Augustine's primary argument is that appropriate corporeal punishment can remove obstacles to rational persuasion and argument. Coercion is ultimately external to persuasion and people cannot be forced to believe; that said, coerced practice and the punishment of attacks on orthodoxy can open many simple people to the possibility of genuine belief, freed from the fear of coercion by Donatist extremists, such as the Circumcellions. As pastoral writings, Augustine's letters are keen to moderate the proportionate use of violence as seen in *Letter 133 to Marcellinus*, which appeals for leniency in the punishment of a group of Donatist clerics who were accused of murder and violence against orthodox Catholic clergy. Marcellinus is explicitly requested to forgo violent and analogous punishment that mirrors the specific violence of the crime:

> I have … learned that most of them have confessed to committing the homicide of the Catholic presbyter Restitutus and the beating of another … and of ripping out his eye and cutting off his finger. Because of this, I have been overwhelmed with the greatest anxiety that your Excellency might determine that these people should be punished by the laws so severely that their punishment will match their deeds. (Augustine 1994, pp. 245–246)

As the confessions were extracted only with beatings, as opposed to the whole panoply of torture that Augustine describes, Augustine trusted that Marcellinus will use a similarly lenient attitude in the violent punishment, whilst not saying that they should not suffer violence at all. Punishment is feature of the fallen world and a necessary corrective to wrong and harm in society. However, Augustine does not present a theory of punishment and associated violence in terms of modern retributivism or consequentialism, even though considerations of desert and of consequences inevitably form part of his pastoral teaching. His primary concern is not the justification of the practice of violence but the challenge of acting within the practice of punishment on the character of the person who must exercise the inevitable violence of the political order. This aspect is also crucial to his account of just war and the appropriateness of war in the face of apparent Christian pacifism. Unlike other modern theologians and Christian moralists, Augustine does not ask whether war or the violence of war is allowed.

Just as there was no monopoly of violence in the Roman Empire, so the prevalence of war and conflict in defence of the Empire was a familiar feature of Roman life, especially in Africa, where the threat of attack from those beyond the border was frequent and proximate. Not only had Rome been sacked by the Goths, but the Vandals from Spain had crossed into Roman Africa and were attacking Augustine's own community, while raids by desert tribes from beyond the southern border had always been a feature of the African provinces of the Empire. War was a fact of life, and consequently soldiering was a familiar and necessary profession. Just as Augustine rejects the idea of fleeing from the fallen world into a Christian utopia, so the order within which the city of God can persist will need those who secure its peace. This is illustrated in Augustine's pastoral advice to Boniface in *Letter 189*, where he supports the young soldier in viewing a military profession as consistent with the duty of Christians by referring to Christ's response to the centurion:

> Do not think that it is impossible for anyone serving in the military to please God. Among those who did so was the holy David, to whom the Lord gave such great testimony. Among them also were many just men

of that time. Among them also was the centurion who said to the Lord 'I am not worthy that you should enter under my roof, but only say the word and my servant will be healed; for I, too, am a man under authority and have soldiers under me: I say to one, "Go", and he goes, and to another, "Come" and he comes, and to my servant, "Do this" and he does it.' (Augustine 1994, p. 219)

This passage, which refers to the Gospel of Matthew, shows how Jesus did not admonish the centurion for being a soldier, but rather acknowledged that he too was 'under authority' and therefore part of the order of peace that is willed for human society. Similarly, Jesus did not deny that the military can be part of that order, so Augustine does not deny the place of the military within the legitimate authorities of the domain of the political. The crucial point here is the absence of any blanket rejection of war and violence, or of a specific command from Jesus to the centurion (and therefore all other soldiers) to put down their weapons and 'turn the other cheek' in the face of violence.

With respect to the conduct of war, Augustine argues that the role of the soldier is that of one who is 'under authority', someone who has a delegated power to kill on behalf of the legitimate ruler who exercises this necessary power to secure peace. Being 'under authority' entails that the soldier, when exercising delegated authority, is not ultimately responsible for actions taken, and therefore can be acting justly by obeying orders, even if the cause determined by the ruler turns out not to be justified. The ruler is ultimately responsible for their soldiers' actions and for the just or unjust killing of others. That said, Augustine does not permit everything in the prosecution of war; the soldier might be required to harm or kill those who harm or kill, but should not will evil against enemies. An honourable soldier is someone with a job to do, but not someone who takes pleasure in violence and the conduct of war. Individual soldiers are expected to obey orders, but they are also expected to act honourably even towards their enemies. Thus Augustine writes:

When fidelity is promised it must be kept, even to an enemy against whom war is being waged ... The will should be concerned with peace and necessity with war, so that God might liberate us from necessity and preserve us in peace. Peace is not sought in order to provoke war, but war is waged in order to attain peace. Be a peacemaker, then, even by fighting, so that through your victory you might bring those whom you defeat to the advantages of peace ... Let necessity slay the warring foe, not your will. As violence is returned to one who rebels and resists, so should mercy be to one who has been conquered or captured. (Augustine 1994, p. 220)

As the goal of war is to protect or restore peace, once peace is achieved, conduct towards enemies should also be directed towards peace, and those who are conquered should not be executed or enslaved. Similarly, the ends of war are limited towards preserving peace and restoring peace when defending against attack. It is not the problem of violence in defending peace that Augustine is primarily concerned with but the vices that are unleashed in the pursuit of war and the exercise of the right to inflict violence.

> What is it about war that is to be blamed? Is it that those who will die someday are killed, so that those who will conquer might dominate in peace? This is the complaint of the timid, not the religious. The desire for harming, the cruelty of revenge, the restless and implacable mind, the savageness of revolting, the lust for dominating, and similar things – these are what is justly blamed in wars. Often, so that such things might also be justly punished, certain wars that must be waged against violence of those resisting are commanded by God or some other legitimate ruler and are undertaken by the good. (Augustine 1994, pp. 221–222)

To this end, Augustine's primary audience is the soldiers tasked with acting under authority and seeking to reconcile in a practical way, in their own professional lives, the demands of being a Christian and being a soldier, as opposed to offering a more formal theory of the moral legitimacy of war in a Christian context. As Augustine takes the problem of war to be an unavoidable fact of a fallen or imperfect world, the focus is primarily on the *jus in bello* (justice in the conduct of war) obligations of individual soldiers and their conduct. As we can see in the passages above, the obligations are more generic virtues of Christian moral life applied to war as opposed to a specific set of norms or principles appropriate to the conduct of war. That said, one can infer from arguments about the appropriate attitude and motives of combatants ideas such as discrimination and non-combatant immunity that play such an important role in later just war thinking. Punishment must be directed at the perpetrators of violence or those 'resisting', and this is a clear indication that it can only be directed at fellow combatants and consequently that non-combatants are immune from punishment. Similarly, 'revenge', 'cruelty' and 'desire for harm' are also unjust motives. If they are allowed free rein, they must undermine the important issue of discrimination in the use of violence. Yet, Augustine is sufficiently realist not to demand (as Aquinas does) that the soldier must not will the death of an enemy in order to fight justly. Instead, Augustine argues that, once subdued, the enemy should be treated as a moral agent, who is after all also acting 'under authority', even if that authority has been misdirected.

When it comes to *jus ad bellum* (or the just cause for war), Augustine's argument is straightforward, given the basic fact overshadowing the discussion, namely the constant risk of attack from beyond the borders of the Empire or the challenge of marauding invaders such as the Goths and Vandals who interrupt peace. The right of war is a necessary tool of political authority to secure and maintain peace, either through self-defence when attacked or by pre-emptively attacking when faced with a significant threat of attack. What is not countenanced is the idea of war as a tool for destroying evil beyond the border, or against those who depart from the teaching of Christianity. Whichever way Augustine's arguments were deployed by later thinkers, no place was left for crusades against infidels or wars against heretics and schismatics. When violence is deployed against the terrorism of fanatical Donatists, Augustine regards this as what we would call a 'police action' and not a 'war on terror'. Only in the most egregious and specific cases can war be an appropriate response to the challenge of sin.

As sin is everywhere in a fallen world, the existence of sin beyond borders would never be a legitimate cause for war, unless it was of such a kind as to threaten peace more generally, such as slaughtering those who are innocent and who can be protected. For example, Augustine's approach would permit intervention to prevent a Rwandan-style genocide because this is a general threat to peace, even if the perpetrators do not intend that it should spill beyond the country's borders. Similarly, Augustine leaves no place for preventive wars that pre-empt a neighbouring power becoming a threat in the future (Doyle 2011). Unlike modern just war theories, Augustine does not presuppose a progressive history that will evolve towards the overcoming of violence and conflict, or that a law of nature will reveal itself in the form of international law regulating and replacing war as a means of resolving disputes. Crucially for Augustine's view of politics, war is a consequence of sin and not merely of the absence of knowledge, or difficulties in coordinating human actions. Attempting to eradicate war, or acting to prevent the rise of threatening powers, would be another example of presuming to understand providence as God's plan for the fallen world. It is as dangerous to presume that war and its challenges do not form part of God's providence as it is to attribute war directly to the will of God. The trials of history and the divine plan that underpins them is ultimately mysterious and it is inappropriate for sinful men to usurp God's judgement in these matters.

As with all violence, the problem posed by war depends upon the purposes for which it is deployed and how those who undertake it act in its pursuit. It is these two dimensions that open up the distinction between *jus ad bellum* and *jus in bello* that plays an important role in subsequent Christian just war theory from Aquinas onwards. Augustine, nevertheless, sets the boundaries and identifies the challenges that remain central to Christian thinking about the role of violence and the conduct of war.

Christianity, Augustinianism and international politics

For many historians of thought, Augustine poses an acute problem in that he is not easily historicised – that is, reduced to a particular historical phenomenon that emerged in an historically contingent linguistic or socio-economic context. He is undoubtedly an historical figure with all the peculiarity and strangeness of his times, and we lose much if we ignore those elements of his thought. Yet (as we have seen above), he was a theologian who reflected on and shaped the Christian tradition. For Christians, this raises the challenge that, in so far as Augustine presented the truth in his teachings about the faith, he has an authority in the present. This is more than just making a claim to transcendental truth as many philosophers fall into that category and yet are not problematically historicised. But Augustine is different because his authority is tied up in a practice and tradition that continues into the present where he is taken to speak to readers as if they were contemporaries. Clearly, this is most obvious in the institutional Church, but I conclude this chapter by showing how his theological voice has been central to thinking about international relations in the 20th and 21st centuries, especially with respect to the challenge of war, violence and just war, or with the challenge of history (Ratzinger 2018). This lasting legacy is illustrated in the discussion of Augustinian ideas in contemporary debates about the place of war in Christian ethics and politics, especially in the context of the War on Terror. It is also evident in the thought of the most significant neo-Augustinian thinker of mid-20th-century politics, Reinhold Niebuhr, whose Augustinian insights have contributed to the development of international relations and a qualified or Christian realist politics.

War and the peaceable kingdom: Augustine and contemporary just war theory

If there is any area where Christian theology and modern international political theory collide, it is the discussion of the war and its necessity or morality. This has been particularly true in the 20th and 21st centuries, which have seen not only unparalleled violence in two world wars, revolutions and their aftermaths but also moves to outlaw war and to subject conflict to regulation by international institutions charged with maintaining peace. Christian theologians have contributed to debates and campaigns for peace, but they have also returned to fundamental reconsiderations of the place of war in Christian practice and judgement. In 1930, at the high point of post-Great War idealism, the Lambeth Conference of the Anglican Communion passed a resolution that: 'This conference affirms that war as a method of settling international disputes is incompatible with the teaching and example of our Lord Jesus Christ' (Lambeth Conference 1930, resolution 25). The debate about the place of war and violence in Christian practice has been most recently challenged by a group of theologians such as the American theologian Stanley Hauerwas, who is a forceful proponent of Christian pacifism as a defining mark of Christian witness. His stance is despite his acknowledgement that the United States professes to be the most Christian of western democracies, whilst also having been at continuous war for the three decades from the end of the Cold War. Hauerwas recognises that Christian pacifism is demanding but remains uncompromising in its support, writing:

> Are Christians not unjust if they allow another person to be injured or even killed if they might prevent that by the use of violence? Indeed, should not Christians call on the power of the state to employ its coercive force to secure more relative forms of justice? Such action would not be a question of using violence to be 'in control' but simply to prevent worse evil.
>
> ... the problem with attempts to commit the Christian to limited use of violence is that they too often distort the character of the alternatives. Violence used in the name of justice, or freedom, or equality is seldom simply a matter of justice – it is a matter of the power of some over others. Moreover, when violence is justified in principle as a necessary strategy for securing justice, it stills the imaginative search for nonviolent ways of resistance to injustice. For true justice never comes through violence, nor can it be based on violence. It can only be based on truth, which has no need to resort to violence to secure its own existence. (Hauerwas 2002 pp. 114–115)

As with Augustine, Hauerwas means by truth the risen Jesus Christ, not an idea or body of principles. But, just as with Augustine, Hauerwas's theological critics have been quick to challenge how quickly this position moves from the complex political judgement of life in a fallen (though ultimately redeemed) world to an injunction towards martyrdom, as the first response to the prevalence of evil amongst us as opposed to the last (O'Donovan 2003, pp. 9–10). This challenge to how a Christian should witness to their faith in the face of violence has become more acute, not less, as modern times have progressed. It has also highlighted the wisdom of Augustine as an important element of that theological and ethical debate. This can be seen particularly clearly in Nigel Biggar's provocatively titled book *In Defence of War* (2013). Biggar takes an unapologetically Augustinian position on the place of war within Christian political judgement. In a strikingly Augustinian move, he criticises Hauerwas for not addressing the relevant scriptural passages about the faith of the Roman soldier who is also 'under authority', the reference that Augustine mentions in *Letter 189* to Boniface. For Biggar, it is striking that Hauerwas, as an evangelical Christian who gives special authority to the Bible, does not give greater weight to the reported words of Christ that do not insist on pacifism or rejection of the soldier's profession. Of course, one can respond that scripture needs to be interpreted in the round and not selectively. But, for evangelical Christians, it is not possible to just ignore reported speech. However, the echoes of Augustine are not simply confined to Biggar repeating this argument. The whole thrust of his book is concerned with showing how it remains possible (even in the

industrial warfare of modern times) to adopt the appropriate Augustinian attitude to enemies and opponents, so that the individual soldier can avoid being
consumed by the lust for violence.

Not all appeals to the authority of Augustine are quite so measured and
nuanced. And, in light of the War on Terror and the associated Gulf Wars, it is
not surprising that theologians and theologically informed political theorists
should turn to Augustine and the classical thinkers of just war theory in search
of practical guidance. Oliver O'Donovan's masterful short book *Just War Revisited* (2003) was published at the time of the second Gulf War but addresses
issues raised by the first Gulf War in 1991. This involved an international
coalition, dominated by the United States but also involving many countries,
intervening militarily to enforce UN Resolutions that followed Iraq's invasion
of Kuwait. O'Donovan's nuanced discussion ranges beyond simplistic accounts of
the justice of war and includes discussion of such vexed but pressing matters as
counter-insurgency war, the development of 'immoral weapons', and the place
of war crimes trials or justice post-bellum. The arguments are problem-focused
in an attempt to inform Christian judgement on unavoidable public and political issues, rather than as an exegetical strategy. But the shadow of Augustine
looms large, not least because O'Donovan rejects the simplistic view of a tradition that is focused on the justice or moral rightness of war.

O'Donovan holds that 'just war theory' is neither a theory nor about the justice of war. Instead, it is an acknowledgement that an absence of peace brought
on by a challenge to peace is a context for necessary action. As with Augustine,
the re-establishment of peace involves the removal of that challenge to it: it is
absolutely not a legalistic right or duty following from a natural or international law. Nor can war be reduced to the just punishment of an injustice within
a legalistic moral order, contrary to the views of new just war theorists such
as Fabre (2012) and McMahan (2009). Just as for Augustine, war is always an
exception and a rupture of order: the practical challenge is to turn that exception to the re-establishment of order and peace. Consequently, war is not something about which there can be a final and complete theory. The ways in which
peace is threatened are many. And so the theologically informed necessity of
judgement about how to confront and respond to each new challenge must
constantly be rethought.

A different type of book that emerged from the same political context was
Jean Bethke Elshtain's *Just War Against Terror* (2003), a polemical response
from the just war tradition to the critics of the War on Terror following 9/11.
Elshtain is an Augustine scholar and eminent political theorist, but in this
politically engaged book she shows impatience with those who argue that the
United States should have stayed its hand and not declared the War on Terror.
Augustine is appealed to directly, as an authority alongside Luther and the German anti-Nazi martyr Bonhoeffer, as Christian authorities for the recourse to
the war when confronted with evil.

[The] point is made most vividly by Luther, with his insistence that there is a 'time of the sword', but it has been widely, if not universally, shared in the historic Church. For Christians living in historic time and before the end of time, the pervasiveness of conflict must be faced. One may aspire to perfection, but living perfectly is not possible. To believe one is without sin is to commit the sin of pride and to become even more boastful in the conviction that a human being can sustain a perfectionist ethic. For St. Augustine, for Martin Luther, and for the anti-Nazi martyr Dietrich Bonhoeffer, the harsh demands of necessity as well as the command of love require that one may have to commit oneself to the use of force under certain limited conditions, and with certain intentions. (Elshtain 2003, p. 101)

Elshtain's argument goes beyond Augustine's writings on war and refers to the broader tradition of just war theory, which includes positions that he does not endorse. Her primary goal is not to explain Augustine's position but to show how the War on Terror can fall within traditional just war theory, given that the primary enemy when she wrote was Al-Qaeda, which is not a state or 'authority' of the relevant kind. In the justification of the war in Afghanistan she argues that, by giving succour and a home to Al-Qaeda, the Afghan state became a legitimate belligerent and target for attack. Similarly, Al-Qaeda breached the requirement to discriminate between combatants and non-combatants by targeting civilians, as in the attack on the Twin Towers.

Elshtain's book is deliberately polemical and intended to engage in public debate rather than the exegesis of Augustine's thought or more scholarly theological debates. But it also reinforces a strong Augustinian message in its account of the enemy of radical jihadi terrorism. She criticises the complacency of the U.S. and European 'liberal intelligentsia', who have forgotten the fundamental Augustinian insight about the nature of the fallen world in their assumption that the forces of law and consensual politics are reducing violence over time and eradicating the need to have recourse to war. This kind of progressivism is precisely the problem, because it cannot make space for evil and its ineradicability from the human condition. In this respect, she argues for the continuing relevance of Augustine's most fundamental teaching and one of Augustine's most important 20th-century followers, Niebuhr.

Niebuhr: neo-Augustinianism and the challenge of history

Reinhold Niebuhr (1892–1971) was an eminent American Protestant theologian and public intellectual during the middle years of the 20th century – a period that covered the Depression and World War II; the Cold War and the U.S. rise to global dominance; and subsequently the civil rights movement and the Vietnam War. He wrote many books, of which the most important for international political theory is *Moral Man and Immoral Society* (1932, reissued 2005). It was written during the collapse of the Wilsonian optimism following World War I and the rise of fascism, Nazism and Bolshevism in Europe. Like E.H. Carr in England, Niebuhr is considered a father of modern international relations as a consequence of his rejection of political and international idealism.

In response to the dark threats of the ideological currents of the mid-20th century, and the historical order in which they arose, Niebuhr resurrects a distinctively Augustinian vision of politics and history that continues to resonate now as Christian realism, manifested in three central positions. Firstly, liberalism and all forms of progressivism are a form of Pelagianism. Secondly, the usurpation of Christ by history must be rejected. Human redemption does not only happen within time and history is not a process that becomes the vehicle of that redemption. Finally, he rejects a naïve pacifism with its associated ideas that education and development will lead to the eradication of war and conflict.

Niebuhr does not write as an historian of thought, or as an academic theologian expounding and explaining Augustine's thought to a modern age. So the question confronting such theologians, about how accurate his depiction of Augustinian realism is, remains tangential. That said, *Moral Man and Immoral Society* does offer a sympathetic interpretation of Augustine's position in Chapter 3. What is most striking is the way in which the challenges that Augustine faced in *City of God* reappear in modern politics, particularly the ineradicability of sin and the prevalence of Pelagian overreach in the progressive political movement of early 20th-century American politics and in the social gospel of liberal Protestantism, as he saw it.

For Niebuhr, the chief failing of liberal Protestantism was its accommodation to post-Enlightenment thought and its abandonment of elements of orthodox Christian teaching about sin and redemption, instead invoking ideas of secular rationalism linked with Christian piety. A focus on loving one's neighbour and care for the poor connected the liberal Protestant social gospel of Rauschenbusch and Gladden with the secular progressive liberalism of pragmatists such as Dewey. Central to this view is the secularisation of sin, which becomes a psychological or sociological category, and the claim that human error is the basis for social and interpersonal conflict and that this is exacerbated by social conditions and personal circumstances. For the advocates of the social gospel, knowledge of the New Testament teaching of Jesus would educate people in how to lead a good life. But, as the substance of that teaching is taken to be consistent with reason or good sense, it converges with the secular morality of progressive liberalism in its focus on individual educational and social improvement and the eradication of the social conditions of vice through public education, poverty reduction and temperance reform (prohibition of alcohol). With progressive legislation and social reform, the conditions of sin and conflict can be eradicated, and social and political harmony can be created. As with the Pelagians in Augustine's time, the exercise of individual will and moral action are seen here as leading to overcoming sin and error. Niebuhr offers a forceful rejection of this naïve optimism:

> What is lacking among all these moralists, whether religious or rational, is an understanding of the brutal character of the behaviour of all human collectives, and the power of all self-interest and collective ego-ism in all intergroup relations. Failure to recognise the stubborn resist-ance of group egoism to all inclusive social objectives involves them [the moralists] in unrealistic and confused political thought. (Niebuhr 2005: xvi)

His point here does not depend upon the Christian doctrine of original sin, although Niebuhr does subscribe to that doctrine. Rather, here he argues that human experience supports the idea that the human inability to coordinate social action and to overcome partial interests has the same effect as orthodox Christian teaching about sin. Whatever their sources, the limitations of human nature undermine political faith in inevitable progress towards human emanci-pation and social well-being. Conflict cannot be designed out of human experi-ence by institutional reform and psychological manipulation, whether that be through welfare states in the domestic context or through Leagues of Nations in the international context. Niebuhr endorses the Augustinian vision as a more realistic account of modern society and politics from which contemporary reli-gion and political philosophy can still learn:

> Augustine concludes that the city of this world is 'compact of injustice' that its ruler is the devil, that it is built by Cain and that its peace is secured by strife. That is a very realistic interpretation of the realities of social life. It would stand in wholesome contrast to the sentimentalities and superficial analyses, current in modern religion. (Niebuhr 2005, p. 46)

Believing in the self-sufficiency of human nature and progress towards human redemption reruns Pelagian heresy in its overconfidence. Niebuhr takes the argument further in challenging historicist political ideologies as dangerous attempts to replace Christ as the source of human redemption. Niebuhr sees the challenge of ideological politics in the 1930s as a reflection of this Christian heresy and in *Moral Man and Immoral Society* seeks to extend that warning into a critique of contemporary political ideology. The fundamental issue at the heart of Augustine's lesson for modern politics is the warning against seeking salvation in and through human history. For progressive liberals, this manifests itself in the faith that historical progress will lead to the steady eradication of conflict and disorder.

But it is not only progressive liberals who offer this faith. It reaches its most stark restatement in the revolutionary politics of Bolshevism, the most recent example of redemptive politics when Niebuhr wrote. The legacy of the 1917 Russian Revolution for European politics, and to some extent for U.S. politics in the depths of the 1930s' depression, provided an unsettling account of redemption in human history, and included that claim that the Marxist materialist dialectic of class conflict in history is the story of human redemption. In this view, the working-out of class revolution will involve the overcoming of all conflict and contradictions through the final class conflict. Here history in this dialectical process usurps the position of Christ as redeemer, with all the dangers this poses to human life by liberating and justifying millennial eschatological violence. The dangers of such false redeemers – or 'Antichrists', to use apocalyptic language – is that they unleash violence and disorder, promising a final overcoming of disorder but without being able to deliver that, and instead creating further violence and destruction. There can be no historical event that redeems the destruction of human lives on the promise of building a better society or a utopia on earth. Such things are always false gods and they need to be recognised as such.

Two conclusions follow from Niebuhr's analysis of ideological political movements in terms of Augustinian theological categories. Either they are genuinely heretical and usurp the place of Christian redemption or, for those who are uncomfortable with the Christian theological perspective, they offer a false optimism about the historical process that can ultimately never be vindicated. Christians and political sceptics alike can therefore converge on a rejection of the political naivety of utopianism, as the danger of creating false gods. In this respect, Niebuhr initiates an anti-perfectionist politics that was to attract many to a sceptical liberalism in the post-1945 period as part of a turn against ideology and ideological politics. There was also rejection of historicism or historical theodicies by thinkers as diverse as Popper, Oakeshott and Berlin. For all of these philosophers, just as for Augustine a millennium and half before them, either history is impenetrable in its logic and meaning or it has no such single or meta-narrative structure: it cannot contain the clue to human emancipation and the overcoming of conflict.

That said, Niebuhr does not retreat in despair or reject the value of political action. Instead, he develops a different perspective on liberal politics that conceives of the constitutional order as a contingent realm in which fundamental disagreements about moral or religious questions can be disciplined, without asserting a political authority to regulate on their truth. Politics becomes a domain of compromise on fundamental questions, a place where temporary or meliorist solutions can be provided for social and economic challenges. Meliorism, or the idea that liberal politics is about fixing or mitigating problems, and not resolving grand issues such as human redemption, became central to the post-war European liberal politics of Popper or Rawls – despite Rawls's anti-Augustinian claim that '[j]ustice is the first virtue of social institutions'. In many respects, this late political liberalism reflects Augustine's own attitude towards politics and the tools of politics, including the deployment of violence and coercion. Whilst Augustine saw political action as an inescapable evil given our fallen natures, he nevertheless also saw politics as necessary and unavoidable.

This Augustinian vision of politics as a response to man's fallen nature is most visible in Niebuhr's rejection of idealism after the 1914–1918 war, and its attempt to regulate and abolish war through the League of Nations. Niebuhr is at his most sceptical on this naïve optimism. He writes:

> This glorification of the League of Nations as a symbol of a new epoch in international relations has been very general, and frequently very unqualified, in the Christian churches, where liberal Christianity has given itself to the illusion that all social relations are being brought progressively under 'the law of Christ'. (Niebuhr 2005: xvii)

Niebuhr does not celebrate war and he shares the Augustinian sense of war as tragic. But equally he thinks that the regulation of international affairs is not straightforward: one cannot simply will the replacement of war with law, as the enthusiasts for the League seemed to believe. The problem of the League and of all such attempts to constitutionalise international politics is that they assume away precisely the partiality and interest-driven character of national politics, so that high-minded idealism is always undermined by the clash of interests between respective ruling classes. Whilst the internal politics of states remains so fraught with class and racial conflict, it is no wonder that international politics should be equally consumed by the passions of national self-assertion and the struggles for recognition that follow from it. The arguments of *Moral Man and Immoral Society* tend towards either a realistic pacifism or qualified support for war as a last resort to defend justice, and they give a profound warning against wars of ideology, such as the 'Christian west' against 'godless Bolshevism'. However, by the time of World War II Niebuhr had become more realist and he supported the war effort as a necessary response to egregious injustice and evil. Similarly, during the Cold War, Niebuhr advocated confrontation with the USSR as a further false god trying to impose its will as the salvation of humanity. His stance made him a central inspiration for the development of the modern discipline of international relations in American political science departments, alongside the former diplomat George F. Kennan and émigré thinkers such as Hans Morgenthau. Yet, Niebuhr was no naïve realist or Cold War warrior. He remained sceptical about the claims of politics, especially during the civil rights struggles of the 1960s and the Vietnam War. Like Kennan and Morgenthau, he opposed this intervention as an unnecessary war of choice based on a false perspective. It was precisely the dangerous form of ideological confrontation between 'western civilisation and godless communism' that he counselled against. Once again, his stance echoes that of Augustine in recognising the politics of imperfection. The danger facing the United States was that of its already strong political exceptionalism becoming a new form of

Constantinianism – a belief that the USA was an empire endorsed and sanctioned by God as his means of redeeming mankind.

This 'middle position' between a sceptical realism and liberal idealism is similar to the 'society of states' view of Wight and Bull in the English School, which itself reflects the similar Christian Augustinianism of Martin Wight and Hubert Butterfield. They reject the hard realism of a Hobbesian view of international politics on the grounds that state sovereignty is an artificial and historically contingent political form. They also reject the idealist view that history is tending towards either a liberal empire backed by American power or, under the guise of globalisation, a world state. Niebuhr is not alone in restating the Augustinian warning against 'Constantinianism' in modern politics, but he is important in reminding modern states that when they confront great evils (such as Nazism and Stalinist Bolshevism) they should not forget their own similar tendency to claim to be a solution to the problem of history. Although Augustine's world is far removed from that contemporary politics and international relations, in one respect at least, his rejection of the 'end of history', he could not be more contemporary.

Bibliography

Essential reading

Augustine. (1994). *Political Writings*, trans. M.W. Tkacz and D. Kries, intro. E.L. Fortin. USA: Hackett.
Augustine. (1998). *The City of God Against the Pagans*, ed. R.W. Dyson. UK: Cambridge University Press.

Secondary reading

Biggar, Nigel. (2013). *In Defence of War*. UK: Oxford University Press.
Butterfield, Herbert. (1962). *Christianity, Diplomacy and War*. UK: Wyvern Books.
Connolly, William, E. (1993). *The Augustinian Imperative: the Politics of Morality*. USA: Sage.
Doyle, Michael W. (2011). *Striking First*. USA: Princeton University Press.
Elshtain, Jean Bethke. (1995). *Augustine and the Limits of Politics*. USA: University of Notre Dame Press.
Elshtain, Jean Bethke. (2003). *Just War against Terror*. USA: Basic Books.
Fabre, Cécile. (2012). *Cosmopolitan War*. UK: Oxford University Press.
Hauerwas, Stanley. (2002). *The Peaceable Kingdom: A Primer in Christian Ethics*. USA: Notre Dame University Press.
Hauerwas, Stanley. (2011). *War and the American Difference: Theological Reflections on Violence and National Identity*. USA: Baker Academic.

Markus, Richard A. (1983). 'Saint Augustine's Views on the "Just War"', in W.J. Sheils (ed.) *The Church and War: Church History*, vol. 20. UK: Oxford University Press, pp. 1–13.

Markus, Richard A. (1988). 'The Latin Fathers', in James Henderson Burns (ed.) *The Cambridge History of Medieval Political Thought c. 350–1450*. UK: Cambridge University Press, pp. 92–122.

McMahan, Jeff. (2009). *Killing in War*. UK: Clarendon Press.

Niebuhr, Reinhold. [1932] (2005). *Moral Man and Immoral Society*. USA: Continuum.

O'Donovan, Oliver. (1996). *The Desire of the Nations: Rediscovering the Roots of Political Theology*. UK: Cambridge University Press.

O'Donovan, Oliver. (2003). *The Just War Revisited*. UK: Cambridge University Press.

O'Donovan, Oliver. (2005). *Ways of Judgement*. UK: W. Eerdmans.

O'Donovan, Oliver; and Lockwood O'Donovan, Joan. (2004). *Bonds of Imperfection: Christian Politics Past and Present*. USA: W. Eerdmans.

Ratzinger, Joseph. [Pope Benedict XVI] (2008). *Church, Ecumenism and Politics: New Endeavours in Ecclesiology*. USA: Ignatius Press.

Ratzinger, Joseph. [Pope Benedict XVI] (2018). *Faith and Politics*. USA: Ignatius Press.

Song, Robert. (1997). *Christianity and Liberal Society*. UK: Clarendon Press.

Williams, Rowan. (2016). *On Augustine*. UK: Bloomsbury.

Suggestion for finding open access versions of St Augustine's texts

Perseus Digital Library, Tufts University
    https://www.perseus.tufts.edu/hopper/searchresults?q=St+Augustine

CHAPTER 4

Machiavelli

Politics and the use of violence

Machiavelli is one of the most controversial of political thinkers. His ideas have many implications for traditional conceptions of politics, such as the role of the common good and the relationship between political power and moral or ethical obligations. In the context of international political thought, Machiavelli is presented as a realist and an originator of the idea of *raison d'état* (reason of state). I claim here that Machiavelli challenges the idea of stable political societies or peoples, and focuses attention on the founding or refounding of political communities in a world of constant change and revolution. This explains his concern with the character of leadership and the ways in which temporary and fleeting political power should be exercised to create and maintain regimes. Rather than steering a careful path around the idea of ethics in politics, Machiavelli explores the nature of political life outside of a moralistic, ethical and legalistic framework. In this way he poses one of the most striking challenges to the conceptual framework of modern politics.

'**Machiavellian** Adjective: Using clever but often dishonest methods that deceive people so that you can win power and control'
(Cambridge English Dictionary)

How to cite this book chapter:
Kelly, Paul. 2022. *Conflict, war and revolution: The problem of politics in international political thought.* London: LSE Press, pp. 105–146.
DOI: https://doi.org/10.31389/lsepress.cwr.d License: CC BY.

Many political thinkers and philosophers have given rise to political nouns to name a body of thought or an ideology. Few have given rise to adjectives in common use for describing a style of political action. None has either been as successful as Machiavelli in this respect, or given rise to a description of political behaviour that is unequivocally negative. The earliest reception of his works was hostile. They were placed on the Roman Catholic Church's index of proscribed books (the Index Librorum Prohibitum) in 1552, within a short time after his death. Since then, Machiavelli has been associated with deceit, duplicity, violence and vice – at least in the traditional moral sense. Indeed, 'old Nick' (often a euphemism for the Devil) is often claimed to be derived from Niccolo Machiavelli. Shakespeare has the Duke of Gloucester refer to 'the murderous Machiavel' (Henry VI) as a source of 'schooling' in a type of politics that is clearly not one that elevates the virtues and wisdom of king-ship. 'Machiavellian' is never used to describe anything other than morally questionable and ambiguous behaviours, however much practitioners of high and low politics might praise the successful deployment of the dark arts of diplomacy and strategy. Historians of ideas spend much time addressing the scholarly question of whether this morally ambiguous characterisation is fair to the historical Machiavelli, who was a Florentine diplomat and humanist scholar. But then, history is rarely fair, and the image or type of the Machiavel-lian person is a recognisable and irreducible figure in characterising political actors and actions.

This figure of the Machiavellian actor is a very familiar one in international politics, statecraft and diplomacy, unsurprisingly, given Machiavelli's profession. However, the role also suits the requirements of high statecraft, which involve, if not lying, then 'economy with the truth', manipulation and compromising of interests. And, of course, when diplomacy either breaks down or needs a bit of momentum, statecraft may involve the deployment of war and violence. Contemporary international politics is full of examples of Machiavel-lian figures such as Henry Kissinger, a scholar, diplomat and U.S. Secretary of State who is irrevocably associated with this style of statecraft, one that is untrammelled by simple moral principles and norms. Although a most sophisticated and erudite scholar, Kissinger was also Richard Nixon's aide responsible for the carpet-bombing of non-belligerent Cambodia, while simultaneously working to withdraw the U.S. from a bloody and futile conflict in Vietnam. He was also central to the United States' engagement with Communist China at the height of the Cold War and the Chinese Cultural Revolution, where both sides pursued rapprochement despite regarding each other's regime as the embodiment of political evil. For Machiavellian figures, the world is never black and white or good and evil, although such concepts are not denied value; instead, the real world of high state politics is one of endless shades of grey. The idea of endlessness as well as the intermixing of light (good) and dark (evil) is important given the Machiavellian image of political activity as constant change, rather than as a series of games culminating in a winner, or else as steady progress towards a single good, such as human fulfilment, justice or some other utopia. For the Machiavellian, politics has a relentlessness about it that makes those not involved in it suspicious.

Indeed, we can see some of this stance echoing in modern popular hostility to politicians as a class apart, pursuing interests that are not those of the regular public. This suspicion and hostility can be the result of the ways in which the activity of politics is conducted. Politicians are never strictly honest; indeed, in many cases their roles require them to be duplicitous. A treasury secretary who was scrupulously honest and frank about economic policy, or a defence secretary who gave straight answers when asked about state secrets, would both be dangerous and self-defeating actors. But suspicions can also arise because politicians seem to reject morality in their actions. The prevention and prosecution of war and the deployment of violence are the most obvious examples of the conflict between morality and politics.

Yet, the same challenge is not simply confined to the highest level of statecraft. Arguably, all politics is a challenge to morality. This can be because normal morality depends on the resolution of some fundamental political questions, or because politics has its own morality, sometimes referred to as *raison d'état*. Alternatively, as Thucydides' realism argues, perhaps politics is just outside the realm of morality, and so here the normal rules of personal behaviour no longer apply. These hierarchical and spatial perspectives on the relationship between moral norms and political action are most obvious in the realm of international politics, where national interests clash in a world without a common international arbiter or possibly international law. Hence, Machiavellianism is most obvious in diplomatists known for their duplicity, such as Molotov, Kissinger, Gromyko or Zhou Enlai. But the international realm only provides a bigger stage for a style of action that Machiavelli claims is ubiquitous to all politics. One of the questions that will come up in this chapter is this: if international politics is beyond the realm of normal morality, why does this not apply to normal 'domestic' politics? It is not obvious that *raison d'état* applies only in a narrowly circumscribed space in international politics. Machiavelli's challenge is that his teaching informs all politics, and not just diplomacy and high statecraft.

Life and times

Niccolo Machiavelli was a profoundly political thinker whose experience in the political service of his native Florentine Republic shaped his thoughts and formed the basis of his conception of political power and agency. His biography thus provides an important context for his thought. So too does the peculiarity of the city politics of Florence and its place in the international context of the 15th-century regional politics of the Italian peninsula. At this time Italy was neither a single kingdom nor what we would now call a state.

Machiavelli was born into a moderately wealthy Florentine family in 1469. His father was an educated lawyer and Niccolo was given a Renaissance humanist education at grammar school. This comprised the cultivation of literary skills through the study and translation of classical authors, and the development of rhetorical and argumentative skills, particularly through learning the great Roman historians who feature so prominently in his later writings and understanding of politics. This humanist training places Machiavelli alongside other humanist thinkers of the pre-Reformation period (such as Erasmus and Thomas More), especially in using the Roman history and letters as sources, rather than the late medieval preoccupation with natural law, Thomist theology (following the thought of St Thomas Aquinas) and scholastic metaphysics.

When the French King Charles VIII invaded the Italian peninsula in 1494, the Medici family fell from power in Florence and the republic was re-established there. Initially the Medicis were replaced by the radical theocratic government of the Dominican friar and preacher Girolamo Savonarola. With Savonarola's overthrow and execution in 1498, Machiavelli entered the service of the republic in the office of second chancery, which involved writing and translating diplomatic documents and official papers. With the subsequent rise of Piero Soderini as *gonfaloniere* (head of Council), Machiavelli was sent on diplomatic embassies to France and Rome, and, most importantly, to Cesare Borgia (the son of Pope Alexander VI), who was waging a campaign in the Romagna region to unify central Italy as a strong kingdom. These missions exposed Machiavelli to the realities of power and the challenges of successful political action, which informed his understanding of political agency. From 1503 to 1506, Machiavelli was responsible for the Florentine militia, an experience that is reflected in his book *The Art of War*.

After a period of relative success for Florence, including the defeat of the Pisans in 1509, the political climate and prevailing alliances changed. An alliance between the Medicis, Pope Julius II and Spanish troops defeated Florence at the Battle of Prato in 1512. Machiavelli's mentor, Soderini, resigned and the republic was dissolved with the return of the Medicis to power. Shortly after, in 1513, a conspiracy against the Medicis resulted in Machiavelli's arrest and subsequent torture – he was hung by the wrists with his arms behind his back, resulting in dislocation and serious pain. His denials of involvement resulted in his being exiled to the family estate near San Casciano, where he took up a focus on writing. It is often claimed that his political writings were part of a campaign design to secure his return to active politics and government service. He certainly continued an extensive correspondence with many political figures. However, the reality of his situation was more complex. If he was seeking rehabilitation, Machiavelli was unsuccessful, despite some embassies for the republic during the later 1520s. Whilst the Medicis retained a dominant role in Florentine politics and held the papacy under Leo X, Machiavelli was never sufficiently trusted to take up a significant role in politics. Instead, exile produced his great political works. In a famous letter he describes his life in exile:

> When evening comes, I go back home to my study. On the threshold, I take off my work clothes ... and I put on the clothes an ambassador would wear. Decently dressed, I enter the ancient courts of rulers who have long since died. There, I am warmly welcomed, and I feed on the only food I find nourishing and was born to savour. I am not ashamed to talk to them and ask them to explain their actions and they, out of kindness, answer me. Four hours go by without my feeling any anxiety. I forget every worry. I am no longer afraid of poverty or frightened of death. I live entirely through them. (Letter to Francesco Vettori)

His works were circulated and discussed amongst friends and patrons, although only *The Art of War* was published in his lifetime. Despite his diminished political authority at the time of his death in 1527, political immortality was imminent.

Thought, theory and works

Machiavelli's most famous books on the art of politics are *The Prince* (1513), *Discourses on the First Ten Books of Livy* (1513–1517), *The Art of War* (1519–1520) and the *Florentine Histories* (1520–1525). He was also author of numerous minor historical writings, as well as major dramatical and literary works, all displaying the skills of a Renaissance humanist as well as those of a trained diplomat and political observer. Each work merits careful attention in its own right, because each is written in its own terms and not as part of an unfolding philosophical system. This poses important interpretative challenges in reading Machiavelli and speaking about his thought or 'theory' as if that were a single body of structured ideas, derived from a shared set of premises and methodology. Much attention in Machiavelli scholarship has been devoted to reconciling the doctrines of *The Prince*, which offers guidance to Lorenzo di Medici on how to acquire and hold supreme political power, with the argument of the *Discourses*, with its defence of republican liberty and politics. Are these different works part of a single grand theory? Or are they occasional works that are not supposed to be linked – the first being an attempt by the author to acquire political office and favour, while the second gives Machiavelli's preferred version of political society and politics? Is the vision of republicanism developed in the *Discourses* modified by that embodied in his other great historical study, the *Florentine Histories*? How does *The Art of War* fit with these dominant works? The relationship or contrast between these works is an historical question: we can legitimately ask what Machiavelli was trying to do with these works and how they fit together.

But in taking this historical approach one must remember Quentin Skinner's salutary warning against the mythology of doctrines, or the crude assumption that an author must have an unfolding theory to be discovered (1969). If a doctrine assumes one interpretation, then the reader or historian will be looking for it at the expense of other explanations of difference and distinction between texts. Skinner warns careful intellectual historians to avoid that error. All that said, the way we read these works does not have to be narrowly historical, with the connections being no more than a shared series of historical problematics. Indeed, we can miss lessons about the way Machiavelli has affected our language of politics by taking too narrow and historical an approach, placing all the emphasis on the original meanings of the author, as opposed to those of their readers across long periods of time. Debunking ahistorical readings is one important task of interpretation. Yet it also risks falsely implying that there is a single true account of Machiavelli's thought that is independent of its political interpretations and uses. Readers can often find a higher synthesis or unity that is immanent in the works, even if that did not cause their production or if it was not the intention of the author. Whilst intentions might be historically singular, thought is not. This book examines paradigms that are more than just the intentions of the author but which remain sufficiently close to the texts, times or thinkers that they can bear the weight of the interpretation. The argument here is that Machiavelli contributes a different and new paradigm of politics and political agency, one that links across and is illustrated by his key works. However, I do not assert the historical claim that Machiavelli was intentionally trying to articulate a single logical theory, unlike Hobbes, for example.

That Machiavelli is novel, iconoclastic and even revolutionary is a familiar argument, although the ways in which he achieves this status are contested. What is certainly clear is that the method and approach of these works are quite different to those of predecessors. Unlike Thucydides, Machiavelli is not an historian. Although Thucydides' *History* has a moral that can be used to support theoretical positions, he intended to do no more than give an account of the war between the Athenians and the Peloponnesians where the narrative is shaped by the direction of events, as it appeared to one who witnessed them. Machiavelli uses history in a way more explicitly directed towards informing political understanding and practice in a world of rapid and continuing change. The historical enquiry is precisely designed to elicit an underlying pattern or explanation of political phenomena:

> Prudent men are in the habit of saying, neither by chance nor without reason, that anyone wishing to see what is to be must consider what has been: all the things of this world in every era have their counterparts in ancient times. This occurs since these actions are carried out by men who have and have always had the same passions, which, of necessity, must give rise to the same results. (Machiavelli 2008, p. 351)

History clearly provides lessons, but Machiavelli is also clear in this passage that the historical record is the basis for reflection and is not self-interpreting. As we shall see later, Machiavelli's method is more complex than simply reading off the historical record because that is contested. It is not misleading to see Machiavelli's writings as contributing to what would now be considered empirical political science. Whilst there is much that distinguishes Machiavellianism and modern behaviouralism, they share an important characteristic in that they take the phenomena of political experience for granted as the object of enquiry. There is no constructive theory of the state or the constitution in Machiavelli's writings, nor is there a prescriptive model of political organisation that the successful politician should seek to achieve. Whilst Machiavelli does support republicanism, his position is not prescriptive – to paraphrase Steven Lukes, for Machiavelli it is 'republicanism for the republicans and cannibalism for the cannibals' (2003). It is for this reason that many commentators spend a considerable effort situating Machiavelli's politics in the context of the Italian city states of the 15th century (Coleman 2000).

Machiavelli's political science is also interesting because it departs from the philosophical or theological meta-narratives that we find in great political philosophers such as Plato, or theologian/philosophers such as Augustine, where there is an underlying philosophical or theological position that explains the order of the universe. Most importantly, Machiavelli's political science denies an ethical or divine order that endorses either a highest good for man or an ideal form of the state. Indeed, it is precisely the absence of such a normative grand narrative that raises the question of whether there is indeed a Machiavellian theory. Many moralistic surveys of western political thinking see the question of political obligation ('Why should an individual obey the state or political ruler?') as the first question of political theory. As we see later with Hobbes, this is a peculiarly modern political question, although it is one that was immanent in Thomistic natural law in the Middle Ages. For Machiavelli, this first question of modern political theory simply does not arise, any more than the question of why one should refrain from taking another's property. For Machiavelli, there is no prior moral obligation here: obedience is commanded by force and violence from the successful incumbent prince or ruling faction amongst the populace. Failure to obey, whilst pondering the reasons for obedience, risks getting hurt and that is the end of the matter.

The very originality of Machiavelli is that he challenges the place of normativity (in the form of law or morality) in thinking about political action. This stance is significant enough, but it is important to see it not as just a sceptical challenge to the philosophy of classical natural law but rather as an assertion of the autonomy of political agency and its priority. What that autonomous activity is, and how it is represented and manifested in the world, is the key to Machiavelli's view. It explains the continuing relevance of his striking and uncompromising view of the demands of politics to contemporary followers. Whilst all of his works do not form parts of a single, grand Machiavellian theory, elements from the major works can be woven into an account of the way Machiavellianism has appeared as an approach to making sense of political action.

Florence, Italy and the wider world

Before interpreting Machiavelli's works in detail, it is worth outlining the peculiar context of his writings. This is not to provide a causal account of his ideas and therefore the elements for understanding his logic and purposes. I follow many scholars, including Skinner (1969; 1984), in rejecting this causal interpretive strategy. Similarly, I do not want to make a strong claim about the Italian cities as the only suitable environment wherein Machiavelli's views make sense (Coleman 2000), although, given his style of theorising, understanding the politics of 15th- and 16th-century Italy does illuminate what is going on in his books. Constant reference is made to contemporary politics in *The Prince* and the *Florentine Histories*, whereas the underlying narrative of the *Discourses* is a contrast between the fortunes of ancient Rome and of the Florentine Republic. The major link between the text of *The Prince* and the context, however, is the book's curious final Chapter 26, 'Exhortation to Liberate Italy from the Barbarian Yoke'. This changes the work into a manifesto and exhortation to a leader (Lorenzo de Medici) to unite Italy against its persecutors, by which he means the Spanish, French and Imperial forces of the Holy Roman Empire. He writes:

> This opportunity to provide Italy with a liberator, then, after such a long time, must not be missed. I have no doubt at all that he would be received with great affection in all those regions that have been inundated by the foreign invasions, as well as with a great thirst for revenge, with resolute fidelity, with devotion and with tears of gratitude. What gate would be closed to him? What people would fail to obey him? What envious hostility would work against him? What Italian would deny him homage? This foreign domination stinks in the nostrils of everyone. Let your illustrious family, then, take up this mission, with the spirit and courage and the faith that inspires all just causes, so that under your standard our country may be ennobled. (Machiavelli 1988, pp. 90–91)

Whatever else is happening in *The Prince*, the argument ends up as a manifesto for change and national unification and liberation, an agenda that inspired later 20th-century thinkers including some perhaps surprising names, such as Antonio Gramsci and Louis Althusser (see below, Revolutionary Machiavellians).

Besides Florence, the important and rivalrous Italian city states of the divided Italian peninsula included Venice, Milan, Naples and Rome. Most of these city states' histories stretched back into the late Roman Empire. Milan was an imperial

capital to which Augustine went to learn from St Ambrose. Venice was the gate-
way to the Eastern Empire in Byzantium and to the civilisation of the eastern
Mediterranean. Although it was the original imperial capital of the empire,
from the 4th century onwards Rome was also the centre of the Christian
world as the seat of the Holy See. The particular histories and rivalries of each
city played a significant role in the unsettled politics of the Italian peninsula,
whether because of their cultural power (Rome), strategic position (Naples and
Venice) or economic wealth (Florence and Milan). This partly explains why
Italy was not a single political entity until the 19th century, and even today is
an unstable state with strong and deep regional divisions. The cities' rivalries
characterise the world in which Machiavelli engaged as a diplomat and politician, as emissary either to Milan or Rome or to the large external powers such
as France, which exploited this instability in order to secure their own political
ends. Wealth, civilisational power and influence were not just the cause of the
unstable geopolitical environment; they also had a significant bearing on
the organisation of political authority and power within these cities.

Whereas France and Spain were in the process of consolidating into major
unified monarchical states, Italian city states were self-governing communes
with republican constitutions and powerful local elites and factions vying to
control those institutions. The sources of those elites and factions, especially
in Machiavelli's Florence, drew on commercial wealth and the protection and
control of trade and manufacture. The great Cosimo de Medici (1389–1464)
was a leading banker. The subsequent accumulations of wealth created commercial oligarchies of families, such as the Medicis in Florence and the Sforzas in Milan. Through their economic and military power these families built
powerful networks encompassing smaller regional cities (or factions within
those cities) that dominated their republican institutions, alongside powerful
guilds of organised producers. Families like the Medicis and Sforzas, or the
Catalan Borgias in Rome and the Romagna, were not hereditarily legitimated
royal families in the sense of France, Spain or England – and it is important to
remember that when reading *The Prince*. However, they managed to function
as hereditary powers all the same. Cosimo de Medici ruled like a king, but was
actually the 'first amongst equals' as head of the Great Council of Florence.

Whilst much of the practical politics of the time has more in common with
Puzo's novel *The Godfather*, these cities were also the site of a considerable
growth in the development of constitutional and legal attempts to constrain
and discipline power, force and violence, especially in the late medieval period.
Jurists such as Baldus de Ubaldus (1327–1400) taught Roman or civil law in
Florence, amongst other cities. He was a major source of the development of
law as a vehicle through which power is exercised and constrained, in a context
where the regulation of economic power, property and personal right was more
important than in the essentially clerical/feudal societies of northern Europe.
This is illustrated in de Ubaldus's distinction between political agency as a consequence of incorporation into a *regnum* (associated with kingly rule) or *civitas*

(the republic or community of citizens). For legalists these are different ways in which political authority can be constituted and both feature in Machiavelli's understanding of political action. But he differs from the medieval legalists and the natural lawyers by focusing on the power or force that underlies these moral and legal discourses, on the grounds that these are merely epiphenomena of real political life.

The struggle for dominance and advantage amongst the regional powers of Italy and the interfering great powers of western Europe – France, Spain and then the Holy Roman Empire – followed the breakdown of a previous local balance of powers. That had been achieved by Cosimo de Medici and Francesco Sforza and it underlay the Peace of Lodi in 1454 between Milan, Florence, Venice, the Papal States and Naples. One of the major destabilising features for such 'balance of power' politics was the position of the papacy. The Pope was not only the ruler of the Church but also a significant Italian prince. However, the choice of Pope lay with the College of Cardinals, reflecting the international character of the Church, so that it became a place where national dynastic interests were played out on the international stage. Following the election of Roderigo de Borgia as Pope Alexander VI and his alliance with Naples (backed by Spain), the King of Naples asserted a claim of right to Milan. Ludovico Sforza formed an alliance with the French King Charles VIII, who was invited into Italy to attack Naples, thus opening Italy to a struggle between France, Spain and the Holy Roman Empire. With France now threatening Florence from the north, Piero de Medici attempted to placate the French by offering them domination of the nearby city of Pisa. But this move only destabilised his rule in Florence and he was overthrown in a popular rebellion by the radical preacher Savonarola. When the French retreated, Florence was placed under a papal interdict (denying the sacraments of the Church – a hugely significant penalty at that time) and Savonarola fell from power and was executed as a heretic. With the establishment of a new Council in Florence, Machiavelli entered political and diplomatic service. Florence then allied with Pope Alexander VI and Venice against Milan, and Alexander's son Cesare Borgia (who features as a hero in *The Prince*) began a campaign consolidating Borgia rule in the Romagna region. At this stage Machiavelli was at the heart of events. As Florence sought to maintain an alliance with France, Machiavelli was dispatched on an embassy to the French King Louis XII in Lyon, followed by a mission to Cesare Borgia. These were the high points of his diplomatic experience and informed his major works.

In 1503 Pope Alexander VI died, and, after a brief succession by Pius III (who was Pope for only 26 days), the papacy went to Cardinal della Rovere as Julius II, an implacable foe of the Borgias. Cesare Borgia had originally hoped to placate Julius, but he failed miserably and was stripped of all offices and imprisoned; fortune had turned against his family. Although Machiavelli was later sent on another embassy to France, the outcome became redundant as

Italy was divided into spheres of influence between France in the north and Spain in the south. Julius took this opportunity to improve his own position and reconquer the Papal States following the fall of Cesare Borgia. However, although the threat from Spain had receded, the position of Florence was not secure because the intervention of the Holy Roman Empire under Maximilian I created further threats in the north of Italy.

The position of Florence and of Machiavelli was rarely secure. In 1508 Pope Julius II brought together France, Spain and Emperor Maximilian in the League of Cambrai to conduct hostilities against Venice, forcing it from the Romagna (the region that was Cesare Borgia's power base). During this period Machiavelli was sent by Florence to Pisa to oversee a siege that resulted in Pisa's capitulation in 1509. Yet, no sooner had Venice been defeated in the wider conflict than Pope Julius broke the League of Cambrai and made peace with Venice, allying Venice with Spain and the Holy Roman Empire against France, which was Florence's protector. Maximilian brought Swiss troops into Lombardy in northern Italy and France withdrew. Florence was now exposed so Pope Julius demanded the removal of Soderini as the head of the Florentine government. Soderini fled and Machiavelli fell from office following the Medicis' return to power. He was subsequently implicated in an uprising, arrested, tortured and only survived and was exiled because Julius II died and was replaced by Pope Leo X (Giovanni de Medici), who decreed a celebratory general amnesty. Despite Machiavelli's efforts until his death, the new Medici Pope distrusted him and imposed unassailable barriers to his return to diplomatic office or a political career.

The struggle for power in Italy continued, albeit complicated by events unfolding to the north of Italy that were to shape the future of European history. This is most obvious in the development of the contest between France, Spain and the Holy Roman Empire. With the accession of the Spanish Charles I to the position of Holy Roman Emperor (as Charles V), in 1519 he consolidated the two powers against the French. Pope Leo X concluded a treaty with Charles to expel the French from Milan and Italy. Subsequent papal reigns were short and so the dynastic implications complicated the politics of the peninsula. In 1523 the new Medici Pope Clement VII allied with France and recaptured Milan, but a year later the French King Francis I was defeated and imprisoned by Imperial forces, though he was released two years later following the Treaty of Madrid. This placed Milan under Spanish influence and confirmed its authority over Naples. Francis quickly repudiated this settlement, however, and allied himself with Clement VII and Venice to drive the Imperial forces out of Italy.

Charles V returned to Italy with German troops, many of whom were now followers of the Reformation leader Martin Luther and not well disposed to any popes. Clement signed a treaty with the Empire but then quickly repudiated it. So the Imperial forces marched on Rome and sacked it in 1527. This attack on the papacy also led to the fall of the Medicis in Florence and a return of republican rule. Yet, Machiavelli was unable to benefit from the change because he died in 1527. The German attack on Rome marked a significant change in the politics of Europe. It became the first part of a civilisational war that was to divide Catholic southern Europe from Protestant northern Europe and to shift the military focus of that struggle from Italy to Germany, a geographical switch that was to have a profound impact on political ideas.

'Teacher of wickedness' – Machiavelli's new science of politics

Given Machiavelli's style of writing, he is both an easy and a very difficult writer to understand. Superficially, a book such as *The Prince* is easy to read and has some simple and clear illustrations. Although longer, the *Discourses* has similar virtues. Yet, the point of these apparently straightforward discussions is a much more complex matter and has led to wildly divergent interpretations and morals. Three dominant contemporary approaches – those of Strauss, Berlin and Skinner – illustrate the problem. Leo Strauss argues that Machiavelli is a 'teacher of wickedness' and a revolutionary thinker breaking with the tradition of classical natural law (1957). Isaiah Berlin (1998) agrees, but claims this change occurs because Machiavelli replaces classical natural law with a different model of political morality, derived from the classical Roman world. Hence, he is not an 'immoralist' – he just advocates a different conception of morality. Quentin Skinner (1978; 2000) identifies a further moral scheme (different to that seen by Berlin), with Machiavelli as a defender of republican liberty. Whilst obscured by the later liberal Hobbesian discourse of negative and positive liberty, Machiavelli's stance nevertheless offers a different way of conceiving of political authority and society. What all three of these perspectives recognise as beyond doubt is that Machiavelli's writings depart significantly from the dominant way of theorising politics in his time; namely, the synthesis of Christianity, neo-Aristotelianism and natural law. Where they differ is whether Machiavelli repudiates Christian natural law, displaces it for a pagan Roman public morality, or rejects the moralisation of politics altogether. The next section explores the ways in which Machiavelli departs from the perspective of Christian natural law.

The 'mirror of princes' and the repudiation of natural law

In our more secular age, Machiavelli's teachings about the status and authority of morality might seem familiar and almost conventional. Yet, such a view risks failing to appreciate just how radical his position was in his own time. The way in which he conceives of the point of politics opens him to the charge of being a teacher of wickedness. The 'mirror of princes' refers to a style of political literature designed to educate and advise the political ruler in the exercise of virtue. Perhaps the most famous classical version is Cicero's *De Officiis* (*On Duties*), which sets out moral guidance for whomsoever would exercise political office. Once political office becomes associated with kingly power, this book serves as a handbook for the good prince. Cicero's example is reflected in many later examples such as Thomas Aquinas's *On Kingship*, Castiglione's *The Book of the Courtier* (1528) or Thomas Elyot's *The Book Named the Governor* (1531), addressed to the English King Henry VIII. This form of literature is vast and by no means confined to the European intellectual tradition. But what all of it contains is an attempt to distil out the virtues of a successful political leader from a wider and more basic moral or ethical perspective on life. In some cases, these works are simply a handbook of the virtues (for anyone), as these might be found in classical Greek thought (emphasising prudence, temperance, courage and justice), or in the primary Christian virtues (such as faith, hope and charity). Alternatively, these works might acknowledge that politics involves difficult choices (including about war and violence) but nevertheless seek to link the demands of political action with the overarching claims of morality.

The situation of political agency or executive power within a hierarchical moral order is best exemplified in Aquinas's *On Kingship*. Thomas Aquinas (later made a Catholic saint) was one of the most important Christian natural law thinkers of the high Middle Ages. His thought (Thomism) brings together Christian revelation with the theology of Augustine and the natural and moral philosophy of Aristotle. For Aquinas, the role of the prince was located within a hierarchical moral order shaped by natural and divine law. The law of nature was discoverable by reason, but it needed supplementation with revealed divine law to give a complete account of the good or goal for humanity. Within that order was the requirement to translate natural law into civil law, or the law of political communities. This in turn left open the requirement to ensure obedience to that law through the exercise of political or executive power. Aquinas is important because he emphasises the prevalence of a rational, law-governed universe that leaves scope for political action exercised by princes. Even a law-governed world will require a person who exercises executive power to secure it, and that is Aquinas's justification for the role of the prince. Yet, equally, the role of the prince and therefore of political executive power is explained in terms of its function within a natural moral order.

Whilst Aquinas's book is the most systematic statement that politics is subordinated to morality, the same stance is a defining feature of all such works. Indeed, Aquinas is in many respects only a more systematic exposition of what is implicit in Cicero, but with the addition of Christian virtues. What the whole 'mirror of princes' literature adds to this formal natural law theory is a stress on how the personal virtue of the prince forms a vital basis for the justification of political rule. The prince exercises executive power within the normative system of natural law, but the moral nature of this argument cannot simply be that it is functional (i.e. the system works) without undermining itself. It is for that reason that the prince should aspire to virtue and nobility and not just rely on the monopoly exercise of force. Nobility, exemplified in the princely virtues, is crucial to the normative justification and legitimation of princely rule. It forms the basis of the consent of the ruled. In this respect, the literature draws on ideas that had been important since Aristotle, and which became increasingly important with the rediscovery of his work in the late medieval period. Machiavelli's humanist contemporaries might have been more comfortable returning to classical historical examples than relying on Aquinas's austere abstract theology. But they would all have accepted the subordination of politics to morality as the premise of this literature.

What is most striking (and shocking for his contemporaries) about Machiavelli's *The Prince* is that his book seemingly conforms with this literature – he is, after all, advising a 'prince', Lorenzo de Medici – whilst completely repudiating its premises. The book's stance is very different to an Aristotelian or Ciceronian account of the virtues. The first 12 chapters discuss the types of principality and how they are acquired, followed by three chapters on military matters comparing the relative merits of mercenaries and citizen armies. Chapters 15 to 19 cover what one might expect from an account of princely virtue, but in fact turn the traditional idea of virtue on its head. The final chapters (20 to 25) provide practical advice to the prince on issues such as the benefits of fortresses and selecting ministers, and the final chapter is the famous exhortation to liberate Italy. What is so striking about *The Prince*'s repudiation of the classical natural law tradition is that it downgrades and marginalises the place of morality in politics, denies that the common good is a top ideal, and transforms the concept of virtue into something like efficacy.

Machiavelli's book begins with a very practical account of the nature of different types of principalities current in the Italy of his day, and how to acquire or retain power in each of them. He does not offer an ideal model of the principality, nor does he attempt a comparative study of European regime types. Instead, he sets out the basis of an answer to Lenin's famous question: 'What is to be done?' The principalities at hand include the papacy and rival city states, such as Venice or Sforza's Milan. And the mixed principalities that he refers to are those allied to larger powers, such France or Spain. By launching straight into a discussion of contemporary Italian politics, he clearly signals a departure from accounts of princely virtue focusing on its moral context. He makes no acknowledgement of the prevailing religious or moral contexts in which the ideal of princely rule would normally be situated. Whilst modern political science presupposes a clear division of labour between the descriptive and empirical science of states and the ideas of political morality and virtue – political science versus political philosophy – Machiavelli does not recognise the distinction.

Many commentators acknowledge the originality of his thought in founding a new science of politics. However, his striking originality is not simply in a focus on the real as opposed to the ideal, since Aristotelian political thought already acknowledges that distinction. What Machiavelli does is *deny* the place of ideal or moral perspectives in addressing the virtues of the prince. It is quite clear that he is not directing attention from the ethical to the practical: complete silence about the claims of natural law as the context for politics signals a denial of it. It is this wilful denial that underlies the claim that he is a teacher of 'wickedness' as opposed to a new type of theorist who shifts attention from the morality of politics to the practical demands of princely action.

He also rejects and denies that the idea of the common good is the key to politics, the second important moral of *The Prince*. The idea of the common good in political philosophy has been central in explaining the point of political action, and therefore its justification. Even when previous theorists had to explain and justify actions that looked 'Machiavellian' (in terms of their duplicity and forcefulness), they excused them in terms of a conception of the common good – which ultimately justified apparent departures from conventionally accepted moral norms as achieving a higher good. For classical thinkers of the Roman era such as Cicero, the common good explains and justifies a lot: it privileges the claims of rulers to obedience even when they require coercive actions such as commanding military service, or the payment of taxes, that may not be in the immediate interests of subjects. The argument is that there is a good that we share through membership of a political society or commonwealth, what Cicero calls the '*res publica*', which it is the task of the prince or ruler to protect and secure. But once again this idea is completely missing from *The Prince*.

Similarly, for Aquinas the prince is often asked to do 'indifferent things' (acts beyond the specifics of the natural law), which may appear to be outside the formal dictates of the law but which are given a moral status by reference to a conception of the common good. In Machiavelli's discussion of examples, there is no attempt to either defend or to demonstrate any conception of the common good. Where interests or an idea of a good or end of action are presented, this is purely in terms of the prince's personal interest and goals. Success or failure is always judged relative to the interests and ambition of the prince, leader or character being discussed. Even in the final chapter's exhortation for a liberator of Italy, the benefits of an end to foreign domination and war are presented largely as opportunities for personal honour:

> I have no doubt at all that he [Italy's liberator] would be received with great affection in all those regions that have been inundated by the foreign invasions, as well as with a great thirst for revenge, with resolute fidelity, with devotion and with tears of gratitude. What gate would be closed to him? What people would fail to obey him? What envious hostility would work against him? What Italian would deny him homage? (Machiavelli 1988, pp. 90–91)

Although a rallying cry for Italy, this exhortation motivates the potential liberator by personal glory and an opportunity for distinction and leadership. Even the liberation from foreign domination is not a clear moral justification for action. The passage clearly indicates that this is also merely another opportunity for a prince to replace the domination of the French or Spanish with that of a home-grown national leader, presumably exercising dominance over the distinct local identities of the Italian city states. Machiavelli's subordination of any traditional conception of the common good to the interest and personal good of an individual prince should not be seen as just replacing a moralistic common good with a more empirical conception as the sum total of the individual interests of those subject to political rule. Such an empirical ideal of the people also plays a very limited role in Machiavelli's thought. Indeed, in most cases, where he refers to the people it is in highly disparaging terms. In the *Discourses* he famously says, '*all men are bad*' [*Discourses* 2008, p. 28], suggesting that an aggregation of individual interests would not have any moral, let alone political, value. In *The Prince* he expands on this, arguing:

> this may be said of men generally: that they are ungrateful, fickle, feigners and dissemblers, avoiders of danger, eager for gain. While you benefit them they are all devoted to you: they would shed their blood for you; they offer their possessions, their lives, and their sons, as I said before, when need to do so is far off. But when you are hard pressed, they turn away. (Machiavelli 1988, p. 59)

The clear implication here is that 'the people' do not offer any basis for formulating a concept of the common good. Instead, they are merely the material with which the successful prince or ruler must work to achieve their own ends and goals. Using a discourse of moral rules and ends may be functional for rulers, helping them to sustain their power. But the common good and other moral ends and rules are not otherwise important. This is a much more convincing ground for arguing that Machiavelli is a teacher of wickedness. He is not merely suggesting that the successful prince must step outside the normal rules of moral action for a greater good: there is no moral good, and this is reflected in the third moral of *The Prince* as a subversion of the mirror of princes, namely his replacement of virtue with *virtu*.

Distinguishing between virtue and the Italian *virtu* is a curious convention
        Machiavelli scholarship, but it is important because it draws attention to the
                virtue as a moral concept connected to classical Greek ethics and to
                        natural law, whereas using the idea of *virtu* shows Machiavelli's self-
                                conception of morality. The subversion of traditional accounts of
                                        Chapters 15 to 19, where the timely use of cruelty and dishon-
                                                and many other things. But the rejection of traditional
                                                        earlier, in Chapter 7, where Duke Valentino (Cesare

Borgia) is introduced as one of his exemplars of the *vir* or man of virtuous action. The chapter contains the famous discussion of Borgia's treatment of his henchman Remirro de Orco:

> Because he [Borgia] recognized that the severe measures that had been taken resulted in his becoming hated by some people, in order to dispel this ill-feeling and win everyone over to him, he wanted to show that if any cruel deeds had been committed they were attributable to the harshness of his governor, not to himself. And availing himself of an appropriate opportunity, one morning the Duke had Remirro placed in two pieces in the square at Cesana, with a block of wood and a blood-stained sword at his side. This terrible spectacle left the people both satisfied and amazed. (Machiavelli 1988, p. 26)

What is most striking about this passage is how central violence is here to Borgia's *virtu*. It is not just that violence is necessary to politics, for even Augustine acknowledged it as a regrettable necessity of a fallen world. Rather, Machiavelli leaves aside any implication of regret or discomfort and instead celebrates the technology of violence – how it is carried out and used to the greatest effect. Also, that effect is not some higher good (such as restricting the violence of criminals or aggressors by creating a fearsome punishment). Instead, the prince's goal is just deflecting blame and feeding the satisfaction and amazement of the people. What is creditable in Borgia is his willingness to act in such an amazing way and be a showman of violence and force to awe his subjects.

Similarly, in the later '*virtu* chapters' what is praiseworthy is how well the successful prince manipulates traditional norms of action such as cruelty and dishonesty. Cruelty is not wrong, but it can backfire and so must be exercised judiciously to achieve the prince's goals in the long term. In this way, *virtu* is much more functional than virtue as a moral concept, and it is closely allied to what Machiavelli clearly suggests are very masculine traits of manly forcefulness and drive. Whilst it would be an oxymoron to speak of the virtue of a torturer, it is certainly feasible to speak of the Machiavellian *virtu* being exhibited by a successful torturer.

Nor is the technology of violence the only element of Machiavellian political science that takes him outside of the normal moral boundaries of action. Machiavelli is equally clear about the primacy of princely prudence (including lying and dissimulation) over honesty. Princes and rulers should not be swayed by the praise and goodwill of the people, who are, after all, also self-deceiving and untrustworthy. Machiavelli is very clear that fear, which lies in the control of the prince, is always a better basis for regime stability than love of the people, which is fleeting. The people are not to be trusted but to be manipulated using the *virtu* of the prince, who is best when he shows regard to how this can be done successfully, for example by killing one's immediate rivals but not depriving their wider families of their wealth. The first can be done quickly and finished cleanly and effectively, whereas dispossessing one's enemy's whole family creates intergenerational resentment and long-term distrust and bitterness. Machiavelli's point is not simply to show that the true virtues of politics are different, because a utilitarian calculus of securing the common good sometimes requires actions that are contrary to normal moral norms. Whatever calculations take place in Machiavelli's economy of force and violence, there is no overarching common good providing any higher-level moral vindication of these types of action. The prince's actions are only vindicated for him by his success.

History, time and change in politics

All political thought is underpinned by a view of history, time and change. In the case of Plato, that is provided via a metaphysical doctrine, whereas for Thucydides it is through the self-conscious recording of the succession of events and their meaning. Whether it is foregrounded as part of a philosophical position or part of the background presuppositions of an account of the nature of political action, the issue of history time and change is ever present. For ancient Greek accounts of the ideal polis (*kallipolis*), there is a need to explain how we can move from where we are to the ideal, as in Aristotle. Alternatively, in Plato we have the corrupt forms of political society as departures from the ideal order, with democracy as the worst type. As we have seen with Augustine, too, the problem of history is central to the political implications of his theology. He explains the fundamental salvation history of humanity as revealed in the Christian Old and New Testaments. But he also addresses those Christians who have tried to read that salvation history onto late Roman imperial history and the triumph of Christianity in the conversion of Constantine. The position of classical natural law combines elements of classical political idealism, especially as exemplified in Aristotle and Augustine's account of theological time and redemption history.

Machiavelli is once again iconoclastic in abandoning the idea of progress implicit in theological time, or the idea of mere temporal succession in the secular world prior to the second coming. Firstly, as we have seen, he separates politics from any narrative of development and perfection. Politics is a morally neutral activity concerned with manipulating power by, or on behalf of, the prince. This might be thought to fit into an Augustinian account of the secular world, where there is no obvious pattern to political events, just a constant succession. But Machiavelli does not simply assert that the historical stage is empty and anything goes. He argues that history has a structure and, if we learn carefully from it, we can be more successful in achieving political ends. Yet, that structure is not teleological and progressive, and thus he clearly departs from classical natural law and emphasises that he is a teacher of 'wickedness' or 'realism', at least against that standard.

Machiavelli's theory of history comes in two parts: a thesis about continuity and a thesis about change. We have already seen that the continuity thesis depends on the view that human nature is broadly constant over time. He asserts:

> that anyone wishing to see what is to be must consider what has been: all
> the things of this world in every era have their counterparts in ancient
> times. This occurs since these actions are carried out by men who have
> and have always had the same passions, which, of necessity, must give
> rise to the same results. (Machiavelli 2008, p. 351)

His science of politics is possible because the motives and springs of human action are constant, therefore the past will provide lessons to an attentive student. Because we can learn from the past, we can search for the best way of mastering circumstances or necessity, and secure the most effective outcomes. However, this possibility of learning from the past raises questions about the problem of historical change. If we can learn from the past by carefully accumulating the lessons of history and common human motives, then a successful education for rulers ought to allow them to apply that accumulated knowledge in ever more successful ways to make historical and political progress. One can raise here the problem of induction that obsessed later thinkers such as David Hume (1711–1776). Hume's point is nicely encapsulated in the example of European biologists inferring that all swans are white based on countless confirmatory observations – until they encountered a single black swan in Australia, thus disconfirming the generalisation.

Unlike Hume, Machiavelli is not looking for law-like generalisations in an explanatory science of politics that holds for all cases, but rather looking for precedents that can be a guide in similar sets of circumstances. If Hume's concerns are applied to Machiavelli, they impact on his fundamental claim that human nature is constant, which itself is a contentious empirical claim. For Machiavelli, this proposition is less a claim derived from experience than a presupposition of historical enquiry. The real challenge to a progressive history for Machiavelli is not the prospect of 'black swan' events challenging his historical generalisations but the more fundamental rejection of a linear and progressive history of the sort that characterises classical natural law, or the linear but non-progressive history of Augustine's secular order. Machiavelli sees the structure of history not as linear but as cyclical. Here he follows a classical Roman tradition going back to Polybius. He does not explain this philosophy of history in a single theoretical discussion, but nevertheless it is clearly manifest when he writes that 'human affairs are always in motion and are either on the rise or in decline' (Machiavelli 2008, p. 150). The presupposition of cyclical change, and the constant rise and fall of principalities and republics, underpins the second major power in both *The Prince* and the *Discourses* operating alongside *virtu*, namely *fortuna* or fortune. Fortuna is the Roman goddess that needs to be both mastered and courted by the prince for success.

Machiavelli's gendered, even sexist, discussion of the struggle between *virtu* and *fortuna* can be disconcerting for modern readers:

> I certainly think that it is better to be impetuous than cautious, because fortune is a woman, and if you want to control her, it is necessary to treat her roughly. And it is clear that she is more inclined to yield to men who are impetuous than to those who are calculating. Since fortune is a woman, she is always well disposed towards young men, because they are less cautious and more aggressive, and treat her more boldly. (Machiavelli 1988, p. 87)

Fortuna is often depicted with a wheel and the idea of the wheel of fortune is a familiar one to this day, although the wheel was also associated with a mode of execution, perhaps just as appropriate, since fortune is not always good. That image of the wheel suggests two important things for Machiavelli: the first is the idea of change being cyclical and the history of political societies being one of rise and subsequent decline and fall; the second is that all political careers potentially end in failure, or avoid that fate only by luck. This logic of movement in history is both inevitable and means that no perfect final state of political order can ever be established. The central message of Machiavelli's political theory is that the combination of *virtu* struggling with *fortuna* is about perpetual movement and change without a final direction or goal for that change – it is anti-teleological.

It is this idea that explains Machiavelli's indifference to the moralistic politics of classical natural law. The challenge of politics is about managing that temporal change in a permanently dynamic process of history. There is no ideal or perfect state free from the tyranny of fortune. As Machiavelli saw in his own experience of diplomacy, the realm of political action does not offer scope for the static exhibition of virtue because the challenge of political agency is constant change. No sooner has one challenge been addressed than another arises and pushes the prince in a different direction. Similarly, the lives of princes and rulers of republics is subject to time and fortune, as illustrated by the rise and fall of Machiavelli's hero Cesare Borgia. Whilst the logic is inexorable – in the struggle between the goddess *fortuna* and the impetuous male prince, fortune will always ultimately win – Machiavelli cautions against fatalism. That said, there is scope for freedom of action: 'I am disposed to hold that fortune is the arbiter of half our actions, but that it lets us control roughly the other half' (Machiavelli 1988, p. 85).

The challenge presented by history and fortune is understanding where one is in the process of rise or decline, and also understanding the tools or strategies appropriate to slowing or accelerating the turn of the wheel of fortune in one's favour. To use another Machiavellian metaphor, how can one deploy dykes and dams to channel the 'dangerous river' of historical events? The study of ancient history is precisely designed to search out examples that might illuminate the present, not in terms of strict precedent for action but in locating the challenges in a judgement about where fortune is leading. The interplay of the two concepts of *virtu* and *fortuna* provide the key to successful political action but also to the choice of examples and the lessons that Machiavelli seeks to elicit in *The Prince*. This is indeed an advice book, or a realist mirror of princes, and not just a disengaged empirical study of political events or good government. As Machiavelli's political world is characterised by relentless temporal change, so the challenge of politics is one of recognising and managing change, and not denying it. The fundamental contrast between Machiavelli and conceptions of politics that follow from natural law, including contemporary moralistic theories such as international liberalism, is that his world ultimately has no place for the rigidities and order of law and morality. At best they could be temporary tools or devices for use by the prince, but in such a role they obviously change their meanings beyond those intended by moralists.

Christianity, religion and patriotism

If political experience is shaped by fortune and by audacity in roughly equal halves, there remains the final question of what place religion plays in Machiavelli's ideas, especially given that he was writing in a culture that was Roman Catholic – and often describing the actions of prominent Catholic Christians such as Popes Alexander VI and Julius II. Had he straightforwardly repudiated Christianity, this would clearly conform to his image as a teacher of wickedness, at least in the sight of many orthodox Christians. Of course, this would also have been a foolhardy stance to take. And Machiavelli does not say that Christianity or religion is false. But what does he have to say on spiritual matters? Does religion have a bearing on his thought, tempering the idea that he is a teacher of wickedness who repudiates classical natural law?

Throughout Machiavelli's life, all the Italian states were Catholic. Indeed, an alternative Protestant strand of Christianity did not develop until the end of his life, within the German principalities of the Holy Roman Empire. Machiavelli gives no clear evidence of atheism and speaks frequently of 'our religion' as a fact of Italian life. In fact, the evidence is to the contrary and by all accounts he was sufficiently observant and died within the Church. We have no evidence of religion forming part of his inner life or conscience, so how far his separation of political thinking from classical natural law illustrates a distance from orthodox belief is impossible to show. Yet, if we turn to his writings, we see a paradoxical view. The discussion of religion, and Christianity in particular, in *The Prince* is coloured by his experience as a diplomat and observer of Cesare Borgia.

Borgia was the son of Pope Alexander VI, and the victim of Alexander's successor but one, Pope Julius II. Alexander and Julius are both deeply political princes in the spirit of Machiavelli's argument, to the extent that one could almost forget that they are also priests and titular leaders of western Catholic Christianity. The analysis of their actions does not rely on analysis of Christian natural law, or even traditional medieval discussions of the relationship between papal spiritual authority and the temporal authority exercised by kings or emperors. As with so much else in classical natural law inherited from the medieval world, this element is notable by its absence in *The Prince*. Chapter 11 is devoted to 'Ecclesiastical Principalities' and concentrates on the problem that popes are weak princes because they are usually elderly when elected, hence they have a short claim on their office and cannot bequeath it to successors. Thus, their fortune tends to be short-lived and destabilising of other nearby principalities because of the ultimately personal nature of alliances and treaties. It is also clear that in interstate politics the papacy is only one prince amongst many, and not the centre of an international political order who can claim political authority on the basis of ecclesiastical office. Throughout this discussion in *The Prince*, Christian revelation or theology plays no part in the argument. When discussing the matter of Church teaching in the *Discourses*, Machiavelli's argument is also non-theological; instead, it is what we would now call sociological:

> ancient religion beautified only men fully possessed of worldly glory, such as the leaders of armies and the rulers of republics. Our religion has more often glorified humble and contemplative men rather than active ones. Moreover, our religion has defined the supreme good as humility, abjection, and contempt of worldly things; ancient religion located it in greatness of mind, strength of body, and in all the other things apt to make men the strongest. And if our religion requires that you have inner strength, it wants you to have the capacity to endure suffering more than to undertake brave deeds. This way of living seems, therefore, to have made the world weak and to have given it over to be plundered by wicked men, who are easily able to dominate it, since in order to go to paradise, most men think more about enduring their pains than about avenging them ... it appears that the world has become soft and heaven been disarmed. (Machiavelli 2008, p. 159)

In this passage Machiavelli's concern is with the sociological effectiveness of religion in sustaining the types of character that will be successful in the field of politics. His simple contrast between the civil religion of the pagans (meaning the ancient Romans) and of contemporary Christians criticises Christianity as creating feeble and weak characters, because of its celebration of humility and its rejection of heroic and martial virtue. This contrast reinforces the subversion of classical moral and Christian virtues in favour of the martial virtue of the Romans. The characterisation of Christian virtues as effeminate is a further illustration of Machiavelli's gendering of moral language and his assertion of the masculine *virtu* as essential for the political success of princes and for stable and successful republics. Consequently, his attitude to the prevailing Catholic Christianity can be considered perfectly consistent with a rejection of moralism and natural law. That said, he is not dismissive of all religion: when outlining the basis of character, he suggests that an appropriate civil religion or patriotic culture is what is needed to sustain political community and, especially, to motivate princes to fight and citizens to serve in the military and so secure their republic.

The paradox of Machiavelli's discussion is that the Catholic culture of his time undermines the martial virtues of a successful prince or citizen and is partly responsible for Italy's weakness. Yet, his discussion of the two popes in 'Ecclesiastical Principalities' presents two martial and aggressive leaders, who, but for the limitations of their terms of office, are highly successful princes in both the political and the military spheres. When these two prelates are contrasted with another ecclesiastical leader, the unarmed Florentine friar–prophet Savonarola, who briefly led Florence between the fall of the Medici and the re-establishment of the republic, we can see that Machiavelli poses a stark choice, although he does not deny the truth of Christian revelation. The choice is between political success in this world, which requires one set of skills and motives, and another set of virtues appropriate to preparing for eternal life. These rival conceptions of character are ultimately incompatible, and one must choose between them. That one must choose is emphasised by the contrast between 'the licentiousness of the prelates and heads of the Church' and the examples of St Dominic and St Francis and their revival of Christianity (Machiavelli 2008, p. 249). As princes, prelates (bishops and popes) are forced to act like Machiavellian princes and therefore to cultivate the *virtu* of the successful prince. The fact that the Church in Italy is a political entity, with all the institutions of a principality, means the prelate becomes a political actor with attention focused on the challenges of history and necessity, as opposed to the life beyond the relentless world of fortune and political change.

What Machiavelli leaves unaddressed is what a prince or a republic should do about the Christian religion, given its effect on the character and virtue of a people. There are certainly passages that celebrate the renewal of Christianity under the militant St Dominic and the mendicant friar St Francis. The new monastic orders they founded were to play a significant role in the Church's expansion into the new worlds of the Americas and the Far East in the following century. And as such they would contribute enormously to the power of the Church and the imperial focus of Christian civilisation under the Spanish and Portuguese.

Apart from that, Machiavelli is largely uninterested in the truths of religion or the gifts of faith in his account of successful political action, precisely because he is focused on the temporally proximate as opposed to eternity. Thus, he leaves open the question of whether the successful prince or republic should shape public education more towards a paganised form of Christianity so as to serve the goals of politics, rather than allow religion to constrain or determine the shape of the prince's goals and ambitions. The overwhelming textual evidence is that religion is to be made subservient to political success, and for the present to triumph over the eternal. This might be the lesson that the modern world is happy to accept, yet it is clear that this is a significant departure from the dominant Christian natural law theory of the age, and a further illustration of how Machiavelli rejects the primacy of morality or religion.

Violence, war and reason of state

Machiavelli clearly does not offer a formal theory of the boundaries and limits of authority, or set out the nature of law within and between political communities. All of this is quite deliberate because his goal is to challenge the idea of a formal model of political relationships from which normative claims can be derived. In this respect he could not be more unlike Aquinas and earlier natural law predecessors, or more different from Hobbes and the state-based theories of international order that were to follow in the next century. Yet, he remains for many subsequent readers one of the most important theorists of international politics, statecraft and diplomacy. Machiavelli gives no analysis or justification of political structures, but when it comes to statecraft and the exercise of political power he is rarely matched. It is precisely this conception of the craft of politics that I consider next. But, given the discussion above, there is no need to worry whether he is moral or immoral, and instead I focus on the most distinctive features of his conception of political practice, namely the deployment of violence in the foundation and maintenance of political institutions.

For Machiavelli, all politics involves the deployment of force because the goal of political action is getting people to do what they otherwise may not want to do. This is almost a formal definition of the idea of power. Yet, Machiavelli is not simply a theorist of power or of the technology of coercion; he is a theorist of the deployment of violence as essential to the technology or instruments of coercing others to do what is willed, either by the prince or by a republic. Violence is not just a sad necessity, as it was for Augustine, or a consequence of war making it the default condition of states, as it was for Thucydides. Violence, and its purposing reason and deployment, is the key to the heart of successful politics, whether of the prince or in a republic. Like other, lesser forms of power or coercion (such as threats or offers), violence is a form of reason-giving. Unlike them, it works indirectly on the will or reason via working on the human body. It can seem the most irrational and primitive of actions. But, for those like

Machiavelli who are attentive to power, it is the most complex and nuanced of reasons, and the way it is deployed has a significant impact on political power and reason-giving, as opposed to other assertions of power that are not central to politics. Later thinkers were to argue that there are other types of violence, whether these be structural or linguistic, that are equally dangerous and coercive. However, Machiavelli subordinates all forms of coercion to physical or bodily violence, which in his view is fundamental and foundational (Frazer and Hutchings 2020).

Violence in The Prince *and the republic*

Machiavelli's most important political works are about how political power is acquired (*The Prince*), how it is maintained (*Discourses* and *Florentine Histories*) and how it is projected externally (*The Art of War*). The answers to each of these questions involve violence. It is from the relationship between his answers to these questions that Machiavelli's central political insights and his implications for thinking about international politics arise.

A misleading way of understanding the works would be to see some as focused on domestic or what becomes known as state politics and others as about international politics. *The Prince*, with its focus on advising a ruler, might seem to have this domestic focus, but that would be to miss the point entirely. The first 12 chapters of *The Prince* are devoted to how principalities are acquired, so we begin from the perspective of the uncertainty and instability of the international political order. The Prince's key task is one of establishing an order or a political entity. Indeed, this is precisely what Cesare Borgia sought to do in bringing order across the Romagna region by binding together a series of small cities and townships into a stable principality with a single unchallengeable source of authority – as opposed to a series of mini principalities ruled by prince bishops, who were not particularly interested in them or able to dominate them. So, the fundamental question at the beginning of *The Prince* is the question of the foundation of a political order.

The question of founding is an ancient subject of political and mythological reflection. Tribes, nations, states and empires have their own foundation myths, examples being the struggle between brothers Cain and Abel following Adam and Eve's expulsion from the Garden of Eden in the Book of Genesis, and in the case of the Rome that between Romulus and Remus. As with Cain and Abel, the founding of Rome also involves the killing of Remus by his brother. Violence and murder are integral to the founding of political authority in these two cases. But both place the founding act in the distant historical past, where it acquires a mythological power, in a way similar to ancient conquests in other foundation myths such as the English realm narrative of William the Conqueror's defeat of King Harold (who died with an arrow in his eye) at the Battle of Hastings (1066). The founding act, whether a murder or a conquest, establishes a constitutive political claim that creates a new political entity – whether of a city, a realm or a kingdom, or indeed what we would now call a state. Any founding story presupposes that the state or political entity did not previously exist. Conquests (as opposed to mythological founding acts) also suggest that there was something prior to the new political entity, whether that is the original Saxon kingdom prior to the Norman Conquest or some other entity.

In the opening of *The Prince*, Machiavelli indicates that this process of founding is not simply primordial and historically rare but something that is frequent and familiar. His opening chapters list the different ways in which principalities can be established drawing on relatively recent historical examples, as opposed to just ancient or mythological cases. The details of this process of founding are also important because they challenge the idea that behind new principalities are relatively stable political bodies with working or challengeable governments. As with his scepticism about the idea of a common good, Machiavelli is similarly sceptical about the idea of a people as a relatively stable body underpinning the possibility of a political community. Machiavelli does not hold the people in high regard as embodying anything of political importance prior to the founding acts of the new prince. Indeed, they merely form a multitude of bodies with contingent connections rather than an actual body politic or a quasi-natural entity, in the way that Aristotle speaks of the polis as a natural community. Peoples are constituted from a multitude by the founding acts of the prince, and therefore the boundaries of political communities (as multitudes of individual people) are constantly open to transformation and change.

Creating a political entity such as a principality involves taking and binding a portion of the multitude together as a new political community – often, at this time, in Italy, Germany and elsewhere, people who share a common language and religion and so might relatively easily transfer from one set-up for political rule to another. This assertion of the absence of any international order that determines the boundaries of political communities, whether as territorial entities or as peoples, is one of the obvious reasons why Machiavelli is characterised as a theorist of realism. Yet, if he is indeed a realist, then his challenge is more radical than simply the claim that there is a society of political communities (states) without hierarchical order, or that there is a state of anarchy between those states. Machiavelli denies that any political entity or people is ultimately stable and permanent because of his theory of history as the cyclical rise and fall of principalities, peoples or ruling powers. This cyclical process means that apparent stability is never firmly established, and order is always temporally contingent, depending upon where one is located on fortune's wheel, whether rising or declining. All systems of international and political order allow for the challenge of change. Yet they also seek to mitigate negative or harmful consequences through mechanisms such as the balance of power and alliances, if not the imposition of a conception of international law. Yet, Machiavelli's account of founding acts, allied with history as cyclical and not progressive, makes that order more uncertain and more deeply contingent or temporary. Underlying his conception of politics, state creation and maintenance, there is not even a regulative ideal of order that political communities or people might work towards. Instead, there is just the relentlessness of change, sometimes for the better and sometimes for the worse. That process is ineradicable, a fact of the world within which state creation constantly occurs. At any stage of history, there will always be those, such as Cesare Borgia, attempting to take the opportunity to build a new principality and dynasty from the disorder of the Romagna, or a Pope Julius II trying to dominate Italy by playing off the great powers.

The first lesson of *The Prince*, then, is that political 'founding' is a ubiquitous act, as opposed to a very special and historically remote act. But that does not make the founding act any more peculiar than the mythological examples. Establishing a new principality is not simply disposing of a predecessor and replacing them on the throne so as to enjoy their wealth and authority. For Machiavelli there is a process of new creation even if this involves just the reassertion of an existing principality amongst the kingdoms of the world. This new creation involves making a people out of a multitude under a ruler with authority, that is, creating a body politic where it did not previously exist. And central to this creative act is the place of violence.

Just as an act of violence imprints force on a human body by destructively marking it, so the founding act of a political order is designed to imprint or mark the body politic in a way that distinguishes it, and gives it its particularity, and for the source of that marking to be the political authority. For Machiavelli, the power to make that mark that stays within memory is central to the claim of a political power to authority over a people. In an act of conquest, the prince might exercise this power directly by crushing and destroying a foe on the battlefield, but this capacity can also be exercised in other ways that are often more spectacular. A good example of this is treatment of Remirro de Orco in the square at Cesana. Borgia's right-hand man and enforcer de Orco was used in pacifying the Romagna, deploying violence against its ruling families to build Borgia's new principality. A forceful and brutal figure in his own right, de Orco was nevertheless brought low by being butchered in the public square. Perhaps the most striking parable in *The Prince*, Machiavelli's message here is nonetheless subtle. A number of elements in the story can be brought out to illustrate the way in which violence, or force against bodies, is used to create political authority.

Firstly, although the act is clearly an expression of Borgia's power against one of his most trusted lieutenants, it is left unclear whether this act was carried out by Borgia himself, who was by all accounts a violent figure when he needed to be. The distance and ambiguity here is important because it clearly links the act to Borgia, but also leaves a certain distance – in the same way that the act of an executioner is that of the prince but not done by the prince. Yet, this is no simple execution, although it has many of the same trappings. There is the sword and the block, and the type of killing has the sort of ritualistic element that was so important to executions of the time. The display of ritualistic power over bodies was an element of the aesthetics of punishment in the early modern world. The infliction of death or pain was an essential part of punishment as an expression of the legal and political power of the prince, but it was only one part of the ritual. The curious lengths to which people in medieval and Renaissance times went in terms of destroying and mutilating bodies was almost as important as the consequence in terms of death and pain. Death and pain were for the victim, but the humiliation and mutilation of the body was for the audience and the crowd – and it was this which demonstrated the peculiar power of the prince in a world in which regular or routine violence was familiar. The need to satisfy and to create awe was essential to assert power and claim authority from those who are left in awe as opposed to just fear.

The ritualistic mutilation of bodies also reflected the religious idea of sacrifice to propitiate a greater power and to restore an order that had been threatened by crime or sin. In the case of Remirro de Orco he had wronged those who stood in the way of Borgia's quest for power, but that wrong was to be partly atoned for by Borgia's ritual sacrifice of his henchman in the public square. But, whilst the death is ritualistic and like an execution, it is also not an execution or a ritual in other important respects. Borgia is able to stand apart from the violence because, although the question of his authorship remains, he is not seen to do the deed. Indeed, unlike an execution or ritual killing, no one is reported as having seen the act itself, but only the choreographed consequence. There is no executioner either, so the act is not simply an extreme example of a capital punishment. It is precisely that ambiguity that creates the necessary awe of the power of Borgia and which elevates him from another local thug into the special class of the prince with charismatic authority.

That assertion of authority, and the command over the people to respect that authority, is prior to the claim to punish breaches of the law and to give justice. And the power to awe the people is part of what binds the multitude into a people with a prince and is the source of the ruler's charismatic power. Throughout this theatrical incident there is no claim to legitimacy based on transferring power from the people to the prince, or the prince deriving power from some other higher authority. The type of action deployed does not just create a strong prudential reason to submit to a dangerous force; it awes the will and the body. Through this physical story it demonstrates how political authority is brought into the world without recourse to moral arguments about the law, or nature, or the common good of the people. The curious violence of foundational political acts binds bodies and stays within the memory of those who are in awe for as long as a prince can maintain that sense of awe. However, as we have seen, that awe is never permanent, hence the possibility of instability. Political authority can often be as short-lived as the natural life of the prince, especially if the princely family is eventually unable to maintain a dynasty, as was the case with Alexander VI and Cesare Borgia.

A similar story about founding violence is also present in the *Discourses*. Machiavelli discusses biblical examples such as Moses, King David and the classical Roman example of Romulus. Rome also periodically reran the founding violence, as with the executions of Brutus' sons following the replacement of the last Tarquin kings after the rape of Lucretia and the founding of the republic. Lucius Junius Brutus led the revolt against the Tarquin monarchy, but he is most famous for sacrificing his own sons to the good of the republic. In the first year of Brutus' term as consul, his sons, along with many aristocrats, become involved in a conspiracy against the republic, whose laws were effectively limiting their freedom. The conspiracy was overheard by a slave and the conspirators were convicted of treason. According to Livy, the punishment involved binding to a stake, stripping for humiliation, flogging and then beheading. It fell to Brutus himself to inflict this vicious and humiliating punishment on his own sons, which he did. This series of executions constitutes the completion of the founding of the republic, or its ritual refounding. This almost religious sacrifice of family blood to the claim of the republic is a key sign of this new political institution, with its authority that transcends even that of Brutus as consul, because it commanded him to exercise the deed. As the original defeat of the Tarquins was a punishment for the rape of Lucretia, so the ritual execution of Brutus' sons involved the new republican body politic ritually purging its old aristocratic authority and power.

Making political communities, whether they be principalities or republics, involves the same ritual purging of what went before to create people as a political body. So physical ideas such as cutting away what is dead or dying, drastically purging and marking the new body, are essential features of creating political authority and distinguishing it from other types of violence. In many respects, Machiavelli's arguments reflect the place of violence and sacrifice that is essential to religion, and especially to the central act of Christianity. Again, because he transposes so much of this feature of popular late Roman religion into his thinking about politics, we should not be surprised at the lack of any explicit discussion of Christianity in his writings.

Founding violence is central to Machiavelli's thought and to his conception of political power, but, as the discussion of Brutus in the *Discourses* makes clear, Machiavelli does not confine the matter to just a single primordial act. Turning to *The Prince*, the issue of founding a refounding is ever present in the context of a world containing weak and declining states. Even in the republic, where he is more concerned with fostering the stability of a political community over time, violence retains a place in refounding, renewing and stabilising authority.

As with the rest of Machiavelli's political theory, the arguments of the *Discourses* arise from reflections on the experience of the Roman Republic and key figures and social forces of Roman history, as discussed by Livy. The examples are the theory, because Machiavelli forcefully asserted that we can learn from them about the stable and permanent passions of men. Of course, examples need to be analysed and questioned, yet they do have a lesson for politics and that is why history is the handmaid of political statecraft. The obvious implication of the *Discourses* is for the domestic stability of a republic devoid of one central ruler, such as Florence. But even here the arguments necessarily have an implication for the shape and conduct of international politics, thus bringing together his domestic experience of being a functionary with the Florentine government and his experience as a diplomat pursuing Florence's overall interests in the context of complex great power politics.

Whereas the international realm provides the stage for an audacious prince to carve out a realm and constitute their own state, the republican sphere involves managing the challenges of domestic politics.

The republican model of a political community – not yet a modern state but neither simply the estate or affairs of a dominant prince – is well suited to exhibiting the forces that drive politics, and that need to be addressed in sustaining a stable political community. Central to Machiavelli's idea of a republic is that of a pluralistic model of the people. A people is not a stable and coherent entity that just needs strong government; it is something that needs to be constantly created and sustained, given the fragmenting forces that are irreducibly present. Just as the prince can make a people, so when this entity is made it will be found to be stratified into distinct classes who are ruled and involved in the process of ruling in different ways. The Roman Republic illustrates the class element of the body politic and the struggles between those forces within the structure of the republican constitution. Similar class interests underpin the Florentine republic and constitution. And much of Machiavelli's republican theory involves comparisons and contrasts between the two, an issue that Machiavelli returns to in his later *Florentine Histories*, which are sometimes said to embody a departure or 'conservative turn' away from his views in the *Discourses* (McCormick 2018, pp. 69–105).

The core problem that underpins the *Discourses* is that of stability and managing change through avoiding corruption. As we have seen, the cycle of time destabilises all things, and corruption is an ever-present challenge to a principality or a republic. Whereas the prince must cultivate personal *virtu* to seize the moment when necessity requires action, the republic seeks to slow the revolution of the wheel of fortune through creating a constitution. For Machiavelli, the constitution is not a founding legal document specifying the distribution of rights and powers but rather a codification of the practical way that those political powers are structured to strike a balance between opposing forces. The forces in a republic are social classes, most importantly the rich and the poor. In the Roman case there were the rival claims of the plebians (the ordinary people) and those of the nobility. In the structure of the Roman constitution these were represented in the political offices of tribunes, senators and consuls.

Machiavelli clearly favoured republican rule over monarchical or other types of rule, but we should be careful not to misunderstand his claim. He does not have a normative ideal state nor a normative view of politics. A successful republic is successful by virtue of one particular good, namely non-domination or republican freedom. Even here the ideal of freedom as non-domination is a functional good that minimises or slows the inevitable challenge of corruption and decline. Unlike later modern conceptions of freedom, which link it to individual agency and human flourishing, for Machiavelli, freedom as non-domination arises when a group of people is not dominated by another group and therefore can be independent (Berlin 1998; Skinner 1997). Domination occurs when whatever rights and liberties a group enjoys are at the discretion of a higher power. This could be a slave under the direction of a master, a principality under the direction of an imperial power, or a class subordinated by another dominant class. On such a view, freedom is not the absence of restrictions on action, as even a Roman slave might have considerable discretion and resources to act on behalf of a master's household. Indeed, many slaves might have been better off than poor freemen in terms of their resources and real opportunities. Nevertheless, the crucial difference is that these 'freedoms' are always at the discretion of a master. Similar issues of status and domination arise in relation to dominant imperial powers and the client relationships that they impose upon small cities or weak principalities.

Within a republic, this issue of domination arises in the struggle between the constituent classes who make up a people within a constitution. The *Discourses* describe the struggle between the ordinary people and the nobility in various republics. The rebellion of the sons of Brutus at the founding of the Roman Republic is an example of the aristocratic elite or nobility trying to overthrow the constraints of the ordinary people's claim to distinction and status. The nobles' appetite for distinction and status is a class manifestation of the *virtu* that Machiavelli seeks in a successful prince. Yet, this kind of *virtu* is manifested in terms of factional self-assertion and domination over others that are precisely the sources of corruption of regimes, through exploitation and disorder within a republic, or the search for militaristic glory and honour in the struggle between republics. Throughout the *Discourses* Machiavelli explores lessons for successful republics and especially the success of Rome as one of the longest-lasting republics – although this too is a republic that eventually collapsed into an empire.

Balance between the powers of the social classes that make up the republic is achieved in a number of ways. The most important condition of a successful republic is an armed citizenry. Since the ancient world, the ability to defend the republic has been a prerequisite of citizenship. The ability to defend the republic, to fight with one's fellows and to be prepared to die for the republic were essential signs of citizenship. This is only possible if the citizenry is armed because it is only in that way that they alone control the destiny of the republic.

As we shall see, Machiavelli is fearful of standing armies and of mercenary troops, because such people can be bought and they tend to prey upon those who rely on them. The Roman Republic went to great lengths to disperse its armies when they were not involved in defence or conquest, as they otherwise could pose significant threats to the city. An armed citizenry is also less likely to be reckless and adventurous as the costs of conflict and war will fall on the citizens and are not just borne by somebody else or external agents. Most crucially for Machiavelli, an armed citizenry can pursue where necessary, and contain when essential, inter-class violence within the republic. This limits the possibility of the nobles employing mercenary forces to tyrannise over the population, since they cannot enjoy the monopoly of violence and force simply through their wealth.

Wealth is also a source of corruption, so Machiavelli is keen that gross inequality does not establish itself within the republic. If inequality is too great, the classes cease to share a common destiny and thus common interests. Ancient history is full of examples of the wealthiest being the object of envy and resentment from the ordinary people, because they can free themselves from the cost of citizenship and assert privacy over public responsibility. For Machiavelli, corruption is largely the result of inequality and the resentments or fears that follow from it. A curious consequence of great wealth is often rich people's strong fear of envy and resentment by the poor majority, which entrenches social division and instability. Whilst the poor fear the wealthy nobles because of their ability to separate themselves and dominate them, so the nobility fears that the poor's envy will in turn threaten them and their wealth, property and advantage. This class tension is ever present in the structure of the Roman Republic and Machiavelli's Florence, and occasionally the tension between social classes does erupt into class violence. The complex lessons of the *Discourses* and of the *Florentine Histories* provide a constant reminder of how close to the surface violence and the resentments that sustain it are in republican politics. But the most interesting and complex issue is not that the eruption of class violence leads to a breakdown of that republic, although it is a temporary breakdown of social balance. Instead, the eruption of class violence is often depicted by Machiavelli as a necessary part of maintaining the stability of a republican order, by challenging the growth of inequality and the subsequent domination and lack of class freedom that follow from it.

Contrary to some idealistic views of republicanism that channel conflict into the deliberative practices of republican government, Machiavelli does not see deliberation as an epistemic process for arriving at the common good, the concept one might find in modern deliberative democrats (Goodin and Spiekermann 2018). Machiavelli is not interested in finding the truth or in constituting the common good through information sharing and deliberation. Instead, his model of deliberation is as a form of conflict and contestation, but one that does not resort to violence. That said, debate can have positive benefits in testing foreign policy and arguments for war (in this he clearly departs from Thucy-dides) or other policy matters. Yet, throughout his writings, the deliberative side of republican politics, and the struggle of speech and ideas, is mirrored by the threat and the reality of violence as a means of securing the republic and restoring balance. As with founding violence in *The Prince* and the *Discourses*, the underlying presence of a threat of violence in the republic is a constant fea-ture of politics. It is not simply a problem that needs to be or can be overcome by republican and deliberative politics. It is something that is integral to repub-lican political life, because disruptive violence is a perfectly sound response to the cyclical problem of domination and corruption that all republican regimes necessarily face.

War and reason of state

The one major work on politics published during Machiavelli's lifetime is the work most obviously related to what we now call international relations and political theory. Yet, *The Art of War* (1519–1520) is a curiously bloodless work from an author who seems adept at handling the issues of violence, force and power, although Clausewitz thought highly of it. The book demonstrates Machiavelli's practical interest in the organisation of military force and its suc-cessful deployment, especially given that he was responsible for the defence of Pisa against siege. The work is much less radical than his political works, and it conveys much of the conventional thinking of a medieval military manual. There are long disquisitions on the ranks, order, organisation and deployment of infantry forces, and discussions of the relative strengths of infantry versus cavalry. There is also some discussion of artillery, but Machiavelli shows little appreciation of what was to become one of the most important developments in military science, namely the deployment of gunpower and the development of handheld firearms. These were starting to be used and were a rapidly devel-oping technology during his lifetime, and they played an important role in the early wars of the Reformation only three decades later.

Central to Machiavelli's work are the various ways of organising the infan-try line in battle so that it can respond to attack, defence and change of cir-cumstances and weaponry, thereby accommodating *fortuna*. Also important are signalling commands to troops and identifying command in the context of battle, such as via the placement of flags and other forms of signalling. All these issues are complicated by later technology, but in different guises remained essential issues of military science that would be familiar to Clausewitz or 20th-century military tacticians. The book has little to say about strategy and there-fore little directly about the place of war in international affairs. In *The Prince*, war provides the opportunity for honour and *virtu* and is almost celebrated as a duty of the prince. And in the republicanism of the *Discourses* war is either a tool helpful for the protection and unification of the republic, or a risk created by overambitious nobles. By contrast, in *The Art of War* the activity of war is seen as a relatively brief series of engagements that test a prince's power or a city's resolve. The model of a duel dominates Machiavelli's military thinking; the rest is about the most prompt and efficient delivery of military force to that political end. War does not dominate that end, as we see from the republican preoccupation with making the war the task of a citizen body as a way of preventing needless wars of personal aggrandisement. Machiavelli is clearly aware of who carries the burden of war, both as soldiers and potential victims.

The one element of *The Art of War* that is repeated in both *The Prince* and the *Discourses* is the discussion of standing armies as dangerous, and the relative merits of citizen armies over mercenaries. Whether in Roman times or in the France of his day, for Machiavelli standing armies were a constant invitation to war and instability, because they have little else to do other than fight and seek rewards from pillaging the people. Both for soldiers in standing armies and for mercenaries, war is their day job. By contrast, citizen armies are more reluctant to fight and bear the costs and inconveniences on their ordinary lives, which are not solely devoted to military affairs. Citizens' livelihoods are based on their land or their trades, and campaigning is a distraction from these, as well as being physically dangerous. Mercenaries are also a problem for republics and princes in that their loyalty is easily bought. They have no shared interest with the republic or the prince, and thus can be as easily paid not to fight, or to change sides, as they are paid to fight and die for their client.

In the struggle for power and founding political acts, the skill of a prince is inspiring followers (and discouraging betrayal) in order to secure their own goals. In this context, the arts of war are important, but in terms of formal military science Machiavelli's concern is much more with the skill of the political agent or of the government of a republic. This fact is important because he does not distinguish the sciences appropriate to domestic politics and those devoted to the international realm. Consequently, he does not develop a formal distinction between the claims of authority governing domestic rule and the needs for effective action amongst states (Meineke [1924] 1957). Meineke and others who see Machiavelli as a founding theorist of reason of state (*raison d'état*) have overplayed the distinction between private or domestic morality and the conduct expected of political leaders. Indeed, whilst it is interesting, Meineke's reading of Machiavelli has more to do with the 'Prussianism' of Meineke's milieu – which spanned the pre-1914 German Reich, the post-war Weimar Republic and the Nazi regime, rather than capturing the reality of Machiavelli's doctrines.

Machiavelli is undoubtedly drawn to quasi-utilitarian discussions of reason of state because of his involvement in, and writings on, the diplomatic challenges facing Cesare Borgia or his own Florence. Yet, a careful reading of Machiavelli's histories, or his large correspondence on diplomatic matters, shows these works are chiefly descriptive and reflective rather than prescriptive or theoretical (Cesa 2014). A reordering of priorities, I suggest, by his radical departure from the superficial niceties of Christian natural law – but in practice the late medieval world was hardly unfamiliar with political and international violence and war. These are best understood not in terms of a two-level or hierarchical discussion of ethics and politics but as the displacement of ethics when thinking about politics and power, and a denial that it can simply be institutionalised in the respective claims of the individual and of the state. Machiavelli does not have a conception of the modern state; his concept *lo stato* is much more ambiguous between politics as an activity, an institutional structure, and different ways of conceiving agency in politics (such as that of the prince, the people and the citizen body). Indeed, given the fundamental lesson of *The Prince*, it is unlikely that Machiavelli would have found Meineke's argument a congenial way of representing his fundamental insights and lessons. His genius, and what made him quite so interesting and important, is that he is not easily disciplined into a philosophical or theoretical straightjacket. This is what makes his legacy so complex and so pervasive in modern international affairs and political thinking.

The long shadow of Machiavelli

Machiavelli wrote at a time of significant transformation in European politics and history in which the idea of the modern state had begun to appear. There was also an important shift in the geographical and ideological context, from the wars of princes to the wars of religion that followed the Reformation in 1517 and are foreshadowed in the Imperial sack of Rome in 1527. Yet, this context can also confuse and obscure the specificity of Machiavelli's legacy in politics and international affairs. It is easy to see him, as does Meineke, as one of the sources of the modern state, in particular the separation of morality from politics in the new science of reason of state that accompanied the possibility of realising autonomous sovereign power. This approach absorbs Machiavelli's ideas into the theory of the modern state, and in contemporary international relations into the state system – with its assertion of autonomy and sovereignty and the absence of any hierarchical authority regulating states. Reason of state, and Machiavelli's role in its emergence, secures his position in philosophical histories of modern politics and its theoretical categories, although it should be noticed that reason of state has other significant original thinkers such as Jean Bodin, whose ideas and politics are different from Machiavelli's (Skinner 1978; Poole 2015). His rejection of classical and Christian natural law is the basis for including Machiavelli amongst the sources of realist theories in international relations, and especially his denial of a higher law or normative order that creates obligations on the prince. Consequently, when early 20th-century thinkers were searching for the foundational theorists of international relations, he was an obvious candidate (Wight 1991; Doyle 1997). The realism versus idealism debate is an important one and certainly has shaped contemporary political and international affairs echoing some Machiavellian themes. However, there are other ways in which Machiavelli has shaped contemporary thinking that are both subtler and more significant than simply lining him up on the side of the 'IR' realists against the 'IR' idealists.

Revolutionary Machiavellians – Gramsci, Althusser and Burnham

The post-war debate between realism and idealism has tended to fit into a broad acceptance of the modern liberal state and the system in which it operates. In the early part of the 20th century, however, there was a curious interest in Machiavellianism amongst those who were seeking the revolutionary overthrow of the state via a communist revolution. This linkage is perhaps not too surprising in the case of the Italian Marxist Antonio Gramsci, who theorised the revolutionary class regime as the 'New Machiavelli' (Gramsci 1971). Gramsci drew inspiration from Machiavelli's account of the founding politics of *The Prince* as a model for the similar founding politics of a new class-state based on the unification of the Italian proletariat and peasantry.

In contrast to classical Leninism, with its top-down direction by the Communist Party, Gramsci is concerned with building a hegemony through the unification of distinct struggles to make the ideas and direction of Marxist Communism culturally dominant. Whilst Gramsci is often credited with a less violent version of revolutionary struggle to that advocated by Lenin, he retained a recognition of the need for foundational violence in building the new order. In this way, he also challenges the non-revolutionary paths to Communism advanced by other socialist and reformist groups. For him, the lesson of Machiavelli is clear – a socialist strategy must do away with the remaining elements of the old regime to secure political stability, in the same way that the prince is counselled to seek security from opponents from the old order, as executing de Orco did for Cesare Borgia. Gramsci also praises the way that Machiavelli, unlike other pre-Marxist thinkers, was not just a writer but was engaged with the politics of creating a people where it did not previously exist. For Gramsci, the leadership role of the Communist Party is that of the 'New Machiavelli' because it also does not inherit a pre-existing people with fixed preferences. Rather, it creates the people by establishing a new social and cultural hegemony, in a way that is analogous to how a people is created through a founding act, and is not a pre-existing constant of politics.

This reading of Machiavelli, as a resource for those who are attempting to make sense of revolutionary politics, is further developed by the great French structuralist Marxist Louis Althusser in his *Machiavelli and Us* (Althusser 1999). Althusser's fascination here is not easily summarised. But much turns on the paradoxical nature of Machiavelli's works, such as the apparent contradiction between the monarchical *The Prince* and the republican *Discourses*, and the radicalism of his method with its unequivocal repudiation of the Renaissance and classical natural law tradition. The things that have shocked many readers are precisely those elements of Machiavelli's thought that make him such a significant figure amongst past thinkers, and such an example for those wishing to defend the brutal reality of Marxist revolution from those who seek to humanise or liberalise his work as a moralistic approach to politics. Machiavelli's repudiation of that pathway opens up a respectable intellectual and practical political tradition, within which contemporary radical revolutionary politics could locate itself.

Machiavelli's preoccupation with force, violence and the act of political founding continued to obsess even former Marxist theorists such as James Burnham, the American Trotskyite, who lost his Marxist faith, worked for the predecessor of the CIA during World War II, and speculated about a new order based on the competition of technocratic elites that had little interest in democracy as anything other than a cover for elite selection and renewal. Burnham's *The Machiavellians* (Burnham 1943) followed his earlier book *The Managerial Revolution*, in which he shifted his allegiance from a Marxist class politics to a new elite politics of technocrats that would lead the new civilisation that was being brought into effect by Leninism in the USSR, fascism and Nazism in Europe and technocratic managerial capitalism in the USA. This theory is satirised in George Orwell's *1984*, where the party has become an end in itself and independent of any ideological substance. Having lost his initial faith in Marxism, Burnham flirted with Nazism as the new order for Europe in the late 1930s. But he was never a true believer and was more interested in the style of politics of technocratic elites as they challenged and deposed the old orders of imperial powers, like Great Britain. *The Machiavellians* links the Renaissance author's thought to a new perspective that Burnham constructed from the work of early 20th-century Italian political economists. Key figures here were Gaetano Mosca, Robert Michels and Vilfredo Pareto (all of whom influenced or were fathers of Italian fascism), with the addition of Georges Sorel's theory of mythical violence. Burnham's book is a curious synthesis of his own intellectual prejudices, rather than a serious historical analysis of Machiavelli or of an historical tradition that can be attributed to him. Yet, like Gramsci and Althusser, he celebrates Machiavelli as a political original who repudiates ethical politics and understands the reality and attraction of power and the necessity of war.

As the Cold War developed and the USSR began to develop nuclear weapons, Burnham changed his views about war, and even proposed a pre-emptive nuclear war with the USSR whilst the USA still had a monopoly of weapons. Burnham's peculiar but influential thought in the 1940s helped shape the realist world view in post-war international relations theory, by addressing approaches to power and war that moved beyond the 'reason of state' realism of the old order (represented by Meineke) or the revolutionary realism that was still tied to official Marxism–Leninism. As new forms of political agency emerged in states that had been transformed by military mobilisation, such as the USA, Burnham's ideas informed those who began to think about America as a capitalist imperial power, especially those who became known as neo-conservatives, who embraced an expansionist view of the USA's destiny, as opposed to the cautious realists, who drew self-limiting conclusions from their political heroes.

Domesticating Machiavelli in contemporary international political theory

The paradigm of realism in modern international theory is obviously shaped by Machiavellian themes and the explanation of reason of state and two-level theories that distinguish diplomatic and political morality from normal everyday morality. But what is also often interesting is the way in which those debates play out in reflections on international politics. Recent books by John Mearsheimer (2011) and Joseph Nye (2020) directly address questions such as why leaders must lie and how to do it effectively, and how leaders cannot simply depart from morality, both of which are deeply Machiavellian issues. Mearsheimer is a tough-minded realist, but in *Why Leaders Lie* he addresses the strategic complexities of not telling the truth and why that is sometimes compelled by circumstance. A particularly interesting example is the case of Saddam Hussein and the non-existent weapons of mass destruction prior to the second Gulf War in 2003. Hussein could not convince the international community that he had fully complied with external sanctions, despite largely having done so, without rendering his regime unstable. Similarly, Hussein's U.S. opponents could not believe him even if he had been telling the truth, nor could they simply confirm that they had been misled by spurious intelligence into a war that cost U.S. lives and money (and thousands of Iraqi lives). The circumstances of effective lying are necessary and ubiquitous in international politics, but they are not purely domestic (as with hiding casualty rates and projections in the Vietnam War to avoid alarming public opinion). Instead, managing deception requires control of events that are actually never in the hands of single agents.

Although less interested in the issue of practical Machiavellianism, Nye is also concerned with assessing the significance of 'morality' for the effectiveness of political leaders, by which he means U.S. presidents since Franklin Roosevelt. His careful and informed study links the categorically different issues of being a good (i.e. effective) president and that of being a good man. For example, by all accounts President Carter was a good man, however one judges his presidency in terms of its effectiveness. Whilst Nye's study appears to challenge the interpretation of Machiavellianism given here, it does follow his thought in emphasising the primacy of the political art of weaving together different policy drivers and interests. Despite all that has been said about the importance of immorality (by conventional standards) in Machiavelli and his celebration of violence and deception, his works are absolutely clear that no ruler should just be a lying brute – that way lies certain instability, chaos and failure, perhaps the key lesson to be drawn from the career of Saddam Hussein.

The most interesting contemporary political theorist who writes in the shadow of Machiavelli but who would not see himself as a simple 'Machiavellian' is Michael Walzer (1973; 1977). He has done so much to re-energise 'just war' theory and is well known for his related discussion of the problem of 'dirty hands'. Walzer's theory of war does not proceed from abstract natural law doctrines, as in Aquinas and followers, but from the practice of war itself. His 'war convention' draws on the way that real-life military conflict throws up dilemmas that shape how we can theorise and regulate war in ways that are understood and considered normative by those who may engage in it. This situated and engaged thinking already echoes Machiavelli's own thought about politics as an irreducibly practical activity. Walzer is also preoccupied with cases where the prosecution of war, or the exercise of political power, necessarily requires departing from otherwise binding moral norms covering the deployment of violence, deception and the imposition of harm. These actions require political leaders to dirty their hands by doing genuinely immoral things.

For Walzer, the political leader has obligations to protect his political community and responsibility for the deploying harm and violence to that end that ordinary individuals do not. These features put the political leader in circumstances where they must act in ways that would otherwise be wrong. Good examples are:

- waterboarding or torturing suspects to foil major terrorist attacks;
- engaging in military actions necessary for state survival that will result in the deaths of innocent non-combatants; or
- requiring soldiers to fight on in such circumstances while planning the state's extrication from a situation – for example, sending soldiers to die in countries like Afghanistan whilst organising a withdrawal.

All these examples are contestable, but each raises the issue of requiring death and harm that would otherwise be considered illegitimate. A hard-headed realist might argue that this is just war and 'people get hurt and die', but Walzer resists the simple realist view, just as he resists the high-minded moralist view that argues that we should never directly do wrong. Key to his thinking about war and international politics is recognising the argument that if they must kill innocents in the pursuit of their objectives, political leaders and their military commands are doing wrong. The interesting question is how we deal with that fact, especially in modern liberal democracies where we want soldiers, officials and politicians who can return to ordinary life without having their characters destroyed by the requirement to deploy violence and inflict wrong. We need people to 'dirty their hands' but we also need them to do it only in ways that do not destroy the integrity of key institutions, political communities or individual citizens.

Two aspects of Walzer's thinking are interesting. Firstly, unlike the abstract and formalist thinking of new 'just war theorists' such as McMahan or Fabre (2009; 2012), he endeavours to structure his thinking within the reality of modern war, as represented in history, autobiography and journalism. So his accounts of dilemmas are real and not simply abstract logical problems. Secondly, he prescribes responses designed to mitigate the evil being done but without dispensing with the evil. An example is provided by the apparent unfairness in the treatment of RAF Bomber Command following the end of World War II. At great personal cost and sacrifice, in 1940–1945 these airmen were required to do things that they considered wrong but necessary during the UK's campaign of terror-bombing against German cities. Pursuing targets that inevitably killed tens of thousands of civilians, many non-combatants and many who are innocent by any standard (such as infants and the old and infirm), the airmen engaged in acts that were wrong and in breach of normal conventions of war. Yet, in the specific circumstances of the time, when Britain was facing the threat of defeat by a terrible enemy, these emergency actions were nevertheless justified. That said, the actions of killing innocents remained wrong, so at the end of the war it was appropriate not to celebrate these actions with campaign medals or the highest honours for leaders like Sir Arthur Harris, who unlike all other major British commanders was not ennobled. Many questions and challenges can be raised against Walzer's specific arguments, but what remains interesting about his way of thinking, and what I think is most Machiavellian about it, is that he offers a complex middle position between the idealism of never doing wrong and the simple realism of having a state-based exemption of reason of state that does not follow the simplistic idea of reason of state.

The most striking feature of Machiavelli's complex writings is not the new concepts and structures that he gives to modern politics, or even the psychological insights that foreshadow later views about leaders and leadership in politics and international affairs, but rather his singular ability to constantly unsettle easy conceptual and theoretical distinctions. This is true whether one sees his writings as lifting the veil from contemporary politics or views them instead as the first shove down the slippery slope to the totalitarianism and brutality of the 20th century, as Leo Strauss did. Whether we see in his work the emerging politics of the modern state or (as some still claim) a noble morality of republicanism and political prudence, he never fails to unsettle. My own view is that this unsettling is partly the consequence of his acknowledgement of the flux of politics and the instability of order. As the turn to the modern sovereign state began in the decades following Machiavelli's death, we see an attempt to secure order in the face of wars of religion and social, political and religious upheaval, through concepts such as the modern sovereign state and the state system based upon it. Yet, what Machiavelli reminds us of is that order is precarious and temporary, and that perhaps the lesson of history in its cyclical form is that a quest for permanent stability is a mistake. In the 21st century, as we see significant challenges to the order that had been constructed since World War II, and perhaps even signs of its abandonment and collapse, it is hard not to regard Machiavelli as a most prescient if troubling guide to thinking about politics and international affairs.

Bibliography

Essential reading

Machiavelli, Niccolo. (1988). *The Prince*, ed. Q. Skinner and R. Price. UK: Cambridge University Press.

Machiavelli, Niccolo. (1989). 'The History of Florence', in A. Gilbert trans *Machiavelli: The Chief Works and Others*, 3 vols, vol. 3. USA: Duke University Press.

Machiavelli, Niccolo. (2005). *The Art of War*, ed. C. Lynch. USA: University of Chicago Press.

Machiavelli, Niccolo. (2008). *Discourses on Livy*, trans. J.C. Bondanella and P. Bondanella. UK: Oxford University Press.

Secondary reading

Althusser, Louis. (1999). *Machiavelli and Us*. UK: Verso.

Benner, Erica. (2015). *Be Like the Fox*. UK: Penguin.

Berlin, Isaiah. (1998). 'The Originality of Machiavelli', in *The Proper Study of Mankind*. UK: Pimlico, pp. 269–325.

Bobbitt, Phillip. (2013). *The Garments of Court and Palace: Machiavelli and the World that He Made*. UK: Atlantic Books.

Burnham, James. (1943). *The Machiavellians*. UK: Putnam.

Cesa, Marco. (2014). *Machiavelli on International Relations*. UK: Oxford University Press.

Coleman, Janet. (2000). *Political Thought from the Middle Ages to the Renaissance*. UK: Wiley Blackwell.

Doyle, Michael W. (1997). *Ways of War and Peace*. USA: Norton.

Fabre, Cécile. (2012). *Cosmopolitan War*. UK: Oxford University Press.

Frazer, Elizabeth; and Hutchings, Kimberly. (2019). *Can Political Violence Ever Be Justified?* UK: Polity Press.

Frazer, Elizabeth; and Hutchings, Kimberly. (2020). *Violence and Political Theory*. UK: Polity Press.

Fuller, Timothy. (ed.) (2016). *Machiavelli's Legacy: The Prince after Five Hundred Years*. USA: University of Pennsylvania Press.

Goodin, Robert; and Spiekermann, Kai. (2018). *An Epistemic Theory of Democracy*. UK: Oxford University Press.

Gramsci, Antonio. (1971). *Selections from the Prison Notebooks*, ed. Quintin Hoare and Geoffrey Nowell-Smith. UK: Lawrence and Wishart.

Lukes, Steven. (2003). *Liberals and Cannibals: The Implications of Diversity*. UK: Verso.

McCormick, John P. (2018). *Reading Machiavelli: Scandalous Books, Suspect Engagements and the Virtue of Populist Politics*. USA: Princeton University Press.

McMahan, Jeff. (2009). *Killing in War*. UK: Clarendon Press.

Mearsheimer, John J. (2011). *Why Leaders Lie: The Truth About Lying in International Politics*. USA: Oxford University Press.

Meineke, Friedrich. (1957). *Machiavellism: The Doctrine of Raison d'Etat and Its Place in Modern History*. USA: Yale University Press.

Nye, Joseph. (2020). *Do Morals Matter?* USA: Oxford University Press.

Orwell, George. (1971). *The Collected Essays, Journalism and Letters of George Orwell: Volume 4 in Front of Your Nose, 1945–50*. UK: Penguin.

Poole, Thomas. (2015). *Reason of State: Law, Prerogative and Empire*. UK: Oxford University Press.

Skinner, Quentin. (1969). 'Meaning and Understanding in the History of Ideas' *History and Theory*, vol. 8, pp. 3–53.

Skinner, Quentin. (1978). *The Foundations of Modern Political Theory*, 2 vols. UK: Cambridge University Press.

Skinner, Quentin. (1997). *Liberty before Liberalism*. UK: Cambridge University Press.

Skinner, Quentin. (2000). *Machiavelli: A Very Short Introduction*. UK: Oxford University Press.

Strauss, Leo. (1957). *Thoughts on Machiavelli*. USA: University of Chicago Press.

Walzer, Michael. (1977). *Just and Unjust Wars*. USA: Basic Books.

Wight, Martin. (1991). *International Theory: The Three Traditions*, ed. Gabriele Wight and Brian Ernest Porter. UK: Leicester University Press.

Winter, Yves. (2018). *Machiavelli and the Orders of Violence*. UK: Cambridge University Press.

Suggestion for finding open access versions of Machiavelli's texts

Online Library of Liberty, maintained by the Liberty Fund
https://oll.libertyfund.org/person/niccolo-machiavelli

CHAPTER 5

Hobbes

Solving the problem of conflict

Thomas Hobbes is one of the first great theorists of the concept of sovereignty and of the modern state. This means that he is also one of the original theorists of the state system that lies at the heart of contemporary international relations. I explore Hobbes's theory of the sovereign state as set out in his book *Leviathan*, and its place in modern international relations theory, both of them shaped by his intellectual context and his wider materialist philosophy of man. Hobbes's account of human nature and the state of nature is important here, as well as his contractarian account of the origin of sovereign power. Hobbes offers an influential account of absolutism that motivates his rejection of international political society derived from early modern papalism. His alternative account of anarchic or sharply rivalrous international relations between sovereign states has greatly influenced contemporary international relations theory, which has absorbed him into the tradition of realism and interstate anarchy.

Thomas Hobbes (1588–1679) is a pivotal figure for both historians of political philosophy and those of international relations and international political theory. For political philosophers, he is the first recognisably modern theorist who developed a civil science based on a human psychology that clearly

How to cite this book chapter:
Kelly, Paul. 2022. *Conflict, war and revolution: The problem of politics in international political thought*. London: LSE Press, pp. 147–178.
DOI: https://doi.org/10.31389/lsepress.cwr.e License: CC BY.

distinguishes humans as they are from an ideal or teleological account of humanity as they ought to be. For Hobbes, the idea of teleological politics is associated with Aristotelianism, and in rejecting it he becomes a modern theorist – standing in contrast to the classical thought of the ancient Greeks, which underpinned the medieval synthesis of Greek thought and Christianity. This modernist form of political science has been seen as either a cause for celebration, because of its liberation from the tyranny of ancient or religious ideas, or else a source of regret because it is an early sign of the decline or decadence of modernity that results in historicism, nihilism and ultimately the totalitarianism of the 20th-century European political experience (Strauss 1953).

As one of the first major theorists of the sovereign state, Hobbes is often located at the beginning of histories of modern political theory that trace the progressive development of the modern European state as a distinct and autonomous political entity. He contributed to the shaping of our contemporary political vocabulary, which sees politics primarily as a domestic matter, operating within a clearly defined political unit that recognises no higher authority or obligation beyond its borders. The sovereign state is the primary way of conceptualising the development of politics in Europe following the end of the European wars of religion, marked by the Treaty of Westphalia in 1648. Attaining statehood is also the aspiration of peoples or nations who do not yet have full political recognition. The Wilsonian fragmentation of the central European empires following the end of World War I, or the continuation of that process in the postcolonial history of Africa, or the collapse of Yugoslavia in the 1990s, all exemplify the clamour of nations and peoples for political recognition as states with full Hobbesian sovereign powers.

The modernity of this process of emerging statehood is exemplified in Hobbes's accompanying naturalistic methodology of civil or political science, which makes no appeals to the ultimate authority of theological revelation, or to a normative or moralised conception of human nature. It builds and explains political institutions taking humanity as it is and the world as we find it. Hence, Hobbes's claim that the domain of politics and the state is an artificial construct, in the sense of being something that is made through human action and not an implication of our nature or of historical or divine purpose. This argument marks an important break with the medieval political theologies that had linked the development of political and legal concepts to theological concepts, and portrayed the development of political history as the history of humanity in the passing times between Christ's resurrection and the end of the world in his second coming. As we shall see, this claim that Hobbes's account stands aside from religious belief can be challenged, when one takes account of the importance of Parts III and IV of *Leviathan*. Yet, it has become a commonplace reading of Hobbes as a thinker indifferent to the claims of revealed religion in politics.

Even if one modifies the crude idea of Hobbes as a theorist indifferent to the claims of religion, his assertion of the priority of sovereignty undermines an important feature of theological politics in pre-modern Europe. It presents conceptual arguments for the ultimate assault on the idea of Christendom as an international polity that took place in the early Enlightenment period. In so doing, his argument becomes an important source for the development of a distinctive state-based model of international relations that constitutes the 'Westphalian order', and which in turn provides the paradigmatic problems and challenges of modern international relations. Hobbes's views on international relations are sketchy and they are primarily implications of his theory of the sovereign state. But they expressly ruled out claims, central to Christendom, that some higher order and authority exists within which subsidiary political units or kingdoms operate. In whatever form international relations is presented, it is instead seen as a system or society of sovereign states that are politically irreducible to any other source of power, such as that of the Pope, or the emperor in the context of the Habsburg lands of central Europe and the Spanish Empire. In the absence of such a top power or authority, the international domain in which states find themselves is one of anarchy. Although I have shown in earlier chapters that intimations of this idea of anarchy are present in Thucydides' and Machiavelli's realisms (although not Augustine's), it is only with Hobbes that we find a clear model of anarchy as a system in the absence of any overarching power and authority. Whether it makes historical sense to impose categorical historical periods on the ideas of individual thinkers, it is indisputable that Hobbes's account of the sovereign state and the anarchical condition between states sets the agenda for subsequent international relations theory as a distinct subject of enquiry – a discipline with its own political theorists and problems challenging the hegemony of modern state-based politics.

Two lives of Thomas Hobbes

Hobbes lived in an extraordinary period of historical conflict and transition. Yet, it is important to refrain from crude causal claims about the relationship between Hobbes's theory and the world out of which it developed. After all, Hobbes had many contemporaries who neither developed statist theories of politics nor rejected Christendom, empire or the primacy of revelation over moral and legal claims. Because Hobbes's theory provides such an exemplary model for analysing and explaining features of the Westphalian order, there is also a particular danger of reifying his theory ('making a thing' of it) or assuming a causal necessity between events and a particular way of theorising them. Keeping this reminder in view, the intellectual context within which Hobbes developed and wrote nonetheless does provide an argument for the peculiar force and salience of his ideas.

Hobbes was born on Good Friday 1588, the year of the Spanish Armada. He studied at Magdalen Hall, Oxford, before becoming a scholar and tutor to the Cavendish family (the Dukes of Devonshire) for most of his subsequent life. This enabled him to travel to Europe and gave him recognition as a gentleman of letters, unattached to a university and thus freed from the professional obligations of religious tests or service. Hobbes completed the first English translation of Thucydides' *History of the Peloponnesian War* (1629), as well as rather less felicitous translations of Homer, but is best known for his account of civil science, which is developed primarily in the *Elements of Law* (1640) and *De Cive* (1642), culminating in *Leviathan* in 1651. The latter remains the greatest work of political philosophy in the English language. Hobbes also published works on optics and mathematics and an important history of the English Civil War, *Behemoth* (1688), posthumously published in 1681. Having lived through the English Civil War, he died during the period of the Exclusion Crisis that led up to the English Revolution of 1688. Whilst his life was that of a scholar and philosopher, it needs to be set against the extraordinary backdrop of European war and scientific revolution that in part explains the characterisation of Hobbes as a source of modernism.

The Thirty Years War and the English Civil War

Hobbes spent much of his early adult life visiting Europe as the companion and tutor to the Cavendish family, and as a refugee from domestic politics. Throughout that period he was simultaneously in close proximity to the Thirty Years War that raged throughout central Europe, Germany and the Dutch Republic, and culminated in a major struggle between the Habsburg Empire and the French. The war began in 1618 with the accession of Ferdinand II to the Habsburg throne of the Holy Roman Empire. Ferdinand was a devout Roman Catholic who sought to impose religious uniformity on all the populations of his lands, in contradiction of the Treaty of Augsburg of 1555, from which the idea of *cuius regio, eius religio* (who rules, their religion) emerged. This brought about conflict with the Protestant provinces of Bohemia. Following the defeat of the Bohemians under Frederick V at the battle of White Mountain, and the persecution of Protestant aristocrats, the war expanded into a full-scale European war with the intervention of the Swedes under King Gustavus Adolphus. The scale of violence, casualties and devastation of civilian life that ensued was not seen again until the last six months of World War II in Europe. Alongside the conflict in central Europe, the Spanish Habsburgs were also waging a major war in the Netherlands against the Dutch Republic. During this second phase of the war, it changed from a civil war within the Austrian Habsburg Empire into a full-scale confrontation between the Protestant and Catholic worlds. The protagonists were the northern European Protestant heartland led by Swedish Lutheranism and the Catholic world of central and southern Europe.

However, from 1630 that clear pattern changed again, with the increasing involvement of the French, allied to Sweden. France, under Cardinal Richelieu, was a Catholic monarchy and a ruthlessly Catholic state, as exemplified by its hostile treatment of its own Protestant Huguenot population. Yet, Richelieu was also concerned about becoming surrounded to the north, south and east by the Habsburg powers of Spain and Austria. In this way, the initial ideological or religious confrontation between Protestantism and Catholicism gave way to a great power struggle between those states aspiring to be the dominant powers in Europe – France and the Habsburgs. Also involved was the weakening of Spain as a major European political land or sea power, because of the rise of the Dutch and subsequently the English maritime empires. From the 1640s, the tide of events turned away from the Spanish and in favour of the French, and then the rise of the Protestant Dutch Republic liberated from the burdens of war. The end of the Thirty Years War is conventionally marked by the famous Treaty of Westphalia of 1648. In fact, there were a number of treaties involved, none of which has a full list of the combatants as signatories. The Treaty of Westphalia represented a new order or a state-based system, with dominant powers vying to ensure the system's stability alongside the dominance of those same powers' long-term strategic interests. This is the political world that Hobbes experienced during his long exile in France before returning to England at the culmination of the English Civil War in 1651.

Compared to the scale and devastation of the Thirty Years War, the English Civil War was something of a sideshow, although it was not unrelated to the inter-dynastic conflicts on mainland Europe: English and especially Scottish armies played a notable part in the Thirty Years War (Wilson 2010). Whereas religious conflict, the assertion of state sovereignty and the emergence of the European state system are the direct legacies of the Thirty Years War, for Hobbes the English Civil War has a much more direct impact within his thought. The *Elements of Law*, *Leviathan* and *Behemoth* were all direct engagements with the war and its legacy. As with the Thirty Years War, the English Civil War has its seeds in post-Reformation disorder, and especially the succession to the English throne of the Scottish House of Stuart. James VI of Scotland was crowned James I of England and his son Charles succeeded him to the throne in 1625. Like his father, Charles I was jealous in the assertion of royal prerogatives and rights and frequently in conflict with Parliament, which had the right of voting money for the Crown or levying taxes. Following the impeachment and execution of George Villiers, Duke of Buckingham, a royal favourite but unsuccessful general, Charles dissolved Parliament and ruled independently from 1629 to 1640. This period of personal rule, coupled with Church reforms inspired by the Archbishop of Canterbury, William Laud, and England and Scotland's withdrawal from the European wars through peace treaties with France and Spain, gave the impression of an increasingly authoritarian regime sympathetic to Catholicism and absolutism (as indeed Charles was).

However, a shortage of money compelled Charles to recall Parliament in 1640. During the following period, Hobbes published the *Elements of Law*, where his thesis of sovereign absolutism and the king's priority over Parliament was first advanced. Given the king's dissolution of the Short Parliament after only a few months, this argument was unpopular, and, fearing the consequences, Hobbes left for France, where he spent the next 11 years until the publication of *Leviathan* and his engagement with the new Cromwellian Republic in 1651. In that intervening period, the Crown and Parliament descended into a civil war that culminated in the capture of Charles in 1646 and his execution (after a trial by the Rump Parliament) in 1649. Subsequently, Oliver Cromwell rose to become lord protector (dictator), following the resignation of Fairfax as commander of the Parliamentary forces, and the defeat of the Royalist forces in Ireland and Scotland. The English Civil War ended in 1651 with the defeat of Charles I's son Charles II at the battle of Worcester. Charles II escaped to France, where he waited for a collapse of the Cromwellian Protectorate. But, with this defeat and the king's patent inability to assert sovereign authority, Hobbes recognised that Charles II was no longer sovereign and that right had passed to Cromwell. In those circumstances, Hobbes returned to England, and with the publication of *Leviathan* in 1651 began his engagement with the new sovereign. Hobbes's consideration of the Civil War was not to end here, however. Despite the restoration of the Stuart line in 1660, he wrote his historical dialogue about the war's philosophical or ideological causes in 1668. *Behemoth* was to be his last major work, although it was not published until 1681, two years after his death and in a period of renewed conflict between the Stuarts and Parliament, which culminated in the Glorious Revolution of 1688.

The birth of modern science and the science of humanity

The claim that Hobbes is the first modern political theorist is also closely connected with the second major context against which his civil science must be read: the birth of the modern natural sciences. Throughout his life Hobbes was associated with thinkers at the forefront of the development of empirical science, such as Francis Bacon (for whom he briefly served as a secretary), William Harvey, Robert Hooke, and Marin Mersenne's circle in Paris, through whom he was introduced to the ideas of Galileo and Rene Descartes. Whilst Hobbes emphasises the importance of empiricism and the lessons of experience, he was also interested in the rationalistic and deductivist philosophy of Rene Descartes, whom he met whilst exiled in Paris in the 1640s. Although we know Hobbes as a political theorist, it was these scientific explorations that were to be the major preoccupation of his time in Europe and they cast a shadow over his political writings such that he is seen as the father of modern political science.

Despite his empirical science interests, Hobbes was not an experimentalist. Instead, he combined the experimentalism of Bacon or Galileo with the rationalism of Descartes. He favoured the model of deductivism derived from Euclid's geometry that underpinned the emerging science of physics (as practised by Galileo, albeit in his case based on his own observations). However, the axioms from this deductivist methodology were rooted in experience; in this way, Hobbes combined the empiricism of Bacon with the rationalism of

Descartes to come up with his own new science. Like Descartes, Hobbes was concerned with securing certainty through logical deduction: something that could not be provided by naïve inductivism. Underpinning this approach was a materialist metaphysics that built on Galileo's insight that the world was comprised of matter in motion. This view of the centrality of motion was reinforced by William Harvey's discovery of the human circulatory system.

From these three sources (materialist metaphysics, empiricism and deductivist inference), Hobbes presents an approach that is known as the resolutive–compositive method. Complex phenomena are explained in terms of the interaction of their simpler elements. The task of scientific explanation proceeds by resolving complex phenomena into their most simple basic units and then logically combining these through a series of deductive inferences. It is important to remember that Hobbes's claim here is a methodological one (about how to understand phenomena) and not an ontological one (about what exists). The key elements are simplification and axiomatisation from which inferences could be made. Theory is then tested against experience. However, as is emphasised by modern positivist theorists, theory itself is not derived from experience – it is constructed (Waltz 1979, pp. 1–17). Carried to its most complete form, Hobbes's approach would reduce all the complex phenomena of the world into the interrelation of the most basic elements of matter in motion. This model has obviously attracted modern naturalistic political scientists, who would like the method and substance of political science to be linked to the more successful natural sciences, such as physics and chemistry. That said, Hobbes's practice is properly characterised as inference from empirically observed axioms (which is reductionist) but tends to proceed to political or civil science from psychology, rather than from physics (Malcolm 2002). Despite the subsequent success of his civil or political science, Hobbes's forays into natural science were both controversial and less successful. He wrote a treatise on optics, but his preoccupation with the geometric method nevertheless resulted in a long, acrimonious and fruitless dispute with John Pell about the possibility of squaring the circle – a mathematical impossibility!

The theory of human nature

In his early writings, Hobbes attempts to link civil philosophy to fundamental materialist metaphysics in a way that is analogous to the derivation of modern political science from physics. However, *Leviathan* begins with the science of human psychology as the fundamental source of his account of human motivation and obligation. This does not mean that he recants the idea that at some level his account of matter in motion can deductively lead to his account of natural law and right. However, for the purposes of Hobbes's civil science, the principles of an empirical psychology are a sufficient explanation and allow for the derivation of political conclusions. The fundamental premises of his psychology are the origin of ideas and beliefs in experience and the origin of action in the motivation to satisfy desires: in short, reason and will.

This approach is solipsistic. Ultimately, mind is only aware of its own contents, namely ideas that are the result of externally caused impressions. Of those external causes the subject of experience (a person) can have no direct knowledge. Knowledge can only be about ideas that result from impressions on the mind, where Hobbes literally means physical marks made on the mind by the impact of things in the world. How these impressions are made must ultimately be a matter of speculation because there can be no direct experience of this relationship. Impressions give rise to ideas and these are the objects of thought and reason. Reasoning itself takes the form of the addition and subtraction of ideas, building from the simplest ideas to the most complex. This process is made public through the medium of language, which primarily consists of names attached to ideas and their relations. In this respect, Hobbes continues the tradition of 'nominalism' that can be traced back to the medieval philosopher William of Occam. One consequence of this nominalism is that it makes moral ideas objects of the mind, as opposed to things in the world, and it opens up the possibility of moral subjectivism and the risk of moral scepticism: Hobbes was not a sceptic and was content for his subjectivism to provide an adequate account of moral truth.

Alongside the account of belief based on experiential impressions, the other main part of Hobbes's psychology is the origin of motives in the will and in desire. All human action, for Hobbes, requires as its efficient cause a passion, which is an exercise of the will towards the thing that is desired. These passions are either appetites or aversions, that is, things liked or things disliked. Appetites tend to move the agent towards the things liked and aversions tend to move the agent away from the things disliked. All subsequent forms of action are merely complex variations of these two basic motivations. Moral ideas, such as the virtues, are therefore the names of tendencies amongst humans to value or be attracted towards certain things or actions, and the vices are the names of tendencies that we disvalue or avoid. Moral judgements are therefore reducible to these observable tendencies amongst human agents. At a fundamental level, ethics is an empirical science based on the tendencies for agents to value or disvalue character traits or modes of action. As we shall see with Hobbes's account of natural right and natural law, at a fundamental level human motivations are fairly constant, yet the contingent variation of circumstances and character allows for a huge variety of subjective desires, interests and wants. These variations in people's situations are also responsible for what Hobbes describes as the variation in manners that account for social and cultural differences (*Leviathan*, Chapter XI). This diversity is limitless because of context and circumstances, but also the fundamental insatiability of human nature. For Hobbes, desires are not few in number and easily satisfied but the heart of a continuous chain of action that accounts for the vitality of human life:

I put for a generall inclination of all mankind, a perpetual and restlesse desire of Power after power, that ceaseth only in Death. And the cause of this, is not always that a man hopes for a more intensive delight, than he has already attained to; or that he cannot be content with a moderate power: but because he cannot assure the power and means to live well, which he hath present, without the acquisition of more. [Chapter XI] (Hobbes 1991, p. 70)

Within this account of the springs of action, Hobbes places considerable emphasis on the idea of man as glory-seeking, and on the idea of vainglory as a source of dispute, and conflict as a feature of human nature. Central to the idea of man being glory-seeking is the way in which status, honour and standing are central to our conception of ourselves. It is an important part of human psychology to be valued by others and accorded status and respect, but Hobbes is also clear that in most cases our sense of our own value is permanently greater than that which others attribute to us. The desire for recognition and acknowledgement of our own merits in accordance with our own valuation of ourselves is an important and irreducible source of conflict and disagreement, as well as a source of motivation to overcome that denial of recognition and value. Glory-seeking is one of the fundamental reasons why there is no natural harmony or order between individuals, where each might intuit their own importance and role for society. In the idea of glory-seeking and the vice of vainglory, where individuals attach a disproportionate significance to their own status and value, Hobbes provides an explanation of why there is no natural order amongst human individuals, in contrast to animal species such as bees. This is also why Hobbes argues that Aristotle's political theory must be wrong because it assumes a natural order or harmony amongst individuals once they are brought together within a rightly ordered political community. For Aristotelians, discord or conflict always reveals a design flaw in a political constitution, whereas for Hobbes the conflict has a different origin. Indeed, conflict is not a flaw at all, but a natural consequence of human psychology in the absence of an artificially imposed order that is created by the sovereign. The remainder of Hobbes's *Leviathan* is an attempt to explain the origin and nature of that order.

The state of nature

The nature of humans is to be always in constant motion, conceived as following a succession of driving appetites or desires ceasing only in death, the ultimate termination of human motion. In Chapter X, Hobbes also provides an extended discussion of the human preoccupation with honour, status and glory. These elements of philosophical egoism are central to Hobbes's account of the natural condition of man and they are supplemented in Chapter XIII with three further dimensions that give rise to his classic account of the state of nature as being a state of war. For Hobbes, political or civil society is not natural but artificial: it is something humans make in order to overcome the consequences of a natural condition without political or civil power. And, if it can be shown that the general features of the natural condition are such that we would always chose to leave it, or submit to political authority as a condition of avoiding it, then he will have provided a motive for a general duty of political obligation, even if the motive is not a sufficient juridical account of political obligation. So Chapter XIII commences with a discussion of equality as a basis for accounting for diffidence, but underpinning this discussion is the prior condition of scarcity.

Scarcity matters because human beings have limitless desires, in the sense of there being no natural limit to human wants. Even if we have enough of our basic needs (such as food and shelter) satisfied, glory and the desire for status, honour and differentiation will always add to our desires. Underlying this idea of scarcity is the finitude of the universe confronting the unlimited scope of human desires. Unless there is either a natural limit to our desires or unlimited material abundance, we will inevitably come into competition with each other for resources and space. Scarcity breeds competition amongst those who are forced to cohabit in relative proximity. Scarcity plus weak motivations to collaborate or cooperate mean that, even when there may be relative abundance elsewhere on the globe, rivalrous competition will arise because of the costs of moving to satisfy our desires. This condition of scarcity leading to competition has now become one of the most fundamental premises of modern economics, and means that humans always have to choose what resources and effort to put into different ends or purposes. If scarcity did not hold, then everyone could have all of the things that they wanted, all of the time, and therefore there would be no need for society or cooperation.

Equality might seem an unlikely next step for Hobbes. Surely, in circumstances of scarcity, some are strong and powerful enough to take what they need and exclude others. If this is true, then, whilst we may not end up with a universal condition of natural sociability, we might still end up with some sort of social order that is imposed naturally by the strongest. However, contrary to this chain of reasoning, Hobbes argues that in the natural condition humans are broadly speaking equal. Clearly, he does not mean that natural inequalities of power do not exist in nature. There will always be the equivalent of a Usain Bolt or Muhammad Ali who can outrun or outpunch others. But, equally, there will be the physically weaker individuals who are intellectually more subtle or sharp; they can use wit, intelligence or guile to overcome the physically strong. Hobbes is yet more radical still, because even the most ordinary individual can have equal power and advantage over the strong or the wise, so that they are never naturally subject. Everyone must sleep some of the time, and even the wise or the physically powerful can become vulnerable to the ordinary and mediocre at such a time. The crucial point that Hobbes is making is a factual one about a rough equality of power as opposed to a moral point about the equality of standing or concern and respect that modern liberal egalitarians argue for (Kelly 2005). In his view, this emphasis on the natural condition of equality leads to the next condition: 'diffidence'.

Diffidence, for Hobbes, does not mean timidity or hesitancy but instead a universal suspicion of (or weak form of paranoia about) other people. In circumstances of natural equality of power, it follows that everyone is under threat from everyone else. This does not mean that we are all negatively motivated towards everyone else or hate. Instead, rough equality of power does undermine cooperative motivations and hence inhibits the formation of any natural permanent society. As everyone could be a potential threat or risk to our own person and possessions, we naturally assume that risk exists when interacting with or confronting others. Thus, competitors become more than a natural fact of scarcity; they become a threat and potential enemy who could threaten our life and estate. Even if they show no signs of behaving in this way, we can never know that they will not do so in the future. Consequently, our behaviour towards others tends to change from competition and wariness towards conflict. We chose to take the advantage whenever it presents itself and before others have a chance to become a threat to us, by which time it could be too late. When diffidence is aligned with glory as the natural desire for status over others, we also move from a situation where the natural condition is one of strong inconvenience and burden to one in which it becomes a permanent situation of potential or actual conflict, or, as Hobbes puts it, a war of all against all.

War, for Hobbes, really is the natural condition, as it does not have to 'consisteth ... in actuall fighting; but the known disposition thereto, during all the time there is no assurance to the contrary' [Chapter XIII] (1991, p. 88). In this sense, war fits the classical realist position of being not something that just breaks out periodically but the natural condition because of fear or threat of inequality or power. For Hobbes, war is not something that can be attributed to bad or fallen character, as it is for Augustine or Machiavelli. Instead it derives from the structure of human interaction in the absence of an imposed order: in this case a political authority or the sovereign.

The interplay of scarcity, diffidence and glory, coupled with equality of power, illustrates the consequences of the absence of political authority and why we would create it if it did not exist. In a wonderful and memorable passage in Chapter XIII, Hobbes describes how political authority is the condition of any of the benefits of society. Society does not create the conditions for its completion in a political order, as Aristotle argued; rather, without political authority there is no society:

> Whatsoever therefore is consequent to a time of Warre, where every man is Enemy to every man; the same is consequent to the time, wherein men live without other security, than what their own strength,

and their own invention shall furnish them withall. In such condition, there is no place for Industry; because the fruit thereof is uncertain: and consequently no Culture of the Earth; no Navigation, nor use of the commodities that may be imported by Sea; no commodious Building; no Instruments of moving, and removing such things as require force; no Knowledge of the face of the Earth; no account of Time; no Arts; no Letters; no Society; and which is worst of all, continuall feare, and danger of violent death; And the life of man solitary, poore, nasty, brutish and short. [Chapter XIII] (Hobbes 1991, p. 89)

This account of the state of nature as being a state of war is an implication of the structure of human interaction, given the minimal universal account of motivations in Hobbes's psychological theory. As such, it can be seen as a hypothetical model. This is certainly something that attracts the interest of modern formal theories of political interaction or international relations, such as the theory of games. Scholars are often keen to distinguish Hobbes's social contract theory from that of his rivals on the grounds that his scheme is a hypothetical or a theoretical model (Boucher and Kelly 1994). Yet, Hobbes is also keen to emphasise the realism of his model and show how it fits historical experience, not as an empirical account of the origin of states but as an account of the condition of man in the absence of political authority:

It may peradventure be thought, there was never such a time, nor condition of warre as this; and I believe it was never generally so, over all the world: but there are many places, where they live so now. For the savage people in many places of *America*, except the government of small Families, the concord whereof dependeth on natural lust, have no government at all; and live at this day in that brutish manner, as I said before. Howsoever, it may be perceived what manner of life there would be, where there were no common Power to feare; by the manner of life, which men that have formerly lived under a peaceful government, use to degenerate into, in a civil Warre. [Chapter XIII] (Hobbes 1991, pp. 89–90)

Although Hobbes's account might work as a formal model, or even as a descriptively accurate anthropology, there is surely something missing in his account that Aristotelians or his medieval followers (the 'schoolmen' that Hobbes hated) would appeal to in order to modify the negative features of the natural condition, namely moral obligation. It is common amongst Hobbes scholars to claim that the state of nature is free of morality, so that there humans are not immoral, but instead neither good nor bad. This simple characterisation has some truth in it, but technically it is not the case that Hobbes's state of nature is a morality-free zone. To see why, we need to turn to his account of natural right and natural law.

The law of nature and the right of nature

The morality that underpins the argument of the state of nature is not addressed until Chapter XIII, in which Hobbes makes a major shift from the classical natural law theory of Aquinas and Vitoria to a modern theory based on natural right. The classical theory asserts the priority of a law that distributes duties, from which individuals can infer rights. On this view, the law of nature distributes duties on everyone not to kill others, and from this one can infer a right to life constituted by being the beneficiary of those duties. In contrast, Hobbes begins with the priority of right over duty and law. In the natural condition, everyone has the power to do whatever is required to preserve themselves, and this is accompanied by a natural liberty. He defines liberty as the absence of 'externall Impediments' to the exercise of our natural powers in action, thus providing one of the classic statements of negative liberty (Berlin 1998, pp. 191–242). To be free, under this concept, is to enjoy the absence of external restrictions on one's power to act. A good deal later in the book, he makes clear that freedom is a characteristic of objects which can move or be hindered from moving:

> *A Free-Man, is he, that in those things, which by his strength and wit he is able to do, is not hindered to doe what he has a will to do.* [Chapter XXI] (Hobbes 1991, p. 146, italics in original)

Standard examples of being hindered in acting would be restraints such as locks and chains or being imprisoned. As we will see later, it does not involve the absence of non-physical constraints such as fear or threats, or the absence of resources. In the state of nature, everyone has the right of nature because they are not under any obligation or duty not to act in a certain way.

Thus, the natural right of nature is a liberty-right that expresses our free power. Importantly, it also places no one else under any obligations to act or forbear from acting any way. This leads to his infamous claim that 'It followeth, that in such a condition, every Man has a Right to every thing: even to one anothers body' [Chapter XIII] (Hobbes 1991, p. 91). In other words, whilst there is a liberty-right to life, this imposes no duties on others not to kill me, and, if another person poses a potential risk to my life, I may pre-emptively kill them, hence the right to 'another's body'. Because the state of nature is characterised by diffidence, where potentially everyone poses such a risk, there cannot be any security. The unrestricted right of liberty creates the absence of security; we can only enjoy secure freedom if we limit our own natural liberty, and this leads to Hobbes's account of the law of nature, which has been the focus of considerable scholarly dispute.

He describes the law of nature as a:

> Precept, or generall Rule, found out by Reason, by which a man is forbidden to do, that, which is destructive of his life, or taketh away the means of preserving the same; [Chapter XIV] (Hobbes 1991, p. 91)

The use of the word 'forbidden' in the quotation raises the ambiguity that scholars have found in his account of natural law morality. In what sense are people forbidden in the state of nature from destroying themselves? If there is a pre-political duty to preserve oneself, such that *not* to do so would be to act unjustly, then his argument for the priority of natural right falls. Yet, Hobbes is quite clear that in the absence of a common power in the state of nature 'nothing can be Unjust' [Chapter XIII] (Hobbes 1991, p. 90). Some scholars have inferred from this that in the natural condition there are no duties and therefore there is liberty but not morality. Others, such as Howard Warrender (1957), have argued that there is a source of duty in the state of nature, namely God, who places us under a direct duty not to kill ourselves as part of His creation. But in the state of nature that duty is incomplete because it has no sanction in this condition; hence, the creation of the sovereign occurs under a duty to complete the moral law. There are many difficulties with this thesis, not the least of which is that Hobbes says nothing to endorse it in his account of obligation. Yet, it remains of interest in that it explains how he might be able to speak of self-destruction as being morally forbidden.

Furthermore, if there are no moral duties in the state of nature, then it is difficult to see how the fundamental elements of the law of nature can be obligation-creating? Hobbes identifies 19 specific laws of nature following from the duty to preserve oneself. All are implications of this primary motive, but three are especially important as they play an important part in his contract theory of sovereign power:

1. We should strive to preserve ourselves, which means that we should strive to maintain peace among ourselves.
2. If others are willing to seek peace, then all should 'lay down this right to all things; and be contented with so much liberty against other men, as we should allow other men against himself'.
3. We should keep agreements.

Hobbes is clear that we can speak of moral obligations in the natural condition if we see that these are derived from the fundamental motive to preserve ourselves. This motive is not an externally imposed duty (like a duty to obey the law of the state) but it is something that is rooted in human nature. To understand why, it should be distinguished from the source of juridical obligations (which is the artificial person of the sovereign). Juridical rights and obligations are the conclusion of his theory of right. But it is equally important that Hobbes does not argue that natural law morality is partial and incomplete, as implied by Warrender. The law of nature is genuinely binding, but this is so only *in foro interno* and not *in foro externo* [Chapter XV] (Hobbes 1991, p. 110). What he means by this distinction is that reason gives us the motive to act in ways that preserve ourselves and other people through the pursuit of peace.

Yet, as we have seen, external circumstances or the structure of human interaction will often give us reason to depart from the law of nature. So this law
creates 'hypothetical imperatives', which for those influenced by Kant's moral
philosophy are the wrong kinds of imperatives because they hold externally
only on certain conditions. Hobbes is not a Kantian and is clear about the
conditional hypothetical character of the law of nature. At the same time, he
does not simply reduce obligation to personal advantage. Whilst it is mostly
the case that humans differ significantly in their judgements and beliefs, Hobbes thinks that in terms of fundamental motives or desires they are broadly
similar. In addressing 'the foole' (or what we would term the free-rider) who
seeks to maximise their own advantage whilst others obey the law, Hobbes's
fundamental point is that our primary motive is not to maximise advantage but
to avoid violent death and preserve ourselves. In that context, the free-rider is
wrong. The conflict of motives is unlike the conflict of beliefs in that its resolution requires security through determination and sanction, by a sovereign civil
power. However, it is important for Hobbes that, whilst the sovereign has the
ultimate authority in determining how morality should be sanctioned, the sovereign is not totally free to decide what the content of morality is. Hobbes's ultimate conviction is that morality is given by our natures. Only the commonality
of our motives to seek peace and self-preservation means that leaving the state
of nature by authorising a sovereign is at least possible, as well as desirable. The
account of natural right as the primacy of liberty and of natural law explains
why we need sovereignty and why it must be absolute.

The creation of the sovereign

The adverse character of the state of nature provides strong reason why people
would leave it, and Hobbes's natural law theory explains why we might be said
to have a duty to leave it. Both arguments are intended to explain the origin and
scope of the powers of the sovereign. Both parts of the argument also emphasise that political authority or sovereignty is an artifice created by humanity
to address the problem of our nature. It is explicitly not an emanation of our
natures, as Aristotle suggests. This artificial character of sovereignty is beautifully captured in the image from the frontispiece of the 1651 edition of *Leviathan*, which depicts a giant body wholly made up of individual human bodies,
with a head and crown and wielding a sceptre and a sword. Beneath this tower-
ing figure of the body politic united under a single head is a further depiction
of an ordered and peaceful realm with well-laid-out towns and cultivated countryside. This famous engraving by Ambrose Bosse provides an iconographic
depiction of sovereignty, and was intended to make the complex argument
accessible to those unable to read the text. If the state of nature is the problem,
then the sovereign is the solution. But how does sovereignty arise? Hobbes has

two accounts. Although they are formally the same, I examine them separately, before addressing the nature and scope of sovereign power itself.

Sovereignty by institution

Hobbes explains the origin of sovereignty by institution in the following way:

> *I Authorize and give up my Right of Governing my selfe, to this Man, or to this Assembly of men, on this condition, that thou give up thy Right to him, and Authorize all his Actions in like manner.* [Chapter XVII] (1991, p. 120 emphasis in the original)

Of course, in arguing this he is not offering a causal explanation. Indeed, given the circumstances of the state of nature and his account of human fear and diffidence, such a causal explanation faces acute difficulties, although he does argue that these are surmountable. Instead, Hobbes's account provides a juridical explanation of political authority within his conception of natural right and natural law. As such, elements of the covenant statement above are crucial for his theory. The first point is that sovereign power is the result of individuals agreeing to give up their natural right to govern themselves. As in the 1651 frontispiece image, the sovereign is made up of individuals and more importantly of the natural rights of individuals. Yet, it is not just the culmination of these individual powers, although it is that too. Instead, it is primarily a *juridical entity* composed of the natural rights of individuals.

The second point in the quotation above is that the wording is that of a covenant or agreement. Individuals agree to transfer their natural rights through this form of words, and the agreement is the legitimate transfer of those rights; they are not simply taken away or usurped. This is the key point of the juridical institution of sovereignty: it is composed of a legitimate transfer of right. Scholars of Hobbes depict him as one of the first great social contract theorists, but it is important to also note that the agreement or covenant is of a special kind. It is not a mutual advantage contract between sovereign and subject, where the subject agrees to give up subjective right in return for security and peace. Hobbes believes that such peace and security will be the outcome of an 'original agreement', but it is not specified in the actual covenant. Subjects expect to benefit, but there is no duty imposed upon the sovereign by the alienation (or irreversible transfer) of subjective right from subject to sovereign. The agreement is not with the sovereign at all and therefore it places no conditions on the sovereign. It is explicitly a mutual agreement amongst all potential subjects to subject themselves to a sovereign. The sovereign as a person is a third-party beneficiary of the agreement and not a direct party to the agreement. The sovereign is the beneficiary of each of us alienating our subjective rights and the agreement is amongst each of us to alienate our rights if all others do so at the same time. The sovereign agrees nothing with their subjects, nor are they asked to. The agreement to authorise a sovereign is what is often referred to as an alienation contract. By this is meant the fact that it is a one-off, unconditional agreement to give up powers that once done cannot be lawfully undone. This is so because when the juridical entity of the sovereign has been created it becomes the formal arbiter of its own rights, powers and jurisdiction. By definition there can be no right or power higher than a sovereign power.

Finally, Hobbes points out the limitation of the powers of alienation of subjective right. The motive for engaging in an agreement to establish a sovereign is the desire to remove ourselves from the 'warre of all against all' in the state of nature, and to exchange unprotected liberty for security and peace. Yet, we cannot be said to place ourselves under a duty to destroy ourselves or to submit to death: this remains part of the law of nature. This does not place a limitation on the powers of the sovereign, for it leaves the juridical authority to create and enforce punishments up to, and including, the death penalty in order to secure civil order. However, that legitimate right of sovereignty does not create a reciprocal duty on an individual to accept death at the gallows, or (in another case) to go willingly to one's death in battle. This is so because the sovereign's right to require obedience ultimately depends upon our overriding right to avoid death.

Thus, Hobbes seeks to provide a juridical account of sovereign power of political authority, rather than a causal theory of the how any particular sovereign state arose in a unanimous alienation contract or agreement. That does not imply he is not interested in the origin of political society, for he does attempt to show that his juridical account of sovereignty is consistent with a causal theory in his second account of sovereignty by acquisition or conquest.

Sovereignty by acquisition

The primordial origin of the first political societies is not Hobbes's primary concern, since this is hard to find in any historical record. There will have been original acts of institution of political societies, however, just as he acknowledges that there are places where the conditions of the state of nature do hold even in his own time, such as uncolonised parts of the Americas. The real issue addressed is a question about the normal way in which most actually existing political societies arose, from force and conquest. Are such cases consistent with a just transfer of right, and therefore the creation of sovereign powers that can in turn claim obedience and rule with legitimacy? Similarly, Hobbes asserts that individuals who are simply born as subjects of sovereign dominion have thereby authorised the alienation of their subjective right to that incumbent sovereign, and therefore have a duty of obedience to it. To understand this argument, we need to turn to Hobbes's account of liberty (in Chapter XXI).

The standard argument against conquest as a case of a legitimate transfer of right is that it involves coercion and therefore the denial of freedom. If one is coerced into acting, then the action is not free and therefore a coerced transfer of right is not a legitimate act. Hobbes contests this view, arguing that it rests on a mistaken understanding of the concept of liberty. He provides a strong negative theory of liberty in which freedom is characterised by the absence of impediments to action: 'LIBERTY, or FREEDOME, signifieth (properly) the absence of Opposition, (by Opposition I mean Externall Impediments of Motion)', and he gives the examples of being 'imprisoned, or restrained, with walls, or chaynes' [Chapter XXI] (Hobbes 1991, pp. 145–146). In the absence of such impediments, a person is free to do whatever she has a will to do. As freedom is a property of objects in motion, impediments are always physical restraints on action. Consequently, an absence of will or a mental feeling of fear of the consequences of acting is not for Hobbes a restriction on the liberty of a person:

> Feare, and Liberty are consistent; as when a man throweth his goods into the Sea for *feare* the ship should sink, he doth it nevertheless very willingly, and may refuse to doe it if he will: It is therefore an action of one that was *free*: [Chapter XXI] (Hobbes 1991, p. 146)

This passage has an important implication that transfers of right based on my fear of the consequences of withholding agreement is a relevant case of free action and therefore a legitimate right-conferring act. In the circumstances of being required to 'consent at the point of a sword', Hobbes is quite prepared to consider such consent a binding transfer of right. In such circumstances, we still have the opportunity to withhold consent, so the action is free. Consequently, just as a highway robber may ask, 'Your money or your life', and acquire a free transfer of property, a conquering power can legitimately acquire the right of sovereign dominion over a people, by offering them a choice between an imposed order or death. Of course, Hobbes also acknowledges that within a state the free transfer of property to a robber in return for life is not a legitimate transfer, because the sovereign will have instituted laws governing the transfer of property. The important point of Hobbes's argument is the parallel between an act of institution and a transfer of right by acquisition or conquest: both constitute free agreements because they are not the result of impediments or obstacles to action. Of course, if someone agrees to subjection at the point of a sword whilst bound to a chair, this would not constitute a free transfer of right, as the possibility of avoiding the obligation is missing. It is the ability to act that is important, irrespective of the cost of the choice or the adverse consequences of trying to avoid making it.

The parallel between an original alienation contract, and an agreement in the face of a conquering power, is completed by the argument that the intention does *not* have to be expressed in the words of a contract. The end or goal of submission to a conquering power, namely peace and order, is sufficient to demonstrate the intention to transfer right, since we all have an overriding motive to avoid a violent death and to preserve ourselves. By linking submission to a dominant power to the transfer of right to a sovereign, Hobbes has answered the challenge of engagement with the newly installed Cromwellian Commonwealth. Having lost the Civil War, the House of Stuart was no longer able to command obedience and in so doing provide peace and security, whereas the Cromwellian army was able to do so. The forces thus became not merely the *de facto* sovereign in the absence of the Stuarts but also the *de jure* or rightful sovereign to which everyone has not only a duty but an interest in submitting to. For Hobbes, the acknowledgement of the Commonwealth was not merely an act of personal prudence on the part of someone who wished to return to England and live a quiet life; it was also a personal duty as someone who was under the jurisdiction of the Commonwealth.

The constitution of the sovereign either by institution or acquisition creates the political society that Hobbes describes as a Leviathan in this famous passage:

> This done, the Multitude so united in one Person, is called a COMMON-WEALTH, in latine CIVITAS. This is the Generation of that great LEVI-ATHAN, or rather (to speake more reverently) of that *Mortall God*, to which wee owe under the *Immortal God*, our peace and defence. For by this Authoritie, given him by every particular man in the Common-Wealth, he hath the use of so much Power and Strength conferred on him, that by terror thereof, he is inabled to *con*forme the wills of them all, to Peace at home, and mutuall ayd against their enemies abroad. [Chapter XVII] (Hobbes 1991, p. 120)

Absolutism and the *Christian Commonwealth*

Although the political authority or the power of the sovereign is a crucial element in the emergence of the idea of the modern state, Hobbes does not really have a specific theory of the state in the way that later thinkers do. He gives no extended discussion of the relationship between constitutional powers, nor is there an outline of the crucial elements (such as the bureaucracy) that play an important role in the work of Montesquieu, Hegel or J.S. Mill. Yet, in the account of sovereignty in the latter part of Part II of *Leviathan* and in Part III, *Of the Christian Commonwealth*, and IV, *Of the Kingdom of Darknesse*, Hobbes sets the parameters for subsequent theories of the state, and for the system or society of states that forms the Westphalian model of international relations.

The central contention of Hobbes's account of sovereignty is that it must be absolutist. It is important to note that this is not necessarily a defence of monarchical absolutism, especially as he offers *Leviathan* as a declaration of engagement with the new Cromwellian Commonwealth. But what is not in doubt is his claim that the sovereign power is unitary, total, indivisible, inalienable and final. Consequently, Hobbes cannot allow for a constitutional division of powers or right of appeal against the final demand of political authority, because that would merely identify where the true sovereign power resides. Nor can the sovereign alienate or delegate powers to an external authority. In this way, Hobbes rules out the idea of sharing power or jurisdiction with a foreign power, such as ceding the power of appointing ecclesiastical offices to the Pope or exempting clergy from civil courts – both key features of Thomas Cromwell's English revolution in government under Henry VIII. Only the sovereign can appoint ministers and political or judicial offices, or confer honours or status on subjects.

For later liberal-inclined constitutional theorists, Hobbes's theory is problematic because it gives the sovereign sole and final (total) authority over the subject and their rights. The sovereign judges all controversies over rights and claims, and decides and imposes punishments and rewards in all disputes. In so doing, the sovereign cannot ever be judged as acting unjustly by his subjects, or be subjected to punishment by them, because by definition it alone determines the content of justice. Also, equally, by definition the sovereign cannot harm his subjects. To judge the sovereign would involve appealing to a private standard outside of the law and consequently would be an unjust act by a subject. This position seems to give the sovereign extraordinary powers, and it has led many to claim that Hobbes is merely providing a cover for tyranny and oppression. Hobbes addresses this point by claiming that cries of tyranny are no more than judgements of sovereign power that a subject either dislikes or finds inconvenient. But his main point is a purely logical point about the nature of sovereign power itself, and not a judgement about the personal character of a particular sovereign prince or a prudential judgement about how sovereign power should be used. To be sovereign, political authority must be final, unified and unchallengeable, and that is why it is considered absolute as it cannot be subject to a higher authority or law as that would, by definition, be the sovereign.

Yet, this does not give a particular prince *carte blanche* to act in whatsoever way they wish. The point of sovereignty is the provision of security and the avoidance of war and conflict, and Hobbes is clear that the prince should be prudent both in the exercise of powers to avoid any collapse back into civil war, and in the exercise of their powers of war in the international realm (an implicit criticism of the Stuarts). Again, whilst the power of war is an inalienable right of sovereignty, the reckless pursuit of war, especially when the prospects of success are uncertain, places subjects in circumstances where they are being required to act against the law of nature and their own self-preservation. The successful sovereign will thus be mindful of the demands of prudent policy, whilst nevertheless enjoying the right of final decision in matters needed to preserve the peace and security of their subjects. What one has a right to do, and what it is wise or prudent to do, are not the same things, but for the benefits of civil peace it is crucial for the sovereign not to confuse these questions.

Historically, the Church had alternative claims to authority apart from the power of the sovereign, so Hobbes's argument is extended in considerable depth in Parts III and IV, which tackle the implications of his theory for religion. These major parts of the text are often glossed over by contemporary students of Hobbes as a mere historical elaboration of the fundamental logic of the origin and nature of sovereignty in Parts I and II. Yet, Hobbes's extensive discussion of the ecclesiastical power and its subordination to the civil sovereign is both a central part of Hobbes's argument and a fundamental illustration of the doctrine *cuius regio, eius religio* (who rules, their religion), derived from the Peace of Augsburg (1555) and which underpins the Westphalian settlement of 1648. The style of Hobbes's discussion in Parts III and IV is also an important illustration of the primacy of his new civil science from within the terms of political theology. Few commentators emphasise the extent to which Hobbes offers his argument as a political theology (although there are exceptions: see Lloyd 1992). Instead, most expositors praise him as one of the first genuinely modern philosophers of politics, someone who decisively subordinates all claims of revelation to the demands of reason.

This is too hasty a dismissal of how central Hobbes's political theology was to his thought. He clearly intended his book to answer those (such as Cardinal Robert Bellarmine) who used scripture and political-theological argument to advance their defence of papal claims to exercise civil and imperial power. Bellarmine (1542–1621) was one of the most important defenders of Catholic political theory following the Catholic Counter-Reformation and the Council of Trent – and Hobbes had actually seen him in Rome in 1614 (Martinich 1992, p. 34). For Hobbes to simply assert the primacy of reason in the face of revelation and scripture would have been a *non sequitur* that would have failed to convince any of his contemporary opponents. It was therefore essential that he show that the argument of the first two books of *Leviathan* is fully consistent with scripture. In addition, he sought to provide the best explanation of the Old Testament account of the Kingdom of God as a limited period of sovereignty over the Jewish people, exercised by Moses on behalf of God until the time of Samuel, when the Jewish people abandoned priestly rule for a civil kingdom. Similarly, in the case of the New Testament, Hobbes emphasises that Jesus Christ's preaching of 'the coming of the Kingdom' is not an historical prediction of a temporal kingdom or state but something precisely different, which inherently leaves the domain of the political for civil sovereigns as part of God's providence.

An important consequence of these arguments is that the nature of ecclesiastical authority is not directly derived from God, or through an intermediate power such as that of the Pope, who for Hobbes is merely another European civil sovereign. It is instead a civil construct for governing religious affairs within a political community, and therefore totally subject to the discretion of the sovereign. In Part IV, Hobbes reinforces this subordination of ecclesiastical power to civil power by supplementing scriptural arguments with scientific explanations of the origins of the idea of spirits and the way these tricks of the imagination are deployed as the cover for exercises of illegitimate political power. Against those who use the claims of scripture and religion as a basis for challenging political authority, Hobbes argues that the only thing necessary for salvation is a belief in the proposition that 'Jesus Christ is Saviour'. The affirmation of this belief is something that is independent of sovereign demands for external conformity. Therefore, no one's salvation can be put at risk by the sovereign demanding a particular form of religious observance or the proscription of it. When properly understood, the minimal demands for salvation cannot be undermined by the sovereign, and thus there can never be a legitimate religious basis for rejecting any claims of the sovereign.

The revolutionary significance of Hobbes's synthesis of civil science with political theology is perhaps lost in the modern world where the claims of revelation are given less credence, at least in the west. Yet, this change is central to the claim of the emerging sovereign state to have the ultimate power to determine the extent and claims of religion within its jurisdiction and territory. Hobbes's argument turns the *modus vivendi* compromises of 16th-century wars of religion into principled claims about the legitimate extent of political authority over the claims of religion. Hobbes undermines the claims of Christendom to be a transnational imperial order that creates the space for local sites of subsidiary rule. And he displaces the complex integration of the 'two cities' (Augustinian) model of politics as the transient secular order awaiting the final reckoning at the last judgement. With Hobbes, the idea of the modern state begins, and with it the idea of the modern state system that is at the heart of international relations.

The Hobbesian tradition in international relations

Although Hobbes's account of the unitary sovereign state provides one of the fundamental building blocks of modern international relations theory, he does not provide extensive discussion of international relations as being (just) the external relations of states. However, he does say things that intimate the direction of such a theory of international politics. Scholarly discussion of Hobbes's international thought tends to discuss those passing references as contradictions of the way that his theory has been used in contemporary international relations theory. I will turn to this aspect in the final section, but first I want to explore here the ways in which Hobbes's arguments have given rise to a distinctive approach in international relations.

Whether the common appropriation of Hobbes is ultimately faithful to the detail of his argument is a secondary matter, unless thinkers who articulate this Hobbesian tradition are simply offering scholarly historical interpretations of Hobbes's argument, which they generally are not. Only in a narrow history of ideas is the authenticity of such interpretations a self-sufficient question. But in Hobbes's case the logic of his theory lends itself to being taken up by other writers, so that such appropriation is particularly important, and a question arises about whether it is potentially legitimate to argue that Hobbes does not have the final word on the implications of his theory. The closest that Hobbes comes to drawing a direct implication of his theory of the state of nature for international relations is captured in the following famous quotation:

> But though there had never been any time, wherein particular men were in a condition of warre one against another; yet in all times, Kings, and Persons of Soveraigne authority, because of their Independency, are in continuall jealousies, and in the state and posture of Gladiators; having their weapons pointing, and their eyes fixed on one another; that is, their Forts, Garrisons, and Guns upon the Frontiers of their Kingdomes; and continuall Spyes upon their neighbours; which is a posture of War. But because they uphold thereby, the Industry of their Subjects; there does not follow from it, that misery, which accompanies the Liberty of particular men. [Chapter XII] (Hobbes 1991, p. 90)

This passage emphasises the most significant lesson that can be drawn from *Leviathan*, namely the account of the natural condition as being one of anarchy. The concept of anarchy has become the primary understanding or challenge to the external relations of the states. By anarchy is meant the idea of a world without hierarchical or vertical authority, that is, the idea of an authority or source of power that exists above the individual units of the international domain. Neither God, through natural law, nor any imperial institution enjoys a right of authority or the power to impose its will on those units namely states. Amongst realist scholars this is both a normative and a descriptive claim, whereas amongst some liberal theorists it is a claim to be assessed empirically but not a normative claim. The factual claim is that there is no such power. The normative claim is either that there is no such authority (realists) or else that there is no such authority but there could and should be (liberals) and so we have obligations to seek it. Although providing some evidence for both positions, Hobbes is primarily appropriated by the realist tradition, especially because the nature of that international anarchy which is characterised as the exemplar of structural realism (Doyle 1997). In Doyle's account, this structural realism is contrasted with the complex realism of Thucydides and the fundamentalist realism of Machiavelli, because it does not depend upon an account of individual motivation or some flaw in human psychology. Instead, it merely and solely depends upon the circumstances or 'structure' of interaction, where the individual can be replaced by a unified state.

International anarchy follows Hobbes's model, according to realists, precisely because, whatever motivates a state's national interest, the circumstances of competition and the absence of a coordinating power create the condition of continual potential conflict, which makes the anarchical condition a state of war. In a strikingly (and deliberately) Hobbesian passage, Waltz makes precisely this point:

> The state among states, it is often said, conducts its affairs in the brooding shadow of violence. Because some state may at any time use force, all states must be prepared to do so – or fall in line at the mercy of their more militarily vigorous neighbours. Among states, the state of nature is a state of war. This is not meant in the sense that war constantly occurs but in the sense that, with each state deciding for itself whether or not to use force, war may at any time break out. (Waltz 1979, p. 102)

Waltz is a particularly good exemplar of the modern Hobbesian tradition because his theory is based on a model of international interaction, as opposed to a series of inferences from experience or an account of history. It is the logic of the model of the state of nature, and whether it is real or not, that is of primary importance to a Waltzian science of international relations. Waltz is not a Hobbesian in the sense of following the historical Hobbes in detail, so the historicity of his appropriation is irrelevant for the purposes of explaining international relations.

International anarchy as the absence of a permanent (as opposed to some contingent) hierarchical power amongst the states is not the only feature of Hobbes's argument in contemporary realist international relations theory. Equally important is the manifestation of what Hobbes calls 'diffidence' in international affairs, that is, not only fear but lack of trust and suspicion, which motivates the desire to strike first. This can be seen most clearly in Herz's (1951) account of the 'security dilemma' and in its most forceful version in the sceptical realism of John Mearsheimer (2014). This is the idea that in circumstances of international anarchy the quest for security by a state impels actions such as building military advantage. This in turn creates risks amongst neighbour states, and consequently leads to reactions that reduce rather than enhance security in a vicious cycle. This is precisely the argument that Hobbes says propels individuals out of the state of nature and into sovereignty, although the very possibility of this in mass settings has been challenged using modern game theory by Jean Hampton (1988). The usual argument against an expectation of states coalescing to enhance their collective security is that effective equality of power does not hold amongst states as it does amongst individuals in the state of nature. For sceptics like Mearsheimer, incentives to collaborate are weakened in a particularly Hobbesian way, so that any contingent order that might emerge within international anarchy is always evanescent and vulnerable to new security challenges. No balance of powers (for instance) is ever sufficient to constrain the threat of conflict for long. On the other hand, Waltz sees the balance of power theory as the key response to international anarchy, and most decisively in the

Cold War context in which he was writing in the balance between the two poles (or power blocks) of the United States and NATO allies versus the USSR and Eastern bloc countries (Waltz 1979).

The most striking disagreement within the Hobbesian tradition of international relations concerns the way in which the theory is supposed to fit actual international politics. It is exemplified by the contrast between the *system of states* theory, of Waltz and hard realists, and the *society of states* model, of Hedley Bull and the English School (Vincent 1981). For Waltz, a theory of international politics requires a model from which law-like generalisations can be derived, and where theories contain non-factual assumptions that must be prior to experience. In this approach, a Hobbesian theory of international politics is a system built on the interactions of stable units (such as states) seeking a balance of power or order. By simplifying experience in this way, he claims to capture what is important in the logic of international politics. What Hobbes's theory does not do, however, is attempt to reflect or explain the many forms of relationship that can exist in an anarchical system of states. For 'society of states' theorists such as Bull, international anarchy does not mean that there are no norms at all operating in the international order. All that is required is that there is no one hierarchical authority with superstate-like powers *imposing* these norms on states and commanding obligation (Bull 2002, pp. 44–47). Unlike Waltz, Bull is interested in how far 'anarchy' is an empirically accurate or realistic description of international politics. In that context, Bull rejects important elements of Hobbes's state of nature, especially his claim that there is 'no place for Industry; because the fruit thereof is uncertain: and consequently no Culture of the Earth; no Navigation, nor use of the commodities that may be imported by Sea' [Chapter XIII] (Hobbes 1991, p. 89). Whilst there is no international order, there has always been international trade and norms that follow from this, which states and peoples (generally) comply with or there is no trade. In this sense, we have not just a state system but a society of states, albeit one that retains international anarchy, hence Bull's famous description of international relations as an anarchical society. For Bull, and those influenced by him, not only does an adequate theory need explanatory power but it must also be descriptively adequate as an account of the world.

Why internationalising *Leviathan* is not possible

With its primary focus on international anarchy as either a system or society of states, the Hobbesian tradition in international relations leaves two questions for Hobbes's theory about why a *Leviathan*-like solution is not feasible in affairs between states. Why is the state of nature argument not global in scope? And why does the logic of the derivation of sovereign not also hold amongst states, giving rise to a global state?

A global state of nature

What the system of states and society of states theorists share is the common assumption that there is more than one state, and this is the legacy of Hobbes's theory. But there remains an important question for his theory: given the logic of his argument, why is there a question about the relation between states? Indeed, why is there not a single global state? Hobbes's argument begins with individuals in a natural condition without a natural order or authority and, whilst he may argue that this is something that holds within his own time amongst the tribes of America, the logical question is why particular states ever arise: why does the state of nature not hold across the world such that the logic takes us from individuals to a global state in one move? Indeed, this is a question that Immanuel Kant asks in his rethinking of the logic of the Hobbesian account of sovereignty. Murray Forsyth also asks this question in an important essay (Forsyth 1979). He seeks to answer it by focusing on changes to the way the state of nature is theorised as Hobbes develops his argument from the *Elements of Law* through *De Cive* to *Leviathan*.

What is certainly clear is that there is nothing in the logic of the argument of *Leviathan*, Chapter XIII, that qualifies the scope of the argument: so, does that mean that there could be such a global state? This is an important question for contemporary cosmopolitan theorists addressing the challenge of globalisation. Hobbes undoubtedly makes many references to the particularity of political communities. And he reinforces the internal/external distinction of modern international politics by including defence against foreign threat as a condition of individuals' submission to the sovereign. Alongside the argument for sovereignty by acquisition, with its focus on conquest by foreign powers, this suggests that Hobbes recognises that state formation takes place within a situation of aspirant but incomplete political communities. That said, all these refences and allusions to the real world of international politics are occasional and not logically entailed by his argument.

Curiously, from the perspective of modern readers, the only part of Hobbes's argument that might be seen to make necessary reference to a pluralism of political states or nations (to use biblical language) is the political theology of Part III. Here we are presented with the biblical order of a plurality of many nations, of which the Kingdom of Israel is one, and by implication, following the post-resurrection new order, another world of separate nations that are yet all subject to the new mandate of Christianity. In responding to the challenge of Jesus Christ's kingship, Hobbes clearly emphasises its extra-political nature, but also that it leaves the plurality of political communities or nations unchanged. This is the basis of his rejection of papal and Imperial claims to domination, as much as Puritan claims to turn the state into a Church or confessional political community. For Hobbes's argument to have any purchase on the Christian imagination of his readers, he has to acknowledge the plurality of nations and hence deny the idea of a world state or empire.

This peculiarly Protestant idea of the providential order as an order of distinct nations explains the inadequacy of many so-called Hobbesian realist international relations theories that simply *assume* the plurality of states as a natural fact and then focus on the systemic effects of that empirical fact. This stance might seem to echo Hobbes's own natural individualism, which also seems to acknowledge the natural fact of diverse human individuals and then model the consequences of their interaction. Yet, the assertion of a plurality of states in the international system is also a normative claim because it singles out some forms of contingent political societies as particularly significant and not just ontologically given. The plurality of nations in Christian theology is not just an observation but involves a normative claim that this is the providential order that needs to be acknowledged, and not usurped by an extra-national power like the imperial claims of the 16th-century papacy. So Hobbes actually links his philosophical and juridical account of sovereignty with a particular view of the providential order.

Although this is largely overlooked in the discussion of Hobbes's ideas in contemporary international relations and in political theory, it preoccupied Hobbes in half of the text of *Leviathan*. And according to some scholars it was an important part of Hobbes's appeal to the radical Puritan elements of the coalition around the Commonwealth Party and Cromwell's Protectorate (McQueen 2018, pp. 105–147). This political-theological claim about the providential significance of the sovereign state, or, as we now know it, the nation state (the sovereign claim of a particular people), remains an enduring part of the justification of state sovereignty in opposition to superstate organisations in the 20th and 21st centuries – even though the original biblical or apocalyptic motivations behind that perspective have long since lost their motivating power.

The (re)assertion of the sovereignty of a nation state against a superstate that curtails national sovereignty has been a curious feature of one of the most significant developments in British politics since the 2016 (Brexit) referendum to leave the European Union, and the subsequent long-running debates about 'taking back' British sovereignty. For the defenders of the UK's decision to leave the European Union, the default argument has been the incompatibility between British national sovereignty and membership of a multistate union that pools sovereignty and accepts the imposition of laws and the adjudication of those laws by the European Court of Justice (the Court of Justice of the EU). This stance was more important than any argument about the relative economic advantages of EU membership versus independence. Sovereignty and not political economy was the critical issue in the run-up to and aftermath of the referendum. As 'Leavers' defended that position of prioritising sovereignty against counterclaims of its economic irrationality, the political-theological aspect of Hobbes's argument has re-emerged. This story could be told from the left-of-centre side of the British ideological perspective using the work of Richard Tuck, who along with Noel Malcolm (see below) occupied a dominant position in British Hobbes scholarship in the late 20th and early 21st centuries.

Tuck was a supporter of Brexit from the left – a position sometimes referred to as 'Lexit' (2020).

An equally interesting example from the right is provided by Noel Malcolm's writing on the future of conservatism. Malcolm is one of the most important Hobbes scholars of his generation, the general editor of *The Clarendon Edition of the Works of Thomas Hobbes* and editor of the definitive edition of Hobbes's *Leviathan*. His well-known essay 'Conservative Realism and Christian Democracy' (1996) was published 20 years before the Brexit referendum debates. It criticises the elision of English conservatism with European Christian democracy, which was advocated by a number of British Conservative Party thinkers and MPs. Malcolm gives a relatively uncontentious account of the development of Christian social democracy alongside – or, in parts of Europe, out of – Catholic social teaching, derived from late 19th-century social papal encyclicals. He next argues that European Christian social democracy might align on some key issues with conservatism, as understood in England. But it fails to acknowledge the most important element of national sovereignty, which is the primacy of the political in it. This is the key danger of European Christian democracy and its dominance within the political structures of the European Union and its advocates' preoccupation with ever closer union and the diminishing of national sovereign competencies.

Malcolm's essay does not advocate leaving the European Union; that is still some two decades away. But it does distinguish between a social approach to politics as derived from Catholic social theory, which explicitly remains silent on the issue of national sovereignty, and the claims of national sovereignty by sovereign peoples as national states. He argues in good Hobbesian fashion that politics is about sovereign powers and tends to particularism amongst people with conflicting identities, whereas Catholicism as a religion that makes universal moral claims is essentially cosmopolitan. It therefore cannot make sense of the primacy of sovereign political claims over those of individuals and social groups. In raising the prospect of a way of understanding politics that does not assume that sovereign political powers are just given in the natural order of history, Malcolm's argument reminds us that sovereignty is an irreducibly normative concept. It is also one in real competition with other ways of conceiving of political and social relationships, whether that be in the context of the British state's relationship with the EU, the British Conservative Party's choices over its fundamental ideological commitments, or Hobbes's argument with his contemporaries about the claims of the sovereign prince over the claims of an international and imperial absolutism based on papal authority. When realist international relations theorists assume the idea of the nation state as a given, they are not merely making an observation statement about the world but are categorising it in a normative way.

Although this political-theological perspective is central to the argument of *Leviathan*, and therefore an important feature of Hobbes's theory of the state and the system of states, it is not a logical implication from the account of sovereign power. To understand this argument, we need to distinguish between two questions that run in parallel through Hobbes's book but which remain distinct. The first is the account of the logic of sovereignty and the second is the origin of the sovereign state. Sovereign power is presented as an answer to the problem of a state of nature, and so the power of sovereignty is as broad as that state of nature. The extent of sovereign power is therefore potentially as extensive as the whole earth, hence the question 'could there be a global sovereign?' For Hobbes, there is no *logical* limitation to the scope of sovereign power. That said, there may be practical limitations to the effective extent of sovereignty, such that the requirements break down; these, however, are practical and empirical (not logical) limitations to sovereignty. Similarly, if the state of nature always arises first in local contexts, because of natural limitations to human interaction, then the problem of the logical scope of sovereignty will not arise as a problem, because it must always be scaled at the size necessary to deliver peace and security. If this small-scaledness is a natural fact or a consequence of divine providence, then there will always be different particular states of nature in different locations, and the problem of a global sovereign will not arise.

Towards a hierarchical world order?

Although the absence of a universal or global state of nature rules out a global sovereign, other scholars have continued to ask why the state of nature between local sovereign powers does not later on create a two-tier logic working towards a global state or some other state-like sovereign order. This model has been most influential amongst those who have tried to theorise an institutionalisation of international peace or global governance. Here the idea is that there is a first-stage covenant between individuals to establish a sovereign state, and then a second-stage covenant between sovereigns to establish a global hierarchical order or world state. We might think Hobbes's theory could entail this because the example of the relations between princes (states) is used as an illustration of how the state of nature as a state of war, the implication being that there is an analogy, and, if the analogy is strict, then the same logic ought to hold.

In this case, Hobbes's argument is much clearer about the analogy not being precise. Firstly, his allusion to foreign princes is to illustrate permanent risk of war, and not the full logic of state of nature itself. So Hobbes does not intend to make the analogy precise enough to warrant the inference of a two-stage logic to his contract theory. More importantly, two fundamental elements of the state of nature do not hold in relations between states. Although individuals clearly fear death (for the most part), they certainly can die and that is not the case with political communities. However, we see the catastrophes that befall peoples, states or nations; they do not die altogether. Wars and revolutions can certainly devastate whole countries, but they do not die completely in the same way that individual people do.

The other element of the state of nature that does not hold between states is the requirement of rough equality of power. Hobbes clearly recognises that this condition does not hold amongst states, and he does not expect it to hold given his argument for sovereignty to transform by acquisition or conquest. In the absence of these elements of the state of nature, the implication of a second-tier agreement does not hold. Without the fear of death and the equality of power making all equally vulnerable, there will always be reasons for princes to seek other ways of securing their position. Sometimes this will be war and sometimes this will be alliances. Those princes who enjoy a natural advantage of power will always seek to structure the terms of interstate cooperation to secure order on advantageous terms for them. This 'realpolitik' is precisely what motivated (Catholic) France's alliance with Sweden and the Protestant powers against the fellow Catholic Habsburgs' empire.

The final point that has been taken as a sign of Hobbes lending support to a view of the international realm as an anarchical society (Bull 2002, pp. 44–47) is the introduction of sociability following the establishment of sovereignty. Hobbes famously characterises the state of nature as a world without commerce, trade, industry and art. So the implication of this stance is that only the creation of a sovereign state allows these evidently important and pervasive activities to flourish. In consequence, the international order is not a world without these important elements of human sociability, even if it is one characterised by the threat of war. Throughout the huge devastation of the Thirty Years War, German and central European industry, art, philosophy and some of the highest achievements of humanity continued to flourish, as did international trade amongst non-belligerents during World War II.

In these circumstances there is the opportunity for cooperation and collaboration across borders as well as competition. As Boucher and Malcolm show, Hobbes was both aware of and involved in colonial trade and commerce (Boucher 1998; Malcolm 2002). This is not just an extraneous biographical fact unrelated to the logic of Hobbes's argument. He is quite clear that international conflict, cooperation and collaboration are shaped by post-state sociability that is absent in the state of nature. This sociability is limited and is insufficient to ensure a permanently pacific international order, but it is not a state of nature (cf. Beitz 1999). So any analogy between politics within states and between states does not hold, nor was it meant to hold.

Overall, Hobbes's great achievement is to provide a unified concept of a sovereign entity that we now know as the state, and to outline the logic of the state system that emerged out of the catastrophe of the European wars of religion. This model is considerably developed and extended by subsequent thinkers, but Hobbes provides its fundamental outline and logic. Whether that system, and the Westphalian order it explains, is stable and permanent is an historical question that Hobbes avoids.

Bibliography

Essential reading

Hobbes, Thomas [1651] (1991). *Leviathan*, ed. R. Tuck. UK: Cambridge University Press.

Secondary reading

Beitz, Charles R. (1999). *Political Theory and International Relations*. USA: Princeton University Press.

Boucher, David. (2005). 'Property and Propriety in International Relations: The Case of John Locke', in B. Jahn (ed.) *Classical Theory in International Relations*. UK: Cambridge University Press, pp. 156–177.

Boucher, David; and Kelly, Paul. (1994). *The Social Contract from Hobbes to Rawls*. UK: Routledge.

Doyle, Michael W. (1997). *Ways of War and Peace*. USA: Norton.

Dunne, Timothy (1999). 'A British School of International Relations', in Jack Hayward, Brian Barry and Archie Brown (eds) *The British Study of Politics in the Twentieth Century*. UK: The British Academy.

Forsyth, Maurice. (1979). 'Thomas Hobbes and the External Relations of States' *British Journal of International Studies*, vol. 5, no. 3, pp. 196–209.

Hampton, Jean. (1988). *Hobbes and the Social Contract Tradition*. UK: Cambridge University Press.

Herz, John H. (1951). 'Idealist Internationalism and the Security Dilemma' *World Politics*, vol. 2, pp. 157–180.

Lloyd, Sharon A. (1992). *Ideals as Interests in Hobbes's Leviathan: The Power of the Mind Over Matter*. UK: Cambridge University Press.

Macpherson, Crawford B. (1962). *The Political Theory of Possessive Individualism*. UK: Oxford University Press.

McQueen, Alison. (2018). *Political Realism in Apocalyptic Times*. UK: Cambridge University Press.

Malcolm, Noel. (1996). 'Conservative Realism and Christian Democracy', in Kenneth Minogue (ed.) *Conservative Realism*. UK: Harper Collins.

Malcolm, Noel. (2002). *Aspects of Hobbes*. UK: Clarendon Press.

Martinich, Aloysius P. (1992). *The Two Gods of Leviathan: Thomas Hobbes on Religion and Politics*. UK: Cambridge University Press.

Newey, Glen. (2008). *Hobbes and Leviathan*. UK: Routledge.

Tuck, Richard. (2020). *The Left Case For Brexit*. UK: Polity Press.

Vincent, Raymond J. (1981). 'The Hobbesian Tradition in Twentieth Century International Thought' *Millennium: Journal of International Studies*, vol. 10, no. 2, pp. 91–101.

Waltz, Kenneth N. [1979] (2010). *Theory of International Politics*. USA: Waveland Press.

Warrender, H. (1957). *The Political Philosophy of Hobbes*. UK: Clarendon Press.

Wilson, Peter H. (2010). *Europe's Tragedy: A New History of the Thirty Years War*. UK: Penguin.

Suggestion for finding open access versions of Hobbes's texts

Online Library of Liberty, maintained by the Liberty Fund
https://oll.libertyfund.org/person/thomas-hobbes

PART II

War, revolution and competition beyond states

CHAPTER 6

Locke

Liberalism and the externalisation of conflict

The second of the great social contract theorists is John Locke. In contrast to his predecessor Hobbes, Locke is considered an early liberal because he argued for a constitutionally limited conception of sovereignty that protects individuals' rights to life, liberty and property. I give an overview of Locke's social contract theory and his account of the constitutional sovereign state. The state of nature, the law and right of nature, and the theory of consent form a central part of the discussion as these are areas where Locke differs importantly from Hobbes.

I also explore Locke's arguments on the right of revolution and the theory of property, which is linked to trade and colonial acquisition. His connection to colonialism and its impact on his theory are discussed in light of what is known as the 'colonial turn' in political theory. I conclude with a discussion of Locke's state theory, his views on the normative status of non-constitutionally limited powers, and the extent to which they should be recognised by legitimate states. Because of his moralistic natural law theory, Locke is often thought of as a source for liberal idealism. However, the chapter concludes with a discussion of his relationship to the realism/idealism distinction and his defence of a militant liberal order in the international realm.

How to cite this book chapter:
Kelly, Paul. 2022. *Conflict, war and revolution: The problem of politics in international political thought*. London: LSE Press, pp. 181–212.
DOI: https://doi.org/10.31389/lsepress.cwr.f License: CC BY.

At the end of his chapter on the English political philosopher John Locke, the author Robert A. Goldwin writes:

> Locke has been called America's philosopher, our king in the only way a philosopher has ever been king of a great nation. We therefore, more than many other peoples in the world, have the duty and the experience to judge the rightness of his teaching. (Goldwin 1987, p. 510)

Amongst historians of political thought, much scholarship over the last few decades has been focused on wrestling Locke's reputation away from those who wish to see him primarily as the philosopher or ideologist of the American founding and the constitutionalism or legal liberalism that follows from that. This effort can take the form of showing that Locke's arguments were engagements in 17th-century political theology and debates that are a world away from the fundamental tenets of liberal ideology – notably, his denial of toleration or civil accommodation of atheists or Roman Catholics. Alternatively, it can seek to show that the American founding was more influenced by the republican heirs of Machiavelli, such as James Harrington and Montesquieu, than by individualist contractarians such as Locke. Some authors have also argued that the very idea of liberalism as a coherent political ideology is problematic before the 19th century.

But what is most interesting about Goldwin's quote above is not simply the allusion to Locke's impact on the domestic constitutional order of the United States but the more general implication that there is something 'American' about Locke. By this, of course, is meant the United States, an association that many American students and scholars recognise but which is also acknowledged in the way in Locke and Lockean liberalism is seen amongst international relations theorists. If Thomas Hobbes is the classic source of modern structural realism, his fellow contract theorist Locke occupies a middle position between realists and idealist internationalists and cosmopolitans. Instead of the international domain being a 'warre of all against all', with every state in constant fear for its security, the liberal vision is one of broadly peaceful competition and occasional cooperation between states pursuing their interests in a world without a permanent international order (Doyle 1987). This cooperation can and does give rise to international institutions and rules that facilitate the mutual pursuit of interest that Joseph Nye and Robert Keohane argue is a better characterisation of international affairs than the narrow security-focused realism of Hobbes-inspired theorists such as Kenneth Waltz (Nye and Keohane 1977).

Within this broadly liberal paradigm, part of which seems to reflect Locke's political theory, there is also a place for hegemonic powers that reinforce the rules of cooperation and collaboration whilst there is convergence of interests between all participants on the scheme of cooperation and the hegemonic power. At least until very recently, during the period when Donald Trump was U.S. president, this coincided with the United States' image of itself as both a partisan actor in international affairs *and* as the guarantor of a rules-based international order in global economy – using its military force to sanction in support of that order rather than simply to pursue its own narrow national interest (Ikenberry 2020). This complex self-image of the United States as the last best hope for a benign liberal order is challenged from all quarters, including within the U.S., since Trump is only the latest manifestation of a nativist and isolationist tradition in U.S. politics. Critics see it as a cynical self-deception, a mask for a disguising a realist and assertive national policy, or a tragic example of Periclean democratic hubris. And, although the U.S. belief is now at some remove from Locke's own thought, it is inevitable that some of this perception is read back into the understanding of Locke's arguments and legacy. Similarly, central aspects of Locke's arguments and philosophical style have a bearing on how liberal aspirations and intentions are perceived when applied to the international realm as the space between legitimate states, and to their relations with illegitimate states or peoples without states.

Locke's arguments most closely connect with the politics of international liberalism in his views on state legitimacy and the claims and normative status of individuals. There is another important element of liberal internationalism that is not directly addressed in this chapter. It draws on Montesquieu and Adam Smith, because Locke was a mercantilist at least with respect to economic policy, and saw global trade in terms of a zero-sum competition. Locke's contribution to international liberalism is chiefly in terms of the architecture and legitimacy of a state-based system of liberal legalism, as opposed to empire or some other structure for state politics (Armitage 2012; Kelly 2015). For contemporary cosmopolitan theorists and revisionist just war theorists (such as Jeff McMahan and Cecil Fabre), Lockean arguments have important normative implications that are to be commended. For others, Locke's arguments contribute an important source of instability in international affairs or (at the most extreme) they undermine the possibility of any international order. Of most interest here is that Locke is both a source of the conceptualisation of the 21st-century liberal order and also a revolutionary challenge to that order with respect to the obligations of individuals and liberal states towards non-liberal regimes.

Living in interesting times – Locke's political life

As in previous chapters, intellectual biography can be of varying use in understanding the arguments and significance of a thinker's international or political thought. In some instances, biography can set a thinker's ideas in the context of a debate or provide a key to unlocking its meaning, and in other cases it is of limited interest. In Locke's case, his biography is most often examined to provide the key to his complex and not always consistent works. In 1689, after returning from exile in Holland, Locke published three great works: *An Essay Concerning Human Understanding*, the *Two Treatises on Civil Government* and the *Letter Concerning Toleration*. The *Essay* is undoubtedly the greatest work of philosophy in the English language and established Locke's reputation as a leading thinker of the European Enlightenment. In it he develops an empiricist psychology that grounds all knowledge in experience. When coupled with the *Letter Concerning Toleration*, with its denial of the political right to impose uniformity of belief or religion, we see the emergence of a liberal enlightened philosophy that provided the philosophical underpinnings of the new science of Isaac Newton. But the radicalism of Locke's philosophy was to prove a problem for his political thought, which was never published in his lifetime under his own name, and which is based on natural law and natural rights. Whether there is a higher synthesis that reconciles the *Essay*, *Letter* and *Two Treatises* remains a major concern for scholars. But each work also gives rise to different emphases in the interpretation of Locke's biography.

In the case of the *Essay*, we might emphasise Locke's interest in medicine and his association with the emergence of empirical science and contemporaries such as Robert Boyle, Leibniz and Newton (Woolhouse 2009). The *Letter* emphasises the significance of Locke's interest in religion and religious accommodation and domestic politics (Marshall 2010). Turning to Locke's *Two Treatises* introduces an international dimension to his political thought, and one that is often overlooked when focusing on the politics of the Glorious Revolution of 1688 (Armitage 2012; Kelly 2015). This issue is becoming increasingly important in the view of many commentators, given the anti-colonial turn in Locke scholarship in the last two decades. This chapter also emphasises the international dimension in Locke's thought, but not simply in terms of his relationship to colonialism.

John Locke was born in Wrington, Somerset, in the west of England in 1632. His father had served in the Parliamentary forces in the English Civil War, and through that service and the patronage of the local MP he was able to send his son John to be educated at Westminster School in London (where he was to witness the execution of Charles I) and then to study at Christ Church at Oxford. Whilst at Oxford, Locke held relatively conservative political views, as evidenced by his argument against religious toleration in the *Two Tracts* of 1660. But he also cultivated an interest in medicine and natural science, which brought him into contact with Anthony Ashley Cooper (the Earl of Shaftesbury), who led the Protestant opposition to Charles II's policy toward Catholic France. Shaftesbury suffered from an abscess on his liver that became the subject of an effective (if improbable) operation conducted by Locke. The success of the operation began a personal and political relationship between Shaftesbury and Locke, which brought Locke into both government service as a commissioner on the Board of Trade and Plantations and secretary to the Lords Proprietor of Carolina, as well as involving him in the radical politics around opposition to Charles II and his Catholic brother James, Duke of York. During this period Locke drafted the *Fundamental Constitutions of Carolina* in 1669 and began his lifelong association with North American colonial administration.

Only Machiavelli, as a diplomat, or Thucydides, as an Athenian general, rivals Locke's practical engagement with international politics. However, Locke's early political career as an associate of Shaftesbury was precarious because of the latter's political hostility to James, Duke of York. With Shaftesbury's fall from favour in 1675 as a result of his opposition to James's accession to the throne (the so-called Exclusion Crisis), Locke took up the opportunity to visit France from 1675 to 1679. He returned to England following a brief return to power by Shaftesbury only to have to flee to the Netherlands in 1683 after the uncovering of the Rye House Plot to assassinate Charles II and James. Locke's friend and political correspondent Algernon Sydney was executed, and Locke rightly feared for his own life in light of his manuscript for the *Two Treatises*, which were written (amongst other things) as a justification of the exclusion of James, Duke of York, from the throne and a popular right to revolution.

For six years, Locke lived in exile and hiding, avoiding spies who sought to assassinate or kidnap him and return him to trial in London. During that time, he was also associated with plotters seeking to overthrow James II as the legitimate monarch and to replace the government. This aspect of Locke's political life has been wonderfully captured by the Locke scholar Richard Ashcraft (Ashcraft 1986). It brings into stark relief the ways in which Locke's arguments challenge fundamental aspects of the state-based system of international relations that we think we have inherited from the late 17th century. Locke denies states' rights and defends intervention by individuals and legitimate states in disputed periods of revolutionary turmoil, in ways that 21st-century theorists would consider a breach of international order or even justifying terrorism.

In 1688, an invasion by Prince William of Orange (the husband of James II's Protestant sister) and an insurgency within England overthrew James II, who fled to France. Locke returned to England but only published his *Two Treatises* anonymously because of fears of their potentially revolutionary message. Locke returned to government service and economic and trade policy. His last active period as a senior official in the new regime was during an important English expansion and imperial consolidation. This process led to the eventual union of 1707 between England and Scotland that fostered the emergence of Britain as a major maritime imperial power in the 18th century, and Locke was for a time at the heart of colonial and foreign policy. He died in peaceful retirement in 1704 in Essex, in the care of his friend and intellectual companion Damaris Masham.

The bloodless so-called 'Glorious Revolution' of 1688 and Locke's place within it both had subsequent impacts on the American founding. Yet, this history has obscured both the revolutionary nature of Locke's liberalism and the extent to which this is also shaped by his international experience and thinking about international affairs. I argue that Locke's focus on the role of the sovereign state within international affairs was always an essential part of his philosophical politics.

The state of nature, natural law, punishment and war

Modern students rarely read the first of Locke's *Two Treatises* for enlightenment and edification. It comprises a long and detailed refutation of Sir Robert Film-er's *Patriarcha* (1680), in which he sought to justify political absolutism as a form of patriarchal rule that can be traced through scriptural sources to Noah's sons. As God had given all dominion over the earth to Adam and through him his sons, so, following the biblical flood, the sons of Noah inherited this divinely ordained right to rule. It is from this that the authority of kings arises, but also, most importantly, their dominion or ownership of the land compris-ing their territory. The ideological value of this argument for the defenders of Stuart absolutism was that it denied the right to taxation by consent. If the king already owned everything, then all so-called private property was really only enjoyed on terms that could be varied without consent. Locke's argument in the *First Treatise* rejects Filmer by providing an alternative reading of scripture.

In the *Second Treatise* he set out to defend political authority as altogether different from the power of patriarchs or fathers. He defines political power as:

> *a Right* of making Laws with Penalties of Death, and consequently all
> less Penalties, for the Regulating and Preserving of Property, and of
> employing the force of the Community, in the Execution of such Laws,
> and in the defence of the Common-wealth from Foreign Injury, and all
> this only for the Publick Good. [II § 3] (Locke 1988, p. 268).

The task of the remainder of the *Second Treatise* is to explain the origin and justification of this conception of political power and its implications. Like his near-contemporary Hobbes, Locke provides an abstract contractarian defence of political power and government, avoiding reference to scripture and drawing on a state of nature, an account of natural law and natural right and a contract or agreement. But there is a great difference between their two views.

The state of nature

Hobbes famously described a state of nature in which the 'life of man [is] soli-tary, poore, nasty, brutish and short', as the basis for his defence of absolute sovereignty. Like Hobbes, Locke seeks to abstract from our experience and to give an account of a world *without* political authority as a reason for creating it: once again, political authority and the state is an artifice of human creation. Locke's account of the state of nature has three important features. Firstly, the state of nature is a 'state of perfect freedom' in which people are free to act and dispose of their own possessions 'within the bounds of the law of nature'. Sec-ondly, there is a law of nature that is binding independently of political power. Thirdly, the state of nature is a 'state of equality', where this is a normative or obligation-creating claim and not merely a descriptive claim. Locke's state of nature departs from that of Hobbes in that it is sociable and includes the acquisition and exchange of property and possessions. Indeed, in Chapter V of the *Second Treatise*, Locke provides a famous account of the pre-political acquisition of private property in land, one that forms an important part of his analysis of colonialism, to which we will return. For Locke, the pre-political world is a world of moral obligations and duties in which all men are free and equal. This is precisely the claim that Filmer sought to deny by emphasising patriarchal or parental subjection as the natural condition.

In contrast, Locke claims that people in the state of nature are both morally free and equal. People are free in the sense of not being subject to the domination or direction of others. But this is not a state of licence where they may do anything they wish: no one is free to kill another human being at will, nor are they free to wilfully destroy anything in nature. As a moral concept, freedom is something that all enjoy as a right of nature, so the state of nature is a condition of moral equality. Individuals in the state of nature are not merely equal in their power to cause harm or threaten others; they are morally equal in having a claim on other agents to act or refrain from acting in certain ways. Locke's argument for this fundamental moral claim of individuals to be free and equal is elusive and controversial; it is introduced in §§ 4–5 with a reference to Richard Hooker's book *Law of Ecclesiastical Polity*. But Locke is aware that a reference to authority is not a philosophical defence of the claim. The argument is developed by linkage to the idea of property: 'For Men being all the Workmanship of one Omnipotent and infinitely wise Maker ... they are his Property, whose Workmanship they are, made to last during his, not anothers Pleasure' [II § 6] (Locke 1988, p. 271).

Locke argues in Chapter V, 'On Property', that the exercise and mixing of labour with unowned nature establishes a *prima facie* claim over the product of that labour. Consequently, if we are created, then our creator owns us, thus precluding any intermediate rights or authority over persons. This right of prior ownership means that human beings do not own their own bodies as persons, at least in the sense of having a freedom to commit suicide. People have a duty to preserve themselves and where possible a duty not to destroy others: this is the foundation of Locke's concept of natural rights.

> Every one as he is *bound to preserve himself*, and not to quit his Station wilfully; so by the like reason when his own Preservation comes not in competition, ought he, as a much as he can, to *preserve the rest of Mankind*, and may not unless it be to do Justice on an Offender, take away, or impair the life, or what tends to the Preservation of the Life, the Liberty, Health, Limb or Goods of another. [II § 6] (Locke 1988, p. 271)

On this argument we are all equal under God. But, of course, this argument depends upon a theistic premise about the existence of a creator, which Locke

was happy to accept as a rational belief but which 21st-century moral individu-
alists find less persuasive. Some scholars have even argued that Locke's *Two
Treatises* was only published anonymously because he was unable to provide a
rational foundation for his fundamental moral convictions that withstood the
challenge of his sceptical and empiricist psychology in the *Essay Concerning
Human Understanding.*

Locke does not provide a simple list of natural rights, but these can be inferred
from his account of what is necessary to preserve life, that is, such things as
the liberty to find sustenance through labour and the means of sustenance such
as food, clothing, shelter, protection. These rights are the basis of claims we
have upon others and they have upon us, and that is the basis of the law of
nature in Locke's theory. But, as we have a duty to preserve ourselves, these
rights are mostly negative rights to be unhindered in the pursuit of food, as
opposed to placing others under a duty to provide it.

> The *State of Nature* has a Law of Nature to govern it, which obliges every
> one: And Reason, which is that Law, teaches all Mankind, who will
> but consult it, that being all equal and independent, no one ought to
> harm another in his Life, Health, Liberty or Possessions. [II § 6] (Locke
> 1988, p. 271)

The law of nature as a law of reason no doubt raises important questions about
moral epistemology that the *Essay* makes difficult to answer. But, leaving that
issue aside, Locke does think that the law of nature creates genuine obligations
by the distribution of duties. Through having a right to life, a person is the beneficiary of all other persons having a duty not to kill them. Similarly, in enjoying liberty, one is also the beneficiary of others having duties not to limit one's
freedom. Yet, that does not mean that Locke has a straightforward beneficiary
theory of rights, because some natural rights (such as the right to acquire property) are liberties that impose no duties on others. They are merely the freedom
of a person to act in a certain way through labouring or appropriating. But,
when one has acquired or laboured, then others are under a duty not to inter-
fere. The point is that the fundamental right is not derived from a prior duty.
Central to Locke's natural law theory is the idea that the violation of a right or a
duty is an objective wrong and as such should be subject to punishment.

Punishment and the executive power of the law of nature

One very important feature of Locke's account of the law of nature is that it
is genuinely a law and not merely a belief about what we should do. As we
have just seen, the law of nature is a sanctioned reason, one for which non-
compliance merits punishment. Law and punishment go together. Yet, more than
this, the law of nature is complete in the state of nature; it is a real law and not

an indication of a law, and that is because it has a real and legitimate sanction-ing power: 'the *Law of Nature* would, ... be in vain, if there were no body that in the State of Nature, had the *Power to Execute* that Law' [II § 7] (Locke 1988, p. 271). That is because everyone in the state of nature enjoys the executive power of the law of nature and therefore '*every Man hath a Right to punish the Offender, and be Executioner of the Law of Nature*' [II § 8] (Locke 1988, p. 272).

It is only through enjoying this executive power of the law of nature that any man in the natural condition can come to exercise power over another person given their natural equality and the duty to preserve one another in the state of nature. When someone harms or kills another, they put themselves beyond the law of nature and become an outlaw. They live outside the law of nature and by another law. We can therefore, regard those who breach the law of nature as akin to a '*Lyon* or a *Tyger*, one of those wild Savage Beasts, with whom Men can have no Society' [II § 11] (Locke 1988, p. 274).

Whilst there is violence and force in the state of nature, this is only legitimate in the form of righteous punishment, otherwise it is precluded by the prior obligation to preserve one another. This executive power of the law of nature gives rise to two specific rights of punishment. Firstly, the right to punishment as restraint, and, secondly, punishment as restitution. The right to restrain is exercised by all people and not merely those who suffer injury or attack at the hands of criminals and outlaws. As we shall see, this third-party right of punish-ment is hugely controversial in international affairs. It can include the imposi-tion of the death penalty on those who threaten or kill. This is the analogy with the lions, tigers and wild beasts with whom one cannot have society. Because people who behave as beasts harm not only their victims but all humankind, so all humankind also share that duty to restrain the threat and danger. Locke particularly singles out death as the appropriate punishment for murder. The defence of killing someone as an appropriate punishment, rather than as a mere side effect of defending oneself and others, is not fully explained. But it is clear from the reference to scripture that Locke's argument depends upon an idea of forfeiture. Does the death penalty apply only to murder?

Locke departs from the strict proportionality of 'an eye for an eye' by arguing that in the case of the lesser breaches of the law of nature appropriate punish-ments may involve judgements of a degree of severity sufficient to make the act 'an ill bargain'. As such, punishment is part retributive and part deterrent. The retributive argument supports the necessity and duty of punishing a breach of the law. On a strict deterrence theory, we might weigh up the cost of punishing against other costs and decide in some cases to withhold punishment because there will be no deterrent effect. However, for Locke, punishment is a duty that falls on us all because of the law of nature, and we do wrong not to exercise that power. The deterrent effect does play a role in deciding the severity and nature of the punishment. There is no simple connection between the nature of the crime and the character of the punishment, the sort of link we might infer from the use of the death penalty to punish murder. It is therefore perfectly possible that the death penalty would be the appropriate deterrent for most crimes against property. Locke was concerned both about the problem of private violence and also about the legitimate exercise of private violence within the executive power of the law of nature (Frazer and Hutchings 2020).

Locke also identifies a further right to reparation. This right is different to the right of restraint, since it may be exercised only by the victim of the crime and not by third parties, as is the case with restraint. The right to reparation allows the victim or injured party to recover what is theirs, either by taking back what was stolen or by recovering its value. This right precludes anyone else from illegitimately benefiting from the proceeds of crime. But it is also important for Locke's later account of the competence of the political magistrate, for only the injured party can decide whether to pursue recovery, and no one else can claim to 'recover' what was illegitimately gained unless it was theirs in the first instance. If the state or third parties sought to recover the proceeds of crime without returning the full value to the original owners, then they too would be guilty of benefiting from the proceeds of crime, and that would put them in breach of the law of nature. The 'strange doctrine' of the executive power of the law of nature is one of the most challenging ideas. While it is clearly one of the building blocks of the idea of political authority, it is also not something that is wholly 'alienable' (i.e. capable of being lost, renounced or transferred). Central to Locke's philosophy is the idea that the pre-political world is moral and that the moral norms in this pre-political world not only create obligations but also carry legitimate sanctions and can displace the claims of politics. This is the genesis of one of the most controversial aspects of liberal universalism in the international domain. But, before turning to that issue, there is one further element of Locke's state of nature theory to address: namely, the place of war.

The state of nature is not a state of war

Locke devotes Chapter III of the *Second Treatise* to the topic of war, and the implication of the discussion for the state of nature is obvious, not least because of the contrast with Hobbes's state of nature picture. In Hobbes's case, war is the absence of law and sovereign authority. For Locke, the absence of sovereign or political authority (as he describes it) is perfectly compatible with sociability, including primitive trade and commerce. War as a phenomenon must be incorporated into the idea of a world that is structured by the law of nature as a fundamental feature of the natural condition. It cannot be explained, as it is for Hobbes, merely as the absence of law and sovereign power.

In II § 16, Locke defines the state of war as a state of enmity and destruction that arises when a person declares by 'Word or Action' a 'sedate setled Design' on another's life (Locke 1988, p. 278). When this design is declared, the person so threatened has the right to destroy that which threatens his destruction, on the grounds that the law of nature requires that all may be preserved.

When a person threatens the life of another, he effectively forfeits his own right to be preserved, and can therefore be killed as one would kill a wild animal or other creature beyond the law. The argument here is similar to the defence of punishment, where inflicting violence and death is justified on the grounds of forfeiture. In § 18, Locke argues that I may kill a thief even though they may not directly threaten my life, because the thief is putting themselves beyond the law of nature by attempting to put me under their power. In restricting my freedom or depriving me of my property, I am entitled to assume that the thief might take away everything else, including my life. As there can be no reparation if the thief does kill me, I do not have to wait for the act and then seek to punish the culprit. The duty of self-preservation entitles me to kill the thief as an unjust aggressor who is effectively waging war with me.

Three important features of the argument follow. Firstly, the state of war is not necessarily a passionate and hasty act such as wantonly striking another. Instead, it is seen as a 'sedate setled Design' on the life of another. Secondly, a threat to the life of another is a legitimate ground for a person to assert their right of self-preservation against the potential aggressor. The aggressor must show or declare his intention to threaten the life of others, but need not have acted on that declared intention to be a legitimate target of defence against aggression. This declaration of intention can be in words or deeds (such as preparing for an invasion to impose Catholicism on Protestant England). But, in contrast to either classical or contemporary realism, the mere existence of an alternative power who could pose a threat is not the expression of a 'sedate setled Design'.

Locke's position rejects the structural threat embodied in the 'Thucydides trap' or security dilemma in the anarchical condition of modern realism. Examples such as Phillip II of Spain's Spanish Armada of 1588 or Louis XIVs support for Stuart absolutism in the so-called 'popish plot' provide Lockean examples of communicated 'sedate setled Designs' – just as for George Kennan it was the USSR's ideological support for global revolution and not simply its military power that made it a military threat. Of course, the reverse of the Lockean position is also a problem for contemporary liberal universalism. If states do not support Lockean natural rights or contemporary human rights (which are not exactly the same thing but are sufficiently close for the argument), then they are liable to punishment and hence threaten in a 'sedate setled Design' a liberal state order committed to promoting universal liberal norms. This is precisely the concern of contemporary critics of a liberal U.S. foreign policy such as John Mearsheimer (2017). They claim that liberal universalism tends to collapse into a security threat to others who fear they may not be regarded as rightly ordered states and peoples. Finally, Locke does not confine the state of war only to rightly constituted authorities such as monarchs or states. In this way he departs from the traditional 'just war' theory of Aquinas or Vitoria, which asserts that only princes can go to war with one another. A state of war can exist between princes, between princes and subjects, and between individuals and non-state groups punishing breaches of the law of nature. This idea has been resurrected by the cosmopolitan just war theorist Cécile Fabre (Fabre 2012). In II § 17, Locke argues that anyone (person or prince) who seeks to put another under his absolute power is effectively declaring war on that person as this involves a declaration of a design on a person's life and freedom. Regimes such as Louis XIV's France were a permanent threat to the law of nature and necessarily posed a 'sedate setled Design' on the rights of others and Englishmen. So the new English state under William III was effectively in a state of nature with France with a possibility of a state of war.

Locke's argument is both an answer to the conflation of the state of nature and the state of war that is to be found in Hobbes and a lesson for international theory. In II § 19, Locke denies that the state of nature is a world of 'Malice, Violence and Mutual Destruction': it is properly understood as a state in which men live without a common superior on earth with the power to judge between them, whereas a state of war is initiated when one uses 'Force without Right' to threaten others (Locke 1988, p. 280). The state of nature can be a state of war but is not identical. Similarly, and importantly for Locke, the state of war can obtain *within* a society or state if its functionaries and rulers use force without right or legitimacy. Locke is quite explicit about this in II § 20, where he writes:

> where an appeal to the Law, and constituted Judge lies open, but the remedy is deny'd by a manifest perverting of Justice, and a barefaced wresting of the Laws, to protect or indemnifie the violence or injuries of some Men, or Party of Men, *there* it *is* hard to imagine any thing but a *State of War*. For wherever violence is used, and injury done, though by hands appointed to administer Justice, it is still violence and injury. (Locke 1988, p. 281)

Locke's state of nature is sociable, moral and not reducible to a war of all against all. In making this claim, Locke does not simply offer the state of nature as a hypothetical model. He draws on the experience of the relations between states and kingdoms as an example of the state of nature. In this respect, his liberal universal order is a more realistic description of international affairs than theoretical realisms:

> That since all *Princes* and Rulers of *Independent* Governments all through the World, are in a State of Nature, 'tis plain the World never was, nor ever will be, without Numbers of Men in that State. [II § 14] (Locke 1988, p. 276)

Between states or rulers there is no higher human legislative institution or world state, but that does not mean that there is no law between rulers. States and princes are not entitled to do anything they wish one with another. When one breaks the natural law, another has a right to go to war to punish the breach of the law of nature. It is only by virtue of this law-governed state of nature that a ruler can punish a non-national for breach of the law and that a resident alien can seek redress for breach of the law in respect of property rights. A non-national engaged in international commerce and trade is entitled to seek punishment for interference with their property or person, even though they have not consented to be ruled by the prince. Keeping faith or keeping contracts is an obligation independent of being members of the same political society. If this were not the case, there would be little reason to engage in international trade and commerce.

Property, territory, colonies and conquest

If Locke's argument were simply to justify legitimate political rule, then the attention that he devotes to the pre-political acquisition of property would be curious. But the fact that he devotes a long and extended discussion to the concept in Chapter V suggests that it has an important place in the argument. This can be best understood if we look at Locke's account of state legitimacy from an external as opposed to the domestic perspective.

Property and territoriality

In the pre-political state of nature, individuals can acquire and enjoy property and possessions under the law of nature. The question for Locke is how access to a common resource for the preservation of our lives gives rise to a private right to exclude others in the enjoyment of property. Near contemporaries of Locke such as Grotius (1583–1645) or Pufendorf (1632–1694) believed in aboriginal common ownership of the world, but this created the problem of how people moved from a common right to private right – including the right to exclude people without violating their natural rights. Locke's revolutionary response avoids this problem by conceiving of the world only as a common resource from which individuals can take in order to preserve themselves under the law of nature. His ingenious move, which has perplexed subsequent scholars, is to argue that the natural condition already contains a form of private property right, namely property in one's own person or body.

We have seen this argument in the context of the derivation of natural rights, where the fundamental premise is that, as all part of creation, we are God's property, which excludes all relations of natural dominion or subordination between people. Having sole responsibility to God for our well-being and agency, we are effectively the owners of our own bodies and what results from our bodily agency, namely labour: 'Man (by being Master of himself, and *Proprietor of his own Person*, and Actions or *Labour* of it) had still in himself *the great Foundation of Property*' [II § 44] (Locke 1988, p. 298). Locke also emphasises labour as the primary source of value:

> I think it will be but a very modest Computation to say, that of the *Products* of the Earth useful to the Life of Man 9/10 [nine tenths] are the *effects of labour*: nay, if we will rightly estimate things as they come to our use, and cast up the several Expences about them, what in them is purely owing to *Nature*, and what to *labour*, we shall find, that in most of them 99/100 [99 hundredths] are wholly to be put on the account of labour. [II § 40] (Locke 1988, p. 296)

The fact that labour is central to Locke's account of value and property is significant for his account of colonial acquisition, but how does it create an exclusive right to things? After all, private property is not simply access to objects in order to secure subsistence. A right to private property, especially if this is to be applied to land, must entail a right to exclude others from what is taken and transformed. How does Locke link labour and exclusive ownership or the transition of a common resource into private property?

The argument from labour provides part of the answer. In a world that is unowned, the transformation of the matter of nature into something valuable by human labour creates a *prima facie* argument for the justice of ownership as control. The crops my labour has grown on the land would not have been there but for the work of clearing, enclosing and cultivating the land. This alone suggests a *prima facie* claim on the product of labour, at least to the extent that no one else can (other things being equal) claim a prior right to that produce. Fairness supports the argument from labour.

But labour is not sufficient for two reasons. Firstly, whilst exercising labour might well create a productive resource that did not otherwise exist, it can at least be asked why that labour is not just wasted effort. Secondly, the enclosure and cultivation of land already assumes a prior right to enclose and exclude and this must assume the land is not previously owned or subject to a prior right. As we have seen, Locke denies that the world is originally owned in common so there must be unowned land for private acquisition. This leads to his adoption of the concept of *terra nullius* (unowned or empty land), which can be traced back to the Roman writer Tacitus, and is the foundation of colonial acquisition. Locke's answer to the first problem is the 'labour mixing' argument:

> The *Labour* of his Body, and the *Work* of his Hands, we may say, are properly his. Whatsoever then he removes out of the State that Nature hath provided, and left it in, he has mixed his *Labour* with, and joyned to it something that is his own, and thereby makes it his *Property*. [II § 27] (Locke 1988, pp. 287–288)

Labour is not only the activity that transforms nature and which creates value; it is also something that can be physically and permanently joined with a thing, so extending the private right to one's body to the thing itself. Thus, by attaching something that was privately and exclusively owned to a common resource,

Locke creates private property in land that is transformed and its produce. Locke adds two important caveats to this basis of right. The first is the 'enough and as good' condition, which entails that all others are not denied the right to access unowned land in order to secure their own subsistence. The second is the 'non-spoilage condition'. No one can exclude others from what is being allowed to spoil and go to ruin. The former constraint is the more important, because it does suggest a problem for future generations arriving in a world where all the valuable and productive land has already been acquired. How could they acquire property and therefore secure their self-preservation? Does this not undermine the right to original acquisition?

Locke's first response is to describe the emergence of the money convention in the state of nature. The adoption of precious metals as a repository of value that can be the basis of exchange creates the possibility of a property right in labour that can be exchanged for wages. In effect, everyone has the ability to acquire property through the sale of their labour, so the 'enough and as good' criterion is satisfied. More interestingly, from the perspective of colonial acquisition, are Locke's many references to North America as a near boundless source of unoccupied land that can be acquired by enterprising people who are prepared to transform brute nature into productive land. Locke believed in the abundance of land in North America whilst recognising the fact of settled societies of the First Nations. Clearly there is a problem about how much territory and land they owned in the context of his account of acquisition. He certainly believed that settled communities such as the Iroquois nation did own property and controlled territory – that did not diminish his belief in the abundance of North America. This is clearly part of the prospectus of the colonisation companies establishing settlement in the new world.

Locke refers to North America as a potential opportunity for initial acquisition, and he also refers to the aboriginal population of Native Americans. Yet surely, if there are such people, then North America is not all *terra nullius* or wasteland free for colonisation, because parts belong to its original inhabitants. Locke's argument seeks to get around this problem through his labour theory of acquisition and the labour mixing argument. The key to this approach is not simply an argument from use but about the nature of that use, where labour transforms nature and creates something new. Native Americans can justly exclude settlers from acquiring towns and villages and cultivated lands around their settled communities. But they cannot exclude settlers taking and transforming lands that they simply use as a common resource. In this way, traditional hunting grounds through which tribal bands roam are not in the Lockean sense 'property', such that an enterprising settler can be precluded from cutting down trees, clearing the land and planting crops.

As many subsequent commentators have argued, Locke may well be stacking the argument in his own favour here with an individualistic and early modern European conception of property that precludes ideas of collective ownership (Arneil 1996). But it is clear that Locke thought that use alone was not a ground for excluding access by the industrious and enterprising to acquire private property. Once that property has been acquired, any subsequent interference with it becomes a breach of the law of nature that can be punished. However, it is the type of use that justifies initial acquisition by colonial settlers and not the defence of that property in just war against assailants.

Conquest and colonies

Locke's discussion of conquest is informed by his theory of property and territory and places a constraint on the colonial acquisition of dominion over native populations. The argument against conquest as a source of legitimate dominion reasserts the claim that political societies can only be founded on the consent of the governed. So, although history might seem to show that many societies appear to arise from conquest and war, this is a mistake that confuses explanation with legitimation and justification. Locke's original contract is primarily concerned with a normative as distinct from a causal process. Conquest does not create political societies; it only destroys them, and we should no more mistake it for creating legitimate political societies than we should mistake the demolition of a house for its construction [II § 175] (Locke 1988, pp. 384–385). In II § 211, Locke argues that the only way in which a political society is dissolved (as opposed to government, which can be dissolved by the people's right to revolution) is through 'the Inroad of Foreign Force making a Conquest upon them' (Locke 1988, p. 406). Consequently, if a conquest is the result of an unjust war, then it creates no more right to property than a thief can obtain by taking it by force. But not all conquests are the result of unjust wars and this has led scholars to speak of a right of lawful conquest in Locke's theory (Ward 2010, p. 287). This form of dominion arises as a result of the punishment of an unjust aggressive war, where invasion is the only way of preventing a 'sedate setled Design' or of punishing a direct attack. In this case, despotic rule is legitimate for a period, but Locke qualifies this right so much as to preclude just conquest as a ground for colonial acquisition or empire. Locke argues that the conqueror in a just war gains no lawful right over those who are engaged in conquest with him. This claim is prompted by risk that foreign backers of the Stuart cause might well expect landed titles in return for their support (Pincus 2009), as was the case with the followers of William the Conqueror in 1066. Furthermore, a just conqueror has an obligation to share the spoils of the just war with his companions, who in so far as they are engaged only in the pursuit of a just war are allowed to recover the cost of the campaign and to recompense any loss that resulted in the war in the first instance.

With respect to those subject to a lawful conquest, Locke argues that despotic rule only extends over those who were actually engaged in the prosecution of an unjust war and not peoples as such. Civilians and non-combatants are not only immune in battle but also not responsible for the unjust war, unless they individually consented to it and participated in it. Only unjust aggressors forfeit their rights because the people cannot transfer an unjust power to their government, as it is not a power they possess. Therefore, it is the prince and his direct servants who must be held responsible for the breach of the law of nature as they have a responsibility to act only to protect civil interests and therefore to reject any illegitimate demands made of them by the people. The people are absolved because it remains the responsibility of government to decline popular demands for unjust aggression.

Those who engage in unjust aggression only forfeit their right to life and liberty: a just conqueror over them gains no right to seize an aggressor's property or that of their descendants or family, and hence wins no long-term territorial rights. Conquest does not circumvent the rights of private property, because these are pre-political. Unjust aggressors can be subject to charge, so that their property can be used to pay reparations for the aggression and for the legitimate costs of its punishment by war and conquest. However, the just conquerors' claim to just recompense cannot be so great as to force the family of an aggressor into death and destitution. In II § 183, Locke considers the case of the relative claims of just reparation and the absolute needs of an aggressor's family, and he concludes that the absolute need should prevail on the grounds of the natural law to preserve (Locke 1988, p. 391). The right to forfeiture undermines the claims of absolutists to base despotic rule on conquest as this only extends over the persons of unjust aggressors and not their property: it cannot give rise to jurisdiction over territory or over a people. To reinforce this point, Locke denies that territorial jurisdiction could be based on just reparation for unjust aggression, for even if reparations were charged to the 'last farthing' they would never extend to the value of the whole country in perpetuity.

Given his peculiar account of property and its relation to territoriality, as well as his practical involvement with the administration of the Carolina Colony, Locke is clearly an advocate of liberal colonialism. Yet, he is also unequivocally not a theorist of empire as that involves the illegitimate extension of sovereign dominion over the colonised. Indeed, by the 1690s, when Locke was a member of the new regime with responsibility for colonies, it was clear that his interest was far more directed towards trade than to territorial acquisition. Nor does he accept that conquest (even in defending against 'unjust aggression' by indigenous populations such as Native Americans) creates a right of dominion by conquest on behalf of settlers. The only grounds for legitimate colonisation are labour and the productivity of settlers in taking unoccupied land into productive use. Consequently, even if one accepts Locke's controversial account of property and initial acquisition, he has still set the bar for legitimate colonial acquisition so high that it probably precludes seeing the extent of colonisation of North America undertaken by Britain and France as legitimate. This has the peculiar consequence of making 'America's philosopher' (Goldwin 1987, p. 510) a critic of the legitimacy of the new post-revolutionary United States of America!

Political society, consent and revolution

The state of nature and the origin of private property are central to the account of Lockean liberal legalism in the international domain. But they are also very important in setting the parameters to the discussion of political authority as an extension or implication of the law of nature.

The original contract and origin of government

The state of nature is both a sociable and a law-governed condition, where primitive forms of property and trade are possible and where there is a genuine sanctioning power of the law of nature in the executive power of nature enjoyed by all individuals. In those circumstances it is not unreasonable to ask the anarchists' question: why, then, do we need any political authority or the state? Locke certainly thinks we do, and much of the argument of the *Treatises* is concerned to vindicate, as well as limit, government. To this end, he deploys the idea of a social contract but again his argument is very different from Thomas Hobbes's.

Although the natural condition is not a war of all against all, for Locke it does involve considerable inconveniences, which can be overcome by submitting to political authority. The greatest of these is the absence of a common and impartial judge. The initial definition of political authority makes it clear that politics is subordinate to the primacy of law and punishment, but, whilst that law has a sanctioning power in the state of nature, it does not have an impartial judge because we are all judge, jury and executioner in our own cases. This problem becomes destabilising when we add the problem of indeterminacy with respect to just or fair punishment. Although murder might warrant symmetrical punishment (a life for a life), when it comes to all lesser offences the justice of retribution and reparation is more complex. This technical absence of an impartial judge then becomes a source of instability where what one person may judge to be an appropriate response to their own case is judged to be an unjust imposition on behalf of another. In this way, we can see how tribal or family feuds could arise especially over land disputes, because of the absence of an authoritative judge. These disputes can escalate into situations that may look like a Hobbesian war of all against all. Yet they differ in that the Lockean problem is not the absence of a just law or rightful punishment but is simply about the fair implementation of these aspects of an objective moral order.

The state or political authority is the idea of a common judge who can determine a civil law with specified sanctions that ensures the just implementation of our natural law rights to enjoy our life, liberty, property and estate. The authority of such a state or common judge can only come from the pre-political authority of individuals to execute the law of nature. Accordingly, the first stage of creating a political authority involves recognising such a power, and this can only be the result of a freely given agreement, hence Locke's turn to the idea of a social contract. Locke's theory is interesting because he also addresses the question of the nature and scope of the group over which such authority can be exercised. The first stage of his contract theory constitutes a people. Only once this is done can there be a second-stage authorising government. The second question can only be answered by the first. So how is a people constituted?

In the state of nature, the absence of an impartial judge matters most to those who are sufficiently close for property disputes or for the burdens of common protection to arise. Owing to such proximity, the initial agreement is to combine the enjoyment of property in land under the authority of a common judge by constituting private estates into a territorially constituted people. Men agree:

> with other Men to joyn and unite into a Community, for their comfortable, safe and peaceable living one amongst another, in a secure Enjoyment of their Properties, and a greater Security against any that are not of it. [II § 95] (Locke 1988, p. 331)

This agreement to form a territorially constituted people is an *alienation* contract as it combines the enjoyment of private property within a political territory. Individuals do not forgo or limit their property rights except the right to subsequently secede with property in land to combine with another state. Once in a territorially constituted political community, real property in land cannot be unilaterally moved to the jurisdiction of another country; this precludes English Catholic aristocrats seceding from Protestant England to place their property under the jurisdiction of the French king. One can leave and take moveable property – but, once constituted as a part of a political community, that is the end of the matter, unless (as we have seen) a state is destroyed by war.

Having constituted itself as a single political community, there is still the question of the constitution or form of government of the state. This is also determined by a contractual agreement, but with the condition that the agreement does not have to be unanimous:

> every Man, by consenting with others to make one Body Politick under one Government, puts himself under an Obligation to everyone of that Society, to submit to the determination of the *majority*, and to be concluded by it; or else this *original Compact*, whereby he with others incorporates into *one Society*, would signifie nothing, and be no Compact. [II § 97] (Locke 1988, p. 332)

The constitution of the state is therefore created by a majority decision amongst a people who have unanimously constituted themselves as a political society. This argument is interesting because it is partly a causal theory of the state that mirrors a possible historical account of actual political communities emerging from tribal alliances and conflict. But it is important to remember that Locke's argument is ultimately an account of how *legitimate* political authority arises. Unless historically emerging political communities have this contractual form, they are not actually legitimate states but simply unjust coercive communities that enjoy no rights or duties from those subject to them, or enjoy no right of recognition from other legitimate states. As such, Locke's rather demanding criteria of legitimacy mean that many (perhaps most) actual states during Locke's time, or our own, will not be legitimate. They are therefore not exempt from the right of third parties to intervene and punish breaches of the law of nature (Simmons 1993, p. 16). This is also why Locke's dangerous doctrine remained anonymous during his lifetime.

Consent and the legitimacy of government

Locke was aware of how demanding his theory was, and the primacy he had given to a moralised notion of political legitimacy under the law of nature, hence the emphasis he places on consent and on prerogative. Prerogative is the discretionary personal power a ruler has to decide how to implement the law or protect civil interests in circumstances where the law or constitution does not prescribe or prohibit action. That said, prerogative has its limits, culminating in the right to revolution, as we shall see in the next section.

The concept of consent plays an important role in Locke's argument because the requirement of legitimacy must be met for all those who fall under political rule. Whilst an original contract amongst those who initially bind themselves into a political community, or who first constitute a state, might well be a source of obligation, how does this affect later generations born into political societies? For Locke, it is fundamental that they can only be subject to legitimate political authority if they too have agreed or consented to that rule. He distinguishes between two types of consent: express and tacit. The former is the most important and easily comprehended, taking the form of oaths of allegiance and office, or the recognition of formal structure, such as engaging in legal processes. This sort of argument is often used to explain how voters in elections can endorse the legitimate rule of a party they have voted against. By engaging in an election, citizens endorse the process for delivering and outcome, as well as expressing their own political preference. The problem with express consent is that it is still only likely to be something a small part of society engage in. To overcome this problem, Locke introduces the controversial idea of tacit consent:

> No body doubts but an *express Consent*, of any Man, entering into any Society, makes him a perfect Member of that Society, a Subject of that Government. The difficulty is, what ought to be look'd upon as a *tacit Consent*, and how far it binds, *i.e.* how far anyone shall be looked on to have consented, and thereby submitted to any Government, where he has made no Expressions of it at all. And to this I say, that every Man,

that hath any Possession, or Enjoyment, or any part of the Dominions of any Government, doth thereby give his *tacit Consent*, and ... Obedience to the Laws of that Government, during such Enjoyment, as any one under it; whether this his Possession be of Land, to him and his Heirs for ever, or a Lodging only for a Week; or whether it be barely travelling freely on the Highway; [II § 119] (Locke 1988, pp. 347–348)

The comprehensive nature of Locke's conception appears to depart from the concept of consent, replacing it with a benefit theory of political obligation where duty is based on the enjoyment of political benefits. This controversial concept has continued to challenge subsequent scholars, but it reinforces the fundamental Lockean premise that political authority is a power that only individuals can place themselves under; it is not a natural condition of natural obligation (see Kelly 2007, pp. 104–112).

It is equally important to note that Locke's argument from consent is a legitimation of political authority and not ultimately individual laws and policies. These will need to be consistent with the demands of the law of nature and natural rights, but Locke is equally clear that there is no simple inference from the law of nature to specific laws and policies. He argues that the government must have prerogative powers to exercise on behalf of the governed in pursuit of and defence of the civil interests and natural rights of the people. To this end, the constitution contains a legislative power to make laws to protect our property, liberty and civil condition, and an executive power to ensure that our political rights and interests are protected. It must remain for government to determine the institutions that protect our rights and the extent of their powers in enforcing and protecting the law. This prerogative is exercised as trust on behalf of those who are ruled.

In the field of international affairs, Locke speaks of a federative power, which is the authority to enter into treaties, alliances and obligations with other states to advance and protect the people's interests. The federative power is exercised at one remove from ordinary citizens because it requires a knowledge and perspective that can only be obtained by those in government. In this way, we can see an implicit defence of a professionalised diplomatic service that informed policy by drawing on the knowledge and experience acquired in embassies and diplomatic missions of the sort undertaken by Locke in his early career. It also suggests that the people as a rightly constituted state acts together in determining the status and relations between political communities. It is for the whole political community to act as one in entering treaties and exercising the power of war and peace conceived of as a state power. These powers are clearly markers of the modern sovereign state.

Implicit in Locke's short statement of the federative power is the idea that interstate war and treaties are reserved powers for the state and not powers to be exercised by private individuals or groups of individuals contrary to the state's will. The creation of private armies and of private engagements with other states for sectional and group benefits are also ruled out as illegitimate. At the same time, Locke acknowledges that the rightly ordered state remains in a state of nature with other political communities especially those that are absolutist and despotic, some of which (such as France) pose a 'sedate setled Design' against the English post-revolutionary order of William III. With respect to external despotic powers, individuals retain their right to execute punishment for breaching the law of nature unless a legitimate sovereign exercises that power on behalf of the body politics using the federative power. Federative power is the special discretionary power the executive exercises with respect to other governments, through either the contracting of treaties or the conduct of war.

Although prerogative and trust are central to effective government, that trust does have its limits. The defence of prerogative is about creating constitutional space in which political judgement can be exercised, but Locke is equally clear that there are strict limits to that prerogative and discretion and there are clear cases when the trust of government is broken. It is in those contexts that we have recourse to a right of revolution.

The right of revolution

The right of revolution is a right both to overthrow a government that acts in breach of its trust on behalf of the people and the right to replace and reconstitute a new government and not merely a right to individual or collective self-defence or resistance. Much of his argument is a defence of revolution from the charge of being an illegitimate rebellion against a divinely instituted government or the wholesale destruction of political society. The discussion of William Barclay's defence of absolutism in §§ 233–235 shows that individuals can replace and not just 'respectfully' resist a tyrant (Locke 1988, pp. 420–423). Yet, Locke also considers the issue of political prudence, namely when to exercise that right and who is to judge when it is appropriate to exercise that right. This issue of political prudence also applies in the case of extending the executive power of the law of nature to international intervention against an unjust and illegitimate third-party government.

Locke's argument is for a right to revolution, a *right* to punish and a putative *right* to intervene; he does not claim that we have a *duty* to do so in either a state of nature or in political society. Who exercises that right and when? In II § 230, Locke addresses the challenge to his theory that it will encourage those with 'a busie head, or turbulent spirit' to seek a change of government every time they disagree with what it does. In such circumstances, the mischief will either grow to an extent where it is recognised as a general threat triggering popular resistance or it will not be seen as a sufficient harm to warrant the greater harm that might follow from its rectification. Two points follow from this discussion that are relevant for extending the argument about revolution and dissolution to international intervention. The first confirms that the balance of harms has an important role in a legitimate decision about whether to punish, rebel or intervene. The second point concerns who should decide.

On this second point, the argument of the chapter on 'Dissolution' is helpfully complex when applied to judgements about whether to intervene or not. Locke makes two claims:

> *The People shall be Judge*; for who shall be *Judge* whether his Trustee or Deputy acts well, and according to the Trust reposed in him, but he who deputes him, and must, by having deputed him have still a Power to discard him, when he fails in his Trust? [II § 240] (Locke 1988, p. 427)

And:

> For where there is no Judicature on Earth, to decide Controversies amongst Men, *God* in Heaven is *Judge*: He alone, 'tis true, is Judge of the Right. But *every Man is Judge* for himself, as in all other Cases, so in this. [II § 241] (Locke 1988, p. 427)

The first passage indicates that the right of revolution is to be exercised by the people, the second passage that the people is composed of an aggregate of individuals who all retain the exercise of their individual judgement. Locke is a reductionist individualist, so no societal judgement exists independently of the individual judgements of those who compose it – there is no will of the people except the aggregation of their individual wills. This, of course, leaves a number of practical and unanswered questions about when the aggregate of individual judgements becomes a judgement of the people. The obvious answer drawing on the argument of § 95 is that the aggregate must be a majority of individuals in the political society, but, equally importantly, there must be a clear sign that the political society and not merely a number of disgruntled individuals such as those with a 'busie head, or turbulent spirit' [II § 230] (Locke 1988, p. 417) recognises that there is a breach of the law of nature and not simply an aggregation of various individual grievances.

Revolution, intervention, and the individual

Locke's discussion of the right of revolution is inextricably linked with international intervention following the 1688 overthrow of James II by the forces of William of Orange and this raises similar questions about when it is legitimate to intervene and who has that right. Given that Locke does allow for a right to intervention, Ward (2010, p. 287), for example, focuses on Locke's reference to the Greek Christians living under the domination of the Turks [II § 192] (Locke 1988, p. 394) as an illustration of where and when one might intervene, who can exercise that right and for what reasons. The answer (drawing on II §§ 8 and 11) is that the right resides ultimately with individuals as it is a right held by individuals in the natural condition prior to the creation of political societies, and it is a right that individuals retain in political society when the powers of government are too remote to enforce prevention, protection and punishment on behalf of the citizen.

Although political societies as states play a non-trivial role in the architecture of international politics, it remains the case that Locke bases his account of political authority on an individual's power under the law of nature. Individual moral power is ultimately at the root of legitimate political power – indeed, for Locke there is no other kind of political power, because anything else is illegitimate coercion and force. Locke's liberalism as applied to political society and the international domain allows for the external judgement and criticism of domestic political arrangements according to the law of nature. This is precisely John Rawls's concern that Locke's account of political society is too naively individualistic to make sense of international politics (Rawls 2007). For Locke it is only in the case of a legitimate and well-ordered political society that there is no scope for external criticism and censure. This is because being well-ordered means being fully compliant with the law of nature and confining the exercise of political power to the protection of people's civil interests. Until there is a just system of legitimate states or a single world state, there remains an individual right to enforce the law of nature.

Locke's individualistic methodology does not appear to preclude any role for the state in the third-party enforcement of the law of nature. Indeed, in the case of William of Orange's intervention in the removal of James II, we are confronted with a state intervening to support the people in re-establishing a well-ordered political society by removing an absolutist government that has put itself into a state of war with the people. The argument is similar to that of the right of revolution, in that there must be a clear majority with a single purpose revolting against the government and appealing to Heaven. In the case of individuals intervening, there is the matter of feasibility. An individual going to war against an unjust state or attempting to punish a breach of the law of nature, however well armed and well intentioned, is unlikely to succeed like an organised political community. But feasibility does not trump what is right.

Locke's legacy in international theory

Standard accounts of international political theory place Locke in opposition to the structural realism of Hobbes's theory (Doyle 1997; Wendt 1999). The Lockean world is not consumed by a preoccupation with war and security threats, but it is a world of anarchy due to the absence of an external overarching power that sanctions international law. Instead, states pursue national interests, in a world of law but without a common police power. Occasionally, this results in conflicts, but when it does the law of nature places strict limitations on either what is permissible as a ground for war (*jus ad bellum*) or what is permissible in the conduct of war (*jus in bello*). Equally, these interests can be pursued in cooperation or in pacific mutually advantageous agreements such as trade. Liberal theorists vary in terms of their emphasis between those who veer towards realism and those at the other extreme who veer towards idealism and the prospect of evolution towards a global rule-governed order. Much contemporary international politics can be seen to reflect that span between pessimist and optimist liberal perspectives on a rule-governed global order. The extension of trade was Locke's primary interest in international politics. In his last major public role as a secretary to the Council of Trade and Plantations, he pursued a mercantilist strategy to expand trade in goods and, more controversially, in human beings in the Atlantic slave trade – which was pursued by colonists in the West Indies and in North America. This aspect of Locke's political activity has ensured that his reputation as a universalist liberal has been challenged in discussions of the colonialist legacy of liberal ideas. Whether or not his fundamental moral and philosophical ideas can consistently support enslavement, he was certainly implicated as a functionary in supporting a regime that condoned slavery and the trade in Africans to North America. This fact might dent the argument that Locke's natural law liberalism lends itself to alignment with idealism, in contrast to Hobbes's alignment with realism. But the simple identification of Locke with idealism over realism misses an important element of his state theory and of his view of international politics.

Hobbes's idea of the state of nature as a state of war is taken as a simple paradigm of the realist view of states in the international system colliding in the absence of global sovereign imposing order. Locke is thought to be different because his view of the pre-political state is a legal and moral world where individuals contract into legitimate political communities in order to secure the enjoyment of their rights and liberties. This has the formal consequence that Locke's cosmopolitan order is one of a plurality of what we now call nation states securing individual rights in a settled jurisdiction and territory, and he is often credited with adding the idea of territoriality to Hobbes's abstract account of sovereignty. However, Locke's theory also has an historical sociological element that recognises that the state as a legitimate political society is not the same thing as a natural community. Natural communities that exercise coercive and absolute power are not the same things as states, and they mostly precede the development of legitimate states. These natural powers and societies can have different forms of coercive rule that force people to submit to them, but they are not in that respect legitimate political societies. The consequence of Locke's uncompromising account of legitimacy is a clear transfer of authority from the ruled to the ruler. This meant that many of the governments of the Europe of Locke's day were not actually legitimate states but simply collections of coerced peoples, or absolutist powers posing a threat to any legitimately constituted state. The Europe of Locke's day was not, therefore, a world of equal states under a law but without a common power to sanction it. Instead, it was a form of the state of nature in which multiple coercive powers existed alongside each other. Some of those powers can be internally focused and not pose a challenge to the Lockean state. They thus did not have a 'sedate setled Design' on the new regime of William III, which presumably Locke thought came close to his ideal because of their absolutist character and proximity other powers (such as France) did indeed pose such a threat of war. One immediate consequence in Locke's political practice was his support for war as a way of containing the unruly power of France on the European mainland, and for competition with France in the colonies in order to ensure trade for the advantage of English merchants. Locke saw trade as a way of spreading the material benefits of creation around the globe, so making goods available in England that climate and geography could not provide. Yet, it is important to remember that he was also essentially a mercantilist who saw trade as a zero-sum competition for wealth.

More importantly, at the level of international theory, Locke saw statehood as an achievement concept and not a natural fact of the international realm. Whereas the Hobbesian schema might be imposed on the plurality of competing powers in the world to give us the state system, for Locke the world was a mixed system of states and of other entities that are not states and have no equal normative or juridical standing. And this lack of standing is not merely a lack of historical development as later liberals might claim – such as John Stuart Mill, who argued that backward barbarisms (such as the Indian principalities under British tutelage) would eventually evolve into states. For Locke, the failing is not developmental but moral. Powers that are illegitimate could become legitimate but, until they do, they fall short of the objective moral order of rightly constituted political societies or states and, therefore, are open to moral challenge. As they technically breach the law of nature in involving illegitimate coercion, they are subject to the natural right to punish breaches of the law of nature derived from the executive power of the law of nature. This individual power is the basis of political right, and, in its transfer to a common judge in the process of a contract to establish civil power, it is given to the government to exercise on behalf of subjects, except where that power is too remote in emergencies or where the right of revolution is exercised against illegitimate rule.

A legitimate political society has a right to exercise that power on behalf of its people and under the federative power to exercise prudence in deciding when to go to war to punish breaches of the law. This condition has the consequence of staying the hand of rightly ordered states in a non-ideal world of illegitimate powers, because no state can have an obligation to ensure that *all* illegitimate coercive governments should be eradicated. However, this idea of international political prudence has precisely the same effect of realism in international affairs. Rightly ordered states have a reason, indeed an obligation, to act, to oppose illegitimate regimes in a precise parallel with Hobbesian states having a reason to go to war to secure an interest or to remove an enemy when they can.

This moralised international order under Locke's scheme opens up the prospect of war and conflict to accelerate the progress of legitimate political communities and the eradication of illegitimate powers that violate the rights of individuals wherever they happen to be. What is clearly missing in Locke's theory and what aligns his theory of the state system under natural law with realism is an international theory of toleration. There is no obligation to acknowledge the standing of regimes and powers that are not legitimate on Locke's theory, only a prudential judgement of when or if, in particular circumstances, to exercise the right of war and the executive power of the law of nature.

The implication of Locke's theory for international politics has been obscured because of the tendency to see his contribution in terms of trade and economic integration, and also because of his successors (such as Rousseau and Kant) being preoccupied with perpetual peace. Yet, Locke's account has remained a contribution to the liberal tradition in terms of what might be characterised as militant or warrior idealism. Conflict for peace and to end war, or to extirpate evils of various kinds, is as old as the Crusades of the Middle Ages, if not earlier. It has also had a more recent manifestation in the militant idealism that was associated with the War on Terror and regime change at the beginning of the new millennium. The end of the Cold War and the emergence of the USA as an unrivalled hegemon in the international realm led many neo-conservative thinkers who combined a militant belief in progress and a commitment to liberal democracy to see an opportunity for accelerating history's march by toppling illiberal undemocratic regimes using military interventions. Their underlying argument was a moral one based on the superiority of democracy as a regime, which was aligned with historical progress and development – misrepresenting Fukuyama's doctrine of the end of history as the triumph of liberal democracy over other regime types (Fukuyama 1992). As liberal democracy was the only good regime, by definition all other regime types were bad regimes and therefore potential enemies that need to be confronted. So this doctrine left no room for neutrality.

The logic of Locke's theory of the state has left this ambiguous and conflictual legacy in a position that is seen as the opposite pole to Hobbes-inspired realism. This tendency of liberalism and liberal internationalism to reveal itself as a fighting creed and a version of Christian millennialism is a particular preoccupation of mid-20th-century Christian realists such as Reinhold Niebuhr, who, whilst not averse to war, were particularly concerned about the idea of using war as a tool for human redemption. Locke's writings on religion and on toleration try to avoid a full-blown Manichean struggle between the forces of good (Protestantism) and the forces of evil (associated with the Pope and Catholicism). This was also precisely what Hobbes sought to avoid by submitting religion to the authority of the sovereign. Yet, the spectre of political Catholicism, especially as embodied in French political absolutism, was for Locke a threat that needed to be contained and confronted. Locke's challenge provides an echo of the way in which many militant liberal internationalists approached the threat of Communism during the Cold War, where the threat was not the doctrine itself but its embodiment in the expansionist absolutism of the USSR.

The Lockean legacy for standard international relations theory still sees the international realm as a realm of state activity, albeit states that are the agents of individual rights and interests. Alongside this view, recent international political theory has manifested a turn to Locke's fundamental moral individualism as part of the cosmopolitan turn that dispenses with the state as a moral agent. This is most strikingly manifest in the work of cosmopolitan just war theorists such as Cécile Fabre. In an extraordinary series of books, Fabre has sought to build a theory of just war on individualistic foundations: 'I articulate and defend an ethical account of war ... by taking as my starting point a political morality to which the individual, rather than the nation-state is central' (Fabre 2012, p. 2). She describes this as a cosmopolitan theory and its similarities with Locke's argument are striking, except that the foundation of her individualist premise does not have Locke's theistic underpinning.

In Fabre's case, as with Locke, the real moral or justificatory work is done by ethical individualism rather than by the contingent nature of political community, which is nothing more than a convenient vehicle for pursuing individual ends. As a consequence, Fabre's grounds for war, such as subsistence wars on behalf of the world's poor, or her explicit defence of an individual's right of war, also resemble and more importantly draw out the individualist implications of Locke's third-party right to punish breaches of the law of nature. In Locke scholarship, the troubling implications of this individualised right are usually overlooked by scholars contextualising Locke's argument. However, for Fabre these implications are celebrated as cosmopolitan rights and duties that are prior to political life and in her argument do not depend on intervening institutions such as the state. The impressive and comprehensive architecture of Fabre's argument – ranging from traditional issues of *jus ad bellum* and *jus in bello* to post-bellum obligations, and most recently the obligations and constraints on what she calls 'economic statecraft', such as sanctions regimes and boycotts – is undoubtedly impressive. But it has not been without criticism.

The fundamental problem underlying Fabre's edifice is the challenge of foundations. Whilst she does address the basis of her rights-based cosmopolitanism, much of the argument depends on the shared intuitions that we find in liberal philosophical culture, which are now no more widespread and certain than Locke's own foundations in Christian rationalism. At the level of philosophical justification, there is a case for appealing to a version of reflective equilibrium between the intuitions of a broadly individualist human rights culture and the implications of those intuitions in the theory, as a way of testing what we ultimately believe. Yet, this method raises a fundamental issue about moral individualism in international affairs. Cosmopolitans and Lockean libertarians have a weak or contingent commitment to the state. In some cases, they challenge it altogether, adopting the tough-minded Lockean position that any state is only morally relevant in so far as it is morally legitimate. In contrast, Kantian cosmopolitans, following an ancient tradition going back to Cicero, see the state or the political association as a necessary element within a cosmopolitan order (Flikschuh 2000). The problem with that cosmopolitan order is that it leaves the state as a necessary moral conception (or achieve-ment concept in terms of Lockean legitimacy) and as an historical and coercive political community that does not necessarily act or conceive of itself as a cos-mopolitan moral association.

The challenge for the cosmopolitan liberal is the relationship between the ideal of the state and the real world of nation states. Individualist cosmo-politans such as Fabre overcome this difficulty by wishing away the problem of the state or association beyond the individual and her claims. The criterion of moral legitimacy for Fabre is individual or human rights and this exhausts the moral terrain. Whilst the primacy of individual human rights does find echoes in the widespread culture of human rights since 1945, or in the more recent development of an international responsibility to protect (R2P), these trends and initiatives have not achieved global dominance. Nor is this just the result of the slow evolution of international affairs. A world made safe for rights in which there are only individuals with rights is a utopian vision so far removed from political experience that one can ask what benefit we derive from conceiving of it. Such a world is very far removed from the one in which we have to live, and the transitioning from the real to the ideal world would be exceedingly costly, even if that idea is thought desirable. The challenge of an individualised global moral order is a fundamental challenge to a liberal international order that is problematic enough. Even the USA, which is seen as, and often presents itself as, the guarantor of a broadly liberal global order, has been wary or even hostile to the extension of individual rights over states' rights, particularly in areas such as the International Criminal Court and global legalism (Posner 2011).

Critics claim that the challenge of Lockean internationalism is that it does not take the challenge of politics seriously. It reduces all issues to moral ones of right and wrong that can be addressed by moral and legal rules and duties. In consequence, it denies rather than responds to the fundamental premise of realists. It also has a further consequence that we can see in both its Lockean and its cosmopolitan variants. If all relevant issues are moralised, then politi-cal experience is reduced to assigning right and wrong and imposing punish-ments or sanctions on those individuals, states, communities and cultures that are wrong. If domestic politics and international affairs are reducible to the requirements of policing the international law (as the surrogate for Lockean natural law), then, rather than creating a 'peaceable kingdom', we create the conditions of instability and chaos that realist theories presuppose, and which was to become the preoccupation of Locke's successors Jean-Jacques Rousseau and Immanuel Kant in the 18th century. In the case of egregious violations of human rights (such as genocide or even just bloody civil wars), liberal orders appear to have an obligation to intervene, which, in the world we find ourselves in, may become a duty of permanent war. When this is coupled with disagreement about fundamental moral, natural or human rights, the individual's right to judge and duty to act creates the further problem of individual interventions in insurgencies or rebellions against unjust regimes.

In the absence of universally shared values, difference and diversity become potential sources of conflict and violence, precisely the problem that the modern European state system developed to try to manage in the 16th century. Whereas an important feature of that settlement was religious toleration, contemporary international liberalism and individualist cosmopolitanism does not have a theory of international toleration; instead, it has only a theory of trade. Locke placed much emphasis on the importance of trade as the principal international activity, as opposed to war. However, his successors tell different stories about how the human obsession with trade, and the journeys undertaken to secure it, contribute to building ties between peoples that unite them in pacific alliances of interest, or whether it is another stimulus for competition and conflict. The question is whether Locke and the liberal internationalism that he inspires is merely a new front in the conflictual international order that the realists predict.

Bibliography

Essential reading

Locke, John. [1690] (1988). *Two Treatises of Government*, ed. P. Laslett. UK: Cambridge University Press.

Secondary reading

Armitage, David. (2012a). *Foundations of Modern International Thought*. UK: Cambridge University Press.

Armitage, David. (2012b). 'John Locke: Theorist of Empire?' in S. Muthu (ed.) *Empire and Modern Political Thought*. UK: Cambridge University Press, pp. 84–111.

Armitage, David. (2017). *Civil Wars: A History in Ideas*. UK: Yale University Press.

Arneil, Barbara. (1996). *John Locke and America*. UK: Clarendon Press.

Ashcraft, Richard. (1986). *Revolutionary Politics and Locke's Two Treatises of Government*. USA: Princeton University Press.

Boucher, David. (2005). 'Property and Propriety in International Relations: The Case of John Locke', in B. Jahn (ed.) *Classical Theory in International Relations*. UK: Cambridge University Press, pp. 156–177.

Buchanan, Allan. (1991). *Secession: The Morality of Political Divorce from Fort Sumpter to Lithuania and Quebec*. USA: Westview.

Doyle, Michael W. (1997). *Ways of War and Peace*. USA: Norton.

Fabre, Cécile. (2012). *Cosmopolitan War*. UK: Oxford University Press.

Fabre, Cécile. (2016). *Cosmopolitan Peace*. UK: Oxford University Press.

Fabre, Cécile. (2018). *Economic Statecraft*. USA: Harvard University Press.

Finlay, Christopher. (2019). *Is Just War Possible?* UK: Polity Press.

Flikschuh, Katrin. (2000). *Kant and Modern Political Philosophy*. UK: Cambridge University Press.

Frazer, Elizabeth; and Hutchings, Kimberly. (2020). *Violence and Political Theory*. UK: Polity Press.

Fukuyama, Francis. (1992). *The End of History and the Last Man*. USA: Free Press.

Goldwin, Robert A. (1987). 'John Locke', in Leo Strauss and Joseph Cropsey (eds) *History of Political Philosophy*, 3rd edn. USA: University of Chicago Press, pp. 476–512.

Ikenberry, G. John. (2012). *Liberal Leviathan: The Origins, Crisis, and Transformations of the American World Order*. USA: Princeton University Press.

Ikenberry, G. John. (2020). *A World Safe for Democracy*. USA: Yale University Press.

Ivison, D. (2010). *Postcolonial Liberalism*. UK: Cambridge University Press.

Ivison, D. (2019). *Can Liberal States Accommodate Indigenous Peoples*. UK: Polity Press.

Kelly, Paul. (2005). *Liberalism*. UK: Polity.

Kelly, Paul. (2007). *Locke's Second Treatise of Government*. UK: Continuum.

Kelly, Paul. (2015). 'Armitage on Locke on International Theory: The Two Treatises of Government and the Right of Intervention', *History of European Ideas*, vol. 41, pp. 49–61.

Keohane, Robert; and Nye. Joseph. (1977). *Power and Interdependence*. USA: Little, Brown.

Macpherson, Crawford B. (1962). *The Political Theory of Possessive Individualism*. UK: Oxford University Press.

McMahan, Jeff. (2009). *Killing in War*. UK: Clarendon Press.

Moore, Margaret. (2015). *The Political Theory of Territory*. UK: Oxford University Press.

Pincus, Steven. (2009). *1688: The First Modern Revolution*. USA: Yale.

Simmons, A. John. (1993). *On the Edge of Anarchy: Locke, Consent and the Limits of Society*. USA: Princeton University Press.

Ward, Lee. (2010). *Locke on Modern Life*. UK: Cambridge University Press.

Wendt, Alexander. (1999). *Social Theory of International Politics*. UK: Cambridge University Press.

Woolhouse, Roger. (2009). *Locke: A Biography*. UK: Cambridge University Press.

Suggestions for finding open access versions of John Locke's texts

Online Library of Liberty, maintained by the Liberty Fund
   https://oll.libertyfund.org/person/john-locke
Also see the Digital Locke Project http://www.digitallockeproject.nl/
The Digital Locke Project presents the first complete text critical edition, based
   on John Locke's manuscripts, of the texts that are related to his most famous
   work, *An Essay Concerning Human Understanding*. The DLP concentrates
   on the material that was produced between the first edition of the *Essay* in
   1689 and Locke's death in 1704.
At the time of writing, there was also a sample of the same edition Professor
   Kelly recommends at:
   http://assets.cambridge.org/97805210/69038/sample/9780521069038ws.pdf

CHAPTER 7

Rousseau

The threat of the international order

In Rousseau's writings, and his influence on international thought and theory, the central concept is sovereignty and its political and international implications. Rousseau focuses on the idea of popular sovereignty, that is, how the concept of sovereign power can be maintained and exercised collectively by a free sovereign people who remain free citizens. In this respect, it is a criticism and a development of the concept as deployed by Hobbes or by Locke.

Rousseau is critical of the concept of state sovereignty as a distinct juridical or law-like entity. Instead, he argues that sovereignty is a power of a people acting in accordance with a general will. In order to be a sovereign people, the citizens need to think of themselves as more than a multitude or collection of individuals trying to secure and protect their private interests. To maintain that idea of a sovereign general will, the people need a strong conception of identity, and to avoid the corrupting power of commercial society and cosmopolitan engagement.

Rousseau's arguments are a precursor of an inward-looking nationalism and anti-cosmopolitanism that has seen a recent recurrence in anti-globalisation movements, political and economic nationalism, national solidarity and the rise of identity politics.

How to cite this book chapter:
Kelly, Paul. 2022. *Conflict, war and revolution: The problem of politics in international political thought.* London: LSE Press, pp. 213–260.
DOI: https://doi.org/10.31389/lsepress.cwr.g License: CC BY.

> My purpose is to consider if, in political society, there can be *any legitimate and sure principle of government, taking men as they are and laws as they might be.* (Rousseau, *The Social Contract*)

Not that long ago, political thinkers and pundits were claiming that the world was entering a new period in which markets would slowly overtake the power of states and we would move into a new global civilisation. This optimism partly followed the collapse of really existing socialism in the USSR in 1991 (Fukuyama 1992). But it had a much deeper root in an amalgam of ideas that had circulated since World War II and which came to fruition in the idea of neo-liberalism or globalisation. These two ideas are not identical, because there have been 'left theories' of globalisation (Held 2005), but they overlap considerably. Both see the extension of global markets and the integration of trade, finance and communications as the irrevocable direction of historical progress.

The neo-liberals, drawing on the ideas of thinkers such as Friedrich Hayek (Hayek 1944; 1960), argue that the market is the only appropriate explanation and system for delivering human well-being, and that it must be protected from distortions created by state activism in the marketplace. Since the rise of Margaret Thatcher in the UK and Ronald Reagan in the USA, this neo-liberal orthodoxy has resulted in pro-market policies of privatisation in domestic politics and the trade liberalisation increasingly breaking down economic borders and culminating in such wider areas as the North American Free Trade Area (NAFTA) and the single market of the European Union. The process of economic integration accelerated as national borders ceased to be barriers to trade in goods or obstacles to the mobility of capital, while in the case of the EU labour could also move across borders. With the subsequent reforms of Deng Xiaoping and the marketisation of the Chinese economy, from the 1990s onwards the triumph of globalisation appeared to have established itself as a global phenomenon, independent of any particular ideological configuration of the state.

The rise of China in the globalised economic order is one of the most striking features of contemporary politics. It challenges one of the fundamental premises of classical liberal free trade theories, but not neo-liberal globalisation. Since the time of Adam Smith (Smith 1776) through to the classic account of Hayek (Hayek 1960), the connection between soft or constitutional government and open markets has been asserted as the condition of economic growth and well-being. Indeed, some commentators have even argued that there is an historical necessity such that opening markets must result in opening political society, and open political societies requires open or free economies. In this account, Smith and Hayek have uncovered the laws of history. The experience of China and contemporary Singapore have become challenges to this simplistic argument. More recently, some thinkers have begun to doubt that the necessity ever made sense, and argue that neo-liberal progressivism was always more of a faith than a reality (Gray 1998; Streeck 2016). In his book *False Dawn* (1998), John Gray aims his fire at the political economy of globalism. More recently, he has set his sights on the associated progressive optimism of those who claim that history is delivering the Enlightenment hope of a more humane and pacific world order (Pinker 2011; 2018) or (to use the phrase of Martin Luther King, repeated by Barack Obama) claim that 'the arc of the universe is long but it bends towards justice'.

Not only has this neo-liberal and Enlightenment optimism been subject to criticism but most recently it has faced a major historical as well as political challenge from the legacy of the 2008 financial crisis and the subsequent rise of economic nationalism and populism – as a result of the economic response to 2008. The 'austerity' agenda in Europe and the attempt by states to prioritise securing global finance has culminated in major challenges to economic globalisation. The Brexit referendum in 2016 and the election of President Donald Trump (with his 'America First' agenda) saw a significant rise in economic nationalism. Countries began retreating from the global order of neo-liberalism in favour of emphasising borders, immigration controls, tariffs and trade wars amongst great powers – precisely the mess that characterised the inter-war period and which inspired the realist critique of idealism by the historian E.H. Carr (Carr 1939). In the UK, the immediate impact of the Brexit process was a withdrawal agreement limiting cooperation and ending the free movement of goods, services and people within the European single market. As political thinkers confronted this historical 'U-turn' in the progress towards a globalised world, they started to see some seeds of this collapse within the very processes of neo-liberal globalisation (with its emphasis on the free movement of capital, goods and labour) and not just the post-2008 austerity agenda. Gray and Streeck argue that globalisation undercuts the cultural presuppositions of the economic order it arises from. And along the way it unleashes political demons that challenge the dominance of western Enlightenment values and progress celebrated by thinkers such as Steven Pinker (2018).

In this context, the ideas of the 18th-century French polymath Jean-Jacques Rousseau emerge as extraordinarily prescient. The 18th century saw the consolidation of European power following the chaos and religious wars of the 17th century, with the rise of the major European powers and empires and the intellectual ferment of the European Enlightenment. Rousseau was part of the enlightened intellectual culture, but he was also one of its most profound critics – understanding the inherent contradictions in the society and intellectual culture of Europe between the end of the European wars of religion and the French Revolution, with its assertion of liberty, equality and fraternity, and the rights of man and the citizen.

Rousseau is one of the most profound critics of social contract theory, whilst also being one of its great exemplars, alongside Hobbes and Locke. He is one of the seminal theorists of liberty at the same time as being considered by some to be a proto-totalitarian (Talmon 1986). And he is undoubtedly a major theorist of democracy. He wrote on many subjects from the origin of languages to botany, and was a significant novelist and writer of operas, as well as making major contributions to western political theory by revolutionising familiar concepts such as sovereignty, the individual and democracy. For our purposes, as an international political theorist, he provides one of the most radical critiques of the international state system that, as we saw, is a legacy of Hobbes. And in doing so he opens up an anti-cosmopolitan theory of international politics that both asserts the primacy of the individual whilst also inspiring the communitarianism and nationalism that has shaped the ongoing struggle between political and economic nationalism, on the one hand, and justice and the universal claims of individuals, on the other.

Throughout this book we are addressing new paradigms of politics that shape the way we think about the international realm. Rousseau is just as original as other thinkers, but he is also closely intertwined with the ideas of Thomas Hobbes and John Locke. So these three chapters can be connected in a way that is different from others in this book. The link is the concept of sovereignty that is central to all three thinkers, as well as the individualist account of sovereign power. But, for all this overlap, and to the extent to which Rousseau is deliberately addressing Hobbes's arguments (as well as those of Grotius, Pufendorf and Locke), he is also criticising the account of sovereignty and its implications in the international sphere. Hobbes leaves open questions about the international realm either as a society or as an antagonistic system of competitive states, and Locke leaves open the right of individuals to exercise their private right towards illegitimate powers. By contrast, Rousseau is very clear about the kind of international realm that emerges from state sovereignty or close alternatives such as national sovereignty that so preoccupy the rhetoric of international politics in the 21st century. Whilst it is always important to remember historical distance and Skinner's (1998) 'myth of prolepsis' (seeing later ideas pre-empted in an earlier age), when one looks at Rousseau's account of the logic of the state system and his assault on the alternative of global cosmopolitanism, it is almost as if he were participating in the debate about the future of globalisation or the terms of contemporary international political theory (Brown 2002; Caney 2005).

The life and writings of an 'extraordinary thinker'

Like Augustine, Rousseau is also the author of a work called *The Confessions* (Rousseau [1770] 1953) and, like Augustine, he makes his own psychological formation one of the cornerstones of his philosophical and social theory. Rousseau underwent a conversion to Catholicism and then a form of reconversion to his previous Protestant faith. So the issue of introspection and self-formation echoed Augustine's own struggle for true self-understanding, and thus their similarities should perhaps not be surprising. However, there the similarities end. Rousseau's philosophy is centred around the claims of the individual as an autonomous being of equal value with other autonomous individuals, a fact that bears some resemblance with the contractarian individualism of Hobbes but which also could not be more different. Rousseau's thought is about the quest for individuality, and, as his late and posthumously published works *The Confessions* and *Reveries of a Solitary Walker* show, this was not just a philosophical endeavour but a personal one, making his autobiography peculiarly important to his thought in a way that is not true for many thinkers of the Enlightenment period.

Jean-Jacques was born in Geneva in 1712 to a modest family, although his mother came from a former patrician family. His mother died following the birth and he was brought up by his father who was a watch-maker – a skilled artisan. The Geneva of Rousseau's birth had since 1541 been the home of Calvinism. Jean Calvin (1509–1564) was one of the leading figures of the Protestant Reformation and the founder of the Presbyterian strand of Protestantism that contrasted with the Anglicanism of the Church of England or the Lutheranism of Germany and northern Europe. Calvin, who had originally been trained as a lawyer, was deeply influenced by Augustine and his views of predestination. Whilst his theology shaped the tradition of Presbyterianism and independent congregationalist Church governance that inspired the Puritans of England and subsequently New England, he also had views on the Church as a full political society, which he realised in the city of Geneva. Geneva was not simply a free imperial city but a Presbyterian polity following structures of government that Calvin set out in the *Institutes of the Christian Religion* (Calvin 1531). Whilst it served as a manual of reformed theology, this text also set out an account of Christian liberty and the structure of the Church. Whilst it offered a democratic form of Church government, it also undermined the idea of categorically separate spheres of life. The civil powers of the government of Geneva were integral to the powers of the reformed Christian community of Geneva – there was no separation between Church and state, even in the attenuated form that existed under the 'two powers' (*regnum*, or the right to exercise political force, and *sacerdotium*, or priestly power) of medieval Catholic political theory.

It was into this strictly governed moral, political and legal order that Rousseau was born. However, in the 250 years between Calvin's *Institutes* and Rousseau's birth, much of the original democratic structure of Church and political life had been replaced with a more oligarchic version of government, which located more and more authority in the hands of a smaller group of leaders. The Petit Conseil, which exercised real executive power, comprised 25 members. As with many republics, the ideal and the reality remained in considerable tension. That said, the ideal of a free political community was to remain central to Rousseau's political thought.

Rousseau had no formal education, but was introduced to reading the classics (especially Plutarch) by his father. Following a violent quarrel, his father was forced to flee Geneva, and Rousseau was sent to live with a pastor named Lambercier, who is most famous for introducing Rousseau to corporal punishment. He was subsequently apprenticed to a master whose brutality caused Rousseau to run away and begin the itinerant lifestyle that was to be his destiny. An early and influential experience came when Rousseau was adopted by Madame de Warens, the widow of a Catholic convert. Madame de Warens took him into her home and eventually her bed. Under her influence, he became a convert to Catholicism, following a period of domestic service in Turin. His time as a domestic servant was not happy and helped shape his lifelong aversion to relationships of dependence and domination. However, his time with Madame de Warens was happy and, apart from other comforts, gave him access to a considerable library that enabled him to cultivate his broad and prodigious intellect.

After a decade under her care, Rousseau launched himself into French literary society and started to make friends with many of the leading figures of the time. In 1742 he befriended Denis Diderot (1713–1784), co-founder of the *Encyclopedie*, which was to play such an important role in French intellectual life in the period prior to the French Revolution. Between 1743 and 1744 he also served as a secretary to the French Ambassador to Venice. In 1745 he also began his lifelong relationship with Thérèse Levasseur, the woman who was to bear him five children, all of whom were quickly dispatched to orphanages. Thérèse was uneducated but loyal and accompanied Rousseau for the rest of his days, eventually becoming his wife.

However, it was Rousseau's literary output on which his contemporary, and subsequent, reputation depended. Although he is now known as a great political theorist, his early works were on music and musicology, subjects on which he contributed to the *Encyclopedie*. His interest in music was not just theoretical; he earned money as a copyist of musical manuscripts and he wrote an important opera, *Le Devin du Village* (1752), which gained considerable fame. His philosophical fame began when he entered a prize essay competition hosted by the Academy of Dijon on whether the development of the arts and sciences had been morally advantageous ('Has the restoration of the sciences and arts tended to purify morals?') – the idea being to celebrate the progress of Enlightenment. Rousseau's prize-winning *Discourse on the Arts and Science* (1749) takes the contrary view, arguing that the advancement of science and knowledge offered by the Enlightenment had actually led to moral corruption and weakening of civilisation and culture. That essay won first prize and its eventual companion, the *Discourse on Inequality* (Rousseau 1755), won second prize in a later competition. Both mounted an attack on the political ideas of the Enlightenment period as exemplified by Grotius, Pufendorf, Hobbes and Locke. The 1750s saw the culmination of his major political writings with the essay *The Social Contract* and *Emile*, a treatise on education and self-culture. He also published a novel, *Julie: The New Héloise*, which became the most popular French novel of its time.

Yet, as his philosophical career flourished, another aspect of his character was to emerge at the same time, namely his almost paranoid sensitivity, one of the less attractive aspects of his character. Rousseau began significant intellectual feuds with the likes of Voltaire, or his former close associates such as D'Alembert and Diderot. These degenerated into actual feuds, which, coupled with his paranoia, required him to flee Paris and then France. He was primarily concerned that those like Voltaire were determined to destroy his reputation. His worries were not wholly baseless, as the banning and public burning of *The Social Contract* and *Emile* (by the Catholic authorities in Paris and the Calvinist authorities in Geneva) confirmed that he was at serious risk. As a fugitive from justice, Rousseau moved to Neuchatel in Switzerland and then in 1766 to England under the protection and support of the Scottish philosopher David Hume. Rousseau settled in Wootton in Staffordshire. Hume was justly famous for his generosity and equanimity, but Rousseau became convinced that Hume was in league with his persecutors, much to Hume's disappointment and pain. Throughout this period, Rousseau continued to write, although not necessarily publish, and he completed his political theory with the application of a regime of equality to different types of society in *The Constitution of Corsica* (Rousseau 1765) and *The Government of Poland* (Rousseau 1771). Both of these works show that Rousseau's philosophy of the general will was no mere utopia but the basis of an egalitarian regime that could exist under certain social conditions. These works also demonstrate that the challenges to a free political community were external. They emphasise the extent to which international relations was an intimate part of his political thought and not simply a further implication of an essentially domestic view of politics, as had been the case with Hobbes.

After the unfortunate break with Hume, Rousseau eventually agreed not to publish further and was able to return to France in 1767. He spent the rest of his life, with Thérèse, studying botany and composing the late autobiographical works such as *The Confessions* (1770) and *Reveries of a Solitary Walker* (1776–1778). His work had always had an autobiographical tone, even when this was partly obscured, as with the 'Profession of Faith of the Savoyard Vicar' in *Emile*. These last works are essential to understanding Rousseau's conception of the individual and his struggle for autonomy that is one of his great legacies to later thought. In 1778 Rousseau suffered a stroke and died.

His subsequent legacy, as an influence on the Romantic movement through artists such as Wordsworth and Goethe, was complicated by the legacy of the French Revolution. Rousseau's undoubtedly revolutionary thought was quickly co-opted into the actual Revolution when his body was transported to Paris in 1794 and interred in the Pantheon. Many of the leading figures of the Revolution (such as Robespierre) had been influenced by Rousseau's ideas, and he was claimed by many factions such as the Jacobins and eventually Napoleon Bonaparte. For subsequent thinkers, this association with a revolution that he did not predict, and which occurred more than 10 years after his death, has coloured his reputation. For thinkers of a conservative disposition, Rousseau is indelibly tainted by the Revolution's excesses, and he was even co-opted by some authors as a founder of the anti-liberal tradition that led to totalitarianism in the 20th century (Talmon 1986). Even some iconic 20th-century liberals such as Isaiah Berlin, who does not go as far as Talmon, nevertheless saw Rousseau's account of 'positive' freedom as a precarious basis for liberal freedom (Berlin 1998). That said, perhaps the most important English-speaking liberal philosopher of the 20th century, John Rawls, took surprising inspiration from Rousseau, especially with respect to the place of a liberal just state in the international order – a philosophical problem that brings us back to the challenges of globalism and economic nationalism.

How should one read Rousseau? One can take a number of perspectives on his work. For some he is a philosopher, but with a curious style. Rawls makes the point that Rousseau's style is something that persists even when he is read in translation (Rawls 2008, p. 192). This is partly the result of the autobiographical and self-exploratory dimension of his thought, even in his most philosophical writings, such as the *Discourses* and *The Social Contract*. But Rawls insists that underlying that personal style there is the familiar logical structure of argument that one would expect from a philosopher; one just needs to read him carefully. However, that is not the only challenge, as, like many great thinkers, Rousseau's works do not all seem to be consistent. For example, he offers a penetrating critique of the social contract tradition of Hobbes, Locke and Pufendorf in the *Second Discourse*, whilst also offering one of the classic social contract theories in another book. Perhaps we should not expect consistency across texts and see each one in its own right. But, given Rousseau's tendency to contextualise his own thinking through engagement with contemporary debates, such as those around the *Plan for Perpetual Peace of the Abbe St. Pierre* (Rousseau 1756), or their interconnection in his autobiographical narrative, it is not wholly persuasive to see each work as an historically discrete artefact, and not part of a single mind engaging with itself and the world.

A further challenge, which I will state and leave unresolved, is the problem of irony in his work. Judith Shklar famously argues that his social contract theory is not to be seen as a philosophical system, even one buried beneath a personal style, as her Harvard colleague Rawls claimed. Instead, Rousseau is an ironist and a utopian, holding up a mirror to the world to challenge what it can be (Shklar 1985). This relieves Rousseau of the demands of rigorous consistency and allows for an ambiguity about which of those positions he states he also actually endorses. At the same time, it makes him a more important, striking and original thinker. Rousseau's ambiguity is precisely what renders his challenge to Hobbes and the juridical contractarians so forceful, precisely because it introduces the element of real-world ambiguity that abstract rationalism tries to eradicate in its search for certainty and precision: a certainty and precision that the real world of politics can never provide.

The Enlightenment and the 18th-century international order

The period of just over a century between the publication of Hobbes's *Leviathan* and Rousseau's *Social Contract* was an extraordinary time of intellectual and political ferment. It is the high point of the European Enlightenment, which saw the extraordinary development of science and philosophy that became the self-satisfied subject of the Academy of Dijon's essay competition. For all its ferocity, the Thirty Years War brought an end to the major religious wars that had marked the century from the European Reformation of Luther and Calvin to the time of Hobbes and the end of the English Civil War. Although it by no means turned Europe into a land of peace and stability, it did allow for the cultural and political rebuilding that ensured the subsequent of growth of philosophy and modern natural science.

The publication of Isaac Newton's (1642–1727) *Principia Mathematica* in 1687 transformed the new science of Galileo and his peers into the modern system of physics that was to dominate until the early 20th century. Newton's mathematical model of the solar system (as the universe) and his derivation of the basic laws of physics, were seen as huge cultural moments that lifted the veil of creation and revealed a rational order to the universe that could be comprehended in a relatively few simple equations. Newton was also one of the inventors of calculus (along with Gottfried Leibniz (1646–1716), with whom he competed for the honour), which provided the mathematical notation by which his laws could be expressed and proved. Modern science has many sources but with Newton a recognisable model of scientific enquiry was developed that would shape the way in which all future claims to knowledge could be vindicated.

Rationalism associated with Leibniz had earlier roots, yet drew its support from the abstract and deductive example of Newton's mathematical physics, as opposed to the empiricism of the English philosopher John Locke, who sought to vindicate Newton's abstract theories by comparing them to human experience and which influenced later Enlightenment thinkers such as David Hume (1711–1776). The conflict between the relative claims of rationalists and empiricists was to dominate Enlightenment philosophy as well as science. Yet, in both cases the model of science as experimental and rational distinguished it from the previous world of religious authority, now associated with the old order of conflict and ignorance. Enlightenment became a new religion, but one liberated from the narrow authority of priests and authorities. And it was this ethic of Enlightenment that shaped the intellectual culture of the early 18th century and its dominant political philosophy, as much as its physical science.

Enlightenment political thought – Pufendorf and Montesquieu

The dominant political philosophy of the late 17th and early 18th centuries was shaped by the new Enlightenment confidence in reason and in reason's claim to provide not only the basis of knowledge but the basis of obligation and law. This is most clearly exemplified in one of the most significant political philosophers of the late 17th and early 18th centuries, Samuel von Pufendorf. Unlike Hobbes or Locke, he is now only read by specialist historians of thought. Although Hobbes had begun the modern social contract tradition and the juridical account of sovereignty (see Chapter 5), his subsequent legacy in Europe was mostly as a materialist metaphysician, whose political theory was overshadowed by the much more influential theories of Locke (see Chapter 6) and Pufendorf, although both took some inspiration from Hobbes.

Samuel von Pufendorf (1632–1694) was a German legal theorist who held a series of academic posts across the various principalities that made up 17th-century Germany. He wrote a major commentary on the work of Hugo Grotius (1583–1645), the Dutch jurist and a contemporary of Hobbes, which was to serve as one of the foundation texts of international law. He distilled his basic response to Grotius's teaching into *De Officio Hominis et Civis* (*The Duty of Man and Citizens*), a 1679 book that was to become one of the most important works of legal and political theory in the 18th century. It influenced Rousseau and Immanuel Kant and many of the American Founders. As an academic and a systematic writer (unlike Hobbes, Grotius or Locke), Pufendorf provided the intellectual curriculum for the study of international law and public law. Like Grotius and Hobbes, Pufendorf derives the idea of sovereignty from the pre-social rights of individuals who constitute themselves as a body politic or political community through a contract or binding agreement that transfers right from the individual to the state as a territorially constituted political entity, and it is through the combination of private possession of property that the territoriality of political communities was created. This emphasis on property, territoriality and sovereignty was either missing or only immanent in Grotius and Hobbes, but it become central to the ideas of Pufendorf. As with Hobbes and Pufendorf on the sovereign state, so both Pufendorf and Locke deploy the concept to pre-political property rights to explain territoriality, as a juridical notion derived from a transfer of individual rights.

The idea of a political community as a juridical entity derived from a pre-political natural law was to shape much of the political language of the 18th century, including the growth of international law as a way of regulating the relationships between juridical states. Unlike in Pufendorf's work, the place of international law in Locke's theory is obscure, albeit not wholly absent (Chapter 6; Kelly 2015). Yet, whilst dominant, natural jurisprudence was not the only significant language of political thought in the early 18th century. Natural jurisprudence had always speculated about the historical origin of political communities and states. Given that Pufendorf and Locke acknowledged significant sociability in their view of the state of nature, in contrast to Hobbes, with property, trade and money exchange, it was only natural that historical and developmental theories would arise explaining the historical as opposed to juridical origins of society, government and moral practices. The Dutch jurist Hugo Grotius had begun his account of a law of nature by noting that society was always present, a fact reinforced in the 'discovery' of new worlds, where some version of society was always encountered, even if, as in the Americas, this was often disparaged as primitive. For Grotius, this natural fact became the basis for his philosophical speculations on the conditions of sociability. For later natural historians of society in the 18th century, such as Montesquieu (1689–1755), the fact of different versions of 'society' became the basis for historical and anthropological speculation about the natural history and difference of societies. Montesquieu's works the *Persian Letters* (1721) and his magisterial *The Spirit of the Laws* (1748) marked a significant departure from the natural jurisprudence of Locke and Pufendorf and were to have an equally important influence on Rousseau and his immediate context.

The *Persian Letters* are written as the correspondence between two Persian travellers in Paris and their Persian home. They allow Montesquieu to reflect on French politics and the rise of political absolutism from the perspective of outsiders. They are both a warning and a brilliant critique of the political absolutism of the French monarchy and the philosophical defence of absolutism in Hobbes's *Leviathan*. The wonderful parable of the Troglodites, a people who are pure egoists with no social motives, is a brilliant critique of Hobbes's state of nature. The Troglodites' indifference to each other and their inability to cooperate lead not to a leviathan but to their dying out in a plague, because they are unwilling to take the advice of physicians. (This story takes on a peculiar poignancy as I write this in the UK's Covid–19 pandemic.)

Montesquieu's *Letters* also use the idea of the 'harem', which is riven by favouritism and intrigue as a model of the dangers of absolutist despotism, a recurring concern of his writings. The *Persian Letters* are part satire of the French monarchy and aristocracy, but they are also a reflection on a type of government that he sees as prevalent in different political cultures – such as those of the Ottoman, Persian and Chinese Empires. In doing this, Montesquieu helps himself to a lot of what has become known as 'colonialist' and 'orientalist' prejudices about these complex cultures (Osterhammel 2018). The ideological and cultural privileging of different civilisations was to become a central element of political thinking in the later 18th and 19th centuries, with the growth of modern trading empires.

The theme of absolutism is also important in Montesquieu's account of different types of government in his major political work *The Spirit of the Laws*, in which the concept of 'laws' is interpreted very widely to include morals, mores and cultural norms, as well as municipal laws and constitutions. Montesquieu sought to root the 'spirit' or the differences in these sources of authority in such things as national character, religion, culture, geography and climate. In this way, he explained why different regimes of law develop in different places and why these regimes are peculiarly suited to different contexts. Such materialist reductionism is taken up by later thinkers to argue for the appropriateness of Protestant forms of Christianity in northern Europe and Catholicism in southern Europe. More controversially, it was used to 'justify' why slavery is a necessary solution to the problem of labour in some climates, and also 'appropriate' for some peoples. Montesquieu does not defend racial slavery, but his arguments open theoretical opportunities for those who do precisely that in the racial theories of the next century.

Montesquieu's typology of political constitutions and regimes, particularly his preference for the balance of powers he finds in the British constitution (which of course is not a written constitution) was to provide many targets of criticism in Rousseau's account of sovereignty in *The Social Contract*. But, alongside his accounts of regimes, Montesquieu also claims that the rise of commercial societies that elevate the idea of 'luxury' and trade between states has a long-term pacific impact. Princes come to compete over luxuries and not through battles and military honour, while the interconnection of states is boosted as a result of trade and capital mobility. The idea that trade tends to encourage peace has become a platitude of international thinking from the 18th century to the present. It became one of the pillars of classical liberal political economy, although it should be noted that Adam Smith was much more sceptical about trade and peace. Whereas Smith was sceptical about the tendency of commercial societies towards cooperation and pacific relations, Rousseau was an even more forceful critic than Smith. He saw commercial society as one of the major negative threats to the modern state system and this is a good starting point for our discussion of his international political thought.

The European state system during the Enlightenment

The Westphalian settlement of 1648 marked the end of the confessional wars of the previous century and a half that had scarred northern Europe, but it certainly did not bring a period of stable peace to the subsequent century spanning the time from Hobbes's *Leviathan* to Rousseau's *Social Contract*. What emerged was a period of conflict and struggle for dominance amongst the new powers of the European continent, and eventually the extension of those European disputes to the wider world through the European empires. The conflicts that persisted retained a confessional element, not least in the struggle between England and France (and, following the unification of England and Scotland in 1707, between Britain and France). Yet, religion was quickly displaced by national and imperial interests, as witnessed in the complex struggle between two Catholic powers France and the Habsburg Holy Roman Empire in the War of the Spanish Succession (1701–1714). Whilst the Treaty of Westphalia is supposed to have ushered in a new world of sovereign states, these states were anything but equal in power, whatever their juridical claims to authority. In the years immediately following Westphalia, the dominant powers were France (under the Bourbons) and the Holy Roman Empire (under the Habsburgs), each positioning for dominance on the European mainland. Alongside these were mercantile powers such as the Dutch Republic, which increasingly saw its interests lying in its extra-European empire. From the fall of the Commonwealth at the end of the Civil War to the subsequent fall of the Stuart Restoration in 1688, England was a peripheral power, only occasionally intervening on the European mainland. Yet, within a short time, by the end of the 17th century, it was to amalgamate with Scotland and emerge as a significant naval power, displacing the position of the Dutch and challenging the French.

The War of the Spanish Succession arose out of a dispute between the Bourbons and the Habsburgs over the claim to the Spanish throne, but it was primarily viewed as an opportunity for one of their empires to establish pre-eminence on the European mainland. The war involved alliances that engaged all of Europe's powers. It was a major and vicious struggle ranging from set-piece European battles such as Blenheim, where the British general the Duke of Marlborough was victorious, to protracted campaigns in the North American colonies between the British, French and Native American allies, and naval battles in the West Indies and the East Indies involving the Dutch versus Britain. By the end of the struggle, France had been contained behind secure borders; the Dutch had been significantly weakened and were being replaced as an imperial and naval power by the British; and the Spanish were reduced to an insignificant European power, although they retained their empire in the Americas.

The redrawing of boundaries and alliances, as well as the positioning of major land powers or naval powers such as Great Britain, established a precarious balance between the main blocs, with the great powers as its guarantors. The concept of the balance of powers was to become an important feature of thinking about international politics in the period leading up to Rousseau's major writings. These powers were protective of their spheres of influence and they exercised some dominance in the politics of the minor allied powers. For many smaller principalities and states, their sovereignty was at best conditional, to the extent that David Hume (1752) saw similarities with the politics of Thucydidean Greece, where Athens and Sparta served as the dominant powers. The European powers of the 18th century also developed a sophisticated military technology and accelerated the development of modern military organisation that was to shape the 18th and 19th centuries. However, at the same time, war remained a brutal and vicious activity with an enormous cost in terms of lives and treasure.

In addition to wars across central and western Europe and in the European colonial possessions, other struggles continued to challenge the boundaries of Europe as both a political and civilisational conflict. The Reformation had internalised military conflict within Christianity between Catholicism and the new Protestant states and republics in a way which finally defeated the idea of Christendom as a political entity. Nevertheless, the challenge posed to Christian Europe from the Ottoman Empire as a last great Islamic political power continued until 1683, when the Siege of Vienna was lifted by Polish and Habsburg forces under the command of the Polish King John Sobieski. The subsequent withdrawal of Ottoman forces from the Danube opened a new period of regime change and state building in central and eastern Europe, although the Ottomans continued to dominate south-eastern Europe for the next two centuries. The external cultural challenge and military threat of the Ottoman Empire thus remained even in the new order of western powers and sovereign states and continued to inspire many thinkers to canvass schemes for perpetual peace. These aimed not simply to eradicate war but also to reorient the focus of conflict from internal territorial disputes within Europe to external and civilisational threats (Hinsley 1962 p. 34).

Plans for developing a lasting peace and international federations to consolidate the position of the major powers became an important new body of political literature that was to shape Rousseau's intellectual world, notably the *Perpetual Peace* (1712) of the Abbe St Pierre (see the next section). Such schemes of federation, with great powers enforcing a guarantee of peace amongst states, were an increasingly common feature of late 17th- and early 18th-century political thinking. Whilst Hobbes's theory of the distinct sovereign state was possibly appropriate for an island kingdom with clear territorial boundaries (ignoring for the moment the complex relationships with Scotland and Ireland, which do not feature in Hobbes's thought), it was more controversial on the European continent, where even the major powers had contested and permeable borders. In this context, the problem of sovereignty was always a claim within a context of proximate and contesting sovereignties, so that the idea of an international system or even federation was always part of Continental thought about the emergence of modern sovereign state.

The final significant feature of the international politics of Enlightenment Europe was the rise of new powers, notably the rise of Great Britain as a major naval and imperial power in the period following the Glorious Revolution of 1688. However, in terms of its impact over the next three centuries, perhaps the most important new power in European politics was the rise of Prussia. Prussia developed from a minor principality, focused on the Baltic Sea and operating in the shadow of the much larger Kingdom of Poland–Lithuania, to a major military power, whose influence and might was still in its greatest period of expansion during Rousseau's lifetime. Under its Hohenzollern rulers, and exploiting a unique tax system to sustain its considerable army, it became a population in service of a military, almost along the lines of the Spartans. The aristocratic military officer class commanded a peasant conscript army that was larger as a proportion of the population and better equipped and disciplined than rival states could manage. Hence, Prussian military and political power was out of all proportion to its population size. As Prussia expanded its influence and territory in conflict with the Austrian Empire and moved against Poland, its military ethos was also complemented by an interest in high culture and Enlightenment thought. This was especially true during the reign during Rousseau's lifetime of Frederick the Great (r. 1740–1786), who was a significant patron of the arts, a musician and a correspondent of Voltaire.

Frederick the Great (1712–1786) was only one further example of the contradictions at the heart of the Enlightenment, between the progress of science and culture on the one hand, and the advance of war, conquest and its inevitable devastation on the other. These twin developments were to shape Rousseau's own ambivalent view of Enlightenment culture and the political theory that was associated with it, namely the sovereign state governing amongst rival sovereign states.

Plans for perpetual peace and the reality of war – Rousseau on St Pierre

An extraordinary passage from the opening of Rousseau's *The State of War* gives one of the most memorable depictions of the horrors of war in western political theory:

> I open the books on rights and morals, I listen to the scholars and legal experts, and, moved by their 'thought-provoking' arguments, I deplore the miseries of nature, I admire the peace and justice established by the civil order, I bless the wisdom of public institutions, and I console myself for being a man by viewing myself as a citizen. Well instructed as to my duties and happiness, I close the book, I leave the classroom, and I look around me. I see poor wretches groaning under an iron yoke, the human race crushed by a handful of oppressors, a starving mass of people overcome by pain and hunger, whose blood and tears the rich drink in peace, and everywhere the strong armed against the weak with the formidable power of the laws.
>
> One can but groan and be quiet. Let us draw an eternal veil over these objects of horror. I lift my eyes and look off in the distance. I see fires and flames, countrysides deserted, and towns sacked. Wild men, where are you dragging these poor wretches? I hear a horrible racket. What an uproar! What cries! I draw near. I see a scene of murders, ten thousand men slaughtered, the dead piled up in heaps, the dying trampled underfoot by horses, everywhere the image of death and agony. This then is the fruit of these peaceful institutions! (Rousseau 2011, p. 255)

Here Rousseau also gives an extraordinary depiction of the experience of many students of political thought confronting the vast chasm between the philosophical studies about states, duties, war and law and the reality of the phenomenon. It serves as important illustration of the tension at the heart of Rousseau's work between his philosophical ambition, engaging with the theories of major thinkers, and his sense of the reality that these theories are supposed to address: the vast personal gap between Rousseau as philosopher and as citizen and historical witness.

At the centre of his most political writings from the 1750s are a number of short works that are consumed by the challenge of the international relations in the modern sovereign state system as defined by Hobbes. Hobbes's political theory does not address the international realm except in passing. It leaves floating a possible implication about whether a further level of contract amongst states might help to eradicate the problem of war between them. Just as the circumstance of war in his original position was the motive to create the sovereign, so could the same conditions obtain amongst states with the continuation of war, beginning a second logic of an international social contract? This is precisely the idea that inspired the development of plans for 'Perpetual Peace', such as that of the Abbe St Pierre in the 18th century. The combination of the logic of Hobbesian sovereignty and St Pierre's writing inspired Rousseau in his most direct reflections on the problem of sovereignty and international politics. During 1756 he wrote two works on St Pierre, although they were published at different times, as the *Abstract of the Project for Perpetual Peace by the Abbe St. Pierre* (1761), which gives an account and makes little commentary, and *Judgement of the Plan for Perpetual Peace* (1782), an analysis and critique of St Pierre's work. During the mid-1750s, Rousseau also wrote *The State of War*, possibly as an unused chapter of *The Social Contract*. This work clearly engages with Hobbes and with the optimism of St Pierre and those who sought to address the horror of war by creating an international federation of states.

Charles-Irénée Castel de Saint-Pierre (1658–1743) authored one of the first formal plans for perpetual peace, an early version of which was first published in 1712. He has had an influence on later schemes for creating international agreements and organisations to prevent war, right up to the 20th-century League of Nations and the United Nations. He proposed a confederation of sovereign European states that bound themselves under a common law forgoing the right to war and submitting disputes to arbitration by a senate of the league, whose decisions were sanctioned by the major powers. Although all members of the league were considered 'equals', clearly some were more than equal in power. The membership of the confederation was to include the European sovereign states but also nearby powers such as Muscovy (the emerging Russian Empire) and 'the Turk' (or Ottoman Empire). The purpose of the League was ultimately to remove a state's right to go to war to expand its territory. So its proposed primary benefit to existing major powers was that it would secure their borders and preclude changes to territory through inter-dynastic marriage and alliance (as, for example, in the War of the Spanish Succession). In turn, this gain would reduce the cost of preparedness for war.

Rousseau's first response was to repeat and outline the main features and benefits of St Pierre's plan in the same way as the student in the opening passage from *The State of War*. However, the more he considered this proposal, the more his judgement was to become harsher. He came to see that not only was the strategy of perpetual peace 'utopian' but it was impossible given the nature of the Hobbesian state system. The book thus became a critique of the 'horrible system of Hobbes' (Rousseau 2011, p. 257). The book is a rejection of Hobbes's claim that war is the natural condition between individuals that can only be resolved by the creation of the sovereign state. Hobbes's account of the state of nature confuses 'natural man' with the idea of man as he exists within civil society, already corrupted by that society. In the natural condition there is no need for war, which is not a 'warre of all against all' but a relation of state power to state power, with each posing a threat to each other because of its efforts to secure and protect its territory and status:

> I therefore call war between one power and another the effort of a mutual, steady, and manifest inclination to destroy the enemy state, or at least weaken it, by all means possible. This inclination put into action is war properly so called; as long as it remains in a state of inaction, it is merely the 'state of war'. (Rousseau 2011, p. 264)

Rousseau's characterisation of the modern state is similar to that of 'offensive realists' like John J. Mearsheimer (2001). States pursue their interests through competition across the board, whether through restricting trade, disrupting international cooperation, or initiating direct military conflict. Within Rousseau's account of civil society, the leaders of the incumbent regime (whether a prince or a republic) are compelled to act by the system – because they will either seek to aggrandise power or be subjected to another's power. This exposes the paradox at the heart of Rousseau's rejection of St Pierre's plan. The very conditions that give rise to the desire for peace and the avoidance of war (namely, the regime of sovereign states seeking protection through advantage) is precisely the reason why such a league could never persist. The dynamic of the state system is inherently one that motivates non-cooperation and non-compliance. In this way, despite offering one of the most striking accounts of the horrors of war, Rousseau leaves us with the prospect of a permanent 'state of war' as the consequence of the state system, and not the state system as the solution to the problem of war. This is Rousseau's most striking statement of an 'offensive realist' position. But, as one would expect with him, it is not his final word or a rejection of the idea of the sovereign state as such, as the next two sections show.

The *Discourse on the Origin of Inequality* and the 'evil contract'

Like the *First Discourse*, Rousseau's short book *Discourse on the Origins and Foundations of Inequality among Men*, was written for a prize competition organised by the Academy of Dijon. It is a complex essay that covers a variety of issues and introduces ways of theorising that were to become important for subsequent political philosophy. Hugely pregnant with ideas, not all of which were original to Rousseau, it raises much that can be challenged and criticised. Much larger books have been written about how to understand this short book. Although I treat the work here as a critique of the social contract tradition (which it is), it is also much more than that, both within Rousseau's 'philosophy' and in subsequent political philosophy, the philosophy of language and historical anthropology. In the introduction, Rousseau distinguishes between natural and moral equality:

> I conceive of two kinds of inequality in the human species: one that I call natural or physical, because it is established by nature and consists in the difference of age, health, bodily strength, and qualities of mind or soul. The other may be called moral or political inequality, because it depends on a kind of convention and is established, or at least authorised, by the consent of men. This latter type of inequality consists in the different privileges enjoyed by some at the expense of others, such as being richer, more honoured, more powerful than they, or even causing themselves to be obeyed by them. (Rousseau 2011, p. 45)

At the outset, Rousseau rejects Hobbes's discussion of equality of natural power and turns Locke's concept of consent to work against the idea of freedom. Whatever else Rousseau is doing, he is clearly critiquing the social contract tradition.

Natural humans and the state of nature

In the classic social contract theories, the state of nature is used to identify the problem that motivates the creation of society and political authority. Humanity's inherent nature is the source of failings that only civil society can compensate for. By contrast, Rousseau argues that Hobbes's account of the natural condition is nothing of the sort. Instead, it is a characterisation of traits that only arise in civil society as if they were natural and pre-social. Rather than being egoistic, appetitive, glory-seeking and diffident creatures in the state of nature, Rousseau depicts a very different individual when all the consequences of socialisation are stripped away:

> I see an animal less strong than some, less agile than others, but all in all, the most advantageously organised of all. I see him satisfying his hunger

under and oak tree, quenching his thirst at the first stream, finding his bed at the foot of the same tree that supplied his meal; and thus all his needs are satisfied. (Rousseau 2011, p. 47)

Not only is the picture of humanity here very different from that of standard state of nature arguments, but a person's relation to nature as well as their own nature is also very different. A key feature of classic social contract theories is competition for resources in order to secure self-preservation, yet here we see limited natural desires that are fully satisfied. Natural humanity lives in circumstances of material abundance and therefore would have nothing to compete over. An individual's body is acclimatised by use so that they can achieve many things that modern people could only achieve with tools and artifice. The individual is physically robust or they would have succumbed to nature in infancy – survival of the fittest, an idea that influences later theories of evolution. The primitive idea of natural adaptation is reflected in the way in which females are suited to carrying young so as to be free to seek sustenance and shelter whilst suckling. Rousseau also suggests that many issues that limit life and create health problems are the result of poor living, excess indulgence or lifestyle in 'civilised' society. The absence gives reason to think that natural humanity is no less healthy, or more likely to lead a stunted life, than those in civil society. In most respects, human beings in the natural condition are similar to other animal species – Rousseau even draws parallels with the orangutan of Sumatra and African gorillas (Rousseau 2011, p. 106). Human nature is not just the animal physicality he describes but also the potential to form ideas and the faculty of 'self-perfection'. Human will and the passions contain the sources of humanity's decline from the nobility of their savage state. Knowledge derived from the senses is something we share with animals – e.g. the smell sense of a predator. When this is coupled with the will, we create conceptions of need and the consequent desires. Admittedly, in the natural condition these are primitive desires:

The only goods he knows in the universe are nourishment, a woman, and rest; the only evils he fears are pain and hunger. I say pain and not death because an animal will never know what it is to die; and knowledge of death and its terrors is one of the first acquisitions that man has made in withdrawing from the animal condition. (Rousseau 2011, p. 54)

The repudiation of the natural fear of violent death is a clear denial of the most important motive in Hobbes's state of nature: to seek peace and leave the natural condition. To fear death, one needs a conception of the self and a sense of either its persistence outside of time or its termination in the face of eternity. Thoughts like these involve complex concepts that a natural human being or an animal would have no need for, because what purpose would complex and abstract thought serve in a world of minimal needs and abundant supply? Language itself is not something that solitary natural humans would acquire, and without language the capacity to reason would also be absent.

In a brief discussion of language, Rousseau makes some profound claims that contradict standard models of language learning, such as those privileging 'ostensive definition' of the sort found in St Augustine or John Locke (which privilege naming). Rousseau characterises language as public practices constituted by rules of grammar, and thus not a private cataloguing of the world of objects. This turn to language is not simply a digression. Rousseau's account of the state of nature may well draw on experience of so-called primitive societies from travel writers and missionaries or biological speculations about evolution, but it is primarily a hypothetical thought experiment taken to its logical conclusion by trying to distinguish and subtract all those things that are a product of sociability. If humans in nature have no need for sociability (except in the most animal respects), then not only will they have no need for language and rational thought or concern for consequences but they will also lack such moral concepts as the capacity to judge ethically and the ability to discriminate between good and evil or virtue and vice. The natural condition is a pre-moral state because there is no prospect of conceptualising moral experience, even if humans have the basis of a moral psychology.

Rethinking self-interest: amour de soi-même *and* amour propre

Whilst humans in the natural condition are primitive, they are not solely animal. There are elements of human psychology that are natural but which only become significant in the emergence of society and in the growth of inequality that follows. Central to human nature is the possibility of perfectibility, understood as the capacity to learn and to improve from learning. In the natural condition there is little occasion for learning; nevertheless, the capacity enables humans to develop strategies to avoid pain and to accommodate risk. However, this is not all. Humanity also has the natural sentiment of pity, which is exhibited in the basic capacity of man to shed tears at suffering and pain – why else, Rousseau asks, would we have tear ducts? Pity is the natural ability to recognise pain and to share in it imaginatively by recognising its occurrence in others. He argues that even the most resolutely egoistic theories of human psychology (such as Bernard Mandeville's *The Fable of the Bees* (1714)) still acknowledge the effect of pity on the hardest hearts. Rousseau's objective is not to develop a full account of morality but to recognise that our natural psychology is more complex than simplistic theories of rational egoism suggest. The rational egoists, such as Hobbes, assume that self-interest is uncontroversial, yet Rousseau draws an important distinction within the concept of self-interest or self-concern:

> We must not confuse egocentrism [*amour propre*] with love of oneself [*amour de soi-même*], two passions very different by virtue of both their nature and their effects. Love of oneself is a natural sentiment that moves every animal to be vigilant in its own preservation and that, directed in

man by reason and modified by pity, produces humanity and virtue. Egocentrism is merely a sentiment that is relative, artificial, and born in society that moves each individual to value himself more than anyone else, that inspires in men all the evils they cause one another, and that is the true source of honour. (Rousseau 2011, p. 117)

All men have a natural desire for survival and to overcome the pain of cold and hunger; they also like pleasure, albeit simple self-referential pleasures. When this is coupled with pity, they have a motive to identify with and feel a repugnance towards pain and suffering. But in nature they have no sense of self with respect to others, because that requires a sociability that is not natural. Once social relations develop, then the sense of self as deserving of recognition emerges, and this is *amour propre*: a sense of what our due is and what we are denied by others or by institutions and social structures.

The *amour propre* concept plays a complex role in the *Discourse*. Whilst Rousseau undoubtedly blames this egoistic conception of self-worth for the growth of vice and inequality, this idea is also at the heart of the claim for equal recognition that he defends throughout his works. It is his own sense of wounded *amour propre* that is revealed in the passages about his time in domestic service in his autobiography *The Confessions*. It is also this sense of what is one's due from others that shapes the emergence of unequal social relations that is institutionalised in the social contract theories he is criticising. The noble savage in the natural condition has no reason to compare themself with others and has only the capacity to see and experience the world through their senses, so the status of others is completely mysterious to them. Yet, this sense of others in comparison to oneself is the primary product of society and the fundamental relationship that underlies moral and political concepts. Once we lose our natural innocence and leave the state of nature, our *amour de soi-même* quickly gives away to *amour propre*.

Contract, coercion and consent

However, given the sufficiency of the state of nature and the apparent perfection of the state of nature with relative abundance, why did we ever leave it? And how did the society that tyrannises us and feeds our *amour propre* originate? The final part of the *Discourse* provides an account of the natural history of society and the emergence of government that is not wholly consistent with the picture of natural man and the state of nature. For Rousseau, civil society is the source of humanity's loss of innocence and explains the subsequent rise of depravity and loss of liberty that culminates in the tyranny of modern governments. They create the inequality of power, status and esteem that exists between rulers and ruled. These fundamental social divisions are in turn the source of so-called virtues that compel governments towards conflict and war and hence explain the perilous state of international affairs. All of this has its fundamental source in the 'evil contract' we enter into when we consent to our own domination.

> The first person who, having enclosed a plot of land, took it into his head to say, 'This is mine', and found people simple enough to believe him, was the true founder of civil society. What crimes, wars, murders, what miseries and horrors would the human race have been spared, had someone pulled up the stakes or filled in the ditch and cried out to his fellowmen, 'Do not listen to this imposter. You are lost if you forget that the fruits of the earth belong to all and the earth to no one!'? (Rousseau 2011, p. 69)

Before all coercion could be brought to bear to sustain regimes of property or personal wealth, humanity must either recognise the claims of private property or not. They might support such claims because of reciprocal advantage, or simply by accepting that our betters have a right to exclude us because we are poor or lesser in some way. It is complicity in acknowledging those structures of inequality that ultimately gives force to the moral language of rights and claims, which in turn can then be backed up with sanctions. If no one recognised those claims, then there would just be force or violence, and the minority would always be subject to the majority. The 'evil' of civil society is that it tricks the majority to subordinate themselves to the interests of the minority.

However, before that confidence trick can be fully played against the many, the advance of society must have already progressed quite far. Accordingly, a speculative history of the growth of society forms the remainder of the book. Once Rousseau turns to why society arises, it is pretty clear that his hypothetical account of the state of nature is not the whole picture. His move does not reinstate the claims of the classic contract theorists, Hobbes, Pufendorf and Locke. Instead, Rousseau argues that individual self-sufficiency is shown to be limited by the challenges posed by nature, and the discovery of ways to overcome competition from other animals. Humans have the capacity of perfectibility so they learn how to overcome competition from animals and enhance the limitations of their bodies by the use of tools. Over time, humans also learn the benefits of limited cooperation following procreation, and so family relations start to emerge. Once this tendency to cooperation has begun and there is a move away from a solitary existence, language and communication develop. With that, further forms of social organisation and burden-sharing begin, as well as the development of concepts that differentiate between humans such as higher, stronger, quicker. These differentiations are then coupled with *amour propre* to become the basis of self-esteem, as well as inaugurating a social division of labour. This process of differentiation takes a long time and in its earliest forms is relatively benign.

Yet, its darker side emerges with the acceleration and institutionalisation of different statuses that follows from the discovery and deployment of technology:

> Metallurgy and agriculture were the two arts whose invention produced this great revolution. For the poet, it is gold and silver; but for the philosopher, it is iron and wheat that have civilised men and sealed the fate of the human race. (Rousseau 2011, p. 75)

Technology is the acquisition and deployment of expert knowledge to transform the world, such as the ability to work metals and the expert knowledge that allowed crop rearing. This is important not simply because it unlocks the potential to transform the world to serve human purposes; for Rousseau, it introduces a transformation of social relations between the holders of knowledge and those who serve it. This is not just the division of labour that Adam Smith marvelled at. It is the division of society that would ultimately end in the class society that exercised Marx and subsequent socialists. Technology has a deeply mixed reputation in modern thought because it both liberates and tyrannises at the same time. Rousseau draws on this ambivalence in his conjectural history of human domination. Agriculture is a strong example, since it clearly requires special knowledge. Similarly, metallurgy involves finding and refining ore, as well as working it into useful tools. In both cases, the technology implies a social organisation of labour that brings with it differentiations such as master and labourer, owner and worker, expert and non-expert.

All of these relationships give rise to differentiations of status that in turn are institutionalised into social classes and stratification, which overcome the simple bases of social organisation such as those based on family relationships. Expertise becomes a basis for social differentiation and domination by the wise, replacing forms of hierarchy based on age and experience. In the next stage, a governing class emerges by exercising control over expert knowledge because they can control the knowledge class. So there is differentiation within differentiation by those who are able to manipulate the metallurgical experts via the creation of expertise in deploying their knowledge, such as using weapons against the weapon makers, or co-opting them into collaboration against others. At each stage, some form of self-subordination continues the substitution of natural liberty to these social tyrannies, but in each case it remains the logic of self-esteem, pride and *amour propre* that is central to this history of the rise and arbitrary concentration of power. This logic of expertise slowly transforms itself into hereditary power as functional skills in working metals or deploying weapons transform themselves into the skills of deploying servants, who in turn identify themselves with extended families and powers. For reasons of efficiency, functional leadership gives way to hereditary leadership and power, which suggests that hereditary monarchy is a relatively late human invention. Alongside these developments in power relations there is the development of moral and political concepts that legitimates what are arbitrary social relation-ships. As status, wealth and power become ever more centralised, increasing inequality in the forms of government with unified and personal sovereignty, such as that held by the French monarch, becomes institutionalised. For Rous-seau, this speculative history culminates in a new form of equality to replace the natural equality of the innocent noble savage. But in this case the equal-ity is not noble. Rather, it is the ignoble equality of equal subjection to the tyranny of political rule.

In the ambiguous ending of the *Discourse*, Rousseau leaves us with a picture of the modern state as one where natural freedom has been replaced by domi-nation. Natural innocence has been corrupted by the pervasive quest for status and honour, a distortion that is only possible because of the extension of ine-quality and domination, which enough people believe (falsely) that they ben-efit from. This quest for status is further extended in the international realm, where sovereign princes seek esteem and recognition through the unending quest for territorial expansion and power. Classic social contract theories pre-suppose this inequality in their accounts of the state of nature, and then attempt to rectify it by seeking consent to precisely the corrupt and dominating social relations that created this state of nature in the first instance. Yet, all the while, a return to natural innocence is not an option, because once the technological bases of social and political differentiation have emerged, the knowledge of that cannot be unlearned. So, does this leave us with the pessimistic conclusion that man is 'everywhere in chains' and humans are condemned to endure their loss of freedom and innocence? As always with Rousseau, the answer is never quite so simple.

The Social Contract

Rousseau is deliberately paradoxical in his political theory. He is both one of the most profound critics of social contract theory and one of its most important or classical theorists, regularly placed alongside Hobbes and Locke in the syl-labus. Yet there is more. Not everyone who reads the complex argument of *The Social Contract* agrees about what they are reading. Is the work an answer to the challenge of the *Discourse on the Origins of Inequality*? Is it a social contract theory at all? Should we read it as a utopia (Shklar 1985), that is, an ideal thought experiment that is designed to show how our politics fails to live up to its potential? Perhaps Rousseau is seeking to show that freedom and sovereignty are incompatible and we can have one or the other but not both. Or is Rous-seau offering us a model of the sovereign state that could be realised? These questions matter a good deal. If Rousseau had stopped with the *Discourse* and *The State of War* he would have made a sufficiently interesting contribution to international political thought by offering a critique of the Hobbesian sov-ereign state. In the rest of this section and the next, I will argue that in fact

Rousseau's *Social Contract* does offer an account of the sovereign state that he thought could and should exist in the world. It is one that has significant implications for international relations, and for international political theory. Here I take Rousseau at his word, whilst acknowledging that this is a risky strategy.

The Social Contract and the general will

'Man was born free, and everywhere he is in chains' (Rousseau 2011, p. 156) – so opens Book 1, Chapter 1 of *The Social Contract*. This is one of the most striking claims in modern political theory. It both sets out the agenda of *The Social Contract* and links the argument to that of the *Discourse*. The noble savage in the natural condition is barely limited in satisfying their minimal wants, and (most importantly) is not subject to the domination of another person. Only with the emergence of social cooperation and civil society does nature give way to the interference of others and our concern for our status in the eyes of others, as the claims of our *amour propre* begin to have force. The *Discourse* ends with the institutionalisation of domination as we become subject to political rules, and also dominated by social mores and standards that reinforce our inequality in the eyes of others. The challenge for Rousseau is whether domination becomes the normal condition of civil society or whether it is possible to be free, whilst still benefiting from society. Before tackling that question, it is necessary to explain Rousseau's concept of freedom or liberty.

His conception of freedom or liberty is not stated in a distinct chapter (as with Hobbes in *Leviathan*, Part II, Chapter XXI). Instead, it is dispersed across all his writings; indeed, his life could be conceived as one long argument for liberty, according to *The Confessions* (Rousseau [1781] 1953). Whether there are two or many conceptions of liberty in his work, Rousseau's position is undoubtedly distinctive and influential. It can be distinguished from Hobbesian negative liberty theories, which reduce freedom to the absence of impediments to action (such as locks and chains). Equally, Rousseau's view is distinct from classical republican theories, which focus on the idea of membership of a political society that is not dominated by an external power. In so far as Machiavelli has a republican theory of freedom, it is a social theory of freedom and, therefore, individual liberty is an implication of membership of a non-dominated political society (unless, of course, you are a slave or a woman). Rousseau's conception is similar to the 'republican' conception of freedom (Pettit 1997; Skinner 1998), yet it differs importantly in being focused on the individual. For Rousseau, individuals are free when they are autonomous or self-governing; that is, when they can act in accordance with decisions and rules that they have set by themselves. They are free from distortion by internal desires as well as by societal forces, or by indirect coercion from the society in which people are forced by popular opinion to live or act in a certain way. Central to Rousseau's argument is the idea of a self that is independent from social conventions and expectations, and the view that obstacles to freedom consist in much more than physical restrictions on action. According to Rousseau, we can be forced to conform, by our upbringing and education, by morality, by social status and by economic factors like poverty or our social class. Poverty does not simply deny people the opportunity to act by restricting the resources available to them; it also shapes our desires and our wants and limits us in aspiration as much as opportunity. As we shall see later, we can also think we are free when we are not, and this is one of the most controversial aspects of Rousseau's thought.

One simple implication of Rousseau's concept of freedom, which is manifest in the short chapters of Book I, is that it is incompatible with the standard arguments from the social contract tradition for the origin of political domination and state sovereignty. No argument that depends on force, conquest or intergenerational agreements can legitimately place a person under the rule of another, nor can freedom be consistent with the idea of alienating our natural liberty in return for security, peace or order. Of course, Hobbes thought natural liberty was greatly overrated and would be happily sacrificed for peace and security, but Rousseau disagrees. A world of Hobbesian subordination is not only risky in the event of the sovereign turning out to be a brutal tyrant; even benign subordination is the denial of all that makes human life bearable and distinctive. A life of subordination is intolerable for Rousseau as a philosophical claim and as a lived reality. He introduces the idea of man's (regrettably Rousseau does tend to mean 'man' and not 'mankind' as a generic category including women) alienation from his true self and from the world, an idea that was to have a significant influence on the young Marx.

In the opening chapters of *The Social Contract*, Rousseau does not deny the idea that some form of Hobbesian or Grotian initial agreement might create the institution of political domination, but this would not only be another example of imposed slavery; it would also not create a genuine people or a body politic. Rousseau clearly identified as inadequate the idea of a multitude gathered under a particular ruler – something familiar from Machiavelli's *The Prince*. He maintains that this remains a mere aggregation of individuals and is not a genuine association or people. So, his fundamental argument against the classical contract tradition is that it does not give rise to a genuinely political society: a people. An association is a people who come together as free individuals, and who retain that freedom whilst constituting a new kind of political community a body politic. In this way, Rousseau's conception of a sovereign people cannot involve the idea of alienating freedom. Nor can it be a completely artificial creation that is distinct from, and dominates, those who have created it – as is the case with Hobbes's state 'leviathan' looming over civil society, as depicted in the 1651 frontispiece of his book.

That said, Rousseau does retain the idea of an original agreement or contract as the basis of his new form of association, which suggests that a people might emerge out of a multitude that was held together and developed over a long period of time, seeing this as a solution to the problem of coordinating self-preservation. Unlike the *Discourse on the Origins of Inequality*, Rousseau does not offer a speculative history of the state. Instead, he moves directly to the point at which an association is constituted, leaving aside whether this happens in an existing multitude or amongst individuals newly thrown together. On one level, none of this matters because Rousseau is not explaining where the state came from; he is concerned with the possibility of legitimate rule amongst a free people. Yet, his argument is also not simply an abstract philosophical one. He intends the idea of a free people to be something that could exist in the world as more than a utopia, so the terms of the agreement are important. He concludes:

> in giving himself to all, each person gives himself to no one. And since there is no associate over whom he does not acquire the same right that he would grant others over himself, he gains the equivalent of all that he loses, along with a greater amount of force to preserve what he has.
>
> If, therefore, one eliminates from the social compact whatever is not essential to it, one will find that it is reducible to the following terms. *Each of us places his person and all his power in common under the supreme direction of the general will; and as one, we receive each member as an indivisible part of the whole.* (Rousseau 2011, p. 164)

At the heart of Rousseau's argument is a simple idea, namely that, if everyone subjects themselves to the domination of everyone else, so that they become dominator and dominated at the same time, then the two statuses cancel each other out – and all domination disappears in a new association of equals governing and being governed at the same time. Central to this idea of a free association is Rousseau's idea of the general will. This is a notoriously elusive concept but it is also his answer to the question of what the sovereign is. The sovereign is the general will: sovereignty exists only when a general will exists because it is a permanent property of a people, as opposed to an aggregation of individuals or a multitude. Only as long as a people has a general will can the people exist as sovereign. Consequently, sovereignty cannot be alienated or transferred to an agent, as Hobbes and Locke claim. To alienate sovereignty is to destroy it. One consequence of this radical claim is that many of the so-called political entities that exist in the international domain are not sovereign states, whatever else they may be. Whilst Rousseau does not explicitly identify the concept of the state and that of the sovereign, as Hobbes does, it is not clear whether he thinks there can be states without sovereignty. If there are such non-sovereign states, then they are diminished things and they have no normative claim to recognition.

The idea of the general will is the solution to the problem of an association as a free people but what exactly is the general will? Rousseau's complex answer to this question is the point of the main body of *The Social Contract*. The most important element of the argument is that it is the source of legitimate rule within a properly constituted people, so there can be no law or political right without the existence of the general will. Yet, if it is a feature of the people properly constituted, it must have some origin in the individuals that makes up the people, consequently the first place to look for the general will is with the individuals who comprise the people. The individuals who constitute themselves into a free association governed by a general will must themselves be able to will that general will. And they must be able to distinguish willing the general will from other kinds of willing. Rousseau's discussion of willing the general will involves distinguishing that will from a private will or from an aggregate or majority will. This involves focusing on the *content or object* of the general will and not a procedural or formal feature of the general will, such as the universalisability test of Immanuel Kant, who builds on Rousseau's insight. Each individual has their own will as the source of action they wish to bring about. That can be wholly private since a person can will the satisfaction of a peculiar desire that they may have but others do not share. So, a private citizen in a democracy who also happens to be a university professor might will that the state provide public support for universities. They may claim that this is a public good and others benefit, but it remains a private act of will because they are ultimately willing the satisfaction of their own particular desire. A private or personal interest is not the general will.

Similarly, a majority might will something that is an aggregation of particular wills because it just happens that a lot of people share the same desires – a majority might will the reduction of taxes as a result of a lot of individuals making judgements about their personal financial positions; this would not be a general will. A majority will is not the general will, so Rousseau believes that the majority will can be trumped by a minority who nevertheless will the general will – on the grounds that the majority is willing as an aggregation of private wills, whereas the minority is willing as engaged citizens and not private individuals who just happen to want the same thing. An example might be where a majority wills to deprive a minority of some of their rights. Of course, this latter claim does seem to beg many questions. It transfers the issue about what it is to will the general will into the question of what it is to will as a citizen. Rousseau does not offer a formal test of the general will, and so we have to search for some examples of what might satisfy that test and he does provide some guidance:

- The general will cannot be represented, so any collective decision that hands political authority to another class, person or body cannot be an example of the general will.
- Similarly, the general will cannot be divided or led to the destruction of the state or body politic; consequently, an act of secession, fragmentation or subordination cannot be an example of the general will. Given that Rousseau

is rather sceptical about the realm of international affairs, this condition might even preclude the sharing of sovereignty under a treaty, as required by modern examples such as the European Union or the International Criminal Court – two highly controversial examples of pooling sovereignty.
- More speculatively, the general will is exhibited in rules and laws that are designed to sustain and protect an association of equals such as equality before the law, and the conditions which sustain that status as political equals, which might include social and economic provisions that prevent dependency and ward off relationships that undermine the commonality necessary for equal citizenship. Judgements about the equal protection of the laws are controversial, but one obvious sign that a general will is indeed general is the absence of any reference to a particular group or to a good or benefit that only advantages some particular individuals or groups of people.

Because the general will is not simply the majority will, we cannot rely on majority decisions to reveal that will, although Rousseau devotes much attention to how it might work in terms of decision rules. Since the general will cannot be represented and neither can it be alienated, that decision process has to be participatory. Consequently, many contemporary commentators have thought of Rousseau as an early proponent of participatory democracy, whereby the interplay of public deliberation and decision-making gives rise to a popular will, free of factions and divisions. His claim that the general will, by definition, cannot be wrong also lends some support to this line of argument as a deliberative decision. Because it is the outcome of a constitutive process, the general will is not the sort of judgement that can be wrong. It is not simply a collective judgement of a matter of fact, such as how best to maximise national income or to defeat an epidemic. Yet some political judgements such as how to secure a state do involve matters of fact so the deliberative model is not a perfect fit. The discussion of the institutions of a free people with a general will soon elides into a discussion of the form of government, which Rousseau is clear is a categorically separate matter from the nature of sovereignty. But, before turning to government, one final element to Rousseau's argument about the general will must be noted.

Rousseau acknowledges that a free people is made up of individuals who have private as well as public and general interests that they can will. Some of these private interests (such as self-preservation and protection) are natural and important, whereas others might challenge the supremacy of the general will. So how does he deal with this potential division in the soul? Firstly, the primacy of the general will suggests that in the original constitutive act our natures change and the priority of individual motives gives way to a new citizen identity. Consequently, we might describe Rousseau's original contract as a 'conversion contract' because the people who emerge from it are transformed into new people, in the same way that it is claimed people who undergo religious conversion (like St Paul) are changed. Precisely how and why this should happen remains a mystery. Yet, Rousseau also suggests that the original agreement does not work by magic, and our private or sectional wills remain operative and sometimes conflict with the general will. When this happens, the law of the state can compel us to act in accordance with the general will, but this creates one of the great paradoxes of Rousseau's argument:

> Thus, in order for the social compact to avoid being an empty formula, it tacitly entails the commitment – which alone can give force to the others – that whoever refuses to obey the general will, will be forced to do so by the entire body. This means merely that he will be forced to be free. (Rousseau 2011, p. 167)

Freedom is constituted by the general will, so if we will an action contrary to the general will we are willing our own unfreedom and we can be made free by the law of the state. This paradoxical statement has proved deeply controversial. Whilst many would agree that the state can compel us to act in our own interest, and prevent us from hurting ourselves or our long-term interests through ignorance, Rousseau goes further in claiming that such coercion is not just good for us but actually makes us free.

Government, the Legislator and the constitution

The problem of the general will persists throughout the remainder of the book but that discussion can be divided into two – namely, the institutional manifestation and conditions of the general will and the social and economic conditions needed, which are discussed in the next section. The institutional conditions introduce a further controversial dimension of Rousseau's argument in the person of the Legislator. The discussion of the Legislator continues the account of the general will but it shifts the attention to the constitution and institutions that sustain a general will as opposed to the content of it. He introduces the Legislator in the following terms:

> Discovering the rules of society best suited to nations would require a superior intelligence that beheld all the passions of men without feeling any of them; who had no affinity with our nature, yet knew it through and through; whose happiness was independent of us, yet who nevertheless was willing to concern itself with ours; finally, who, in the passage of time, procures for himself a distant glory, being able to labour in one age and obtain his reward in another. (2011, p. 180)

And:

> The Legislator is in every respect an extraordinary man in the state. If he ought to be so by his genius, he is no less so by his office, which

is neither magistracy nor sovereignty. This office, which constitutes the republic, does not enter into the constitution. It is a particular and superior function having nothing in common with dominion over me. (2011, p. 181)

Rousseau speaks of the Legislator having godlike properties. However, the comparisons to the near-mythic status of Lycurgus (the lawgiver for Sparta) or Solon (the lawgiver for Athens) should not mislead, as the substantive point is familiar in more modern examples. The most important point is that the Legislator is the source of the constitution whilst not being an active part of the state or sovereign. In this way, they stand outside the state, in the same way that the Founders of the U.S. Constitution are outside the constitution itself. (In the USA, the original intent of the drafters of the Constitution is given an almost sacred status by some conservative jurists such as the Federalist Society.) Or perhaps they resemble Mustapha Kemal in the Turkish Republic, where his lead and influence were seen as outside the constitution of the state but the constitution derives its standing from such a figure. By being outside the constitution, the Legislator can give a constitution whilst not being involved in its interpretation or application; that task remains for the magistrates in Rousseau's theory, or judges in modern constitutions, whose power is constituted and also circumscribed by the constitution. By legislating and departing from the scene of politics, the Legislator cannot act contrary to the general will, because they cannot take sides or prefer a particular view or party. Yet, the most important function of the Legislator is that they can become an impartial or extra-political focus for the identity and character of a people, and in so doing provide content to the general will.

So, one further answer that Rousseau gives to the question 'what is the general will?' is what is prescribed by the constitution, which gives the transgenerational character to a people. Allegiance to the constitution derived from the near-sacred character of the Legislator is reinforced by the way in which the Legislator is regarded, and the way in which the constitution shapes the character of the citizen – thus ensuring the stability of the people overtime. Stability arises from the moral socialisation of people into allegiance to the institutions of the state. But for this path to succeed the state must be constituted in a way that gives priority to the constitution as the institutionalisation of the general will. There cannot be opportunities for factions or parties to emerge in Rousseau's general will. This is a challenge for Rousseau because he also thinks that an elective aristocracy is the best form of government for a free state.

Elective aristocracy might be thought to mirror the form of representative democracy that emerged in the 19th century, but Rousseau is not sympathetic to the British constitution that so impressed his predecessor Montesquieu. To prevent parties or factions, his constitution precludes intermediate associations between the people and the government, which would provide the social basis of differentiation and faction. Any group that limits or selects membership within the body politic is inimical to the general will and must therefore be abolished or proscribed. This rules out churches, guilds, trade unions, societies, fraternities, and institutions like universities unless they are vehicles of the sovereign. Especially controversial in his own lifetime were his views on religion, which resulted in his being condemned by both the Catholic Archbishop of Paris and the Calvinist authorities in Geneva and his subsequent flight from France. The chapter on 'The Civil Religion' (Book IV, Chapter VIII) makes the case that a religion or public doctrine is an important mechanism for educating and socialising citizens and for holding together a body politic as a single transgenerational entity but, in arguing for the value of religion on sociological or political grounds, he explicitly rejects the claims of Christianity as a candidate for a civil religion.

Rousseau distinguishes three basic types of religion: the religion of man, the religion of the citizen and the religion of priests. The religion of man is, according to him, the essential doctrine of Gospel Christianity. It is concerned solely with the meaning and direction of the individual's life, and so has no political significance. He suggests that this was the position of the early Christians in the Roman Empire until their numbers became significant. The religion of the citizen is the pagan religion of the ancient world, which is confined to a political society. The gods here are purely local, yet devotion to them sustains the moral and cultural ties that enable citizens to love, serve and ultimately die for the republic. The religion of the citizen is different from the religion of man or primitive Christianity because it is not reductively individual or universal. That universal aspect of Christianity becomes problematic when it is linked with the third type of religion, that of priests. Once a priestly caste exists within a political society – and Rousseau acknowledges that this is something Catholic Christianity shares with Japanese Shintoism or Tibetan Buddhism – there is a rival hierarchy and society within the state, which nurtures difference between believers and unbelievers, as well as an alternative claim to authority and rule. In this respect, Rousseau's hostility to priestly religion echoes that of Hobbes in *Leviathan*, Part IV.

Rousseau's argument against intermediate associations and churches has made him subject to the charge of 'totalitarianism' by some later scholars, since it is precisely this subordination of everything to the state or the party that is the hallmark of a totalitarian state. The constitution succeeds by becoming a focus for the attention of citizens in deciding how to act in ruling themselves or choosing their magistrates; it also shapes their idea of themselves as a free people. Whilst freedom is a virtue of citizens and not simply of republics, Rousseau links the republican ideal with his commitment to individuality by suggesting that the character of the genuinely free person is achieved in a life lived with others, as part of a free people. This communitarian dimension of freedom is further developed in Rousseau's account of the sociological and economic conditions of a free people.

The conditions of a free people

The constitution is one source of the uniformity that is necessary to ensure the triumph of the general will over particular interests on the part of citizens. But Rousseau was also concerned that the constitution needed to be set in an appropriate social context, one that would ensure social uniformity and undermine factions and parties. The structure of society embodied by the political constitution is designed to make people citizens, but this cannot be done if they are geographically dispersed over very large areas. The size of a political community is important in terms of binding together a single people. Rousseau is clear that not all existing 'states' can be sovereign peoples because some are simply too large, and in those circumstances empire is as much political development as one can expect. A free society requires the sort of identification that is only possible amongst those who actually do interact and identify as fellow citizens, or at least could do so in certain circumstances. A free sovereign people must therefore be small and concentrated, as in his example of the island of Corsica. Most of the 'states' of Europe of Rousseau's day would fail this test and could not sustain a stable state. However, size is not the only geographical constraint represented by the example of Corsica. The territory of a sovereign people cannot have natural features or barriers that subdivide a people and create the potential for local identities to divide a group. In this way, Rousseau pre-empts a concern of many modern nationalists, who argue for secession and self-determination because of geographic barriers between them and the wider society of which they are a part. Corsica has the advantage of being a modest-sized island, which creates a strong bond between those who share the island and those inhabitants from Italy or France. Rousseau also has in mind the cantons of Switzerland and his own city of Geneva. They are not islands, but nevertheless they have strong natural physical boundaries formed by mountain ranges and lakes. States that extend beyond such natural boundaries and a small size are soon corrupted and become despotisms.

Geography is not everything. The economic and social character of the society has to sustain relationships of rough or approximate equality if people are to see themselves as sharing a common fate and common responsibility. The biggest threat to such rough equality is the challenge of commercial society. This aspect of Rousseau's argument connects with his account of the sources of war and his rejection of the benefits of commercial society championed by earlier thinkers. For instance, Montesquieu had argued that the preoccupation with luxury would lure a ruling class away from war and conquest and that trade would create transnational bonds of interdependence. For Rousseau, however, both of these features of commercial society are threats to freedom and independence. The growth of a commercial class or traders would not only undermine rough material equality but create factions and divisions in society. Rousseau's argument echoes the experience of Thucydides' Athens, where family and commercial ties undermined the cohesion of the Athenians and encouraged political adventurism over the protection of the sectional interests in the polis. In Rousseau's Europe, most disputes between states had their source in struggles to dominate and control trade, or to secure and sustain colonies and colonial benefits. A free society cannot have colonies that remain subordinate to the mother country and trade. And the protection of trade is a perpetual source of international conflict and also division within a state.

The Social Contract concludes with an indirect response to the challenge of St Pierre's *Plan for Perpetual Peace*. Instead of seeking a federation of states sanctioned by the large military powers, Rousseau claims that sovereignty is achieved by autarky or the withdrawal, as far as possible, from international relations. Free states should be relatively self-sufficient and willing to defend themselves from external threats and attacks. Otherwise they should be indifferent to international affairs and seek isolation and self-sufficiency, as opposed to cooperation. The more states seek to integrate and cooperate, the less likely they are to be free. Although his kind of freedom may come at an economic cost, Rousseau is absolutely clear that economic inequality is perhaps the greatest threat to freedom amongst individuals and within societies, a lesson that is being rediscovered in the writings of the contemporary economist Thomas Piketty (Piketty 2013; 2020).

Rousseauean international relations – Corsica and Poland

In 1764 the island of Corsica requested France for assistance in its struggle for independence from Genoa. Rousseau was approached for help in drawing up a political plan for the Corsican nation, which was subsequently published as the 'Constitutional Project for Corsica' (Hoffman and Fidler 1991). A short time later, the Polish Count Wielhorski sought Rousseau's advice on a plan for Polish independence from Russia. Rousseau's contribution, completed in 1772, became the *Considerations on the Government of Poland* (Hoffman and Fidler 1991). Both requests are a testimony to the impact of *The Social Contract* and to the fact that Rousseau's ideas were not considered to be hopelessly idealistic or utopian. Neither work is a constitution of the sort one might hope from a Rousseauean legislator, yet they reinforce arguments that are familiar from *The Social Contract*, in which Rousseau had already mentioned Corsica in his discussion of the right size of a free state or people. What is interesting about them is not simply that they illustrate his views on the social, economic and cultural conditions of a free state and people; they also provide the best evidence of his views on international relations and the problem of war and conflict in the European state system. Whilst the modern state system is the source of international conflict and war, the state (properly understood as a free people or a people under a general will) is the solution to that war and conflict. Unlike Hobbes or even the later thinker Immanuel Kant, Rousseau does not see that solution in terms of extending the architecture of juridical sovereignty into an international federation or plan for perpetual peace. He sees peace as achieved through the rejection of any cosmopolitan idea of an order of rightly constituted states. In contrast to a cosmopolitan order, he posits a series of militant republics or national communities, which look inward for legitimacy and stability and which challenge the international realm as a source of corruption and disorder.

So Rousseau encouraged the Corsicans to turn their geographical independence to their advantage by seeking economic and political self-sufficiency or autarchy, and also taking cultural independence as a basis for separation from the corruptions of international society. The familiar idea of society as a source of corruption is contrasted with the authentic (albeit hard and hand-to-mouth) existence of independent farmers and fishermen on the island of Corsica. Independence is not achieved by claiming recognition in the world of affairs but by cultivating the resilience of an independent people, indifferent to the struggles of others. Rousseau offers a warning example of the Swiss, who as independent farmers and citizen soldiers were corrupted by the engagement of Swiss mercenaries in international affairs and the subsequent impact of wealth and luxury in corrupting their martial independence:

> these rustic men, whose knowledge at first did not extend beyond themselves, their mountains, and their huts, learned to know other nations by defending themselves against them; their victories opened the neighbouring frontiers to them; their reputation for bravery gave princes the idea of employing them. They began to pay the troops they had been unable to conquer; these worthy men, who had so well defended their own liberty, became the oppressors of the liberty of others.
>
> ... Imperceptibly they were debased, and were no longer anything more than mercenaries; a taste for money made them feel poor; contempt for their way of life gradually destroyed the virtues that same life had engendered. (Hoffman and Fidler 1991, p. 152)

Corsica can avoid this because it has the advantage of being an island; the crucial point is not just geographical separation but economic and cultural independence.

This argument is further emphasised in the *Considerations on the Government of Poland*. Unlike Corsica, Poland was a large continental territory with a proud national history and a 'home' territory that had been fought over by large and militarily powerful neighbours: Prussia, Russia and the Austrian-Hungarian Empire. (Indeed, beginning in Rousseau's lifetime and finishing 17 years after his death, between 1764 and 1795, these three powers completely carved up the Polish lands between them, abolishing its state.) Given Rousseau's views about the size of political communities, Poland was obviously unpromising as a free people. Nevertheless, Rousseau thought there were ways in which a free

Poland could assert its national independence. He emphasises a number of things that were considered important by later movements for national liberation in the 19th century. He encourages the rejection of cosmopolitan fashion and language and emphasises the value of national dress, styles of address and institutions. The education of Poles should focus on their national history and achievements as well as its literature and language – ideas that were to be celebrated by Romantics in the early 19th century. Yet the real challenge comes from Rousseau's account of what Polish freedom and independence would involve. As a large but dominated state, he argues that Polish national freedom is not best achieved by asserting itself on the international stage but rather by forgoing those opportunities for competition that it is ill-suited to win. Again, by seeking self-sufficiency and avoiding luxury and wealth, the Poles can make themselves less attractive to external exploitation and also free themselves from the ties of commerce and trade that undermine national authenticity. Rousseau offers an argument familiar from later nationalist leaders that to attain national freedom it is worth forgoing the wealth and the goods celebrated by others. The most striking feature of his suggestions for Poland concerns its military organisation and strategy. Rousseau follows the usual republican argument about citizen militias being preferable to standing armies. He too says that military organisation is a bond of peoples as common citizens. However, he differs strikingly in his view of the military tactics that should be employed by this citizen militia:

> I should like them above all to practice for lightness and speed, learning how to break off, disperse, and regroup without difficulty or confusion; to excel in what is called guerrilla warfare, in all the manoeuvres appropriate to light troops, in the art of inundating a country like a torrent, or striking everywhere without being struck, of continuing to act in concert though separated, of cutting communications, of intercepting convoys, of charging rear-guards, of capturing vanguards, of surprising detachments, of harassing large bodies of troops … and learn … to conquer and destroy the best-disciplined armies without ever joining battle and without leaving them a moment's respite. (Hoffman and Fidler 1991, pp. 188–189)

For an author who emphasises the pity of war, Rousseau comes close to describing the form of guerrilla war that Goya celebrated in *The Disasters of War*, his etchings of the struggle against the Napoleonic forces in Spain a generation later. Whilst the Poles would never defeat the Russians or the Prussians in a formal conflict, their struggle should reflect their national advantage of character in conducting a conflict on their own terms and raising the cost of invasion and domination to an unsustainable level. In arguing for national struggle for survival, as opposed to wars for territorial aggrandisement (which had been important in Poland's past history), Rousseau introduces a new dimension to the consideration of war. He does not develop this further but it becomes an important part of 19th- and 20th-century discussions of wars between nations and peoples, confirming the vicious picture of conflict that he described in the opening section of *The State of War*. His argument for independence and national self-determination, as a rejection of the Hobbesian state system, with its perennial wars between powers, concludes with a picture of the free people as a fiercely independent military power that prefers to avoid conflict and international relations, whilst it is prepared to defend itself to the last and with all its resources. For those who seek to characterise Rousseau as a moralist who subverts Hobbes's theory of sovereignty for his account of a free people bound by a general will, he concludes with a dark vision of a world in which free peoples struggle to assert themselves from powers that are inimical to national independence.

Rousseau's complex legacy

Whilst scholars are keen to categorise Rousseau's legacy for international relations (Doyle 1997, pp. 136–160; Hoffman and Fidler 1991), he remains an uneasy fit for the usual categories of realist or idealist. He is definitely not a liberal (although see Rawls 1999 below). Indeed, it is precisely this studied ambiguity that makes his work so interesting, challenging and important. Many major political concepts emerge from his thought in a new light, such as sovereignty and liberty. His critiques are never simply for or against, as we find with other thinkers discussed in this volume. He reshapes Hobbes's concept of sovereignty and Locke's concept of liberty in new and insightful ways. In doing so, he never wholly rejects them, so we end up combining the juridical idea of sovereignty from Hobbes with an ethical dimension that Hobbesian realists thought they had been liberated from. Similarly, he links freedom with an approach that becomes communitarianism in the hands of later philosophers. And, whilst he emphasises the social conditions of group and individual freedom, he remains enough of a moralist for his impact on the subsequent development of nationalism to be both sociological and ethical: a tension that has remained at the heart of subsequent theories of nationalism. Rousseau's immediate impact was coloured by his appropriation by the Jacobins during the most violent periods of the French Revolution, and all subsequent interpretations have had to wrestle with that. In the 20th century, that issue has been a source of contestation amongst those who have seen Rousseau as a source of liberal values of freedom and solidarity.

Totalitarianism and nationalism

Political theory always reflects the climate in which it is written and this is as true of philosophical analysis and construction as it is of historical scholarship and writings about past political and international thinkers. How that past is interpreted, and how thinkers are categorised in terms of the big debates, is an undoubted fact and concern for subsequent scholars and students who seek to implicate or liberate thinkers like Plato, Marx and Hegel from responsibility in the horrors of totalitarianism, Hitler's death camps and Stalin's Gulags (Popper [1945] 2011). The post-World War II period saw the development of theories such as totalitarianism by political thinkers such as Hannah Arendt (Arendt 1951). The concept began as reflections on the experience of Nazism and its death camps and quickly incorporated Stalinism as a further iteration, as the Cold War engulfed political thinking from the late 1940s. Although Rousseau was not originally considered a 'totalitarian' in Karl Popper's work or Arendt's oeuvre, it was not long before his writings were incorporated into the pre-histories of the main ideological opponents in the Cold War. This process was either relatively crude, as in the case of Jacob Talmon's *The Origins of Totalitarian Democracy* (Talmon 1986), or more nuanced, as in the case of Isaiah Berlin's essay 'Two Concepts of Liberty' (Berlin [1958] 1998).

Talmon provides a subtle reading of Rousseau at the same time as he also offers the most Procrustean interpretation of Rousseau's general will and his claim that one can be forced to be free. Talmon linked these ideas to the claims of modern totalitarian states through a simple genealogy that saw the extreme coercion of Stalinist class politics and purges as inherently part of trying to achieve the collective freedom of the proletariat. By implication, they also became an excuse for the acute suffering of the present as a condition of later collective liberation.

Isaiah Berlin also explored the coercion implied by the general will and realising one's true interests only by acting according with the law, and distinguished it from the gap between people's felt interests and the empirical frustrations that are created by external impediments. Berlin's account focused on distinct concepts and traditions of 'positive and negative' liberty. His original 1958 lecture became one of the major texts of post-war liberal political theory. It presents itself as a conceptual distinction, but, in reality, it is also the categorisation of distinct traditions of thought about freedom. By implication, although not expressly stated, Berlin also thinks there are good (negative) and bad (positive) versions of the language of liberty. Negative liberty can be traced to Hobbes and consists in the absence of restraints on action, whereas positive liberty, traced to Rousseau, consists in having a free will. For Berlin, the problem with positive liberty theories is that they open themselves to a capacious account of the obstacles to a free will – these can be real things, like the absence of education, but they can also involve the absence of false consciousness, something that can only be removed by the direction of a vanguard party leading a whole people to see their true and objective class interest.

Whilst coercive class politics was one of the more obvious threats within Berlinian positive liberty theories, it was not the only danger that arose from

Rousseau's account of the general will. Talmon and Elie Kedourie also saw Rousseau's account of the conditions of the general will as resulting in a dangerous ideological nationalism (Talmon 1981; Kedourie 1960). Rousseau was not the only source of nationalism and Kedourie was not so simplistic as to lay all the flaws of nationalist politics at his feet. Nevertheless, he makes the case that Rousseau's account of the conditions necessary to sustain a general will, and therefore a free political community, quickly transform themselves into the basis of an ideology of nationalism – the claim that in principle the state and the nation should coincide and be self-determining. In Kedourie's view, this was what inspired President Woodrow Wilson's destruction of the great multinational empires of Austria–Hungary in Europe and the Ottoman Empire in the Middle East at the end of World War I. In the former Ottoman lands, this unleashed generations of Arab nationalism and instability in the multi-ethnic and multinational states of that region. Similarly, nationalism created the disorder of interwar central Europe and national grievances fuelled the rise of Nazism during the interwar period. Debates about the concept of the nation between functionalists (Gellner 1983) and ethno-nationalists (Smith 1986) take us far beyond the ideas of Rousseau himself. Yet, the basic functionalist view is that nations arise with the modern state as the mechanism to sustain and reproduce state power, rather than being founded on an historically primordial conception of a people. This does reflect Rousseau's view of the conditions of the general will and his attempts to institutionalise that in Corsica and Poland.

Where Rousseau's ethical ideal of a free people has played more of a role is (surprisingly) in the thought of Isaiah Berlin and some of his students on the compatibility between nationalism and liberalism. Berlin's support for Zionism and the state of Israel as an ethical as well as political project meant that he thought a simplistic opposition between liberalism and nationalism was incorrect. It masked a reality in which a broadly liberal conception of national identity was not only possible but where (properly understood) any viable regime needed a conception of national identity to bind its people in a common ethical community. Berlin's thought on liberalism and nationalism has had an impact on his students such as Yael Tamir and David Miller, who have subsequently developed sophisticated theories of national identity (Miller 1995) and liberal nationalism (Tamir 1993) in books of the same name. Neither thinker provides interpretations of Rousseau. However, they both explain and justify the ethical value of national identity in Rousseauean terms, as the conditions of a free people. Their works, and those of other liberal nationality theorists, have been a significant source of theorising about self-determination, secession (Buchanan 1991) and territoriality (Moore 2015). But the turn towards national self-determination has also reopened a perennial issue raised by Rousseau – and that is the balance between the claims of ethical communities and those of cosmopolitan theories of universal rights that discard the notion of ethical community as a fundamental property altogether. This issue replays in moral and political theory, in the struggle between national economies and globalisation in the world economy.

Justice versus globalism – Rawls and Rousseau

Given the multivalent character of his writings, Rousseau's legacy in international relations is ambiguous. Yet, in contemporary international political thought the most surprising resurgence of Rousseauean ideas, about an ethically sanctioned autarky as opposed to liberal cosmopolitanism, is within liberalism itself. It follows the publication of John Rawls's *The Law of Peoples* (Rawls 1999). Rawls is the undeniably dominant figure of late 20th-century English-speaking political philosophy and his work is known widely beyond the usual disciplinary boundaries of academic subjects. Yet, the Rousseauean turn in his thought came as a surprise to many of his early students and followers. They had tended to see Rawls's views on justice as embodying a global cosmopolitanism. This view was an extension of a naïve reading of Rawls's argument as simply grounded in Kant's ethical theory. (In fact, Kant's political theory is much less universalist than Rawls's work, and is itself indebted to Rousseau (Flikschuh 2000).) In order to understand that view of Rawls, it is necessary to begin with a brief overview of his theory of justice as fairness.

When first published in 1971, Rawls's massive book *A Theory of Justice* was hailed as a rebirth for classical political philosophy, after several decades in which logical positivism and ordinary language philosophy had cast doubt on the possibility of there being any more major works of moral or normative political theory. Yet, it is very clear that Rawls's book is anything but an analysis of the concept of justice. Instead, he follows a tradition, going back to Cicero, that sees justice as the first virtue of social and political institutions, and consequently an account of justice as a theory of a just society or 'scheme of social cooperation'. In place of the reigning utilitarianism of much English-speaking political theory, Rawls recovers the idea of the social contract as a way of representing a just political order – following the tradition of Rousseau in *The Social Contract*. The premise of Rawls's theory is similar to Rousseau's, in assuming the equal standing and value of all persons, and that the task of a theory of justice is to create a scheme of social cooperation between free and equal subjects who nevertheless disagree about ultimate ends or 'conceptions of the good'. In this way, equality and the distinct value of persons is an ethical commitment, and not simply a methodological device, as it is in Hobbesian contract theory. Yet, if individuals are free and equal, and we cannot assume that they already share a single conception of the common good, how can we explain a scheme of social cooperation that recognises that fundamental equality of status? Central to Rawls's idea of justice is the concept of fairness and he famously describes his theory as 'justice as fairness', using the analogy of a game.

The argument proceeds along the following lines. We begin with the idea of reasonable disagreement that characterises modern societies. We do not all share the same values or views about how society should be organised – there are atheists and Catholics and liberals and conservatives. We cannot just pick a set of ultimate values as the basis of social cooperation. Why would a Catholic accept a scheme chosen by atheists and vice versa? If we cannot begin with the end of social cooperation, can we focus instead on some rules that do not presuppose, or are neutral between, various ultimate ends? Rawls's intuition is that we can, as long as those rules are seen as fair, just as in a game we can accept the outcome even if we lose, as long as the rules by which that outcome is determined are fair.

The rest of the argument of *A Theory of Justice* is about explaining and defending how the rules that would be required to make a scheme of cooperation are fair, and showing how those rules are to be derived. To answer both of these questions, Rawls deploys the idea of a social contract. Firstly, as with Rousseau, it is used to present a just political order as a scheme of cooperation that would be agreed between free and equal subjects. Secondly, it is used as a decision procedure for deriving the principles of a just order. Because Rawls does not assume natural equality in the same way as Hobbes, or posit any initial simple equality of wealth and resources, he conceives of individuals being free and equal through the idea of an equal set of primary goods. These are rights, liberties, income, wealth and the social bases of self-respect. The idea is that these are goods that we all want, whatever else we might want, because they make possible the equal chance of leading valuable lives for each of us. This equal treatment is ensured by these primary goods being distributed according to two principles of justice and these are that:

> First: each person is to have an equal right to the most extensive scheme of equal basic liberties compatible with a similar scheme of liberties for others. Second: social and economic inequalities are to be arranged so that they are both (a) reasonably expected to be to everyone's advantage, and (b) attached to positions and offices open to all. (Rawls [1971] 1999, p. 53)

These principles are ordered in 'lexical priority' (in the same way words are ordered in a dictionary) so that the distribution of basic liberties in the first point cannot be traded against inequalities of wealth, welfare or status. Much of the debate on Rawls's theory concerns these distributive principles, but we are still left with a question about their derivation and status as fair principles, and not simply the political prejudices of a privileged Harvard professor. To resolve this problem, Rawls deploys the second social contract argument in this theory, namely the original position and the veil of ignorance.

The 'original position' is a hypothetical thought experiment that represents a fair initial agreement between equals, and therefore one that can be the basis for a fair scheme of social cooperation. Representative individuals have to choose those principles that should regulate the terms of cooperation between them. Each individual is assumed to be motivated to seek the best outcomes for herself or himself. Rawls assumes modified rational egoism for his account of individual psychology in the original position. However, if we are each motivated to seek our own advantage, then we will exploit our unequal bargaining positions, and surely this could not give us fairness. To address this, Rawls introduces the idea of a 'veil of ignorance', as a result of which the participants in the original position are denied knowledge about the particularities of their own identities such as their age, gender, endowments, skills, and conception of the good (religion, morality, political beliefs). They are also denied information about the particularities of their society, their social position within it, and the level of development of their society. Deprived of such information about ourselves, we cannot make choices that advantage ourselves over other individuals. If we cannot advantage ourselves, we will chiefly choose equality. Where we do choose inequality, we will only allow it in cases that benefit the worst-off individual, should I turn out to be that person. Again, this concept of the original position as a model of a fair scheme of social cooperation has inspired a whole cottage industry of scholarship. But, for our purposes, the most interesting discussion of Rawls's theories has been about what its implications are for international or global justice.

A *Theory of Justice* says surprisingly little about the international domain, because it deliberately addresses the subject of justice in a closed domestic society. This did not stop scholars considering the application of Rawls's method to the wider world. Just as one could ask why Hobbes's social contract does not apply immediately to the whole world, so one might argue the same of Rawls: why is there not an original position from which the principles of justice can be justified globally? This question was taken up most famously by Charles Beitz in his book *Political Theory and International Relations* (Beitz 1979). Beitz argues that Rawls's model applies in the international realm for two reasons. Firstly, the global distribution of resources is arbitrary and so a matter of justice in the same way that the individual distribution of natural abilities is arbitrary. Secondly, international trade and connectivity create a single scheme of social cooperation, and therefore raise claims of justice. Whilst this international cooperation is not complete (since not every country trades with every other and some countries such as North Korea self-isolate), in general in the modern world there is enough cooperation to create this single scheme. Therefore, by analogy, Rawls's approach can be generalised.

The challenge for Beitz is whether the global original position is a second level of contract between states, or whether it should be a single initial global agreement. In later writings, Beitz eventually adopts a cosmopolitan view of the initial global original position, such that all the elements of social justice apply universally. In this respect, his position mirrors that of Thomas Pogge (Pogge 1989), who argues that it is individuals' fundamental capacities that make them participants in the relevant context of justice, and not their membership of states or political communities. This global cosmopolitanism denies the ethical significance of states or associations, and it has become the basis of much contemporary international political theory. But it was rejected by Rawls in his last major work, *The Law of Peoples* (Rawls 1999), where he criticises these cosmopolitan readings of his theory and re-emphasises the Rousseauean tenor of his theory.

The Law of Peoples is an explicitly Rousseauean text. Rawls begins the work with an acknowledgement of Rousseau's thought, exemplified in the opening epigraph of this chapter, as a model of the kind of realistic utopia he is trying to justify. A realistic utopia is supposed to take human beings as they are and conceive of 'institutions as they might be'. This is not an acknowledgement of humanity's flawed nature, as one might imagine from standard realist theories like Hobbes or Machiavelli, but rather a Rousseauean acknowledgement that mankind's moral properties of freedom and equality are realised in a particular form of association, such as Rousseau's social contract or a Rawlsian just scheme of social cooperation. What international institutions there might be are then going to be shaped by the priority of these 'well-ordered' and just peoples. It is important to note that Rawls is concerned with 'peoples' and not with the standard units of international politics such as states or nations. States and nations might be well-ordered societies or regimes of justice, but they are not so by definition. Therefore, it remains an open question how far Rawls intends *The Law of Peoples* to apply to existing states and nations. In this way, his argument mirrors Rousseau's with respect to the European state system of his own day.

The second important Rousseauean element of *The Law of Peoples* is how different it is from the idea of 'justice as fairness' within a scheme of cooperation. The fundamental issues of justice are addressed within single schemes of cooperation amongst a people in each society. Consequently, there is no difference principle or redistribution between peoples in the international realm, and it is this that has upset most of his followers. How could a theory of justice not apply to the egregious inequalities that exist between rich and poor countries? Although Rawls does not put it this way, social justice seems to be essentially a domestic matter. And, given the hypothetical nature of the agreement amongst well-ordered peoples, the work to achieve social justice is done at the primary agreement stage. This, of course, leaves open the question of unequal natural assets amongst political societies. Yet, because Rawls is not attempting to vindicate the actual state system, he ignores those inequalities, and partly explains them away on the grounds that the wealth of nations is mostly accounted for in terms of their intellectual capital and social choices. At the second level of agreement between just, liberal peoples, the outcomes are rules for governing the interrelations of just societies and their coordination and process for resolving disputes. He lists eight principles of justice that shape relations amongst free and democratic peoples:

1. Peoples are free and independent, and their freedom and independence are to be respected by other peoples.
2. Peoples are to observe treaties and undertakings.
3. Peoples are equal and are parties to the agreements that bind them.
4. Peoples are to observe a duty of non-intervention.
5. Peoples have the right to self-defence but no right to instigate war for reasons other than self-defence.
6. Peoples are to honour human rights.
7. Peoples are to observe certain specified restrictions in the conduct of war.
8. Peoples have a duty to assist other peoples living under unfavourable conditions that prevent their having a just and decent political or social regime. (Rawls 1999, p. 37)

These principles are more or less those listed in Immanuel Kant's *Perpetual Peace* (1795), which speaks of republics in light of Rousseau's ideas of free autonomous communities bound by a general will. The main lesson of *The Law of Peoples* is that it obligates just peoples to recognise the equal status of other just peoples in an engagement. But this is not all there is to Rawls's *The Law of Peoples*. The second section concerns non-ideal theory, or what happens when just regimes confront regimes that are not just. This is an issue that was particularly pressing given the claims of many 'liberals' and supporters of human rights to use military power to promote their values. If there is a just order and some regime refuses to implement it, then why is this not a legitimate basis for intervention? For Rawls, this is both a theoretical question, given that some regimes might approximate being well-ordered without being fully liberal, and it was a political challenge in the late 20th century, when liberal ideas potentially had the unchallenged power of western military might behind them. (That situation did not endure into the 21st century.)

Rawls seeks to shift the discussion in international theory from the idea of justice in the international realm to one of toleration. The virtue of toleration is useful because it recognises the claims of individuals and societies to pursue goals and values that are unjust or wrong to liberals, but it does not respond to that by proposing the eradication of those others's goals and values. Europeans learned to live with each other by tolerating religious difference (*cuius regio, eius religio*), so that Protestant and Catholic states stopped using religion as a basis for war, without conceding the truth of their own confession. The precise measures of tolerance that are appropriate depend on the character of non-liberal societies. Rawls sets out a hierarchy descending from reasonable liberal peoples, through decent societies (those who have a decent consultation hierarchy, i.e. have a good government but are not democratic), to outlaw states, burdened societies and benevolent absolutisms. The point of the hierarchy is to show that there are many ways in which political societies can depart from a liberal ideal without warranting external intervention and reform.

Although Rawls's *The Law of Peoples* seems to have moved quite far from Rousseau, the fundamental moral of his position is clearly Rousseauean. What Rawls sees as justice, and Rousseau sees as living as free equals, requires individuals to constitute themselves as a community under a general will and with the passion and commitment to defend that ideal. Like freedom for Rousseau, justice cannot be imposed from outside a state – it must be willed into existence by a people, and without that it disappears. Rawls had served as an infantryman in World War II, and he retains Rousseau's scepticism about war, force and violence. He also takes Rousseau's view that apparently benign motives, such as willing peace and justice in the international realm, can quickly be perverted in the context of international politics to achieve quite the reverse. So, whilst Rawls alludes to Kant's *Perpetual Peace*, his own view of international political theory is actually much closer to the scepticism of Rousseau's response to Abbe St Pierre.

Conclusion

Rousseau, Hobbes and Locke are the three great thinkers of the modern sovereign state and the international system of states that arises from it. Yet, whilst they use superficially similar concepts (such as the state of nature, individual, sovereign, and state of war), they are radically different in the way they substantiate these concepts. Rousseau deliberately subverts Hobbesian concepts and his contract method by setting his thought in a unique political context of modern European history, and showing that this context shapes the relationships that Hobbes describes as abstract philosophical and juridical relationships. Rousseau also subverts Locke's idea that individuals possess rights and duties that can be asserted against others outside of a political community. To liberate these concepts from their particular context is the radical strategy of Rousseau's writings: a strategy so radical for some of his readers that it is considered a departure from the realism at the heart of Hobbes's politics, or the idealism and moralism at the heart of Locke's. Yet, Rousseau does not think that he is rejecting the possibilities of real politics in favour of utopianism. Individual freedom and political rule are compatible, but rendering them so is a profound ethical and political challenge.

Rousseau makes the radical claim that sovereignty is an ethical achievement, only possible amongst a people bound together by a general will. Similarly, individual liberty or freedom is only possible in a people bound together by a general will. Freedom is only achieved in a community of a certain kind, sovereignty is manifested only by a community of a certain kind, and not all political entities are free peoples of the relevant sort. In introducing this radically new idea of a free people as an association of free individuals constituted by a general will, Rousseau introduces a new political idea that remains both inspiring and challenging to this day. It reappears in some form when political communities seek to protect their independence by taking a stand against the impact of alien powers from beyond the political, economic and cultural borders of their political community, This is an anti-cosmopolitan stance that unites many of those on both the political right and political left (Deneen 2018).

Bibliography

Essential reading

Rousseau, Jean-Jacques (1991). *Rousseau and International Relations*, ed. S. Hoffman and D.P. Fidler. UK: Clarendon Press.

Rousseau, Jean-Jacques. (2011). *The Basic Political Writings*, ed. D.A. Cress, intro. David Wootton. USA: Hackett.

There are numerous equally good translations of Rousseau's *Political Writings*; this is the version referred to in the text and to which page numbers correspond).

Secondary reading

These works are either referred to or have directly influenced the arguments in this chapter. It is not a comprehensive guide to the scholarship on Rousseau.

Arendt, Hannah. (1951). *The Origins of Totalitarianism*. USA: Schocken Books.

Arendt, Hannah. (1963). *On Revolution*. UK: Faber and Faber.

Beitz, Charles R. (1979). *Political Theory and International Relations*. USA: Princeton University Press.

Berlin, Isaiah. (1998). *The Proper Study of Mankind*. UK: Pimlico.

Bertram, Christopher. (2004). *Rousseau and the Social Contract*. UK: Routledge.

Bertram, Christopher. (2012). 'Rousseau's Legacy in Two Conceptions of the General Will: Democratic and Transcendental' *Review of Politics*, vol. 74, pp. 403–420.

Buchanan, Allan. (1991). *Secession: The Morality of Political Divorce from Fort Sumpter to Lithuania and Quebec*. USA: Westview.

Caney, Simon. (2005). *Justice Beyond Borders*. UK: Oxford University Press.

Carr, E.H. [1939] (2016). *The Twenty Years' Crisis 1919–1939*. UK: Palgrave.

Cohen, Joshua. (2010). *Rousseau: A Community of Equals*. UK: Oxford University Press.

Deneen, Patrick J. (2018). *Why Liberalism Failed*. USA: Yale University Press.

Fabre, Cécile. (2012). *Cosmopolitan War*. UK: Oxford University Press.

Flikschuh, Katrin. (2000). *Kant and Modern Political Philosophy*. UK: Cambridge University Press.

Gellner, Ernest. (1983). *Nations and Nationalism*. UK: Blackwell.

Gray, John. (1998). *False Dawn: The Delusions of Global Capitalism*. UK: Granta.

Hayek, Friedrich A. (1944). *The Road to Serfdom*. USA: University of Chicago Press.

Hayek, Friedrich A. (1960). *The Constitution of Liberty*. USA: University of Chicago Press.

Hinsley, Francis H. (1962). *Power and the Pursuit of Peace*. UK: Cambridge University Press.

Kedourie, Elie. (1960). *Nationalism*. UK: Hutchinson.

Kymlicka, Will. (1995). *Multicultural Citizenship*. UK: Oxford University Press.

McMahan, Jeff. (2009). *Killing in War*. UK: Clarendon Press.

Miller, David. (1995). *National Identity*. UK: Oxford University Press.

Moore, Margaret. (2015). *The Political Theory of Territory*. UK: Oxford University Press.

Neuhouser, Friedrich. (2013). 'Rousseau's Critique of Inequality: Reconstructing the Second Discourse' *Philosophy and Public Affairs*, vol. 41, pp. 193–225.

Osterhammel, Jurgen. (2018). *Unfabling the East: The Enlightenment's Encounter with Asia*. USA: Princeton University Press.

Pettit, Philip. (1997). *Republicanism: A Theory of Freedom*. UK: Oxford University Press.

Piketty, Thomas. (2013). *Capital in the Twenty-First Century*. UK: Harvard University Press.

Piketty, Thomas. (2020). *Capital and Ideology*. UK: Harvard University Press.

Pinker, Stephen. (2011). *The Better Angels of Our Nature: Why Violence Has Declined*. UK: Penguin.

Pinker, Stephen. (2018). *Enlightenment Now*. UK: Penguin.

Pogge, Thomas. (1989). *Realizing Rawls*. USA: Cornell University Press.

Popper, Karl. [1945] (2011). *The Open Society and Its Enemies*. UK: Routledge.

Rawls, John. (1999). *The Law of Peoples*. UK: Harvard University Press.

Rawls, John. [1971] (1999). *A Theory of Justice*. UK: Harvard Belknap Press.

Rawls, John. (2007). *Lectures on the History of Political Philosophy*. USA: Harvard.

Shklar, Judith. (1985). *Men and Citizens: A Study in Rousseau's Social Theory*. UK: Cambridge University Press.

Smith, Anthony D. (1986). *The Ethnic Origins of Nations*. UK: Blackwell.

Sreenivasan, Gopal. (2000). 'What Is the General Will?' *Philosophical Review*, vol. 109, pp. 545–581.

Streeck, Wolfgang. (2016). *How Will Capitalism End?* UK: Verso.

Talmon, Jacob. (1986). *The Origins of Totalitarian Democracy*. UK: Penguin.

Talmon, Jacob. (1981). *The Myth of the Nation and the Vision of Revolution*. UK: Secker and Warburg.
Tamir, Yael. (1993). *Liberal Nationalism*. USA: Princeton University Press.
Wokler, Robert. (2001). *Rousseau: A Very Short Introduction*. UK: Oxford University Press.

Suggestions for finding open access versions of Rousseau's texts

Online Library of Liberty, maintained by the Liberty Fund
   https://oll.libertyfund.org/person/jean-jacques-rousseau
also Marxists Internet Archive
   https://www.marxists.org/reference/subject/economics/rousseau/index.htm

CHAPTER 8

Clausewitz

The professionalisation of war

In histories of political thought, Clausewitz is a rare and unfamiliar figure. When he is discussed, it is mostly as a footnote to discussions of the state, or as a marginal figure who is chiefly of interest to a small professional readership concerned with strategy and military affairs. Instead, I bring Clausewitz into the foreground of international political thought by arguing that his great work *On War* is as much a work of political theory as any of the other texts discussed here. Clausewitz played a central part in the climate of state and military theory that grew up in 19th-century Prussia in response to the French Revolution, the idea of the rights of man and the citizen, and the subsequent wars for national liberation by the French republic, which transformed into the long-lasting Napoleonic War. The methodology of Clausewitz's military theory was a development of a new policy science. His account of the concept of war and the place of *genius* and *friction* align with a Romantic critique of crude Enlightenment rationalism. His concept of the 'paradoxical trinity' covers the interplay between the people, the army and the government. Critics have asked whether there is actually one trinity or two different 'trinities' at play in Clausewitz's work. Either way, the 'trinity' illustrates the deep interplay of (historic or popular) hatreds, chance, and reason or considered policy as the dynamic forces that explain war and drive international relations. Clausewitz also analysed the priority of offence and defence in the conduct of military operations. Finally, I discuss Clausewitz's influence in an age that followed him, characterised by increased violence and scale of war.

How to cite this book chapter:
Kelly, Paul. 2022. *Conflict, war and revolution: The problem of politics in international political thought*. London: LSE Press, pp. 261–304.
DOI: https://doi.org/10.31389/lsepress.cwr.h License: CC BY.

[I]t is clear that war should never be thought of as something autonomous. (Clausewitz 1984, p. 88)

The modern discipline of international relations grew out of the traumatic experiences of World Wars I and II. From the middle years of the 1914–1918 conflict there was an upsurge of interest in plans for perpetual peace and a desire to seek a modern version in the post-war settlement, implemented via the League of Nations. These plans to arbitrate between interstate disputes failed to address the chaos that led up to World War II in 1939. Finding a better solution preoccupied key figures in international relations' refounding as a discipline focused on better understanding the actual conduct of interstate politics and mitigating its consequences (Carr [1939] 2016). The first founding can be seen as a key source of idealism and normative international relations, and the second as the founding of realist international relations, given the failure of naïve idealism. At the heart of both approaches is the problem of war and how it can be contained.

The disciplinary conflict between idealism and realism reflected the extraordinary manifestation of war as an historical activity in the 20th and into the 21st centuries. In just over a century the rapid technological advancement of military means and capabilities transformed the 19th-century experience of war. The century began dominated by a traditional technology of bayonet charges, rifles and artillery. By 1918 the means of war had expanded to include poison gas, motorised artillery, tanks, machine guns and aircraft. Aeroplanes engaged in traditional duels in the sky in dogfights, whilst giant airships brought war to domestic populations with the aerial bombing of towns and cities. By the end of the 1939–1945 war the expansion and development of technology included jet propulsion, rockets and nuclear explosives. These developments appeared to have rendered the practice of traditional warfare redundant, because nuclear and thermo-nuclear weapons upset the point of war as an assertion of state power through the idea of 'mutually assured destruction' (MAD). Yet, whilst the Cold War appeared to have replaced the idea of a 'hot' or direct conflict between the ideological adversaries of the liberal democratic west and Communist east, more conventional wars continued to be waged, by the great powers in Korea and by proxies almost everywhere else. The collapse of the USSR and the end of the Cold War in 1989 did not see a move towards peace but only a resurgence of war as a tool of global pacification in the two Gulf Wars (1991 and 2003) and the 'War against Terror' following 9/11. War remains prevalent in the early 21st century, as it was in all previous periods. Despite many attempts to displace the preoccupation with war in political and international theory, the central significance of interstate and guerrilla conflicts has not reduced there either.

The obsession with war in international theory is a legacy of the dominance of realism as an approach in international relations and the idea of state sovereignty in political theory and philosophy. War remains a problem that different styles of political thought try to manage, contain and eradicate or limit. For Hobbes, the state is the bulwark against the ever-present threat of war. For Locke, a properly constituted state defends against the challenge of unrestrained absolutism (which often fuels wars). For Rousseau, war is a consequence of the international system. War is also a central part of the moralist tendency of much political theory, where the interesting questions are about how it should be disciplined and used within a moral and ethical context. It is no coincidence that just war theories prioritise the concept of justice over war.

Despite the best efforts of Machiavelli, political theory and international theory still presuppose that wars need to be specially justified before the tribunal of justice or interest. This can obscure an important set of questions about what war is and how one should actually theorise it as a recurring feature of human experience, and not an aberration that arises solely from the failure of politics.

When philosophers and political theorists write about war, it is usually as a distraction from something more important, whereas soldiers, especially generals, tend to write about their own direct experience. Soldiers tend to be practical individuals (until very recently always men), a welcome trait because when they get things wrong people literally get hurt. Yet, that also means military thinkers rarely achieve a sufficiently disengaged experience to generalise usefully about war, over and above a reflection on a particular strategy or set of tactics. They tend to alternate between an historical perspective, on the one hand, and a practical manual on the other, and so they speak to narrow audiences.

The genius of Clausewitz is that he theorises about war in the context of practical military experience, but without collapsing into the perspective of an historian. Whilst high-level strategic thinking is part of his great 1832 book *On War*, his genius is to say something general about the activity of war, the profession of arms, and the place of wars and military conflicts in the conduct of states and the relations between them. More importantly, in so doing Clausewitz introduces a style of political thinking that should be characterised as the technology of the state – the application of science to a practical policy problem. This technocratic approach to politics first appeared in the late 18th century under the heading of 'police' or what would now be considered public policy, and went on to have an impact on political thinkers as diverse as Jeremy Bentham and George Friedrich Hegel. The approach expanded rapidly in the 19th century, when the state claimed many new competences in spheres of policy that were almost unheard of before, like welfare and mass education. Policy-relevant thinking developed first and most extensively out of the work of military thinkers. Clausewitz recognised war as perhaps the oldest and most distinctive activity of political communities, and yet also placed it in the broadest contemporary context. He saw modern war is an activity only made possible by the new bureaucratic states and the system of relations that they entail. This is what makes Clausewitz's great work not just an adjunct to regular political thought, or one amongst the many founders of modern military strategy. It is instead a significant contribution to understanding the effective pursuit of politically set policy, albeit by other means.

Life and career

Clausewitz's is an intriguing figure because he was an academic soldier in a military culture where even staff officers were mostly involved in practical teaching and conducting field rides for the youth of the Prussian aristocracy, from whom the senior officer class were drawn. His interests were broad and philosophical, as well as practical and historical, and his model of science as a systematic ordering of knowledge was comprehensive. Like his philosophical contemporary Hegel (who died in the cholera pandemic that swept through Berlin in 1831 and probably also killed Clausewitz), he sought to comprehend an activity and mode of practical experience, rather than deduce campaign success from a series of empirical premises derived from military history and local geography. Yet, Clausewitz was also a practical soldier. Throughout his life and career he sought a general command in the field and not just a post in the lecture room of the staff college.

Carl was born in 1780 into the relatively modest middle-class Clausewitz family, which had some military and academic connections. His father had been commissioned as a junior officer in the Prussian Army as a result of Frederick the Great's relaxation of the barriers on entering the Prussian officer corps during the Seven Years War (1756–1763). However, he was retired out of the army at the end of the war as Frederick sought to reassert the social exclusivity of the Prussian officer corps to the landed nobility or *Junkers*. Clausewitz followed his father's profession and obtained a commission into the 34th Infantry Regiment at the age of 12. Yet, he was already pursuing wide and disciplined reading that was to form the basis of his writings later in life. He first saw military service at the early age of 13, during the Prussian Army's 1793 role in containing and forcing back the new French army of the First Republic.

With the end of that period of active campaigning along the Rhine and in the Vosges, the next five years of his early career were spent in garrison duty in a small town, a posting made bearable for him by access to the library of Prince Henry, brother of Frederick the Great. Clausewitz made good use of this time with systematic study that brought him to the attention of his superiors, and in 1801 he entered the Kriegsakademie, or War College. At the time this was led by General Gerhard von Scharnhorst, an enterprising and important military thinker and reformer. Unlike most of the senior Prussian officers, Scharnhorst was an artilleryman, rather than an infantry or cavalry soldier. He was also a Hanoverian, rather than Prussian, yet his authority was derived from success in the field. Clausewitz soon became a protégé, and his intellectual and practical ambition made him an ally in the reform of Prussian military culture and the organisation of the Prussian state, within which the military class was so central. The challenge Scharnhorst wrestled with was the rise and success of the new French Revolutionary armies. On the face of it these defied aristocratic conventional wisdom about military organisation, command structures and the class of officers. Many of the leading French generals had risen from nowhere. In addition, French modes of organising supply, administration and planning were radically different, yet French armies achieved considerable success.

However, the most important factor that attracted Scharnhorst's attention was the transformative role played by the revolutionary ideology or national 'spirit' of the French troops. Their Revolution had unleashed a powerful ideological factor that motivated these armies in a struggle for liberation against the established power of the old order. The place of war and the role of the state and nation in the new order unleashed by the French Revolution were to form the backdrop of Clausewitz's own thinking about war.

Clausewitz graduated in 1803 (top of his class) and became adjutant to the son of his regiment's colonel in chief. He also met Marie von Brühl, who became his wife after an extended courtship. Marie played an important part in his life as an intellectual companion. (It was under her direction that Clausewitz's extensive writings were edited and published as *On War* in 1832, not long after his death.) Clausewitz's new commission was to be tested when Prussia went to war with France in 1806. He served in the Battle of Jena-Auerstedt and was captured following defeat. Captivity for senior officers was a relatively benign affair at this time, and the most senior were often effectively returned following a ransom. Clausewitz remained in captivity until 1808 and acquired a lifelong hostility to the French that was to inform his subsequent career. After his return from captivity, Clausewitz rejoined Scharnhorst, who was now based in Königsberg reorganising the Prussian Army, and continued to serve as his loyal reforming ally.

Yet, when Prussia concluded an alliance with France in 1812, Clausewitz took the extraordinary step of resigning his commission and joining other Prussian officers now in the service of the Russian emperor, Alexander I, just as Napoleon was commencing his campaign in Russia. In this capacity, Clausewitz took part in the great Battle of Borodino in 1812. Although Napoleon's armies won a technical victory over General Kutusov here, and went on to occupy Moscow, the battle marked the high point of the French armies' Russian campaign. The Russian forces survived to harry and destroy their enemies in their long winter retreat back to the western borders. Clausewitz was also the intermediary in organising the capitulation of the Prussian forces serving with France and their going over to the Russians. This important act began the alliance of Russia, Prussia and Britain that led to Napoleon's eventual defeat in 1815 at Waterloo.

Despite this new alliance, Frederick William III did not readmit Clausewitz into the Prussian Army until 1814, and always denied him a major field command. He returned to Berlin as director of the War College, but was not given any role in the further reform of the military or Prussian state. It was during this period that he began drafting *On War* and his studies of the Napoleonic campaigns. In 1830 he was assigned to an artillery command in Breslau following fears of a new war after uprisings in Paris and Poland. But the war never came and instead Clausewitz's last enemy was the cholera epidemic. He was charged with organising a *cordon sanitaire* to prevent the Berlin epidemic spreading out into Germany, but instead he fell victim to the disease and died in 1831.

Although the subsequent reputation of the book later grew to be considerable, for some time after its publication it had only a limited impact and Clausewitz was overshadowed by others. When his reputation first began to be recovered, it actually was due to a misreading of Clausewitz as the philosopher of Prussian militarism, a creed that was to reach its reputational nadir during World War I. In fact, Clausewitz was anything but a caricature unthinking Prussian militarist, but neither was he a liberal democrat. He was a technocratic soldier with an understanding not only of the art of war but more importantly its place in the new bureaucratic state that emerged in Europe in the aftermath of the French Revolution and the defeat of Napoleon. His recognition of war as the fundamental technology of the modern state makes him especially relevant in our own time, as new conceptions of the site of politics emerge.

Prussia and political theory: *On War* in context

Clausewitz's dual identities as a patriotic Prussian and a soldier were to become inextricably connected in European history in the 19th and early 20th centuries. Some later critics have accused Clausewitz of being the theorist of 'Prussianism', a militaristic and authoritarian ideology of politics that was linked to Kaiser Wilhelm II's brutal policy in World War I, and was later seen as enabling the worst excesses of Nazism during World War II. But the main culprits behind 'Prussianism' are not exclusively military figures. The great German philosopher G.W.F. Hegel (who taught at Berlin University in the latter years of Clausewitz's life) was also criticised by L.T. Hobhouse and Karl Popper for justifying the same culture of militarism and politics of authoritarian nationalism, with its prioritisation of reason of state over morality and ethics (Hobhouse 1918; Popper 2011). The Prussian ideology was one of the targets against which the modern liberal democratic view of the state developed in 20th-century Anglo-American thought. The convergence of the character of the Prussian state, and its link to one of the high points of German philosophical culture, forms the central context for understanding Clausewitz's work.

Clausewitz was born in the last years of the rule of Frederick II, or Frederick the Great, who consolidated the territory and the power of Prussia in his 46-year reign through a series of wars, which left his kingdom a major European power and a site for the emergence of a resurgent German political culture. The Hohenzollern kingdom emerged from a small Baltic duchy with its capital at Königsberg. It was characterised by a distinctive administrative culture and taxation system that allowed the state to sustain a standing army that was disproportionate to its size and those of its neighbours. The large size of the military and its officer class integrated the landed nobility into a distinctive military culture that was also reflected in the personal character of Frederick the Great's predecessors. Frederick's father applied military-style discipline to the education and sometimes brutal upbringing of his son. Owing to the size of its military, and the dynastic opportunism of its royal family, Prussia was heavily involved in the European wars of the 18th century that saw the slow eclipse of Poland–Lithuania as a major central European power – squeezed between Russia, Austria and the rise of Prussia. Frederick the Great's own career was dominated by his success in the Silesian wars of the 1740s and 1750s against Austria that absorbed parts of contested Polish territory into the Prussian kingdom. The latter part of these conflicts was an extension of the War of the Austrian Succession and the Seven Years War. The demands of the Seven Years War relaxed the rigid class basis of the Prussian officer class (thus enabling the rise of Clausewitz's own father, noted above). However, this process was temporary and subsequently reversed: Prussia remained a rigidly stratified and ultra-conservative political culture.

However, Frederick the Great was not merely a militaristic monarch. He was also a patron of the arts and philosophy and encouraged the growth of an intellectual culture that challenged the dominance of France as the leading exemplar of European Enlightenment. He invited the French philosopher Voltaire to live with him at his palace at Sanssouci near Potsdam, and Frederick was as famous for his intellectual salons and dinners as he was for his exploits on the battlefield. He surrounded himself with a male court and, though married, he was almost certainly homosexual and died childless. He was succeeded by his nephew, who inherited a powerful central European state that through dynastic connections was consolidating many of the German principalities into a single political unit, and a vibrant philosophical culture that would lead European thought in the reaction against the legacy of the French Enlightenment in the wars of the French Revolution.

This late flowering of German Enlightenment thought began with Immanuel Kant in the East Prussian city of Königsberg, and continued in Berlin with his successors and Clausewitz's contemporaries, J.G. Fichte and G.W.F. Hegel. These thinkers, in turn, provided the inspiration for the Romantic movement, as a reaction against the abstract individualism of Kant's ethical theory or the French 'rights of man and the citizen' that became the battle slogan of the French Revolutionary armies. This Romantic movement contributed a new interest in subjective experience, creativity and the ideal of genius. It also directed attention to the contexts in which genius and creativity take place, such as our relationship to nature, and to the languages and cultures within which identities are formed and through which artistic creativity is expressed. This attention to culture and language prompted the development of theories of nationality and national identity, which in turn inspired the political ideology of nationalism that developed as reaction to the universalism of the rights of man.

Immanuel Kant (1724–1804) was undoubtedly one of the greatest philosophers of any age. Beginning with the *Critique of Pure Reason* (1781), his critical philosophy transformed subsequent western philosophy. In this work Kant set out to establish a Copernican Revolution in philosophy that changed the way in which the basic questions of metaphysics and epistemology were understood. His predecessors had sought to derive a secure basis for knowledge through a priori deductions from reason (Descartes), or through sense experience (Locke and Hume), which resulted in a stand-off between rationalism and empiricism. Kant sought to overcome this opposition by a transcendental argument that presupposed the possibility of knowledge, and sought the conditions of that knowledge in an account of the rules of understanding that order our experience. This process sidestepped the traditional problem of scepticism, which denied the possibility of certain knowledge, by arguing that scepticism is not genuine but simply a consequence of misleading philosophical theories. Kant's solution to the problem of knowledge was to show how the human mind orders experience through the application of rules of understanding to sensible intuitions, so that we can have certain knowledge about the world. This shift of attention to the structure of understanding of the knowing subject entailed a distinction between the world as experienced (the phenomenal world) and the world of things in themselves (the noumenal world), about which we can have no direct experience. The 'two worlds' view and the primacy of the subject (or knower) was to transform subsequent philosophy as his successors challenged or developed these views. With its possibility of an unconditioned subject beyond the world of experience and knowledge, the two worlds view also opened up Kant's account of moral philosophy – because it rendered possible an account of freedom (and therefore moral responsibility) in a world of causation and necessity that had otherwise seemed to threaten the possibility of free agency. Kant's moral philosophy of unconditional duties has also been a perennial starting point for all subsequent non-naturalistic theories of morality. His theory of moral agency is related to but does not prescribe his account of political philosophy, which was his third major contribution.

Where his moral theory is an account of internal freedom and the moral agent's ability to engage in free moral judgement and action, Kant's political philosophy posits a world of free individuals. Their agency and claims to freedom and property (that follows from that agency) presuppose the idea of an omni-lateral power (one that applies to and includes all individuals within its scope) that determines the extent of those claims of subjective rights as public rights. Kant's political theory argues that the claim of freedom and equality that is central to previous social contract theories presupposes the necessity of a state, as the omni-lateral power that determines individual rights claims. This idea, that the state was the presupposition of freedom and equality and that political obligation was a precondition of free agency, was the beginning of a tradition of state theory that was closely associated with Prussia. It was also attractive to the official conservative political culture of the Prussian kingdom, because it overthrew the idea of a fundamental confrontation between the claims of the state and the rights of man. Although Kant's philosophy was revolutionary, his politics certainly was not.

That said, it did transform the philosophical landscape of his successors, J.G. Fichte and Hegel, both of whom continued and extended the idea of the state as the solution to the problem of individual rights and political obligation. Fichte's philosophy developed as a reaction against Kant's dualism between the phenomenal and the noumenal. Fichte replaced it with an idealist philosophy of consciousness that rejects the need for an account of the noumenal world as a grounding of consciousness. This rejection of the grounding of consciousness was taken up by Hegel in his philosophical logic. For both Fichte and Hegel, the idea of the phenomenal world arises from the activity of self-consciousness itself. Similarly, the idea of the moral self as a free agent is something that emerges within consciousness from the confrontation with another conscious mind or self, against which it must define itself through a process of recognition.

Fichte and Hegel also agreed on seeing the emergence of the idea of the self-conscious agent as an inherently social phenomenon. This shifts the focus of philosophical thinking from the isolated subject as an individual to the importance of the communitarian conditions for identity and self-hood. Once again, the shift in perspective is from self-conscious individuals in a state of nature, seeking to explain and create social relations such as the state, to the new idea of subject or individual as a social creation emerging in a context, with others. Fichte's metaphysics of morals is obscured by his relationship with Kant and his contemporary Hegel. But his importance in political thought is illustrated in his lectures, *Addresses to the German Nation* (1808), in which he defends the importance of German national identity in the face of the universalism of the rights of man, and because of his theory of state. On the nation and nationalism, Fichte is interested in the idea of language and culture that is central to the ideas of J.G. Herder, another contemporary of Kant, who found his way to Berlin and who developed theories of language and culture as the vehicles through which identity and thought is constituted.

Fichte's concern is to encourage a literature and culture through which the spirit of a people could be articulated in its distinctiveness and peculiar genius. The emphasis on culture and language was to inspire a turn to history and to the folk culture of a people. Two of the vehicles through which that culture is defended are the education system and the civic and political rights of the state. The state that emerges in Fichte's writings is different from Kant's ideas. It is not solely focused on providing a constitutional context for secure individual freedom. Fichte is more concerned with the justification for the state to limit personal freedom through paternalism or state actions so as to improve the condition of its subjects, rather than just protecting them from each other and external international threats. In particular, he emphasises the police function of the state, which is confined not to internal security but to what we would now consider the remit of social and public policy – indeed, it is the root from which the word 'policy' is developed by later thinkers. Policy, and police, is also the category into which Clausewitz links his theory of war as a policy instrument.

The communitarian or contextualist account of the emergence of human subjectivity also played a central part in Hegel's thought. G.W.F. Hegel is second only to Kant in the pantheon of great German philosophers and political theorists. His political philosophy is to be found in *Elements of the Philosophy of Right* (1821), where he argues that the historical process of the emergence and development of freedom culminates in the idea of the state. For Hegel, the state is both a set of bureaucratic institutions of government and law, which in turn regulate and direct powers such as the military and the police powers of the sort favoured by Fichte. However, Hegel also saw the state as the culmination of an ethical story, and the entity through which our situated freedom is actualised or made possible in the world. He goes beyond Kant's idea that the state gives determinacy to right by arguing that the state brings together natural relationships and sources of obligation (such as the family) with those of civil society in a new synthesis, which alone makes a full ethical life possible. Once again, freedom and moral agency are only made feasible by our duty to submit ourselves to the state and its constitutive power. History and reason are integrally linked in the development of the state and its institutions.

Much of the subsequent debate around Hegel's theory of the state concerns what he meant by describing it as the culmination of the teleology (or purpose) of history – the 'state is the end of history'. Did this mean that all subsequent historical experience was included within the idea of the state as the mode of public experience? Alternatively, as Hegel's progressive followers and critics suggested, was the state the current stage of historical progress that will only be transcended in a direction that remains obscure, possibly towards a post-state cosmopolitan order? Since the 19th century, progressive and conservative liberals have differed in their interpretations of Hegel's implications for the ideal of freedom and agency. The solution to this debate takes us beyond Clausewitz's context, yet one essential element of Hegel's story brings us back to Clausewitz and his specific teaching. Hegel's theory of international relations and international law provides an account of war as part of the rationale of the state system. War is not an unfortunate consequence of the state system that needs to be overcome by plans for perpetual peace or cosmopolitan order but a necessary requirement for the internal order of the particular state, ensuring the reality of the identity-creating factors of the ethical life made possible in the modern state system. War becomes the highest goal of the modern state and the medium through which it reproduces itself and asserts its claim to recognition in the world.

The political and intellectual contexts in which Clausewitz's thought was formed, and in which he began to write his masterpiece, combined Prussian military experience and culture with ideas refined through the highest development of late Enlightenment German philosophy, and where war is transformed from a recurring problem into the ethically sanctioned highest goal of the modern state system. Once great philosophers such as Hegel had secured the place of war in the ethical and political reason of the state, it remained for Clausewitz to provide the scientific analysis and account of the phenomena of war to fit that high intellectual challenge. War needed to be understood in its totality and that is the task of *On War*: it is also why Clausewitz's book could not be a manual of practice or a series of reflections on recent battles. His genius was to see the challenge of thinking about war in this new way.

The problem of Clausewitz's *On War*

On War is a long and complex book on a relatively new subject. However, the book is made more complex because Clausewitz worked on it for a long time and it remained incomplete at the time of his death. He had discussed the plan for the work extensively with his wife, Maria, and she saw it to publication. Although he began work on the material for the book in 1816, he wrote an important note in 1827, suggesting a significant reworking of the conception of the book. Only Book I was complete to his satisfaction and for Book VIII in particular he emphasised the importance of his insight into the relationship between war and politics or policy. The 1827 note, the large body of material and the obvious questions about consistency make the book difficult to comprehend and have raised serious questions about how it should be interpreted. Because the book sets a template for a new way of thinking about military affairs, it cannot simply be set in a context of other similar-type works to settle these fundamental questions of interpretation. Successors write in Clausewitz's shadow in a similar way to philosophers writing after Plato or historians after Thucydides. These great texts provide a point of reference and a key to style and method, even when the task of a successor is to differentiate their view from and to criticise the great texts. Clausewitz sets out to provide a comprehensive theory of war and, in so doing, to offer more than reflections of past military history. His theory of war is intended to be comprehensive, and not one merely specific to a particular time and place. In this way it aspires to be scientific. In order to understand that claim, and to distinguish it from interpretations that could distort what Clausewitz is saying, it is necessary to reflect on his methodology or philosophical presuppositions before turning directly to the object of enquiry.

In setting out his comprehensive scientific theory of war, Clausewitz draws on his experience in the field, his wide reading of military history and his understanding of late Enlightenment philosophy and science. He was also addressing a challenge posed by contemporary military thinkers such as H. Dietrich von Bulow, author of *The Spirit of the Modern System of War* (London, 1806) and Antoine Henri de Jomini in *The Summary of the Art of War* (New York, 1854). Both writers developed a mechanical or 'geometrical' conception of the science of war in their reflections on the experience of the late 18th century and French Revolutionary wars. Central to the geometrical approach was a familiar dichotomy between science and art that was deployed in policy discussions by many late Enlightenment thinkers. At around this time, the English utilitarian philosopher Jeremy Bentham (1748–1832) was drawing a distinction between the science and art of political economy. The former concerned the principles of a mechanical explanation of behaviour, drawn from the rational modelling of human experience. The aim of this science was to determine the causal relations of properties such as supply and demand. The art of political science was to translate this scientific explanation into distinct policies, such as whether to regulate the maximum level of interest that the law allowed to be charged, or the levels at which tariffs should be set.

In the case of military science, von Bulow and de Jomini also sought to explain the nature of action in war and reduce it to a series of principles from which practical inferences could be drawn by commanders. The aim of this science was to comprehend the possibilities of war and provide commanders with manuals for action that were derived from these basic principles. In particular, von Bulow developed the idea of the line operation and the conduct of war as an account of possible manoeuvres around that line. As the technology of war had developed, armies were constrained by logistical problems of lines of supply. In order to advance, armies required that bases of supply, or depots, be established, and these in turn dictated the direction of attack against an adversary. Using 'geometric' reasoning, von Bulow argued that the army must confront its adversary at an angle of 90 degrees from the line. Geometry became a model of scientific explanation for these thinkers because it was formal and deductive. It had also been the science of spatial relations from the time of the ancient Greeks and so captured their view of the essence of military affairs as the movement and deployment of forces in space. The main challenge for opponents was to attack the adversary's line of supply and depots using skirmishing and therefore reduce the need for direct confrontations. The consequence of this 'geometric' science was to result in a mechanical approach to the order of battle, and (according to von Bulow) a reduction in the need for direct confrontation and instead a preference for skirmishing tactics. An enlightened science of war would be one that reduced the occasions and amount of violence to the minimum necessary to achieve one's end, with the possibility that the effective deployment of force could in principle serve as a checkmate, as if war were a giant game of chess.

This 'geometric' approach was developed further by de Jomini, who was to be Clausewitz's chief rival as the leading strategic thinker for the remainder of the 19th century. De Jomini expanded on von Bulow's approach with a more sophisticated account of the war of manoeuvre. He deployed ideas such as 'interior lines', which allowed for shorter and quicker logistical supply within an enclosed area than was possible outside it, making the area easier to defend. De Jomini's work is full of illustrations representing how various configurations of interior lines might be deployed. In the context of Napoleon's campaigns, he sought to show that this kind of strategy allowed a smaller force to concentrate and defeat larger armies by dividing them. These 'geometrical' approaches were enormously popular because they seemed to uncover the universal laws of military conflict. Especially with de Jomini, they appeared to show, firstly, how these laws explained the success of Napoleon's campaigns and later how his strategy might be defeated. The 'geometric' approach laid out a science of war in terms of a set of universal laws that all conflict followed, and which could be the basis of manuals for the conduct of war and the training of officers who would be adept at applying these lessons. It was precisely this conception of military science that Clausewitz sought to expose and replace. He challenged not only the substance of von Bulow's and de Jomini's laws of war but their very conception of a science of war that was simple, mechanical or geometric and reducible to an easily taught art. He writes:

> If one has never personally experienced war, one cannot understand in what the difficulties constantly mentioned really consist, nor why a commander should need any brilliance and exceptional ability. Everything looks simple; the knowledge required does not look remarkable, the strategic options are so obvious that by comparison the simplest problem of higher mathematics has an impressive scientific dignity. Once war has actually been seen the difficulties become clear; but it is still extremely hard to describe the unseen, all-pervading element that brings about this change of perspective. (Clausewitz 1984, p. 119)

By contrast, Clausewitz had indeed seen war and knew why it was never so simple or reducible to a mechanical science. Such a mechanical or geometrical way of thinking ignored the two concepts that Clausewitz saw as essential to comprehending the reality of war and therefore any attempt to claim knowledge about it; these were the ideas of friction and of genius. He confronts his predecessors with the paradoxical claim that:

> [e]verything in war is very simple, but the simplest thing is difficult. The difficulties accumulate and end by producing a kind of friction that is inconceivable unless one has experienced war. (Clausewitz 1984, p. 119)

The attempt to abstract principles of manoeuvre from the messy reality of the human experience of war left the impression of armies moving in a vacuum without any resistance. Yet, for Clausewitz, the more one considered the reality of war, the more one saw every single moving part of a complex military engagement being beset by countervailing forces and obstacles.

The concept of friction is not given a simple definition or a single illustration, but it reappears in numerous examples throughout the work. Weather can be source of friction, with rain slowing the movement of infantry columns, baggage and supply trains, or creating muddy conditions preventing the deployment of cavalry. At the individual level, rain can frustrate the effective use of muskets or artillery, while fog and battle smoke simply deny a commander sight of his troops and their deployment. Real war is beset with opportunities for friction to frustrate the plans of 'paper wars'. Acknowledging the impact of friction is not a counsel of despair or a denial of initiative, because the task of the commander and his forces is to confront and overcome the constraints that friction imposes. Friction is a reality of war but the challenge is to recognise it in strategy and tactics. A true account of war cannot simply abstract a pure science from this messy world of experience without at the same time denying the reality of the experience of which one is seeking knowledge. Such a science is a distortion of the object of experience and therefore cannot be a basis for knowledge. The science of war thus cannot be reducible to a few simple rules and principles in a manual that commanders can learn and consult.

This loss of simplicity is not only an acknowledgement of the complexity of human experience; it also has implications for humans acquiring knowledge of war, which introduces the second major concept at the heart of Clausewitz's theory: the role of genius. Against the tendency of Enlightenment thinking to emphasise rule-following and the application of knowledge, the character of the genius played an important part in the Romantic reaction. It was peculiarly appropriate for an age of military thinking that was shaped by Frederick the Great and Napoleon Bonaparte, two epic figures who appeared to embody historical transformation and who fascinated Clausewitz and his contemporaries. Genius, and its character, was an issue of the age, fascinating political philosophers such as Hegel and Fichte, or great artists such as Goethe and Beethoven. The genius was not a rule-follower but an agent who through his originality (it was always a he) transformed knowledge, experience and the world. The genius is a central figure in the aesthetic theory of Immanuel Kant's *Critique of Judgement* (1790), a work that Clausewitz would have been familiar with (Echevarria 2007, pp. 108–111).

For Kant, what is distinctive about the genius is that he brings a new 'rule to art' to a problem or situation, and thus transforms the way in which it is seen and in which it is subsequently practised. In music, for instance, Beethoven established new ways of going on with received forms such as the symphony, quartet and sonata. This is the act of giving a new rule to art: a way of setting out a new way of doing things but within a practice, activity or body of knowledge that was already in existence. Genius presupposes the activity or practice of an art or knowledge, but is not dominated and limited by that practice in the way that a virtuoso concert performer, or someone who is excellent in applying the rules, might be. This idea of the creative artist who goes beyond the rules was an important cultural trope, especially in the hands of philosophers and artists.

Yet, in the context of military affairs and conduct, such a view can be problematic. For some of Clausewitz's contemporaries, military geniuses such as Frederick the Great or Napoleon are almost incomprehensible to military science and need to be passed over as magical or semi-miraculous figures. Whilst not diminishing their extraordinary achievements, however, Clausewitz seeks to understand the character of the military genius:

> 'genius' refers to a very highly developed mental aptitude for a particular occupation … What we must do is to survey all those gifts of mind and temperament that in combination bear on military activity. These, taken together, constitute *the essence of military genius*. We have said *in combination*, since it is precisely the essence of military genius that it does not consist in a single appropriate gift – courage, for example – while other qualities of mind or temperament are wanting or are not suited to war. Genius consists *in a harmonious combination of elements*, in which one or the other ability may predominate, but none may be in conflict with the rest. (Clausewitz 1984, p. 100)

The discussion of military genius involves a review of both intellectual virtues and virtues of character (such as courage or confidence). In combination, all are essential to the military genius, but the appropriate combination of these qualities is also relative to the role of the individual, whether a field officer leading a small group or the commander-in-chief conducting whole armies in a major campaign. Having moved from mechanical and abstract conceptions of the science and art of war, Clausewitz seeks a deep and nuanced account of psychology of the military genius, and not just an account of the things that the soldier, general or commander-in-chief should know. He is concerned with moving beyond the idea that the military genius combines courage with knowledge, and instead offers an account of the character of mind of the military genius.

He begins with a discussion of courage and analyses its sources. With respect to the intellect, Clausewitz distinguishes between two essential features or qualities: *coup d'oeil* and determination. The former is an account of that capacity to retain the 'light of truth' in circumstances where quick and confident analysis and decision is required. He likens the capacity to an 'inward eye' that sees a pattern or relationship with aspects of knowledge and experience that are needed for 'rapid and accurate decisions' in circumstances where knowledge and the truth matter but where time and circumstances deny the possibility of considered deliberation. This confident ability to 'see and understand' circumstances, opportunities and risks enables the military genius to respond to chance: it takes previously learned experience but assimilates it into the new circumstances with confident judgement and decision. As such, *coup d'oeil* is more than just knowledge or intelligence, but it is also more than just reckless decision and quick judgement. The risk of being wrong or failing to appreciate the challenge of circumstances also requires an aspect of intellectual courage that Clausewitz describes as determination. This is the intellectual courage to take responsibility for difficult decisions and hold to them. A virtue of the intellect is also the possession of stable emotions and firmness of character so as to suppress doubt and fear of being wrong. Clausewitz remarks that junior officers who show this virtue of mind and character often lose it when promoted to more senior positions, out of fear of being proved wrong.

Other aspects of the character of the military genius that Clausewitz relates to the danger, uncertainty, exertion and chance or war are energy, firmness, staunchness, emotional balance and strength of character. Each of these is given an extended discussion in Book I, Chapter 3. Yet, it is not the details of the examples that matter but the way in which Clausewitz explores the interrelationship of these elements of character in his account of the circumstance of war. The issue of genius is discussed throughout the book, but the relevant chapter in which the concept is introduced concludes with a clear attempt to bring the idea down from the near-miraculous character attributed to Napoleon or Frederick by their followers, to a conception that is appropriate to the seriousness of the task of military leadership.

> If we then ask what sort of mind is likeliest to display the qualities of military genius, experience and observation will both tell us that it is the inquiring rather than the creative mind, the comprehensive rather than the specialised approach, the calm rather than the excitable head to which in war we would choose to entrust the fate of our brothers and children, and the safety and honour of our country. (Clausewitz 1984, p. 112)

What Clausewitz's theory of war is seeking is not a set of rules or principles that can be applied, or a simple character profile that could be used for assigning rank and promotion, but an account of the interrelationship and ordering of the elements of experience that are required in the intense circumstances of war. Clausewitz is not seeking to replace geometry with another master science (such as psychology) in his account of war. Instead, his ambition is to bring all the elements appropriate to understanding the experience of war into a coherent and ordered body of knowledge. He sought to emulate the great Prussian philosopher Immanuel Kant, who had not sought to enumerate all that we can know, or (following the sceptical tradition) list all that we do not know. Instead, he sought to save metaphysics and epistemology (the theory of knowledge) by providing an account of how that experience must be ordered so as to count as knowledge. Similarly, with Clausewitz the task is to provide an account of ordering the totality of experience that makes up our knowledge of the phenomenon of war in its most complete form. In order to understand the method and point of *On War*, we should see it as akin to the approach in Kant's *Critique of Pure Reason* and his *Critique of Judgement* applied to the phenomena of war.

The object of enquiry – what is war?

To ask what the object of enquiry of a theory of war is might seem an odd question. Surely, everyone knows what war is. Yet, whilst history and experience might seem to render that question redundant, the history of political and military thinking brings it back to the fore and explains why it is such an important question for Clausewitz to answer in his new theory of war. Writing on war was not a phenomenon unique to the European Enlightenment. The Greeks and Romans, as well as Renaissance writers, had written histories of wars and conflicts. And political thinkers such as Machiavelli wrote on the theory of war itself. However, much of this writing was concerned with the organisation of armies and was self-consciously backward-looking, drawing on the history of Roman warfare: something that was of particular interest to Machiavelli. Even with the development of new technology, early modern military writings were effectively drill manuals, or focused on specialist 'sciences' such as siege warfare or fortification.

Early modern political theorists such as Hobbes were no better in their conceptualisation of war as generalised individual violence. The natural condition might have been 'a war of all against all' but this left the nature of war general, vague and ultimately unhelpful for the modern scholar of war, although it at least acknowledged the essential place of violence. As modernity and technology advanced, so the understanding of war began to shift from a problem of the organisation of armies into the new science of operations, to which Clausewitz's opponents, von Bulow and de Jomini, contributed so much. The focus on operations inspired a preoccupation with movement, logistics and lines of supply, and the organisation and utilisation of space – to the extent that this, in turn, was transformed into a science of movement that displaced the fundamental fact of war. It was this fundamental fact, the one that we are most familiar with, that Clausewitz sought to return to the centre of attention in his definition of the object of enquiry.

> War is nothing but a duel on a larger scale. Countless duels go to make up war, but a picture of it as a whole can be formed by imagining a pair of wrestlers. Each tries through physical force to compel the other to do his will; his *immediate* aim is to *throw* his opponent in order to make him incapable of further resistance.
> *War is thus an act of force to compel our enemy to do our will.*

Force, to counter opposing force, equips itself with the inventions of art and science. Attached to force are certain self-imposed, imperceptible limitations hardly worth mentioning, known as international law and custom, but they scarcely weaken it. (Clausewitz 1984, p. 75 italics in original)

He continues:

Kind-hearted people might of course think there was some ingenious way to disarm or defeat an enemy without too much bloodshed, and might imagine this is the true goal of the art of war. Pleasant as it sounds, it is a fallacy that must be exposed:
… It would be futile – even wrong – to try and shut one's eyes to what war really is from sheer distress at its brutality. (Clausewitz 1984, pp. 75–76)

These two passages reinforce Clausewitz's primary insight that war is about violent conflict between opponents. Whilst in exceptional circumstances manoeuvre alone might compel an enemy to do as we want, it is violent force applied to the bending of the will of another that makes war distinctive. Violence and the risk of violence are of the essence of war and are what military action is for – everything else is contingent upon these. The advancement of military science is not concerned with the reduction of violence in the exercise of force, and it is a great error to consider the goal of military science as the eradication of brutality and suffering, or with disguising it and masking its necessity. Attempts to conduct conflict with the limitation of force are invitations to failure, not marks of civilisation and superiority over barbarians or the savage past. Reliance on war as a tool of policy requires this direct confrontation with its reality as concentrated violence directed at forcing the will of an opponent. As a soldier, Clausewitz is not afraid to advocate or exercise violence, but he is concerned that those who command violent conflict do it without deceiving themselves about the possibility of humanising the suffering and brutality that war results in.

Alongside the emphasis on violence, and even the prospect of concentrated and massive violence, the main message of this definition is the link of war with the idea of the duel. Clausewitz conceives of war as an aggregation of individual duels between opponents, with the idea of a duel as the central act of war. The duel is a particular type of violent act or combat, but it contains important elements that can be lost in the image. Indeed, it is interesting that Clausewitz uses the wrestlers as his illustration. The wrestlers are opponents in a structured combat – indeed, in the sport of wrestling, that structure is taken to the point of an art – but even outside the sport of wrestling there are important elements not to lose sight of. The wrestlers engage each other in the most basic form of combat, where the only weapon is the use of one's body against an opponent.

There is a form of equal recognition that is central to the struggle as the opponents have the same capacity to harm. A duel between a wrestler and an opponent with a sword, spear or gun would not be a duel. In the formal world of 18th-century duelling, one of the opponents would choose weapons, but they must both use the same weapon. So, combat is different from Hobbes's world of the 'war of all against all', where by definition one can confront a stick with a sword, or a sword with a gun, or kill one's opponent by stealth whilst they are sleeping.

The image of the duel is of structured combat where the opponents have accepted conflict and confront each other; this simple point reveals an essential feature of war and of the duel as an act between two opponents to seek to defend their honour. A war arises when an opponent is recognised as an opponent and confronted as such. Combatants are central to the idea of war and it is from this basic idea that we can distinguish non-combatants when discriminating amongst those who may be attacked. Whilst the modern progress of war has extended the idea beyond the duel to include those who sustain a war effort, the justification for attack requires the linking of an activity to supporting an attack. Attack and defence are interconnected in a single struggle. If an opposing state marches its army into a neighbour, but the neighbour chooses to acquiesce, then there is no attack and no defence. Consequently, whatever the political motive behind the act, it is not war, in the same way that an insult that goes unmarked is not a combat, nor is a unilateral blow to a bystander. Not just any violence will do to initiate or constitute a combat.

Central to the formalised rules and rituals of 18th-century duelling is the historically ancient and basic act of giving violence in a mutual combat where the parties accept each other and deploy equal violence as the means of seeking satisfaction. There are many ways in which disputes can be resolved and satisfaction sought and given, but combat is an ancient and perhaps primordial form. The duel is not just interpersonal combat; it also involves the re-establishment of honour, and that is also a feature of why it is a ritualised act of violence between opponents. For Clausewitz, wars are the ways in which kings, nations, people and individual armies seek to preserve their honour, with combat as the test. The rituals that shape and govern this modern practice of war are shaped by international law and custom, but, as Clausewitz emphasises, these are 'imperceptible' and weak when set against the primary feature of war, namely its violence. Once again, Clausewitz packs a lot into this short mention of international law and its limitations.

The right of war is a right of states or political communities and not something that is conferred by a higher legal authority. So the relevant laws or rules or norms are those mutually recognised by the rival parties as part of the honour code of militaries. Just as, in the wrestling bout, there are minimal rules that exclude weapons or deceit, so in wars there are mutually binding rules of conduct that militaries accept and place upon their own behaviour. The laws of war concern the conduct of war by respective militaries, or what are called by just war theorists the rules of *jus in bello*. These are principles that are policed by respective militaries themselves, and not by an external or over-arching power. The treatment of combatants, the wounded, prisoners of war and the observance of surrenders and armistices, and the distinction between combatants and non-combatants are all part of the scarcely observable laws and customs that shape war. Breaches are a matter of honour and are therefore enforced by the respective armies and not by international courts or tribunals. Most militaries remain jealous of these privileges to this day, with their own courts martial having primary responsibility for any breaches of the laws of war. Clausewitz does not acknowledge a higher law of war that might cover the justice of going to war or *jus ad bellum*. The right of war is effectively a state right and therefore not a moral duty on states: states can refuse combat or assert neutrality. War is an instrument of state policy to ensure a state interest, and as such it is for a state and it alone to go to war, by accepting combat in the case of invasion and attack, or initiating combat and attack itself, for whatever the relevant policy reason might be. Just as modern war is a more formalised version of the primordial combat of a duel, so modern war brings into play the institutions that exercise this role – states and armies.

War is, then, an act of force to coerce the will of an opponent. Of its nature, war inherently employs violence, although in rare circumstances its effects can be achieved with minimal violence. However, even in this case the threat of recourse to violence is the central task of war. Clausewitz was dismissive of what he described as wars of observation, where armies skirt each other but seek to avoid a conflict or confrontation. Such acts are only wars by analogy since the possibility of conflict remains but it is not exercised. In the new world of war by mass armies unleashed by Napoleon, a planned war of observation is exceedingly unwise as a policy. These elements of combat and violence come together most forcefully in Clausewitz's account of a successful struggle. In the case of the wrestlers that he uses as the example of a duel, the winner manages to throw and dominate his opponent. In the case of war, the victory is more complex and must aspire to be more permanent,

> for if war is an act of violence meant to force the enemy to do our will its aim would have *always* and *solely* to be to overcome the enemy and disarm him.
> ... The fighting forces must be *destroyed*: that is, they must be *put in such a condition that they can no longer carry on the fight*. Whenever we use the phrase 'destruction of the enemy's forces' this alone is what we mean. (Clausewitz 1984, p. 90)

Clausewitz warns that war is never final, in that an enemy (state or people) is never wholly annihilated such that it cannot arise in the future as an adversary. Yet, in confronting an enemy, the task is indeed to destroy an enemy army's ability to pose a threat. In this way, Clausewitz brings out what is essential to the nature of war. One can only compel an enemy to do one's will when that enemy's army cannot offer further resistance. When we read this phrase as a mandate in light of 20th-century history and alongside Clausewitz's reference to the necessary brutality of war, this can appear callous and morally problematic. But we must be careful that Clausewitz is referring to the destruction of an enemy's fighting forces as a potent threat and opponent, and not the individual destruction of each member of the enemy's armed forces. Clausewitz is not counselling mass slaughter. There will be other ways in which armies are destroyed as fighting forces and through which they are actually or effectively disarmed. It remains for a commander to judge how his tactics or strategy achieve that goal of destroying an enemy's forces. This will often depend on the context and, as Clausewitz argues in Book VIII, the policy that is behind the war in the first instance. That said, Clausewitz does not ultimately baulk at the necessity of destroying an opponent's army through the act of killing their soldiers in combat; this is ultimately what war is all about.

The use of concentrated violence to disarm and destroy one's opponent raises a further issue that is central to Clausewitz's account of war and which has raised confusion about the typology of war especially in the final Book VIII of *On War*. At the beginning of Book I, Clausewitz writes:

The maximum use of force is not incompatible with the simultaneous use of the intellect. If one side uses force without compunction, undeterred by the bloodshed it involves, while the other side refrains, the first will gain the upper hand. That side will force the other to follow suit; each will drive its opponent towards extremes, and the only limiting factors are the counterpoises inherent in war.
This is how the matter must be seen. (Clausewitz 1984, p. 75–76)

From this brief passage, the discussion of different types of war emerges. In Book VIII, the discussion begins with a distinction between 'absolute' and 'real' wars and in Books VI and VII Clausewitz suggests (although he does not use the term) that there are limited wars. When this is coupled with his idea of 'wars of observation', it appears that there are a number of types of war and thus no single object of enquiry. That fact is problematic because Clausewitz makes clear that he is offering a universal and general theory of war that fits the variety of historical experiences. Underlying military history there is a single object of study that links what happens in different historical epochs from the Greeks to the present. There are things that can be said, about all wars, but which do not reduce the idea of war to a mechanistic account of deployment of forces. The consistency of the theory is a major issue and was one of the concerns that Clausewitz claimed motivated his reconsideration of his theory in the note of 1827 that was appended to the publication of *On War* by his wife. But the issue of consistency is not the only concern, as the terminology of 'absolute' versus limited war has been central to the understanding of the book in light of the experience of war in the early 20th century. 'Absolute' war can appear to open the way to the totalitarian conceptions of total war mobilisation by a society, and so it needs to be understood appropriately.

In fact, Clausewitz uses the idea of 'absolute' war as a philosophical term of art and not as an instruction for the deployment of unrestricted force and violence. The term implies a complete and unconditional understanding of the concept of war and this unconditionality is illustrated in the logic of escalation that he identifies in the passage above. As the task of war is to apply enough force to destroy an enemy, there is a clear logic of escalation. The amount of force needed is whatever is the quantity necessary to overpower an enemy and to which they cannot respond. When translated into historical or contemporary political experience, this can seem deeply unnerving. Clausewitz's point is that there is no limit to the amount of force that needs to be deployed to defeat an enemy, other than that amount which is totally overwhelming. This idea brings with it images of mass waves of attack, relentless barrages of artillery and of course, in our own day, the overwhelming response to nuclear attack in the idea of MAD.

Critics of the murderous wave assaults in the trench battles of World War I or of the logic of nuclear deterrence see the source of their problems in Clausewitz's idea of 'absolute' war. The logic of escalation is built into the conception of war as the deployment of concentrated violence to destroy an enemy. However, as I have mentioned, this is a logical or conceptual point not a moral or practical one: we must remember that Clausewitz wants to educate his military readers, but not offer them a manual for campaigns and actions.

Thus, when he appears to distinguish limited wars or engagements in the extended development of the argument, he is not falling into a contradiction. What is the limitation of the logic of escalation and how is that consistent with his clear statement about the concentration of massive force? Clausewitz answers this question with his distinction between 'absolute' and 'real' wars in Book VIII. He is not, in fact, offering an account of different types of war, but qualifying the application of escalation logic in the context of a real world of conflict characterised by friction. Committing enough force to overthrow an enemy remains a central conceptual insight of war as a violent conflict, but the reality of translating that idea into concrete actions in 'real' wars of the kind that had been fought against Napoleon recognises the constraints and limits on escalation created by the forces of friction.

It is not always possible to escalate, or even to bring to the field, the planned resources for an engagement, because of logistical constraints. The reality of war is that mess of friction that he had referred to in rejecting the mechanistic and geometric approach to war. Friction is not the only feature that constrains the logic of escalation. Equally important is a new dimension with which Clausewitz has become most closely associated, namely policy or the political purpose for which a war is being fought. Central to the final Book VIII of *On War* is Clausewitz's insight that:

> War is merely the continuation of policy by other means ... The political object is the goal, war is the means of reaching it, and means can never be considered in isolation from their purpose. (Clausewitz 1984, p. 87)

To make sense of particular wars, we do not need a typology of different wars, Instead, we must understand the interplay of the fundamental forces that shape all wars and their applications of violence. This brings us to the heart of Clausewitz's theory, namely the 'paradoxical trinity'.

The two versions of the trinity?

The image of the trinity is one of the most important in Clausewitz's work. It forms the centrepiece of his theory of war, as opposed to his definition of the object of enquiry. Trinitarian thinking is deeply rooted in western political thought because of its echo of the fundamental basis of Christian theology (which distinguished three personalities of one god – God the Father, God the Son (Jesus Christ), and God the Holy Spirit). Even with the retreat of explicitly Christian thinking as the only language of political philosophy, the idea of the trinity remained central, not least in the dialectical logic of Clausewitz's most famous contemporary amongst philosophers in Berlin in the 1820s, namely G.W.F. Hegel. Clausewitz would have been aware of Hegel's work, even if he did not directly draw on it. The image of the trinity is, therefore, central to the understanding of Clausewitz's thought but also fraught with difficulty because of its resonances from philosophy and theology.

Contemporary scholars and critics of Clausewitz have also struggled with the idea of the trinity and its implications for understanding the place of war in political ideas and most importantly in making sense of his famous claim that 'war is merely the continuation of policy by other means' (Clausewitz 1984, p. 87). The reason for this controversy is that the preliminary account of the 'paradoxical trinity' has two distinct faces:

> War is more than a true chameleon that slightly adapts its characteristics to the given case. As a total phenomenon its dominant tendencies always make war a paradoxical trinity – composed of primordial violence, hatred and enmity, which are to be regarded as a blind natural force; of the play of chance and probability within which the creative spirit is free to roam; and of its element of subordination, as an instrument of policy which makes it subject to reason alone.
>
> The first of these three aspects mainly concerns the people; the second the commander and his army; the third the government.

> The passions that are to be kindled in war must already be inherent in the people; the scope which the play of courage and talent will enjoy in the realm of probability and chance depends upon the particular character of the commander and the army; but the political aims are the business of government alone. (Clausewitz 1984, p. 89)

In the first statement, Clausewitz draws on motives, virtues or passions and presents the trinity as an interplay of psychological forces whether understood as elements of the individual psyche or as collective psychological forces of a people. The second statement links these to distinct institutions or bodies, such as the institutions of the state and government, the army, and a body such as the people, conceived of as a collective entity. Clausewitz does not specify the precise relationship between these two faces of the trinity or explain whether they are in fact two distinct trinities, but, in debates about the relevance of his thought for contemporary politics and military affairs, a distinction and prioritisation of one over the other is often emphasised as crucial to understanding his true meaning (Fleming 2016, pp. 49–78). For some commentators, the psychological elements have priority and are only illustrated by their contingent institutional manifestation – whereas for others the interplay of the institutional manifestations is precisely what makes Clausewitz interesting to political theorists as well as students of military affairs and strategy (Howard 2002).

The emphasis on psychology, passion and motive is precisely what allows one to liberate Clausewitz from being an historically conditioned theorist of 19th- and early 20th-century war, and no more than an historical curiosity when viewed from the present. Because Clausewitz aspired to provide a universal theory of war, and not merely one for his own age, there is much to recommend the emphasis on the first face of the trinity. That said, there is also good reason to see the two faces as interconnected and inseparable. In this way, Clausewitz's argument echoes Plato's division of the soul and the state in his *Republic*, where the tripartite division of the soul or psyche is reflected in, or illustrated by, the functional differentiation of classes in the polis. The larger object is used to illustrate and illuminate the smaller, namely the individual soul.

That this analogy helps us illuminate Clausewitz should be unsurprising, because it is reworked in different forms throughout the history of philosophy and political theory, and is certainly partly echoed in Hegel's political thought. The one crucial difference from Plato, and similarity to Hegel, is that Clausewitz follows the latter in seeing a dialectical interplay between the elements, as opposed to a hierarchical ordering of the sort that would be found in Plato and would have been appreciated by some of Clausewitz's more authoritarian Prussian audience. For Plato, the task of the philosopher-king is seeking the right ordering of the state to reflect the right ordering of the soul, with reason dominating over the passions and desires, and rule thus confined to the class or strata of society who are wisest. For Clausewitz, on the other hand, the interrelationship is dynamic and (unlike Hegel) also non-teleological. There is no final pattern of relationship between these elements that is being sanctioned or chosen by the logic of history.

Hatred, enmity and the people

Clausewitz has already emphasised the importance of force and violence to the concept of war, but in the trinity he emphasises that this is not simply a strategic choice. Rather, it has its roots in fundamental enmity and that is most associated with the idea of the people. The idea of the people is usually overlooked or downplayed in traditional military thought. The people are clearly essential as a source of recruits and of supply, but beyond that they are at best ambiguous and at worst a threat. No army can survive without manpower and a supply of new blood, just as no large modern army can be sustained in the field without provisions, which in turn depends on a population producing a surplus of food and resources. The genius of the Prussian state was that its social structure supported its military through its tax structure and its culture of military service amongst a largely agricultural population, with a semi-feudal notion of service. Yet, whilst the people are essential to a military, they are also a problem. Frederick the Great's wars had faced population shortages and the (strictly temporary) relaxation of the social status needed to enter the officer class noted above. The effort to re-establish the social hierarchy of the Prussian military, by once again confining staff positions within the nobility, reflected the ambiguous status of the people. They were necessary but also a risk.

The spread of the French Revolution and its culture of the rights of man was a further illustration of the problem of the people. In Prussian thinking, egalitarianism was not consistent with the necessity of order and hierarchy, upon which a military culture depended, and the spread of egalitarian ideas was also a challenge to domestic political order. The military was not only for fighting extra territorial wars but also the primary institution through which the power of the state was projected onto its subjects, who were ruled. The people were potentially an unruly body that threatened political rule and the institutions through which it was exercised as much as it sustained them. In Clausewitz's day, the primary police function of a state was exercised by the military. His own death, following the establishment of a *cordon sanitaire* to contain cholera epidemic in 1831, illustrated the breadth of that police function, which was not confined to simply suppressing domestic violence.

The place of the people is important in Clausewitz's account of the trinity for another reason, inspired by his great mentor. Scharnhorst had seen the importance of national cohesion and identity in transforming a republican people that the Prussians considered unruly into a revolutionary fighting force under Napoleon and his generals, one that quickly threatened the entire political order of Europe. Where conservative politicians and thinkers saw the end threat, Scharnhorst and Clausewitz perceived the new force that could transform an unruly rabble into a people that could be motivated to fight en masse with such success. The reaction against the 'rights of man and the citizen' was not just a reactionary return to the *ancien regime* but a recognition of the power of national culture and spirit as a unifying force of a people. Clausewitz was familiar with Fichte's *Addresses to the German Nation* (1806), which were influential in inspiring a German nationalism that contradicted the universalist and cosmopolitan claims of the French Revolution. Indeed, he corresponded with Fichte, who argued for a revitalised educational culture that focused on national literature, the German language and history. These were all ideas that chimed with the growing Romantic cultural reaction against the late Enlightenment that was associated with the French encyclopaedists and Rousseau.

The place of national culture is important for Clausewitz, but he does not simply refer to it as a source of unification or collective motivation. Instead, he sees it as a source of opposition, enmity and conflict. The ideology of the 'rights of man and the citizen' was responsible for an enormous amount of violence and conflict, but at its heart it expressed a fundamentally cosmopolitan idea of universal community, one in which conflict and war were an exception. For Clausewitz, conflict, opposition and hatred were natural features of group differentiation, whether that was explained in terms of nation, tribe, clan or family. Hatred and enmity are fundamental features of human experience that manifest themselves in group opposition and hostility. Differing groups stand in opposition to one another and from that emerges the conflict that causes war. The idea of the nation is only the most recent historical manifestation of this idea of differentiation and enmity at the heart of conflict and war. Throughout history humans have opposed each other in groups and consequently fought each other.

The important theoretical claim that Clausewitz is making here in stressing the idea of the people and of enmity within the trinity is that conflict is not simply a tool of reason, or a strategy deployed to achieve national interests that are created and shaped by the circumstances of the state system. At the heart of human experience is something more fundamental and visceral than a clash of interests, and that is enmity and hatred, which lead to violence and killing. Without this enmity, war would not exist as a persistent feature of human experience. It is the failure of political theories, particularly social contract and natural law theories, to recognise this that results in their denial of war and their attempts to discipline it out of existence with state power and theories of perpetual peace. The emphasis on enmity and hatred can also be contrasted with Hegel's attempt to sanitise war within the dialectical logic of history. For Hegel, the rationale of war is that it binds an ethical community together in confrontation of an enemy, and it is the mechanism through which political communities or peoples gain recognition as states by other states. Whilst this is perfectly consistent with Clausewitz's argument, it is important that he does not seek to redeem violence and hatred with any such higher teleological purpose. War is essentially an expression of violence.

Chance, probability and creativity: the general

If the people provide the motive for military action and the resources in terms of personnel and supply, the army and the person of the commanding general provide the will behind an army's actions. In this aspect of the trinity Clausewitz focuses attention on chance, probability and freedom as the defining features of military experience, thereby turning the discussion of genius and of friction in the direction of the army itself. The limitless sources and combinations of factors that cause friction, deny the possibility of any mechanical and formal science of military affairs, and render useless any attempt to construct a manual of advice for the conduct of war. Risk and uncertainty are ineradicable features of war and the permanent challenge of military command. In explaining the history of wars and campaigns, the factors of chance and probability play an important part in accounting for the outcomes, whether success or failure. Hatred and hostility are insufficient to account for the act of war or its conduct and outcomes. Yet, Clausewitz is not merely alluding to the messiness of historical experience, as his careful choice of the concepts of chance, probability and freedom suggests.

The concept of chance is a reminder that the world is complex and unpredictable. Although science delivers laws that govern the movement of objects, it is rarely so specific that it can guide the conduct of an engagement or campaign. It is only in very specific tasks, such as siege warfare or the detailed use of artillery, that mathematical precision is relevant. In most cases, the number of constituent elements of an action are so great as to introduce the prevalence of chance as opposed to certainty. Clausewitz's account of military genius holds that the ability to see or intuit patterns and opportunities is the best that can be hoped for, not a deductive science.

That said, the allusion to probability is both a contrast with deductive certainty and yet also a recognition that chance can be quantified and understood. It is not the case that all is chaos and uncertainty so that no one is ultimately responsible for conduct and action. The military genius needs judgement and the ability to weigh probabilities and chance in directing action. Judgement can be improved and honed through study, experience and the relevant application of skills and techniques, as long as one understands that these are tools for fixing problems and not ways of unlocking the fundamental structure of reality. Clausewitz also emphasises the role of creativity and freedom and in so doing he is making space in his account of war for the special role of the military and its generals in the conduct of war, operating between the pressures of a people with its popular hostility and the rational policy of a government or state.

Armies take on the institutional exercise of violence on behalf of a people against external enemies, and occasionally against internal factions. The army has a peculiar role in exercising this power of consolidated violence and therefore in the conduct of war. The army and the general have the skill and competence to exercise this judgement about how to act, but they must also have the freedom to challenge an opponent. Most importantly, in going to war, the army and its general must be able to respond to an attack in the appropriate way. War cannot be conducted by a committee of experts remote from the field, precisely because of the influence of chance, uncertainty and friction. The field general must have the freedom and discretion to apply battle plans, and to vary them, according to the disposition of the terrain and opposing forces, but also according to the element of friction. This requirement that the army is freed from the impatient hostility of a people, or the concerns of a government, is an important part of strategy. It does not mean that the army is totally independent of external factors – the whole point of the trinity is to emphasise the ineradicable interconnection of the three parts. And Clausewitz says nothing that would support later ideas of total war, or the subordination of all aspects of social and political life to the claims of the military and its conduct of war, popularised by Erich Ludendorff following the German defeat in World War I.

The military is always connected to the other dimensions of the trinity, yet it is essential that the military has sufficient autonomy and freedom to act and to adjust strategy in the response to circumstances. When this freedom and agency is curtailed, armies are defeated and war plans fail. The challenge, especially for a state or government, is how much freedom and autonomy can be given and ought to be given. In learning from the past and planning for the future, a military leadership will always be seeking maximum freedom to accommodate to circumstances, but also seeking to limit the freedom and opportunities of opponents. The accommodation of freedom and agency on behalf of an army, with the claims of the wider interests and concerns of a people and state brings us to Clausewitz's third dimension.

Reason, policy and the state

The claim of reason or its embodiment in government or the state as policy is the final key element of the trinity. Chapter III of Book VIII provides an historical outline of the evolution of war in the context of state and government power, culminating in the emergence of the state in the early modern period and its approach to war and the organisation of the military. Translations of Clausewitz sometimes differ over the question of whether the key term should be 'politics' or 'policy'. I use them interchangeably, but acknowledge that Clausewitz is primarily concerned with that aspect of politics which occurs within government agencies or bureaucracies, and which we refer to when discussing public policymaking. This executive focus can be opposed to a broader conception of politics that might involve popular deliberation and tend towards democracy. Clausewitz was not a democrat. That said, he does acknowledge the popular political forces unleashed by the French Revolution and their impact, and therefore the ambiguity in how he uses politics or policy does capture an important part of his discussion.

The issue of politics or policy was always involved in some respects in the history of war. But its centrality is most striking in the modern period following the European wars of religion, where the visceral hatreds that motivated whole populations gave way in the 18th century to a more constrained or aristocratic view of military action, captured in the following quotation:

> War thus became solely the concern of government to the extent that governments parted company with their peoples and behaved as if they were themselves the state. The means of waging war came to consist of the money in their coffers and of such idle vagabonds as they could lay their hands on either at home or abroad [to serve as soldiery]
>
> ... The enemy's cash resources, his treasury and his credit, were all approximately known; so was the size of his fighting forces. No great expansion was feasible at the outbreak of war. Knowing the limits of the enemy's strength, men knew they were reasonably safe from total ruin; and being aware of their own limitations, they were compelled to restrict their own aims in turn. Safe from the threat of extremes, it was no longer necessary to go to extremes. (Clausewitz 1984, pp. 589–590)

Policymaking in the modern state is increasingly a matter for an administrative or bureaucratic elite that, whilst working for the monarch, tends towards an interest of its own. This technical interest begins as a way of protecting the interests of the monarch, but in practice it becomes a distinct political interest of the state different from the person of the prince. Consequently, motives such as honour and pride give way to calculations of interest and judgements of relative risks. In terms of strategy, the impact of politics turns war into a limited game that is not consumed by absolute gains such as the conquest, assimilation and destruction of enemies. Especially in the 18th century, war involved limited objectives that were sufficient to support the other tools of policy, such as diplomacy, and in this way limited war emerged. Limited war is only limited in terms of its contribution to policy – the actual engagements through which it is carried out retain the fundamental logic of escalating force to defeat he enemy, and its brutal violence. The limitation is that the task is to take a piece of territory, destroy a fortress, or attack a city in order to leverage a political and diplomatic result, rather than to destroy an army or defeat an enemy state so that it can no longer pose a threat.

The government recognises the ongoing nature of conflicts and disputes within the external state system and, therefore, needs to ensure the supply of military forces, economic power and diplomatic support to sustain its position. Armies take time to rebuild and to train, and their total destruction in a defeat not only limits the power of a prince or monarch but puts the legitimacy of the government at risk. In this way, the bureaucratic class and its interests in the long-term administration of the state place a constraint on the escalation of military action and force, thus limiting the idea of absolute war. Clausewitz does not pass judgement on this change in history, or mourn the loss of a more heroic age when armies served the honour of monarchs or peoples. His only concern is to understand the changing historical circumstances of war and the increasingly important place of policy in shaping war and conduct. Although he does not make the connection, it is clear that Clausewitz's idea of the task of military theory is one further consideration alongside other policy sciences such as economics. Sustaining a war requires a productive population with an economic surplus and sufficient population surplus to engage in war. But, as Adam Smith is quick to point out in *The Wealth of Nations* (1776), political economy is just as likely to encourage conflict as provide the resources and capacity to engage in conflict. The development of the modern state system has transformed the nature of war by turning the conduct of war into a policy science of using the limited state resources available to gain maximum advantage or to defer conflict, until such a time as the relative balance of forces are rendered equal by circumstances, such as territory gains or diplomatic alliances.

Whilst the logic of war entails the escalation of force, the policy context restrains that escalation, and this brings a new requirement to the thought of the military leader. Policy is not merely external to the general's thinking – one of the factors outside the conduct of war. Instead, it must now become central to the context in which strategy, war planning and the conduct of operations are shaped. It is in this context that Clausewitz emphasises the continuity of war and policy when he asserts that 'war is merely the continuation of policy by other means'. War is one of the policy tools of the modern state and its exercise should be seen as the extension of that policy agenda in circumstances where other policy tools are no longer appropriate or sufficient. In making this claim, Clausewitz is asserting the case for the permanent importance of war in a world where theories of perpetual peace, or arguments about the demands of political economy, constantly confront the state and its policymakers. War and the capacity to wage it effectively must remain a power of the state. Yet, they involve interests and motives that will often conflict with other policy goals and thus require careful political engagement on behalf of the military to ensure that its power and capacities are protected.

This raises the question of the relationship between the military and the other constitutive powers of the state. When monarchs ruled and wars were small and vicious but a continuation of sovereign will, the prince was the commander-in-chief, and the state and the military were one. However, with the development of modern states and government bureaucracy, the military is removed from the direct will of sovereign action. This raises the constitutional question of the place of the military in relation to sovereign power and the development and pursuit of policy. The relation between civilian and military power in government is as fundamental to the modern state as the relationship between civilian and ecclesiastical power in early modern politics, but with consequences that are far more proximate and urgent. The issue had been masked by monarchs exercising supreme military command, sometimes successfully, as in the case of Frederick the Great. Yet, even in Clausewitz's day the U.S. Constitution's subjection of the military to ultimate civilian control, or the rise of a figure such as Napoleon who subordinated civilian authority to the military and eventually assumed the former as emperor, made the question of the relation of political and military power a very real issue.

Clausewitz's proposed solution is to incorporate the commander-in-chief into the cabinet, the central decision-making body of executive government. He says:

> If war is to be fully consonant with political objectives, and policy suited to the means available for war, then unless the stateman and soldier are combined in one person, the only sound expedient is to make the commander-in-chief a member of the cabinet, so that the cabinet can share in the major aspects of his activities. But that, in turn, is only feasible if the cabinet – that is, the government – is near the theatre of operations, so that decisions can be taken without serious loss of time.
> ... What is highly dangerous is to let any soldier but the commander-in-chief exert an influence in cabinet. It very seldom leads to sound vigorous action. (Clausewitz 1984, pp. 608–609)

The commander-in-chief is therefore essential for the successful articulation and implementation of policy, but he should not dominate. The commander-in-chief will be just as prone as a regular general to escalate sufficient force to defeat an enemy. But in the domain of politics that impulse needs to be tempered by the objective, as well as the resources that are available for all aspects of state policy. There is a fine balance between asserting the legitimate interests of the military in the conduct of policy by other means, ensuring the effective conduct of war, and ensuring the long-term stability and security of the state. It is this concern that underlies Clausewitz's hostility to any soldier but the commander-in-chief being involved in policy or the cabinet.

In the light of subsequent history, and the charge of 'Prussianism' made against both Clausewitz and the German military in World Wars I and II, it is worth acknowledging his important subordination of the military to the broader interests of the state. This idea is central to the place of the military in modern liberal democratic societies. But one should note that this subordination is not peculiar to liberal democracies and is equally familiar in party states. Perhaps the most egregious example was the later oath of allegiance that the German officer corps made to Hitler as the personification of the racial state. Clausewitz is aware that simple constitutional provisions mask the complex way in which this alignment of policy and military interest is best achieved, and there is no final balance of the elements of the trinity in a single institutional structure.

The emphasis on policy in Book VIII explains the emerging importance of conflicting pressures on strategy and action in the context of the modern state system, which for Clausewitz explains the prevalence of 'real' and limited war over 'absolute' war. But Clausewitz did not think that absolute war was only a logical possibility that was increasingly never revealed in historical experience because of cost and competition with other policy agendas. The experience of the French Revolution and of Napoleon had broken the political confines of the late 18th-century state system:

> War, untrammeled by any conventional restraints, had broken loose in all its elemental fury. This was due to the peoples' new share in these great affairs of state; and their participation, in turn, resulted partly from the impact that the Revolution had on the internal conditions of every state and partly from the danger France posed to everyone.
>
> Will this always be the case in future? From now on will every war in Europe be waged with the full resources of the state, and therefore have to be fought only over major issues that affect the people? (Clausewitz 1984, p. 593)

Of course, Clausewitz does not answer this question, nor could he. But the recognition of the persistent possibility of absolute 'people's wars' in a world where the political power of the masses or people is unleashed on an unprecedented scale remains one of the central challenges of war ever since. In light of the 20th-century experience of mass war in Europe and beyond, this looks a particularly prescient observation. However, one should not lose sight of the primary lesson of the Clausewitzian trinity, namely that the complex interplay of hostility, chance and policy can adapt to new circumstances and challenges. His brief and prescient history of conceptions of war leading up to Napoleon is not meant to suggest a teleology of history. The state system has its logic, but there is no claim that the state system and the idea of interstate war is the only form of war in future. The trinity explains the forces that shape modern war, and the elements of the trinity support concerns about the dangerous tendency of the forces unleashed by the French Revolution. But Clausewitz is not a crude reactionary, or a fatalist who saw mass society as eradicating the state-based order.

The means – the practical conduct of war

For all the theoretical sophistication of Clausewitz's conception of war, he was also a practical man and an experienced soldier, and this is reflected in his comprehensive discussion of the conduct of war. He had marched through the

Rhineland and the Vosges as a young soldier and his writings retain the detailed observation of landscape and territory and its influence on the deployment and ordering of troops. The vast majority of *On War* is devoted to expanding on his primary ideas in considerable detail and from all relevant perspectives. Although military technology has transformed the task of war-fighting, the fundamental ideas about the orientation to troops in a landscape (with its opportunities and constraints) remain as insightful as when it was first written.

Clausewitz's observations about crossing a marsh or swamp using planks are no doubt outdated, because modern troops have more technological fixes to those challenges. But his appreciation of the way in which features of landscape impact on the fundamental objective of the engagement is not simply an artefact of the limit of technology. Marshes and swamps, forests, rivers, mountains and fortresses all feature as specific problems and opportunities in defence or attack. There is also considerable discussion of supply, billeting, guarding and moving troops. Clausewitz was a continental soldier, and for him war was conducted by armies on land, engaged in taking and holding territory as a means of destabilising and destroying an enemy. There is nothing in his book on naval warfare or operations, or about amphibious operations such as invasions – a source of engagement that is as old as Greek warfare. We can only speculate whether Clausewitz thought naval warfare fell within or outside the broad categories of his military theory, namely the engagement viewed from the perspective of offence and defence. That said, the notion of the engagement, the concentration of force and the centre of gravity, as well as the priority of defence over attack, have as much relevance to naval warfare as land warfare, although the details about applying these ideas in such a context are lacking.

The organising categories of the detailed discussion of particular issues reinforce the methodological point that strategy, tactics and the conduct of war cannot be reduced to a mechanical or geometrical science or a set of universal principles, as de Jomini claimed. The interplay of hostility, chance and policy impacts on all wars, but in different ways. Yet, whilst there are no universal principles, the emphasis on conflict is central, especially in the overriding preoccupation with the 'Engagement' as the centrepiece of discussion. Clausewitz says, 'Fighting is the central military act: all other activities merely support it ... Engagements mean fighting' (Clausewitz 1984, p. 227). Although war tends to be seen in terms of a single great engagement, the reality of war, according to Clausewitz, comprises a large number of engagements. The task of the strategist is to link these large and small engagements into a single coherent major engagement that relates all action towards the fundamental task of defeating the enemy. From the perspective of policy, the enemy is defeated when they are no longer able to sustain conflict, whether in terms of pursuing its initial attack or, if in a defensive war, its inability to withstand the force of the attacker.

Because the task of defeating an enemy involves putting him 'at such a disadvantage that he cannot continue fighting' (Clausewitz 1984, p. 231), the general must find the point at which maximum force can be concentrated on the enemy's 'centre of gravity'. The 'centre of gravity' is an extension of the metaphor portraying the engagement as a duel between wrestlers. The concentration of force and the centre of gravity are important once one ceases to believe that there is an underlying mechanism that rules out the impact of chance and circumstances. If the outcome were always decided by the relative number of forces, then most wars would either not take place or would involve little actual conflict and violence. Where those numbers are deployed and concentrated is important for equalising a conflict in which the opponents are not exact equals. Yet, the 'centre of gravity' can itself become a mechanical device (contrary to Clausewitz's intention) if one fails to recognise that it is ultimately a metaphor, or at best the subject of a difficult and uncertain judgement. It is also something that cannot be predicted with accuracy or a certain high probability without recognising the constraints and opportunities that terrain, supply and personnel provide or the consequences of friction.

The importance of the engagement and the search for an opponent's 'centre of gravity' can also support a common military prejudice in favour of attack or offence over defensive war. By contrast, Clausewitz seeks to divert attention from the priority of offence over defence, although he discusses the considerations relating to both at considerable length. Indeed, Clausewitz gives good reason for considering defensive war the priority. Offence might well seem the most important form of conflict, because it involves bringing concentrated force to bear on what is perceived to be an enemy's centre of gravity, whereas defence appears to be passive. Yet, this prejudice is just that, for a proper defence also requires bringing concentrated force to the weak point or centre of gravity of an attacker. This weak point may only appear once an attacker's supply lines are extended to their limits, as happened in the Russian campaign against Napoleon. Here the defenders' strategic retreat and use of the vast battle space of the Russian interior overextended Napoleon's supply, and consequently reduced the force of his attack to the point where it was not able to do more than technically defeat the Russians at Borodino, and therefore did not achieve a decisive outcome. In the new context, and against an opponent that was only willing to give battle on its own terms, the strategy and tactics that had proved so successful previously for Napoleon and his armies were undermined.

The example shows that, for Clausewitz, the defending power has a priority, in that it must give war by returning conflict. Whilst this decision is rarely as stark as in the Russian campaign, it remains for the defending power to decide when to deploy its force. If it is appropriately constituted, the defenders can do that by absorbing the attacker's strikes until such a point that its force is exhausted. At its most extreme, this can result in battles of attrition, where the goal is to run down the forces and materiel of the opponent, until a time when they are no longer able to continue the campaign. Whilst effective defence requires distinct strategies to exhaust an opponent's attack, the fundamental logic of attack and defence remains the same; that is, destroying the forces of the enemy and rendering them unable to continue hostilities.

The capacious logic here, combined with the encyclopaedic detail, is what makes *On War* such a rich and enduring work for soldiers and scholars alike. The book's fundamental insight about the centrality of violence and force to the modern state system, and to the task of politics and policy, is also something that is overlooked by modern political theorists who concentrate only on reaching agreement between states via deliberation. Most importantly in an era that continues to seek the Enlightenment ambition of a world without war and conflict, and with effective institutions for perpetual peace, Clausewitz provides an essential corrective. He also provides a recognition of the limitation of reason in human affairs, but also the requirement of reason in acting on passion and sentiment. In this respect he is amongst the most important political thinkers of the international order.

The legacy of *On War*

Clausewitz gains from being one of those thinkers about whose thought a little is widely known but who suffers from most of those people not having much idea of his complex arguments or actually having read his book. This has an unfortunate impact on any account of his reception and influence, because much scholarship here tends to quickly collapse into counterclaims that he did not really say many or most of the things that he has either been accused of or credited with (Bassford 1994). In short, there is no substitute for careful reading. That said, even the less-than-accurate readings and interpretations of his work have an important impact on the way in which modern war and the state are understood. Most interesting discussions of the problem of war are still framed by the theory of Clausewitz.

The immediate reception of Clausewitz's *On War* was muted. The book was initially overshadowed by the work of his rival as the leading post-Napoleonic War strategist, Antoine Henri de Jomini (1779–1869). A Swiss-born soldier in Napoleon's army, his *The Art of War* was required reading amongst the officer class in Europe and in the United States during the 19th century. It was read by the young officers at West Point who were to face each other in the U.S. Civil War, perhaps the first modern industrial war. However, Clausewitz's reputation later rose significantly as a consequence of its association with Field Marshal Helmuth von Moltke (1800–1891), who reformed the strategy and organisation of the Prussian Army, and then the Grand Army after German unification. Von Moltke was one of the outstanding military leaders of the mid-19th century and played a significant role in the war over Schleswig-Holstein with Denmark in 1864, and the Austrian-Prussian War in 1866, before his signal triumph in the Franco-Prussian war. Von Moltke was a strategic genius in his own right but had been a student at the War College when Clausewitz was director, and he was seen as a disciple of Clausewitz. In particular, he was taken to exemplify a rejection of the formalistic approach to a war of manoeuvre that was associated with de Jomini in favour of Clausewitz's strategic flexibility. It was through this association with German success that Clausewitz's ideas attracted the attention of Von Moltke's disciples and the strategic thinkers and staff colleges, which produced not only a wider audience for the book but translations of into French and English. The rapid success and challenge of Prussian strategy became a focus for opponents and allies alike. So began the legend of Clausewitz as the theorist of Prussianism and a Prussian way of war, a legend that was to become controversial following the next major European war in 1914–1918.

One consequence of the experience of World War I on British intellectual life was a reaction against the philosophical idealism prominent in late 19th- and early 20th-century politics. This had much to do with the reputation of Hegel and Fichte and their influence on British idealists such as F.H. Bradley (1846–1924) and Bernard Bosanquet (1848–1923), especially the claim that their philosophies subordinated the individual to the state. The idealists viewed the state as an ethical community in which personal and group identity is revealed, and so it was easy to caricature German idealism as a source of Prussian militarism and aggression that had 'caused' the Great War. Clausewitz has almost nothing to do with this debate, but it was possible to read his trinity of state, army and people as vindicating the kind of state worship that was attacked by critics of idealism and all things Prussian. For instance, the liberal thinker L.T. Hobhouse opens his book on *The Metaphysical Theory of the State* with the following claim, having watched a Zeppelin raid on central London from his home in Hampstead Heath:

> As I went back to my Hegel my first mood was one of self-satire. Was this a time for theorizing or destroying theories, when the world was tumbling about our ears? My second thought ran otherwise. To each man the tools and weapons that he can best use. In the bombing of London I had just witnessed the visible and tangible outcome of a false and wicked doctrine, the foundations of which lay, as I believe in the book before me. To combat this doctrine effectively is to take such a part in the fight as the physical disabilities of middle age allow. Hegel himself carried the proof-sheets of his first work to the printer through streets crowded with fugitives from the [battle]field of Jena. With that work began the most penetrating and subtle of all the influences which have sapped the rational humanitarianism of the eighteenth and nineteenth centuries, and in the Hegelian theory of the god state all that I had witnessed lay implicit. (Hobhouse 1918, p. 6)

For those interested in challenging the philosophical presuppositions of the model of politics that had resulted in the Great War, it was easy to see the alignment of the state and army over the people, or Zeppelin raids on civilian populations, as an example of absolute war, as perfectly illustrating the legacy of Hegel and Fichte, translated into a doctrine for the Prussian military by Clausewitz.

Yet, there are elements in this example that do connect with Clausewitz's view of absolute war or a people's war. The German air raid on London was on a civilian target and therefore broke the taboo that war is a professional affair between uniformed combatants. As with other developments in the Great War, the aerial attack that triggered Hobhouse's anger indicated a shift between the elements of the trinity from the armies to the peoples. This hostile interpretation of Clausewitz was not, however, confined to the philosophers and political theorists, who are generally not well disposed to war. It also manifested itself through selective interpretation, in a criticism of the impact of Clausewitz's ideas on both the Axis and Allied military leaderships. Here a different facet of Clausewitz's theory was the chief target.

Clausewitz was claimed as a key source for the strategy of bringing massive concentrations of force to bear in single engagements that led to the failed military tactics and strategy of the trench warfare of the Western Front, with its stalemate, limited impact and mass slaughter. This line of criticism was deployed by the British strategic thinker Basil Liddell Hart, who experienced combat in the Battle of the Somme and who rejected what he considered to be the failed frontal assault strategy of the British and French in favour of his own indirect strategy. The failed strategy concentrated massive force at supposed points of weakness with the view to breaking the enemy in a decisive engagement. In the context of the static war of the Western Front, it was claimed that this would result in a breakthrough. However, the great battles, such as that of the Somme, failed to achieve this goal and resulted only in the mass slaughter of troops for little military benefit. Liddell Hart argued that the considerable improvement of military technology (especially artillery, machine guns and poison gas) had rendered this so-called Clausewitzian strategy redundant. In this new context he ridiculed Clausewitz as the 'Mahdi of mass and mutual massacre' (Liddell Hart 1933, p. 120).

In place of this direct mass assault, Liddell Hart advocated an indirect approach, which avoided confrontation at the point of the enemy's forces but instead focused on the periphery as the way to the centre. He also urged reliance on small-scale deployments and confrontations. In the context of a European war, this should result in Britain avoiding a major land campaign with the kind of mass mobilisation and frontal assaults that led to the Battle of the Somme and instead relying on its naval power, with interventions and campaigns at points of weakness and at times of advantage to knock out the allies of Britain's adversaries, such as the ill-fated Dardanelles campaign against Turkey. In the years following the Treaty of Versailles, Liddell Hart's ideas were taken up by those who feared that another mass land campaign would be politically unacceptable and equally ineffective, as well as those who advocated new transformative technologies such as air and tank warfare.

For a time, Liddell Hart had a significant impact on British strategy and his ideas were favoured by Neville Chamberlain in the interwar period. Yet, by the time World War II started in 1939, his approach had been repudiated by the strategy of a land campaign with France in support of Poland. Liddell Hart was always a controversial figure amongst strategists and he was especially protective of his own reputation – to the extent of taking credit for the strategic achievements of others. In particular, he claimed credit for new thinking on armoured and tank warfare that was said to have inspired the German blitzkrieg, which avoided concentrated frontal assault in favour of rapid mobility. Liddell Hart dressed up his own strategic opposition to the 1914–1918 legacy in terms of an opposition to Clausewitz. But, in reality, the contrast is superficial because Clausewitz was a far more nuanced thinker and less rigid or even 'Prussian' than Liddell Hart claimed. Yet in the end the dispute was not really about the interpretation of Clausewitz's theory but more a claim that the nature of war had radically changed and so Clausewitz's theory was no longer appropriate to a new kind of technologically advanced warfare begun in World War I and brought to completion in World War II, with the development of air power, rockets and nuclear weapons.

With the extension of military technology apparently rendering armed confrontation on a battlefield irrelevant, the post-1945 world posed a significant challenge to those who claimed that Clausewitz's message had continued relevance. In a world where the belligerents were grouped under the nuclear umbrellas of the United States and the USSR, which guaranteed MAD and the impossibility of surviving let alone winning a nuclear confrontation, the fundamental Clausewitzian insight of war as an instrument of state policy no longer seemed plausible.

However, the invention of nuclear and thermo-nuclear weapons did not lead to the abandonment of war and the consequent necessity for states to have sound military strategy. The Cold War stand-off between the west and the Communist bloc did not eradicate war or war planning. The Korean War of 1950–1953 was a major but traditional military confrontation, albeit partly conducted through proxies. The North Koreans relied on Soviet airpower and Chinese forces after the initial success of the multilateral United Nations forces led by the USA in containing and rolling back the invasion. The Korean confrontation was contained within a traditional interstate war format, although the United States was content to act as the dominant leader of a multinational coalition. More importantly, despite the ill-advised urgings of General Douglas MacArthur (and others) for a nuclear attack on China, it was a war that did not escalate into nuclear exchanges, especially as President Truman removed MacArthur from command. The Korean conflict ended in an armistice and the final resolution of the war is still an issue today in international politics.

What this illustrated was that conventional war was not irrelevant, whether conducted under the guise of multinational alliances or using other proxies. It required the continuation of a state-centric model of strategy and war. War plans for conventional confrontations between Soviet and NATO forces on the European continent continued to be made throughout the next four decades.

Yet, more interestingly even in the field of nuclear conflict, the idea of war being a policy that might be pursued even with the devastating power of nuclear weapons continued to preoccupy some strategic thinkers. Not everyone was sceptical of the idea that a nuclear war might be winnable. In the early 1950s, some intellectuals, such as the game theorist John van Neuman and the physicist Edward Teller, advocated a pre-emptive American attack on Stalin's Russia, before it could build up nuclear forces. Later, others (such as the physicist Herman Kahn), argued that there could be some political gain from engaging in a nuclear war.

A question will always remain whether the strategy of fighting a nuclear war was offered in good faith or whether it was only intended to support the idea of deterrence – where the ultimate goal is not to have to exercise the deterrent power and therefore never put to the test the premise that there is a winnable nuclear war. Many advocates of the idea of tactical nuclear war (deploying only smaller battlefield nukes) were, no doubt, following the strategy of deterrence and MAD, even if their personal views were that the devastation of all-out nuclear war was unthinkable. If there is still any conceivable world in which nuclear war-fighting is a genuine policy option for a state, then there is scope for Clausewitz to inform that thinking.

Alongside the strategists who argued for a winnable nuclear war, others saw Clausewitz informing strategy where nuclear technology made outright conflict unviable. Of particular interest here is the French liberal-realist Raymond Aron (1905–1983), who recognised Clausewitz's injunction to see war as an element of policy, and to also recommend other options when that policy tool is unviable. He closes his study of Clausewitz and his lessons for modern strategy with a recognition that, alongside the complex ways in which Clausewitzian war remains viable, there is also the need to look at other state policy options, short of direct conflict that are necessitated by nuclear technology. Writing in the 1970s, these ideas included strategic limitations on nuclear forces and diplomatic controls over the proliferation and acquisition of nuclear weapons by new powers (Aron 1970). The diplomatic contests over strategic arms limitation agreements became a new form of policy confrontation that resulted in policy as 'war by other means', where actual conflict would have been self-defeating. For Aron there was no reason to regard this as a betrayal or denial of Clausewitz's wisdom, as opposed to its sensible extension beyond the battlefield arena. What Aron did not live to see was a series of developments that led to a major transformation of strategic thinking that extended beyond the problem of accelerating technology.

Whilst the Cold War limited direct interstate conflict, and obscured it behind multistate ideological alliances, it remained the case that the USA and USSR were the main protagonists in a major ideological and military confrontation. States, militaries and peoples remained essential elements of thinking about strategy whether in the context of war as a policy or through strategic diplomacy, as Aron had suggested. Yet, what we now know as the final phase of the Cold War, and the eventual collapse of the USSR, brought to the fore a transformation in military strategy that became known as the revolution in military affairs. These authors explicitly rejected what they claimed are the fundamental building blocks of the Clausewitzian view. Central to this approach is the work of Martin van Creveld (Van Creveld 1991) and Mary Kaldor (Kaldor 2012).

It is important to appreciate the complex events that led to this new thinking. The 1980s began with the Soviet invasion of Afghanistan, inaugurating the last phase of proxy conflict between the USA and USSR. However, it also coincided with the revolution in Iran and the overthrow of the shah, who was a U.S. ally, in favour of the Islamic Republic in Iran. The early stages of the revolution involved the humiliation of the United States with a siege of the U.S. embassy in Tehran and a failed rescue attempt by special forces. This debacle in turn contributed to the fall of President Carter and his replacement by President Reagan. He began a new period of hawkish foreign policy against the traditional threat of Communism, but also a new cultural struggle against the Islamic Republic. What began as a Cold War confrontation unleashed forces that transcended the simple world of ideological power-block confrontations. In time, they led to a proliferation of proxy conflicts from central America to the Soviet border in central Asia, as well as the new civilisational conflicts predicted by Samuel Huntington (Huntington 1996). President Reagan accelerated a nuclear arms build-up that had begun under President Carter, but he also pursued conflicts against 'the forces of communism' in central America by funding and supplying military uprisings against left-leaning popular regimes such as the Sandinistas in Nicaragua, and directly against the Soviets in Afghanistan through supporting guerrilla warfare by the Islamic mujahideen militias.

At this time, war was being outsourced to private and non-state actors who were also not strictly national liberation movements. The war in Afghanistan became a guerrilla war of attrition that sapped Soviet morale and was seen by many as a Russian 'Vietnam'. However, when the Soviets withdrew their troops, the power vacuum was filled by a tribal and confessional civil war. It was only stabilised in turn with the rise of the Taliban regime of Islamist ultra-conservatives and warlords, who nonetheless provided a safe haven for the radicals of Al-Qaeda. Al-Qaeda were the Islamist terror group responsible for the 9/11 attacks in New York and Washington, DC, in 2001. It was itself an outgrowth of the radical jihadist fighters who had learned their trade alongside the special forces and security force militias that had supported the Afghan war against the Soviets and been directed by the American CIA or Pakistani intelligence.

The USSR's 1988–1989 retreat from Afghanistan was quickly followed by the fall of the Berlin Wall in 1989 and the collapse of the USSR in 1991 into its component republics (still dominated by Russia), after the reform movement led by President Gorbachev failed to hold the multinational state together. With the implosion of the USSR and the collapse of the security block built around Soviet power, the international regime appeared to have fundamentally changed. Borders were redrawn (mostly peacefully) in the former Soviet space. Other national and religious conflicts grew in apparent fulfilment of Huntington's predictions of a new confrontation between Islam and the west. The USA's overwhelming military power in the new global situation also seemed to endorse Francis Fukuyama's claims about 'the end of history'.

Many military thinkers and strategists claimed that the challenge of this new world 'disorder' would not create a peace dividend through disarmament. Instead, it ushered in an increasingly chaotic and violent world where military power appeared more relevant than ever, and in ways that did not fit the decades of traditional war planning or even the planning for counter-insurgency wars against national liberation groups. It was in this context that Martin van Creveld's *The Transformation of War* (van Creveld 1991) appeared. Van Creveld is an eminent military historian who set about rethinking war in the new contexts that he argues Clausewitz failed to capture. His wide-ranging book does not simply argue that we are in new circumstances, because he acknowledges that the conventions of traditional war associated with Clausewitz had been under siege for some time and that the phenomenon of war had always defied systematisation. The central theme of his book is to demolish the central components of the trinity by undermining and problematising the ideas of the state, the army and the people as the central nexus of thinking about war. Each of these were shown to be unstable and transforming as a result of the impact of new conflicts, powers and opportunities. 'Who fought whom, how, and for what?' could no longer be seen in terms of the interplay of the fundamental elements of Clausewitz's trinity. Furthermore, trinitarian thinking was in danger of obscuring the challenges that military planners and strategists actually needed to address the problem of conflicts in the future.

Van Creveld's wide-ranging reflections are supplemented in the 'new war' literature by Mary Kaldor's *New and Old Wars* (Kaldor 2012). A British social theorist, as opposed to a military historian or strategist, Kaldor came to the subject following her involvement in the politics of the European peace movement. At the centre of her key book is an extended case study of the conflict in Bosnia–Herzegovina following the break-up of the former Yugoslavia. She argues in considerable detail that the motivations, actors and context of this conflict overturn the central elements of the trinity. The conflict involved identity groups and irregular militias that often had as much to do with organised crime as they did with the former Yugoslav army. The conflicts took place in a contested space that was also part-regulated by international organisations, such as the UN peacekeepers and NATO forces acting under a UN mandate. It also operated in the shadow of Russia as the traditional guarantors of Serbia and Orthodox Christians in the Balkans.

This intense local conflict also took place within a globalising world economy, with an apparently emerging cosmopolitan order that was replacing the bipolar world of the Cold War.

Her case study is supplemented by consideration of the 'War on Terror' and the ill-fated 'traditional' wars that were fought by the U.S. military and allies in Afghanistan and in Iraq as a result of 9/11. The conflict between the violent groups in Bosnia–Herzegovina, those in the tribal and warlord struggles in sub-Saharan Africa, or with the global Islamic terror groups Al-Qaeda and later ISIS, all required a cosmopolitan order in which traditional war between states and state armies was replaced by a vision of international collaboration in peace-building and enforcement – in which major national armies would deploy troops in conflicts that were remote from their immediate national interest. This radical approach to new wars was aligned with movements for preventive wars, and the coercive 'responsibility to protect' (R2P) populations against violence from their own state. It was also associated with significant alternative approaches to cosmopolitan regulation of a globalised economy, attempting to eradicate some of the sources of international conflicts, such as significant coerced population movements or the global drugs trade.

In the eyes of the new war theorists, the Clausewitzian trinity failed because it assumed that the state, the military and the people were stable and given objects of enquiry, rather than contingent and fluid entities that were rapidly disappearing in a new world of disorder. States were always controversial actors in the context of an unequal global order, but they were facing new challenges. These could be benign, as with the pooling of sovereignty in a supranational unions such as the European Union in reaction to economic globalisation. Similarly, international partnerships to regulate trade such as the WTO were claimed to produce benefits for all their signatory states. However, new challenges could also be malign in terms of the impact of identity politics attacking the national coherence of traditional nation states, and with the fall of the USSR, the rightsizing of borders and the reassignment of populations. Militaries were just as problematic, because of the rise of heavily armed militias, deploying weapons that had traditionally only been available to national armed forces. As the proliferation of high-calibre weapons continued, the idea that the national army was able to assert the state's monopoly of violence within a territory could also collapse. This was especially acute in regions where natural resources or narcotics meant that private groups could finance armed forces to equal the quality of states.

Yet, even with respect to military power the challenge was not simple disaggregation. Political alliances and sovereign unions meant that collaboration between national armies continues, either through peacekeeping or warfighting such as in the first and second Gulf Wars. The third pillar of the people was always the most precarious. The identity of a people was a perennial issue for political thinkers, and it was also one of the issues that Clausewitz was most concerned with. Nations, ethnicities, cultures and religions have always been sources of identity and unity, or fragmentation and diversity. For the new war theorists, a new wave of diversity and fragmentation (made possible by cosmopolitanism) has complicated the interests that underpin policy and the identities of the peoples that engage in conflict. The world of globalisation has accelerated these tensions in ways that require a different conceptualisation if we are to make sense of and manage the conflicts of the future.

As with all revolutions in thought or intellectual disciplines, this intervention also spurred a reaction. In this case, a resurgence of interest in Clausewitz occurred, seeing him either as a thinker whose fundamental ideas are distorted by interpreting him as advocating a rigorous structural trinity in his theorising of war or as someone who has a much richer and nuanced view of war that captures precisely many of the challenges that the new world disorder poses (Strachan 2007; Fleming 2013). At the same time, the world order fails to follow the desired pattern of human predictions. The second Gulf War may have been a poor response to a global terror group, but the defeat of Saddam Hussein's Iraq showed that there remain some fundamentals of interstate conflict and the deployment of mass force. Similarly, the long post-crash period, from 2008, has also reinvigorated nationalist populisms that have challenged the institutions of the international order in favour of national self-assertion, especially amongst the larger military powers such as the USA, China and Russia. The current era may well have new and perhaps ever more complex sources of military conflict. But there are also familiar elements that link the exercise and deployment of concentrated violence to political agendas by states and by groups that claim political legitimacy. Whilst Clausewitz does not provide a prescriptive policy science to deal with all such future developments, and indeed warns against such a narrowly rationalist view of war, his work remains an important challenge to other aspirant accounts of the deployment of violence for political and policy ends and one from which we continue to learn.

Bibliography

Essential reading

Clausewitz, Carl von [1832] (1984). *On War*, ed. M. Howard and P. Paret. USA: Princeton University Press.

Secondary reading

Aron, Raymond. (1983). *Clausewitz: Philosopher of War*, trans. C.C. Booker and N. Stone. UK: Routledge and Kegan Paul.
Bassford, Christopher. (1994). *Clausewitz in English*. UK: Oxford University Press.

Carr, E.H. [1939] (2016). *The Twenty Years' Crisis 1919–1939*. UK: Palgrave.

Creveld, Martin van (1991). *The Transformation of War*. USA: Free Press.

Echevarria II, Antulio J. (2007). *Clausewitz and Contemporary War*. UK: Oxford University Press.

Echevarria II, Antulio J. (2017). *Military Strategy: A Very Short Introduction*. UK: Oxford University Press.

Fleming, Colin M. (2013). *Clausewitz's Timeless Trinity*. UK: Routledge.

Gallie, W.B. (1978). *Philosophers of Peace and War*. UK: Cambridge University Press.

Gat, Aron. (1989). *The Origins of Military Thought: From the Enlightenment to Clausewitz*. UK: Clarendon Press.

Gray, Colin S. (1999). *Modern Strategy*. UK: Oxford University Press.

Grayling, Anthony C. (2017). *War: An Enquiry*. UK: Yale University Press.

Handel, Michael I. (1988). 'Clausewitz in the Age of Technology' *Journal of Strategic Studies*, vol. 9, pp. 51–92.

Hobhouse, Leonard T. (1918). *The Metaphysical Theory of the State: A Criticism*. UK: George Allen and Unwin.

Howard, Michael. (2002). *Clausewitz: A Short Introduction*. UK: Oxford University Press.

Kaldor, Mary. (2012). *New and Old Wars*, 3rd edn. UK: Polity Press.

Paret, Peter. (2007). *Clausewitz and the State*. USA: Princeton University Press.

Popper, Karl. [1945] (2011). *The Open Society and Its Enemies*. UK: Routledge.

Strachan, Hew. (2007). *Clausewitz's On War: A Biography*. USA: Grove.

Zamoyski, Adam. (2018). *Napoleon: The Man Behind the Myth*. UK: Collins.

Suggestions for finding open access versions of Clausewitz's texts

The Clausewitz Homepage is edited by Dr Christopher Bassford
https://www.clausewitz.com
Also archived via Marxists Internet Archive
https://www.marxists.org/reference/archive/clausewitz/index.htm
In addition, *On War* is available at:
https://antilogicalism.com/wp-content/uploads/2019/04/on-war.pdf

CHAPTER 9

Lenin and Mao

Revolution, violence and war

Whilst Marx undoubtedly had a significant impact on the development of social and political theory, it is through his followers, especially
Lenin and Mao, that his doctrines have had the greatest impact on
international thought and affairs. Marx theorised (for some, predicted)
the revolutionary overthrow of capitalism, but it was actually Lenin in
1917 and Mao in 1949 who presided over the two great socialist revolutions of the 20th century. Their writings on the theory and practice of
revolutionary politics have also had the most impact on modern international political thinking. I briefly discuss the Marxist framework, but
then focus on Lenin's theory of the vanguard party as the vehicle for
establishing a dictatorship of the proletariat – a conception that took
seriously the idea of dictatorship. Lenin's theory also saw imperialism as
the latest ('highest') phase of capitalism and he frankly recognized the
role of violence in the revolutionary overcoming of the state.

Turning to Mao, his thought transforms Lenin's legacy in the specific context of the Chinese struggle against Western imperialism. Mao's
thought identifies the peasant masses as a revolutionary class in a way
that transforms his account of revolution. Mao's influential writings on
revolutionary war stress the role of guerrilla forces. Lenin and Mao's
thinking about the practice of revolutionary politics has reshaped contemporary political and international theory.

How to cite this book chapter:
Kelly, Paul. 2022. *Conflict, war and revolution: The problem of politics in international
political thought.* London: LSE Press, pp. 305–367.
DOI: https://doi.org/10.31389/lsepress.cwr.i License: CC BY.

The party was to be a kind of universal machine uniting social energies from every source into a single current. Leninism was the theory of
that machine, which aided by an extraordinary combination of circumstances proved effective beyond all expectation and changed the history
of the world. (Kolakowski 2005, p. 686)

The Marxist tradition has posed perhaps the most significant challenge to the
model of international politics as a system or society of sovereign states, especially Marxism–Leninism (ML), which became the official ideology of the
USSR from 1917 to 1989. ML's revised version, Maoism, still officially forms
the basis of the state ideology of the People's Republic of China. Whatever its
superficial legal status as a union, the USSR was effectively a single state. And
preserving the unity of the People's Republic has been perhaps the most important single plank of the Chinese state ideology. Yet, the impact of Marxism–
Leninism in global politics has transcended the boundaries of realist theories of
the international realm as a system of states of differing size and power.

Throughout the Cold War, up to the collapse of Soviet power in 1989 (followed by the formal collapse of the USSR in 1991), the USSR represented itself
as an example of 'socialism in one country', operating in a holding position
until the final collapse of capitalism. The USSR was the primary model of a rival
ideology to capitalism, one that transcended borders, ethnicities and nationalities. It claimed to inform and direct the historical process of global revolution
that was the inevitable consequence of the material contradictions at the heart
of capitalist modernity. As such, it also claimed to reveal the true nature of
international politics masked by the state system, or its transformation in the
nationalist and postcolonial struggles that followed the break-up of western
empires from 1945 onwards. Until the mid-1970s, the ideological stand-off
between the western capitalist powers and global communism included China
(and smaller countries such as Cuba and Vietnam) as simply offshoots of the
USSR. This global stand-off was a dominant concern of much international
relations theorising and the preoccupation of western foreign policy, to the
extent that classical concerns with individual states' interests and competition
were absorbed into a hyperrealism based on a clash of ideology.

Amongst the architects of post-war international relations in the United States
were figures like George F. Kennan. He advocated containment of the USSR
and its eastern European satellites, on the grounds that they were motivated by
an inherently expansionary ideology, one that could only be contained and not
brought into a stable scheme of mutual cooperation by the traditional tools of
diplomacy or economics. Of course, war remained a theoretical possibility, but
because the USSR was a nuclear power it was not a realistic military option.
Some realist theories sought to dispense with official political ideologies as a
superficial manifestation or projection of state interests and power (a view that
is curiously similar to the materialism of Marxist theory). But most western
theorists took the Marxist–Leninists at their word and saw their opponent as

a single global ideological adversary with only superficial local variation. The idea of a 'domino theory' was used to justify confronting Marxism–Leninism in Vietnam from 1955 to 1975, as well as other regional conflicts. It assumed a monolithic ideological opponent despite the other factors that are now seen as crucial in understanding these events.

The fall of the Berlin Wall in 1989 and collapse of the Soviet bloc in Europe are often seen as the beginning of a new era of post-ideological politics. Yet, it also marked the rise of China as a global economic power. Following the leadership of Deng Xiaoping (regarded in China as Mao's equal in shaping the country's political and economic destiny), China began to exercise a significant global influence. Many observers saw China as moving away from any continuing adherence to Maoism/Marxism–Leninism into just a form of capitalist authoritarianism as its economy grew very rapidly and it took an ever larger place in global trade. China joining the World Trade Organization in 2001 (agreeing to respect western patents and other trade rules) became one of the main stabilisers of the global financial system during the global financial crisis in 2008 (Tooze 2018, pp. 239–255). But, following the rise of western populism and the Trump presidency's effective withdrawal from most of the institutions of the global economic order for a time (2016–2020), many western observers have re-emphasised China's continuing communist system in language once again reminiscent of the Cold War – a stance driven by some political leaders and movements who never really abandoned the idea of a global conflict between the west and communism.

Marxist approaches are important in their own right, and undoubtedly have a claim to be considered central to understanding contemporary international relations and international and political theory. However, since I do not aim here to provide a comprehensive chronological overview of international thought, my primary focus is on Lenin and on Mao. Both are undoubtedly world historical figures associated with major revolutions and with the politics and tragedies of 20th-century history. Yet, many Marxists and non-Marxist scholars alike will argue that both are surely second in rank as political theorists to Marx himself. If one wants to understand Marxism–Leninism, does one not need to focus on Karl Marx himself – or at least the later Marx's writings with Friedrich Engels?

My response to that obvious question has several aspects. Marx is undoubtedly a major political and social theorist but as a political thinker or as an international thinker he is most interesting when viewed through the theories of his followers. Secondly, Marx is a central figure around whom a very broad tradition of thought and politics has grown up, with many variants. So it is very difficult to make definitive statements about Marx's own views without taking sides on political interpretative debates within that tradition. It is no more straightforward to state uncontroversially what an orthodox Marxist political theory is than it is to state what an orthodox Catholic political theory is, because both are families of theory and ideas in continual conversation dialogue and debate.

Even in Lenin's lifetime there were fierce debates within the Marxist tradition about whether he was a 'revisionist' (a charge that became akin to naming someone a heretic in Catholic thought) because he moved beyond Marx and Engels and sought to adapt their theory to new circumstances. Lenin refused to accept that charge and was quick to defend his own orthodoxy against others, whom he in return charged as revisionists. Later the same challenge faced Mao as he was accused of departing from orthodox Marxism–Leninism as defined by Lenin's successor as Soviet leader, Stalin. In consequence, it would be easy, but not informative, to be drawn into interesting debates about whether Lenin or Mao was an orthodox Marxist or revisionist.

A third (perhaps most significant reason) for focusing on Lenin and Mao is not just their success as the political architects of the two globally significant Marxist revolutions in 1917 and 1949. Both are thinkers who saw the primary task of politics itself as progressing revolution and so they developed diverging but complementary approaches to thinking about politics, institutions and agency in the context of revolution. As well as historical agents they were theorists whose prescriptions looked beyond the structure of the nation, the state or the global state system. They also thought about the place of the Communist Party as the site of politics and its peculiar role in relation to the institutions of the capitalist state system. Both also addressed the character of the revolutionary class, in Mao's case replacing the industrial proletariat by a revolutionary peasantry. They examined the tasks and internal organisation of the party in relation to the revolutionary class. And they explored the conduct of revolution in detail, including the use of violence and war. Because they confronted the revolutionary moment, whether it turned out to be Marx's final crisis of capitalism or not, both thinkers became central in rethinking international politics, raising immense issues about totalitarianism and the destruction of human rights and stimulating the external criticism of these developments. Both their bodies of thought also raise issues about the underlying economic imperialism of the current globalised world. In the chapter's conclusion I also argue that some elements of Lenin's and Mao's fiercely activist and ruthless styles of party organisation, and their stress on the character of politics as revolutionary destruction, have been transferred from the Marxist tradition into the radical transformation of the political system by revolutionary terrorists. These themes have even influenced those on the populist right who believe in the creative destruction of neo-liberal globalism as a prelude to re-establishing political order and authority.

Two revolutionary lives

The personal and political context of Vladimir Ilich Ulyanov (whose revolutionary name was Lenin) was shaped by two important factors. The first and most obvious was the socialist tradition following Marx and Engels (who were close intellectual as well as political collaborators) and the Second International. But his Russian heritage was equally important. He was born into the Russian tsarist empire at the height of its expansion, and not a mature European nation state or even a colonial maritime empire like Britain or France, where the main implications of imperialism were obscured in domestic politics by occurring beyond their borders. The tsarist empire was different. It was the third largest in history after the British maritime empire and the Mongol empire. The tsar's sway spanned the Eurasian landmass from eastern Europe to the Pacific Coast. Indeed, until 1867 it included what after its sale to United States became the state of Alaska, plus the Aleutian Islands and settlements on the North American continent as far south as northern California (Lieven 2003). To the west, the Romanov tsars expanded their swallowing of much of Poland, the Baltic states of former Poland–Lithuania and Finland. Until its final collapse during World War I in 1917, the tsarist empire was an expansionary one. It constantly pushed the boundaries of its territory and influence, particularly with respect to its borders with neighbouring empires such as the declining Ottomans and in the 19th century with the British in the 'great game' played out on the northern borders of the British Indian empire and the western reaches of the Chinese Qing Empire. The form of government appropriate to this enormous territorial scale is another feature distinguishing the tsarist apparatus from a European nation state. Even with the strongly hierarchical structure of a monarchical empire, the formal centralisation of authority meant that the actual site of political authority was always remote. That changed the way power was exercised and authority was communicated, even after the invention and spread of the telegraph and the railways.

Yet, the main distinguishing feature of empires over republics and principalities was their necessary pluralism and diversity. Whilst the Russian people dominated, they were only one of many ethnicities and nationalities that formed the empire. And, whilst Russian Orthodoxy was a defining feature of Romanov rule, it was only one of many religions throughout the empire, which encompassed a significant Jewish population in the west, and animist paganism in Siberia and the far east. The Islamic central Asian khanates were also brought under Russian dominance throughout the 19th century. Geographical, cultural, religious and linguistic diversity shaped the political experience of the world into which Lenin was born in April 1870 in Simbirsk, a town on the Volga River about 700 km from Moscow.

During the 18th century, Russia became an increasingly important power within European politics and in the early 19th century it played a critically important role in the defeat of Napoleon's imperial projection of the legacy of the French Revolution. However, whilst Great Britain, France and Germany followed the Napoleonic Wars with a period of industrial, commercial and social transformation, Russia fell behind. The 19th century was a period of cultural uncertainty marked by a struggle between European reformers known as 'westernisers' (such as Alexander Herzen), and 'Slavophile' thinkers (such as Dostoevsky) who championed Russian culture and civilisation against the decadence of European rationalism. This debate shaped the way in which Russian thinkers responded to and engaged with currents in European politics such as the rise of socialism. It was also linked to concerns about why and if Russia was different in terms of its stage of industrial development from the Marxist perspective, and consequently whether it had reached the material conditions for proletarian revolution that orthodox Marxists associated with highly industrialised economies such as Britain, Germany and France. Whether Russia was ready for a proletarian workers' revolution was certainly an issue that shaped Lenin's life and thought, but other types of revolution (such as peasant uprisings, populist insurgency, criminal partisans and terrorism) were very familiar in Russian political life. Russian contemporaries of Marx and Engels, such as the anarchist Bakunin (1814–1876), preached revolutionary violence and assassination as political tactics that have become part of the character of the modern terrorist. Lenin's elder brother was executed after being implicated in a terrorist plot and this was one of the events that turned the young Vladimir Ilich Ulyanov to revolutionary politics.

His law studies at Kazan University were interrupted after he was expelled for agitation against the tsarist government, but he continued to study, eventually becoming an external student of the University of St Petersburg. His move to St Petersburg marked his formal commitment to revolutionary and socialist politics. He was subsequently arrested and exiled to Siberia, where he continued his work as a revolutionary and began his career as a socialist theoretician studying the social and economic development of Russia. After exile in Siberia, he became an exile in Europe from 1900, visiting London and Paris and settling in Switzerland after a brief return to Russia between 1905 and 1907 (following the revolution of 1905). He became a leading voice of the Russian social democrats (Marxists), a publisher of clandestine journals and a socialist organiser or professional revolutionary. During this period, he engaged with leading figures on the European left such as the German social democrats Karl Kautsky and Rosa Luxemburg, but always primarily focused on debates amongst the Russian social democrats. When this group split into two over revolutionary tactics, he became leader of the activist and hard-line Bolshevik faction, bitterly opposing the larger Menshevik faction, who saw the Russian industrial working class as yet too small to sustain an immediate socialist revolution.

The onset of the Great War in Europe and the failure of a European proletarian revolution in the face of mass war posed a critical challenge for many on the left. The workers of the world had patently ignored Marx and Engels's call to unite and cast off their chains in favour of nationalist war mobilisation. Lenin and his party were one of the few socialist groupings across Europe to take the unpopular route of utterly opposing the war as an imperialist confidence trick. Three years after hostilities began, in February 1917, the collapse of the Russian war effort and the tsarist regime led to a revolutionary government from February 2017. Lenin returned to St Petersburg, arriving on a sealed train at Finland Station (arranged by the German Secret Service). He mobilised all the Bolshevik forces to undermine the Mensheviks' government, with a St Petersburg *coup d'état* in October 1917 that set off a wider Bolshevik revolution. The enormous challenges of leadership and conduct of the revolution, including the Russian Civil War of 1917–1922 and fighting off multiple hostile forces, consumed Lenin's intellectual and physical energies until his death in 1924. He was eventually succeeded as unchallenged Soviet leader by Joseph Stalin. Stalin's long and brutal leadership, combined with his espousal of 'socialism in one country', has cast a long shadow over Lenin's legacy, especially questions about whether the brutal and systematic violence of Stalin's regime was always immanent in Lenin's ruthless views of the party, state and revolution, or whether Stalin betrayed Lenin's revolution. This is a large and complex scholarly question that goes well beyond the remit of this chapter, but I do explore the central place that violence occupied in Lenin's thought and practice.

Like Lenin, Mao Tse-Tung (Máo Zédōng) was born into the last years of the Qing Empire (1644–1912). Born in 1893, Mao was brought up in a regime that, unlike that of the tsars, was in terminal decline. The Qing Empire had Manchu roots from beyond the northern border, as opposed to the Han Chinese Ming Dynasty that it had displaced and defeated. In its heyday in the 18th century, the Qing Empire was expansionary and extended far into central Asia, as well as exercising suzerainty over Tibet and much of what is now Myanmar. This populous and wealthy empire used the longest continuous literary civilisation and the mandarin educational and bureaucratic system as essential parts the Qing state. Yet, in the 19th century the empire-state had already entered a period of decline leading to its 1912 collapse, often associated with the insistent incursions of the rising western imperial powers, especially following the 1868 Meiji Revolution, which rapidly built up nearby Japan as a modern military power. However, China's long-term decline and collapse were more complex and had roots in a population explosion, and a fiscal crisis, as well as an economy that did not industrialise. A series of 19th-century wars, mostly fought by the British to extend their drug trade into China (the so-called Opium Wars), did stimulate some reform processes, particularly in the military. But the catastrophic defeat of the recently modernised Qing army by the Japanese in 1895 led to the further loss of Taiwan and the growth of Japanese influence in northern Korea, beginning the end of the Qing Dynasty. Further weakened by foreign intervention following the populist Boxer uprisings against foreigners in 1900, the dynasty finally collapsed in 1912. It was replaced by an unstable republican regime nationally, with powerful regional warlords. Mao's educational and political formation was closely tied to the intellectual and political struggles that were unleashed in this period.

Whilst the Qing Empire was wealthy and powerful during its 18th-century high point, Qing China overwhelmingly remained a peasant agricultural economy, a peasant world that still by 1900 hardly differed from that experienced by the ordinary Chinese over many centuries. Mao was born in Hunan province, as opposed to an east coast city, so as a child he would have seen little of the slow industrialisation that was taking place, or even much of the western influence that came from missionary activity or trade. The pace of life was dictated by nature and the long-established culture and conventions of Chinese peasant life, which were ultimately to play an important part in his approach to Marxism–Leninism and to his own revolutionary thought and practice towards the end of his life. For the few more middle-class people, education played an important part in social mobility in this largely Confucian culture. But it was the highly literary classical education that alone gave access to the Qing bureaucracy, and not a modern scientific or technical education.

Mao's education included a traditional literary formation that enabled him to become an accomplished poet. But at schools in Changsha (the capital of Hunan province) he never cultivated the skills of a traditional literati. Nor did he confine his quest for learning to either classical literature or the new learning coming from the west, such as recently translated works by Adam Smith, Charles Darwin and Herbert Spencer. Liberated from the demands of peasant life when his father became relatively wealthy, Mao pursued his education, interrupted by a brief period in the republican army. By August 1918 he had arrived in Beijing with an opening as a clerical assistant in Beijing University Library. For the next few years, Mao shuttled back and forth between Beijing and Changsha as he was introduced to Marx's writings and cultivated his interest in revolutionary socialism. He became involved in the organisation of the fledgling Communist Party of China, which was steered from Moscow by the Communist International. The early and mid-1920s saw Mao engaged in organisational activity and research in the countryside amongst the peasants whilst the party formed part of a popular front with Sun Yat-Sen's Guomindang (KMT).

This temporary coalition was always unstable, and it collapsed spectacularly in 1927 when Chiang Kai-Shek became leader following Sun's death. Chiang sided with local warlords and sought the defeat of the Communists and opened a long period of civil war that spanned the period until the establishment of the party state as the People's Republic in 1949. During this time, Mao rose within the ranks of the Communist Party leadership, especially after the Long March, when the party relocated its military and political headquarters and core armies and personnel from the more developed south-east China to the rural far north-west to evade pursuing Guomindang armies. This became an iconic event in the mythology of the new party state, and Mao marked himself out as a charismatic leader as well as theorist of revolution and especially revolutionary war. The mythology of Mao the revolutionary leader is brilliantly captured, if not actually created, for western readers in the Canadian journalist, Edgar Snow's (1938) book *Red Star over China*. Following the expulsion of the Japanese in 1945, a resumed Chinese civil war ended in 1949 with the communist armies occupying all of China, and expelling Chiang Kai-Shek's remnant forces to Taiwan.

Like Stalin, and far more than Lenin ever did in the USSR, Mao came to dominate the party state and to represent the 1949 revolution, but, as with Stalin, he could not exercise such extraordinary power and influence without allies and supporters. In the subsequent 27 years until his death in 1976, his relationship with the rest of the party and its leadership was neither straightforward nor simply dictatorial. These years saw a rush to modernise and industrialise, leading to both extraordinary economic change as well as devastation, violence and famine under the Great Leap Forward agricultural collectivisation push from 1957 to 1960.

Mao's ideas of peasant war were also put to effective use (albeit with high casualties) in pushing back the US-led United Nations army in the Korean War (1950–1953). The death of Stalin and the rise of Khrushchev (1894–1971) marked a significant break in the communist world, and the rise of Chinese communism as a focus for attention by revolutionaries throughout the world. The final decade of Mao's life was shaped by his unleashing of the Cultural Revolution, in which the masses and especially young people were encouraged to turn against and question the institutionalised leadership of the Party. Armed with Mao's *Little Red Book* and inspired in huge rallies, a spirit of unrestricted revolution and revolutionary violence was again unleashed against all aspects of society including within the party itself. Key leaders were killed or subjected to humiliation and re-education ('criticism'), which often broke them physically. The violence also tore through ordinary life, with families destroyed as children denounced parents; school pupils denounced and sometimes killed teachers. 'Bourgeois' occupations, such as science, intellectual work or high culture, were particularly suspect, with universities and other institutions closed and their staff sent to work in the fields. To many outside analysts, this unleashing of revolutionary violence simply confirmed the extreme nature of communist ideology. For others, the idea of total revolution was inspiring, whether to groups seeking to overthrow colonial domination in South East Asia, or amongst western radicals challenging the cultural hegemony of capitalism (Lovell 2019). Following Mao's death and the fall of the 'Gang of Four', a ruling clique in his later years, the new party leader, Deng Xiaoping, began a process of economic liberalisation that transformed China into a global economic power. How far any of Mao's legacy remains important in the Chinese Communist Party's rule across subsequent decades is deeply contested, but it clearly remains a party state. And, beyond the boundaries of the People's Republic, Mao's style of politics is still prevalent, perhaps most clearly in the rise of political populism.

Mao's legacy as a political actor is unquestioned, however one judges it. But his legacy as a political thinker is more ambiguous, especially outside of China. Whereas Lenin, Trotsky, Gramsci and others still feature in lists of PhD dissertations in the west, with waves of revisionist scholarship either saving them from the judgement of history or condemning them as moral monsters, Mao's work is less well studied. Much of this is due to the availability of quality texts in translation beyond the relatively small number of Mandarin speakers. Whilst he was a prolific writer, Mao does not have substantial contributions to the central questions of Marxist theory, choosing to defer to the classic statements of Lenin or Stalin. His writings are heavily influenced by China's historical and cultural experience: Mao was a careful student of classical Chinese thought, even though he often disparaged it in polemics, and he was an accomplished poet. His most influential works were often essay-style addresses or speeches to party organisations that are hard to generalise from. His most influential work, *Quotations from Chairman Mao Tse-Tung* or the *Little Red Book* (Mao 1966), is a series of selections from such works designed to give an overview of his ideas. It is not a systematic work, and, like a religious catechism, it is a series of statements and aphorisms, rather than developed arguments. Yet, on the specific challenges of the conduct of a revolutionary war against imperialism, his works from the mid-1930s are substantial contributions to thinking about the conduct of revolution. They influenced later revolutionaries from Che Guevara to many radical European leftist sects, as well as East Asian national liberation struggles. It is in these works that Mao develops the vision of revolution as an anti-imperialist war, and that are central here.

Marx: the essentials

What matters for our purposes is the thought of Lenin and Mao, and not whether they were authorities on Marx's thought or the source of significant distortions of his ideas. Many scholars of Marx have spent considerable effort freeing the interpretation of his thought from the legacies of his major followers. Although Lenin and Mao became significant theorists of revolution in their own right, they nonetheless retained a strong commitment to what they took to be the central tenets of Marxism as the framework for their thought. So, many key concepts or positions defended by Marx and Engels are central to situating the context of Lenin and Mao's revolutionary theories, and I briefly outline them here.

Historical materialism

Marx saw himself as the successor to the great German philosopher G.W.F. Hegel (1770–1831) and many of his early ideas are best seen as a revolutionary transformation of Hegel's philosophy of history. For Hegel, history is ultimately the history of thought and ideas and their progressive development through a dialectical process (the development of ideas through overcoming opposition or contradiction). Institutions and actions are instances of that overarching conflict of ideas. The process of dialectic seeks a complete and consistent understanding of human experience (often referred to as spirit or *Geist*) and so there is a direction or pattern to history that underpins all moral, political and social progress. Marx and his student friends (who became known as left-Hegelians) liked the concept of dialectical development. But they objected to the way Hegel's philosophy of history was employed as a justification of the policies and authority of the Prussian state. Instead, they argued for the radical transformation of Hegel's philosophy of history into an account of human liberation.

Marx's breakthrough as an independent philosopher came about through his rejection of the inherent idealism of Hegel's thought, which held that ideas drive history. Marx substitutes a materialist conception of history and human experience in place of Hegel's idealism. He develops this in a number of works, some of which he did not publish, such as *The German Ideology* (1846). However, historical materialism underpins his most famous work, *The Communist Manifesto* (1848) and his great later work *Capital* (1867). Put simply, Marx saw that social and political life was not becoming more rational as a result of philosophical progress but more conflictual and chaotic. The scope of this crisis was accelerating as modernity and industrialisation were developing across Europe. It was precisely the core character of that process, which he called the capitalist mode of production, that was the driving force of conflicts between social classes in societies, and the source of the different political and ideological disputes that followed from that conflict.

To really understand social and political conflict, one needs to focus on its material conditions, that is, its productive forces and the consequent relations of production. In the first instance, that means that societies and human relationships are shaped by the technology of the society, which enables humans to sustain their existence and reproduce their society. For much of human history, technology had been limited by human or animal physical power, and consequently society was largely agricultural, with only limited industrial production. With steam power, and eventually electricity, production shifted to cities and towns. People were liberated from the land, but capitalism created a new despotism of factory-based wage labour in poor conditions for minimum wages. This material base of society then shaped the relations of production, which have a dominant role in shaping individual identities. Modern urban-industrial societies create propertyless factory workers in large numbers, and factory and capital owners in ever smaller numbers. These two groups become Marx's proletariat (working class) and capitalists. The forces and relations of production constitute the historical mode of production. Marx saw history as a succession of modes of production and not merely philosophical systems, and his own time as the triumph of the capitalist mode of production displacing the prior feudal mode of production.

Marx's theoretical life work was the analysis of the capitalist mode of production in his book *Capital* (1867) and its subsequent unpublished volumes. Central to this analysis is his theory of ideology and the claim that the economic base of society shaped (or determined) the superstructure of that society. By this he meant that the political, legal, cultural and philosophical ideas of a society must ultimately reflect the economic or material power relations in that society. New philosophical ideas are therefore not ways of reconciling prior conflicts within a philosophical synthesis but reflections of those power relations. They must either act as justifications and rationalisations of these power relations or be attempts to critique and overthrow them. Thus, the struggle between conservative and liberal forces in Europe following the French Revolution was, for Marx, nothing more than the consequence of the economic transformation of Europe by the triumph of mature capitalism.

Crisis and revolution

The first part of Marx's revolution in thought was the material analysis of society and social relations. However, he also saw a material dialectic in the historical progress from one mode of production to the next, and this was to be the most important part of his analysis for his successors. The conflict of ideas and political arguments that we find at the heart of political life is only a superficial sign of the fundamental conflict that lies at the heart of the mode of production, and it is only the resolution of this conflict that ultimately leads to the transition from one to the next. One might see the arguments of social contract theorists from the 17th century on as reflecting the emergence of a new capitalist mode of production out of the old feudal order (Macpherson 1962). Central to Marx's theory of historical change is crisis and revolution. Crisis tendencies arise as technology develops and opens up the possibility of further social and political change. Marx saw these tendencies in the way that capitalism accelerated industrialisation and urbanisation, bringing more people into factory-based production, which in turn had an impact on the market for the goods that capitalism produced. The process of exploitation of labour power is vital to create the surplus value that form the capitalists' profits, and competition between capitalists results in the progressive impoverishment of the industrial workers. Although mechanisation opens up enormous productive potential, it paradoxically accelerates the immiserisation of the mass of factory workers, who presumably would otherwise form the potential market for capitalist products. This exploitative logic of capital accumulation creates a contradiction at the heart of the mode of production that must lead to its overthrow and replacement.

The important point about this crisis tendency, and why Marx saw it as ineluctably creating a revolutionary moment, is that crisis is inherent in the material conditions of the mode of production. Therefore, it cannot be addressed by any form of political settlement between labour and capital, as many optimistic 19th-century novelists (such as Disraeli, Dickens or Gaskell) or utopian thinkers (such as Owen and Fourier) hoped. The logic of exploitation was structural and not personal or alterable. It could only be overcome through fundamentally changing how work and the economy are organised to the new relations of production made possible by the advance of technology. This crisis-induced overthrow of the relations of production is precisely what Marx meant by the idea of revolution, and it is the inevitable condition of historical change. Although Marx is permanently associated with the concept of revolution, he actually says little about it, because he is more concerned with the material logic of the crisis tendencies in capitalism. Despite his journalistic leanings, this is also why he is less interested than many of his contemporaries in the minutiae of 19th-century politics.

Class politics

The concept of revolution applies to Marx's analysis at a number of levels. However, the most familiar one is the analysis of transformative political struggle through class conflict. The concept of a social class is an important feature of his analysis of the superstructure of a society. Marx is not an individualist, nor is he an unambiguous humanist, unlike utilitarians and natural rights theorists. Like Hegel, he thinks that an individual's identity, aspirations and political interests are socially constituted, but, unlike Hegel, he also thinks that the social constitution of identity is shaped by one's position in the mode of production. The opposing class interests of workers and capitalists shape their respective identities and their relationships. They can have no common interest and therefore there is not much for a politics of bargaining and compromise to address. Instead, the members of both classes are in mutual and irreconcilable opposition to one another. This is why Marx is so dismissive in *The Communist Manifesto* of types of socialism that seek to overcome social conflict through achieving political compromise. It is also why his followers considered the most devastating criticism was to be called a revisionist – i.e. someone who thought that political reform could replace or avoid the need for revolutionary conflict.

The concept of class is a complex one in Marx and Marxist thought. It is used to explain the (fundamental) identities or interests of the proletariat, the agents of revolutionary transformation. It is not intended as a celebration of the folkways of the urban working class, because those will be overcome once capitalism is overthrown. But it does establish a hierarchy within identity that explains political, national or gender struggles as ultimately reducible to the structures of economic power and interest that are shaped by the capitalist mode of production. Revolution is a consequence of class conflict brought about by the material crisis tendencies within the capitalist mode of production. Those crisis tendencies work themselves out in history through the vehicle of the mutual opposition of classes. So classes are the real agents in history and not individuals ('great men') or nations. Consequently, the goal of revolutionary transformation is not to end individual suffering and misery but the overthrow of the structures of domination that are at the heart of capitalism. Human liberation is the liberation of the working class from capitalist domination. Ending class domination will directly result in an improvement in most individuals' well-being. But it is class liberation that matters, because without it no individual goods, rights or interests are possible. Marx's focus on classes as the primary agent in history as opposed to individuals has led to numerous problems for subsequent Marxists. It would be wrong and foolish to accuse Marx of being indifferent to individual human suffering. It is crucial to remember that most of Marx's writing was in the light of the failure of the liberal wave of revolutions across Europe in 1848, and the brutal suppression of the Paris Commune in 1870. As a result, he thought that only the complete overthrow of the underlying material structure of capitalism would enable any genuine human emancipation. Despite all of this, Marx uses the concept of class as an analytical tool to explain the structure of politics and the revolutionary crisis facing capitalism. But those looking to *The Communist Manifesto* for a political programme will be disappointed. It devotes considerable attention to criticising those socialists who have a plan for revolution, or who think they are best placed to direct and lead the working class to triumph. Marx's ambiguity about how class politics should be conducted left considerable room for his followers to disagree about what his legacy was and how the communists should conduct themselves.

Communism

Marx's historical materialism explains the rise and nature of capitalism and why its inherent crisis tendencies must lead to revolution. What follows on from that revolution? Marx's answer is communism, but what does he mean by that? The name suggests the holding of property and organisation of the economy in common (and the abolition of private ownership), but in a very general way. Towards the end of his life, Marx gave some brief outlines of what a communist society might be like, but he was always cautious about prescribing the conditions of life under communism. The main reason for this reticence was that the revolutionary transformation from capitalism would create new forms of social life but it also would transform the lives of people and their social interactions in fundamental ways. In his approach, this material transformation must overcome ways of thinking about human nature and society's interests that are merely the inheritance of the capitalist mode of production. There is no constant and trans-historical human nature that persists through the various historical modes of production. That said, some things can be said of communism in terms of absences of essential features of the capitalist mode of production. Wage labour will be abolished as a result of socialised production and thus there will be no private property or money as a means of resource allocation. With the abolition of private property and the democratisation of ownership, social class will be abolished, because the fundamental relationship of domination of worker by capital owners disappears. In this respect, a communist society will be a society of equals.

Marx was not a utopian thinker who imagined a post-capitalist society. He took exception to those early socialist utopians who thought that a better society merely needed an exercise of imagination. Instead, for Marx, what replaces capitalism must be better simply because it overcomes the contradictions of capitalism in the struggle between labourers and owners of capital. The precise form that emancipation will take is not something that can be derived by philosophical speculation. Instead, it will be worked out in the practical struggle of revolutionary change. As Marx famously said in the 'Eleventh Thesis on Feuerbach' in *The German Ideology*, '[p]hilosophers have hitherto only interpreted the world in various ways; the point is to change it' (McLellan 2000, p. 173).

Marx and Engels chose to use their leadership in the Second Communist International to support the revolutionary overthrow of capitalism by defending the forces of the working class from those who claimed to have plans and blueprints for a new society, or who said that they had a better understanding of the requirements of revolutionary change than the proletariat itself. This theoretical legacy later inspired both Lenin and Mao, the two most significant leaders of Marxist revolutions. Yet, Marx's studied ambiguity about the character of revolutionary politics and the building of a communist society left both these successors with multiple challenges and opportunities to shape the conduct of revolutionary change and impose their own orthodoxy on Marx and Engels's thought, which the original thinkers may not have shared or appreciated. The concepts and positions involved in the ideology of Marxism–Leninism and then Maoism were not inherent in Marx's own work.

Lenin and the party – 'what is to be done?'

Lenin wrote on Marxist theory in a style affected by Friedrich Engels's quest to make Marxism into a science. Yet, the primary assumption behind Lenin's work was that Marx and Engels had provided the theoretical framework to understand history, so that the task was no longer to seek how to understand the world but to change it. He accepted the materialist theory of history, the inevitability of the collapse of capitalist modernity and its replacement by communism, and the class analysis of politics and revolutionary change. Theory was important because 'without revolutionary theory there can be no revolutionary movement' (Lenin 1988, p. 91). But, for a Russian professional revolutionary, this theory only set the framework – it did not prescribe what is to be done. This question was the starting point of Lenin's life work and the title of one of his most famous works. It is also the work in which the idea and character of the Marxist professional revolutionary is first defined. Lenin's contribution to theory concerns the role and task of the professional revolutionary.

Lenin's serious engagement with Marxism began during his studies in St Petersburg and developed in his exile in Siberia, where he spent time studying the Russian economy and especially its relative development on the path to mature capitalism. Given the orthodox Marxist account of historical development, it was necessary for economies to go through the stage of capitalist development to the point where a genuinely revolutionary transformation was possible. The problem for many subsequent Marxists was that Russia still appeared superficially to be a peasant economy, and consequently largely without the necessary revolutionary class of the proletariat or industrial workers. The question of development was not simply one of political economy but manifested itself in the political and revolutionary struggles of Russian life. There had been a long history of peasant revolts against the Russian nobility and state that had uniformly been brutally suppressed. By the 1900s, there was also a long sequence of radical challenges to the tsarist autocracy that manifested itself in populist uprisings and revolutionary assassination and terror, of the sort that had led to Lenin's brother's execution. Yet, the presence of radical violence was not enough to trigger a revolutionary moment, as Marx had warned in *The Communist Manifesto* (1848). Bomb throwing, assassination and uprisings were all very well, but, unless they were manifestations of the inevitable uprising of the working class, they stood little change of success. The material conditions needed to be in place for a genuinely revolutionary moment as opposed to another ill-fated coup or uprising, like the Paris Commune of 1871. An appropriate grounding in theory was necessary to understand that part of the logic of history. The risk for the proletariat was being constantly led into premature uprisings by anarchists, populists and terrorists – such ungrounded and ill-fated rebellions only had the effect of allowing the forces of the capitalist state to strengthen and reassert their power.

When Marx and Engels wrote of 'the Communist Party' in their 1848 *Manifesto*, they were referring to all those who took the side of the working class in the impending struggle with the capitalist bourgeoisie. To express a preference for the communists was to take a side. What it did not mean at that stage was to be a member of a single, hierarchical political organisation of the sort we now associate with political parties, either in one-party states or multiparty democracies. The move towards this modern understanding of a political party was developing in the period following the death of Marx, especially in countries like Britain and Germany with modernised political systems and where the question of who represents the working class began to emerge. It was in this context that Lenin's earliest writings on political organisation were written – and later consolidated into his pamphlet, *What Is to Be Done?* On leaving Siberia for exile in Switzerland, Lenin began to establish himself as a leader of the Russian social democrats (another name for the communists) and to transform that group into a structured organisation that became recognisable as a political party.

The significance of Lenin's pamphlet can be lost in its involvement in detailed historical context and debates. However, Lenin sets out a number of fundamental elements of the revolutionary movement and its conception of, and approach to, politics. The party is composed of a small group of professional revolutionaries. They are the vanguard leading the proletariat, but they do not themselves have to be part of the industrial working class. The party should be built as a centralised, clandestine and hierarchically organised authority, in the pursuit of revolution. Its objective is the emancipation of the proletariat, the cultivation of class consciousness and the overthrow of class domination once and for all. The party is not about social reform. Consequently, bourgeois values such as democracy, liberty, equality and rights are of secondary importance to Lenin and any professional revolutionary. Thus, Lenin uses this pamphlet to make the case for a significant transformation of Marxist theory, one in which the party takes a leadership role for the working class by directing it towards revolution:

> Only a centralised, militant organisation that consistently carries out a social-democratic policy and satisfies, so to speak, all revolutionary instincts and strivings, can safeguard the movement against making thoughtless attacks and prepare attacks that hold out the promise of success. (Lenin 1988, p. 198)

Lenin begins his defence of the party in the context of working-class politics in the late 19th century. The belief that the working class are the agent of revolutionary change has given rise to a mistaken belief that industrial workers must be left to work out their transformative role themselves, and not be misdirected into coups and utopian reform projects. However, as the working class developed a self-consciousness in countries like Britain or Germany, it was diverted by earlier reformist ideologies that had sought to better the conditions of the working class through social reform and labour representation. Policies such as labour legislation (including the right to strike, factory regulation and social welfare reform) all appeared to offer the short- or medium-term route to improve the conditions of the labouring poor. They might also avoid out-and-out conflict with the coercive powers of the state, such as the military and the police. Exponents of this view claimed that the interests of the working class were best served by the self-organisation of trades unions, labour representation committees, and making alliances between these bodies and radical intellectuals – such as the Fabians in Britain, who continued the tradition of radical liberal and utilitarian reformers from the early 19th century.

For Lenin, the lure of the trade union model of working-class politics was a dangerous deceit because the conflict between the interests of labour and capital were mutually antagonistic and irreconcilable. Perhaps it was his experience of a more violent autocracy in Russia that reinforced his suspicion of bourgeois concessions as superficial and temporary, but Lenin remained convinced that the working class were in a mortal struggle with capital that could only end in the overthrow of capitalism. His understanding of Marxist theory convinced him that the key to the emancipation of the working class was through the revolutionary overthrow of capitalism. But he recognised that the proletariat, which carried that historical role, was not always well placed to understand its historical significance. The first task of the party was to lead the working class in the direction of its true interests by building a revolutionary class consciousness. This seemingly original departure from Marx's theory of ideology was made possible, according to Lenin, because the professional revolutionaries possessed a revolutionary theory. The theory was the key to understanding class politics and the material struggle between labour and capital, and it was vindicated because it emerged from the material conditions of conflict and historical change. It was not just a free-standing theory about change but something that was given by the material logic of history. Lenin did not just have a faith in Marx's theory; he genuinely believed that Marx had unveiled the logic of history in the same way that Darwin and other scientists were unveiling the logic of biological change.

Two things follow from this transformative insight. Firstly, to avoid the corruption of class interests by labour and trade union politics there needed to be a dedicated revolutionary vanguard who understood and were fully committed to the task of revolution and not reform. Secondly, that group would not be swayed and corrupted to the short-term gains offered by reformist or liberal politics but would work to direct the working class towards its own interest, namely the overthrow of class domination and the ultimate emancipation of humanity. Lenin writes that 'we must have people who will devote themselves exclusively to social-democratic activities and that such people must train themselves patiently and steadfastly to be professional revolutionaries' (Lenin 1988, p. 188). Who were these people? This question is particularly important because it has a direct bearing on the authority of Lenin and his colleagues, and indeed of the master theoreticians Marx and Engels (who was actually a Victorian capitalist). As we have seen, Lenin first became a revolutionary at university and during his captivity in Siberia. His move to exile placed him at the heart of a group of émigré intellectuals and revolutionaries, none of whom were industrial workers. Running risks and producing clandestine newspapers and pamphlets bridged the gap with industrial workers, but it did not really ground these people within the working class. Consequently, for Lenin the professional revolutionary vanguard could be drawn from the educated working class, but it could equally be drawn from university students and intellectuals. This stance linked his ideas to the long-standing views of intellectuals and students as those who had broken their ties with their birth origins and become devoted to the universal cause of emancipation. But, again, what must now link and discipline these individuals is their adherence to Marxist doctrine, as opposed to a subjective or personal sympathy with the plight of the urban poor or the lives of the workers.

The task of this group is to be guided by revolutionary theory so as to become a revolutionary movement and to lead the working class in their historical role. It cannot be sentimental, or become preoccupied with the living conditions and welfare of the workers and the poor. As a scientific socialist, Lenin's concern is not with the welfare of the aggregate of working men and their families – that is the fundamental difference between reformist and trade unionist labourism and his professional revolutionaries. The beneficiaries of the revolution were never expected to be assignable individuals within an aggregate social class. The working class is not simply the group of all the industrial labourers who do not own capital. From an historical point of view, those individuals gain their significance through their class position. Moral considerations about the rights or welfare of individuals are merely a diversion from the fundamental power relations that exist between classes. Lenin does not devote much attention or moralistic concerns to the welfare and rights of workers, except as offering objective evidence of the need to overthrow class exploitation. The professional revolutionary is therefore attentive to the dangers of sentimentalism and simplistic moralism, and the way these can be exploited by the capitalist class to co-opt the leaders of the labour movement.

> For it is not enough to call ourselves the 'vanguard', the advance contingent: we must act in such a way that all the other contingents recognise and are obliged to admit that we are marching in the vanguard. And we ask the reader: are the representatives of the other 'contingents' such fools as to take our word for it when we say that we are the vanguard? (Lenin 1988, pp. 147–148)

Lenin's professional revolutionaries are the group who serve as the vanguard of the working class, not just those who identify with the interest of the working class. The party is an advance contingent because it leads the proletariat in the direction of its own world historical interest by being the repository of their class consciousness. The role of the working class is being the agent of the overthrow of class domination. As such, their class interest is different from the perceived interests of the members of the proletariat as a contingent collection of individuals.

Individual members of the proletariat might be content with shorter working hours, higher wages, paid holidays and better housing. Yet, a focus on those individual interests leads only to class exploitation and failure, and this is why Lenin thinks the workers need a professional vanguard who become the 'head' of the workers as a political movement. This clearly shifts the focus of revolutionary politics away from any preoccupation with short-term material gains and political positioning within the domestic systems of capitalist states. The politics of Fabians, reformers and trade unionists or labour parties is ultimately epiphenomenal (secondary to the real politics of class conflict) and, as such, a distraction. In exercising its leadership role, the vanguard must therefore co-opt and control the other manifestations of working-class politics and direct them towards the ultimate goal, which is not reconciliation with the capitalist system and its state but their overthrow.

This form of revolutionary politics has several consequences. Firstly, as Lenin's career prior to 1917 shows, it focuses a lot of attention on asserting its leadership amongst the working-class movement, and defeating the other 'contingents'. From an external perspective, this can make revolutionary politics look preoccupied with factional status and position, as opposed to concrete reform. Yet, for Lenin and his professional revolutionaries, and from the point of view of history, this politics of status and position is far more important than seeking the election of labour representatives. The ultimate task of the revolutionary party is to safeguard against 'thoughtless attacks and prepare attacks that hold out the promise of success' (Lenin 1988, p. 198), by which he means seeking the objective opportunities to accelerate revolutionary transition. For Lenin and his professional revolutionaries, there was no question that capitalism was heading to its ultimate crisis and therefore was not reformable; the question was readiness to exploit those moments that might expose the final transition.

To this end, the party needed professional revolutionaries, and to conduct its affairs in a clandestine and conspiratorial fashion to avoid infiltration by the tsarist secret police, who were keen to disrupt its activities and personnel. Once the party became the primary focus of political activity, then the training and disciplining of its militant membership would be part of its reason for existence. The party was tasked with distinguishing genuine revolutionaries from either those who were weak in their revolutionary commitment or (more seriously) spies, traitors and collaborators who infiltrated the party to disrupt it. A perennial feature of this form of class politics is the assertion of authenticity amongst the membership and the rooting-out of collaborators. Although this type of political activity may again seem obsessively inward-looking, it is actually of fundamental importance, given the party's historic role and the relative insignificance of individuals in achieving that goal. The later Soviet history of purges and intra-party violence is already built into the logic of the party in its vanguard role. The necessity for discipline and authority also manifests itself in Lenin's indifference to internal party democracy and his preference for a centralised and hierarchical leadership.

'the broad democratic principle' will simply facilitate the work of the police in carrying out large scale raids, will perpetuate the prevailing primitiveness and will divert the thoughts of the practical activists from the serious and pressing task of training themselves to become professional revolutionaries to that of drawing up detailed 'paper' rules for election systems. (Lenin 1988, p. 200)

To ensure the appropriate direction of the party, Lenin rejects what he calls 'the broad democratic principle' – the idea that authority is dispersed throughout the party and decisions are based on elaborate constitutional ('paper') rules. Such a form of governance opens the party to manipulation by the secret police and others who wish to frustrate its success. For Lenin, it was this unnecessary preoccupation with party constitutions and procedures that was such a feature of the trade union politics that he rejected. Instead, the party needed a centralised form of authority and leadership, coupled with absolute discipline in the implementation of decisions. His preferred form of politics was that of a strong executive prerogative, as opposed to a constitutional and constrained form of politics designed to spread the legitimacy of decisions. This executive conception of politics has become a perennial feature of revolutionaries of left or right and more recently of the resurgence of populism. It appeals to the idea that politics is about getting the job done and not endlessly discussing process, but it also fits well with agendas that are simple and unitary, whether this be in wartime or in responding to an emergency. The crisis of late capitalism is effectively a permanent emergency and the task facing the revolutionary party is overthrowing the system, so superficially there is little scope for complex policy agendas and the weighing of conflicting but necessary ends. As Lenin moved from being a clandestine revolutionary to being the leader of an actual revolution, and a government enmeshed in a civil war from 1917 to 1922, the task of deciding became more pressing, as the choices became more complex.

Who forms that centralised party leadership? This issue remains an opaque question in *What Is to Be Done?*, although it was to become a hugely important issue as Lenin moved from leading one faction in the complex world of anti-tsarist Russian politics to leading the Bolshevik revolution some 15 years later. He writes of party political authority being in the hands of a small central group, but there is no clarity on how small that group should be, or on the nature and authority of leadership. His own position as a dominant figure amongst a leadership group suggests that a small group is possible, but the problems that arose following his premature death in 1924 illustrate the cost of that ambiguity – as Stalin came to replace him. For many subsequent communists, Stalin betrayed the legacy of Lenin by consolidating rule in his own hands as a permanent dictator. Other communists took the orthodox line of the party, which claimed that Stalin was simply fulfilling the inherent logic of Lenin's account of party leadership with its clandestine and centralising decision-making processes.

What Is to Be Done? was published in 1902, shortly before the abortive rebellion of 1905 and long before the momentous events of World War I and the collapse of the tsarist autocracy. Since Lenin was a practical revolutionary, his thought developed in the light of experience, and during the 1917 Revolution and the civil war that development was to accelerate significantly. Yet, the principal elements of his theory of the party, and its dominant position in his thinking about political agency, did not change. The party and the conduct of politics were centralised, clandestine and conspiratorial, with primary focus directed at enemies of the party outside and inside the party structure. To describe politics in this way is not to offer a partisan caricature of Leninism, because this form of conduct was the necessary consequence of the party's historical role and purpose. The party and its goal as the class-conscious leader of the proletariat was all that mattered to Lenin and his close followers, as it was ultimately the reality of politics liberated from the distortion of the bourgeois state. As Hannah Arendt, no friend of Lenin, pointed out, despite the sloganeering of the 1917 Revolution and its cry of 'All Power to the Soviets' it was the consistently claimed purpose of the Bolsheviks to 'replace the state machinery with the party apparatus' (Arendt 1963, p. 269).

As the history of the USSR unfolded in the aftermath of the revolution, the Communist Party remained the principal site of politics, despite the addition of state institutions in the intervening years. What happened within the party and its leadership always dictated what happened in the world's first communist state. A striking feature of Lenin's early account of the revolutionary party is how little he says about the state, the international order, and the territorial dimensions of international politics. As the revolution of 1905 failed, and the tsarist autocracy reasserted its position up to 1914, it became clear that the final crisis of capitalism was still over the horizon and that Russia's international context was as important as the domestic struggle against the tsarist regime. The revolution in other countries that Marx had envisaged on the verge of triggering the world uprising against capitalism had failed to materialise, and the system that showed all the tendencies of crisis also demonstrated a curious resilience. It was precisely this challenge that led Lenin to examine how capitalism was adapting and transforming itself in a new form that Marx could not have fully appreciated, namely imperialism.

Capitalism, imperialism and the nation

Lenin's short pamphlet *Imperialism, the Highest Stage of Capitalism* was published in 1916 following an intense period of study from 1915 onwards. This was the height of World War I, with the launch of the British spring offensive on the Somme in order to relieve the unrelenting pressure of German attacks on the French army at Verdun. On the Eastern Front, the Russian army was in retreat from Poland and facing challenges in the south created by Romania's entry into the war alongside Austria–Hungary and Germany. The stalemate on the Western Front, with increasing carnage and limited or no prospects of breakthrough, represented war at its most brutal and futile. This was the context for Lenin to address the nature of capitalism and its new form as imperialism. Although the text attempts a social scientific analysis of a new social form, the work's significance (in both Lenin's thought and the prospects for proletarian revolution) is far more than the sum of its tables charting external investment and returns on capital would suggest.

Lenin was convinced that capitalism was in the midst of its final crisis and the revolutionary's task was to exploit the opportunities that this crisis posed for a complete overthrow of the forces of the bourgeoisie concentrated in the modern state system. As the ill-fated revolutionary uprising of 1905 had shown, the forces of the capitalist state (in this case the tsarist autocracy) were resilient. Yet, for Lenin, this simply meant that the revolutionaries needed to show care in seizing their moment and not be forced into precipitate actions when the time was not right. The tasks for formation and mobilisation of the workers continued to be the primary goal of the class-conscious vanguard leadership. Whilst Lenin focused this activity within the Russian Social Democratic Party, he at first understood his work as continuous with that taking place throughout the mature capitalist economies. The revolutionary moment was structural and not simply national. When the working classes of the mature capitalist economies were at the right stage, they would trigger a worldwide revolution. This might begin in one country but that would signal a rapid spread across the united working class, who shared more in common as members of an economic class than they did as members of a state.

By 1915, Lenin had realised this was a naïve view at best, because the workers of the world had enthusiastically gone to war against each other. More importantly, the leadership of the various national social democratic parties, including such venerable figures as Karl Kautsky in Germany, had voted to support the war effort once war was declared. Lenin remained opposed to the war and a committed internationalist who preferred to work for Russia's defeat. Yet, he saw how the labour movement was co-opted into the mass mobilisation for the war, with one nation's workers co-opted into a war with their fellow workers. For him, a civil war within the proletariat was unconscionable, but a civil war within the capitalist class was another matter. The capitalist class had an interest in co-operating amongst themselves to defeat a socialist revolutionary uprising. But, if capitalists were threatened by other capitalists, then competition and struggle were indeed inevitable, an important tenet of the Marxist analysis of class struggle. Some socialists asked why the workers of Germany had gone to war with the workers of Britain or France, as opposed to manifesting class solidarity and pursuing a Europe-wide general strike, as some (such as Jean Jaurès in France) had hoped. But for Lenin this was not the real issue.

Instead, he asked why the capitalist class had entered into and still pursued such a brutal civil war between national capitalisms. To answer this question, one needed to understand how capitalism had developed since the end of the 19th century. Lenin saw the answer in terms of a development towards a globalised form of capitalism that he descried as imperialism. His analysis is also intended to show that this development does not stave off the final collapse of capitalism but instead is a sign that the mode of production is entering on a final crisis moment. Although superficially a technical study of modern imperialist capitalism, Lenin's work remains an optimistic one from the point of view of revolutionary consciousness. The apparent collapse of revolutionary consciousness amongst the workers across all combatant countries, in favour of backing patriotism and extreme militarism, was only superficial: history was all going to plan.

Imperialism was not a new phenomenon, but it had grown in significance in the late 19th century, with economic arguments used to promote and rationalise what some countries had been doing for centuries. With the incorporation of the British East India Company into the British state after 1857, and the declaration of Queen Victoria as Empress of India in 1876, the idea of Britain as a world imperial power grew from a political fact into a self-ascribed ideology. Advocates of imperial expansion in Africa and South East Asia formed a new political voice that challenged the prevailing ideology of free trade guaranteed by the Royal Navy, which had ensured Britain's global presence. The opening up of continental (and not just coastal) Africa in the mid-19th century to the major imperial powers of Britain and France, alongside new competitors like Belgium and Germany, and the older Portuguese presence, began a scramble for Africa. This attempt to partition the whole continent into European-owned territories became an important contributory factor in the path to war. The United States also began its expansion into the Philippines and Cuba. To the defenders of imperialism, such as Milner and Rhodes in Britain or Theodore Roosevelt in the USA, the justifying argument was not simply national pride and assertiveness but economics. Traditional colonialism secured tariff-controlled markets of traditional colonialism. But the new imperialism sought control of access to supplies for resources essential for modern economies, such as oil and rubber, as well as new sources of cheap labour. Colonialism was not just an opportunity to resettle surplus populations in the metropolitan countries that had grown significantly during industrialisation. It was also an opportunity to export capital into new markets where investment returns would be better than could be gained in the mature markets of the old capitalist powers, as with the British banks building railways across Latin America.

Lenin drew on the analysis of heterodox economists like J.A. Hobson (1858–1940), who was also to influence John Maynard Keynes, and Rudolf Hilferding (1877–1941) in seeing the financialisation of capitalism. But he rejected the implication that this trend could postpone the long-term crisis of capitalism. All the major theorists of imperialism recognised the transformation of modern industrialised economies away from being heterogenous collections of industrial capitalists with interests in particular manufactures and industries competing vigorously with each other for market share. As industrial economies mature, the logic of capitalism is towards creating monopolies within national economies, and the diversification of firms' ownership across industries through financial capital. The real powers of the new era were not the original industrial magnates of a single industry town but instead those who dominated whole industries. Through diversification of share ownership, these hegemonic figures also increasingly dominated multiple related industries – for example, steel magnates having an interest in railways as a primary consumer of steel as well as coal. The exploitation of other raw materials was increasingly essential for the development of the chemical industry or more advanced forms of engineering. These fields relied on metals such as nickel or chrome (especially important for the modern arms industry) as much as iron and steel. The new metals were often not available in large deposits in Europe, but they were plentiful in Africa, Canada or Australia, which powerfully drove imperial expansion.

Capitalism begins its transition to imperialism as it matures, and the process of industrialisation and urbanisation is completed. The further development of capitalism is always driven by the capitalists' need for profits, and now requires security of supply for all basic raw materials, encouraging internationalisation because they are dispersed across the world. However, domestic rates of profit in metropolitan core countries are at risk from growing international competition (by other countries' monopolies) and fully mobilised domestic markets. The opportunities for domestic exploitation of labour are diminished, but this falling rate of profit now does not lead to the revolutionary moment that Marx and Engels expected. Instead, the opportunity for overseas investment and expansion to defer the crisis exists, and opens up new opportunities for capital in terms of investments in overseas industry and development. Building railways in imperial possessions, colonies and spheres of influence is a simple example of the opportunities for exploiting new markets for goods, such as steel and machinery. It also provided opportunities for investing capital in new companies exploiting the new possessions, and all with the added advantage of cheap labour to exploit.

As the returns on capital invested overseas become increasingly important for economies such as Britain, the political imperative to protect it rises. The state extends its reach either through direct takeovers of territory, as in India and Africa, or indirectly through building dominant economic control, as in South America. This logic of imperial expansion extends the life of mature capitalism and postpones a domestic revolution, a change that is captured in Lenin's quotation from a speech by a leading British imperialist, Cecil Rhodes, in which he campaigns for empire as a solution to domestic social unrest. The opportunity to exploit native labour in imperial possessions and colonies would raise the relative standard of living of the domestic working class in the metropolitan country and undermine their self-perception as the most impoverished class. Below the industrial workers of European industrial economies there was always 'the wretched of the earth' in the colonies.

> My cherished idea is a solution for the social problem, i.e., in order to
> save the 40,000,000 inhabitants of the United Kingdom from a bloody
> civil war, we colonial statesmen must acquire new lands to settle the
> surplus population, to provide new markets for the goods produced in
> the factories and mines. The Empire, as I have always said, is a bread
> and butter question. If you want to avoid civil war, you must become
> imperialists. (Lenin 1978, p. 75)

The growth of imperialism amongst the established capitalist economies displaced the traditional land powers of continental politics. Whilst the maritime power of Britain was important, it had been peripheral to the important
European power struggles of France, Russia, Prussia and the Austro-Habsburg
empire in the 19th century. The United States' rise as a solely hemispheric power
(following the Monroe Doctrine) had made it marginal to European politics.
Yet, with the transformation of capitalism into imperialism, Lenin identifies
Britain, America and Japan as major imperial powers (a particularly prescient
judgement in light of later 20th-century history). Like the United States and
Britain, Japan had rapidly risen to become a modern industrial power with
ambitions across north-east Asia in China, Manchuria and Korea, but also
with a powerful and modern navy that had already inflicted a major defeat on
Russia (one factor triggering the abortive 1905 revolution).

> Capitalism has grown into a world system of colonial oppression and of
> financial strangulation of the overwhelming majority of the population
> of the world by a handful of 'advanced' countries. And this 'booty' is
> shared between two of three powerful world plunderers armed to the
> teeth (America, Great Britain, Japan) who are drawing the whole world
> into war over the division of their booty. (Lenin 1978, p. 11)

The rise of new capitalist imperial powers was not without war and conflict,
because the control of imperial possessions and the sea lanes necessary for
imperial trade and protection often gave rise to boundary disputes. In addition,
there were conflicts between the old traditional powers and new rising powers,
as with Japan's aggressive interventions into China or the far east of the tsarist
empire with the Russo-Japan War of 1904–1905. It is not a surprise that naval
power was a key feature of imperial power and the naval arms race was one
further destabilising fact in the run-up to war in 1914. But Lenin was not only
interested in the fact of imperialism as a new form of what we now call global
capitalism. His concern was not just to show that imperial expansion was a feature of the modern world order and a potential source of the world war going
on around him. He primarily sought to show that imperialism remained locked
within the crisis logic that historical materialism predicts, so that the proletarian revolution (although it was seemingly overtaken by and lost to patriotism
and military mobilisation) was actually still inevitable.

The advocates who celebrated imperialism as a positive development of a globalised political economy failed to see that the long-term tendency towards national monopoly fuelling imperialism was also leading to conflict between imperial powers. Imperial powers could not live in harmony with other imperial powers because they competed for territory to colonise and resources to monopolise. In fact, Lenin points out, all that imperialism manages to achieve is to spread the crisis of capitalism from the territorial states of Europe into the wider world, hence globalising the crisis of capitalism. Imperialism defers the final collapse in time, and spreads the crisis out in terms of space and territory, but at the end of this temporal and spatial extension there remains a final conflict and a global revolution. Nor had imperialism deferred revolution by a long stretch of time. Lenin's main concern was to show that it had accelerated the revolution into a global conflagration – because imperial dominion had imposed the conditions of crisis on still developing economies that on their own would not yet have reached sufficient maturity to form part of crisis capitalism.

Lenin's theory of imperialism had significant implications for understanding the international order and the tensions within it. Rather than a system of states of differing sizes, the global order was made up of very unequal capitalist imperial powers, constantly jostling each other to secure the interests of their globally dispersed capital. The (nation) state was no longer the highest stage of political development but the plaything of larger global capitalist powers. However, this displacement of the state by imperial powers was also a source of potential crisis because the very size and scale of imperial powers made them vulnerable to the pressures of traditional empire where the centre exert its authority through military force, violence and coercion of the peripheries. The instability of such imperial powers was illustrated by nationalist uprisings. These had proved a recurring problem for the continental great powers of the Europe in the 19th century and they were again emerging in Europe leading up to 1914. They also played a part in the internal power structures of colonies and possessions, which in turn made imperial power unstable. For example, throughout World War I Britain faced uprisings in Ireland and in India, and the Austro-Hungarian Empire was riven by national claims for self-determination.

Lenin was also interested in the plight of nationality, not just as an epiphenomenal diversion from the true politics of class, as classical Marxist theory maintained. Nations served as a vehicle through which the pressures of class conflict manifested themselves in territorially dispersed empires, Nationalism was a sign of how capitalism had sought to disrupt class interests by creating the national enmities and oppositions that manifested themselves in the willingness of European workers to slaughter each other on the battlefields of the Western and Eastern Fronts. According to Lenin, this fact should not have been a surprise to professional revolutionaries. He did not endorse nations and nationalism as an autonomous source of political allegiance and agency. But he thought that the emergence of national struggles was an essential element of global class struggle and that national movements could be incorporated into the mobilisation of revolutionary forces. At the same time, he was equally aware of how national sentiment could be mobilised by the forces of reaction to frustrate the revolutionary change. Consequently, in practical politics it was essential for the party and professional revolutionaries to be at the vanguard of nationalist movements as well as class struggle.

For many social democrats, the apparently easy diversion of the workers into supporting patriotic militarism caused a crisis of confidence. Yet, Lenin was able to see this as a vindication of his fundamental class analysis of politics and revolutionary change. Lenin's theory globalised the revolution and considered the way in which the territoriality of revolution must necessarily extend beyond the realm and structure of the nation state, which is always only a contingent manifestation of western capitalism. The state is merely the vehicle through which capitalist power is exercised against the interests of the workers whether on a national or an imperial scale. The state is an instrument of coercion, domination and violence and so it can only be dealt with through its violent destruction.

'The state and revolution' – Lenin and violence

The central elements of Lenin's argument about the role of party, the crisis of capitalism and imperialism as a sign of the new globalised nature of capitalist power and consequently the extension of revolution beyond national boundaries seem to omit or downplay the role of state. Yet, the state remained an important challenge for Lenin's account of revolution, especially during the establishment of the new revolutionary regime in Russia after 1917.

The revolution in Russia began after significant defeats for the Russian army on the Eastern Front in 1916 and early 1917. The prospect of a military mutiny led to factions in the Duma (or Russian Parliament) taking control of the government and the subsequent abdication of the tsar and royal family: this was the February revolution. During this time, when a provisional government sought to establish itself, Lenin was at first still an exile in Switzerland. He quickly returned to St Petersburg, but due to the war had to proceed through Germany, which was still in conflict with Russia. The German authorities no doubt hoped to force Russia out of the war, which would allow them to concentrate all their forces on the Western Front. So they facilitated his return via a sealed train that took him through Germany and then to Helsinki in Finland, from where in April he began his famous journey to St Petersburg's Finland Station, a journey often seen as the opening of the Bolshevik revolution. On his arrival in St Petersburg, he took up the leadership of the Bolshevik faction, but was unable to spend all his time in St Petersburg – because he was being pursued by opponents within the provisional government as well as by the military leaders, who hoped to overthrow the provisional government and re-establish the tsarist regime. During the extraordinary turmoil of mid-1917, Lenin wrote another book, *The State and Revolution*. This was not a manifesto for his subsequent conduct of the revolution, but it does address issues of political organisation, governance and the place of the state in a new revolutionary order. As with many of Lenin's theoretical writings, it is a reflection on the works of Marx and Engels, and most explicitly on their views of the 'dictatorship of the proletariat' and the place of the state and violence in revolution. I noted above that Marx and Engels actually said very little on the theory and practice of conducting a revolution, yet that that is precisely the situation in which Lenin found himself. He felt it was essential to ground the new experience and policy in aspects of Marx's thought. Once again, the question is not whether Lenin was an accurate expositor of Marx and Engels but what these reflections tell us about the state, governance within a proletarian revolution, and the conduct of revolution.

The problem of the state

Along with orthodox Marxism, Lenin had a complex relationship with the idea of the modern state as the primary institutional structure of politics. The essential Marxist position is that the state developed as a mechanism for constraining and reconciling the conflicting interests of labour and capital, worker and capitalist, within the capitalist mode of production. Accordingly, it inherently reflects the dominance of capital over labour. It institutionalises that domination through its coercive mechanisms, which are primarily the police, the military and more recently the security services or a counter-revolutionary secret police. Unlike social democrat revisionists in Germany and trade unionists and Fabians in Britain (who had sought a parliamentary path to socialism by working within the state on labour reforms and welfare policies), Lenin's experience as a clandestine professional revolutionary facing the tsarist autocracy was of the state in its pure aggressive role, as the direct enforcer of capitalist power. The constant fear of police agents infiltrating the Bolshevik Party, or attempting to subvert party members, was an everyday experience for the professional revolutionary, and the reality of Lenin's career in 1905–1917. Even the collapse of the tsarist regime and the start of the provisional government left hostile state forces in the military and the secret police confronting Lenin and his colleagues after his return to St Petersburg in April 1917. The logic of his *Imperialism, the Highest Stage of Capitalism* was that these military and police functions would grow in all states under the demands of imperial rule, just as they had always been dominant in imperial states such as Russia. Similarly, as the crisis tendencies emerge even with the extension of global capitalism, the concessions towards labour that the revisionists relied on would be withdrawn and shown to be a sham. And the mechanisms of direct coercive rule developed in the colonies would be repatriated for dealing with the domestic proletariat.

Thus, for Lenin and his cadre of professional revolutionaries, the state was and remained an enemy. However, it was also a fact. So the question remained how to reconcile the state with the Marxist commitment to the dictatorship of the proletariat. Marx had retained some anarchist tendencies in his thought, which reinforced the view that the central functions of state power would be overcome by technological advances. So the governance of men by coercive means was replaced by the 'administration of things', a largely evolutionary process impelled by technological development. By contrast, Lenin was confronted with a coercive state in a major war that would not just disappear. Furthermore, his own theory of the party suggested that he took seriously the idea of the 'dictatorship of the proletariat' as an actual political dictatorship stage in revolutionary change, and not just as a metaphor akin to Rousseau's 'general will' suggesting the end of dictatorial power. In contrast to these more philosophically nuanced readings of Marx, Lenin's view of the challenge of overcoming the power of the state through proletarian agency is clear:

> The doctrine about class struggle, when applied by Marx to the question of the state and of socialist revolution, leads necessarily to the recognition of the *political rule* of the proletariat, of its dictatorship, i.e. of power shared with nobody and relying directly upon the armed forces of the masses. The overthrow of the bourgeoisie can be achieved only by the proletariat being transformed into the *ruling class*, capable of crushing the inevitable and desperate resistance of the bourgeoisie and of the organising of *all* the labouring and exploited masses for the new economic order.
>
> The proletarian needs state power, the centralized organisation of force, the organization of violence both to crush the resistance of the exploiters and to *lead* the enormous mass of the population – the peasantry, the petty bourgeoisie, the semi-proletarians – in the work of establishing a socialist economy. (Lenin 1992, pp. 24–25)

Engels had hoped for the 'withering away of the state' under socialism. But, for Lenin, this was first going to require direct, coercive action by the proletariat under the leadership of the party. This action was going to have a forceful and violent character because the state itself was a vehicle for violence, either against the domestic proletariat or internationally against the imperial powers and perhaps the proletariat of other states. The challenge was not simply to defeat the forces of the state in battle, although that was to become a pressing challenge during the 1917–1922 civil war, but to deal with the way that the capitalist state had created counter-revolutionary and reactionary consciousness amongst the people. Capitalist power was exercised in the interests of a small group of people, but the instruments of that power were considerable numbers of ordinary people drawn from the working population and peasantry as soldiers, and from the petit bourgeoisie in terms of police and government functionaries in the bureaucracy and legal system. Even with the effective work of a revolutionary party leading the cultivation of class consciousness amongst the workers and peasants, it was too simple an idea to imagine that a completely mobilised proletariat would withdraw from the institutions of a capitalist state, leading to its implosion and the consequent emergence of a proletarian dictatorship. This hope was naïve and not the historical reality that Lenin faced.

Party, state and bureaucracy

The October Revolution of 1917 that brought Lenin to power was the result of an armed insurrection in St Petersburg that overthrew the provisional government of Kerensky and formally placed power in the hands of the workers' councils, or soviets, that had been organised and led by the Bolshevik Party. Lenin had announced the replacement of the state by the soviets with his rallying cry of 'All Power to the Soviets' in an article in the party paper *Pravda* in July 1917. Although a rallying slogan, this claim is also important because it indicates the way in which Lenin and the Bolsheviks intended to deal with the power of the state. The provisional government had struggled to establish its authority because it confronted a divided opposition to the old regime and its residue in the key institutions of the state, in particular the army and the Church. This situation confirmed Lenin's view that the state was a problem to be confronted in revolution, but that left the issue of how to do governing and governance. The dictatorship of the proletariat entailed that all power must lie with the revolutionary working class, but that still left pressing practical questions about how that power is constituted in political institutions and how it is exercised. Even the anarchists had structures of power and organisation when they enter the field of combat and political action. The fragmentation of the tsarist army created the opportunity for Leon Trotsky to develop the organised workers into a Red Army. During the revolution and the subsequent civil war, this became a formidable fighting force. Yet, all of this simply re-emphasised the need for some structure of authority and a mechanism for government.

Lenin's solution was the soviets or workers' councils. These would be locally organised and would take on the tasks of administration. In this way, the workers would displace the petit-bourgeois class of professional managers and administrators and democratise the practice of governing.

> Capitalist culture has *created* large-scale production, factories, railways, the postal service, telephones and so forth, and *on this basis* the great majority of the functions of the of the old 'state power' have become so simplified and can be reduced to such very simple operations of registering, filing and checking that those functions will become entirely accessible to all literate people, that these functions will be entirely performable for an ordinary 'workman's wages' and that these functions can (and must) be stripped of every shadow association with privilege or peremptory command. (Lenin 1992, p. 40)

Capitalism itself had developed the style of bureaucratic administration that had simplified the tasks of government so that they could be democratised and there was no need for expertise. The passage above also shows that the modern state had relatively limited state-wide functions beyond the instruments of coercion, confined to such things as transportation and the postal service. Lenin has little to say about regulation or about welfare provision. In urban areas the soviets would take over aspects of local government covering such things as public health, water and sewerage.

But Lenin did not at first see the national organisation of a complex economy as the pressing task of the revolution – that was dominated by sheer survival, and consequently his focus was on the coercive structures of former state power such as the army. However, as the immediate threat to the revolution from military attacks by former tsarists and from western powers' allied armies both receded, the challenges of the New Economics Policy became more pressing – and, with that, domestic opposition from peasants, landowners and the business classes. This exposed tensions inherent in Lenin's initial commitment to transferring all power to the soviets.

The ideal model of the soviet was as a council of workers with a commitment to equal status and a belief in relatively equal competence, directly exercising executive power. In reality, they were far less democratic and egalitarian. The real focus of power within them was always the Bolshevik Party and the soviets were only authoritative to the extent that the party exercised leadership within them. This guiding role was also centralised and directed by the party leadership, and ultimately by Lenin and his closest allies, such as Trotsky in the conduct of the civil war. This tension between the potential for democratic governance and centralised authority is also manifest in Lenin's generally disparaging remarks about democracy:

> Democracy is a *state* which recognises the subordination of the minority to the majority, i.e., it is an organisation for the systematic use of *violence* by one class against another, by one section of the population against another. (Lenin 1992, p. 73)

Democracy only has value and authority when it results in decisions that accord with the dictates of the party, the class-conscious leaders of the revolutionary masses. Majorities and minorities are not in themselves of any significance because the majority will can be distorted by class interests and by reactionary or counter-revolutionary will, as can the interests of the minority. In Rousseauean terms, the class consciousness of the vanguard is the general will, whereas the aggregate interests of party members or the proletariat is merely the will of all. The prevalence of counter-revolutionary consciousness amongst the population, and opposition from the beneficiaries of the old order, posed serious problems for the revolutionary leadership. The conduct of revolution required iron discipline and a lack of sentimentalism. There must be a forceful response to counter-revolutionary insurrection, even when that began amongst workers or others committed to revolution but who had deviated from the central direction of the party leadership – as in the infamous Kronstadt naval uprising, which was brutally suppressed. This tension between the objective needs of the revolution, as defined by the party and its leadership, and the popular will of the workers' councils, led to the need for institutions of coercion and discipline. These increasingly came to define the structures of the Leninist party state, as with the Cheka, the forerunner of the KGB, founded by Felix Dzerzhinsky, a former Polish aristocrat turned communist. The Cheka served as Lenin's secret police, disciplining the party and rooting out counter-revolutionary sentiment wherever it arose.

Violence and the conduct of revolution

Whilst tight organisation and strict bureaucratic discipline became distinctive features of the revolution, the other striking feature of the new Soviet order was the place of violence as a tool of revolution and regime-making, a feature that was to persist in the institutional history of the USSR. Everyone is now aware of the vast purges and executions of the Stalin years (Solzhenitsyn 1974), but much scholarship is still preoccupied with whether that violence was imminent in Lenin's revolution or whether it was added by Stalin to the party structures that he inherited. Whatever the truth of the relative moral culpability of Stalin over Lenin, it remains clear that violence was always a necessary tool, and not merely a contingent consequence of Lenin's revolutionary overthrow of the tsarist state. The violence of the immediate revolution, the subsequent civil war and the subsequent implementation of the New Economic Policy was real and appalling in its scale and magnitude. Lenin might have argued that the fact of violence was unexceptional, since violence is prevalent in human history, and had escalated radically during World War I and the subsequent disorder in central and eastern Europe that followed it (including a bitter frontier war between the Soviets and Poland). To understand his theory, though, the real question concerns his attitude to violence as a tool of choice for accomplishing revolutionary politics and accomplishing social change, and how this fits into his vision of the new society.

The place of violence as a tool of politics has to be set against two fundamental issues that are often overlooked in popular judgements of revolutionary politics: firstly, the status and dignity of persons, which we characterise most commonly as human rights (a discourse that only came into its own after World War II); and, secondly, the state as a site of violence. Post-Enlightenment thought in Europe and political ideologies place the individual at the heart of the defence of political agency, with the state as a guarantor of peace and stability. Marxists distance themselves from this tradition, on the ground that it is merely a rationalisation of the interests of the dominant class. Marxist thought – and Lenin's is no exception – abandons the central position of the individual in moral and political theory. This does not mean that the lives of individual human beings do not matter – indeed, it would be hard to explain what is wrong with class domination without linking it in some way to the lives and well-being of persons. That said, structural power relations shape the ideological and the material conditions in which individuality is formed.

Consequently, Lenin is not a fundamental humanist, in this sense – the value of human lives is derivative from the collectivities within which those lives become concrete and real. Class establishes the hierarchy of relationships between individuals that determines ultimate value, and so exploiters are not of equal value to the exploited. Thus 'moral' egalitarianism prior to the state of communism (as the only form of society that could make egalitarianism possible) is fundamentally abandoned. The rights or status of the exploiters and their agents are not of equal concern and value to the agents of revolutionary change. This argument does not entail that the exploiters should always be subject to violence. But it does mean that, should this be so, it can be justified in terms of legitimate punishment or as the consequence of other legitimate emancipatory actions such as the civil war. There are no human rights, as such, that limit the revolutionary struggle for emancipation from exploitation. And, secondly, there is no limit on the conduct of that struggle: there is no scope for 'just war' arguments in the conduct of revolution.

The absence of a theory of liberal or human rights does not automatically entail violence and killing; something else is required for that, and it follows from Lenin's theory of the state. The fundamental issue is that the state is the vehicle for containing class conflict in the interests of the capitalist class. It is not an impartial legal institution but an instrument of class domination with coercive powers monopolising violence in the interests of the capitalists. The overthrow of capitalism will involve the overthrow of the capitalist state and that entails direct confrontation with the instruments of state violence such as the police, judiciary and military. All of these instruments are controlled and exercised in the interests of an ever-narrower social group of capitalists. Yet, in practice they also co-opt a very large number of people into the maintenance of capitalist power, creating temporary interests in maintaining the regimes that grant them privileges, employment and even subsistence.

Crude Marxist theory suggests that the progressive immiseration of the proletariat during the final stages of capitalist crisis would break the bonds of attachment to the capitalist state. But Lenin argues that the development of advanced capitalist states as imperialist states shows that process is unreliable for achieving rapid change. The proletariat, at the direction of the vanguard party, therefore, needs 'state power, the centralized organisation of force, the organization of violence … to crush the resistance of the exploiters' (Lenin 1992, p. 25). Accordingly, the revolutionaries need to infiltrate the institutions

of the workers' state so as to build a class consciousness amongst its functionaries, but also that (like the capitalist state) it must use similar powers against
those who resist the revolution. Consequently, violence against opponents
remains a principal tool of revolution.

The challenge of capitalist state power has two dimensions, one repressive
and the other ideological. Firstly, there is the direct confrontation with the
counter-revolutionary forces that we see in the early stages of Lenin's revolution and the civil war. These issues were addressed by the formation of the Red
Army under Trotsky's direction and later by creating police functions for the
new regime, such as Dzerzhinsky's Cheka. Both are involved in enforcing
the will of the vanguard party and its instruments, the soviets. Those who stand
in the way of the will of the party need to be defeated, because there cannot be
any compromise with capitalism.

The second challenge of capitalist power is the legacy of its ideological force
on those who were implicated in its exercise, either as direct functionaries or
as beneficiaries of capitalist power. Many of this large class have a weak attachment to the previous state but a correspondingly weak commitment to the
revolution, and they are therefore potential counter-revolutionary opponents.
Whilst the revolution is proceeding, the development and spread of revolutionary consciousness is spreading, but that process is made difficult because of
the prevalence of pre-revolutionary consciousness. By definition, this is something that also needs to be defeated. Replacing the consciousness of the previous regime requires making new 'men' (a new humanity). But it cannot be
achieved overnight or even in a relatively short period, as Lenin appreciated
in the course of making revolution. However, if the process of making the new
humanity of the revolution is a long-term process, perhaps spanning generations, then the prevalence of counter-revolutionary consciousness is a persistent threat. The difficulty and timescale of such a cultural/ideological change
are compounded by the fact that the process of revolution will only be complete
when it has occurred everywhere. So the revolution was under constant threat
from counter revolutionaries, both at home and abroad.

These internal and external threats place the revolution on a constant war
footing with its opponents and this shapes the institutional organisation of
the state mechanisms used to deliver the dictatorship of the proletariat. Lenin
never completed *The State and Revolution*, since it was superseded by the reality of the unfolding revolution. He died in 1924 whilst the revolution was in its
infancy and was confined to the territory of the former Russian Empire. The
Russian revolution did not immediately trigger a global revolution, and ineffective Bolshevik-style 1919 uprisings were put down in Germany and Hungary.
The USSR's isolation was to create problems for Lenin's successors and for the
revolutionary movement, not least the question of whether a proletarian revolution could succeed if it were confined to only one country (however large).
As early as 1919, the 'Comintern', or Third International, was established in

Moscow to promote global revolution through supporting genuinely revolutionary groups and agents throughout the world. The clandestine activity of professional revolutionaries that had characterised Lenin's early life became a career path for world revolutionaries. They went to Moscow to absorb doctrine and to perfect key skills, or they were influenced by Moscow-trained agents, tasked with founding communist parties across the world. Lenin's successors, especially Stalin, became the leaders of a global movement based in the world's first socialist state. But the relationship between Moscow and those other parties was to become a complex issue, especially with the rise of communist parties in countries that were also seeking to overthrow the dominance of western imperial powers. This issue was particularly important for the second leader of a communist revolution and the only figure to rival Lenin in this role, Mao Tse-Tung.

Revolution and the challenge of imperialism – the development of Mao's Leninism

As with Lenin, the challenge of imperialism was central to Mao's political and revolutionary theory, but in ways that extended beyond Lenin. His thought encompassed the difficult relationship between leadership of the first socialist revolution and the subaltern status of the Chinese Communist Party, until its triumph in 1949 and Mao's separation from the dominance of Moscow in the 1950s. Lenin saw imperialism as the most recent development of global capitalism that explained the resilience of the European capitalist powers and the onset of an inter-capitalist war. For Mao, imperialism was the lived experience of his political formation, from the impact of Japanese expansionism in the 1890s and the western imperial 'concessions' on Chinese territory that persisted beyond the republic and World War I. These treaty-based limitations of Chinese sovereign power reinforced China's subordinate status at the hands of the superior military might of western powers. Although China's dealings with the western powers were disguised in the form of legal agreements, they reflected the unequal capabilities of the respective parties. China was forced to accept conditions that were nationally humiliating, and which continued to complicate international relations into the late 20th century, especially with regard to Hong Kong.

Mao's intellectual formation was also deeply influenced by the wider imperialism of ideas as much as the exploitative power of economic imperialism. His early education in classical Chinese thought was supplemented by influential western thinkers as China opened to the west and recognised the relative success of western economic and technological development. Many Chinese thinkers turned to western ideas for theories of modernisation to account for China's relative decline since the early 18th century, and to search for a manifesto for rapid technological and social change. This ambition was further inspired by the Japanese crash course in modernisation. In a few short decades, this led Japan from almost complete cultural and economic isolation to becoming a modern military power that could decisively defeat the Russian tsar's navy in 1905. Marxist ideas were part of that western-fuelled ferment of thinking about modernisation. However, from 1917 onwards, Marxism (under Lenin's leadership) ceased to be just a theory of modernity and became a global revolutionary project directed from Moscow. The survival of the October Revolution and the Red Army victory in the civil war provided evidence for Lenin and his followers that their particular analysis of the challenge of late imperialist capitalism as a revolutionary moment was correct, and gave them an authority over communists in all parts of the world. Lenin had shown the way, and his leadership mantle was subsequently assumed by Stalin. Other, less developed communist struggles had to follow that lead and acknowledge the authority of Moscow. The Bolshevik revolution and the 'Moscow line' provided an undoubted template for successful struggle, to be followed by loyal communist cadres throughout the world. Mao was initially no exception in this mould, although the peculiar circumstances of China's path to revolution were to challenge that loyalty to Moscow.

The fortunes of China's small domestic Communist Party changed following its expulsion from the cities of the eastern seaboard by Chiang Kai-Shek. As the party and its forces retreated deep into the countryside, the character of its role as a proletarian revolutionary party changed. There was an increasing focus on the peasantry as a revolutionary class, alongside the urban proletariat. This inspired different responses from the leadership of the party, and it was in this context that Mao emerged as an increasingly important figure. China's situation shaped his early theoretical writings. The Communists' move from a civil war against the Guomindang (KMT) to an imperial/colonial war against the Japanese from 1937 also transformed attention away from the directions coming from Moscow to the struggle for survival against a technologically advanced foreign foe. Mao's theoretical works are relatively unsophisticated endorsements of Leninism in terms of fundamental theory and analysis. Texts such as 'On Contradiction' (1937) are basically explanatory essays applying Leninist concepts to China's experience. Underlying this apparent deference, there remained the obvious fact that the 'Moscow line' was another western importation, offering their wisdom for China's redemption. And, whilst Mao stayed loyal to Stalin's role as the supreme leader of the global revolution, it was also clear that his own thinking was more deeply focused on the particular challenges of the Chinese experience. For him, the Soviet model was only a model at the most general level. Mao's loyalty was no more than a form of filial piety, which he did not feel for Stalin's successors, especially after having led his own successful revolution with the declaration of the People's Republic of China in 1949. The challenge of imperialism was not just exposed by Leninist analysis. It was something that was reinforced by the Comintern and its interwar focus on Europe as the primary site for the continuation of the proletarian revolution.

Imperialism had echoes within the language and structures of the global revolutionary movement and its attitude towards the underdeveloped economies of the Far East.

Building a revolution in China required Mao to focus on the particular challenges of an undeveloped peasant economy that had been the site of a major war theatre from 1937 to 1945, as well as a two-decade civil war stretching before and after the conflict. The realities and legacy of imperialism encouraged Mao to look to the 'contradictions' within China's recent political and historical experience for signs of the revolutionary possibilities and strategies. In turn, these new opportunities changed the Communist emphasis to liberating the masses from the tyranny of imperialism and its political forms throughout East and South East Asia. Central to Mao's revolutionary theory was the place of the peasant masses and their relationship to the party.

The role of the peasants

The peasantry appear early on in Mao's writings, largely as a result of his early familiarity with peasant life as child and as a result of fieldwork amongst the peasants recounted in his 'Report on The Peasant Movement in Hunan' (1927). The peasants were to retain a special and elevated place in his thinking that is novel within Marxism. For Marx and Engels, the agricultural peasantry were a leftover of the incomplete modernisation of western capitalist societies. The growth of the urban-industrial bourgeoisie was displacing them as an important force in history. The peasantry remained largely trapped in a feudal mode of production, and as such a potential reservoir for reactionary armies, such as the French forces that suppressed the Paris Commune. For Lenin, the situation was more complex, given the huge relative size of the peasantry compared with the still-small industrialised proletariat in Russia. In his address at the Finland Station, he evoked themes that could appeal to farmers as well as workers:

> The people need peace; the people need bread; the people need land. And they give you war, hunger, no bread ... We must fight for the socialist revolution, fight to the end, until the complete victory of the proletariat.

Set against that, though, was the peasants' potential as a counter-revolutionary force, evident especially during the civil war and the New Economic Plan period.

For Mao's China, the peasantry formed the majority of the population and, without a process of rapid industrialisation, that was likely to remain the case for a long time into the future. (China did not become a majority urban population until about 2000.) This obviously raised a central Marxist question: was China remotely close to the historical-material conditions essential for a proletarian revolution? Furthermore, the limited size and extent of the industrial proletariat challenged the idea of a sufficiently developed revolutionary consciousness amongst the masses or within the proletariat itself. The educated offspring of the small bourgeois class might be the basis of a revolutionary intelligentsia that could be incorporated into the party, but they too were few in number. Mao first made sweeping statements in 1927 about the role of the peasants as a revolutionary class:

> The present upsurge of the peasant movement is a colossal event. In a very short time … several hundred million peasants will rise like a mighty storm, like a hurricane, a force so swift and violent that no power, however great, will be able to hold it back. They will smash all the trammels that bind them and rush forward along the road to liberation. They will sweep all the imperialists, warlords, corrupt officials, local tyrants and evil gentry into their graves. Every revolutionary party and every revolutionary comrade will be put to the test, to be accepted or rejected as they decide. There are three alternatives. To march at their head and lead them? To trail behind them, gesticulating and criticizing? Or to stand in their way and oppose them? Every Chinese is free to choose, but events will force you to make the choice quickly. (Mao 1966, p. 53)

The peasants are the undoubted vehicle of revolution in China because of their numbers as the foot soldiers of the revolutionary struggle, and because they became the key basis for supply of the Communist Party as it retreated deep into the countryside during the 1930s civil war, moving ever further away from the urban centres that were held by the Guomindang Nationalists.

But how does this conveniently activist stance fit within the Marxist framework? Can a revolutionary status of the peasantry be retained within a Marxist–Leninist framework? Mao's slender ventures into theoretical work aimed to interpret orthodox Leninism in a sufficiently broad light so as to encompass a revolutionary role for the peasants. Contradictions remain the motor of historical change and development in Leninist thought. But for Mao these need to be seen as the actual material contradictions of Chinese society and not some idealised or generic view of the contradictions found in late 19th-century European economies. The struggles of China's peasants against exploitative landlords were the basis for the fierce class oppositions necessary for revolution. These contradictions were exacerbated by the interference of foreign imperial powers such as Britain, France, Germany and Japan – all of whom sought to keep China weak in order to exploit labour and resources, whilst at the same time dominating domestic markets for manufactured goods.

The normal process of material development within an economy that (in an earlier age) would have resulted in industrialisation, urbanisation and the development of a proletarian class (with the appropriate class consciousness) was thus frustrated by imperialism. Mao and his colleagues recognised that a proletarian consciousness was latent, rather than developed, in China. But this was precisely because of the impact of imperialism. Imperialism might have appeared to postpone the development of revolutionary consciousness until such a time as domestic capitalist modernisation had taken place in China. Yet, Mao was to argue that this was not the case at all, because imperialism had the effect of shifting the burden of being the revolutionary class directly onto the peasants themselves. In countries like China, imperialism was unleashed in a form that accelerated Lenin's insights, and arguably shifted the site of global revolution to those imperial possessions. The advantage of the peasantry under imperialism was that they did not have a pre-revolutionary consciousness that needed to be overcome to make them the vehicle of the revolution. Nor were China's peasantry potentially counter-revolutionary, although some of the small-landowning peasants posed that risk. Indeed, the significance of the 'Report on the Peasant Movement in Hunan' (1927) was precisely to show that the peasants had already demonstrated their ability to function as a revolutionary class and not merely an obstacle to change as a leftover from feudalism.

In a later piece from 1958, Mao explains why the peasants remain an important revolutionary class:

> Apart from their other characteristics, the outstanding thing about China's 600 million people is that they are 'poor and blank'. This may seem a bad thing, but in reality, it is a good thing. Poverty gives rise to the desire for changes, the desire for action and the desire for revolution. On a blank sheet of paper free from any mark, the freshest and most beautiful characters can be written: the freshest and most beautiful pictures can be painted. (Mao 1966, p. 16)

Mao's claim about the peasants being 'poor and blank' is an important clue to his thinking. The 'blankness' is the absence of any developed counter-revolutionary consciousness that might pose an opposition to the consciousness-leading role of the party. The party cadres, or local party leaders, had to direct the masses of the peasants so that they were not victims of counter-revolutionary ideologies and forces such as the Nationalist Guomindang. This was to be achieved by party cadres immersing themselves in the lives of peasants and in their local struggles, and learning from that experience. Because of their material conditions, namely grinding poverty, the peasantry are constantly open to the message of the revolutionary party.

Mao emphasises the struggle against poverty in a way that departs from orthodox Marxism. For European Marxists, poverty was merely a consequence of the fundamental exploitative relations of mature capitalism, whereas exploitation was the real issue. For Mao, exploitation remains important but poverty becomes a direct driver of revolutionary consciousness and the opportunity to eradicate it the motive for revolution. This is especially so because the structure of imperialism made the sources of exploitation ever more remote from the experience of the exploited, in ways that were not true of more traditional (and inherently local) feudal exploitation. Poor peasants, seeking to improve their desperate material condition, had a sufficient motivation for revolutionary action, so long as it was subject to the discipline of the party. For all of Mao's celebration of the peasants and their experience, the leading position of the party remained unchallenged in his thought. A centrally organised and disciplined party of professional revolutionaries, on Lenin's template, was never challenged by Mao, however much it needed to be accommodated to the circumstances of China's peasant economy. The relationship between the peasants as the revolutionary class in China under imperialism and the party was to be one of Mao's constant preoccupations, even into his later years and the Cultural Revolution.

The peasants, the masses and the challenge of liberalism

Mao's focus on the extreme poverty and unremitting labour of the peasants struck a chord with other Asian and African national liberation struggles, which saw the interests of the imperial powers as the source of domination over the people, and their complete exclusion from the benefits of economic development. Yet, his position also raised complex issues for a Marxist revolutionary. Whilst the material conditions of the oppressed is an obvious feature of exploitation, the Marxist tradition has always rejected the idea that their hostility to capitalism is a moral condemnation, or one that is reducible to capitalism's denial of rights of individuals, or judgements about the low welfare levels of masses of individuals. If the key problem was the denial of rights, then rights could be extended; indeed, radical liberals made precisely this argument. What is wrong with capitalism is that in its primitive forms it fails to recognise the equal human rights of all. The liberal solution is political emancipation and the extension of rights. For other liberals (such as the utilitarians, influenced by Jeremy Bentham and J.S. Mill) the issue was not rights but low social welfare and its maldistribution across people. In each case, the solution was not revolution and the overthrow of the capitalist system but reform and redistribution, leading erstwhile revolutionaries into the Marxist heresy of revisionism.

For Mao, the problem of poverty is the common motivating force of the peasantry and this deprivation has its roots in the system of private landlords owning almost all property in land. But focusing on peasant poverty is not a concession to individualism and liberalism, because in China poverty is a unifying force within the revolutionary class, and it is class struggle that ultimately matters. For Mao, his turn towards the peasants is a further, double-emphasised rejection of liberalism and individualism. In a short piece entitled 'Combat Liberalism' (1937), Mao rejects the idea of the individual as a rights bearer and liberal ideas such as free speech and discussion. These ideas are a form of 'petty-bourgeois selfishness' that places the claims of the individual above those of the unity of the party and the revolutionary collective. Mao praises discipline above the assertion of self or freedom, and advocates the overcoming of the personal perspective as a potential threat to the interests of the revolutionary class or its party. The disciplined party member subordinates their personal interest to the interest of the peasant masses and the party as its leader. They overcome the idea of a person as the subject of rights or welfare that preoccupies liberal thinkers.

Mao's focus on the extreme and pervasive poverty of the peasants, and their 'blankness', is a celebration of the impersonality of class membership and the overcoming of the idea of the subject of liberal moralism. He is indifferent to the claims of individuals and sees the world in terms of these classes in conflict. Whilst this stance is common to all Marxists, it is more extreme in the case of Mao because China's peasants lack the formation of western conceptual superstructure, such as Christianity, which legitimised social relations by appealing to a world beyond time in which all individuals' lives would be redeemed and all injustices would be rectified. This strong form of anti-humanism, and the denial of the subject as a bearer of rights or interests independently of their class position, was later to inspire many radical French social theorists during the heyday of the Cultural Revolution.

An absence of concern for the individual members of the peasantry and the need to suppress any liberal individualist prejudices amongst the party cadres are both celebrated in Mao's account of the violence of the peasant associations against landlords and others in his 'The Peasant Movement in Hunan' (1937). The revolutionary spirit of the peasants is demonstrated by the ways in which they use violence to overcome injustice. But Mao also uses these stories of punishment – many of which were to become commonplace during the Cultural Revolution – to silence those who argue against the peasants' violence and what he calls the 'Going Too Far' misconception. In a famous statement reproduced in the *Little Red Book*, Mao claims:

> [A] revolution is not a dinner party, or writing an essay, or painting a picture or doing embroidery; it cannot be so refined, so leisurely and gentle, so temperate, kind and courteous, restrained and magnanimous. A revolution is an insurrection, an act of violence by which one class overthrows another ... Without using the greatest force, the peasants cannot possibly overthrow the deep-rooted authority of the landlords which has lasted for thousands of years. The rural areas need a mighty revolutionary upsurge, for it alone can rouse the people in their millions to become a powerful force. (Mao 2014, pp. 18–19)

For Mao, the peasants have the advantage of being a mass that is united by its common experience of poverty and being blank in terms of different ideological accounts of its own condition (which might otherwise have tended to fragment that common class identity). Mao does not deny that there are sources of fragmentation and false consciousness amongst the peasants. Indeed, he recognises the different layers of class identity from the peasantry through the feudal classes to the urban proletariat. But he claims that the peasant experience was the most authentic, to the point that he feared that the revolutionary consciousness of peasant fighters was corrupted by too much time in the urban areas during the conduct of revolutionary war. The authenticity of peasant revolutionary consciousness made it particularly appropriate for party cadres to lead it in its struggle against the imperialist global order. For Mao, the real risks of fragmentation, corruption and false consciousness are more pressing within the party itself, and the experience of the peasants is presented as a model for party discipline.

The mass line and the party

The peasantry as a revolutionary class is Mao's response to the challenge of whether a genuine Marxist–Leninist revolution was possible in China. Fundamentally, the peasants provided the mass support that supplemented the proletariat in creating a genuine revolution. In this he distances himself from Lenin, whereas in his commitment to the central political agency of the party he remains an orthodox Leninist. The party has an exclusive mission as the vehicle for political action and a role in leading the masses in their revolution. This, of course, raises the question of the relationship between the peasant masses and the party – given Mao's celebration of the revolutionary actions of the peasant associations in his 'Peasant Movement in Hunan' (1927) report, where the associations acted independently of the party and its cadres.

The answer to this question is complex, especially given the way in which Mao created a leadership cult around himself early in his career and exploited this at various times to challenge rivals and potential successors. He also flirted with using populism against the party bureaucracy at a number of points following the 1949 establishment of the PRC, and most significantly during the Cultural Revolution. Mao followed Stalin in his conception of personal leadership, but, like Stalin, he remained enough of a Leninist to leave the authority of the party unchallenged. Where he differed from Lenin was in the way he linked the party to the masses. For Lenin, the relationship between the party and the proletariat was a hierarchical and centralist one: the party was the arbiter of the consciousness of the proletariat, and so the unchallenged leader of the workers. For Mao, there is a more complex and less hierarchical relationship between the party and the peasant masses, which is manifested in the idea of 'the mass line' and which is captured in the following passage from the *Little Red Book*:

> In all the practical work of our Party, all correct leadership is necessarily 'from the masses, to the masses'. This means: take the ideas of the masses (scattered and unsystematic ideas) and concentrate them (through study turn them into concentrated and systematic ideas), then go to the

masses and propagate and explain these ideas until the masses embrace
them as their own, hold fast to them and translate them into action, and
test the correctness of these ideas in such action. Then once again concentrate ideas from the masses and once again go to the masses so that
the ideas are persevered and carried through. And so on, over and over
again in an endless spiral, with the ideas becoming more correct, more
vital and richer each time. Such is the Marxist theory of knowledge.
(Mao 1966, p. 57)

The mass line is both an account of the revolutionary legitimacy of a policy and
action and an account of party discipline. In terms of legitimacy, the masses are
seen as the active agent in revolutionary change and the party cadres need to
embed themselves in their midst in order to learn from them how to advance
the revolution. In doing this the party cadres must avoid two errors: 'tailism'
and 'commandism'. The former is the idea that the party cadres must just follow
whatever the peasant masses appear to be doing, as the tail of an animal always
follows it wherever it goes. This failing misunderstands the dynamic relationship between the masses and the party, whose task it is to lead the revolution
by its professional service of the revolution. The critique of 'tailism' is also an
assault on a naïve form of direct democracy, where the opinion of the masses
at a given point becomes the will of the people, which it is the party's task to
receive and implement. Mao was no democrat. Policymaking is a dynamic relationship between the masses and the party, where the party develops and sys-
temises the ideas of the masses, and then disseminates them through education
and propaganda. The important point here is the proximity and interconnect-
edness of the party and the masses.

It is equally important to avoid a second failing that is common for any technocratic policy elite or group of professional revolutionaries, namely 'commandism'. This is the idea that the party cadres or the party central leadership
have a special technocratic role independently of the masses, and are able
to direct the masses towards their real interests. It is a persistent danger for
Leninist parties, which are by definition a professional revolutionary elite. Mao
was suspicious of the tendency of a revolutionary intelligentsia to capture the
party, and later its bureaucracy, so as to impose its own ideas on the masses
as their class interest. His experience with the peasants in Hunan exposed a
populist tendency that was lacking in Lenin and especially Stalin (who used
the secret police as the primary vehicle for intra-party discipline). Mao also
used secret police tactics and had similar enforcers. But he retained and cultivated a direct line of communication to the masses over the heads of key
rivals, echoing the idea of populist leadership expressing the authentic voice
of the people against a corrupt political elite. It is in this context that the mass
line becomes a form of party discipline.

The assertion of the revolutionary authority of the masses as the ultimate
source of policymaking was reinforced by the use of re-education amongst the

peasants, as well as self-denunciations and the use of punishments that had their roots in the peasant associations. Mao's report on the 'Peasant Movement in Hunan' (1927) described the wearing of conical paper hats as a ritual humiliation, and that became a familiar sight during the purge of the party leadership and bureaucracy in the Cultural Revolution of the late 1960s. Similarly, the return to the land to work amongst the peasants was both a standard punishment for party cadres with erroneous tendencies in their political thinking, and a way of disciplining the urban youth, who went from city schools and universities to work with the peasants in the fields. The unleashing of popular violence was often celebrated as part of demonstrating mass revolutionary spirit, but it remained something that Mao controlled carefully. Whilst there is undoubtedly a populist tendency in his thought and leadership style, this was to reinforce his position within the party, and not to undermine the position of the party as the vehicle of political and military control of the masses.

For all of Mao's celebration of the masses, the doctrine of the mass line does not liberate them from party discipline, or recognise the people as a totally independent source of power. As with most populists (who appeal to an ideal of the people as the basis for their claim to power), the masses were not vested with a distinct authority, nor did they have a clear and conscious identity that could exercise any authority independently of the party: 'if the masses alone are active without a strong leading group to organize their activity properly, such activity cannot be sustained for long, or carried forward in the right direction' (Mao 1966, p. 58). So Mao remained a revolutionary committed to overthrow the existing imperialist order as a condition of emancipating the masses. Indeed, towards the end of his life it was clear that revolution was not just a protracted event prior to the institution of a dictatorship of the proletariat and socialism. Instead, it was a continual process whereby new contradictions would emerge from society that needed to be overcome by revolutionary struggle. His model for that revolutionary struggle was inextricably linked to the protracted revolutionary war that dominated his life until 1949.

Violence and the conduct of revolution

Perhaps Mao's most well-known phrase is that 'Every Communist must grasp the truth: "Political power grows out of the barrel of a gun"' (Mao 1966, p. 28). It became a global revolutionary slogan in the 1960s and 1970s amongst new Maoist communist groups in the west and in the developing world. They reacted against the sclerotic statism of the USSR as much as the imperialism of the United States at war in Vietnam. Mao appeared to offer a more authentic revolutionary spirit, one that was detached from the second-class capitalism of the post-Stalin USSR, and more appropriate for the rising peoples of the postcolonial world. His aphorism reflects the importance of the protracted war against the Kuomintang, regional warlords and the Japanese in building a revolution and a unified state in China. Yet, Mao's realist claim is also a familiar one about the nature and constitution of political power in a violent conflict.

From the mid-1920s to the late 1940s, China was in a state of constant war. Across five earlier decades, too (1859–1916), China had barely seen a period of sustained civil peace due to the wars and uprisings that marked the decline of the Qing Dynasty and foreign incursions, plus the chaos of the first republican regime of Yuan Shikai. Consequently, the Chinese revolution was not an uprising within a stable but capitalist state; it occurred within a territory that had a disputed government, imperial interference from European powers, and few of the trappings of an effective state. It was only in the last years of the revolutionary wars following the defeat of Japan (1947–1949) that the Communists' struggle with the Kuomintang became a genuine civil war between a government and a civil opponent seeking to overthrow it. Unlike the Bolshevik revolution led by Lenin, there could be no simple seizure of power. Both Mao's communists and his KMT opponents, led by Chiang Kai-Shek, built their political power in the context of mutual struggle and war against a foreign power. Also, whereas a bitter civil war followed after Lenin's seizure of power in a *coup d'état* (and as Russia withdrew from World War I), Mao's revolution was forged throughout in the context of pre-exiting war. In consequence, Mao's early and most important writings on revolution are writings on war. In these works he carved out a reputation as one of the most important theorists of war in the 20th century, abandoning the Clausewitzian model of war. His approach came to shape thinking about colonial wars of liberation, insurgencies and the organisation of terrorist wars into the 21st century.

Revolutionary war in China – rejecting the Clausewitzian trinity

Like Lenin, Mao was a careful reader of Clausewitz. He fully understood how the challenges of a revolutionary war, especially one conducted in the context of a huge territory such as China, without a strong central state opponent, could not fit into the principal categories of a Clausewitzian war. Although many of his writings on revolutionary war are directed at the specifics of the struggle against Japan, and were written to help the party and its army to understand the new challenges of the conflict, he also contested three central elements of the Clausewitzian view – Clausewitz's 'trinity' of war-shaping forces; the importance of territoriality; and the impossibility of a war of annihilation.

For Clausewitz and his followers, war was an activity pursued by relatively stable modern states to achieve state interests. Even the American Civil War was a war of secession between two self-proclaimed states. Although this idea was tested severely during World War I's mass conflicts, it still remained the model for most military strategists and high commands. Yet, Mao saw that many of its presuppositions failed to apply in the context of a revolutionary war. Clausewitz's trinity of state (or government), army and people placed most emphasis on the state as the source of policy. The army was the institution that pursued and implemented policy in war, by the concentration and application of overwhelming violence in engagements where rival armies confront each other.

For Mao, the role of the state gave way to that of the people: 'The revolutionary war is the war of the masses; only mobilising the masses and relying on them can wage war' (Mao 1966, p. 40). This does not challenge the idea that 'war is the continuation of politics' (Mao 1966, p. 30) but it transforms the substance of the claim. The mass of the people is the source of the revolution and therefore war is their policy, as opposed to the professional armies of the imperialist powers, who are obeying the orders of their superiors, whatever their view of their orders might be. According to Mao, this gave the Chinese an advantage over the Japanese Imperial Army, and it underpins his confidence in the long-term victory in that conflict. By exercising the power of war against imperialist aggression, the whole population assert themselves as a people with a single revolutionary will, and overcome the contradictions that existed in the fragmented and weakened state of China before the revolutionary war. The people are also the source and sustenance of the army and eventually of the new revolutionary state that was to be built following victory in the civil war in 1949.

In this way, Mao reverses the order of the Clausewitzian trinity, with the people given priority over the state but close parity with the army. The relationship between the people and the army should be close and carefully cultivated, unlike Clausewitz's suspicion of the people as a potentially unruly threat to military professionalism and discipline. For Mao, the people provide the manpower and the supply and provisioning of the army. The relationship between the army and peasants was something that the party sought to cultivate to ensure those logistics. Given that much of the war involved movement, Mao argued that this connection proved an advantage over both the Japanese and their puppet occupation government, as well as over the Kuomintang, who could not rely on such support outside of some urban areas and were often seen as alien and hostile occupying forces.

The relationship between the army and the people was also more nuanced than the Clausewitzian ideal. Mao was determined to build a professional revolutionary army and saw the necessity of confronting the Japanese and the Nationalists during the civil war in traditional engagements, using all the technology of modern warfare. This would take time and resources but was always vulnerable to the progress of events. So the boundaries between the masses and the army remained fluid, particularly during guerrilla war and strategic defence and retreat. The regular army units would sometimes need to disperse and engage in guerrilla actions alongside irregular peasant fighters. They could often disappear into the peasant masses until the opportunity to re-form emerged. This fluid identity was not seen as a threat to military discipline and order but as an essential response to the temporal and spatial dimensions of the revolutionary war.

Territoriality and protracted war

The exploitation of territory for strategic advantage is an essential feature of the Clausewitzian model of war, but it has a different role in revolutionary war. The theatre of the Chinese revolutionary war was huge in size, and this transforms the idea of territoriality and replaces it with the people. The revolutionary people are not responding (just) to territorial incursion, and the goal of conflict is not simply to expel the external invader and return to a territorial *status quo*. Of course, the imperialist powers, whether Japan or the western powers in their treaty 'concessions' areas, are a threat to the masses. However, Mao saw the real threat in the idea of imperialism not the temporary incursion. In 'On Protracted War' (1937) he saw the struggle against Japan as a contribution to the class struggle of Japanese people against their military and imperial elite. The goal of victory was as much the overthrow of the imperial power through revolution in Japan as it was the expulsion of an alien, occupying force.

The narrative of occupation was to become a more important issue in the long-term legitimation of the PRC regime, but it was not high on the agenda of Mao and the party. Furthermore, where for Clausewitz taking and holding territory was essential to the defeat of an opponent, it became less important in the revolutionary war. Indeed, when confronting the 'encirclement and suppression' strategy of Chiang Kai-Shek's army, the Communists' key strategy was not to hold territory and be vulnerable to encirclement but rather to be mobile and avoid it. This stretched the supply and communication lines of the opposing army and exploited the depth of space made possible by the vastness of the Chinese interior.

Mao was determined to counter the overly traditional view of some of his colleagues who saw the loss of territory as a failure. Against that view he developed the concept of the 'strategic retreat' as an active (rather than passive) strategy, because it denies the enemy the opportunity to take and hold territory and to concentrate forces for a massive attack. Territory is transformed from being one of the goods that the military strategy is designed to secure and protect. Instead, it becomes one of the weapons used to diminish the advantages of a technologically advanced and numerically superior enemy. By spreading the theatre and extending lines of supply and communication, the superior advantages of the imperialist army are weakened, and the defensive strategy of the revolutionary army is transformed into an offensive one. The central concept is movement, which again weakens the control of the battle space by the superior force.

Alongside the spatial dimension of territoriality, Mao also explores the temporal dimension of the revolutionary war in the appropriately named 'On Protracted War' (1937). He emphasises here that the time dimension of a revolutionary war is different to that of a Clausewitzian war, which is concentrated and time-limited. The ultimate goal of the revolutionary war is the creation of a revolutionary people and the overthrow of the imperialist order. The immediate focus of that might well be the incursion of Imperial Japanese forces in

1937. Yet, even at that time, Mao saw this as only a dimension of the wider revolutionary struggle against imperialism as a social form of late capitalism. As the peasant masses were the revolutionary people, they had an historical role that was not dependent on the success or failure of individual military engagements. The final overthrow of the forces of imperialism might take a long time. Indeed, if one links the agrarian war, struggles against the warlords, and actions against the Kuomintang and Japanese as a single anti-imperialist struggle, it clearly lasted more than three decades. Throughout that time, the Chinese masses were developing their revolutionary consciousness and identity as a people. Thus, the passage of time was an advantage to the revolutionary forces, whereas the constant attrition against an apparently undefeatable army sapped the morale, resources and will amongst those forced to defend imperial interests.

This is not simply a naïve denial of the suffering of revolutionary forces in this protracted struggle, although Mao could appear rather cavalier about the well-being of the individuals who made up the peasant masses, the guerrillas and the regular army. Rather it was a reassertion of the class-based conception of political change that underlay Mao's account of the war. The struggle is not between aggregates of individuals whose welfare is being pursued or protected by war; it is about the inevitable overcoming of historical contradictions in China. A failure to defeat imperialism prolongs the exploitation that underpins the present conflict and promises only further conflict in the future. Furthermore, the people have nowhere to retreat to in order to avoid that conflict, unlike a temporarily invading army that is limited by the resources and manpower it can devote to this specific engagement. Time was on the side of the Chinese people, and their numbers were also a key advantage. They were able to absorb losses much more effectively in their own territory than an invading power, who faced the risk of domestic uprising or opposition from waging a protracted war of attrition.

Justice and a war of annihilation

Unlike Clausewitz, and perhaps surprisingly given Mao's rejection of the moral categories of liberal individualism, he nevertheless speaks of revolutionary war as being a just war:

> History shows that wars are divided into two kinds, just and unjust. All wars that are progressive are just, and all wars that impede progress are unjust. We communists oppose all unjust wars that impede progress, but we do not oppose progressive, just wars. Not only do we Communists not oppose just wars: we actively participate in them. (Mao 1966, p. 27)

What makes a war just or unjust is where it stands in the court of history. Wars such as World War I are considered unjust because they were between imperial powers vying for positional advantage in the exploitation of the masses. A war to overthrow imperialism is both just and required, because it removes exploitation and domination. The justice of war is defined in terms of the interests of the revolutionary class or people, and not in terms of the individual rights and interests of members of that class. For Mao, even more than for some western Marxists (like Louis Althusser), the concept of the individual as a site of moral concern is completely absent: he does not even attempt a derivation of moral significance from class position. The justice of going to war (*jus ad bellum*) is settled by the historical role of class agency in terms of the revolutionary overthrow of exploitation and domination.

Mao has less to say on the just conduct of war (*jus in bello*). The emphasis he places on class interest, and on the masses as the arbiters of that – see his discussion of punishments by the peasant associations in 'The Peasant Movement in Hunan' – suggests that the concept of justice in the conduct of war gives way to the justice of the struggle. This is further illustrated by the place of annihilation in his concept of revolutionary war. However, even here we need to be careful not to introduce inappropriate moralistic concepts into Mao's thought. The concept of annihilation means total destruction of the enemy and is familiar from Clausewitz. The task of an engagement is to annihilate the enemy as an opponent by destroying its capacity to fight or oppose the will of the victor; it does not necessarily mean killing all of the enemy. But, in the context of a revolution, it makes no sense for one's opponents to be stopped and disarmed if they are then able to regroup and re-enter the field at some stage. Whereas Clausewitz saw war as a relatively frequent activity amongst states who may be frequent belligerents, Mao inevitably saw the revolutionary war as existential.

The imperial classes need to be overcome once and for all in order for the revolution to be effective, and so the annihilation of the fighting power of the opponent is only one element of their annihilation. The long-term overcoming of a class opposition completes the process of annihilation and, as with Lenin's view of overcoming the state, this might require a considerable amount of violence and death. But there is another equally important part of this process of annihilation that has more relevance in relation to the immediate engagement. The forces of the imperialists are ultimately drawn from the people. Even in the case of the war against the Japanese, Chinese forces of the collaborationist regime of Wang Jingwei formed an important part of the forces in the field. These troops could be annihilated by being turned to the interests of the revolutionary people and incorporated into the regular Red Army or into guerrilla forces that continued the war. The total annihilation of such forces was also important because it was a major source of supply of materiel in order to continue the conflict and arm the people. The nature of revolutionary war entails that annihilation is the only appropriate long-term response to an enemy, and that it is always justified to use as much force and violence as necessary to overcome this enemy.

Guerrilla wars

Mao's account of guerrilla war was to be one of his most closely studied works on war and revolution, not least because of the importance of such forces and operations in the anti-colonial wars of liberation following the end of World War II. Guerrilla warfare was not new or unique to China. The name goes back to the insurgent and irregular groups who fought the French occupying forces in Spain during the Napoleonic Wars. Mao's famous essay 'On Guerrilla Warfare' (1937) locates the rise of this mode of combat within a history of war from the time of Clausewitz, but stresses the new importance of guerrilla operations within the context of revolutionary wars against imperialism. Guerrilla wars are asymmetric at the most fundamental level. Armies are often unequal in numbers, resources or technology, without being fundamentally unmatched. Napoleon showed how a numerically smaller army could still defeat a larger one. The asymmetry of numbers was overcome by skill, initiative and the drive of senior commanders. Yet, even in such cases the opponents are still fundamental equals in being national armies with populations, governments and resources behind them. The fundamental asymmetry for Mao is that the revolutionary army is not simply less well equipped or less professional than its imperialist opponent, but it is unequal or different in kind. Writing about the relationship between regular forces and guerrilla forces, Mao emphasises that guerrilla forces are appropriate for the period prior to the building of a sufficiently powerful regular army. Guerrillas are both a tactic for conflict in a revolutionary war and a stage in the building of a revolutionary army, which will eventually subsume the guerrilla forces as part of the centrally controlled military. His discussion of guerrilla warfare covers who the guerrillas are, how they are controlled, what they are for, and how they fight.

Who are the guerrillas? This question is important because military hierarchies are traditionally hostile to irregular forces, which they regard as tricky to distinguish from bandits and rabbles, hard to discipline, and difficult to bring within an ordered battle plan. This discomfort was equally felt by senior Chinese commanders, who were concerned with growing the professionalisation of an effective People's Liberation Army, and party leaders, who feared losing party control over such groups. Mao's lecture defends the necessity of guerrilla forces to the party and shows how they come under the central authority of a mass party revolution. The guerrillas are drawn from seven sources:

a) From the masses of the people.
b) From regular army units temporarily detailed for the purpose.
c) From regular army units permanently detailed.
d) From the combination of a regular army unit and a unit recruited from the people.

e) From a local militia.

f) From deserters from the ranks of the enemy.

g) From bandits and bandit groups. (Mao 2014, p. 82)

There is a relationship here with regular forces, including regular forces from the opposing side who have deserted or been captured and changed side. But the most important source is the mass of the people and those from the locality in which the guerrillas operate, whether these individuals are from regular forces, militias or local bandits with knowledge and experience of the terrain in which they operate. The ultimate legitimacy of these forces is their link to the people, who will support, shelter and supply them during their operations. This link to the people is especially important because it enables the forces to maintain constant activity and movement, whilst remaining rooted in a source of supply and personnel. In addition, it reinforces morale and the guerrillas' motivation to act in defence of the people they live and fight amongst.

How are guerrillas controlled? As a Leninist, Mao was always concerned with maintaining the party's authority amongst the people and exercising firm central control. That said, in the case of guerrilla forces he was not only prepared to relinquish central direction but required the guerrilla forces to act independently.

> In guerrilla warfare, small units acting independently play the principal role and there must be no excessive interference with their activities. In orthodox warfare particularly in a moving situation, a certain degree of initiative is accorded subordinates, but in principle, command is central-ized. This is done because all units and all supporting arms in all districts must co-ordinate to the highest degree. In the case of guerrilla warfare, this is not only undesirable but impossible. Only adjacent guerrilla units can coordinate their activities to any degree … But there are no strictures on the extent of the guerrilla activity nor is it primarily characterized by the quality of co-operation of many units. (Mao 2014, p. 68)

This discretion was partly a response to the necessity of the battle space, where the guerrilla forces do not control communications, supply or access to link up with the regular units. Instead, guerrilla forces are expected to create their own initiative and to operate independently within the broad remit of annihilating the enemy's forces and frustrating its ability to concentrate forces for a strike. Mao's guerrilla units were expected to function as small independent armies with their own command structure and plans of engagement that are dictated by the proximity to the enemy in their particular space, and by the resources, terrain and opportunities that are available. The duration and success of a guer-rilla unit is down to the commanders and the population that sustains it. Mao did not see such units as merely dispersed forces of the regular army that would be recalled and reunited after a successful engagement. The life and duration of guerrilla forces would be determined by the concentration of forces facing it. The independence of the guerrillas' command and battle plans meant that a unit being destroyed or its commanders captured or killed could not comprise the central strategy. This part of Mao's theory was to have a considerable influence on the development of terrorist and insurgent operations in later wars, and in shaping the cell structure of revolutionary political groups in the late 20th century.

What are the guerrilla forces for? Mao summarises their tasks as follows:

> to exterminate small forces of the enemy; to harass and weaken large forces; to attack enemy lines of communications; to establish bases capable of supporting independent operations in the enemy's rear, to force the enemy to disperse his strength; and to co-ordinate all these activities with those of the regular armies on distant battle fronts. (Mao 2014, p. 69)

These types of tactic achieve two main strategic ends. The first is to diversify away from the fundamental objective of a Clausewitzian strategy of concentrating lethal force onto the enemy so as to achieve its annihilation. When a smaller and less powerful force confronts a stronger force, it instead needs to diminish the major power. The goal is not victory or defeat but attrition as a means of annihilation. In a regular conflict, time and personnel are the basic limitations on waging a war of attrition. Yet, in the context of the anti-imperialist war in China, those constraints did not apply to the communists or to the guerrilla groups. Dividing and harassing the enemy's supply lines and communications limit the possibility of concentration, and increase the 'friction' that Clausewitzian generals so feared. A dispersed but active enemy is also harder to concentrate on because there is always more than one point of contact. Mao's strategy is a textbook inversion of the central tenet of Clausewitzian strategy.

The second end of guerrilla strategy is building a mass revolutionary army by training non-regular soldiers to fight the imperialist forces, but also to recognise the context of the imperialist war. Propaganda is one of the central tasks of the guerrilla forces. Propaganda by deed occurs in engaging with the enemy, but their wider propaganda war is advanced by organising the peasant mass as a revolutionary force with the party at its head. As his discussion of 'Protracted War' shows, Mao saw the military campaign against Japan, and later against the Kuomintang, as part of the wider struggle for the liberation of the masses. Building an army and building a revolutionary people went hand in hand and, in Mao's account of guerrilla conflict, this was as important as the harassment of occupying forces.

How do the guerrillas fight? The common image of the guerrilla army is of poorly armed but highly motivated columns of peasant soldiers. Yet, Mao also makes clear that effective guerrilla forces need to fight a sophisticated war deploying communications equipment and the materials necessary to destroy supply routes (such as bridges, roads and railways), as well as engaging in direct attack on the enemy: 'a demolition unit must be organised in each regiment' (Mao 2014, p. 90). This is a model that was to be copied by special forces and commando groups in subsequent wars and in colonial wars in pursuit of the guerrillas and insurgents, as commanders realised that one way to defeat guerrilla forces was to copy and fight like guerrilla forces.

The theatre of engagement for guerrilla conflict is determined by the enemy's deployments. Consequently, guerrilla units are constantly active and mobile, probing the weak points of enemy supply lines and forces but also avoiding the encirclement and suppression tactics of anti-guerrilla operations by regular armies. However, central to Mao's thinking about guerrilla forces and operations was the idea of base areas where they could supply, recuperate, establish medical services and engage in training and propaganda. As Mao writes, 'Propaganda is very important. Every large guerrilla unit should have a printing press and a mimeograph stone, they must also have paper on which to print propaganda leaflets and notices' (Mao 2014, p. 91).

Guerrilla operations require the capacity to fight without a rear area: this is an advantage for guerrillas, but it is also a challenge. So Mao insists that the long-term success of guerrilla operations require base areas that are carefully chosen and can be easily defended. Mountainous areas were ideal as they served as natural fortresses against which regular troops were less effective and not easily concentrated. But the base area also needs to be able to supply food and shelter, as well as additional recruits and space for training. So, whilst mountainous areas are preferable, Mao does not exclude 'plains country' or 'river, lake and bay' areas. The point of contrast between base areas and guerrilla areas is that in guerrilla engagement the task is never to take and occupy territory. Guerrilla units will hopefully establish ties with the local population and benefit from it, but the point is not to hold and defend territory, so the normal distinctions between defensive and offensive operations do not apply to guerrillas: every attack is also a retreat. Base areas are different since these are held in order to sustain the long-term possibility of guerrilla operations and to provide the economic support that a complex campaign relies on. The defence of base areas also creates opportunities for guerrilla units. The base area serves as a target for the enemy, but because of its location it should ideally divide the enemy's forces in seeking to overcome it, unlike a fortress, where defence is concentrated within it. This fragmentation of the enemy's forces allows guerrilla units to weaken supply lines and communications, making direct conflict more successful when finally required.

The focus on guerrilla war should not distort the historical understanding of the Red Army as a regular army in conflict with the Japanese Imperial Army or the Nationalist Army between 1945 and 1949. The Red Army fought regular engagements and built itself into a large and powerful fighting force, even if it did not always prevail in the field. The guerrilla forces played an important part in the struggle against Japan and the Nationalist forces, vindicating much of what Mao argued in 'On Guerrilla War'. However, the long-term importance of that work is not solely its role as a rallying cry, or as a statement of strategy, but rather its long-term impact as a model for subsequent guerrilla, insurgent and 'terrorist' fighting and organisation in the future. Mao was an important figure in the reshaping of military strategy and tactics following World War II and in the context of the nuclear age that rendered problematic, if not impossible, the large-scale wars of position and manoeuvre that were familiar from eastern Europe, and from the Chinese war of 1937–1945. The insurgents in the colonial wars for South East Asia, ranging from the collapse of the Dutch and French Indo-Chinese empires to the Communist insurgency against the British in Malaya, all adopted aspects of the cellular division of authority and the tactics that the communist guerrillas had deployed against Japan and the Nationalists. As western militaries were forced to confront the tactics of guerrillas, they adjusted their own tactics accordingly, often deploying counter-insurgency methods that mirrored precisely those deployed by their guerrilla opponents.

Leninism and Maoism in the modern era

The legacy of Lenin and Mao is the main legacy of Marxism on 20th-century politics and international affairs, however unfair that attribution to Marx might be in the view of some Marxist scholars. Lenin and Mao have dominated the theory and conduct of revolutionary politics, even amongst their opponents and those tasked with confronting their challenge politically or militarily. In international affairs they enjoy the peculiar status of being both a problem with which international theorists have to wrestle and a source of ideas that have informed the way in which political and internationalist theorists make sense of world politics. However much anti-Marxist critics of Lenin like to depict him using the racially loaded idea that he is 'Asiatic' and not therefore truly western, an increasingly important recognition has developed that sees Lenin and Mao are representatives of different hemispheres and cultural presuppositions. A racially loaded characterisation as 'Asiatic' is irrelevant when applied to Mao, who was Chinese and deeply proud of that, combining a strong nationalist streak with his revolutionary communism. This brief concluding section distinguishes how Leninism and Maoism are still a problem for international affairs from their contribution to international political theory.

Leninism and Maoism as an international problem

From the very beginning, revolutionary Russia (which soon became the USSR) was a challenge to the western global order. Lenin's 1917 withdrawal from World War I destabilised the previous British–French–Russian alliance against

Germany and Austria at time of uncertainty for the western powers, prior to the arrival of U.S. forces on the battlefield. Western powers were quick to intervene in the revolution and the civil war, partly in order to retain some eastern pressure on Germany and Austria, as well as destabilising the communist regime that threatened to spread revolution across the rest of Europe. Though real, the threat of such interventions was negligible in the first years of the regime, because it was preoccupied with surviving the civil war and seeking economic stabilisation. By the time of Lenin's death in 1924, his successor, Stalin, was on the way to exercising a dominant position over the USSR and its foreign policy.

Throughout the pre-1941 period of Stalin's rule, the fundamental policy direction was ensuring the stability of the USSR above all else, despite Moscow offering support for nascent communist parties beyond its borders through the Comintern. Communism remained an expansionist and revolutionary creed, but the focus of communists and fellow travellers was supporting the interests of the USSR against its neighbours and imperialist rivals. Stalin claimed to continue the direction of the revolution that had been set by Lenin, however much later historians have sought to separate their positions.

In these years, many western intellectuals visited the USSR and saw a new society, albeit one that was strictly controlled and carefully presented to the outside world. The USSR remained a potential modernist utopia in the eyes of many, especially following the economic collapse of 1929 and the great depression of the 1930s. It attracted overt support from intellectuals, as well as the covert support of those who were to become Soviet agents and assets. The fortunes of the USSR during the 1920s and 1930s became part of the backdrop of E.H. Carr's *The Twenty Years' Crisis* (1939). This is one of the founding texts of the realist tradition in international relations, because it sought to overthrow the post-Versailles idealism of the League of Nations.

Yet, whilst some intellectuals saw the USSR as a beacon for the future, others observed the disturbing conduct of the USSR from the inside and began to turn away from the Soviet world view. The experience of the Spanish Civil War (as depicted by George Orwell and Arthur Koestler) began to undermine the faith of many socialists that Soviet communism was anything other than a new source of tyranny. Anti-communism was fuelled by former communists such as James Burnham, who retained a belief in technocratic government but without the millennialist belief in a future revolution.

For intellectuals on the right, Soviet Marxism was an atheistic and 'Asiatic' doctrine that threated western civilisation, or what came to be known as 'Judeo-Christian' values. This concern with godless communism led many on the right to flirt with fascism and in some cases Nazism, as a restraining force to combat Bolshevism. The experience of World War II complicated how the role of the USSR was understood in global affairs. Stalin at first joined Hitler in partitioning Poland, following the Molotov–Ribbentrop pact in 1939. When Hitler attacked the USSR in mid-1941 (to Stalin's initial disbelief), the USSR became a British ally of necessity, later joined by the USA after Japan's attack at Pearl Harbor in December 1941 and Hitler's declaration of war on the USA. In the European theatre, the USSR provided the manpower to sap the strength of the Wehrmacht, following its defeat at Stalingrad in 1943. At the end of the war, Soviet armies dominated much of eastern and central Europe, and the Red Army was established as the only rival to US military power. The brief alliance of convenience soon gave way to a Cold War between the capitalist west and the communist east that dominated international politics until the fall of the Berlin Wall in 1989 brought an end to the Warsaw Pact. The USSR broke up into its constituent republics in 1991 and Russia re-emerged as a chastened and economically weak state, but one with a huge nuclear arsenal.

The Cold War dominated the post-war study of international relations, and much of the demand for international relations scholars was shaped by the rapid change in circumstance from 1945 to 1948. A key figure at this time in US politics was George F. Kennan (1904–2005), a career diplomat with experience in the Moscow embassy before World War II and one of the leading academic Soviet watchers. He shaped US post-war strategy with his 'Long Telegram' of 1946 and an article, 'The Sources of Soviet Conduct', in *Foreign Affairs* (1947), famously published anonymously as by 'X'. Kennan argued that the logic of Soviet policy was relentlessly expansionist, but that the Soviet state was insufficiently strong in economic terms to carry this through to world domination. This made the USSR an unstable adversary and risked a collapse into a further war that was doubly problematic once the USSR acquired nuclear weapons. Kennan's response was not to seek the ideological or military defeat of the USSR but to operate a policy of containment. For many anti-communists, this failure to advocate communism's defeat seemed just a form of accommodation to a bipolar world. To many observers, Kennan was a classic Cold Warrior, providing a justification for the long-term US engagement in Europe, whereas for more militant anti-communists he was almost an appeaser.

The implications for realism in international relations followed from Kennan's rejection of the ideological and military defeat of communism, and its replacement with a technical policy problem that saw expansionism as the issue and left the judgement of the evils of the regime to the popular press. Military planners and the new strategy scholars still sought to construct policies and plans for undertaking a limited nuclear war against the Soviets, or mutually assured destruction. But Kennan's influence, and the new realism that had grown across the political spectrum since Carr's 1939 essay, transformed itself into the dominant paradigm of international relations, where all questions were either about the truth of realism or why realism was inadequate.

In all of the changes after 1945, China and Mao's legacy were seen in the terms of the global ideological struggle between the west and communism, to the point that few scholars took China's revolution seriously as anything other than an extension of the global expansionism of the USSR. Interestingly,

Kennan did not have this simplistic view of China and East Asia. He was a sufficiently sophisticated student of Soviet affairs to appreciate that Mao was not simply a delegate of Stalin or just following the Moscow line. Indeed, Kennan became increasingly sceptical of the 'domino theory' model of Asian national liberation struggles, which led to all such anti-colonial wars being seen as continuations of Soviet efforts at domination. The Korean War (1950–1953) was complex. It involved (unacknowledged) Soviet military support and massive Chinese forces intervening to save the North Koreans from defeat. So it appeared to reinforce the model of an expansionist ideology, but without taking account of the difference between communism as a globally expansive doctrine and the USSR being an expansionist power.

China's 1949 revolution and the subsequent cult of Mao certainly had a significant impact on anti-imperialist and anti-colonial struggles but, apart from intervening in Korea when U.S. forces under MacArthur neared the Chinese border, China otherwise fought only small border wars with India in the 1950s and in the 1960s with the USSR. The Chinese also helped the North Vietnamese struggle to expel the French in the 1950s, and at first also backed the North and the Viet Cong battle in the 1960s against the USA and South Vietnam (although they withdrew from this from 1968 on). In no other respect did China engage in expansionist military adventures (Lovell 2019).

Much international relations scholarship on China continued in a Cold War intellectual frame, although Mao's China failed to behave according to the expectations of scholars. It was only in the 1960s that scholars began to take a serious interest in the domestic base of Mao's mass revolution, as opposed to the broader Soviet-dominated geopolitical framework. The significance of China in international affairs changed radically with its opening to the USA and President Nixon's subsequent visit to meet Mao in 1972. The USA's approach to China was originally conceived as a way of dividing the communist 'bloc', exploiting the growing hostility between China and the USSR that had increased since the death of Stalin. US–China relations remained cool until the end of the Cultural Revolution, following the death of Mao in 1976 and his eventual replacement by Deng Xiaoping (1904–1997).

Deng was a colleague and rival of Mao who became the most important subsequent leader of the PRC, and came to enjoy a respect amongst Chinese people that was equivalent to or greater than that in which Mao is held. Although an uncompromising Communist leader who was prepared to use the PLA against the protesters at Tiananmen Square in 1989, he also opened up the Chinese economy to global trade and investment, leading to the spectacular rise in Chinese economic power over the following 40 years. Yet, whilst the crisis year of 1989 saw the beginning of the collapse of the USSR, Deng's China survived Tiananmen Square and went on to achieve spectacular economic growth. China rose from a developing state to a regional power and hundreds of millions of Chinese people left the countryside to move into the new industrial cities, with many also moving out of poverty into middle income status. Eventually China grew into a global manufacturing hegemon that threated U.S. economic domination as the largest global economy, a status that China has already assumed.

With China's ascent, international relations scholars have turned their attention from its role as a communist state to simply regarding it as a global superpower that has displaced the USSR and any other imperial power and which now confronts the USA as a challenger if not yet quite an equal. The study of China–U.S. relations centres on concerns about how this bipolar rivalry will impact on peace, international political economy and regional and global international relations. For a sub-discipline that since the 1940s has focused on U.S. power and its impact on the world, this is a big change. China remains an authoritarian, one-party and communist state, albeit one that Mao would have found in some ways incomprehensible. Yet, for all its transformations since Mao and Deng's time, the basic structures of the state and party, and their interrelations, are still much as Lenin or Mao would have expected a party state to be.

Conclusion: imperialism, party politics and war

The communist threat, the rise and decline of the USSR and the spectacular rise of the PRC to world power status have been normalised in international relations thought. Yet, both Lenin and Mao set out to challenge the state-focused idea of international order, and to replace it with different conceptions of the context, site and ends of political power, now reshaped by the concepts of imperialism, party-centralism, and the organisation of war in very different forms from the Clausewitzian trinity. Both men's accounts of imperialism, party organisation and discipline, and the conduct of revolutionary and guerrilla war have had a huge influence on subsequent theorists within the socialist tradition. Much subsequent western Marxism has been a struggle to transcend the bounds of Lenin's legacy, with his critics seeking either to rehumanise Marxism–Leninism or to broaden its remit into cultural struggles, as was the case with Antonio Gramsci and his followers. Similar arguments can be made about Mao and his influence on socialism in Asia and the developing world. These impacts would be important enough given the impact of Leninism and Maoism on the 20th and 21st centuries. But it would distort the significance of their thought to confine a consideration of later impacts just to the socialist tradition. The key concepts deployed and developed by Lenin and Mao have had as much significance beyond Marxism.

Lenin was not the first thinker to describe imperialism as a new economic form and he acknowledged both the non-Marxist J.A. Hobson (1858–1940) and the Austrian Marxist Rudolf Hilferding (1877–1941) in his work – unlike his Marxist contemporary Rosa Luxemburg (1871–1919), who is not mentioned. Lenin gave important additional impetus to the concept in international politics and relations. Imperialism was an account of why revolution was no longer a solely national issue and why capitalism was able to accommodate its crisis tendencies. Yet, the phenomena of capitalist development on a global stage and operating beyond the context of the nation state did not need to be linked to the logic of dialectical materialism as a source of contradictions that would require overcoming in a revolution. The Marxist–Leninist acknowledgement of the development of capitalism as the driver of all social relations was useful even without positing a necessary historical crisis.

As former communists (such as James Burnham) lost their revolutionary faith, they retained the basic material analysis of society and the recognition of new social and political forms that followed the international growth of the capitalist society. The Cold War world created the circumstances in which the new international power of the USA was coupled with an extension of American economic interests. Many scholars might have described the USA as a benign empire that helped underpin the global economic order, but it was nevertheless seen as an empire – with its combination of economic power opening up national markets to its own advantage, and with its overwhelming military might (Ikenberry 2001). The Leninist and Maoist stories of how this economic form led to war might not have applied directly given the United States' role as a power without an economic challenger, although the USSR restrained its global military power. But the way the U.S. exercised its interests in destabilising or changing regimes that were not to its economic interests (e.g. in Iran or Chile) suggested that international political economy could be understood through concepts such as imperialism, by both its friends and its foes.

With the collapse of the USSR as a restraint on U.S. power in 1991, the USA was the leader of a unipolar, although not necessarily a peaceful world, as the Middle East saw a number of major traditional-style wars. The same period also saw the high point of economic globalisation with the offshoring of manufacturing jobs into high-skilled but low-wage economies (like India, China and Vietnam), and the hollowing-out of the domestic manufacturing economies within western democracies. What Lenin and Mao saw as the detachment of capital from the nation state, and its consolidation in international hands, became the phenomenon of globalisation. Its exponents claimed that it was the only realistic model of the global economy and a fact that domestic political regimes needed to reconcile themselves to (Held 2004). Yet, as the global financial crash of 2008 and its long-term consequences have shown, the new model of a 'weightless' economy of global financial capitalism was not without its own crisis tendencies. These were especially manifested in the growth of populism, 'democratic backsliding' and economic nationalism after 2016. But they were also illuminated by the rise of China as a global economic power, and the lender of last resort to the global economy following 2008. From the 2010s onwards, China also built up its military and made territorial claims in the South China Sea, and over Taiwan. So it is by no means clear that rival economic imperial powers will not come into conflict through trade and technology wars, even if not outright military conflicts.

In addition, illuminating the broadest phenomena of contemporary global politics, Lenin and Mao's writings on party organisation and in Mao's case the organisation of guerrilla war have had a considerable impact beyond the confines of Marxism–Leninism, on the micro-organisation of political power and its exercise. The ideal of ruthlessly disciplined and tightly organised parties of professional party functionaries has become normalised across all political regimes, to the extent that we can forget how much of that tendency has its roots in Lenin's *What Is to Be Done?* Mass parties, whether in one-party states or in multiparty democracies, are dominated and controlled by inner cores of professionals, who largely direct rather than respond to the aspirations of the broader membership. The more authoritarian the regime, the more the Leninist model of parties is the norm, as illustrated by nationalist populists such as the Ba'ath Party in Egypt, Syria and Iraq. In populist regimes, these cores of professional cadres (a term widely used by the Maoists) are central to the leader's authority in a loosely organised mass party. Similar structures may also be formed by 'entryist' groups seeking to wrest power from the mass membership, as seen in the fragmented politics of the left after 1968 in Europe. The secretive centralised character of some of these groups led them to shift from political struggle within a political system to revolutionary struggle against a settled political system. Some went further into the politics of terrorism and insurrection, which also drew on aspects of Mao's theory of guerrilla war. So-called Maoists of the radical European left were often tightly organised but decentralised to avoid infiltration and decapitation strategies by police and security services.

For those that became terrorists, such as the Baader–Meinhof Group in Germany, the Red Brigades in Italy, the Provisional IRA, and various Palestinian terrorist groups, the strategy of decentralised cell-structures with only the loosest of central direction allowed them to develop successful operations that withstood infiltration or wider failure to gain support, for a time. This strategy has reappeared most recently and effectively in global-reach terrorist groups such as Al-Qaeda and ISIS (outside its doomed caliphate in Iraq/Syria). In those cases there is no strict central command or strategic leadership but instead a fiercely activist brand identity that is adopted locally to recruit and inspire those who work in strictly isolated cells. All of these phenomena extend, develop and modify ideas and forms that have their roots in Lenin and Mao's political and organisational writings on the conduct of revolution. Whilst revolution remains a political aspiration for some, or a problem that militaries and security forces need to understand in order to confront, both sides will turn to Lenin and Mao for insights, rather than to Marx.

Bibliography

Essential reading by Lenin

Lenin. (1978). *Imperialism, The Highest Stage of Capitalism*. Russia: Progress Publishers.

Lenin. (1988). *What Is to Be Done?* ed. R. Service. UK: Penguin.
Lenin. (1992). *The State and Revolution*, ed. R. Service. UK: Penguin.

Essential reading by Mao

Mao. (2014). *Selected Works of Mao Zedong*. Marx-Engels-Lenin Institute.
Mao. (1967). *Selected Military Writings of Mao Tse-Tung*. China: Foreign Language Press.
Mao. (1966). *Quotations from Chairman Mao Tse-Tung* [*The Little Red Book*]. Beijing.

Secondary reading

Ali, Tariq. (2017). *The Dilemmas of Lenin*. UK: Verso.
Avineri, Shlomo. (1968). *The Social and Political Thought of Karl Marx*. UK: Cambridge University Press.
Claeys, Gregory. (2018). *Marx and Marxism*. UK: Penguin.
Harding, Neil. (1977). *Lenin's Political Thought, vol. 1: Theory and Practice in the Democratic Revolution*. UK: Macmillan.
Harding, Neil. (1981). *Lenin's Political Thought, vol. 2: Theory and Practice in the Socialist Revolution*. UK: Macmillan.
Harding, Neil. (1996). *Leninism*. UK: Macmillan.
Ikenberry. G. John. (2001). *After Victory: Institutions, Strategic Restraint and the Rebuilding of Order after Major Wars*. USA: Princeton University Press.
Katzenbach Jnr, Edward L.; and Hanrahan, Gene Z. (1955). 'The Revolutionary Strategy of Mao Tse-Tung' *Political Science Quarterly*, vol. 70, pp. 321–340.
Kolakowski, Lezek. (2005). *Main Currents of Marxism*. USA: Norton.
Lovell, Julia. (2019). *Maoism: A Global History*. UK: Bodley Head.
McLellan, David. (2000). *Karl Marx: Selected Writings*. UK: Oxford University Press.
Ryan, James. (2011). '"Revolution Is War": The Development of the Thought of V.I. Lenin on Violence, 1899–1907" *The Slavonic and East European Review*, vol. 89, pp. 248–273.
Ryan, James. (2012). *Lenin's Terror and the Ideological Origins of Early Soviet State Violence*. UK: Routledge.
Schram, Stuart. (1990). *The Thought of Mao Tse-Tung*. UK: Cambridge University Press.
Snow, Edgar. (2018). *Red Star over China*, ed. J.K. Fairbanks. UK: Grove.
Solzhenitsyn, Alexander. (1974). *The Gulag Archipelago*. USA: Harper Collins.
Spence, Jonathan D. (1990). *The Search for Modern China*. USA: Norton.
Spence, Jonathan D. (1999). *Mao*. UK: Weidenfeld and Nicholson.

Tooze, Adam. (2018). *Crashed: How a Decade of Financial Crises Changed the World*. UK: Penguin.

Suggestions for finding open access versions of Lenin's and Mao's texts

Lenin
Marxists Internet Archive
https://www.marxists.org/archive/lenin/index.htm

Mao
Marxists Internet Archive
https://www.marxists.org/reference/archive/mao/index.htm
A 1963 edition of the *Selected Military Writings of Mao Tse-Tung* is in the
Marxists Internet Archive at:
https://www.marxists.org/reference/archive/mao/selected-works/military
-writings/mao-selected-military-writings-1963.pdf
And *Quotations from Chairman Mao Tse-Tung* is at:
https://www.marxists.org/ebooks/mao/Quotations_from_Chairman_Mao
_Tse-tung.pdf

CHAPTER 10

Schmitt

The danger of the international liberal order

Carl Schmitt rejects the optimism of the contemporary liberal internationalist view of the global order that has been dominant since 1945.
Schmitt is an uncompromising conservative thinker who has influenced
theorists of the left and right. He analyses the international state system as
a bulwark against the violence and conflict that underlies the universalist
and globalist tendencies of liberal and revolutionary politics. His ideas
are a response to the decline of European power, the rise of Cold War
ideological opposition, and the emergence of new global hegemons such
as the United States. Schmitt provides both a critique of liberal optimism
and globalisation, and at the same time he attempts to salvage essential
concepts such as sovereignty, war and enmity, as a way of disciplining
politics and responding to the decline of state power. Schmitt is critical
of liberal democracy. He sees the concept of 'the political' as centred on
what sovereignty is and where it resides, following the abandonment of
liberal popular sovereignty theories and nationalism. These views are the
foundations for his critique of global liberalism and international law.

Sovereign is he who decides on the exception. (Carl Schmitt)

One way of writing a contemporary history of international political thought
would see the progressive triumph of a broadly liberal and more internationalist global order liberating itself from the legacy of an increasingly outdated

---

How to cite this book chapter:
Kelly, Paul. 2022. *Conflict, war and revolution: The problem of politics in international
political thought*. London: LSE Press, pp. 369–408.
DOI: https://doi.org/10.31389/lsepress.cwr.j License: CC BY.

Westphalian world order centred around states. Increasingly porous economic borders and more pacific relations between political communities accentuate the forces of integration that follow from a globalised world and shared knowledge, leading to progress towards the universally desired goals of peace, stability and a reduction in violence. That, at least, is the 'desire of the nations' expressed by many political optimists and shared by commentators and opinion formers such as Francis Fukuyama and Stephen Pinker (Fukuyama 1992; Pinker 2011; 2018). In more theoretical realms, this narrative has been accompanied by the growth in philosophical cosmopolitanism that has challenged liberal theory for not being sufficiently radical in its individualism (Pogge 2007; Singer 2004). Key liberal theorists, such as John Rawls and Michael Walzer, have sought to rein in this overweening hubris, much to the disappointment of their followers. Yet, Rawls and Walzer still leave us with a more modest yet nevertheless broadly liberal 'end of history' including some version of a globally pacific society of states.

Beyond the realm of theory, the post-1989 world order has, however, been more complex. Patterns of development remain as uncertain as ever, with the Trumpist transition of the USA in 2016–2020 away from being an assertive but potentially benign liberal Leviathan, conferring international order in return for accommodation of its interests (Ikenberry 2012; Nye 2015). Even after Trump's departure, the USA remains a more unpredictable and potentially more diffident international actor. A unipolar international system looks to be gone for good, given China's rise, and, given the potential poles, multipolarity seems neither attractive nor problem-free. The prominence of nation states in responding to the global financial crisis of 2008–2010 and the Covid–19 crisis in 2020–2022 both suggest that the states system is not giving away to a new order. But nor is it being completed by any coherent new assertion of the logic of state sovereignty, despite the efforts of Britain to 'take back control' from the European Union.

Thinking beyond the state system has become a pressing task for many international political theorists, especially focusing on international society as a system built from pooled state sovereignty, and thinking beyond the boundaries of liberal ideas of individual rights, domestic and international legality, and free and open trade. The salience of these topics has reignited interest in thinkers who challenge the fundamental terms of contemporary political and international thinking. None is more challenging or more controversial than the German jurist and political thinker Carl Schmitt (1888–1985). His intellectual and political biography, as well as his practical judgement, makes him a difficult thinker to handle, let alone to learn from. Yet, his work is enjoying a major resurgence of interest precisely because of the radical way in which he critiques the fundamental terms of liberalism and the modern state order. He argues that these conceptual forms are not merely inadequate to the world we confront but, more importantly, that they are also a source of conflict, disorder and violence, rather than the solution to a disordered world. The trenchancy of this argument takes Schmitt beyond the usual claim that liberal concepts are implicated in colonialism, patriarchy or other sources of oppression. For Schmitt, liberalism is not only conceptually inadequate; it is dangerous – liberalism is the enemy. Yet, whilst rejecting the domestic and global liberalism and the intellectual and political structures that underpin it, such as modern political economy, he seeks to retain and conserve important political ideas, such as sovereignty, but liberate them from false notions such as the nation state, the national economy and the people. That argument and his remarkable account of politics and international relations are the focus in this chapter.

Schmitt: life and work

Carl Schmitt was born in 1888 in Plettenburg in Westphalia to a Catholic family living in a predominantly Protestant region of the newly united German Empire or Reich. The empire's set-up still retained some legacy of the patchwork of religiously divided principalities in Germany's post-Westphalian order, from which the Prussia-dominated empire emerged. His family's religion marked Schmitt out as an outsider in ways that shaped his subsequent intellectual development. Coming of age in the late Wilhelmine Empire, Schmitt graduated in law at what was then the German University of Strasbourg in 1915. During the 1914–1918 war he joined the general staff of the army in Munich, charged with implementing martial law. For much of the latter part of the war, Germany was effectively ruled by an authoritarian and military government under Hindenburg and Ludendorff. With the German army's collapse on the Western Front and the Armistice of November 1918 Germany was plunged into a period of political chaos and violence, as the new Weimar Republic, with its democratically elected political parties, struggled to survive and fill the space left by the demise of the imperial and military regimes.

The fledgling republic's struggle for legitimacy was not simply against the real threat of communist revolution but also from conservatives and Catholic conservatives, who were deeply suspicious of liberal and democratic government. The Weimar Republic's strongest opponents were also the remnants of the army and irregular anti-communist militias (the Freikorps), from which the Nazi Party was to emerge over subsequent decades. In this context, Schmitt began his first public career as a leading academic public lawyer and author. He championed the critique of constitutional liberalism through a number of books such as *Political Romanticism* (1919), *Political Theology* (1922) and *The Crisis of Parliamentary Democracy* (1923). In these rhetorically sparkling, incisive and provocative essays, Schmitt established his credentials as a major theorist of the Weimar Constitution. What particularly marked out his contribution was his profound scepticism and hostility to liberal constitutionalism and his assertion of the centrality of politics to public law and the constitution, in opposition to the normativism of liberal positivists such as Hans Kelsen. Schmitt's fundamental objection to liberal constitutionalism was not simply a technical issue of jurisprudence but rested on its failure to take seriously the politics of constitutionalism such that it undermined its own ability to protect itself from threats and challenges. This was an acute weakness in the context of the deeply divided Weimar state, which faced a punitive and destabilising Versailles Treaty with multiple adverse economic and political consequences for Germany (Keynes 1919). These threats and challenges finally manifested themselves in the rise of the NSDAP, or Nazi Party, which took power with conservatives' connivance in 1933.

Throughout the 1920s, Schmitt was a leading figure in the political debates of late Weimar and an increasingly important political theorist, publishing his seminal *The Concept of the Political* in 1932. Although he was not himself a Nazi at this time, he was associated with the right-wing conservative government of Franz von Papen, who brought Hitler into government. The forcing through of the 1933 Enabling Act that effectively did away with the Weimar Constitution and gave dictatorial powers to Hitler and the Nazis marked a turning point in Schmitt's life and career. Schmitt joined the Nazi Party in May 1933 after it had already taken power, and was quickly rewarded with an appointment as state councillor for Prussia and to a prestigious professorship at the University of Berlin. This was the high point of Schmitt's public legal and political career as he became what was referred to as 'the crown jurist' of the Reich.

Schmitt's association with Nazism is a complex matter. He was certainly a party member and directly participated in the assertion of Nazi control over society, including the burning of law books by Jewish scholars and the harassment or isolation of Jewish academics. Like the philosopher Martin Heidegger, who also threw in his lot with the Nazis in 1933 as the rector of Freiburg University, Schmitt's reputation is permanently coloured by this association. Yet, more than Heidegger, Schmitt's association was directly political. The question of whether or not he was a Nazi in terms of a full intellectual engagement with that ideology is less clear. Indeed, as early as 1936 he aroused the suspicions of the SS, who accused him of being an opportunist Catholic thinker who was insincere about his racial anti-Semitism. Schmitt was protected from the full implications of this suspicion, but he withdrew into academic writing for the remainder of the war. In particular, he began his writings on international politics, which was to mark his second major career in the late Nazi and post-war period.

With the defeat of the Nazis, Schmitt was arrested and interned but released without charge in 1947. His own reflections on that period, such as *Ex Captivitate Salus* (1947), present him as someone wronged by victor's justice. Schmitt refused de-Nazification and was thus barred from returning to university teaching. The remaining decades of his long life nevertheless allowed him to exert a considerable influence over young German scholars of history and politics as well as a wide range of international thinkers, who disseminated his ideas on the Cold War and international politics. Although a non-person in anglophone academia, he continued to lecture in Francoist Spain, where the lectures that formed his late work *The Partisan* (1963) were first delivered. Yet, it would be seriously misleading to see his influence as enduring only in the remaining fascist states. Although his name was rarely mentioned, students of his work in political science, history and international relations (such as Raymond Aron, Hans Morgenthau, Reinhart Koselleck and Hannah Arendt) extended his influence across the modern social sciences. At the time of his death in 1985, Schmitt had become a revered thinker for both the political hard left and hard right, both of which shared his hostility to constitutional liberalism and the political and economic order that went with it. This response has only grown stronger in recent years.

The dark legacy of Schmitt's anti-Semitism

As anglophone scholars began to recover Schmitt's ideas from the 1970s onwards, a frisson of transgressive excitement was associated with someone who had come so close to one of the darkest manifestations of political power. This no doubt helped encourage many students bored by triumphalist liberalism or the collapse of 'really existing Marxism' to turn to his writings. For others, such as Stephen Holmes, Schmitt's legacy and teaching are fatally undermined by the enormous lapse of political judgement demonstrated by his engagement with Nazism (Holmes 1993). A debate has raged over whether Schmitt was merely an opportunistic lawyer who feigned Nazism for professional preferment and a quiet life, or whether he is someone whose ideas must be infected by their association with one of the vilest regimes in history with its legacy of murderous anti-Semitism. Perhaps even more than with Heidegger, whose philosophy is metaphysical and more remote from practical affairs, the question of whether Schmitt's writings are implicated in the evil of holocaust is a serious question. Surely someone who has shown such a failure of practical judgement can hardly be a guide to the failings of liberalism (Kelly 2005, p. 6).

However, many Schmitt scholars have dismissed simplistic denunciations of his work and legacy by showing how he was accused by the SS of not being a real Nazi and failing to demonstrate a commitment to racialist anti-Semitism (Bendersky 2014). Similarly, Schmitt personally did help Jewish scholars (such as Leo Strauss) and he had Jewish friends, albeit that they seem to have been abandoned during the Nazi period. After the war he also sustained a philosophical and theological correspondence with the Jewish theologian Jacob Taubes. All of this, along with an impatience with drawing simplistic moral judgements about those who had to live with the Nazi regime and not just read about it, somewhat limited the adverse effect of Schmitt's past on the appraisal of his work, as with Heidegger.

Yet the recent publication of Heidegger's *Black Notebooks*, Schmitt's *Glossarium* (a sort of commonplace book) and his diaries have all shown a more deeply problematic aspect of his attitude to Jews, as something that went beyond an ultra-traditionalist Johannine Catholic Christianity (see Ratzinger 2018). (Johannine Christianity gives a central place to the Gospel of John with its particularly hostile account of the Jewish authorities). In the case for the prosecution, Raphael Gross's detailed discussion of Schmitt's private intellectual world shows a person with deeply questionable animosities towards Jews, including those of his own association. These attitudes cast a darker shadow over his thought and legacy. Gross is careful to avoid the charge that Schmitt was a Nazi thinker in any formal sense, and he acknowledges that Schmitt would have had nothing but contempt for the biologically reductionist components of Nazi race theory. Yet, it remains the case that, in light of the substance and the language of the diaries, it is hard to find any way of describing Schmitt other than as an unrepentant anti-Semite. Gross continues:

> Without a doubt, Schmitt's many layered and deeply rooted antisemitism also intensified his alignment with Nazism in 1933 in an essential way. In 1932 it was not at all clear whether Schmitt would emerge as a radical National Socialist. But his antisemitism – we see this precisely in the diaries – was already very radical long before 1932; it was hatred, a daily obsession with what he considered the true enemy ... Against this backdrop, I find it difficult ... to imagine how contemporary political theory could profit from Schmitt's work. Continuing to assimilate and use ideas without an acknowledgement of the strong role antisemitism played in them means passing on elements of that same conceptual substance – albeit for the most part in encoded form. (Gross 2016, p. 111)

In this book I do not mean to celebrate the arguments of any of the thinkers discussed. So, in that sense, I could attempt to avoid Gross's charge. Yet, even adding Schmitt to the canon of international political thought undoubtedly gives some form of intellectual respectability to his thought, and thus risks the 'passing on of that conceptual substance'. In light of Gross's comprehensive indictment, I do not seek to explain away this dark legacy of Schmitt's life and thought. He was an anti-Semite and, whilst that does not follow logically from his conceptual distinctions and dichotomies, it is hard not to read many of them without hearing echoes of his anti-Semitism. Similarly, he may not have been a Nazi in an racial-ideological sense, but he was still an active member of the Nazi Party and remained active for longer than Heidegger. These facts need to be constantly borne in mind, whilst recognising at the same time that Schmitt raises important and complex challenges for both liberal legal and political philosophy and for international relations. These challenges do not disappear just because of his deeply flawed character. We do not gain greater insight into those arguments by downplaying the character of the author, just as we cannot understand them better by reducing their discussion to a moral judgement about the character of their author.

Anti-liberalism

Throughout Schmitt's career, one constant thread in his philosophical work and his career as a public lawyer was his critique of, and contempt for, liberalism as a political ideology, and liberal constitutionalism as a jurisprudential philosophy. This aspect of his thought has attracted adherents on the political left as much as the right, but it has also attracted the attention of political liberals themselves, because of its force and incisiveness. A number of his early works bring together both his jurisprudential and his political arguments and provide an important context for his subsequent major works *The Concept of the Political*, *The Nomos of the Earth* and *The Partisan*.

Bourgeois parliamentarism

As a public lawyer, Schmitt's understanding of liberalism is derived from an historical and sociological understanding of its key institutions in the practice of liberal constitutional states. He does not begin with philosophical speculations about the abstract moral foundations of liberalism. In his later speculations on Hobbes's philosophy, written during his fall from grace under the Nazis, Schmitt emphasises the methodological individualism of liberalism and therefore places Hobbes as one of its founding thinkers. Yet, Schmitt is generally sceptical and dismissive of the claims of morality as a foundation for law and political science. He begins his critique of liberal constitutionalism as part of his response to the 1919 Weimar Constitution with a focus on the central institutions of liberal politics. *The Crisis of Parliamentary Democracy* (1923) provides a forceful analysis and critique of the internal contradictions at the heart of liberal politics: he sums up the critique in a way that will be familiar to many conservative critics of parliamentary or congressional politics today:

> There are certainly not many people today who want to renounce the old liberal freedoms particularly freedom of speech and the press. But on the European continent there are not many more who believe that these freedoms still exist where they could endanger the real holders of power. And the smallest number still believe that just laws and the right politics can be achieved through newspaper articles, speeches at demonstrations, and parliamentary debates. But this is the very belief in parliament. If in the actual circumstances of parliamentary business, openness and discussion have become an empty and trivial formality,

> then parliament, as it developed in the nineteenth century, has also lost
> its previous foundation and meaning. (Schmitt 1988, p. 50)

The fundamental problem of parliamentarism is twofold: firstly, the claim to achieve democratic representation, and, secondly, the epistemic effectiveness of parliamentary politics in the process of policy- and lawmaking. Parliaments developed from being advisory councils to a sovereign monarch into an authoritative source of legislation. The challenge to them has grown since the 19th-century expansion of the franchise along democratic principles, such as equal representation and equal voice in legislation. Institutionalising these principles in any effective way is deeply problematic, because the possibility of direct inclusion of citizens has to give way to some form of representation. In turn, this opens the Rousseauean challenges around the general will being represented by a particular minority group (parliamentarians and ministers) forcing the majority to be free. The idea of democracy as 'an assertion of an identity between law and the peoples will' (Schmitt 1988, p. 35) is essential for the democratic legitimacy of legislation, but it presupposes a unitary concept of the people that can be said to have a single will.

Liberal parliamentarism is an institutional response to that democratic challenge. The general will or the authority of law and policy can be justified if it emerges from an institutional process that approximates free and uncorrupted democratic deliberation. Such a process is characterised by features such as the election of representatives, open public deliberation on the floor of Parliament, and the separation of powers between legislation (which requires careful deliberation) and the executive (which needs to be able to act promptly in the face of pressing political issues). A free press that reports these deliberations to the electorate allows them to hold the representative legislators to account. 'Parliament is accordingly the place in which particles of reason that are strewn unequally among human beings gather themselves and bring public power under control' (Schmitt 1988, p. 35). Schmitt clearly interprets liberal democracy as having an epistemic (or knowledge-generating) function, as well as a legitimating function, in a way that is similar to leading 19th-century defenders of liberal democracy, such as John Stuart Mill. Yet, for Schmitt, this liberal optimism masks the reality of parliamentary politics in modern states and exposes the weakness of liberalism as a basis of constitutional politics. His critique is obviously coloured by the difficulties of the early Weimar period, but it remains a familiar feature of realist political science and the critique of liberal democracy.

Liberal parliamentarism requires that individual voters are 'particles of reason', so that their pooling together and sorting into sets with shared views combines to reveal the truth about politics and law. Similarly, representatives within the parliamentary chambers are also individual 'particles of reason'. However, for Schmitt the reality of politics is that it has become distorted by economic interests and the emergence of political parties that coalesce around interest groups in society. Far from being a world of discrete individuals bearing their own partial share of the general will, the preferences and cognitions of individuals are now shaped by conflicting social and political interests, which configure public policy through bargaining and temporary coalition-forming. Similarly, the press, rather than being the 'tribunal of public opinion' (as thinkers such as Jeremy Bentham had hoped) has become just another vehicle through which party and sectional interests are combined and compete.

In the earlier 21st century, one might think that this realist account of parliamentary politics is actually familiar, and we should just abandon the hubris of liberal democracy and accept the institutions we have as they are – because, for all their manifest flaws, they are preferable to much else on offer. But Schmitt's argument is subtler than simply exposing the hollowed-out reality of contemporary parliamentary politics. For him, what it actually exposes is the way in which 'technology', by which he means the manipulation of interest and experience, has taken over political action. Manipulative politics allows expert practitioners to exploit institutional processes and rules to win in controlling legislation and policymaking. But, whilst game-playing can make for successful political actions (in terms of getting laws passed), it creates precisely the sort of scepticism and denigration of politics that populists criticise. And it raises questions about the legitimacy of all legislation that emerges from such factionalised politics. For Schmitt, this manipulative politics undermines political unity because it opens up deep fissures within political society, creating instability and insecurity, and undermines any idea of a public interest.

Dictatorship and decisionism

The essay on *Dictatorship* [1921] grew out of an earlier legal brief that Schmitt had written on the scope of emergency powers embodied in Article 48 of the 1919 Weimar Constitution – which conferred powers upon the Reich president to act in the case of an emergency, including the suspension of the constitution and rule of law. Schmitt's longer work is a history of the political idea of dictatorship in European political thought from the Roman law to the present. Unlike many of Schmitt's other works, it is not polemical, and it subordinates rhetorical flourishes to scholarly arguments. The main body of the text develops the distinction between the commissarial and sovereign conceptions of dictatorships (discussed below). In light of the subsequent collapse of the Weimar Republic in 1933, and fascist and later Nazi regimes operating as dictatorships from the 1920s through to 1945, the text is prescient and controversial. Yet, Schmitt's argument suggests that the concept of the dictator and dictatorial powers are actually central to constitutionalism and state theory in order to address the importance of emergencies. The concept of 'emergency', and who decides what it is and when it arises, is for Schmitt the central political challenge facing constitutionalism and the central defect in liberal thinking.

Liberal theory since the time of Locke had sought to constrain the arbitrary exercise of political power through the concept of law. Law specifies what it is permissible for individuals to do with their liberties, but, more importantly, it sets the limits of executive political power, in reaction to monarchical absolutism. Subsequent liberal theory developed and extended this legal limitation of the political through its emphasis on the separation of powers and the rule of law. In the context of the republican overthrow of the military-monarchical order of the Wilhelmine Reich following the end of World War I, the debate between constitutionalists and absolutists coincided with the division between the Lockean emphasis on freedom and the Hobbesian emphasis on order. Yet, Schmitt's argument is no mere preference for order and Hobbes over Locke and freedom. Rather, it is an account of the conceptual incoherence at the heart of liberal constitutionalism, because of its attempts to eradicate politics from constitutionalism and law.

The historical narrative of *Dictatorship* demonstrates that the idea of extra-constitutional powers has been recognised within conceptions of the state or political unit going back to the Roman Empire. *Commissarial* dictatorships refer to the specific powers conferred on a figure to suspend the constitution or regular functioning of political and legal power in order to defend that power against potentially overwhelming threats. This commonly arises in circumstances of civil war or protracted external war, where the normal functioning of legally constituted powers is confronted by exceptional challenges. Central to the idea of the commissarial dictator is the specific recognition of the sorts of emergency that the dictator's powers are required to address, and in consequence the circumstances in which those powers cease and return to the constitution.

> In practice [*in concreto*] the commissary dictatorship suspends the constitution in order to protect it – the very same one – in concrete form. The argument has been repeated ever since – first and foremost by Abraham Lincoln: when the body of the constitution is under threat, it must be safeguarded through a temporary suspension of the constitution. Dictatorship protects a specific constitution against an attack that threatens to abolish this constitution. (Schmitt 2014, p. 118)

This suspension of law and the constitution nevertheless remains part of the concrete reality of a legal system, because all legal systems presuppose the idea of a normal condition in a homogenous society in which it is valid. Exceptions from that normal condition require the powers needed to return to the normal condition. Consequently, the idea of an exception is central to (helps to define) the idea of a normal constitutional order. This entails that no normative system can be fully specified so that the law applies in all possible circumstances. There is always an element of decision about the implementation of any norm that cannot be specified by that norm. So formalistic accounts of legal validity, such as that of Hans Kelsen, leave out of the account the irreducibly political role within the law that determines the nature and scope of its implementation. That power is primarily exercised by judges in normal circumstances. Yet, at the most fundamental constitutional level, determining what counts as an emergency and what counts as 'normal' conditions can only be a political act, located outside the constitution in order to protect the constitution itself. This is what Schmitt means when he argues in *Political Theology* that 'the Sovereign is he who decides on the exception' (Schmitt 1988, p. 5).

In the constitutional debates over the scope of emergency powers, Schmitt also advances the more radical idea of a sovereign dictator. The sovereign dictator differs from the commissarial dictator because they are not confined to the protection of a specific constitution that must at some point be reinstated at the end of the emergency. The sovereign dictator draws their authority not from the terms of the actual constitution but from some future constitution that will come into effect:

> sovereign dictatorship ... does not *suspend* an existing constitution through a law based on the constitution – a constitutional law; rather it seeks to create conditions in which a constitution – a constitution that regards itself as the true one – is made possible. Therefore dictatorship does not appeal [for its justification] to an existing constitution, but one that is still to come. (Schmitt 2014, p. 119)

This might seem an abandonment of legality and the assertion of pure power, something that is captured in the negative connotation of dictatorship following the experience of the Nazis. But Schmitt insists that the idea can nevertheless be considered constitutionally valid, if it is exercised in respect of a constitutional power that is immanent in a foundational political power within society.

The theory of *Dictatorship* is central to Schmitt's critique of liberalism because it emphasises the primacy of politics, including the fundamental political act of deciding the exception to the constitution and rule of law in the face of emergencies. Doing so also decides the scope of the limits of constitutional powers over the attempts of liberalism to subordinate political power to regulation and the law. In asserting the primacy of the political over law, rights and private interests, Schmitt does not fall back on a crass realism of power politics. But, if the political is not merely power, what is it?

Political theology

The most contested and complex element of Schmitt's critique of liberalism concerns the status of political theology. He published a book entitled *Political Theology* (1922) and returned to the subject again towards the end of his life. In the early work, which contributes to his account of sovereignty, he asserts that '[a]ll significant concepts of the modern theory of the state are secularised theological concepts' (Schmitt 1988, p. 36) but he leaves this idea unexplained. As an historical claim, it has an obvious appeal. It draws attention to the problem of secularisation (unlinking from a religious basis) as the undermining of the motivational power of those theory of the state concepts. It is also worth debating his proposition as an explanatory historical thesis. Yet, his claim does not have an obvious normative force. It does not entail that we should return to those religious theological premises, but neither does it clearly state that we can rethink politics without acknowledging that source. He does not offer a theological reading of those political concepts in the way that Hobbes or some contemporary political theologians do (O'Donovan 1996). It is important also to emphasise that Schmitt never claims to be a Catholic political theorist, unlike the French philosopher Jacques Maritain (who influenced papal policies). Nor does he write from a Catholic political perspective in his major writings, despite his early association with the Catholic Centre Party in the early years of Weimar. Schmitt's own relationship to Roman Catholicism is highly particularistic (Mehring 2017) and not much can be inferred from it. Despite this ambiguity, the idea of Schmitt's theory as a political theology has gained much prominence, especially following the work of Heinrich Meier (1995; 1998).

Central to Meier's thesis is a claim about the form of Schmitt's theory and not its confessional content. The contrast between a political theologian and political philosopher concerns the fundamental approach to the idea of truth and the task of the theorist. The philosopher, as represented by the character of Socrates, seeks human wisdom in the world through the exercise of critical reason. All knowledge claims are subject to this critical challenge. In consequence, knowledge and wisdom are hard to come by, except in the negative sense of knowing the limitations of reason and the elusiveness of truth. The political theologian starts with the priority of faith in a revealed truth and their task is to defend and explicate that truth, and to criticise beliefs opposed to it. In contrast to the philosopher's ideal, a political theologian is always engaged within the struggle of truth for acceptance. This has an important impact on the way in which theoretical arguments are to be understood. The open quest for knowledge through enlightenment, debate and deliberation is only going to be a qualified and limited good for the political theologian, since it can prove useful to the dissemination of truth. But the discovery made by this method and its authority is always qualified. A political theologian will always be sceptical and dismissive of liberal philosophers with conducting an impartial quest for the truth. For the political theologian, the truth is a given, and its authority is independent of the individual reason and mind.

This reading of Schmitt helps explain his approach to liberal argument, which is one of dismissal and derision, but it also explains his own non-liberal conservatism. Schmitt is not merely a liberal conservative with a scepticism about rapid change (like Edmund Burke). He is, as he constantly claims, more in sympathy with Catholic reactionaries such as Louis de Bonald (a philosopher counter-revolutionary during the French Revolution), Juan Donoso Cortés (a 19th-century Spanish aristocrat who defended dictatorship) and Joseph de Maistre (a defender of monarchy as divinely sanctioned). These latter writers all defend revealed truth and its concrete instantiation within the Roman Catholic Church in the face of individualism and liberalism following the French Revolution. The truth of revelation is already there and does not need explication, but the opponents of that truth need to be politically confronted and their ideas defeated, by whatever means.

As a conservative, Schmitt opposes the optimism and progressivism of liberalism. For him, the idea of history as progressive is one of the liberal doctrines that is most subject to challenge from a political-theological perspective. For liberals (from Hegel through Mill to Stephen Pinker), history is the unfolding of human progress and enlightenment in opposition to religion and superstition. But for Schmitt this is just hubris. History is simply a period of change and passing away. It has no purpose or end, and no triumph of any particular political order can be inferred from it. In this respect, Schmitt's philosophy of history is similar to that of post-Augustinian Christianity. The truth of revelation is complete and fulfilled and secular history is simply the period of change preceding the second coming or Parousia. He emphasises this interpretation of his thought by alluding to the character of the Katechon (from 2 Thessalonians 2). The Katechon (restrainer) is a figure who emerges to preserve the Christian age by challenging those forces that seek to accelerate the end of time through the offer of utopianism. The Katechon struggles with the Antichrist as a force that seeks to usurp Christ's role as arbiter of the end of time. Whether Schmitt genuinely believed what underlies this mystical and apocalyptic language, it does serve as a metaphor that makes sense of an anti-teleological view of history, with its frequent but dangerous and violent attempts to bring it to an end in a utopian final political order. The obvious candidate for the 'end of history' in Schmitt's lifetime was that offered by Bolshevik revolution, but Schmitt also saw this threat of a dystopian 'end of history' as being implicit in the liberal faith in progress. As an extended metaphor for the challenge of history in liberal modernity, political theology and the recovery of secularised theological concepts are essential to understand the character and tragic risks of utopian schemes. Progress is the enemy in political theology and progress is a permanent danger. The apocalyptic language of the Antichrist is perhaps the only way of recovering the violence and evil that is unleashed by revolution, whether that be in 1789 or 1917 – liberalism or Bolshevism.

The Concept of the Political

Central to Schmitt's critique of liberal politics is his assertion of the fundamental role of political decisions: something that is often described as 'decisionism'.

He does not want to replace the liberal rule of law and rights with pure power, but that leaves open the question of what 'the political' is, if not unrestricted power and the pursuit of interest. How do we make sense of ideas such as sovereignty in a world in which traditional contract theories or theories of popular sovereignty are shown to be self-defeating? It is in answer to this question that he develops his famous argument about the concept of the political.

Friends and enemies

Adjectival nouns such as 'the political' are a scourge of academic prose – the political what? But, for Schmitt, the choice is important and specific. He begins his important short work *The Concept of the Political* (1932) by distinguishing between the political and the state. The state is an institutional structure that has emerged in European history, but it is not definitive of the political, although it may well be the site for most political action. The substance of that political action is the usual source of accounts of the political, whereby politics is reduced to something else such as class interests, economic power, national culture, or in the contemporary world gender or other identity categories. For Schmitt, the challenge of liberalism is its reduction of politics to something more important, which in turn creates the weaknesses of liberal constitutions in recognising and confronting existential challenges. The question of 'the political' arises in the context of what Schmitt calls an age of neutralisation, that is, an age in which an underlying conceptual scheme is giving way to a new one, in which important concepts become detached from their origins. This is most obviously the case with respect to secularisation, which undercuts the foundations of concepts of political authority and order.

However, the issue is not simply the rise of secularisation but rather the competition between different alternative conceptual schemes for making sense of human experience. These might be 'morality', 'economy' or 'technology', by which Schmitt thinks of the recasting of fundamental authority in terms of technocratic and scientific domination and elitism. The analysis of bourgeois parliamentarism shows how liberal parliamentary politics is consumed by economics and morality. Economic interests both fuel liberal globalisation and the class conflict theories that are at the heart of Marxism and social democracy. Moralism is the implication of the individualist reductionism of liberalism, translating every struggle into a conflict of individual rights. Ultimately, this must diminish political power and relationships, by creating conflicts between individuals with rights and state power that seeks to curtail those rights. For Schmitt, liberalism tends to collapse into libertarianism, with its identification of the state as the greatest threat to individual freedom and standing.

In contrast to this tendency to economic or moral reductionism, Schmitt offers a non-reductive account of the relationship of the political in terms of the 'friend/enemy' distinction: 'The specific political distinction to which political actions and motives can be reduced is that between friend and enemy' (Schmitt 1996, p. 25). The distinction is not a definition and it remains open to others to challenge his identification of politics with another criterion. But it is offered as a criterion for identifying the specifically political features of human experience and for contrasting those with others, in the same way that the opposition between good and evil provides the ultimate criteria in the moral sphere or mode of experience, or the opposition of beauty and ugliness operates in aesthetics. In this respect the political appears as one criterion amongst many, and Schmitt even concedes that it can manifest itself with respect to the substance of economics or art or morality. Yet there remains something distinctive about the political, in that its objective autonomy 'becomes evident by virtue of its being able to treat, distinguish, and comprehend the friend-enemy antithesis independently of other antitheses' (Schmitt 1996, p. 27). It is important not to be misled by this into thinking that Schmitt is merely offering a further distinction to add to those of good versus evil, or beautiful versus ugly, so that one could subordinate the political to the moral. For Schmitt, the challenge of liberalism or romanticism (with its aesthetic view of the world) is not that it makes a different philosophical choice but that it denies the political altogether, or tries to discipline it out of existence with moral constraints and legal regulations. The priority of the political is boldly asserted over other such distinctions on the grounds of the intensity of the friend versus enemy distinction:

> The political is the most intense and extreme antagonism, and every concrete antagonism becomes that much more political the closer it approaches the most extreme point, that of the friend-enemy grouping. (Schmitt 1996, p. 29)
>
> ... The friend, enemy ... concepts receive their real meaning precisely because they refer to the real possibility of physical killing. War follows from enmity. War is the existential negation of the enemy. It is the most extreme consequence of enmity. It does not have to be common, normal, something ideal, or desirable. But it must nevertheless remain a real possibility for as long as the concept of enmity remains valid. (Schmitt 1996, p. 33)

The priority of the political is that it is existential and it threatens the possibility of killing and not just violent death. No other distinction has this priority. For instance, once economic competition develops to the point of the threat of killing, it has ceased to be economic and has become political. The defence of trade, markets or resources is no longer an economic matter if it becomes the basis of a friend/enemy opposition. The same argument applies to religion. Once a faith turns the distinction between the elect and the non-elect, Christian and non-Christian, damned and saved, into one of mortal enmity, it ceases to be religious and theological but is political. It is precisely the recognition of this transition that led to the subordination of questions of faith to the claims of the political state following the European wars of religion.

Although the threat of war and killing is potential and not always actual, echoing Hobbes's account of the state of nature, Schmitt is clear to distinguish his dichotomous friend/enemy opposition from the Hegelian dialectical opposition between the master and slave, which results in an overcoming of negation in a higher mode of being and experience. The struggle with enemies is not a metaphor for identity formation: it is not part of a dialectical process leading to reconciliation. For Schmitt, the threat of war and the requirement of killing one's enemy is not a philosophical dialectic of history. It is an existential opposition that leads nowhere, beyond the defeat of one's enemy or the enemy's triumph. Schmitt rejects historical teleology and the friend/enemy distinction is not an attempt to explain historical political change, although relationships of enmity will certainly be part of descriptive history.

Having identified the relationship of friend/enemy, Schmitt devotes much of *The Concept of the Political* to explaining the precise significance of the distinction. As Gabriella Slomp (2009) points out, there is little discussion of the concept of friendship, which is an irreducible part of the distinction, despite the fact that friendship has been central to understanding political society from the time of Cicero. For Schmitt, though, the relation of political friendship is something that has to be inferred from that of political enmity. It is, however, clear that the relationship distinguishes the internal perspective (friends) from the external (enemies). Consequently, Schmitt gives a very specific and public account of the relationship of enmity. As part of his rejection of the reductionist individualism of liberalism, he denies that enmity is a psychological relationship between individuals. Nor is it reducible to the economic category of competitor in market relations. 'The enemy is not merely any competitor or just any partner in a conflict in general. He is not the private adversary whom one hates' (Schmitt 1996, p. 28). It might well be the case that feelings of hatred follow from the relationship of enmity, but it is not essential to that relationship. Nor does it follow that hatred is always associated with enmity. For all the examples of hatred of the enemy that is found in accounts of the war against Japan, or by veterans of Vietnam, there are many examples of respect for the enemy in even the most brutal and bloody battles of World War I. The enemy is a distinctly public category, that Schmitt identifies using a Latin distinction between *hostis* and *imicus*. The *hostis* is an adversary with whom one can face mortal struggle without the feeling of hatred; the *imicus* is a hated and personal adversary. Whilst it is difficult to keep these ideas apart in the human psyche, it is easier to see distinction empirically, especially when the relationship is distinguished from morality with its necessity of characterising the friend as good and the enemy as evil. Indeed, for Schmitt it is one of the achievements of the modern idea of politics that it can separate itself from this sort of moral reductionism.

The state and war

Although the concept of the political is prior to the idea of the state, the state is the primary vehicle through which that relationship is realised in the world. Much of *The Concept of the Political* is a continuation of Schmitt's critique of theories and ideologies that weaken the state by denying the distinction between friend and enemy, and failing to see the state as the place within which friendship is defined through confrontation with external enemies. The most important consequence of this insight is that it challenges the liberal constitutional prejudice that the state or political power is the enemy that needs to be contained by the rule of law or by the internal balance of factions within a liberal party system. As these threats are primarily ideological creations of liberals, or of Marxists (with their conception of class conflict), the primary political task is that of building a unity around a concrete version of the friend/enemy distinction by holding to the irreducibility of this relationship as an existential challenge for a political community. In this respect, identification of an external enemy is a unifying feature of a community as a political community. By this Schmitt does not mean that enmity with the French is essential or definitional for being British or German. But he does mean that having a mortal external opponent is what makes a community into a political community. And, where that political community has achieved statehood, it is what sustains it as a community.

For this reason, Schmitt (like Hobbes) is sympathetic to authoritarian and unified government. It is also why he is so critical of pluralism as a threat to, or denial of, the state. In a critique of the English pluralists G.D.H. Cole and Harold Laski, Schmitt argues that pluralist theories do not have a theory of the state because they reduce the political community to a set of overlapping plural communities with conflicting claims to authority. Hence, they deny the idea of unitary political authority. Cole and Laski saw the primary political threat as coming from the modern authoritarian state, as opposed to an external enemy. But in so doing they undermined the possibility of an ordered arbitration of the claims of these different communities, which is to invite chaos and disorder. At its worst, this disorder can result in civil war, a concept that Schmitt does not like – because war ought to be an extension of politics, and therefore presuppose a state or a new emergent state distinguishing itself through the political criterion of friendship and enmity. By contrast, a civil war is a 'dissolution of the state as a political entity' (Schmitt 1996, p. 46). The problem of pluralism is not simply theoretical incoherence but political risk, because a pluralist state would be subject to constant external threat without having the coherence needed to defend and assert itself.

The demand for unitary decision and unity in the community at the heart of a political theory of the state manifests itself clearly in the political decision to identify *domestic enemies* of the friendship that binds a state together as a political community. This fundamental power of decision is obscured by pluralist and liberal theories, which see the political threat in the state itself. By contrast, Schmitt concludes that the fundamental political criterion of friend/enemy must underlie a constitution in order to answer the fundamental question of when an exception to constitutional rule arises and what counts as an emergency. The criterion of the political explains the priority of that sovereign decision, and also gives it content within a particular political community. Here the relationship identifies the nature, boundary and membership of the political community, or who is subject to defence through the use of violence and who is the enemy that must be confronted through the use of violence and war.

Schmitt's *The Concept of the Political* is a critique of political pluralism as an account of the state and of domestic politics (to the extent that he argues pluralist theories do not really have a theory of the state). But, whilst he opposes pluralism within the political community or state, he defends pluralism as characteristic of international relations. This is in contrast to liberalism, which defends pluralism at the state level but favours universalism at the level of the international and global. In order for there to be political friends, there cannot be permanent enemies within a state and consequently there must be unity. But, in order for such unity to exist, there must be external enemies, and therefore at least one other political community. Pluralism at the international level is a consequence of the concept of the political. The logic of the state system is a world of particular states or international pluralism. This necessity of international enmity is what is misunderstood by pacifists following World War I and the attempts of the League of Nations to eradicate war between nations in favour of a humanitarian world order. The termination of a war between different states would not lead to world peace but to a peculiar kind of war:

> Humanity as such cannot wage war because it has no enemy, at least on this planet. The concept of humanity excludes the concept of the enemy, because the enemy does not cease to be a human being – and hence there is no specific differentiation in that concept. That wars are waged in the name of humanity is not a contradiction of the simple truth: quite the contrary, it has an especially intensive political meaning. When a state fights its political enemy in the name of humanity, it is not a war for the sake of humanity, but a war wherein a particular state seeks to usurp a universal concept against its military opponent. At the expense of its opponent it tries to identify itself with humanity in the same way as one can misuse peace, justice, progress, and civilisation in order to claim these as one's own and to deny the same to the enemy. (Schmitt 1996, p. 54)

The argument here is twofold. In practice, a war for humanity would not be between the universal category of humanity and its enemy but merely a disguised form of regular warfare, with a political community using the category of humanity to demonise its enemy. Global or humanitarian wars are just a cover for the imperial ambitions of particularly strong states. Schmitt notes that imperial expansion has been defended in terms of defending humanitarian or universal or civilisational values from the time of the Romans. However, the use of the universal category of humanity changes the character of the war, precisely by demonising the enemy, who by definition cannot now be 'human' and does not merit the respect of fellow human adversaries. This dehumanisation of the enemy raises the prospect of the wars of annihilation that characterised imperial expansion in North and South America and more recently Africa, as well as the European wars of religion.

Whilst the book is primarily focused on the need to sustain a strong and decisive conception of the state, and to defend it from internal weakness of the sort that blighted the Weimar Constitution, it concludes with a pessimistic view of international politics and the rise of a new imperialism, emerging under the guise of liberal economic globalisation. The themes of this pessimism came to form the basis of his last major works written following his fall from grace with the Nazis after 1936 and in the face of Nazism's ultimate defeat by the Allied powers, especially the United States and the USSR. These replaced the old imperial European great powers in shaping a new world order, or what Schmitt describes as a new nomos of the earth.

The Nomos of the Earth and International Law

The Nomos of the Earth in the International Law of the Jus Publicum Europaeum was written between 1942 and 1945 (nomos is an ancient Greek term for a body of law or convention governing human behaviour). Schmitt drew on material on the concept of Großraum (literally 'great spaces') written in the late 1930s and on the discriminating concept of war. His book was published in 1950 at the height of the Cold War. It can be seen as a continuation of the *Concept of the Political* since it does not repudiate the friend/enemy criterion of politics. Yet, it is also a development of his ideas in the face of the continuing challenge of universalism (in the form of international law) and the new ideological confrontation of the capitalist versus the communist world. This polarity threatens the stability of enmity as focusing on an adversary, as opposed to a hated opponent. Schmitt makes a change of style or methodology in the face of the abstract universalism that was shaping the new liberal world order, now placing emphasis on the idea of a 'concrete order' as the site of theorising international law. This brings out his stress on territoriality and situatedness in understanding the idea of a concrete order that alone makes sense of the concept of law. Schmitt remains a jurist and, whilst he is a critic of the direction of modern international law, he is not a crude sceptic, nor even a positivist who argues that without a legislator there is no law. That said, the peculiarity of international law only works within a domain of international politics that must have some boundaries between those within and those without. The book is an attempt to situate the idea of international law within a concrete order, and to analyse the challenges that arise from the transformation of that order – which Schmitt thinks are exemplified by the retreat of the European state system, which he describes as the *jus publicum Europaeum*.

Territoriality and conquest and law

The Nomos of the Earth is a form of history of the idea of an international or global law and the conception of order that it emerges from. It is a 'form' of history because Schmitt is offering an interpretation of concept formation, one that ranges widely over sources and subject fields in a way that a traditional history of a legal or political concepts would find challenging. His intention is to problematise the perspective that sees law either solely as the authoritative norms of a sovereign lawgiver or (as in natural law) as the implications of a moral or ethical conception of human nature. In a striking statement he claims:

> the earth is bound to law in three ways. She contains law within herself, as a reward of labour; she manifests law upon herself, as fixed boundaries; and she sustains law above herself, as a public sign of order. (Schmitt 2006, p. 42)

His history begins with a controversial account of the meaning of the Greek term *nomos*. This is usually interpreted as law or convention, in contrast to the rival idea of *physis* as nature. For Schmitt, the idea is however connected to the 'taking' or appropriation of land in a way that reinforces his claim about the earth containing law within itself: 'land appropriation [is] the primeval act in founding law' (Schmitt 2006, p. 45). This founding act has an internal and an external perspective: firstly, it creates claims of ownership with attendant ideas of distribution over how much an appropriative act can claim, and on what terms against whom within a community. This claim is originally a communal one, even if the subsequent distribution is individualised. Individual claims always follow from a prior communal claim.

This is an interesting inversion of the Lockean account of colonial acquisition. For Schmitt, the English settler could only 'take' land in North America because the English power had defined the site of taking as *terra nullius*. Externally, the community's act of appropriation makes claims about what is free to be appropriated and what is owned, against those who make rival claims. Appropriation or taking brings with it ideas of what land can be acquired, owned and ordered. A history of international law is therefore ultimately a history of land appropriations within which this fundamental source of law is based, and in which conceptions of territoriality and geography are essential and not accidental. Order or nomos is therefore always territorially bounded, and international law develops from the problems of determining boundaries and overlapping claims amongst appropriator jurisdictions. It also presupposes those outside of these orders, who are within the realm open to taking, or who place limitation on takings. It is, however, the dawn of modernity, exemplified in this case by the discovery of the New World of the Americas and the practical demonstration that the world was a globe, which raised the significance of a territorially limited world.

The globe as a potential challenge to order emerges in a number of ways. Firstly, Schmitt draws attention to the idea of *rayas* as divisional lines between Portugal and Spain arbitrated by Pope Alexander VI, marking the respective spheres of influence for colonial expansion. These are examples of emerging law or order within a global context. Similarly, the Anglo-French conception of amity lines is also raised as an example to the territorially bounded nature of interstate jurisdiction. This is the idea that the terms of treaties between such powers holds within Europe but not necessarily beyond it, so that conflict between these European powers in 'the Indies' does not necessarily constitute a treaty breach between them.

Secondly, Schmitt raises the challenge posed by the sea as a natural boundary to territorial order and a realm within which unbounded claims to right and competence are exercised. The contrast between land and sea powers is as old as that between Athens and Sparta, but it remains a persistent preoccupation for Schmitt, since it is linked to the development of universalist or globalist claims on the part of mercantilist sea-based powers.

Thirdly, Schmitt draws attention to the rise of the concept of humanity as a juridical notion in the 'just war' theory of the Renaissance thinker Francisco de Vitoria. The concept accommodated natives or indigenous peoples whose status could not be derived from their juridical or theological standing within the Order of the European colonialist states. From Vitoria onward, ethical significance was derived from being part of the created order even prior to membership of Christendom through baptism. These ideas of taking/occupation, just war and the boundlessness of obligation that arose from the law of the sea shaped the development of international law amongst the European powers and informed the writings of the political theorists of the early modern period. They create the understanding of international order embodied within the *jus publicum Europaeum*.

The crisis of the *jus publicum Europaeum*

The key argument in *Nomos of the Earth* is an account of the *jus publicum Europaeum* as an idea of the international public law for the European states of the Westphalian order. The main features here are familiar from previous thinkers, with Schmitt offering careful, if sometimes controversial, readings of the ideas of Grotius, Pufendorf, Locke and Rousseau as theorists who articulated the elements of the European order that lasted from the mid-17th century to the late 19th century. This order emerged from the Thirty Years War and withstood the challenge of the French Revolutionary wars in the early 19th century. Central to this world was the equal recognition of the claim to sovereignty amongst the major European powers, and the transformation of war as a policy tool amongst those powers for settling disputes between sovereigns. It is in this context that some of the elements of the criterion of the political emerge, such as the 'bracketing of war' or the distinction of war as a legitimate power of states exercised under commonly understood rules, and the understanding of enmity as adversarial rather than an opposition of hatred. Here, Schmitt's thought clearly reflects his reading of Clausewitz on the regulation and professionalisation of war as an extension of policy. Once again, the contrast between the territorially contiguous land powers and the sea power of Great Britain plays an important part in the narrative. The law of war and its international regulation are most appropriate to the land powers and the conduct of their conflicts, because these presuppose spatial limitation and territoriality – whereas the sea power and the domain of the sea do not recognise the same idea of territorial exclusivity, and the constraint that this places on jurisdiction.

The central thesis of Schmitt's argument is that international law grew as the public law of the European state system and the great powers that sustained it. Indeed, it was precisely in this capacity as a guarantor of territoriality and the arbiter of changes to borders following wars that the idea of the great powers emerged 'as the strongest participants in this common spatial order' (Schmitt 2006, p. 190). Great power status is not only a matter of power but the end or purpose to which this is exercised in sustaining a common territorial order from which that power emanates.

The substance of the *jus publicum Europaeum* is concerned with the matter of war, with territorial change and acquisition and with the continuity of regimes and the matter of succession. Whilst the primary context for this law is the European continental land mass, the nomos of the *jus publicum Europaeum* extended beyond the geographical boundaries of Europe into the space of European colonies. These were understood as effectively extensions of European territoriality and subject to the same norms that applied within this peculiarly European family of nations, with its set of related but rivalrous great powers.

The challenge for the *jus publicum Europaeum* arises when this law is detached from its territorial context and abstracted into an international law that no longer relates to the understanding of European civilisation and culture. The central claim of *The Nomos of the Earth* is that international law is always the law of some geographically limited and territorially bound order; therefore, there is no completely abstract international law. Any new 'nomos of the earth' must be that of some new emerging order and Schmitt sees this in the displacement of 'Europe' by the United States:

The first long shadow that fell upon the *jus publicum Europaeum* came from the West. The first characteristic indications became visible with the growing power of the United States, which could not decide between *isolation* behind a line separating itself from Europe and a global, universalist-humanitarian *interventionism*. (Schmitt 2006, p. 227)

This detachment begins with the rise and assertion of United States power with the 1823 Monroe Doctrine and continued with the U.S. recognition of the Congo Society's flag in 1884 and therefore a new state on African soil. The Monroe Doctrine asserted a sphere of influence – the western hemisphere – within which the United States would not tolerate any further extension of European wars and colonial conquests there. On one level this was an act of isolation from the wars of the 'Old World' and led to a strong tradition of political isolationism in U.S. politics. Yet, at the same time, according to Schmitt, it was an assertion of U.S. power in the world by marking its own sphere of influence within an entire hemisphere (going well beyond the immediate borders of the USA), which it regarded as its own peculiar responsibility. In so doing, Secretary of State James Monroe was imposing a clear limit on the scope of the *jus publicum Europaeum* as a source of international law or a nomos of the earth.

The second issue was part of a complex discussion of the division of the Congo Basin in the 1880s by the European great powers and Belgium's claim to sovereign acquisition. By recognising the claim of one of the colonial societies as a new state, the U.S. was ignoring the claims of the *jus publicum Europaeum* over the territorial claims and annexations of European powers. The American intervention and its unilateral act of recognition defined a capacity to set boundaries on the European powers. It was not simply a prelude for the new assertiveness of the U.S. on the world stage but a particular assertiveness that is conflicted between universalism and isolationism: something that still characterises U.S. foreign policy today (Kagen 2018). The challenge of universalism is most explicit in the idea of a discriminating concept of war and global legalism, and the challenge of isolationism behind the Monroe Doctrine and the division of the world into global spheres of influence underlies Schmitt's idea of the Großraum (or global blocs).

The discriminating concept of war

Central to the idea of the *jus publicum Europaeum* was the idea of 'bracketing war' and its regulation together. Schmitt characterises this process without recourse to moral conceptions and he is dismissive of the moralisation of war – as we have seen in his earlier account of territorial conquest and the claims of indigenous Americans under Vitoria as 'humans'. The concept of *jus* is a primarily juridical notion, even for Aquinas and the Thomists. Therefore, it needs to be distinguished from the all-encompassing rise of morality following the individualistic turn of modern natural law, exemplified by Locke's theory of the morality of war as a punitive power derived from individual rights. Yet, the moral regulation of war is often claimed as one of the highest achievements of international liberalism, as exemplified by the Nuremburg Tribunals (1945–1946), and their predecessors following World War I.

Schmitt's preoccupation with attacking the aspiration to legally regulate war and to criminalise the idea of 'aggressive' war is coloured in the eyes of his critics by his own experience, not least because it also appears in a brief he wrote in detention following the defeat of Nazism. 'The International Crime of War in Its Particularity As Opposed to War Crimes' (Schmitt 2014) was written in response to Justice Robert Jackson, the chief prosecutor for the U.S. during the Nuremburg Trials. Schmitt particularly argued that no crime can deserve a punishment when it was not a crime at the time the act took place (*nulla crimen, nulla poena sine lege*), and this and his broader brief remain serious arguments with respect to the legitimacy of subsequent war crimes trials.

Schmitt begins his account of the law of war within the idea of the *jus publicum Europaeum* as he understood it. The idea of war as a regulated activity grew up within the Westphalian state system following the European wars of religion in the 17th and 18th centuries. Schmitt regarded these wars as the archetype of moral wars in which the enemy was not a mere *hostis* (or adversary) but an *inimicus* (the subject of hatred), concepts that were also central in his account of the *political*. Essential to this idea of enmity, and to the modern legal regulation of war, is that of a military enemy as an authorised adversary, exercising the right of states to pursue war. The concept of the *political* is thus projected outwards to the international realm because the enemy is an external threat to the political claims of a state. Schmitt is clearly drawing on the Clausewitzian idea of war as an extension of the political, or a technical power of states to pursue their policy agendas. War is therefore a defining feature of state power in the *jus publicum Europaeum* and it is to be contrasted with the ideological and political wars of religion that shaped the Reformation period. For the opponents in those conflicts, the enemy was absolute: there could be no settlement between Catholic or Protestant, or between both creeds and the Anabaptist revolutionaries. One side could only win by converting or annihilating the enemy. In both cases, the key issue is not defeat, after which an enemy can go home, but destruction, after which they cease to exist. The moralisation of war imposes the concepts of good and evil on enemies and this turns that political relationship back into an existential relationship of victory or annihilation.

Whether Schmitt is right about 18th-century wars as professionalised extensions of political powers, he certainly claims that the regulation of war is of a different order to claims about good and evil. Of course, war can introduce great evils, especially as technology advances. According to Schmitt, this is what led to international regulations amongst the European powers of certain kinds of technologies, such as explosive bullets or flat-headed bullets known as 'dum-dums' that create more grievous wounds. Similarly, the conduct of war can result in breaches of the standards of military behaviour that are generally accepted, such as the torture or summary execution of prisoners. These issues of *jus in bello* are again regulated by interstate agreements such as the Hague Conventions. But the crucial feature of these *jus in bello* cases is that they fall to the state to enforce and prosecute. This does indeed happen as shown by the United States' trial of William Calley for the Mai Lai massacre in Vietnam, or prosecutions of British soldiers for breaches of laws of war following the second Gulf War.

What is not captured here is the idea central to modern 'just war' theory of the *jus ad bellum* or sanctions against the crime of war itself. For Schmitt, this is an incoherent notion that has its roots only in the victor's moral judgement of their opponents following World War I, and it has much to do with the fundamental flaw of the Versailles Treaty that followed the armistice. If war is a legitimate Clausewitzian extension of state power, then it is not a moral notion, and its onset cannot be considered unjust without a globally accepted conception of justice. This is precisely what Schmitt rejects as a matter of fact in the case of the crime of aggressive war. No such crime was accepted by the parties to World War I or II and, consequently, whatever else one might think of the Nazi leadership (a subject on which Schmitt is remarkably quiet), they were not in that case in breach of the law. Justice Jackson was acutely aware of this problem and sought to locate the relevant crime in international agreements such as the Geneva Protocols, the Versailles Treaty and the Kellogg–Briand Pact of 1928. Schmitt argued that the latter contained so many qualifications and contradicted so many provisions of other treaties that it could not be considered an authoritative source of law.

But Schmitt's argument is more than just that there was no agreed law against waging a war of aggression. For him, the very idea is incoherent and dangerous because it would eradicate the idea of a pluralised international domain, such as the state system that underlay the *jus publicum Europaeum*. The criminalisation of war would entail the eradication of a plurality of political communities. They would instead be subject to an order that could legislate against war and punish crimes under that order. Such an entity would be more than the loose federation of the League of Nations or the United Nations – it would be a single political community but one without the fundamental features of a political community, namely radical difference, and enmity as hostility. It would be an inhuman Manichean world of two fundamental categories of person, namely the good and the evil. This echoes Schmitt's concern with the claims of Bolshevik class war as a reintroduction of religious war by other means. The liberal aspiration to eradicate war in this way unmasks the hidden millenarianism of liberalism as an alternative source of the end of history.

Schmitt's argument might seem rather exaggerated, but the argument is illustrated by the fate of neutrality in the new discriminating concept of war. If an act of war is aggressive (and therefore by its nature unjust), what possible grounds could there be for asserting neutrality? One might plead poverty as a poor country, but could one not have a right of neutrality on the issue? If international relations becomes the domain of good and evil, then there can be no principled arguments for toleration or containment of regimes, as George Kennan claimed with respect to the USSR. There must always be the potential to confront and defeat wrong and evil. There must always be an authority to whom one can appeal for a judgement of when a war is aggressive – after all, hardly any state, even the Nazi state, claims not to be defending something in having recourse to war; aggression is always a matter of perspective. In medieval Europe, that power was potentially the authority of the papacy. And in the *jus publicum Europaeum* that power was the consensus of the major European powers. But, with the collapse of that order through the rise of the global liberalism, who is the relevant authority?

Where could that new authority or nomos possibly reside? One possible answer is in the United Nations as a potential international federation or (to its critics) a global superstate. Yet, Schmitt's point is not simply to worry about the United Nations as a potential liberal global superstate but rather that such institutions fail to achieve global pacificism. Instead they actually become a mask for enmity and conflict, just as the modern state of the Weimar Constitution was a plaything of economic and social conflict between classes and factions. Conflict is an ineradicable feature of human experience and central to that is conflict between organised groups, which is characterised as war. To overcome that conflict, human beings would need to become different to what they are. This potentially limitless remaking of humanity is what lies at the heart of liberalism, at least according to Schmitt. In this it usurps religion, but without the disciplining function that religion has. For Schmitt, the challenge for the future in seeking a new nomos of the earth is avoiding reincurring the experience of the European wars of religion.

Großraum and the new nomos of the earth?

The concept of Großraum has an ambiguous role in Schmitt's late thinking on international order, not least because it was used in the late 1930s by Schmitt to give a legal framework for Hitler's expansionism in Europe in the run-up to World War II (Schmitt 2011). But even in this context it should not be confused with superficially similar concepts such as *Lebensraum* (literally 'living room') which played a role in Hitler's racialist theory, and which the Nazis did not derive from Schmitt. Schmitt's Großraum means the idea of a greater space (an extended territory) in which a dominant power exercises an authority beyond that of regular sovereignty over smaller states, without at the same time fully denying the sovereignty of those states. In the closest that Schmitt offers to a definition, in *Nomos of the Earth* he writes:

The territorial status of the controlled state is not changed if its territory is transformed by the controlling state. However, the controlled state's territory is absorbed into the spatial sphere of the controlling state and its special interests, i.e. into its spatial sovereignty. The external, emptied space of the controlled state's territorial sovereignty remains inviolate, but the material content of this sovereignty is changed by the guarantees of the controlling power's economic Großraum. (Schmitt 2006, p. 252)

The core idea is of a major power exercising a veto over the exercise of the sovereign powers of a minor state in its proximity (somewhat like the Chinese imperial concept of suzerainty). So it is a political constraint on the exercise of the legal sovereign power of that state, rather than a legal denial of that sovereignty. Originally this was a feature of the great power order of the *jus publicum Europaeum*, but it was transformed by the exercise of the Monroe Doctrine of 1823. That greatly expanded a traditional conception of local concerns into the idea of a hemispheric exclusion of the 'Old World' from the Americas.

From a defensive viewpoint, the primary drivers for the extension of Großraum thinking was the expansion of economic interests with trade and economic development. The scope of a major state's interests extended beyond those of territoriality and included the rights of succession and government stability of neighbouring states, as well as access to markets, sources of supply and trade routes. With industrialisation in the 19th century, the control over and ownership of international capital in rail networks, access to river ports and ownership of natural resources central to new heavy industry all extended the concerns of state interest beyond geography as a source of boundaries and borders. Economics moved from a private matter into a central part of state relations and became a source of conflict. A striking example of how economic networks and organisation gave rise to an extension of national interests beyond state boundaries is J.M. Keynes's *The Economic Consequence of the Peace* (Keynes [1919] 2015). Whilst Schmitt rejects the idea that economics is the primary driver of political and legal relationships, he is clear that the 19th century saw a transformation of state interests. Industrialisation and economic development led to the consequent shift from states being largely agricultural economies to their being commercial and industrial economies that rely on the import of raw materials to sustain expanding populations.

The challenge of the Monroe Doctrine was that it involved a much larger territorial claim than normally associated with Großraum, as traditionally understood. If it is interpreted as an isolationist act or a retreat behind a boundary, it raises a challenge to access to resources (especially in Latin America), which are crucial to the developing European economies. It is therefore a potential threat to them, and certainly a risk to European liberal ideas of free trade and open economies. Here Schmitt was writing in the aftermath of the global wave of protectionism that had scarred the 1930s, in which tariff walls and the need to secure access to essential resources (such as wheat, oil and metals) became an existential challenge to modern states. However, there is also the danger of 'economic' thinking driving a universalism of trade and markets and challenging borders and sovereignty. One possibility is that the Monroe Doctrine becomes just a first step on the way to a universal global order by one political society, driven by its own economic and commercial interests. Here the issue is the scale of the claim to control access to a hemisphere. When cast in spatial terms, it is greater than even the extended economic networks of a large country like the USA in relation to its neighbours. There is no necessary universalism in the Monroe Doctrine's assertion, unless it is coupled with the universalist legalism of the discriminating concept of war. But equally, for Schmitt, there remains an open question about how large a Großraum can be before it ceases to represent a particular spatial order, and instead becomes a genuine claim to be a nomos for the whole of the earth or a global political order.

The Nomos of the Earth does not end with a concrete conclusion about how the new world order should be understood. Schmitt offers three alternative pathways:

- a global state;
- a continuation of 'balance of power' thinking amongst macro-alliances, with technical changes to the balance of power components, such as the USA usurping the earlier British responsibility for the free seas; and
- a new global order of several Großraums balancing each other.

The first is seen as the most problematic because it threatens the chaos of an end of history. The second is the Cold War balance between the west, now under U.S. dominance, and its confrontation with the Soviet enemy. The third assumes a more complex view of regional global Großraum confronting each other and is part an acknowledgement of the rise of Asian powers that do not fall under the dominance of western order. Japan's failed attempt to build up an Asian empire only opens the way for the possible rise of China. (Schmitt's book was published in 1950, only one year after the Chinese Communist Party took power.)

It remains part of Schmitt's 'concrete order' thinking that the new 'nomos of the earth' can only be seen in intimations and challenges. The dominant post-war source of those changes was the United States and its Cold War role, so that Schmitt's speculations are oriented towards the direction of U.S. thinking. Interestingly, despite the USSR's undoubted role in the destruction of Nazi Germany and its proximity to Schmitt, he has nothing to say about the threat of Soviet communism as a candidate for the new world order. Perhaps this is because the USSR represents raw military power and not an attempt to reorder the world as a global legal order. The challenge of the USSR simply represents a continuation of the political as a struggle between friend and enemy. The risk for Schmitt is not the commonly perceived one of nuclear war, which he did not think would bring war to an end in a universal conflagration. Rather, it is the rise of global order and the overthrow of politics, which might bring an end to interstate warfare but would not bring an end to violence and disorder.

The Partisan

Amongst the many challenges that the Cold War posed to the international order was the consequence of nuclear weapons undermining the possibility of future significant interstate wars occurring on 1914–1918 or 1939–1945 lines. The inconclusive confrontation of the Korean War was partly the result of the wider fear of escalation into a nuclear conflict by both of the major ideological powers. The risk of accidentally falling into the global conflagration remained real, and theoreticians explored the security dilemma as a technical problem in decision theory. However, Schmitt did not regard nuclear weapons as signalling the end of war or a fundamental constraint on his theory of politics as mortal confrontation between friend and enemy. Whilst most theorists of international relations were looking at the rise of American power and the ideological confrontation between the U.S. and USSR, Schmitt turned his attention to new types of conflict and belligerence in his *Theory of the Partisan* (Schmitt 2007 [1963]). Although the lectures were intended as an extension of the argument of *The Concept of the Political*, they came to be seen as a prescient account of the rise of new kinds of conflict such as the urban terrorism of the 1960s and 1970s. They have also informed the understanding of non-state threats posed by the global terrorism of Al-Qaeda in the early 21st century.

Schmitt is not simply concerned with new forms of violence but with those that can be seen as specifically political, and therefore are not the chaotic and ever-present forms of violent human behaviour that are regulated within domestic legal systems under the heading of crimes. Partisan violence and action might well need to be criminalised, but it is categorically distinct from ordinary criminality. It has a political dimension and authority amongst those who are involved in it. As we have seen, political action is concentrated on the idea of the state in most of modern European history, yet it is not identical with state action, and hence the concept of the political is not reducible to the theory of the state. In his major works, Schmitt was concerned with violence from the perspective of states and the systems that states form through their actions in the international domain. However, in the *Theory of the Partisan* he returns to a category of political action that he had ignored, although not necessarily denied, in his earlier work.

The partisan exercises political violence on behalf of a political community but they are not a regular state actor and in particular do not form a part of the regular military powers of the state exercising political force within a 'bracketed' conception of war. That said, a partisan is not merely a single individual exercising violence. Schmitt illustrates this partisan relationship with what he calls the classic *telluric* (tied to the soil or territory) partisan of the Spanish guerrilla war against Napoleon, or the Russian irregular fighters against Napoleon, and also against the German invasion from 1941 to 1945. The problem is that military authorities are hostile to affording irregular partisans recognition and protection under the laws of war. Anti-partisan campaigns by military forces are notoriously brutal and involve hostage-taking, summary execution and torture. In consequence, partisan warfare is total and the enmity of the partisan for their enemy is absolute, especially given its *telluric* or territorial dimension. In the classic cases, the partisan is fighting an occupier, often after their state and its regular army have been defeated. Although this should bring the conventional war to an end, this does not happen for the partisan, who continues the struggle against the occupier from within the civilian community. In many cases, the partisans are remnants of the defeated army that fight on, but they also include civilians and those previously considered non-combatants because of their age, status and social role. It is precisely this *telluric* dimension that is at the heart of Schmitt's interest, because it emphasises the concrete experience of partisans as political actors. They have a total attachment to the political territory of the community, even when the institutions of the state have been defeated or compromised through occupation and collaboration.

Partisans assert an irreducible political claim through the connection to land and territory, their assertion of absolute and unconditional enmity towards their opponents, and their total commitment to the political assertion of or defence of their community. The classic partisan is the freedom fighter struggling against an occupying power and continuing the political struggle on behalf of a political community with a compromised state structure. Whilst conventional military authorities are hostile to or lukewarm about partisans, their claim to act on behalf of a political community in seeking its liberation and emancipation has become a recognised and distinct form of political violence. However, whilst exhibiting a kind of nobility, the *telluric* partisan is also dangerous because of their tendency to absolute enmity. This always escalates the type of and scope of violence that they exercise, and inspires more counter-violence in response – thus putting pressure on the bracketing of war as an attempt to humanise it.

Schmitt also traces the development of the partisan away from a spatially limited belligerent into a global belligerent, under the influence of Lenin's doctrines of global revolutionary struggle. The modern partisan is shaped by Lenin's and Mao's ideas in the struggle against a global and universal enemy, such as capitalist imperialism and colonialism in the case of Mao's theory. Schmitt saw Mao's thinking as containing within it the elements of *telluric* partisanship, especially because he fought a civil war against nationalists and colonial powers, as well as exhibiting a reluctance to submit to Stalin and Moscow as a new communist imperial power. That said, the commitment to revolutionary violence and the absolute enmity of the colonial and imperialist power of capitalism also continued Lenin's push towards a genuinely global struggle against a global enemy. Although the enmity of the global partisan is universalistic, it primarily serves as an obstacle to recognising the more insidious and dangerous global power of global capitalism. This does not imply that Schmitt has become an enemy of capitalism, but it does reflect his thesis that violent struggle will always erupt against the claims of a universalistic order that denies the pluralism of the political. In this sense, if universalism is the metaphorical Antichrist for its attempt to build Heaven on earth and usurp the rule of God, the global partisan is the Katechon or restrainer of the Antichrist and the guarantee of an open and undetermined history and therefore human experience.

This apocalyptic idea of partisan as the opponent of an alien, faceless and tyrannising global order proved attractive to radicals in the 1960s and 1970s such as the Baader–Meinhof gang in Germany and the Red Brigades in Italy. They sought to fight the global capitalist system through terror and the tactics of partisans: kidnapping, torture, murder and symbolic acts of destruction. It also impacted on the practice of otherwise *telluric* partisans such as the Provisional IRA or the Palestine Liberation Organization (PLO), who extended their wars to take action beyond the territorial community they sought to liberate from colonialist domination and aggression. Schmitt's speculations on the development of the criterion of the political in a globalised world also take on a stark significance in the War on Terror after 9/11. However, for Schmitt the key significance of partisan actions was as a sign of the irreducibly belligerent character of human experience, even in an age where conventional wars had been rendered problematic by nuclear weapons. The tendency to distinguish friends from enemies manifested in these new partisan forms shows how central the concept of the political is, as it manifests within new forms of order within and beyond the nation state that is transformed by an international legal order and economic and cultural globalisation. The open question Schmitt leaves is whether this turn from regular to irregular war reopens the kind of enmity that characterised the pre-modern world of religious wars of annihilation.

Schmitt in contemporary international theory

Despite his presence at the foundation of the modern post-war sub-discipline in America and Europe, through his connection with Hans Morgenthau and Raymond Aron and their students, Schmitt is frequently 'rediscovered' as a potential classic of international relations theory (see Odysseos and Petito 2007). Both Morgenthau's and Aron's relationships with Schmitt went back to their pre-war education and academic career. Although Morgenthau was left with a poor impression of Schmitt's character, this does not seem to have been a consequence of the anti-Semitism that Gross catalogues. Yet, that fact, along with his complicity with the Nazi state, explains the absence of Schmitt at the forefront of the giants of the subject, despite the context of the Cold War backdrop to post-war international politics. This was also true in political theory.

Until relatively recently, Schmitt was not read, except as a footnote in the history of ideas of late Weimar Germany, despite the fact that he remained an unacknowledged interlocutor of Leo Strauss, Herbert Marcuse, Eric Voegelin and especially Hannah Arendt – whose work is focused on the task of expunging violence and enmity from an account of the political. Schmitt is rarely if ever mentioned, but he is her constant challenge.

This tendency to avoid acknowledgement of his work has not stopped other scholars constructing family trees that tie Schmitt to contested policy choices in recent international politics. A particularly egregious example is the linking of Schmitt via Leo Strauss and his students to the 'Project for the American Century' that was implicated in advocacy for, and response to, the second Gulf War. For those who wanted to criticise the policy, what better argument could there be than one that linked the war to a former Nazi via an esoteric émigré political theorist (albeit a Jew)? Care needs to be taken in tracing the impact of Schmitt's thought on theory or policy in international relations, although it is undoubtedly the case that Schmitt's ideas and conceptual distinctions are there. This is especially true amongst realists trying to transcend economic determinism or the formalism of Waltz-type systems theory, in the face of the end of the Cold War and the collapse of the Westphalian order.

A clash of civilisations?

The challenge of the end of the Cold War and the collapse of the USSR is best exemplified in two opposing articles: Francis Fukuyama's 'The End of History' in *The National Interest* (Fukuyama 1989) and Samuel P. Huntington's 'The Clash of Civilisations' in *Foreign Affairs* (Huntington 1993). The former predicts the triumph of western capitalism and the nation state because globalisation and the convergence of human interests have undermined the sources of ideological conflicts. Although this draws on the ideas of Alexandre Kojeve (who in turn was associated with Schmitt), this argument for a universal triumph of economic liberalism could not be further removed from Schmitt's anti-liberalism. Huntington's article, on the other hand, can be seen as a direct application of Schmittian categories to the post-Cold War world and a rejection of the optimism that underpins Fukuyama's historical projection. In both cases, the article was followed by a book-length expansion of the argument, but in neither case does the more careful examination have the polemical force of the original articles (Fukuyama 1992; Huntington 1997).

Huntington's essay was designed, in an almost Schmittian style, to both analyse and provoke those who, in their excitement at the collapse of the Berlin Wall and the end of the Cold War, really did think we were entering the end of history, at least in the sense of a new period of universal pacifism and consumption. In shattering this optimism, Huntington wrote, presciently, that:

In the coming years, the local conflicts most likely to escalate into major wars will be those, as in Bosnia and the Caucasus, along the fault lines between civilisations. The next world war, if there is one, will be a war between civilisations. (Huntington 1993, p. 39)

The concluding section of the essay is therefore a warning to those who assumed that the end of the Cold War would result in a significant 'peace dividend' and thus legitimise a transfer of resources away from defence and military spending towards domestic consumption or tax cuts. Coupled with the rise of the neo-liberal preference for a small state apparatus, the end of the Cold War was seen by many as an opportunity to cut back on the size of the state and rein in the behemoth of the 'military industrial complex'. In light of this, observers, many of whom were on the left, read Huntington's essay as a plea from within a conservative political constituency to maintain high levels of military spending, using the advent of a new external enemy as the rationale. With the collapse of any serious *ideological* opponent as a candidate for the enemy (so conceding Fukuyama's main point), Huntington turned to the new identity politics to find that enemy. His innovation was to extend identity politics beyond the reach of national cultures, which was the familiar currency of intra-state multiculturalism (Kymlicka 1995). Instead, Huntington focused on the broader transnational identity frameworks upon which culturalism drew.

Central to civilisations is religion, or proxies for religion such as Confucianism in the case of China and East Asia. Civilisational conflict has been masked by the ideological oppositions of the Cold War, but with the end of that ideological conflict brought about the long-term oppositions of value and ideas that drive conflict and opposition could reassert themselves. Religion-based conflicts have been brought back into focus, especially in territorial regions where civilisations confront each other, and in states that are mixed. The emerging examples that Huntington alludes to have become classic examples of inter-ethnic conflict such as the former Yugoslavia, Ukraine and the Middle East conflict between Israel and Palestine. More importantly for international affairs in the subsequent decades, he identifies a conflict between global Islam and the west, and the rise of China as the next major fault lines in world politics. He presciently argues that the rise of these two forces in politics challenges the presumption of liberalism, that economic modernisation will be accompanied by soft or constitutional democratic government, as opposed to authoritarian capitalism.

Huntington's thesis does not mention Schmitt, but it has been read by critics and supporters (including some Schmitt scholars) as exemplifying Schmittian themes (McCormick 1993). The most obvious is the identification of an external enemy as an irreducible feature of international politics. With the disappearance of the USSR as an objective enemy, the new enemy of the west is a civilisational opponent with whom one confronts mortal struggle, hence the allusion to future wars as civilisational. With this notion of enmity and confrontation, Huntington emphasises that the end of the Cold War is not the end of war. Although neither the essay nor his later book expands on the idea of war in history, it is implicit in Huntington's argument that war is an ineradicable feature of international politics, and not merely a technical problem to be overcome by diplomats and policymakers. This is a familiar classical realist position, yet it is also a specifically Schmittian realism in that it does not see war as a problem that can be resolved, managed or contained. War is an existential feature of the human condition, which is linked with the deepest ways in which humans have tried to make sense of that condition, namely through religion.

Equally important to the identification of the enemy is the idea of civilisations as concrete orders. In this way, Huntington goes beyond identity politics by concentrating on value systems that have an institutional and a territorial manifestation. This analysis actually becomes a bit tenuous in relation to Confucianism, and more broadly it has been subject to much criticism from specialists and sceptics alike. Yet, it does have force in contrasting western Christianity against the orthodoxy of the eastern churches, or Islam against the west, or Islam against Hinduism in South Asia. The values of these systems are related to institutions of law and governance, as well as having broad territorial boundaries and concentrations that can give rise to a history of confrontation and conflict. Huntington does not abandon the idea of the state or even a qualified system of states within this world of conflicting civilisations. But he does identify major and intermediate powers as central to the political organisation of civilisations, echoing Schmitt's idea of Großraum or territorial orders in which these powers dominate and set the terms of other state's powers. Obvious examples in Huntington's essay are the USA, China and, in the case of eastern Christian Orthodoxy, Russia. Islam as a religion does not have a central dominant state, but it is a site of conflict for that dominant position. We might see the obvious candidates for dominance as Saudi Arabia (containing the Islamic holy places and a centre for Sunni Islam) or Iran (a strong centre of Shia Islam). Yet, again presciently, Huntington draws attention to the position of Turkey in central Asia (with its Ottoman legacy and modern success) as a potential civilisational power.

Huntington is careful to present his theory of civilisational conflict as an analysis and description of emergent empirical patterns in international affairs at the turn of the millennium. Civilisational preference might indeed account for the different approaches of Russia and Turkey to the first Gulf War, and the hostility of Russia to western action against Serbian forces in Bosnia and later with respect to Kosovo. What is unclear is whether he is also affirming a normative claim, that civilisational preference and opposition should shape U.S. or western policy in the future. This has become one of the most deeply contested features of Huntington's argument. In one passage of the essay he does come close to endorsing civilisational preference, not simply as an explanation but as a justification for policy.

Muslims contrasted Western actions against Iraq [in the 1991 Gulf War] with the West's failure to protect Bosnia against Serbs and to impose sanctions on Israel for violating U.N. resolutions. The West, they alleged was using a double standard. A world of clashing civilisations, however, is inevitably a world of double standards: people apply one standard to their kin-countries and a different standard to others. (Huntington 1993, p. 36)

He is clearly suggesting here that actions favouring civilisational preference are what will happen, a fact of life. Therefore it is something that we might as well recognise in constructing international policy. The decades since the 1990s have seen significant debates in U.S. and western international policy between those defending an evolving global order and those acknowledging different and ineradicable sites of conflict precisely as Schmitt would have predicted. Huntington provides one possible avenue through which a new 'nomos of the earth' emerges. Yet, his is not the only Schmittian way, as we can see if we look at the distinct but related critique of global legalism.

Global legalism

The challenge to global legalism has become a contested element of international law and human rights thinking, especially in the USA. Although he is by no means the only critic of global legalism, the American jurist Eric Posner has become an important figure in this critique (Posner 2011). Once again, I do not wish to identify Posner as a self-confessed apostle of Carl Schmitt – he is not. Posner's work can be located within venerable traditions of American jurisprudence and political science which emphasise Hamiltonian federalism and scepticism about judicial activism. That said, in writings with his colleague Adrian Vermeule, Posner does draw on Schmitt's critique of liberal constitutionalism in relation to the emergency powers of the U.S. presidency, which have become particularly important in the context of the War on Terror.

Challenges to the idea of international law are familiar within realist international relations theory and policy, and its associated moral scepticism also generates a scepticism about human rights. The specific critique of global legalism is not simply a rehash of realist moral scepticism and an assertion of statism that one might find in Morgenthau or George Kennan. Instead, it is a specific extension of the issue of judicial activism to the international realm. Judicial activism occurs when judges make law themselves in their adjudication and application of the law to new cases. For strict legal positivists and realists, judges make new law in adjudicating hard cases and hence can usurp the prerogatives of legislatures. This creates the problem of the democratic legitimacy of judicial review within liberal constitutions. If judges directly make laws, then the issue of their authority to do so is raised. Within this complex set of debates, Schmitt's early work on *Dictatorship* (1921) and the concept of sovereignty in *Political Theology* (1922) argues that all constitutions and legal systems ultimately depend on a fundamental political act. Within a stable political community, that political act can be provided by democratic institutions, or an elected executive power such as the U.S. president. In American constitutional politics, Posner and his colleagues have been associated with defending a broad and unconstrained interpretation of presidential powers. But in the field of international law there is no such political structure that legitimises the lawmaking behind international law and adjudication.

For critics of global legalism such as Posner, the problem is not just the absence of a global state with political structures but furthermore the absence of any legitimate political context that can ground the practice of international jurists. This makes them into a professional elite abstracted from the social practice and the profession of lawyers operating within national, state or municipal legal systems. Alternatively jurists become merely functionaries (bureaucrats) of an autonomous system in the international realm. Much of Posner's argument is an empirical account of international law and decisions that shows that they are merely an extension of the political interests of dominant states or the result of coalitions of states collaborating to achieve shared national interests – e.g. other states often gang up to limit the legitimate power of the United States. If a coalition dominates, then it is best to see those interests stated clearly so that governments can be held politically accountable. If a single state dominates, then global legalism is no more than an abstract form of international moralism. Posner has interesting critical discussions of the recent growth in international tribunals for prosecuting human rights violations in Rwanda or the former Yugoslavia, as well as a critique of the near-'sacred' status of the Nuremburg War Crimes Tribunal following World War II. These discussions echo Schmitt's own (perhaps self-serving) critique of victor's justice. More importantly these developments rest on a 'discriminating concept of war' that assumes a just global order.

The challenge of global legalism is that it is not actually a concrete order but instead an abstraction of global liberalism. In his *The Perils of Global Legalism*, Posner includes a final intriguing afterword, 'America versus Europe'. Here he suggests that there are two perspectives on global international law that are in conflict as candidates for what Schmitt would describe as a new nomos of the earth. Posner does not argue that the European form of global liberalism poses the existential challenges that one could infer from Schmitt's political/theological speculations. But it does threaten the integrity of sovereign powers by separating law from democracy or popular government, and placing the two in conflict. Posner's position is not merely a restatement of U.S. hegemony within the post-Westphalian state system and the advantages of a unipolar world. It also challenges the immanent historicism of international law as the next phase of progressive evolution towards a world without war, or without political communities locked in conflict.

A war on terror: Schmitt, partisans and global terrorists

The debates within the U.S. government and amongst American constitutional theorists over the extent of presidential power in the face of the terrorist attacks of 9/11 and the subsequent 'War on Terror' has also raised the spectre of Schmitt as an éminence grise behind the voices backing ultra-realism. A good example is the brief written by a former deputy assistant U.S. attorney general, John Yoo, on the scope of the Geneva Conventions with respect to the treatment of terror suspects and detainees. He is also particularly associated with the controversial advice that governed U.S. military and intelligence services practice under President George W. Bush on the use of the euphemistically named 'enhanced interrogation techniques' (including waterboarding, stress positions and sleep deprivation). Yoo argued for the narrow interpretation of the idea of prohibitions of torture in the Geneva Conventions that made this approach legitimate. Once again, it is important to remember that the president's right to exercise emergency powers is an original feature of the U.S. political system that is set out in the Federalist Papers and was also exemplified in President Lincoln's suspension of the fundamental legal doctrine of habeas corpus during the U.S. Civil War. That said, Schmitt's preoccupation with emergency powers in his account of the sovereign dictator, as well as his theorising of the modern partisan, undoubtedly shaped the American understanding of the response to the War on Terror. And even critics of U.S. strategy and policy are inclined to appeal to Schmittian concepts and language to characterise and critique policy positions and the public rhetoric surrounding the 'War on Terror'. Indeed, that very language is a clear rejection of the alternative line of criminalising global terrorism, with its implications for a global police action, one that brings with it intimations of a global legal order that many U.S. policymakers have sought to resist in asserting the primacy of U.S. political interests and capabilities to act.

Whether Schmitt's ideas directly shaped policy decisions within the U.S. about how to deal with jihadi terrorism, his concept of the partisan does have implications for how such terrorists are to be understood. Al-Qaeda's Islamic jihadism rejected attachment to any given place, and proclaimed the idea of a worldwide caliphate as a deferred ideal. It is a clear exemplar of Schmitt's global partisan waging a 'just war' without boundaries. On the other hand, the adherents of ISIS are a mixture of the global and the *telluric* or territorially based partisan. In a rejection of Al-Qaeda's refusal to declare the realisation of the caliphate, the leadership of ISIS in Iraq and Syria did just that, establishing a territorial caliphate as a place and entity. Within its territory, ISIS fighters took on many of the features of Schmitt's *telluric* partisans, fighting occupiers and external aggressors (Gerges 2016). The two Islamic movements share the features of global partisanship in their total enmity of their opponents. The struggle is not one that can end in a new political compromise but must involve the annihilation of their enemy. This perhaps explains the extraordinary brutality and theatrically gruesome violence of ISIS towards its opponents

(Gerges 2016). ISIS can only triumph when their enemies are completely anni-hilated, and with that any conception of the political within the caliphate. To this extent, the caliphate is not another political community but is genuinely an attempt to replace the political with a divine order. That the Kingdom of God would be the outcome of such a horrendously brutal and violent process is perhaps a fitting illustration of Schmitt's political/theological warning about human capacities for evil and against dangerous forces that wish to bring his-tory to an end, what he refers to – using Christian apocalyptic language – as the coming of Antichrist.

Conclusion

Schmitt's dark and ambiguous past and his illusive and eclectic style make him an attractive yet dangerous thinker both to a resurgent conservatism that is trying to avoid the liberal reductionism of neo-liberal capitalist triumphalism and to a western left that is seeking to expose the real face of its enemy as again more than just the legacy of Edmund Burke or Adam Smith. In a world where history has lost its place as a supplier of meta-narratives of progress, redemp-tion and justice, Schmitt's willingness to use apocalyptic terms to confront the challenge of nihilism makes him a profound challenge to the limited vision of technocratic international relations and political science. His committed views also contrast with the apparent emptiness of much applied ethics and liberal political philosophy. Whether he has any answers to give, his challenge to contemporary international, political and legal theory is as a provocation to confront the ways in which the hidden legacies of our conceptual frameworks expose the real and ambiguous nature of human experience, and the unavoid-able requirement to conceive of a political response. Yet, he also remains a challenge because so many people still remain spellbound by the allure of vio-lence and channelling conflict to enhance their own agenda or conception of political action.

Bibliography

Essential reading

Schmitt, Carl. (1988). *Political Theology: Four Chapters on the Concept of Sove-reignty*, trans. George Schwab. USA: MIT Press.

Schmitt, Carl. [1923] (1988). *The Crisis of Parliamentary Democracy*, trans. E. Kennedy. USA: MIT Press.

Schmitt, Carl. (2006). *The Nomos of the Earth in the International Law of the Jus Publicum Europaeum*, trans. G.L. Ulmen. USA: Telos Press.

Schmitt, Carl. [1932] (2007a). *The Concept of the Political*, trans. George Schwab. USA: University of Chicago Press.

Schmitt, Carl. [1963] (2007b). *Theory of the Partisan*, trans. G.L. Ulmen. USA: Telos Press.

Secondary reading

Gerges, Fawez A. (2016). *Isis: A History*. USA: Princeton University Press.

Gross, Raphael. (2007). *Carl Schmitt and the Jews: The 'Jewish Question' the Holocaust and German Legal Theory*. USA: University of Wisconsin Press.

Gross, Raphael. (2016). 'The "True Enemy": Antisemitism in Carl Schmitt's Life and Work'. *The Oxford Handbook of Carl Schmitt*. UK: Oxford University Press.

Hooker, William. (2009). *Carl Schmitt's International Thought: Order and Orientation*. UK: Cambridge University Press.

Huntington, Samuel P. (1993). 'The Clash of Civilisations' *Foreign Affairs*, vol. 72, no. 3, pp. 22–49.

Huntington, Samuel P. (1997). *The Clash of Civilisations: And the Remaking of World Order*. UK: Simon and Schuster.

Keynes, John Maynard. [1919] (2015). 'The Economic Consequences of the Peace', in Robert Skidelsky (ed.) *The Essential Keynes*. UK: Penguin.

Loughlin, Martin. (2018). 'Why Read Carl Schmitt', in Christoph Bezemek, Michael Potacs, Alexander Somek (eds) *Vienna Lectures on Legal Philosophy*, vol. 1. UK: Hart, pp. 49–67.

McCormick, John P. (1993). 'Carl Schmitt: The Age of Neutralisation and Depoliticisation' *Telos*, vol. 96, pp. 130–142.

Meier, Heinrich. (1995). *Carl Schmitt and Leo Strauss: The Hidden Dialogue*. USA: University of Chicago Press.

Meier, Heinrich. (1998). *The Lesson of Carl Schmitt: Four Chapters on the Distinction between Political Theology and Political Philosophy*. USA: University of Chicago Press.

Meierhenrich, Jens: and Simons, Oliver. (2016). *The Oxford Handbook of Carl Schmitt*. UK: Oxford University Press.

Muller, Jan-Werner. (2003). *A Dangerous Mind: Carl Schmitt in Post-War European Thought*. USA: Yale University Press.

Odysseos, Louiza; and Petito, Fabio. (2007). *The International Political Thought of Carl Schmitt: Terror, Liberal War and the Crisis of Global Order*. UK: Routledge.

Posner, Eric A. (2011). *The Perils of Global Legalism*. USA: University of Chicago Press.

Schmitt, Carl. [1919] (1986). *Political Romanticism*, trans. Guy Oakes. USA: MIT Press.

Schmitt, Carl. [1923] (1996). *Roman Catholicism and Political Form*, trans. G.L. Ulmen. USA: Greenwood Press.

Schmitt, Carl. (2011). *Writings on War*, trans. Timothy Nunan. UK: Polity Press.

Schmitt, Carl. [1921] (2014). *Dictatorship*, trans. M. Hoelzl and G. Ward. UK: Polity Press.

Schmitt, Carl. (2015). *Dialogues on Power and Space*, ed. Federico Finchelstein, Andreas Kalyvas, trans Samuel Garret Zeitlin. UK: Polity Press.

Schmitt, Carl. (2015). *Land and Sea: A World Historical Meditation*. USA: Telos Press.

Schulman, Alex. (2012). 'Carl Schmitt and the Clash of Civilisations: The Missing Context' *Journal of Political Ideologies*, vol. 17, no. 2, pp. 147–167.

Slomp, Gabriella. (2009). *Carl Schmitt and the Politics of Hostility, Violence and Terror*. UK: Palgrave.

Walt, Steven M. (2005). *Taming American Power*. USA: Norton.

Walt, Steven M. (2018). *The Hell of Good Intentions: America's Foreign Policy Elite and the Decline of U.S. Primacy*. USA: Farrar Straus and Giroux.

Suggestion for open access further reading on Carl Schmitt

Carl Schmitt
Entry in the *Stanford Encyclopedia of Philosophy*
https://plato.stanford.edu/entries/schmitt

CHAPTER 11

Conclusion

Realisms in international political theory

Most accounts of realism in international relations draw on conceptions of international theory that expressly react against early 20th-century idealism. They only turn to the past to find big thinkers who support the insights of contemporary theory and ideology in international affairs and international relations theory. The so-called 'classical realists' E.H. Carr, Reinhold Niebuhr and Hans Morgenthau set an agenda for post-1945 international relations theory that is partly vindicated by association with thinkers such as Augustine and Machiavelli. Even the so-called English School theorists such as Hedley Bull (Bull 1977) and Wight draw on an historical 'tradition' of realism against which they develop their conception of the international realm as an anarchical society, by contrasting it with a realist state system that can be traced to Thucydides, Machiavelli and Hobbes. Some of the thinkers here will be familiar from discussions in works by Wight (1991), Doyle (1997) or Boucher (1998), I have not sought to write another history of that side of the argument. And I have also discussed thinkers such as Locke, who is a mainstay of accounts of idealism or moralism, as well as ambiguous thinkers such as Augustine and Rousseau. Yet, all that aside, there is undoubtedly a question to answer about the relationship between the broad sequence of thinkers considered here and the perennial interest in realism in international relations, and that question cannot just be given a yes or no answer.

In this chapter, I explain why this book has equivocated about whether it is simply considering a realist canon. At stake is the role of realism in international

---

How to cite this book chapter:
Kelly, Paul. 2022. *Conflict, war and revolution: The problem of politics in international political thought.* London: LSE Press, pp. 409–428.
DOI: https://doi.org/10.31389/lsepress.cwr.k License: CC BY.

relations theory and how international political theory contributes to challenging its hegemony. To that end I consider realism as a specific doctrinal position (or even an ideology) and I define that conception in terms that will support my equivocation. However, I also want to address the development of a new 'realist' challenge within contemporary political theory or philosophy with which I am more sympathetic and to which the canon discussed here clearly contributes. These two realisms are not unconnected, but neither are they strictly related by implication. At best they share a 'family resemblance' rather than a methodology or common set of problems. Some commentators argue that the new 'realist turn' in political theory is actually older than the 'classical realism' of 20th-century international relations theory. Whether that is true or not, it has important implications for the ambition of international political theory and especially some of its recent preoccupations. Because the 'realist turn' is still defining itself, it does not yet have a settled position that can be given a history – another reason for not offering this book as a history of realist international relations. That said, I do wish to make a concrete claim that helps to clarify what is at issue in that realist perspective, and consequently makes relevant some of the thinkers covered here (such as Locke) who would not normally be associated with my realist approach to politics. The new realists are insufficiently explicit about their statism – and it is this which underpins their hostility to and reticence about acknowledging the place of violence in what they like to describe as 'the first political question', following Bernard Williams (2005).

I begin with an outline of realism in contemporary international relations theory, or what is sometimes known as the 'Westphalian system' (Brown 2002). I next give an account of international political theory (IPT) as a critique of that position, and summarise three of the most important IPT perspectives – as a prelude to outlining the 'realist turn' in political theory and philosophy. The final section focuses on the central challenge facing a more realist IPT, namely the relationship between legitimacy, violence and the site of politics.

The Westphalian system

One of the central charges of the great classical international relations theorists of the 20th century against their opponents in the interwar period was that their academic preoccupations overlooked the urgent realities of real politics, such as the rise of Nazism and the threat of Stalinist communism. Refining complex normative international institutions was all well and good, but in the meantime things were happening that did not fit those normative theories, and were urgent and dangerous. Realism accepts that urgency and keeps its eyes close to the foreground, largely ignoring what may be happening over the horizon. Those interested in international affairs are always preoccupied with a realistic perspective on what is happening in the world here and now. So it is not surprising that realism should claim to be the default position of international relations. Yet, one of the perennial features of academic life, as opposed to political practice or journalism, is a concern with the underpinnings of an activity or a mode of experience. Perhaps in fields of the natural sciences (such as physics) this is not done by most physicists themselves but by mathematicians or philosophers. However, in all other subjects, scholars in general have views about those presuppositions and thus about how their practice should be conducted. Debates about methods of enquiry are a perennial subject of concern in history, literary studies, political science and international relations. Indeed, in political science, the preoccupation with the presuppositions of the activity and its object of enquiry is the professional terrain of political theorists, who (to the frustration of political scientists) are never satisfied with accounts of the object or method of their discipline. In the same way, within international relations, international theory is its own variant of that sub-discipline.

As international relations has come to distinguish itself within (or even outside) the rest of political science, the perspective of realism has come into its own as both a default theoretical position that scholars can defend or challenge, and also an account of the object of enquiry that international relations scholars can be expert in, as opposed to other aspects of political science generally conceived. These patterns explain the prevalence or hegemony of realism, but also the often-remarked fact that it is deeply contested as a single position (Bell 2009). Realism is always a construction, but some elements are commonly shared by the different 'realist' theorists. These elements are often grouped into the idea of the Westphalian system (Brown 2002), and include:

- a state-based system and the so-called 'domestic analogy';
- positivism and the rejection of normativity;
- the primacy of power politics; and
- conservativism with respect to international affairs, by which I mean a preference for the status quo over reform (rather than conservatism as an ideological position).

Each of these traits is an important target of criticism by IPT.

The Westphalian system and the 'domestic' analogy provide useful touchstones in international relations and political theory. For both, the 1648 Peace of Westphalia can conveniently be used to mark the beginning of the modern sovereign state and the consequent state system. Under the two treaties involved, a distinction is made between the idea of the state as responsible for internal political order within its territory and the subject of relations between state, assigned to the remit of diplomats and soldiers in practice or of international relations theorists in academic studies. The domestic analogy fits with the treaties' determination that the religion of a people within a particular state or territory was a strictly internal concern and not a matter for war or dispute between princes, an idea clearly echoed in the arguments of Thomas Hobbes. For later international relations theory this provided a foundational distinction within the emerging discipline of political science between the study of politics within states and that between states. The domestic analogy had the effect of reinforcing a states-based view of politics and enshrining it within political science. Questions of constitutional design, voting systems, political rights and welfare provision were all considered domestic matters, to be explained by domestic forces within a political territory or tradition. What international relations theorists contributed was an understanding of a different set of questions that covered the relations between these internally self-sufficient domestic states. As international relations is concerned with a world of many states, it could not be reduced to a simple extension of national political interest, even in the case of the most powerful nation states.

The Westphalian analogy emerges whenever one thinks of domestic political agendas. Just as the 1648 Peace made the issue of whether a state was Catholic or Protestant a domestic matter, so in the modern world the question of whether a state is democratic or authoritarian is a domestic matter. For instance, it is not for a state to use political power beyond its borders so as to advance socialised health care, social democracy, or the removal or racial limitations of voting rights. But this ethos of self-limitation by states is only one part of the analogy. Underpinning the constraint on the ambition of politics that manifests itself in an ideology of states' rights, there is also the structural ordering of the international systems. The world is essentially a world of states, each with their own settled national interests, confronting an international domain of other states, each with their own national interests. Whilst Hobbes's idea of natural equality may not hold between these states, there is equally no natural and permanent hierarchy in international affairs. Nor are there any unambiguous sources of authority that have legitimate claim over the national interests of any state. Central to all conceptions of realism is the idea that the fundamental object of study is a world of states, and the forces or norms that govern their interaction in the absence of a natural or authoritative order. What kind of system emerges from this interaction is the subject matter of international relations. Debates within it are between different accounts of that order. Liberals see the mutual advantage of states leading to a broadly rules-based order that allows for the benefits of public goods and economic growth. So-called English School theorists explain how the international realm is a society but not a political order with a settled coercive power. Lastly, realists see the international order as a world of anarchy, contingency and power politics. For them, the international realm is best characterised in terms of conflict, the potential for war and the contingency of peace and order.

So, realists are suspicious of those who see order and rules emerging spontaneously out of interactions. Peace is the exception that needs explanation and conflict and war, or the permanent potential of such conflict, is the normal state of international affairs. The main arguments amongst realist thinkers are about whether this world of international anarchy is merely the result of historical experience, or whether there is a causal story about the nature of conflict following from states pursuing mutually conflicting interests without a tendency towards stable equilibrium. This explains the realists' claim to be focused on the facts of the matter, and not some ideal or utopian vision of how the world might be if certain conditions could be made to hold. This is connected to the second important feature of realism as an international relations theory.

Positivism is a methodological position that claims to focus solely on empirical facts as the object of scientific enquiry, and to seek to understand the relationships between those facts. Positivism in the social sciences aspires to the status of natural science with a stable object of enquiry that is independent of the values and aspirations of the enquirer. For a chemist, an element such as carbon is what it is, irrespective of the values, hopes and ambitions of the chemist. What a chemist analyses and the claims they make about the properties of this element are unaffected by whether they personally are a Marxist–Leninist or a Catholic Royalist. The object of enquiry is indifferent to the values of the enquirer, and how it behaves is fully conditioned or determined by causal laws and canons of scientific explanation. Of course, the real world of science is actually much more complex. Philosophers of science argue deeply about the nature of natural kinds, causal laws and the stability of the objects of scientific enquiry – think of the uncertainty principle in quantum mechanics. Yet, the aspiration to be a positive science, and to avoid collapsing all questions into questions about normative values, remains a central ambition of much social science.

Classical realists (such as E.H. Carr and Hans Morgenthau) had profound philosophical reasons behind their realism, which were linked to the ideas of Marx, Nietzsche and Weber and their critique of conventional moralism, rather than drawing on conceptions from the natural sciences. By contrast, neo-realists (such as Kenneth Waltz) have been far more interested in modelling international relations on a scientific methodology, one that privileges formal modelling and deductive inferences in theory development, rather than historical and empirical speculation. Carr and Morgenthau respond to Weber's post-Nietzschean idea of a disenchanted world that cuts them off from the possibility of normative foundations, whereas Waltz's ambition is to provide robust explanatory claims that are empirically true irrespective of the claimer's values. Thus, a positivist stance can be a consequence of indifference to the claim of individual or collective values, in the same way that economics proceeds without reference to concepts like justice. Alternatively, as in the case of Carr and Morgenthau, positivism can be the tragic consequence of the retreat of values and the problem of nihilism. Whichever metaphysical foundation is chosen here, realism abandons an appeal to values in explaining international politics.

Accordingly, a realist account of the international system rejects the credibility of questions about how international affairs *ought* to be conducted, and normative issues about how states *should* pursue their interests in competition with other states. If there are laws in the international realm, these will be causal laws about empirics, describing the relationship between states pursuing their interests, or statistical correlations derived from the empirical data. They are not rules or principles that prescribe how states should behave and what should happen to them when they fail to live up to those rules. If in practice international affairs operate with some normative rules, or states choose to comply with sets of values, these are things that need to be explained in terms of some prior non-normative value. They are not pre-given principles that shape the claims of the primary actors in the international realm, namely states. Consequently, the realist is concerned with the prior question of why states might choose to comply with international laws that govern the conduct of war, rather than the moral question of whether and under what circumstances war is permissible. Foundational normativity does not exist. And non-foundational (caused) normativity needs to be explained in terms of some other non-normative property or factors. This methodological prioritisation of the positive over the normative, whatever its philosophical grounding, is responsible for the two remaining dimensions of the Westphalian system and realism: power politics and conservativism.

Power politics is a feature of realism because (in the absence of normativity or values being a source of motivation) the only reason for individual, group or state actions is the pursuit of interests or the satisfaction of desires. In the case of individual persons, the satisfaction of desires is the achievement of one's interests, because there has to a positive account of interests that is based on a natural property such as desire. Although states are different from persons, for realists they are similarly motivated by a natural property such as the aggregation of individual interests as the interest of the people, or the identification of the national interest with the interests of the ruling class or leadership. In each case, the motivation for action is again the satisfaction of desire or the pursuit of interest. Reason plays a role in satisfying one's desires or pursuing the national interest. But that role is purely a strategic calculation about how to best secure that interest, not in terms of deciding what that interest or desire should be. Consequently, whilst the chosen course of action can be rational or irrational, desires and interests are not.

The issue of power arises because states or rulers must pursue their national interest in a world where other states do likewise. In international affairs, there is no set of rules that naturally coordinates individual actions and interests (akin to a legal system that coordinates individual actions within a state). So each state is free to pursue its interest, as it sees fit, all of the time. Yet, without natural coordination we face a world of competition and potential conflict, with only our own power to fall back on to get other states to act within our interests, or to prevent them from acting contrary to our interests. Power in this case is the ability to get others to do what we want, and for the realist that is all there is to fall back on, in the case of international politics. Power can be seen to have many dimensions, including the soft power of some states that cause oth-ers to want to imitate and align with them. But in the end power is that ability to get others to do what one wants or needs and, if that is not through dialogue, deliberation or imitation, then it can only be done through a threat of force. Realists tend to dismiss or overlook many of the subtle 'faces of power', in order to concentrate on its simplest and most striking forms such as military force and violence. This is partly a conceptual point, because, if the desire is to get others to do one's will, then force is a paradigm case of so doing. The concepts of power and force are therefore fundamental ones in realist theory.

However, the focus on power in realism is not merely an analytical and pos-itivist point. The importance of power is not only conceptual but empirical. Much of history is the history of states going to war with other states to settle disputes or pursue interests that cannot be derived from persuasion, diplomacy or deceit. Realism has come to dominate international affairs, not just because of its theoretical parsimony and simplicity but because of its usefulness for policy science in international affairs such as security studies, diplomacy and strategy. Two of the most well-known realist thinkers in post-war United States international relations were George Kennan, who argued for containment of the USSR, and Henry Kissinger, who advocated that the U.S. use military force overtly and covertly alongside diplomacy to secure its interests as the guarantor of international order. Kissinger's reputation was as a modern 'Machiavellian', willing to deploy power in whatever way is necessary, the archetypical power politician, avoiding difficult questions about the morality of war, violence and conflict. By contrast, Kennan was a very different character. His strategy caused many political critics to argue that he was 'soft on Communism'. Kennan was undoubtedly a realist, but one who saw the strategy of diplomatic and military containment of Soviet and Marxism–Leninism expansion as a way of exercis-ing power with the best likelihood of success. He regarded his more fiercely 'anti-Communist' critics as preoccupied with the pursuit of a perverse ideology, rather than recognising the claims of power and its strategic exercise.

Conservatism is the last dimension of realism. It follows from the state-based vision of international relations, denying any priority of normative values and principles, and the preoccupation with the effective manipulation of power. This conservatism is the most important trigger behind the growth of IPT as a critique of the hegemony of realist international relations. This is a small 'c' conservatism, not an ideological position – although it is sometimes associ-ated with political conservatism, because big 'C' conservative parties in many democracies support the military, and during the Cold War were keen to con-front their ideological enemies.

However, the main challenge of conservatism in realist international relations is that it tends to reflect the domestic analogy at the heart of the state system. International politics is always about a state pursuing its national (inter-nally set) interest in the context of other states doing likewise. The resulting division of labour between domestic and international politics means that many pressing issues that affect peoples are consigned to the domestic realm and most importantly to domestic resolution. The task of international relations is limited to securing the peaceful relations between states, and managing whatever international rules and institutions states have jointly created to serve their respective interests. The primary challenges of international politics are maintaining the international status quo from threats to stability as a result of changing balances of power and shifting alliances. At one level, this might seem a noble enough ambition given the costs of war and the breakdown of international order – a point that stands to the credit of realists such as Carr, Morgenthau, Niebuhr or Kennan. Yet, at the same time, this preference for the status quo has the effect of marginalising any new challenges, such as the provision of global public goods like dealing with the consequences of climate change. Equally, realism's preference for the status quo can become the basis for an ideological preference for asserting sovereignty over relying on mutually beneficial cooperation. This risks reifying what were only ever temporary and contingent features of (past) political experience.

This tendency to see international relations as a fixed set of technical problems thrown up by an international order with a particular (unchanging) character has made politicians and diplomats overly cautious in dealing with international problems that do not easily fit into this paradigm. This is especially the case when these problems are shaped by structural or external forces, or where the resolution of those problems is hampered by the preoccupation with the easy categorical distinction between the domestic and the international. Such issues as famines (in Bengal in 1943 and 1971, or the subsequent Bangladesh Famine of 1974) fell outside this distinction between the domestic and the international. Indeed, it was their salience that forced moral questions onto the agenda of international relations, and served as one of the main inspirations of IPT from the 1970s onwards. This convergence between a unique upsurge of interest in normative political theory and acute international problems transformed international relations as a subject and created one of its most vibrant and interesting sub-fields.

International political theory as critique

The convention of crediting John Rawls with rescuing political theory or philosophy from its near death at the hands of logical positivists and Oxford ordinary language philosophy goes back to Peter Laslett. It has come under considerable critical scrutiny in recent years by genealogies that have sought to question the hegemonic status of Rawlsian liberal-egalitarianism (Forrester 2019). It is certainly the case that plenty of important political theory was being done – although less so amongst analytical philosophers than the convention suggests. Yet, what is unquestionable is the explosion of interest in normative questions that coincided with Rawls's publication of *A Theory of Justice* (Rawls 1971) and the subsequent debates it inspired. Political philosophy and theory was not only fashionable but also, it appeared, urgent. This was a period of extraordinary intellectual output that coincided with important and pressing issues in international politics. The background was the high point of the Cold War, with troubling confrontations across the 1970s and '80s. From the mid-1960s the U.S. as guarantor of the liberal democratic order was also mired in domestic civil rights disturbances and constitutional struggles and in an ill-fated war in Vietnam. The war tore apart American university campuses, not least because of the draft (compulsory U.S. military service selected by lot). Domestic issues in the United States always became international issues, because of its central place in international alliances and the domestic politics of all liberal democratic states. At first, the domain of the international itself came into play when assessing Rawls's claim to apply the concept of the social contract only to a 'closed domestic society' – which seemed to endorse one aspect of the state-centric approach of realism, albeit decisively abandoning its positivism.

Although Rawls wrote important essays on practical political issues such as civil disobedience, his primary work was his major grand theory of justice as fairness. The motivations behind this book are complex, but amongst them was a desire to provide an alternative to utilitarianism as the basis for public judgements of morality and justice, yet without relying also on an ethically realist account of natural law or natural rights. If there are to be person-protecting rights that limit the application of expedience or utility, then these need to be derived from a source of authority that all of us could reasonably accept, within a context of multiple ideas about the best form of life.

Rawls accepted the fact of pluralism (or reasonable disagreement) about what constitutes the good life and how one should live. But he nevertheless argued that we can arrive at principles of right (a basis for law and civil rights) that protect the fundamental dignity of free and equal persons. The theory is therefore critical of the prevailing technical policy language of utilitarianism, yet it also sought to provide a stable (liberal) basis for the intuitions that underpinned the widespread human belief in fundamental rights for each person to be treated as free and equal citizens. These intuitions were brought together and reconciled in a conception of political society as a fair scheme of social cooperation, that is, as a social contract shaped by two principles of justice. The first Rawlsian principle distributed a set of basic liberties to each, and the second ensured that any economic inequalities permitted were so structured as to benefit the worst off and to reflect fair equality of opportunity. Although Rawls is concerned with vindicating the claims of political philosophy and justifying normative principles, his argument was also seen as providing a justification for liberal political policies, of the sort that underpinned Lyndon Johnson's Great Society programme in the USA (1964–68), or the British welfare state according to writers like Anthony Crosland.

In this respect, Rawls's theory was contradicted by the libertarian theory of Robert Nozick in his 1974 book *Anarchy, State and Utopia*, which argued that positing any central distribution of goods that involved seizing from individuals the product of their own labour was inherently unjust. Nozick was also a significant philosopher seeking to test the limits of normative political theory (and not simply a libertarian ideologue). Within a short period, much of the Rawls versus Nozick debate involved taking sides in an ideological debate about redistribution within states, and consequently also between them. With the rise of the new right and the political success of Thatcher and Reagan in the early 1980s, political philosophy became more deeply politicised than had been expected. Political theorists continued to discuss Rawls versus Nozick debates in ever more technically sophisticated arguments about the metric of social justice.

Political theorists in political science departments no doubt place Rawls's *Theory of Justice* as the central text of the resurgence in normative theory. However, two other works also emphasised the extent to which that explosion of interest was always international and came to have a powerful influence on IPT. Peter Singer's (1972) essay 'Famine, Affluence and Morality' was published in the new journal *Philosophy and Public Affairs* in the wake of the Bengal Famine of 1971. And Michael Walzer's (1977) book *Just and Unjust Wars* (Walzer 1977) was a second path-breaking intervention in international affairs. It raised the prospect of justifying normative claims about the justice of war and the rights and wrongs of humanitarian intervention. Both interventions obviously challenge the normative silence and conservatism of realist international relations theory. Whilst some political philosophers became obsessed with the foundationalist debates about the possibility of grounding normative theories of justice, others with an interest in international affairs looked to these new theories to challenge policy and broaden the agenda of the study of international affairs beyond the relations of states and the distribution of power.

Singer was an uncompromising but sophisticated utilitarian philosopher who had made his name arguing for animal liberation. His essay on famine argued that individuals could be shown to have a duty to assist the poor and suffering by making personally insignificant spending choices so as to support famine relief charities that would collectively have significant impacts on overall global well-being. Singer showed that utilitarianism could be freed from the taint of being a technical 'Government House' morality and instead be a radical and transformative ethical theory for guiding personal actions that would fit with times. More importantly, Singer also offered an account of moral obligations that took *no* account of states, nations or peoples, by claiming that moral obligations are urgent, overriding and indifferent to the distribution of political sovereignty and responsibility. In one short essay, Singer rejected both the claims of states and the positivist denial of normativity. In response to his examples of famine relief, it was just implausible for realists to offer a metaphysical account of why there could not be universal moral obligations to people confronting undeserved suffering. His issue-driven approach to moral and political philosophy was to be a major inspiration behind the movement towards 'applied ethics'.

For most of the 20th century, moral philosophy written in English focused on second-order ethical questions about the meaning and status of moral claims, especially in the light of logical positivism and ordinary language philosophy, which reduced normative claims to expressions of subjective preference or emotion. Philosophy, as a discipline, was considered to have very little to offer to substantive questions about how to live or what to do when faced with choices over valuable ends. Most philosophers were prepared to retreat to an analysis of the meaning of moral concepts and the conditions for their correct application. Singer's approach chimed with an age that was impatient with these technical and interminable disputes about emotivism, prescriptivism and descriptivism as accounts of the meaning of moral judgements, and instead wanted theorists to engage with the big issues of the day – such as the justice of war and military conscription, the regulation of private behaviour, or when it is legitimate to disobey the state or the law.

Although his argument is importantly different to Rawls's, Singer also draws on what he takes to be the widely shared intuition that individuals and their standing matter, at least when confronted with avoidable suffering. This approach is given a strikingly cosmopolitan direction in his 2002 book *One World: The Ethics of Globalisation*, where the ethical status of individuals and their well-being was taken to be definitive of the claims of intermediate institutions such as states. These only have moral standing in relation to individual interests and well-being (a direction that Rawls refuses to take; see Chapter 7). The new millennium began with a cosmopolitan optimism that soon gave way to more traditional concerns about states, war and conflict following 9/11 and the second Gulf War. Yet, this cosmopolitan optimism was not only challenged by a resurgent realism but was also confronted within IPT itself by the work of Michael Walzer, the third of our major sources of IPT.

Walzer had established his name with his *Just and Unjust Wars*, but he had also contributed to the methodological debates surrounding Rawls and his approach to political theory. Whereas Rawls and Nozick both began from a methodological individualism, Walzer returned to a different approach associated with Aristotle, Hegel and Marx that was to become known as communitarianism. His *Spheres of Justice* (1983) also defended a pluralist notion of 'complex equality' against Rawls's assumption that his 'primary social goods' could encompass all that mattered to peoples or groups. Communitarianism began as a critique of Rawls's methodology and for the best part of a decade the brightest and best minds struggled with the liberalism versus communitarian debate. Yet this superficially methodological debate disguised an underlying and important normative defence of political communities and associations, if not states as such. Walzer, and those influenced by him, such as David Miller (Miller 1995), Yael Tamir (Tamir 1993) and Margaret Moore (Moore 2015), became associated with a resurgence of interest in ethical nationalism. Nations could be seen as ethical communities within which individual identities (conceptions of the self) emerged. So national communities are constitutive sources of value, and not just instrumental goods.

Nationalism studies, which had become theoretically marginalised inside sociology or history departments, now became a central problem for IPT, as the claims of nations gave rise to further debates about self-determination, secession, national preference and, most recently, the rights of migrants. Many of these debates exposed fundamental differences of value and philosophical method. Walzer is always careful to ground his ethical positions in historical experience and in terms of the moral realities that practitioners faced. In *Just and Unjust War* he seeks to understand the perspective of those engaged in the task of fighting wars and defending the interests of a people. So his primary concern is the way in which the war convention should be understood amongst military personal and citizens, rather than an ideal and abstract legalist perspective that sees all war as morally compromised and thus never just. His approach can be contrasted with individualist cosmopolitans, such as Cécile Fabre (Fabre 2012) or Jeff McMahan (2009), who address the challenge of war from the perspective of first principles, and who deny any moral status to political communities such as states.

IPT remains a vibrant field of enquiry. Much of the focus of recent work has concentrated on debates about membership and the relative claims of individuals and political associations, whether peoples, nations or states. To this extent, IPT has offered a robust critique of classical realism except for the most die-hard positivists. It has also forced mainstream international relations theorists to raise their gaze from interstate politics to the challenges of global public goods and individual welfare and rights. Yet, IPT's success has not been left unquestioned. Some of the more radical and strident claims of global cosmopolitanism have contributed to a backlash within political theory against abandoning sensitivity to the claims of political virtue and obligation by reducing political theory just to applied ethics and questions of individual good. This backlash has been characterised as the 'realist turn' and introduces our second conception of realism: the one that is most appropriate to the narrative of this book.

The realist turn in political theory

The political theorists who have taken the 'realist turn' are aware that the concept of realism is both ambiguous in philosophy and conceptually loaded in IPT and international relations. The central idea of the turn is to assert the relative (or total) autonomy of politics in political theory. As 'political' political theory is not ideal as the name for an approach or school, realism is the preferred option. As with all new movements in political theory or international relations, much of the writing in this idiom concerns its distinction from other forms. That said, a number of scholars have been concerned to show that this approach is not just a methodological correction to the overambition of cosmopolitan individualism, but is also a perspective from which a different type of normative theory can be conducted (Philp 2007; Sleat 2016). This idea of realist political theory as a different way of doing normative political theory was also the ambition of one of its most important theorists, Bernard Williams, although he did not live to deliver fully on that ambition (Williams 2005; Hall 2020).

Williams's most famous insight is to distinguish political realism from moralism and to assert the priority of the 'first political question' as the basic legitimation demand. Moralist approaches to political theory can take two forms. The *enactment model* is exemplified by the applied ethics approach of Singer, where political prescriptions are derived from pre-political ideals, such as universal welfare, equality or autonomy. This form of political theory is the founding ambition of journals such as *Philosophy and Public Affairs* addressing policy and politics with the best outcomes of moral philosophy. The *structural model* alludes to the kind of grand theorising favoured by Rawls and his liberal-egalitarian followers. In this instance, permissible political conduct is limited by the prior demands of a theory of justice, an account of autonomy or a set of pre-political rights. In both cases, the challenge is the priority of moralism, that is, the subordination of politics to ethics and morality. This accusation may seem to echo the argument against the attempted subordination of idealism to the reality of power politics that is familiar from Carr or Morgenthau. Yet, Williams does not deny the possibility of normative political theory in favour of positivism or amoral scepticism, whatever some of his philosopher colleagues may have thought. His primary concern is to distinguish genuine political claims from ethical or moral claims, and to show that political life can create obligations and reasons that are prior to moral judgements and reasons. Characterising the domain of the political was an ambition that he did not live to deliver upon. But asserting the priority of the 'first political question' was a preoccupation of his later years and led to his most important writings on political theory, which defend the claim of legitimation over moral justification. The first question of politics concerns the legitimacy of political authority, or why we should recognise the claims of political authority. This question is prior to the moral question of political obligation – 'Why obey the state?' – because it can be given a number of answers that are not necessarily moral. More importantly, it requires an answer before one can ask moral questions of political authority, such as the justice of its distributions and use. To subject political institutions and relationships to the priority of morality has the paradoxical consequence of leaving all existing political societies illegitimate. If political obligation or legitimate submission is only appropriate to just institutions, then there are no genuine political societies, a point acknowledged in very different ways by Augustine and John Locke (see Chapters 3 and 6). If we do recognise the claims of the political in real life, and Williams suggests we do most of the time, then they cannot depend on the priority of answering a moral question about justice or right: that way lies anarchy. Williams makes much of this question of theoretical priority, partly because of his scepticism about the two dominant ethical positions in contemporary moral theory (utilitarianism and Kantianism).

Other thinkers weave different strands of argument into the question of the priority of the political. For many critics, the lack of historical awareness in contemporary political philosophy is itself a fundamental problem. The idea that a perennial philosophical question about justice could be finally settled is itself problematic for many theorists. Does Rawls's theory really settle the question of justice once and for all? Forever could be a very long time. Contextualist theories, such as Walzer's communitarianism, are much more sensitive to the claims of history. They acknowledge that moral questions of justice, right and equality must be given answers that are sensitive to the historical conditions in which they are asked. Although he is not a realist in any straightforward sense, Walzer's work (and that of many influenced by him) does contribute to the 'realist turn', at least by raising the problem of historical contingency or even relativism in respect of fundamental moral and political values.

This historical challenge to the possibility and desirability of a final answer to the problem of justice finds one of its most strident defences in the work of Raymond Geuss. Although Geuss acknowledges some debt to Williams, his dismissal of the claims of morality over politics has more to do with Marx and Nietzsche. Geuss is a relentless critic of the attempt to build politics on the ethics of Immanuel Kant, as he claims (with some justification) that Rawls seeks to do. But, for Geuss, Kant is not the highest expression of Enlightenment morality; he is merely a late Prussian thinker, obsessed with trying to salvage an unattractive variant of Christian piety. Following Nietzsche, one of Geuss's heroes, he argues that moral philosophies are simply the dead politics of the past exercising a kind of tyranny over us, in the way that in Nietzsche's view the weak use morality to dominate the strong (Rossi and Sleat 2014, p. 692). For Geuss, morality and ethics are no better than an historically contingent ideology that has its own history and power relations that serve some interest. His hostility to Rawls (and the tradition of theory that he began) is that this is just one further manifestation of bourgeois class morality. But, if all is politics, then morality can give it no advice. Whatever normative component there is for political theory to provide has to be found within political activity itself. Geuss gives the imperialist ambition of liberal-egalitarian philosophy its most brutal kicking.

There is another important strand of criticism offered by those who do not accept Geuss's Nietzscheanism, and that is the challenge of multiple value systems coexisting. This problem of value pluralism is not new in contemporary political philosophy. It was the central preoccupation of Isaiah Berlin, who had an influence on Rawls's philosophical formation (Berlin 1998). Berlin was not a relativist, nor was he a moral sceptic like Geuss, but he was a staunch defender of the view that moral values and systems were plural: this is true whether we are discussing individual values (such as liberty, equality and solidarity), or moral systems (such as liberalism, nationalism or Christianity) (Hall 2020). Values may be combined in different ways, but they cannot be reduced to a simple unity without some remainder, or having to make tragic choices. Similarly, different value systems may partially overlap, but they too are never completely commensurable. For value pluralists, political choice and disagreement are inevitable consequences of modern and diverse societies. Yet, even within non-pluralist societies (such as revolutionary Iran), Berlin would argue that there is still the problem of pluralism between theological liberals and hard-liners. Pluralism is an ineradicable feature of moral experience. But, if pluralism is the reality of moral experience, it cannot then be appealed to to settle political disputes between different values and principles.

The challenge facing the liberalism of Rawls and his followers is to ground a fair scheme of social cooperation that can establish principles for governing this empirically evident pluralism, or what Rawls call the fact of reasonable disagreement. The point of the liberal turn to social justice is to establish claims of right (or justice) that can reconcile the different conceptions of the good (or conceptions of value and the good life) of free and equal individuals. Yet, the problem with this approach, for realists, is that it assumes that a rational consensus can be provided for those principles of right, when that is precisely what the value pluralist claim denies is possible. Can one make a categorical distinction between the right and the good that does not beg the question? The theory of justice helps itself to precisely that consensus when it claims it is possible in order to justify the priority of social justice over a politically imposed conception of the common good. Indeed, Geuss's point is that liberal egalitarians just pick their preferred settlement and impose it on everyone else. However, William Galston argues that the fact of pluralism does not have to involve the claims that there can be no normative consensus, although he does argue that this will not be permanent and final as a conception of justice claims. It will emerge from a political process and draw on the values internal to that process, such as the constitutional culture of a particular society (Galston 2002). Realist political theory is much closer to the actual politics of really existing societies and far less ambitious or utopian than much of the normative political theory published over the last five decades.

Legitimacy, violence and the site of politics

The 'realist turn' in contemporary political theory provides an important corrective to the ambitions of individualist cosmopolitanism to reduce all political questions to moral or ethical questions, leaving political theory only the technical task of delivering on the answers. And, whilst it is undoubtedly connected to some of the deflationary claims of the great 20th-century classical realists (such as Carr, Morgenthau and Niebuhr), realist political philosophy does not abandon normative theorising altogether in favour of positivism. Indeed, many such as Matt Sleat (2016) and Edward Hall (2020) argue that the influence of Williams provides a useful redirection for normative political theory rather than a retreat into the history of ideas or methodological criticism. There is no reason for political theory of a realist orientation to fall victim to Procrustean positivism, or to conservativism – although these authors also make space for a genuinely conservative approach to political thinking that has not been seen since the work of Michael Oakeshott in the 1950s (Oakeshott 1962). In the field of the history of political thought, this 'realist turn' is also valuable in opening up new discussions of major past thinkers who do not fall within the param- eters of the 'rise of the modern state' or the debate between 'cosmopolitans and communitarians' about the theoretical starting point for normative theory.

However, there are also two dimensions of traditional IR realism and of the new realist political theory that this book challenges or seeks to expand on. The first is the state-based focus of politics and the second is the place of vio- lence. For the first issue here, many histories of political thought and of IPT address the rise and rationale of the modern state system and the relations that exist between those states. These histories can be teleological, addressing the emergence of the state system as a consequence of an historical process such as historical materialism, as we find in Carr. Alternatively, moralist theories could explain the growth of this system as the development of the idea of natural law and natural rights, and of the institutions necessary to realise and sustain them. One of the reasons for insisting that this book is not a simple history of realist international theory is my strong desire to challenge that kind of teleological history, when applied to the institutions of the state system or to the ideologi- cal and philosophical justifications of it. Yet, the new 'realist turn' in political theory also has a tendency to assume the primacy of the state as the vehicle through which political questions arise, or to take them for granted in ways that overlook the contingency of the form of modern politics. At its worst, this can result in an unquestioning acceptance of conceptions of the domain of the political that are either conservative in their endorsement of the status quo or utopian in their sympathy for a correct type of political institution – republi- canism. This challenge is nicely captured in a quotation from Matt Sleat:

> One of the central truths of politics is that there is a difference between the ability to rule and the right to do so, that might does not equal right and that politics is not the same as successful domination. Any claim to be ruling politically will need to make some appeal to principled grounds on which such rule is exercised – principles that should be intelligible to both the rulers and the ruled such that it can be recognised as a form of politics rather than sheer domination. (Sleat 2016, p. 32)

Implicit in this view is a conception of the people that remains sufficiently stable and coherent for it to have a 'politics', whilst also being sufficiently pluralist for the 'consensus' view of political legitimation to not hold. Perhaps the argument is that the emergence of political communities is an historically contingent matter, and so not one for political theory. Indeed, one of the reasons for privileging the 'first political question' of the legitimation of power over the moral question of justice is precisely that the question only arises in the face of an entity within which politics can emerge. Yet, one of the reasons for turning to international theory is to see the variety of sites where politics can arise, and how even in the modern world it is not obvious that that question arises only (or even mostly) with states. IPT, when viewed over a long period of time, illustrates the different forms (which I have called paradigms) in which politics can manifest itself, and consequently how that process of legitimation also varies.

The second issue concerns the primacy of legitimation, and the place of violence within it. Violence has been a constant companion of each of the thinkers discussed in this book. In some cases, it was the threat that was constantly below the surface (as in Thucydides) or a perennial feature of the fallen world (Augustine and Schmitt). Violence can also be the problem that the sovereign state exists to discipline and constrain (Hobbes and Clausewitz) or something that the state unleashes (Locke, Rousseau and Clausewitz). But violence can also be part of the process of legitimation itself (as in Machiavelli, Lenin and Mao, and Schmitt). In this respect the perspective of IPT is more useful for broadening the scope of a new political theory than a conception of political theory that assumes stable political entities, whether states or republics.

Sleat is right to draw a conceptual distinction between the power to rule and the right to rule: a punch in the face might give one 'a reason' but not the right kind of reason in seeking to answer the basic legitimation demand. The ability to deploy violence and force is not itself a legitimating reason without further explanation. But that does not mean we must follow Hannah Arendt's rejection of all violence and force, and so see politics and its legitimating strategies solely in discursive terms (Arendt 2005). Hobbes's account of sovereignty by acquisition does seem to suggest that force and its threat are a legitimate reason if a reason is a simple cause of action, but this is not the only way in which violence works in the process of legitimation. Machiavelli's *The Prince* offers a different way in which violence and force can provide a legitimating reason of the relevant sort that is not reducible to a calculation of interest: it can 'satisfy and amaze', as did the violence against Remirro de Orco's body. To claim that this sort of action cannot legitimate political authority involves an implicit moral claim that violence is unacceptable, and that can only depend on a moral judgement and not a conceptual distinction.

The important point about Machiavelli's discussion (and those of Lenin, Mao and Schmitt) is that all of them challenges the sufficiency of discourse or argument in the process of legitimating power. What Machiavelli shows is that how legitimation works and to whom it is directed cannot be settled so easily. And if we turn from Machiavelli's *The Prince* to his republican theory, we can see that the simple contrast between the ideal of republicanism and the immanent violence of the modern nation state is also far from uncontroversial. History shows that politics is not only set in a context where violence was more prevalent than it has become in the modern state, but that it is often an integral part of how political legitimacy is conceived.

Conclusion

This book is a textbook designed to introduce and raise issues that are addressed in detail in other places, as opposed to a narrow research monograph that raises and answers a single question or set of questions from the scholarship. So this concluding essay cannot answer all of the complex issues that emerge from the challenges of IPT to the hegemony of realism. Nor can it resolve the realist political theory challenge to the unreality and unpolitical direction of much contemporary political philosophy, especially in its cosmopolitan form that rejects any ethically significant entity beyond the human individual. IPT has been liberated from a narrow statist politics by its engagement with the explosion of normative political theory from the mid-1960s onwards. Yet, it has also lost sight of the importance of politics and the ambiguity surrounding the nature of that activity.

In setting out a canon of thinkers that can contribute to contextualising modern debates in IPT, I hope to have provided a resource for that specific sub-discipline and for realist political theory more broadly by bringing questions about the nature of the political (the place where political relationships arise, as well as the nature of those relationships) to the foreground. This contribution contrasts particularly with many western histories of political thought that tend towards identifying the progress of history towards the free and equal subject, liberated in a cosmopolitan global order and freed from the tyranny of arbitrary institutions such as states – accounts that place liberal democracy as the end of history and the last human.

I also hope to have challenged the horizon of realist political theory with its preoccupation with the fact of disagreement amongst a people. The perspective of the international as a starting point is valuable because it begins with the question 'amongst whom do the problems of politics arise?' rather than simply treating the international realm as the last part of a state theory. In so doing, it opens a challenge to some aspects of the 'new realist' political theory, with its rejection of violence in accounts of legitimacy (Sleat 2016; Hall 2020). The place of violence in politics and its consistency with an understanding of what are genuinely political relationships are challenges posed to all political theory by Hannah Arendt. Arendt has not featured in my story with a distinct chapter, but in many respects her challenge and that of another great but non-canonical thinker Frantz Fanon (Fanon 2001) have haunted all of the discussions throughout this book. I will not make the grand claim that the ubiquity of violence is the fundamental problem facing IPT. But I will conclude with the Augustinian insight that violence remains an ineradicable feature of human experience whatever other more benign and favourable goods political life and international politics may bring. Therefore, it should not be denied.

Bibliography

Arendt, Hannah. (2005). *The Promise of Politics*. USA: Schocken.

Bell, Duncan. (2009). 'Introduction: Under an Empty Sky – Realism and Political Theory', in D. Bell (ed.) *Political Thought and International Relations: Variations on a Realist Theme*. UK: Oxford University Press, pp. 1–25.

Berlin, Isaiah. (1998). *The Proper Study of Mankind*. UK: Pimlico.

Brown, Chris. (2002). *Sovereignty, Rights and Justice: International Political Theory Today*. UK: Polity Press.

Bull, Hedley. (2002). *The Anarchical Society: A Study of Order in World Politics*, 3rd edn. UK: Palgrave.

Fabre, Cécile. (2012). *Cosmopolitan War*. UK: Oxford University Press.

Fanon, Franz. (2001). *The Wretched of the Earth*. UK: Penguin.

Forrester, Katerina. (2019). *In the Shadow of Justice: Postwar Liberalism and the Remaking of Political Philosophy*. USA: Princeton University Press.

Galston, William. (2002). *Liberal Pluralism: The Implications for Value Pluralism for Political Theory*. UK: Cambridge University Press.

Geuss, Raymond. (2005). *Outside Ethics*. USA: Princeton University Press.

Hall, Edward. (2020). *Value, Conflict and Order: Berlin, Hampshire, Williams, and the Realist Revival in Political Theory*. USA: University of Chicago Press.

McMahan, Jeff. (2009). *Killing in War*. UK: Clarendon Press.

Miller, David. (1995). *National Identity*. UK: Oxford University Press.

Moore, Margaret. (2015). *The Political Theory of Territory*. UK: Oxford University Press.

Nozick, Robert. (1974). *Anarchy, State and Utopia*. UK: Basil Blackwell.

Oakeshott, Michael. (1962). *Rationalism in Politics*. UK: Methuen.

Owens, Patricia. (2009). 'The Ethic of Reality in Hannah Arendt', in Duncan Bell, *Political Thought and International Relations: Variations on a Realist Theme*. UK: Oxford University Press, pp. 105–121.

Philp, Mark. (2007). *Political Conduct*. UK: Harvard.

Rawls, John. [1971] (1999). *A Theory of Justice*. UK: Harvard Belknap Press.

Rossi, Enzo; and Sleat. Matthew. (2014). 'Realism in Normative Political Theory' *Philosophy Compass*, vol. 10, pp. 689–701.

Singer, Peter. (1972). 'Famine, Affluence and Morality' *Philosophy and Public Affairs*, vol. 1, no. 3, pp. 229–243.

Singer, Peter. (2002). *One World: The Ethics of Globalisation*. USA: Yale University Press.

Sleat, Matt. (2013). *Liberal Realism: A Realist Theory of Liberal Politics*. UK: University of Manchester Press.

Sleat, Matt. (2016). 'Realism, Liberalism and Non-Ideal Theory Or, Are there Two Ways to do Realistic Political Theory?' *Political Studies*, vol. 64, pp. 27–41.

Tamir, Yael. (1993). *Liberal Nationalism*. USA: Princeton University Press.

Walzer, Michael. (1977). *Just and Unjust Wars*. USA: Basic Books.

Wight, Martin. (1991). *International Theory: The Three Traditions*, ed. Gabriele Wight and Brian Ernest Porter. UK: Leicester University Press.

Williams, Bernard. (2005). *In the Beginning was the Deed: Realism and Moralism in Political Argument*, ed. Geoffrey Hawthorne. UK: Cambridge University Press.

References

Primary texts (by chapter order)

Thucydides. (1972). *History of the Peloponnesian War*, trans R. Warner, ed. M.I. Finley. UK: Penguin.

Augustine. (1994). *Political Writings*, trans. M.W. Tkacz and D. Kries, intro. E.L. Fortin. USA: Hackett.

Augustine. (1998). *The City of God Against the Pagans*, ed. R.W. Dyson. UK: Cambridge University Press.

Machiavelli, Niccolo. (1988). *The Prince*, ed. Q. Skinner and R. Price. UK: Cambridge University Press.

Machiavelli, Niccolo. (1989). 'The History of Florence', in A. Gilbert trans *Machiavelli: The Chief Works and Others*, 3 vols, vol. 3. USA: Duke University Press.

Machiavelli, Niccolo. (2005). *The Art of War*, ed. C. Lynch. USA: University of Chicago Press.

Machiavelli, Niccolo. (2008). *Discourses on Livy*, trans. J.C. Bondanella and P. Bondanella. UK: Oxford University Press.

Hobbes, Thomas [1651] (1991). *Leviathan*, ed. R. Tuck. UK: Cambridge University Press.

Locke, John. [1690] (1988). *Two Treatises of Government*, ed. P. Laslett. UK: Cambridge University Press.

Rousseau, Jean-Jacques (1991). *Rousseau and International Relations*, ed. S. Hoffman and D.P. Fidler. UK: Clarendon Press.

Rousseau, Jean-Jacques. (2011). *The Basic Political Writings*, ed. D.A. Cress, intro. David Wootton. USA: Hackett.

Clausewitz, Carl von [1832] (1984). *On War*, ed. M. Howard and P. Paret. USA: Princeton University Press.

Lenin. (1978). *Imperialism, The Highest Stage of Capitalism*. Russia: Progress Publishers.

Lenin. (1988). *What Is to Be Done?* ed. R. Service. UK: Penguin.

Lenin. (1992). *The State and Revolution*, ed. R. Service. UK: Penguin.

Mao. (2014). *Selected Works of Mao Zedong*. Marx-Engels-Lenin Institute.

Mao. (1967). *Selected Military Writings of Mao Tse-Tung*. China: Foreign Language Press.

Mao. (1966). *Quotations from Chairman Mao Tse-Tung* [*The Little Red Book*]. Beijing.

Schmitt, Carl. (1988). *Political Theology: Four Chapters on the Concept of Sovereignty*, trans. George Schwab. USA: MIT Press.

Schmitt, Carl. [1923] (1988). *The Crisis of Parliamentary Democracy*, trans. E. Kennedy. USA: MIT Press.

Schmitt, Carl. (2006). *The Nomos of the Earth in the International Law of the Jus Publicum Europaeum*, trans. G.L. Ulmen. USA: Telos Press.

Schmitt, Carl. [1932] (2007a). *The Concept of the Political*, trans. George Schwab. USA: University of Chicago Press.

Schmitt, Carl. [1963] (2007b). *Theory of the Partisan*, trans. G.L. Ulmen. USA: Telos Press.

Secondary reading

Ali, Tariq. (2017). *The Dilemmas of Lenin*. UK: Verso.

Allison, Graham. (2017). *Destined for War*. USA: Houghton Mifflin.

Althusser, Louis. (1999). *Machiavelli and Us*. UK: Verso.

Arendt, Hannah. (1951). *The Origins of Totalitarianism*. USA: Schocken Books.

Arendt, Hannah. (1963). *On Revolution*. UK: Faber and Faber.

Arendt, Hannah. (2005). *The Promise of Politics*. USA: Schocken.

Armitage, David. (2012a). *Foundations of Modern International Thought*. UK: Cambridge University Press.

Armitage, David. (2012b). 'John Locke: Theorist of Empire?' in S. Muthu (ed.) *Empire and Modern Political Thought*. UK: Cambridge University Press, pp. 84–111.

Armitage, David. (2017). *Civil Wars: A History in Ideas*. UK: Yale University Press.

Arneil, Barbara. (1996). *John Locke and America*. UK: Clarendon Press.

Aron, Raymond. (1983). *Clausewitz: Philosopher of War*, trans. C.C. Booker and N. Stone. UK: Routledge and Kegan Paul.

Ashcraft, Richard. (1986). *Revolutionary Politics and Locke's Two Treatises of Government*. USA: Princeton University Press.

Avineri, Shlomo. (1968). *The Social and Political Thought of Karl Marx*. UK: Cambridge University Press.

Barry, Brian. (1965). *Political Argument*. UK: Routledge and Kegan Paul.

Bassford, Christopher. (1994). *Clausewitz in English*. UK: Oxford University Press.

Beitz, Charles R. (1979). *Political Theory and International Relations*. USA: Princeton University Press.

Bell, Duncan. (2009). 'Introduction: Under an Empty Sky – Realism and Political Theory', in D. Bell (ed.) *Political Thought and International Relations: Variations on a Realist Theme*. UK: Oxford University Press, pp. 1–25.

Bell, Duncan. (2018). 'Realist Challenges', in R. Eckersley and C. Brown (eds) *Oxford Handbook of International Political Theory*. UK: Oxford University Press, pp. 641–651.

Benner, Erica. (2015). *Be Like the Fox*. UK: Penguin.

Berlin, Isaiah. (1998). 'The Originality of Machiavelli', in *The Proper Study of Mankind*. UK: Pimlico, pp. 269–325.

Bertram, Christopher. (2004). *Rousseau and the Social Contract*. UK: Routledge.

Bertram, Christopher. (2012). 'Rousseau's Legacy in Two Conceptions of the General Will: Democratic and Transcendental' *Review of Politics*, vol. 74, pp. 403–420.

Biggar, Nigel. (2013). *In Defence of War*. UK: Oxford University Press.

Bobbitt, Phillip. (2013). *The Garments of Court and Palace: Machiavelli and the World that He Made*. UK: Atlantic Books.

Booth, Wayne C. (1979). *Critical Understanding: The Powers and Limits of Pluralism*. USA: University of Chicago Press.

Booth, Wayne C. (1988). *The Company We Keep: An Ethics of Fiction*. USA: University of California Press.

Boucher, David. (1985). *Texts in Context*. Netherlands: Martinus Nijhoff.

Boucher, David. (1998). *Political Theories of International Relations*. UK: Oxford University Press.

Boucher, David. (2005). 'Property and Propriety in International Relations: The Case of John Locke', in B. Jahn (ed.) *Classical Theory in International Relations*. UK: Cambridge University Press, pp. 156–177.

Boucher, David; and Kelly, Paul. (1994). *The Social Contract from Hobbes to Rawls*. UK: Routledge.

Brown, Chris. (2002). *Sovereignty, Rights and Justice: International Political Theory Today*. UK: Polity Press.

Brown, Chris. (2015). *International Society, Global Polity*. UK: Sage.

Brown, Chris; and Ainley, Kirstin. (2005). *Understanding International Relations*, 3rd edn. UK: Palgrave.

Brown, Chris; and Eckersley, Robyn. (eds) (2018). *The Oxford Handbook of International Political Theory*. UK: Oxford University Press.

Buchanan, Allan. (1991). *Secession: The Morality of Political Divorce from Fort Sumpter to Lithuania and Quebec*. USA: Westview.

Bull, Hedley. (2002). *The Anarchical Society: A Study of Order in World Politics*, 3rd edn. UK: Palgrave.

Burnham, James. (1943). *The Machiavellians*. UK: Putnam.

Butterfield, Herbert. (1962). *Christianity, Diplomacy and War*. UK: Wyvern Books.

Caney, Simon. (2005). *Justice Beyond Borders*. UK: Oxford University Press.

Carr, E.H. [1939] (2016). *The Twenty Years' Crisis 1919–1939*. UK: Palgrave.

Cesa, Marco. (2014). *Machiavelli on International Relations*. UK: Oxford University Press.

Claeys, Gregory. (2018). *Marx and Marxism*. UK: Penguin.

Cohen, Joshua. (2010). *Rousseau: A Community of Equals*. UK: Oxford University Press.

Coleman, Janet. (2000). *Political Thought from the Middle Ages to the Renaissance*. UK: Wiley Blackwell.

Collingwood, Robin G. (1939). *An Autobiography*. UK: Clarendon Press.

Collingwood, Robin G. (1993). *The Idea of History with Lectures 1926–1928*. UK: Oxford University Press.

Connolly, William E. (1993). *The Augustinian Imperative: The Politics of Morality*. USA: Sage.

Creveld, Martin van (1991). *The Transformation of War*. USA: Free Press.

Dahl, Robert. (2015). *On Democracy*, 2nd edn. USA: Yale.

Deneen, Patrick J. (2018). *Why Liberalism Failed*. USA: Yale University Press.

Doyle, Michael W. (1997). *Ways of War and Peace*. USA: Norton.

Doyle, Michael W. (2011). *Striking First*. USA: Princeton University Press.

Dunne, Timothy (1999). 'A British School of International Relations', in Jack Hayward, Brian Barry and Archie Brown (eds) *The British Study of Politics in the Twentieth Century*. UK: The British Academy.

Echevarria II, Antulio J. (2007). *Clausewitz and Contemporary War*. UK: Oxford University Press.

Echevarria II, Antulio J. (2017). *Military Strategy: A Very Short Introduction*. UK: Oxford University Press.

Elshtain, Jean Bethke. (1995). *Augustine and the Limits of Politics*. USA: University of Notre Dame Press.

Elshtain, Jean Bethke. (2003). *Just War against Terror*. USA: Basic Books.

Fabre, Cécile. (2012). *Cosmopolitan War*. UK: Oxford University Press.

Fabre, Cécile. (2016). *Cosmopolitan Peace*. UK: Oxford University Press.

Fabre, Cécile. (2018). *Economic Statecraft*. USA: Harvard University Press.

Fanon, Franz. (2001). *The Wretched of the Earth*. UK: Penguin.

Finlay, Christopher. (2019). *Is Just War Possible?* UK: Polity Press.

Fleming, Colin M. (2013). *Clausewitz's Timeless Trinity*. UK: Routledge.

Flikschuh, Katrin. (2000). *Kant and Modern Political Philosophy*. UK: Cambridge University Press.

Forrester, Katerina. (2019). *In the Shadow of Justice: Postwar Liberalism and the Remaking of Political Philosophy*. USA: Princeton University Press.

Forsyth, Maurice. (1979). 'Thomas Hobbes and the External Relations of States' *British Journal of International Studies*, vol. 5, no. 3, pp. 196–209.

Frazer, Elizabeth; and Hutchings, Kimberly. (2019). *Can Political Violence Ever Be Justified?* UK: Polity Press.

Frazer, Elizabeth; and Hutchings, Kimberly. (2020). *Violence and Political Theory*. UK: Polity Press.

Freeden, Michael. (1996). *Ideologies and Political Theory a Conceptual Approach*. UK: Oxford University Press.

Freedman, Lawrence. (2013). *Strategy: A History*. UK: Oxford University Press.

Fukuyama, Francis. (1989). 'The End of History?' *The National Interest*, vol. 16, pp. 3–18.

Fukuyama, Francis. (1992). *The End of History and the Last Man*. USA: Free Press.

Fuller, Timothy. (ed.) (2016). *Machiavelli's Legacy:* The Prince *after Five Hundred Years*. USA: University of Pennsylvania Press.

Gaddis, John Lewis. (2018). *On Grand Strategy*. UK: Allen Lane.

Gallie, W.B. (1978). *Philosophers of Peace and War*. UK: Cambridge University Press.

Galston, William. (2002). *Liberal Pluralism: The Implications for Value Pluralism for Political Theory*. UK: Cambridge University Press.

Gat, Aron. (1989). *The Origins of Military Thought: From the Enlightenment to Clausewitz*. UK: Clarendon Press.

Gellner, Ernest. (1983). *Nations and Nationalism*. UK: Blackwell.

Gerges, Fawez A. (2016). *Isis: A History*. USA: Princeton University Press.

Geuss, Raymond. (2005). *Outside Ethics*. USA: Princeton University Press.

Goldwin, Robert A. (1987). 'John Locke', in Leo Strauss and Joseph Cropsey (eds) *History of Political Philosophy*, 3rd edn. USA: University of Chicago Press, pp. 476–512.

Goodin, Robert; and Spiekermann, Kai. (2018). *An Epistemic Theory of Democracy*. UK: Oxford University Press.

Gramsci, Antonio. (1971). *Selections from the Prison Notebooks*, ed. Quintin Hoare and Geoffrey Nowell-Smith. UK: Lawrence and Wishart.

Gray, Colin S. (1999). *Modern Strategy*. UK: Oxford University Press.

Gray, John. (1998). *False Dawn: The Delusions of Global Capitalism*. UK: Granta.

Grayling, Anthony C. (2017). *War: An Enquiry*. UK: Yale University Press.

Gross, Raphael. (2007). *Carl Schmitt and the Jews: The 'Jewish Question' the Holocaust and German Legal Theory*. USA: University of Wisconsin Press.

Gross, Raphael. (2016). 'The "True Enemy": Antisemitism in Carl Schmitt's Life and Work'. *The Oxford Handbook of Carl Schmitt*. UK: Oxford University Press, pp. 117–146.

Habermas, Jürgen. (1998). *The Postnational Constellation*. UK: Polity Press.

Habermas, Jürgen. (2005). *Old Europe, New Europe, Core Europe*, ed. Daniel Levy, Max Pensky and John C. Torpey. UK: Verso.

Hall, Edward. (2020). *Value, Conflict and Order: Berlin, Hampshire, Williams, and the Realist Revival in Political Theory.* USA: University of Chicago Press.

Hampton, Jean. (1988). *Hobbes and the Social Contract Tradition.* UK: Cambridge University Press.

Handel, Michael I. (1988). 'Clausewitz in the Age of Technology' *Journal of Strategic Studies*, vol. 9, pp. 51–92.

Harding, Neil. (1977). *Lenin's Political Thought, vol. 1: Theory and Practice in the Democratic Revolution.* UK: Macmillan.

Harding, Neil. (1981). *Lenin's Political Thought, vol. 2: Theory and Practice in the Socialist Revolution.* UK: Macmillan.

Harding, Neil. (1996). *Leninism.* UK: Macmillan.

Hauerwas, Stanley. (2002). *The Peaceable Kingdom: A Primer in Christian Ethics.* USA: Notre Dame University Press.

Hauerwas, Stanley. (2011). *War and the American Difference: Theological Reflections on Violence and National Identity.* USA: Baker Academic.

Hayek, Friedrich A. (1944). *The Road to Serfdom.* USA: University of Chicago Press.

Hayek, Friedrich A. (1960). *The Constitution of Liberty.* USA: University of Chicago Press.

Herz, John H. (1951). 'Idealist Internationalism and the Security Dilemma' *World Politics*, vol. 2, pp. 157–180.

Hinsley, Francis H. (1962). *Power and the Pursuit of Peace.* UK: Cambridge University Press.

Hobhouse, Leonard T. (1918). *The Metaphysical Theory of the State: A Criticism.* UK: George Allen and Unwin.

Hooker, William. (2009). *Carl Schmitt's International Thought: Order and Orientation.* UK: Cambridge University Press.

Howard, Michael. (2002). *Clausewitz: A Short Introduction.* UK: Oxford University Press.

Huntington, Samuel P. (1993). 'The Clash of Civilisations' *Foreign Affairs*, vol. 72, no. 3, pp. 22–49.

Huntington, Samuel P. (1997). *The Clash of Civilisations: And the Remaking of World Order.* UK: Simon and Schuster.

Ikenberry, G. John. (2001). *After Victory: Institutions, Strategic Restraint and the Rebuilding of Order after Major Wars.* USA: Princeton University Press.

Ikenberry, G. John. (2012). *Liberal Leviathan: The Origins, Crisis, and Transformations of the American World Order.* USA: Princeton University Press.

Ikenberry, G. John. (2020). *A World Safe for Democracy.* USA: Yale University Press.

Ivison, D. (2010). *Postcolonial Liberalism.* UK: Cambridge University Press.

Ivison, D. (2019). *Can Liberal States Accommodate Indigenous Peoples.* UK: Polity Press.

Kagan, Donald. (2009). *Thucydides.* USA: Viking Penguin.

Kaldor, Mary. (2012). *New and Old Wars*, 3rd edn. UK: Polity Press.

Kant, Immanuel. [1793] (1991). 'Perpetual Peace', in H.S. Reiss (ed.) *Kant Political Writings*. UK: Cambridge University Press.

Katzenbach Jnr, Edward L.; and Hanrahan, Gene Z. (1955). 'The Revolutionary Strategy of Mao Tse-Tung' *Political Science Quarterly*, vol. 70, pp. 321–340.

Kedourie, Elie. (1960). *Nationalism*. UK: Hutchinson.

Kelly, Paul. (1999). 'Contextual and Non-Contextual Histories of Political Thought', in J. Hayward, B. Barry, and A. Brown (eds) *The British Study of Politics in the Twentieth Century*. UK: British Academy, pp. 37–62.

Kelly, Paul. (2005). *Liberalism*. UK: Polity.

Kelly, Paul. (2007). *Locke's Second Treatise of Government*. UK: Continuum.

Kelly, Paul. (2015). 'Armitage on Locke on International Theory: The Two Treatises of Government and the Right of Intervention', *History of European Ideas*, vol. 41, pp. 49–61.

Keohane, Robert; and Nye. Joseph. (1977). *Power and Interdependence*. USA: Little, Brown.

Keynes, John Maynard. [1919] (2015). 'The Economic Consequences of the Peace', in Robert Skidelsky (ed.) *The Essential Keynes*. UK: Penguin.

Kolakowski, Lezek. (2005). *Main Currents of Marxism*. USA: Norton.

Kuhn, Thomas S. (1962). *The Structure of Scientific Revolutions*. USA: University of Chicago Press.

Kymlicka, Will. (1995). *Multicultural Citizenship*. UK: Oxford University Press.

Lasswell, Harold. (1936). *Politics: Who Gets What, When and How*. UK: McGraw Hill.

Lewis, David Malcolm; Boardman, John; Davies, John Kenyon; and Ostwald, Martin. (1992). *The Cambridge Ancient History, vol. 5*. UK: Cambridge University Press.

Lloyd, Sharon A. (1992). *Ideals as Interests in Hobbes's Leviathan: The Power of the Mind Over Matter*. UK: Cambridge University Press.

Loughlin, Martin. (2018). 'Why Read Carl Schmitt', in Christoph Bezemek, Michael Potacs, Alexander Somek (eds) *Vienna Lectures on Legal Philosophy*, vol. 1. UK: Hart, pp. 49–67.

Lovell, Julia. (2019). *Maoism: A Global History*. UK: Bodley Head.

Lukes, Steven. (2003). *Liberals and Cannibals: The Implications of Diversity*. UK: Verso.

Lyotard, Jean-Francois. (1984). *The Post-Modern Condition: A Report on Knowledge*. USA: University of Minnesota Press.

Macpherson, Crawford B. (1962). *The Political Theory of Possessive Individualism*. UK: Oxford University Press.

Malcolm, Noel. (1996). 'Conservative Realism and Christian Democracy', in Kenneth Minogue (ed.) *Conservative Realism*. UK: Harper Collins.

Malcolm, Noel. (2002). *Aspects of Hobbes*. UK: Clarendon Press.

Markus, Richard A. (1983). 'Saint Augustine's Views on the "Just War"', in W.J. Sheils (ed.) *The Church and War: Church History*, vol. 20. UK: Oxford University Press, pp. 1–13.

Markus, Richard A. (1988). 'The Latin Fathers', in James Henderson Burns (ed.) *The Cambridge History of Medieval Political Thought c. 350–1450*. UK: Cambridge University Press, pp. 92–122.

Martinich, Aloysius P. (1992). *The Two Gods of Leviathan: Thomas Hobbes on Religion and Politics*. UK: Cambridge University Press.

McCormick, John P. (1993). 'Carl Schmitt: The Age of Neutralisation and Depoliticisation'. *Telos*, vol. 96, pp. 130–142.

McCormick, John P. (2018). *Reading Machiavelli: Scandalous Books, Suspect Engagements and the Virtue of Populist Politics*. USA: Princeton University Press.

McLellan, David. (2000). *Karl Marx: Selected Writings*. UK: Oxford University Press.

McMahan, Jeff. (2009). *Killing in War*. UK: Clarendon Press.

McQueen, Alison. (2018). *Political Realism in Apocalyptic Times*. UK: Cambridge University Press.

Mearsheimer, John J. (2011). *Why Leaders Lie: The Truth About Lying in International Politics*. USA: Oxford University Press.

Mearsheimer, John J. (2018). *The Great Delusion: Liberal Dreams and International Realities*. UK: Yale University Press.

Meier, Heinrich. (1995). *Carl Schmitt and Leo Strauss: The Hidden Dialogue*. USA: University of Chicago Press.

Meier, Heinrich. (1998). *The Lesson of Carl Schmitt: Four Chapters on the Distinction between Political Theology and Political Philosophy*. USA: University of Chicago Press.

Meierhenrich, Jens; and Simons, Oliver. (2016). *The Oxford Handbook of Carl Schmitt*. UK: Oxford University Press.

Meineke, Friedrich. (1957). *Machiavellism: The Doctrine of Raison d'Etat and its Place in Modern History*. USA: Yale University Press.

Miller, David. (1995). *National Identity*. UK: Oxford University Press.

Moller-Okin, Susan. (2013). *Women in Western Political Thought*. USA: Princeton University Press.

Moore, Margaret. (2015). *The Political Theory of Territory*. UK: Oxford University Press.

Morley, Neville. (2014). *Thucydides and the Idea of History*. UK: I.B. Tauris.

Muller, Jan-Werner. (2003). *A Dangerous Mind: Carl Schmitt in Post-War European Thought*. USA: Yale University Press.

Muthu, Sankar. (2012). *Empire and Modern Political Thought*. UK: Cambridge University Press.

Neuhouser, Friedrich. (2013). 'Rousseau's Critique of Inequality: Reconstructing the Second Discourse'. *Philosophy and Public Affairs*, vol. 41, pp. 193–225.

Newey, Glen. (2008). *Hobbes and Leviathan*. UK: Routledge.

Niebuhr, Reinhold. [1932] (2005). *Moral Man and Immoral Society*. USA: Continuum.

Nozick, Robert. (1974). *Anarchy, State and Utopia*. UK: Basil Blackwell.

Nye, Joseph. (2015). *Is the American Century Over?* UK: Polity.

Nye, Joseph. (2020). *Do Morals Matter?* USA: Oxford University Press.

Oakeshott, Michael. (1962). *Rationalism in Politics*. UK: Methuen.

Oakeshott, Michael. (1983). *On History and Other Essays*. UK: Blackwell.

O'Donovan, Oliver. (1996). *The Desire of the Nations: Rediscovering the Roots of Political Theology*. UK: Cambridge University Press.

O'Donovan, Oliver. (2003). *The Just War Revisited*. UK: Cambridge University Press.

O'Donovan, Oliver. (2005). *Ways of Judgement*. UK: W. Eerdmans.

O'Donovan, Oliver; and Lockwood O'Donovan, Joan. (2004). *Bonds of Imperfection: Christian Politics Past and Present*. USA: W. Eerdmans.

Odysseos, Louiza; and Petito, Fabio. (2007). *The International Political Thought of Carl Schmitt: Terror, Liberal War and the Crisis of Global Order*. UK: Routledge.

Orwell, George. (1971). *The Collected Essays, Journalism and Letters of George Orwell: Volume 4 in Front of Your Nose, 1945–50*. UK: Penguin.

Osterhammel, Jurgen. (2018). *Unfabling the East: The Enlightenment's Encounter with Asia*. USA: Princeton University Press.

Owens, Patricia. (2009). 'The Ethic of Reality in Hannah Arendt', in Duncan Bell, *Political Thought and International Relations: Variations on a Realist Theme*. UK: Oxford University Press, pp. 105–121.

Owens, Patricia; and Rietzler, Katharina (2021). *Women's International Thought: A new History*. UK: Cambridge University Press.

Paret, Peter. (2007). *Clausewitz and the State*. USA: Princeton University Press.

Pettit, Philip. (1997). *Republicanism: A Theory of Freedom*. UK: Oxford University Press.

Philp, Mark. (2007). *Political Conduct*. UK: Harvard.

Piketty, Thomas. (2013). *Capital in the Twenty-First Century*. UK: Harvard University Press.

Piketty, Thomas. (2020). *Capital and Ideology*. UK: Harvard University Press.

Pincus, Steven. (2009). *1688: The First Modern Revolution*. USA: Yale.

Pinker, Stephen. (2011). *The Better Angels of Our Nature: Why Violence Has Declined*. UK: Penguin.

Pinker, Stephen. (2018). *Enlightenment Now*. UK: Penguin.

Plamenatz, John P. (1963). *Man and Society*, 2 vols. UK: Longmans.

Pogge, Thomas. (1989). *Realizing Rawls*. USA: Cornell University Press.

Poole, Thomas. (2015). *Reason of State, Law Prerogative and Empire*. UK: Oxford University Press.

Popper, Karl. (1959). *The Logic of Scientific Discovery*. UK: Routledge.

Popper, Karl. [1945] (2011). *The Open Society and Its Enemies*. UK: Routledge.

Posner, Eric A. (2011). *The Perils of Global Legalism*. USA: University of Chicago Press.

Ratzinger, Joseph. [Pope Benedict XVI] (2008). *Church, Ecumenism and Politics: New Endeavours in Ecclesiology*. USA: Ignatius Press.

Ratzinger, Joseph. [Pope Benedict XVI] (2018). *Faith and Politics*. USA: Ignatius Press.

Rawls, John. [1971] (1999). *A Theory of Justice*. UK: Harvard Belknap Press.

Rawls, John. (1999). *The Law of Peoples*. UK: Harvard University Press.

Rawls, John. (2007). *Lectures on the History of Political Philosophy*. USA: Harvard.

Rossi, Enzo; and Sleat. Matthew. (2014). 'Realism in Normative Political Theory' *Philosophy Compass*, vol. 10, pp. 689–701.

Ryan, James. (2011). '"Revolution Is War": The Development of the Thought of V.I. Lenin on Violence, 1899–1907" *The Slavonic and East European Review*, vol. 89, pp. 248–273.

Ryan, James. (2012). *Lenin's Terror and the Ideological Origins of Early Soviet State Violence*. UK: Routledge.

Said, Edward. (1979). *Orientalism*. UK: Penguin.

Schmitt, Carl. [1919] (1986). *Political Romanticism*, trans. Guy Oakes. USA: MIT Press.

Schmitt, Carl. [1922] (1988). *Political Theology: Four Chapters on the Concept of Sovereignty*, trans. George Schwab. USA: MIT Press.

Schmitt, Carl. [1923] (1988). *The Crisis of Parliamentary Democracy*, trans. E. Kennedy. USA: MIT Press.

Schmitt, Carl. [1923] (1996). *Roman Catholicism and Political Form*, trans. G.L. Ulmen. USA: Greenwood Press.

Schmitt, Carl. (2006). *The Nomos of the Earth in the International Law of the Jus Publicum Europaeum*, trans. G.L. Ulmen. USA: Telos Press.

Schmitt, Carl. [1932] (2007a). *The Concept of the Political*, trans. George Schwab. USA: University of Chicago Press.

Schmitt, Carl. [1963] (2007b). *Theory of the Partisan*, trans. G.L. Ulmen. USA: Telos Press.

Schmitt, Carl. (2011). *Writings on War*, trans. Timothy Nunan. UK: Polity Press.

Schmitt, Carl. [1921] (2014). *Dictatorship*, trans. M. Hoelzl and G. Ward. UK: Polity Press.

Schmitt, Carl. (2015). *Dialogues on Power and Space*, ed. Federico Finchelstein, Andreas Kalyvas, trans Samuel Garret Zeitlin. UK: Polity Press.

Schmitt, Carl. (2015). *Land and Sea: A World Historical Meditation*. USA: Telos Press.

Schram, Stuart. (1990). *The Thought of Mao Tse-Tung*. UK: Cambridge University Press.

Schulman, Alex. (2012). 'Carl Schmitt and the Clash of Civilisations: The Missing Context' *Journal of Political Ideologies*, vol. 17, no. 2, pp. 147–167.

Shklar, Judith. (1985). *Men and Citizens: A Study in Rousseau's Social Theory*. UK: Cambridge University Press.

Simmons, A. John. (1993). *On the Edge of Anarchy: Locke, Consent and the Limits of Society*. USA: Princeton University Press.

Singer, Peter. (1972). 'Famine, Affluence and Morality' *Philosophy and Public Affairs*, vol. 1, no. 3, pp. 229–243.

Singer, Peter. (2002). *One World: The Ethics of Globalisation*. USA: Yale University Press.

Skinner, Quentin. (1969). 'Meaning and Understanding in the History of Ideas' *History and Theory*, vol. 8, pp. 3–53.

Skinner, Quentin. (1978). *The Foundations of Modern Political Theory*, 2 vols. UK: Cambridge University Press.

Skinner, Quentin. (1997). *Liberty before Liberalism*. UK: Cambridge University Press.

Skinner, Quentin. (2000). *Machiavelli: A Very Short Introduction*. UK: Oxford University Press.

Sleat, Matt. (2013). *Liberal Realism: A Realist Theory of Liberal Politics*. UK: University of Manchester Press.

Sleat, Matt. (2016). 'Realism, Liberalism and Non-Ideal Theory Or, Are there Two Ways to do Realistic Political Theory?' *Political Studies*, vol. 64, pp. 27–41.

Slomp, Gabriella. (2009). *Carl Schmitt and the Politics of Hostility, Violence and Terror*. UK: Palgrave.

Smith, Anthony D. (1986). *The Ethnic Origins of Nations*. UK: Blackwell.

Snow, Edgar. (2018). *Red Star over China*, ed. J.K. Fairbanks. UK: Grove.

Solzhenitsyn, Alexander. (1974). *The Gulag Archipelago*. USA: Harper Collins.

Song, Robert. (1997). *Christianity and Liberal Society*. UK: Clarendon Press.

Spence, Jonathan D. (1990). *The Search for Modern China*. USA: Norton.

Spence, Jonathan D. (1999). *Mao*. UK: Weidenfeld and Nicholson.

Sreenivasan, Gopal. (2000). 'What Is the General Will?' *Philosophical Review*, vol. 109, pp. 545–581.

Strachan, Hew. (2007). *Clausewitz's On War: A Biography*. USA: Grove.

Strauss, Leo. (1957). *Thoughts on Machiavelli*. USA: University of Chicago Press.

Strauss, Leo. (1978). *The City and Man*. USA: University of Chicago Press.

Strauss, Leo; and Cropsey, Joseph. (1987). *History of Political Philosophy*. USA: University of Chicago Press.

Streeck, Wolfgang. (2016). *How Will Capitalism End?* UK: Verso.

Talmon, Jacob. (1986). *The Origins of Totalitarian Democracy*. UK: Penguin.

Talmon, Jacob. (1981). *The Myth of the Nation and the Vision of Revolution*. UK: Secker and Warburg.

Tamir, Yael. (1993). *Liberal Nationalism*. USA: Princeton University Press.

Tooze, Adam. (2018). *Crashed: How a Decade of Financial Crises Changed the World*. UK: Penguin.

Tuck, Richard. (2020). *The Left Case For Brexit*. UK: Polity Press.

Vincent, Raymond J. (1981). 'The Hobbesian Tradition in Twentieth Century International Thought' *Millennium: Journal of International Studies*, vol. 10, no. 2, pp. 91–101.

Voegelin, Eric. (1952). *The New Science of Politics: An Introduction*. USA: University of Chicago Press.

Walt, Steven M. (2005). *Taming American Power*. USA: Norton.

Walt, Steven M. (2018). *The Hell of Good Intentions: America's Foreign Policy Elite and the Decline of U.S. Primacy*. USA: Farrar Straus and Giroux.

Waltz, Kenneth N. [1979] (2010). *Theory of International Politics*. USA: Waveland Press.

Walzer, Michael. (1977). *Just and Unjust Wars*. USA: Basic Books.

Ward, Lee. (2010). *Locke on Modern Life*. UK: Cambridge University Press.

Warrender, H. (1957). *The Political Philosophy of Hobbes*. UK: Clarendon Press.

Wendt, Alexander. (1999). *Social Theory of International Politics*. UK: Cambridge University Press.

Whitehead, Alfred North. (1929). *Process and Reality: An Essay in Cosmology*. USA: Macmillan.

Wight, Martin. (1991). *International Theory: The Three Traditions*, ed. Gabriele Wight and Brian Ernest Porter. UK: Leicester University Press.

Williams, Bernard. (2005). *In the Beginning was the Deed: Realism and Moralism in Political Argument*, ed. Geoffrey Hawthorne. UK: Cambridge University Press.

Williams, Rowan. (2016). *On Augustine*. UK: Bloomsbury.

Wilson, Peter H. (2010). *Europe's Tragedy: A New History of the Thirty Years War*. UK: Penguin.

Winter, Yves. (2018). *Machiavelli and the Orders of Violence*. UK: Cambridge University Press.

Wokler, Robert. (2001). *Rousseau: A Very Short Introduction*. UK: Oxford University Press.

Woolhouse, Roger. (2009). *Locke: A Biography*. UK: Cambridge University Press.

Zamoyski, Adam. (2018). *Napoleon: The Man Behind the Myth*. UK: Collins.

Zerelli, Linda. (2008). 'Feminist Theory and the Canon of Political Thought', in John S. Dryzek, Bonnie Honig and Anne Phillips (eds) *The Oxford Handbook of Political Theory*. UK: Oxford University Press, pp. 106–124.

Press

Suggestions for finding open access texts for the major authors covered in *Conflict, War and Revolution*

Research credit: Heather Dawson, LSE Library

If you do not currently have access to a university library that holds the same editions of works by the major thinkers that Professor Kelly references in his textbook, here are our suggestions for finding *free and open access copies* of these thinkers' major works. Below we cover:

- Primary sources for the major works of each main thinker. There are also a few cases where the same sources that Professor Kelly recommends are freely available. But mostly you will need to operate with earlier or different editions.
- Some general sources, which may also be relevant for accessing other literatures about these thinkers as well (secondary sources).

Bear in mind that, if you have access to a public library or a university library, most of them will now offer access to e-book packages. These are great because they allow cross-searching of many titles. In larger public libraries you may be able to find there the same sources that Professor Kelly recommends.

Free open access websites are increasing in number but they are not always perfect. What is available is affected by copyright regulations and so it may differ from country to country. Items can also be removed at short notice – so if you can download a useful source it is best to do it straightaway and save to a PDF library on your PC.

When reading digital texts, it can be helpful to use the computer's 'find' function to quickly find key passages and concepts that you are interested in. But be careful to read around the passages you identify (both before and after) so as to ensure that you understand the author's argument and its context fully.

Bear in mind also that most freely available editions are older versions, and so more modern translations or editions may give a different slant to the author's view, or even a different translation of an author's key concepts. So always check the bibliographic details for the date. If there are any apparent divergences between your text and Professor Kelly's analysis, bear in mind that he is using the most modern and best-regarded editions.

1. Suggestions for individual authors

Thucydides
https://openlibrary.org/books/OL5471702M/History_of_the_Peloponnesian
_War
This is the same edition that Professor Kelly recommends:
Thucydides. (1972). *History of the Peloponnesian War*, trans R. Warner ed. M.I. Finley. UK: Penguin.

St Augustine
https://www.perseus.tufts.edu/hopper/searchresults?q=St+Augustine

Machiavelli
Online Library of Liberty. This is maintained by the Liberty Fund
https://oll.libertyfund.org/person/niccolo-machiavelli

Hobbes
Online Library of Liberty https://oll.libertyfund.org/person/thomas-hobbes

John Locke
Online Library of Liberty https://oll.libertyfund.org/person/john-locke
Also see the Digital Locke Project http://www.digitallockeproject.nl/
The Digital Locke Project presents the first complete text critical edition, based on John Locke's manuscripts, of the texts that are related to his most famous work, *An Essay Concerning Human Understanding*. The DLP concentrates on the material that was produced between the first edition of the *Essay* in 1689 and Locke's death in 1704.
At the time of writing, there was also a sample of the same edition that Professor Kelly recommends at:
http://assets.cambridge.org/97805210/69038/sample/9780521069038ws.pdf

Rousseau
Online Library of Liberty.
https://oll.libertyfund.org/person/jean-jacques-rousseau
also Marxists Internet Archive
https://www.marxists.org/reference/subject/economics/rousseau/index.htm

Clausewitz

The Clausewitz Homepage is edited by Dr Christopher Bassford
  https://www.clausewitz.com
Also archived via Marxists Internet Archive
  https://www.marxists.org/reference/archive/clausewitz/index.htm
In addition, *On War* is at:
  https://antilogicalism.com/wp-content/uploads/2019/04/on-war.pdf

Lenin

Marxists Internet Archive https://www.marxists.org/archive/lenin/index.htm

Mao

Marxists Internet Archive
  https://www.marxists.org/reference/archive/mao/index.htm
A 1963 edition of the *Selected Military Writings of Mao Tse-Tung* is in the
  Marxists Internet Archive at:
  https://www.marxists.org/reference/archive/mao/selected-works/military
  -writings/mao-selected-military-writings-1963.pdf
And *Quotations from Chairman Mao Tse-Tung* is at:
  https://www.marxists.org/ebooks/mao/Quotations_from_Chairman_Mao
  _Tse-tung.pdf

Carl Schmitt

Entry in the *Stanford Encyclopedia of Philosophy*
  https://plato.stanford.edu/entries/schmitt

2. Good general sources of open access materials worth trying

All of these services will return some sources for some of the thinkers above.

Directory of Open Access Books

https://www.doabooks.org
This is a service of the OAPEN Foundation that works with publishers to increase discoverability. The Directory of Open Access Books is a joint service of OAPEN, OpenEdition, CNRS and Aix-Marseille Université, provided by the DOAB Foundation. It searches across thousands of books from a range of publishers.

The Internet Archive

https://archive.org/about

Gallica

https://gallica.bnf.fr
Digital library of the Bibliothèque Nationale de France. Provides free access (in French) to thousands of full-text historic French-language books, journals

and newspapers from the library. Mostly it houses older and out-of-copyright editions.

The Online Books page
onlinebooks.library.upenn.edu
Excellent index to over three million free e-books that is maintained by Penn University. It includes links to both individual titles and large e-book directories.

Perseus Digital Library Project Tufts University
https://www.perseus.tufts.edu/hopper/searchresults?q=Thucydides
Covers the history, literature and culture of the Graeco-Roman world.

Index